T0265272

Get the eBook FREE!

(PDF, ePub, Kindle, and liveBook all included)

We believe that once you buy a book from us, you should be able to read it in any format we have available. To get electronic versions of this book at no additional cost to you, purchase and then register this book at the Manning website.

Go to https://www.manning.com/freebook and follow the instructions to complete your pBook registration.

That's it!
Thanks from Manning!

Acing the CCNA Exam

Volume 1
Fundamentals and Protocols

Jeremy McDowell

MANNING
Shelter Island

For online information and ordering of this and other Manning books, please visit www.manning.com. The publisher offers discounts on this book when ordered in quantity.

For more information, please contact

Special Sales Department
Manning Publications Co.
20 Baldwin Road
PO Box 761
Shelter Island, NY 11964
Email: orders@manning.com

Manning Publications Co.
20 Baldwin Road
PO Box 761
Shelter Island, NY 11964

Development editor: Connor O'Brien
Technical editor: Jeremy Cioara
Review editor: Kishor Rit
Production editor: Kathy Rossland
Copy editors: Alisa Larson and Kari Lucke
Proofreaders: Melody Dolab and Katie Tennant
Technical proofreader: Munish Kaushal
Typesetter: Tamara Švelić Sabljić
Cover designer: Marija Tudor

ISBN 9781633437678
Printed in the United States of America

brief contents

contents

preface

In 2018, as a junior high school English teacher in the city of Kobe, Japan, I found myself at a crossroads. What I had originally intended to be a brief teaching stint in Japan had stretched into four years, and I was reaching the limit of my stay. I was in Japan on the Japan Exchange and Teaching (JET) Programme, a program sponsored by the Japanese government to bring recent university graduates to Japan to teach English for up to 5 years. As my tenure neared its end, I pondered my next step.

Being fascinated with computers since childhood, I found the field of IT a natural choice. I was no computer wizard—I had no experience in programming or anything of the sort—but after some searching, I stumbled upon the Cisco Certified Network Associate (CCNA) certification. If the stories were to be believed, getting CCNA certified was the gateway to a promising career in IT with a decent salary and plenty of room for growth. After a bit of studying, I was hooked! Peering under the hood of networks like the internet—an ubiquitous part of the modern world—was (and still is) endlessly fascinating.

Fast forward a year to 2019, and I was a network engineer at the world's leading colocation data center and interconnection provider! I share my personal story here to emphasize that, with no formal education or previous experience on the topic, I was able to self-study, get certified, and make a 180-degree career change to enter the IT industry. And my story is no exception; I hear such stories from students all over the world on a daily basis.

You will occasionally encounter naysayers who downplay the value of the CCNA these days. One common argument is that, with the rise of cloud services like Amazon Web Services (AWS) and Microsoft Azure, there is less demand for network engineers; students should pursue cloud providers' certifications instead. I couldn't disagree more;

connecting the complex multicloud infrastructure used by many modern enterprises is no simple task, and we need network professionals more than ever.

Studying a particular cloud service provider's solutions before learning the fundamentals of networking is simply putting the cart before the horse—a house built on sand. The same can be said of pursuing the field of cybersecurity before grasping basics like networking. Network fundamentals are foundational knowledge for any IT professional, and the CCNA exam tests and certifies not only that you understand the fundamentals, but also that you have the skills to apply them in real networks. In our increasingly interconnected world, such knowledge and skills are invaluable—my story, and countless others' stories, prove that.

This book—consisting of two volumes—is the culmination of insights gained from countless interactions with many thousands of students of my CCNA video course, refined and expanded to offer a comprehensive resource. For countless people—including myself—becoming CCNA certified has been truly life changing. There will be struggles and setbacks, but if you're looking to make a change in your life and career, I can't recommend the CCNA enough, and I hope that this book will inspire and empower you to pursue and achieve your CCNA certification.

acknowledgments

Writing and publishing a book is a major undertaking—certainly not something I could have done on my own! I'd like to thank everyone who contributed to this book in one way or another, directly or indirectly.

Thank you, to everyone at Manning who has worked hard on this book; there is a lot of behind-the-scenes work that goes into publishing a book. I'd like to thank my editor Connor O'Brien most of all for his valuable feedback on each chapter of this book. The book has turned out far better than it ever could have without his detailed reviews and guidance.

Thank you, Andy Waldron, acquisitions editor at Manning, for giving me a chance to write this book. I reached out to a few publishers about writing a CCNA book, and Andy was quick to respond and express his interest. After a few quick calls, the contract was signed, and the rest is history!

Thank you, Jeremy Cioara, for your contributions as technical editor for the book. Jeremy Cioara is an author, educator, and business owner known for his ability to simplify complex technical concepts into entertaining and practical explanations. He brings more than two decades of experience, a love of learning, and a keen eye for detail.

Thank you, all of the reviewers, for your time and valuable feedback at each stage of the process: Amit Lamba, Andrea Cosentino, Casey Burnett, Eder Andrés Ávila Niño, Emmanuele Piccinelli, Emilio Grande, Gavin Smith, George Gyftogiannis, Glen Thompson, Greg MacLean, Jeremy Chen, John Bisgrove, John Guthrie, Jose Apablaza, Narayanan Seshan, Nghia To, Paul Love, Pedro Seromenho, Raghunath Mysore, Simone Sguazza, Sushil Singh, Vladislav Bilay, and Zachary Manning. Special thanks go to Munish Kaushal, my technical proofreader, for your careful reviews of the many (very many!) figures, commands, and examples in this book.

I'd also like to thank everyone who has supported Jeremy's IT Lab during the past five years. It's because of all of you that I can pursue my dream as a job—for that, I am forever grateful. Writing a CCNA book would never have crossed my mind without your support. Special thanks go to those on the Jeremy's IT Lab Discord server for being a totally awesome and supportive group, always willing to lend a hand and lift each other up (without forgetting to have fun).

Finally, thank you, my friends and family who have supported me in my personal life during this process; writing a book is a major time commitment and often means neglecting the more important parts of life. Thank you, Miki, for your understanding and constant encouragement during my long work hours throughout the whole process, and thanks, Mom and Dad, for your support and encouragement as always.

about this book

Acing the CCNA Exam was written with one goal in mind: to help you prepare for and successfully pass the CCNA exam. It begins from zero and assumes no previous knowledge, covering network fundamentals and every CCNA exam topic step by step.

Who should read this book

As an exam study guide, this book is for anyone who wants to pass the CCNA exam and attain their CCNA certification. If that's you (good choice, by the way), you've come to the right place! Even for those who already have their CCNA or are already working in the field, this book will be a useful resource for reference, covering key network protocols and how to configure them on Cisco routers and switches.

How this book is organized

The CCNA exam is quite wide in scope, and as a result, this book is divided into two volumes. This is volume 1, consisting of 24 chapters arranged across 6 parts:

- Chapter 1, separate from the main 6 parts, serves as an introduction to the CCNA exam: what it is, why you should get CCNA certified, and advice about how to study for the exam.

Part 1 lays the foundation of networking concepts, introducing how networks operate at a basic level, the devices that form a network, and the protocols that govern communication:

- Chapter 2 introduces some of the different types of devices, such as routers and switches, that make up networks, and the roles of each.

- Chapter 3 covers the different cables, connectors, and ports that are used to physically connect devices to form a network.
- Chapter 4 covers the TCP/IP model, a network "blueprint" that conceptualizes the various functions involved in network communications.
- Chapter 5 introduces the command-line interface (CLI) of Cisco routers and switches—the text-based interface that we will use to interact with and configure them throughout this book.
- Chapter 6 focuses on the role of Ethernet switches in facilitating communications within a local area network (LAN).
- Chapter 7 covers Internet Protocol version 4 (IPv4) addresses; these are how computers identify each other on a network.
- Chapter 8 focuses on the interfaces that connect Cisco routers and switches and how to configure them.

Part 2 delves into how data navigates through complex networks, focusing on routing principles, the end-to-end journey of a data packet, and segmenting a network with subnetting:

- Chapter 9 covers the fundamentals of routing—the process by which routers forward packets to destinations in remote networks.
- Chapter 10 is a deep dive into the various processes involved in delivering a message from one host to another, reviewing the key concepts covered up to this point.
- Chapter 11 introduces subnetting, which is the process of dividing a larger IP network into multiple smaller networks.

Part 3 focuses on technologies and protocols used by switches to facilitate their role in forwarding frames in an efficient, reliable, and secure manner:

- Chapter 12 covers virtual LANs (VLANs), which are used to segment a LAN for improved efficiency and security.
- Chapter 13 explains Dynamic Trunking Protocol (DTP) and VLAN Trunking Protocol (VTP), which play key roles in the configuration and management of VLANs.
- Chapter 14 introduces Spanning Tree Protocol (STP), a protocol that ensures a loop-free topology in Ethernet LANs.
- Chapter 15 delves into Rapid Spanning Tree Protocol (RSTP), an evolution of STP that provides faster convergence.
- Chapter 16 discusses EtherChannel, a technology that combines multiple physical links into a single logical unit to increase bandwidth while providing redundancy.

Part 4 covers key protocols used by routers—dynamic routing protocols to enable automatic and adaptive packet forwarding, and first-hop redundancy protocols to provide a reliable gateway for hosts in a LAN:

- Chapter 17 introduces dynamic routing, focusing on the various protocols that enable routers to communicate with each other and dynamically build their routing tables.
- Chapter 18 focuses on Open Shortest Path First (OSPF), the most common dynamic routing protocol used by routers within an organization.
- Chapter 19 explains first hop redundancy protocols (FHRPs), which provide continuous network availability by allowing routers to coordinate and provide a redundant default gateway.

Part 5 introduces the next generation of the Internet Protocol, IPv6, designed to overcome the limitations of IPv4 and support the internet of the future:

- Chapter 20 covers IPv6 addressing, detailing the structure and various types of IPv6 addresses.
- Chapter 21 delves into familiar routing concepts from an IPv6 perspective, focusing on configuring IPv6 static routes.

Part 6 explores the role of the Layer 4 protocols TCP and UDP, as well as how to use IP access controls lists (ACLs) for filtering and securing network traffic:

- Chapter 22 discusses Transmission Control Protocol (TCP) and User Datagram Protocol (UDP), the core protocols of the Transport Layer.
- Chapter 23 introduces standard ACLs, which identify and filter packets based on their source IP address.
- Chapter 24 covers extended ACLs, which provide more granular traffic filtering based on IP addresses, port numbers, and protocol types.

Additionally, there are four appendixes, each of which should prove helpful in your exam preparation:

- Appendix A is a reference table that lists the CCNA exam topics and which chapters of each volume cover each topic.
- Appendix B is a reference table that lists the Cisco IOS CLI commands covered in each chapter of this volume, with a brief description of each.
- Appendix C consists of several quiz questions for each chapter of this volume. I recommend using these questions to test your understanding after studying each chapter, and then doing the same for review as necessary.
- Appendix D lists the correct answers to the chapter quiz questions in appendix C and gives a brief explanation for each answer.

If you are just beginning your CCNA studies, I highly recommend starting from volume 1 (this volume) and reading the chapters in order; each chapter builds upon the previous ones, assuming familiarity with all preceding material. However, if you are using this book as a secondary resource (having already completed another course of study, such as my video series), feel free to treat the book more as a reference guide. In this case, you can directly consult chapters that address specific areas you want to focus on. Appendix A will be particularly useful for this targeted study, as it lists which chapters in which volume address each CCNA exam topic.

About Cisco CLI commands and output formatting

This book contains many examples of Cisco command-line interface (CLI) commands and output in examples and in line with normal text. These examples are formatted in a `fixed-width font like this` to separate it from ordinary text, using the syntax conventions shown in the following table. Code annotations accompany many of the code examples and highlight important concepts. Where necessary, the code has been reformatted to accommodate the available page space, and where code wraps, we've used line-continuation markers (➥).

Table 1 CLI syntax conventions

Convention	Description
`Standard text`	Command prompts and CLI output not typed by the user.
`Bold text`	Commands and keywords as typed by the user.
`Italic text`	Arguments in a command for which you supply values.
[**x**]	Square brackets indicate optional elements, such as optional keywords.
. . .	An ellipsis indicates that output has been abbreviated/omitted.
|	Pipes (vertical bars) are used to separate mutually exclusive elements, as shown in the following two conventions (square brackets and curly braces).
[**x** | **y**]	Optional alternative elements are enclosed in square brackets and separated by pipes.
{**x** | **y**}	Mandatory alternative elements are enclosed in curly braces and separated by pipes.

Each command in this book will be explained as it is introduced, but you can refer to this table as needed for clarification. The following examples demonstrate some of these different syntax conventions:

- **show ip interface** *[interface]*
  - You must type **show ip interface** and then optionally provide a value for the *interface* argument.
- **vtp version** {**1** | **2** | **3**}
  - You must type **vtp mode** and then the keyword **1**, **2**, or **3**.

- **`switchport trunk allowed vlan`** `[`**`add`** `|` **`remove`** `|` **`except`**`]` *`vlans`*
  - You must type **`switchport trunk allowed vlan`**, optionally specify one of the listed keywords, and then specify a value for the *`vlans`* argument.
- `R1(config-if)#` **`interface g0/1`**
  - The command prompt `R1(config-if)#` was displayed, and the user typed the command **`interface g0/1`**.

liveBook discussion forum

Purchase of *Acing the CCNA Exam* includes free access to liveBook, Manning's online reading platform. Using liveBook's exclusive discussion features, you can attach comments to the book globally or to specific sections or paragraphs. It's a snap to make notes for yourself, ask and answer technical questions, and receive help from the author and other users. To access the forum, go to https://livebook.manning.com/book/acing-the-ccna-exam-fundamentals-and-protocols/discussion. You can also learn more about Manning's forums and the rules of conduct at https://livebook.manning.com/discussion.

Manning's commitment to our readers is to provide a venue where a meaningful dialogue between individual readers and between readers and the author can take place. It is not a commitment to any specific amount of participation on the part of the author, whose contribution to the forum remains voluntary (and unpaid). We suggest you try asking him some challenging questions lest his interest stray! The forum and the archives of previous discussions will be accessible from the publisher's website as long as the book is in print.

Other online resources

There is no shortage of helpful resources for CCNA students online. I have collected some of my recommended resources (video courses, practice exams, etc.) on my website at https://www.jeremysitlab.com/ccna-resources.

Another page that every CCNA candidate should have bookmarked is the official exam topics list at https://learningnetwork.cisco.com/s/ccna-exam-topics. This is where you can find what Cisco expects you to know to pass the CCNA exam.

Finally, I recommend bookmarking Cisco Certification Roadmaps at https://learningnetwork.cisco.com/s/cisco-certification-roadmaps. This page will give you information about Cisco's yearly certification review process. If there are any scheduled changes coming to the CCNA exam, they will be listed on this page well in advance.

about the author

JEREMY MCDOWELL is a senior network engineer from Canada, living and working in Japan for over 10 years. After graduating with a bachelor of music degree from the University of Toronto, he taught English in Japan for five years before entering the networking industry in 2019.

Combining his knowledge of networking with his teaching skills, Jeremy has helped thousands of students study for and pass the CCNA exam through his YouTube channel Jeremy's IT Lab, which currently has over 340,000 subscribers.

about the cover illustration

The figure on the cover of *Acing the CCNA Exam*, titled "Maître d'école," or "Teacher," is taken from a book by Louis Curmer published in 1841. Each illustration is finely drawn and colored by hand.

In those days, it was easy to identify where people lived and what their trade or station in life was just by their dress. Manning celebrates the inventiveness and initiative of the computer business with book covers based on the rich diversity of regional culture centuries ago, brought back to life by pictures from collections such as this one.

1 Introduction to the CCNA

This chapter covers

- What is the CCNA?
- Why study for the CCNA?
- How to study for the CCNA

In this chapter, we will take a look at the CCNA exam itself, why it's valuable, and how you should go about studying for it. If you are interested enough in the CCNA to buy a book about it, chances are you already have a basic idea about what the CCNA is. You also certainly have your own reasons for wanting to study for the CCNA. However, I hope this chapter helps clarify some doubts you may have and encourages you to continue down the path to achieving the CCNA certification.

1.1 What is the CCNA?

The Cisco Certified Network Associate (CCNA) is an entry-level networking certification by Cisco Systems, and it is also the name of the exam you have to pass to become CCNA certified. The CCNA exam tests a candidate on various aspects of networking, such as IP addressing, wired and wireless network connections, routing and switching packets across a network, network services, security fundamentals, network automation, and many more. The various topics of the CCNA exam are organized into six logical domains.

1.1.1 The six domains of the CCNA exam

The six domains tested on the CCNA exam and their relative weightings are as follows:

- 1.0 Network Fundamentals—20%
- 2.0 Network Access—20%
- 3.0 IP Connectivity—25%
- 4.0 IP Services—10%
- 5.0 Security Fundamentals—15%
- 6.0 Automation and Programmability—10%

Within each of the domains, there are various topics and subtopics. If you are planning to take the CCNA exam, it is a good idea to know exactly what Cisco expects of you. Fortunately, Cisco has you covered; you can view the CCNA exam topics list on the Cisco Learning Network at http://mng.bz/AdVx.

Looking at the list of exam topics at the start of your studies might be a bit intimidating. If you are like I was when I started studying for the CCNA in 2018, you might have heard of an IP address before, but everything else on that list seems like a foreign language. Rest assured that if you follow volumes 1 and 2 of this book from start to end and take your time to understand the concepts, you will be fluent in the language of networking. You won't be an expert, but you will have the foundational knowledge and skills necessary to take on the CCNA exam and enter the world of network professionals.

I have heard the CCNA described as "a mile wide and an inch deep." Objectively speaking, that statement is true. The CCNA covers a wide variety of topics related to the field of networking, and as an entry-level certification, it does not dig deep into many nitty-gritty details, especially compared to Cisco's higher-level certifications like Cisco Certified Network Professional (CCNP) and Cisco Certified Internetwork Expert (CCIE). However, do not let this statement make you underestimate the CCNA or think it is trivial. It is often more difficult to wrap your head around a topic for the first time than it is to dig deeper once you already have a grasp of the fundamentals, and the CCNA certainly includes plenty of new topics for an aspiring engineer to understand. The CCNA is also much more comprehensive and challenging than comparable entry-level networking certifications like CompTIA's Network+.

Although the CCNA is a vendor-specific certification (as opposed to a vendor-neutral certification like Network+), it is the de facto industry standard entry-level certification in the networking industry. In addition to testing your skills at configuring and troubleshooting Cisco routers and switches, the CCNA tests your knowledge of the fundamentals of networking. Modern networks use a variety of standard protocols that apply regardless of which vendor's device is running them. IP (Internet Protocol) is IP; it does not matter whether it is being used by a Cisco router, an Apple iPhone, or a Windows PC. The CCNA requires a combination of theoretical knowledge of standard protocols, as well as practical application on Cisco devices. That makes it one of the most respected and desired entry-level certifications not just for network professionals but also for IT professionals in general.

1.1.2 Format of the CCNA Exam

The CCNA is a 120-minute exam covering the six exam topic domains previously listed. The majority of the questions are multiple choice, but you can expect questions of various formats, such as

- *Multiple choice, single answer*—The question won't state "select one," but you'll only be able to select one option at a time.
- *Multiple choice, multiple answers*—The question will clearly indicate how many options to select: "select two," "select three," etc.
- *Drag and drop*—In these questions, you are required to move items or options from one part of the screen to another to correctly answer the question. This can involve matching terms with definitions, sequencing steps in a process, etc.
- *Lab simulations*—In these questions, you will log in to and configure Cisco routers and switches in a simulated network.

Cisco has a short video summarizing each of the four question types. I recommend taking a look to familiarize yourself with the question types and the exam interface: http://mng.bz/ZEpA.

When taking the CCNA exam, questions are randomly selected from a large pool, so no two test-takers will have the exact same experience. This applies to both the types and order of questions, as well as their distribution across the six exam domains. Although the exam topics list is divided into six sections, the exam itself is not. You will receive a set number of questions and have 120 minutes to answer them, managing your time as needed. And here's an important point: after you answer or skip a question, *you can't go back!* Don't make the mistake of skipping a difficult question with the intention of answering it later—this is not possible.

EXAM TIP Effective time management is crucial for success on the CCNA exam. Some questions, particularly lab simulations, demand more time than others, so it's important to allocate sufficient time for these questions. The challenge lies in not knowing the exact number of lab simulation questions or their placement within the exam. For example, if you only have 1 minute left and the final question is a lab simulation, it's unlikely you'll be able to finish the question, resulting in lost points. My recommendation is to answer the more straightforward questions confidently and move on—avoid spending excessive time second-guessing yourself. If you don't know the answer, select one and move on—there is no penalty for guessing.

Cisco keeps the exact contents of the exam and the grading scheme tightly protected, but the general consensus is that the lab simulations are more heavily weighted than the other question types. There's a study tip: when studying for the CCNA, never skip the lab exercises! Whether the lab simulations on the exam are more heavily weighted or not, hands-on practice is still essential for studying.

Exam scenarios

Throughout the book, you will find several exam scenarios that present questions similar to what you might find on the CCNA exam. Note that these aren't actual CCNA exam questions. The contents of Cisco's exams are protected by a nondisclosure agreement (NDA) that you must accept before taking each exam. Violating the NDA will result in Cisco banning you from their certification program. This includes accessing leaked exam questions to prepare for an exam; don't do it!

1.1.3 Scheduling and taking the exam

The CCNA exam, administered by Cisco's testing partner Pearson VUE, can be taken either at an authorized test center or online. To schedule the exam, visit CertMetrics (https://cp.certmetrics.com/cisco/en/login). If you don't have a Cisco account yet, you'll have to make one; just click Sign Up, and make an account.

Once logged in to CertMetrics, click Schedule Now to proceed to the Pearson VUE website, where you can find the CCNA exam under Proctored Exams. Here, you can choose between taking the exam at a test center or online.

Some prefer to schedule the exam at the start of their studies and build a study plan based on that date. However, if this is your first time taking a certification exam, I advise against this, as the time required for preparation can vary depending on factors like your work and educational background and the amount of time you can dedicate to studying.

> **NOTE** The CCNA is not held on specific dates; you are free to schedule and take the exam at any time throughout the year. Online exams are available 24/7 (depending on the availability of proctors), but in-person exams depend on the test center's availability.

Both test center and online exams are proctored to ensure exam integrity. At a test center, staff will be present to monitor you. If you take the exam online, a proctor will confirm that you have a suitable testing environment before the exam (possibly asking you to remove objects around your desk or walls) and monitor you via webcam and microphone during the exam. For details about online testing, check out Cisco's page here: http://mng.bz/RZvv. If you can't secure a quiet, private location for at least 2 hours, I recommend taking the exam at a test center—any unexpected disturbances (such as another person entering the room) could result in your exam being canceled.

1.2 Why get CCNA-certified?

Every day, thousands of people worldwide decide to begin their journey to becoming CCNA-certified. There is a good reason for that: although these days there are many competitive players in the field of networking, Cisco is still the industry leader by far. Enterprises all over the world, large and small, use Cisco devices in their networks, so it makes sense that those enterprises would want to hire people competent with Cisco devices. A job search on LinkedIn for "CCNA" gives many tens of thousands of results in the United States alone, and that number multiplies to hundreds of thousands worldwide.

Whether you are already in the field of IT and looking to move up the ladder to a new position or are new to the field and looking for your first job in IT, the CCNA can give you a major career advantage. A CCNA-certified person should be ready to take on job roles like network technician, network support engineer, network/systems administrator, junior network engineer, and many more. Aside from the immense value of the information you learn and the skills you acquire, simply having the CCNA on your resume is a big help in getting past the so-called HR filter and actually getting the interview. Getting a job in IT without any experience can be difficult, but being CCNA-certified will greatly improve your odds.

Although the CCNA is a networking-focused certification, it is valuable not only for those aiming for networking-specific roles. Networking is one of the foundational skills of IT, so your CCNA studies will serve you well regardless of your path. CCNA-certified professionals often move on to careers in cybersecurity, cloud, systems engineering, and other areas of IT.

Whatever your reasons are for wanting to become CCNA-certified, I promise you that you won't regret it. IT is competitive, with many eager individuals all over the world looking to join the field. The CCNA will help you differentiate yourself and stand out from the crowd.

1.3 The structure of this book

The official CCNA exam topics list divides the topics into six logical domains. However, for a student beginning their CCNA studies, studying the topics in order from top to bottom is not ideal. Each CCNA instructor (myself included) structures their book or course differently, but no course (that I am aware of) follows the order of the exam topics list. At a very high level, the two volumes of this book cover the exam domains in the following order:

- 1.0 Network Fundamentals and 3.0 IP Connectivity
- 2.0 Network Access
- 3.0 IP Connectivity (again)
- 4.0 IP Services
- 5.0 Security Fundamentals
- 6.0 Automation and Programmability

However, you will find elements of multiple domains throughout all parts of both volumes of the book. If you are just beginning your CCNA studies, I recommend studying this book in the order I have written it; each chapter assumes you have already studied the previous chapters, so jumping around is likely to result in confusion. However, appendix A includes a chart that you can use to cross-reference the CCNA exam topics and the chapters in volumes 1 and 2 of this book. The chart should prove useful when reviewing specific exam topics before the exam.

Figure 1.1 depicts a sample network and highlights some of the various devices and protocols that make the network work. This is only a small selection of the topics we'll delve into in this book. If you're a newcomer to networking, you might have only heard of a few of the highlighted technologies (and probably aren't sure how they actually work). However, at the end of both volumes of this book, you'll be able to explain all of these technologies and more.

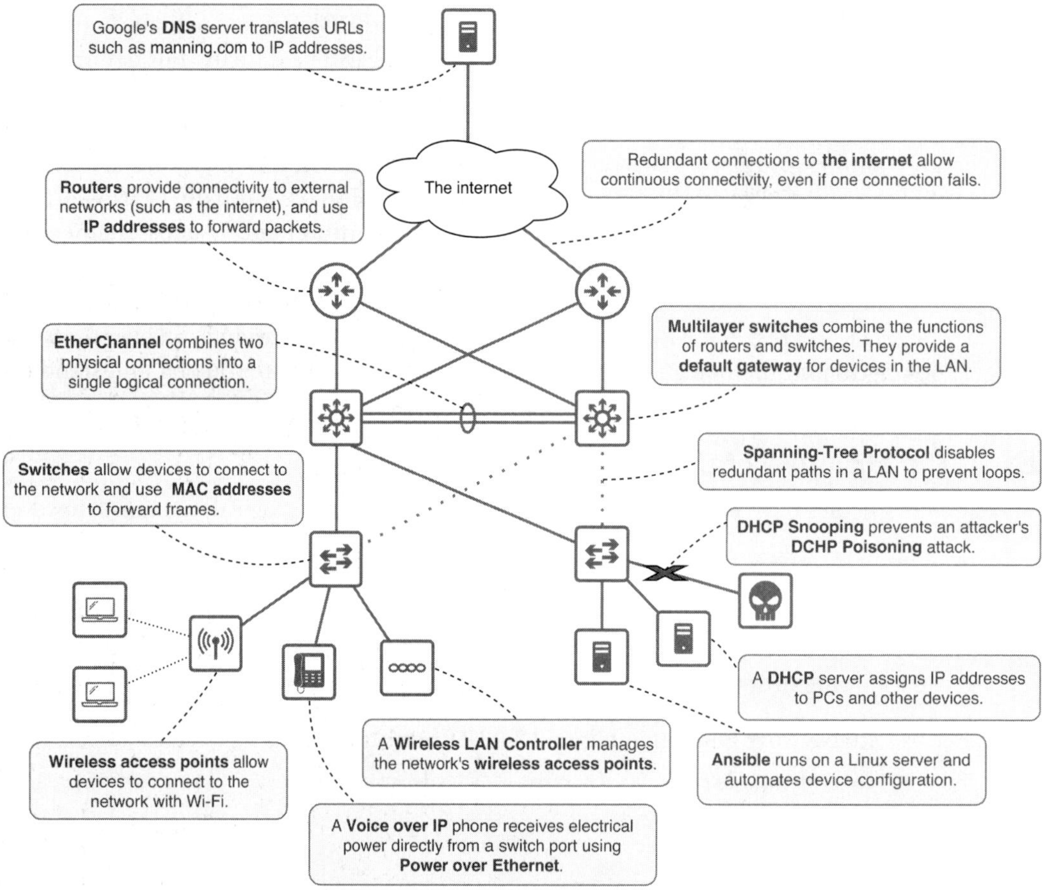

Figure 1.1 A local area network (LAN) connected to the internet (as represented by the cloud icon). Various devices (routers, switches, etc.) and protocols (DHCP, DNS, etc.) are highlighted. We will cover all of these technologies and more in this book's two volumes.

1.4 How to study for the CCNA

The CCNA is a demanding exam that requires an understanding of various complex concepts, how they relate to each other, how to practically apply them in a network, and how to troubleshoot them when things go wrong. An optimal CCNA study plan should therefore take advantage of multiple resources such as a book, a video course, and practical lab exercises. Let's examine each of these resource types and their role in effectively preparing for the CCNA exam.

1.4.1 Using a book

For many CCNA candidates, a book is where they start their CCNA studies, and for good reason. The written word is a powerful medium for conveying technical information. I want to emphasize that studying from a book differs from simply reading from a book. While you study from a book, stop occasionally to think about what you've just read. Take notes. Try to explain the concepts you are learning. Be an active learner, and you'll be able to get the most out of this book and others. You don't get more out of a book by simply reading through it multiple times. You get more out of a book by being an active learner rather than a passive learner.

1.4.2 Using a video course

A video course allows you to cover the same material studied in a book from a different angle. It's common to hear that videos are good for developing a general understanding of a particular topic, and books are good for digging into the details. The extent to which that is true depends on which book and which video course you are using, but I would generally agree. While you don't have to use both a book and a video course, my own experience and the experiences of many others suggest that it is beneficial. Use this book in combination with a video course of your choice, and you'll be able to take advantage of the strengths of both mediums.

1.4.3 Lab exercises

Lab exercises (labs) are an essential part of any CCNA study plan. *Labbing*, a common bit of IT jargon, is a term that means getting hands-on practice with the technology you're studying. Because this book is about the CCNA, in this context, labbing means practicing configuring Cisco routers and switches. Although there is a lot of theoretical information covered in the CCNA, it's all for the purpose of being able to apply your skills in a real network, so labbing is an essential part of studying for the CCNA.

There are a few options available for CCNA lab practice: physical hardware, network emulators, and network simulators. Let's take a look at each option and why I recommend using a network simulator (Cisco Packet Tracer) for the CCNA.

The first option is to use physical hardware—real Cisco routers and switches. While this may seem like the ideal approach, it is not the one I recommend for your CCNA studies. It certainly is valuable practice for an aspiring network engineer to connect and configure real physical network devices, but in terms of cost and convenience, this approach is not the best. To buy all of the necessary hardware would be cost prohibitive for most—likely many thousands of dollars. Second-hand hardware can be more affordable (you could probably assemble a viable home lab for under $1,000), but it is still too expensive for many. Second-hand devices also often run old software versions, which may not accurately represent the behavior of more recent devices.

Another option is to use a network emulation platform such as Cisco Modeling Labs (CML). CML uses virtualization technology to run virtual routers and switches, enabling you to build and run virtual networks on a personal computer or server. These virtual devices run real Cisco IOS (Internetworking Operating System, not to be confused with Apple iOS, which runs on iPhones) and allow you to configure nearly anything you would be able to on a physical Cisco router or switch. Although I would recommend this approach over physical hardware, I still do not think it is ideal. While cheaper than hardware, CML still costs around $200 per year. Additionally, running these virtual labs can require a lot of CPU and RAM resources, so unless you already have a powerful computer, you might have trouble running networks with more than a few virtual devices.

These reasons are why I think Cisco Packet Tracer is the best option for CCNA lab practice. Whereas CML is a network emulator that uses virtual machines to run real Cisco IOS, Packet Tracer is a network simulator. It is software that simulates the function of Cisco network devices but does not actually run real Cisco IOS. This makes Packet Tracer very lightweight—you do not need a powerful computer to run even very large simulated networks. Best of all, it's free. I'm all for investing money in your studies when necessary (I'm certainly glad you invested in this book!), but when a tool like Packet Tracer is available for free, it's hard to argue against it. Figure 1.2 shows a screenshot of a lab in Packet Tracer.

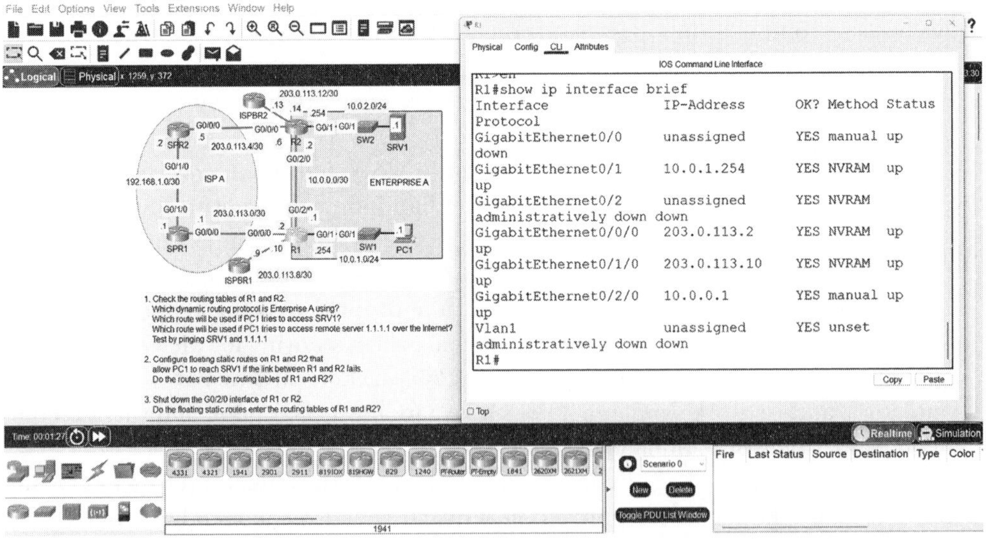

Figure 1.2 A lab in Cisco Packet Tracer. On the left is the network diagram with the lab's instructions below it, and on the right is the CLI of one of the devices in the network.

NOTE Go to http://mng.bz/2Kra to download Packet Tracer for free (click Sign Up if you don't have a Cisco account). That page also includes links to free courses from Cisco that guide you through how to download, install, and use Packet Tracer.

Although I recommend Packet Tracer, there are certainly downsides to it. Because it doesn't run actual Cisco IOS but rather a simulated version of it, there are plenty of features and configuration commands that Packet Tracer doesn't support. Packet Tracer only supports what its developers have programmed into it. That means that there will be some instances where a configuration command I show in this book cannot be used in Packet Tracer. However, Packet Tracer was developed as a tool for CCNA labs, so the vast majority of what we will cover in this book is supported. For studies beyond the CCNA, however, you should look into one of the other two options.

Most CCNA courses include lab exercises with them; they are essential practice. My video course includes lab exercises that will help solidify the concepts you've studied and build your networking skills. You can access it for free on YouTube at http://mng.bz/1G9q.

1.4.4 Using multiple resources together

So you've got this book, you've decided on a video course, and you've installed Cisco Packet Tracer on your computer for labs. Now what? While there is no single correct answer for how to approach your studies, the following are a couple of ideas.

One option is to focus exclusively on this book at first. Read a chapter, take notes, try to explain the concepts in your own words, and try out the configurations in Packet Tracer. Then, progress to the next chapter, and repeat the process until you have completed both volumes of this book. After that process, you may very well be ready to take on the CCNA exam, but there's also a chance that there will be some gaps in your understanding of the concepts. To fill in those gaps, you can then follow the same process with a video course of your choice.

A second option is to use multiple resources at the same time. Study a chapter from this book, and then study the equivalent section of the video course. Do the labs provided in the course, move on to the next chapter of the book, and then repeat the process.

As I mentioned previously, there is no single correct answer. You might have to experiment to find the approach that works best for you. I will emphasize one point, though: don't forget to do labs! Networking is a skill, and no skill can be developed only by reading a book. You have to get your hands dirty and apply what you've learned.

Summary

- The CCNA is an exam and certification by Cisco Systems. It is the de facto industry standard entry-level networking certification.
- The CCNA exam topics are divided into six domains: network fundamentals, network access, IP connectivity, IP services, security fundamentals, and automation and programmability. Each domain contains various topics and subtopics.
- The CCNA exam is 120 minutes in length and consists of a variety of question types: multiple choice, single answer; multiple choice, multiple answers; drag and drop; and lab simulations.
- Exam questions are randomly drawn from a large pool. Question types, order, and distribution across the exam domains are random, so each test-taker will have a different experience.
- After answering or skipping a question, you can't go back. Don't skip a question with the intention of answering it later—this is not possible.
- Don't be afraid to guess if you don't know the answer to a question on the exam. There is no penalty for incorrect answers.
- The CCNA exam is administered by Pearson VUE and can be taken at an authorized test center or online.
- Enterprises of all sizes use Cisco devices and seek CCNA-certified engineers. The knowledge and skills gained in the CCNA apply to all areas of IT—not just networking.
- Study resources (including this book) do not teach the CCNA exam topics in order, from top to bottom. Rather, each instructor teaches the topics in the order they believe to be best. Use the appendix at the back of this book to cross-reference the CCNA exam topics if necessary.
- Multiple study resources (book, video, labs) should be used together to solidify what you learn.
- Labs can be done with physical hardware, an emulator (such as Cisco Modeling Labs), or a simulator (Cisco Packet Tracer).
- Cisco Packet Tracer is the best option for CCNA labs because it is free, easy to set up, and supports most of what is needed for the CCNA.
- Do your lab exercises!

Part 1

Network fundamentals

Welcome to the first leg of your journey into the intricate world of computer networking. In this first part of the book, we will set the stage for your understanding of how networks like the internet work, forming a foundation we will build upon throughout the rest of this book. When learning any new subject, the fundamentals are key, and networking is no exception. We'll start in chapter 2 by examining the various kinds of devices that form networks: routers, switches, and firewalls—the devices that form the underlying network infrastructure—as well as the clients and servers that communicate over that infrastructure.

In chapter 3, we'll see how we can connect those devices with copper and fiber-optic Ethernet cables. Chapter 4 takes a theoretical approach, covering the TCP/IP networking model; this is the blueprint of the internet and most modern networks, providing a theoretical framework for understanding how different network protocols function and interact. Chapter 5, on the other hand, is very hands-on; we will connect to the command-line interface (CLI) of a Cisco router and navigate through its basic command hierarchy. If you're new to CLIs, you'll feel like you've hacked into the matrix! The CLI can seem like a maze at first, but with a bit of hands-on practice, it will soon feel like a second home.

In chapter 6, we will begin delving into how networks actually enable devices to communicate with each other, focusing on how switches facilitate communication within a local area network (LAN). Then, chapter 7 addresses one of the most important topics in all of computer networking: Internet Protocol (IP) addresses. Just as a house needs an address to communicate via physical mail, a computer needs an IP address to communicate via digital messages over a network. Finally, chapter 8 focuses on Cisco router and switch interfaces, which are used to connect these network infrastructure devices.

2 Network devices

This chapter covers

- The definition of a network
- Types of network devices, including clients, servers, switches, routers, and firewalls

This chapter is a high-level introduction to networks and some of the different types of devices that compose them. After looking at what a network is, we will examine clients, servers, switches, routers, and firewalls. We will look at the basic roles of each of these types of devices in a network, but we won't get into any details about how they actually perform these roles—we've got the rest of the book to do that! By the end of this chapter, you will be able to identify each of the network devices in figure 2.1 and briefly explain their respective roles.

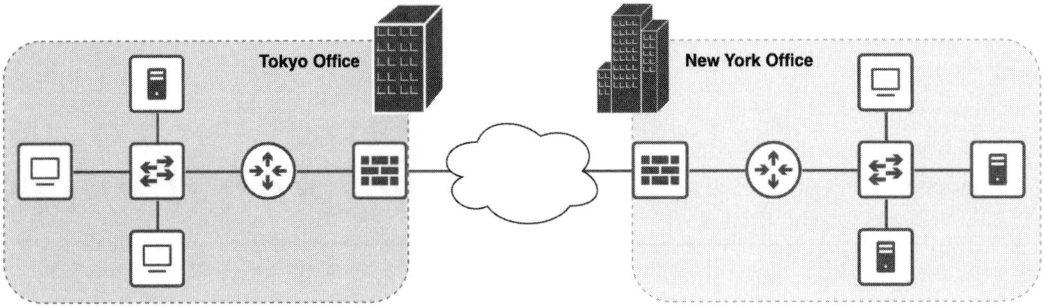

Figure 2.1 An enterprise network connecting multiple offices over the internet

Each office in figure 2.1 is a *local area network* (LAN), a group of interconnected devices in a limited area such as an office. Within each office in the diagram, you can find the kinds of network devices we will look at in this chapter: clients, servers, switches, routers, and firewalls. The connection *between* offices is called a *wide area network* (WAN)—a network that extends over a large geographical area (such as between cities). In volume 2 of this book, we will cover several WAN connection types. The internet, as represented by the cloud icon in figure 2.1, is just one of the options for connecting remote locations.

2.1 What is a network?

What is a network? As a general term, *network* can refer to many different things. A system of railways connecting towns and cities is a network. The veins and arteries in our bodies can be called a network. A group of people, such as business associates, can also be called a network. What do these all have in common? They are all about connecting people or things. In this book's two volumes, we are looking at a specific kind of network: a *computer network*—a network that connects computers. A computer connected to a network can be many different things, including

- A personal computer connected to the internet via a home network
- A television that connects to the internet to stream Netflix
- An iPhone connected to the internet via wireless 5G
- A YouTube server that streams videos to devices all over the world
- An enterprise's servers that store private files and data
- A security camera that saves footage to a server

We can define a computer network as a telecommunications network that allows nodes to share resources. That definition is certainly short and sweet, but you might be left with a couple of questions, like "What is a node?" and "What is a resource?"

A *node* is any device that connects to a network. It includes the previously listed examples, like a personal computer or an iPhone, as well as the network infrastructure that connects the devices—the routers, switches, firewalls, and various other types of devices that make up the network.

A *resource* is anything that can be accessed or used over the network. For example, if you use a web browser such as Google Chrome to access manning.com, the webpage that appears on your screen is a resource shared over the network. It is a file located on a server somewhere on the internet, and that server shares the webpage with the device you use to access the website. However, resources aren't just files. There are countless examples, but here are a few:

- A printer that is connected to the network and shared by users in an office
- An online game server that supports multiplayer gaming
- Cloud-based software like Gmail and Microsoft 365

2.2 Types of network devices

The previous discussion of nodes and resources leads us to this section. Let's look at the types of nodes that share resources over a network, as well as the types of nodes that comprise the network infrastructure that facilitates the sharing of resources.

2.2.1 Clients and servers

First, we will look at the nodes that share resources over a network: clients and servers. We cannot understand one without understanding the other because they are defined by their relationship with each other: a *client* is a device that accesses a service provided by a server, and a *server* is a device that provides services for clients. Figure 2.2 shows the icons for clients and servers that we will be using throughout this book.

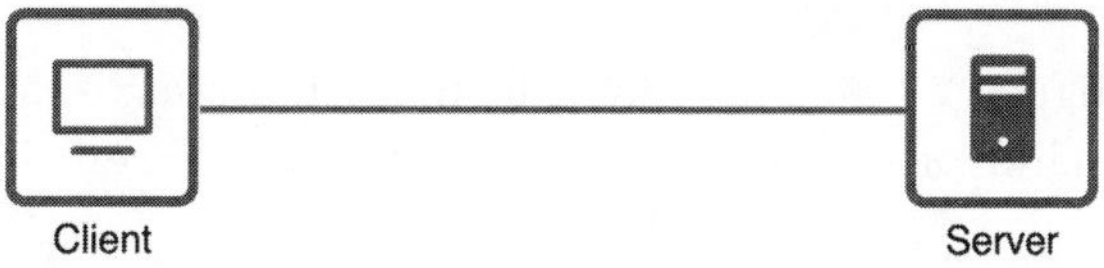

Figure 2.2 Icons representing a desktop computer and a file server. Icons like these are commonly used in network diagrams to represent clients and servers.

It's important to note that clients and servers aren't specific types of physical devices. Rather, they are roles that can be assumed by a variety of devices. If a device provides a service, such as hosting a webpage, that device is functioning as a server. If a device accesses a service, such as retrieving a webpage from a server, that device is functioning as a client.

> **NOTE** The term *server* is also used to refer to a kind of device—a very powerful computer designed to be able to provide services to many clients, such as a You-Tube server streaming video to thousands of clients over the internet. However, almost any kind of device can function as a server, so it's better to think of a server as a role, not a specific kind of device.

Let's list a few examples of client–server pairs:

- *Client*—A network-enabled TV that streams a movie on Netflix
- *Server*—A Netflix server that hosts the movie and sends it over the network

- *Client*—An iPhone scrolling through X (formerly Twitter)
- *Server*—X servers that host the tweets and send them to the iPhone

- *Client*—A PC accessing an Excel spreadsheet located on an enterprise's server
- *Server*—An enterprise's server containing spreadsheets and other internal files

Almost any node can be both a server and a client, depending on the context. For example, in a home network, it's possible to share files among devices. You can transfer a movie file from one PC to another PC in the network. In that case, the PC where the movie file is located is a server, and the PC accessing the file is a client. If the file was shared in the opposite direction, the server and client roles would be reversed. And both PCs would be clients when they are accessing websites over the internet. Figure 2.3 shows a client–server relationship between two PCs.

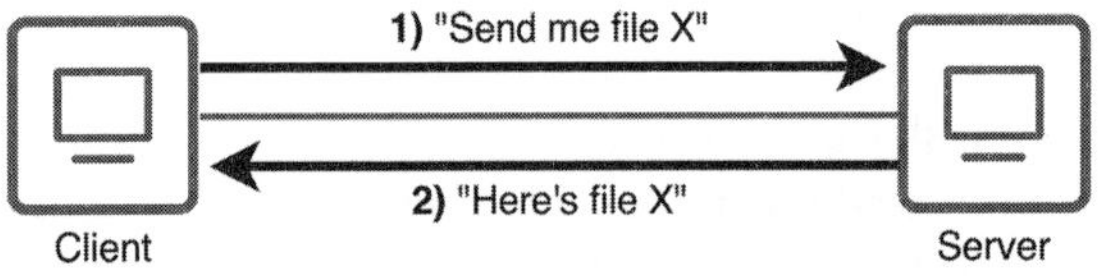

Figure 2.3 Two desktop PCs sharing a file. The PC on the left is functioning as a client, and the PC on the right is functioning as a server.

> **NOTE** Both devices in figure 2.3 use the client icon to emphasize that they are both PCs—the same kind of device—but their roles are different in this exchange.

Sometimes a network is as simple as two devices directly connected to each other. However, this type of connection is rare. To expand the network and allow more devices to communicate with each other, we need some specific types of devices to act as the network infrastructure and facilitate that communication.

Client and server nodes are often called *endpoints* or *end hosts*. These are general terms for devices that communicate over a network, as opposed to the network infrastructure devices that connect the end hosts.

2.2.2 Switches

Let's build out the network further by connecting our end hosts to a *switch*, as in figure 2.4.

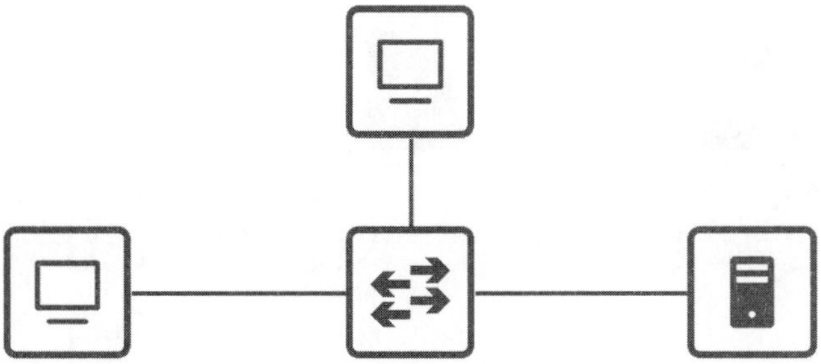

Figure 2.4 Three end hosts connected to a switch

Devices connected to a switch are able to communicate with each other via the switch. Note that they do not typically communicate with the switch itself—the switch only serves as infrastructure over which communication can occur.

The role of a switch is to connect devices within a LAN. For example, all of the PCs, security cameras, printers, servers, and other devices in an office are probably connected to one or more switches. For this reason, it's common for switches to have many ports for end hosts to connect to—usually from 24 to 48 per switch.

> **NOTE** A *port* is a physical connector on a device. Devices are physically connected by connecting one end of a cable to each of two devices. A port serves as the interface between one device and the other devices in the network. For that reason, the terms *port* and *interface* are often used interchangeably.

Switches use a variety of technologies to facilitate communications between the devices connected to them. In chapter 6, we will begin to learn exactly how switches do this. For now, it's sufficient to know their basic purpose. Note that the role of a switch is not to provide connectivity between LANs or to external networks. For example, you would not connect a switch directly to the internet. For that, we need another type of device.

2.2.3 Routers

So far, we've connected end hosts to a switch to allow them to communicate with each other. Switches provide connectivity among devices within a LAN, but chances are we want our end hosts to be able to communicate with external networks, too. For example, for end hosts to communicate over the internet, we need a device that provides connectivity between LANs and the internet. That type of device is called a *router*. Figure 2.5 shows how routers are used to connect LANs to external networks, such as the internet.

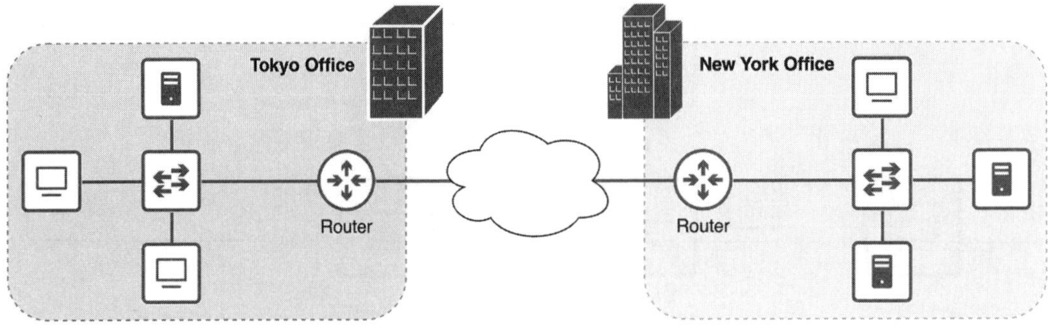

Figure 2.5 Two LANs connected to the internet via a router at the edge of each LAN

> **NOTE** A cloud icon is used in a network diagram to represent parts of a network that are unknown or unimportant to the diagram. For example, a cloud is often used to represent the internet. For the purpose of figure 2.5, we just need to know that the two LANs are connected to the internet. We do not need any details about what the internet (a very large and complicated network) actually looks like.

Routers are not used to connect many end hosts within a LAN. Instead, they are placed at the edge of a LAN and used to enable communications between LANs and external networks, such as the internet.

Like switches, routers use a variety of technologies to play their role in the network—facilitating communications between LANs. We will begin to look at how routers work in chapter 7, which covers IP addresses.

Wireless routers

You might be wondering, "If that's a router, what is the wireless router that connects my home network to the internet?" A wireless router (also known as a *Wi-Fi router* or *home router*) is not just a router; it's a multifunctional network device that combines the roles of multiple different network devices.

These devices typically fill the roles of a router, switch, wireless access point (to provide Wi-Fi connectivity), and firewall all in one device. They are perfect for a *small office/home office* (SOHO) network with only a few users. However, in enterprise networks, it's simply not feasible for a single device to fulfill all necessary roles.

2.2.4 Firewalls

Devices in the two LANs in figure 2.5 are perfectly capable of communicating with each other and with other devices over the internet. However, by allowing our devices to communicate over the internet, we are exposing them to potential security risks.

The internet is a large public network, and anyone can connect to it, whether their intentions are good or not. To protect our networks, we should make use of *firewalls*. Figure 2.6 shows how firewalls can protect networks by denying certain kinds of network traffic.

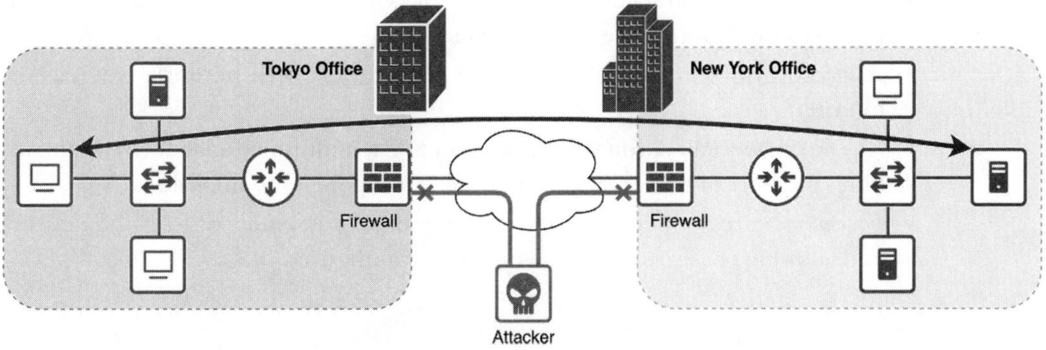

Figure 2.6 A firewall between each LAN and the internet secures the network. Network communications between the two LANs are allowed, but malicious traffic from an attacker is denied.

You have probably heard the term *firewall* before regarding a piece of software on your PC. For example, Windows PCs use Microsoft Defender Firewall by default. This kind of firewall is a *host-based firewall*. It examines network traffic entering and exiting the host device and then decides to allow or deny (block) it. It makes these decisions based on a set of defined rules. However, this is not the kind of firewall you need to know for the CCNA. The kind of firewall we will cover is the *network firewall*.

A network firewall is a separate hardware appliance that serves a purpose similar to a host-based firewall but on a larger scale. It inspects all traffic entering and exiting a network and decides to allow or deny it based on a set of configured rules.

Firewalls are not a major focus of the CCNA. We will cover some of their functionality in chapter 11 of volume 2, which covers security concepts, but the majority of this book will focus on the previously discussed two device types: routers and switches.

Summary

- A *local area network* (LAN) is a group of interconnected devices in a limited area, such as an office.
- A *wide area network* (WAN) is a network that extends over a large geographical area, such as between cities.
- A computer network is a telecommunications network that allows nodes to share resources.
- A *node* is any device that connects to a network: a personal computer, an iPhone, a router, etc.
- A *resource* is anything that is shared over a network, such as a web page.

- Various types of network devices are used to facilitate network communications.
- *Clients* and *servers* are defined by their functions in relation to each other: clients access services provided by servers, and servers provide services for clients. Most types of devices can be both a client and a server.
- *Switches* provide connectivity between devices in a LAN. They typically have many ports (24 to 48) for devices to connect to.
- *Routers* provide connectivity between LANs and external networks, such as the internet.
- A *wireless router* (Wi-Fi router/home router) is a multifunctional device that combines the roles of router, switch, wireless access point, and firewall.
- *Firewalls* secure the network by inspecting traffic that enters or exits the network and allowing or denying it based on a set of configured rules.

3 Cables, connectors, and ports

This chapter covers

- The specifications and standards that allow computers to communicate
- The fundamentals of traffic over a network
- Types of wired connections and cabling standards
- The uses of unshielded twisted pair and fiber-optic connections in networks

In chapter 2, we looked at a few diagrams showing network nodes connected with cables. In this chapter, we will look at the specific kinds of cables, connectors, and ports used to make those connections. These topics are part of section 1.0, Network Fundamentals, of the CCNA exam. Specifically, we will cover aspects of exam topic 1.3, which is as follows:

- 1.3 Compare physical interface and cabling types
  - 1.3.a Single-mode fiber, multimode fiber, copper
  - 1.3.b Connections (Ethernet shared media and point-to-point)

In the past, there have been many different ways to connect devices, and there still are. However, in modern networks, *Ethernet* reigns supreme and is by far the most common connection type. Perhaps you have heard of Ethernet before in reference to *Ethernet cables.* Ethernet is not one single thing but rather a collection of standards for physical wired connections as well as rules for communicating over those connections. In this chapter, we will look at two different kinds of physical connections between devices: those using copper cables and those using fiber-optic cables.

3.1 Network standards

In modern networks, someone in an office using a Dell PC connected to a Cisco switch can communicate with another person using an Apple MacBook connected to the Wi-Fi in Starbucks. The data is sent over the internet, possibly traveling over the infrastructure of multiple Internet Service Providers (ISPs), which use entirely different hardware. How is it possible that all of these devices, made by different companies, can communicate with each other? For this modern miracle, we can thank *standards*: sets of technical requirements and specifications that define the rules of communication in networks.

To demonstrate why these rules of communication are important, let's forget about computers for a second and think about direct communication between humans. If an English speaker uses English to speak to a person who only understands Japanese, there isn't going to be any communication at all. Each language, English and Japanese, has a different set of rules about how information should be communicated between people. Unless both speaker and listener agree on the rules, communication doesn't happen.

Even if both parties understand English, they must agree on the medium of communication. If person A writes a message on a piece of paper, but person B closes their eyes and tries to listen to the message, the result is the same as in the previous example: communication doesn't happen. For humans to be able to communicate with each other, we must agree on both the rules of communication and the medium of communication.

The same can be said of computers. For two computers to communicate, they must adhere to the same rules of communication—for example, how to format data when sending it over the network. There must also be rules governing the medium of communication: specifications for physical cables, connectors, and ports, as well as radio waves used in wireless communications.

There are several governing bodies that define the standards used in computer networks, and I'll be mentioning a couple of them throughout this book's two volumes. The main one relevant to this chapter is the *Institute of Electrical and Electronics Engineers* (IEEE, pronounced I-triple-E). In 1983, the IEEE first defined the *IEEE 802.3* standard, better known as *Ethernet.*

> **NOTE** The IEEE also defines the IEEE 802.11 standard, better (but not officially) known as *Wi-Fi.* IEEE 802.11 wireless LANs are a major topic of the CCNA exam and are covered in part 4 of volume 2 of this book.

Ethernet is not a single standard but rather a family of standards that define both physical aspects of network connections as well as how data should be formatted into messages to be sent over the network.

3.2 Binary: Bits and bytes

Terms like *bit*, *byte*, *megabit*, *megabyte*, etc. might be familiar to you, even if you're not entirely sure what they mean (I certainly wasn't before I started studying networking). You might even use the terms yourself, referring to a *gigabit internet connection* or a file that is *X gigabytes in size*. Depending on your age, you might even reminisce about your *56k* (kilobit) internet connection.

To understand what these terms mean, we must define the term *bit*. A bit is the most basic unit of information used by computers. The word *bit* is simply a blend of the words *binary digit*. *Binary* is a number system that expresses all values using only two digits: 0 and 1. A *byte*, on the other hand, is simply a unit of 8 bits. Eight bits are equal to 1 byte.

Binary is the language of computers. They compute in binary, and they communicate in binary. Everything you see on a computer screen or hear from a computer speaker is a series of 0s and 1s interpreted by a computer and presented to you in a human-understandable format. That includes applications, photos, videos, songs, this book if you're reading it in an electronic format, and everything else a computer does.

The CCNA, as a networking certification, is all about how computers communicate; that's what networking is. When two computers connected by a cable communicate with each other, they are sending each other long (*very long*, by human standards) series of bits (0s and 1s) over that cable. In modern networks, they often send these bits at the rate of *billions* (with a "b") per second. Exactly how these 0s and 1s are conveyed depends on the medium. For example, 0s and 1s can be communicated over copper wiring by modifying the voltage of an electric signal between the two devices. Voltage "x" represents a value of 0, and Voltage "y" represents a value of 1. Figure 3.1 illustrates this concept; as the router sends 1 byte of data to the switch via the cable connecting them, changes in the voltage of the signal are used to communicate values of 0 and 1.

> **EXAM TIP** Understanding the binary number system is very important for the CCNA exam. In future chapters of this volume, we will cover how to count in binary and how to convert between binary and other number systems like decimal and hexadecimal.

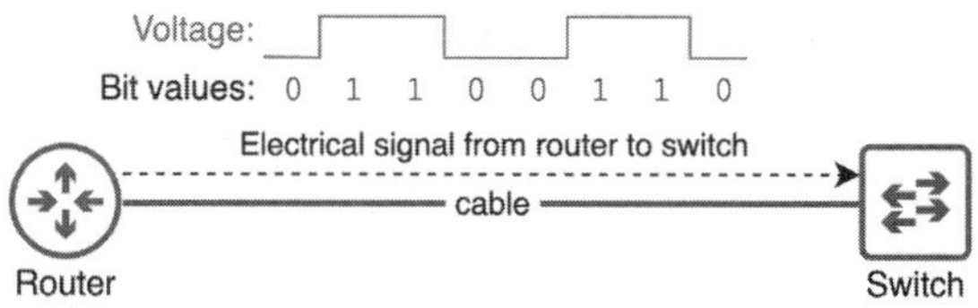

Figure 3.1 A router sends 1 byte of data to a switch. Changes in the voltage of the electric signal indicate values of 0 or 1.

We measure the speeds of network connections by how many bits can be transmitted per second over the connection. However, due to the incredible speeds of computer networks, we express these rates using larger units like *kilobits*, *megabits*, and *gigabits*. The following are some common units of measuring bits:

- 1 kilobit (kb) = 1,000 (thousand) bits
- 1 megabit (Mb) = 1,000,000 (million) bits (1,000 kilobits)
- 1 gigabit (Gb) = 1,000,000,000 (billion) bits (1,000 megabits)
- 1 terabit (Tb) = 1,000,000,000,000 (trillion) bits (1,000 gigabits)

Network speeds are then stated as *X bits per second* (bps)—for example, 56 kilobits per second (56 kbps), 100 megabits per second (100 Mbps), 10 gigabits per second (10 Gbps), 1 terabit per second (1 Tbps), etc.

1,000 or 1,024 bits?

There is some confusion over whether 1 kilobit is 1,000 bits or 1,024 bits, 1 megabit is 1,000 kilobits or 1,024 kilobits, etc. The definitions listed previously are correct, and they are the terms you should know for the CCNA. The 1,024 values are a result of the binary (base-2) number system; 2^{10} is equal to 1,024. The correct terms for the base-2 values are

- 1 kibibit (1,024 bits)
- 1 mebibit (1,024 kibibits)
- 1 gibibit (1,024 mebibits)
- 1 tebibit (1,024 gibibits)

3.3 Copper UTP connections

The CCNA requires you to know about two kinds of wired connections: those using copper cables and those using fiber-optic cables. First, we will look at copper cables. This is the kind of network cable most often called an *Ethernet cable*, although the Ethernet standard makes use of both copper and fiber-optic cable types. Before we examine a copper Ethernet cable itself, let's look at the connector at the end of the cable as well as the port it connects to on a network device, both of which are pictured in figure 3.2.

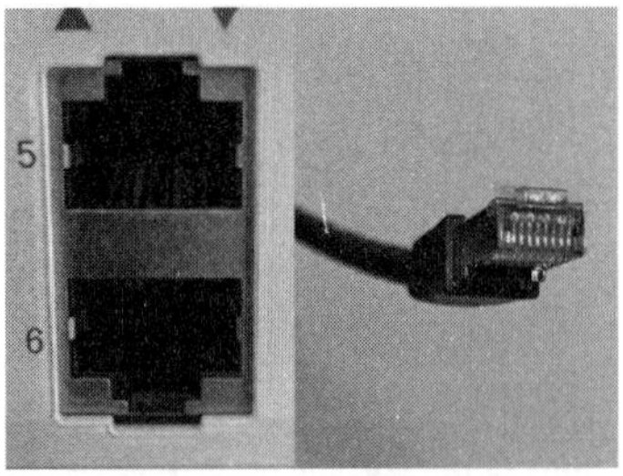

Figure 3.2
Two 8P8C ports on a Cisco switch (left) and an 8P8C connector on a copper UTP network cable (right)

Figure 3.2 shows the *8 position 8 contact* (8P8C) connector of an Ethernet cable on the right. The name refers to the fact that there are eight pins on the connector: one for each of the eight wires inside of the cable. These connectors allow the cable to connect to ports like the ones shown on the left of figure 3.2. Another name for this kind of connector is *RJ45* (RJ stands for *Registered Jack*); strictly speaking, this name is not correct, but it is commonly used when referring to Ethernet cables.

The type of cables used for these connections are called *unshielded twisted pair* (UTP) cables. There are also *shielded twisted pair* (STP) cables, but they are less common, so I will refer to them as UTP throughout this book. Each UTP cable contains eight individual wires inside, twisted together to make four pairs. Let's examine the meaning of UTP:

- *Unshielded*—The wires do not have a metallic shield around them. This shield can reduce *electromagnetic interference* (EMI) but is not present in UTP cables.
- *Twisted pair*—The eight wires in the cable are twisted together to form four pairs of two wires each. The twisting of the wires reduces EMI between the wires of each pair.

3.3.1 IEEE 802.3 standards (copper)

The IEEE defines various standards for Ethernet connections that support different speeds, cable types (copper or fiber-optic), and distances. Each standard is referred to by a few different names:

- One name is derived from the maximum supported transmission speed.
- The name of the IEEE *task group* that defined the standard is also used to refer to the standard itself. These names begin with IEEE 802.3, followed by a letter.
- The third name is an informal name given by the IEEE that indicates both the speed and cable type (standards for copper cabling end with *T*).

IEEE working groups and task groups

The IEEE assigns *working groups* to develop specific technologies. The two main working groups relevant to the CCNA are 802.3 (tasked with developing the Ethernet standard for wired networks) and 802.11 (wireless LANs, also known as Wi-Fi).

Within each working group, *task groups* are assigned to revise and continue developing upon the original standards. Each time a task group is formed, it is assigned a letter in serial order (i.e., 802.3a to 802.3z). Once all of the letters are used, an additional letter is added (i.e., 802.3aa to 802.3az). At the time of writing, 802.3dk is in development.

Table 3.1 lists some examples of Ethernet standards using copper cabling. Take note of the three names for each standard, as listed previously.

Table 3.1 A handful of Ethernet standards

Speed	Speed-derived name	IEEE task group	Informal name	Maximum cable length
10 Mbps	Ethernet	IEEE 802.3i	10BASE-T	100 m
100 Mbps	Fast Ethernet	IEEE 802.3u	100BASE-T	100 m
1 Gbps	Gigabit Ethernet	IEEE 802.3ab	1000BASE-T	100 m
10 Gbps	10 Gig Ethernet	IEEE 802.3an	10GBASE-T	100 m

EXAM TIP For the purpose of the CCNA exam, there is no need to memorize the IEEE task group names associated with each standard. You should be aware of the *speed-derived* and *informal* names, however.

Each of these standards supports a maximum cable length of 100 meters. Attempts to use UTP cables longer than the listed maximum can result in signal attenuation and decreased performance. Maximum cable length can be a problem for copper UTP connections. As you'll see in section 3.4, increased maximum cable length is a major advantage of fiber-optic cables over copper UTP cables.

NOTE The cables used in the aforementioned Ethernet standards are not actually defined by the IEEE but rather by two other organizations: the *Electronic Industries Alliance* (EIA) and the *Telecommunications Industry Association* (TIA). So the name "Ethernet cable" isn't very accurate because the cables, although used by Ethernet, are not defined by IEEE 802.3.

The standards for these cables are given names like *Category 5*, which is often shortened to *Cat 5*. Table 3.2 lists some cable standards that can be used with the aforementioned Ethernet standards.

Table 3.2 Common UTP cable standards

Speed	Ethernet informal name	Cable name
10 Mbps	10BASE-T	Cat 3
100 Mbps	100BASE-T	Cat 5
1 Gbps	1000BASE-T	Cat 5e
10 Gbps	10GBASE-T	Cat 6a

3.3.2 *Straight-through and crossover cables*

Although these days all UTP cables used for network communications have four pairs of wires (eight wires), not all of the Ethernet standards use all four pairs of wires:

- 10BASE-T uses two pairs (four wires).
- 100BASE-T uses two pairs (four wires).
- 1000BASE-T uses four pairs (eight wires).
- 10GBASE-T uses four pairs (eight wires).

Each wire inside of the cable is connected to one of the eight pins of the 8P8C connector. For devices to communicate over these wire pairs, each wire pair forms an electrical circuit between the two connected devices. In 10BASE-T and 100BASE-T connections, it is very important to use the proper cable to ensure that the wires connect the pins on one end of the connection to the correct pins on the other end of the connection. To facilitate that, there are two kinds of cables we can use: *straight-through* and *crossover*. These cable types differ in which pins on one end of the cable connect to which pins on the other end of the cable.

STRAIGHT-THROUGH CABLES

10BASE-T and 100BASE-T use two wire pairs, one for each direction of communication. The two wire pairs are

- The pair connected to pins 1 and 2
- The pair connected to pins 3 and 6 (yes, it's 3 and 6, not 3 and 4)

This is shown in figure 3.3, in which a PC and a switch are connected via a UTP cable. Pins 1 and 2 on the PC connect to pins 1 and 2 on the switch. Likewise, pins 3 and 6 on the PC connect to pins 3 and 6 on the switch.

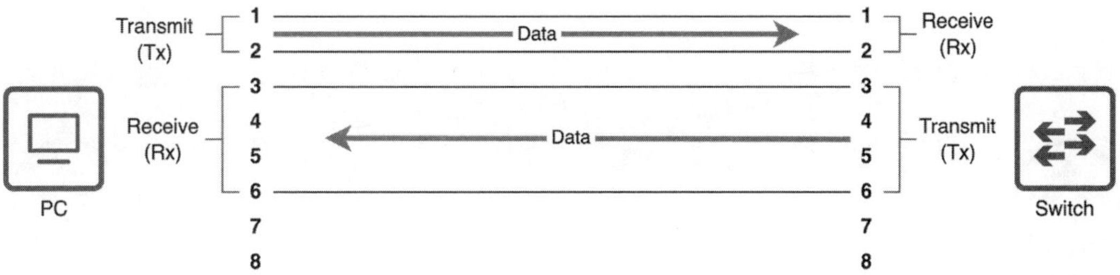

Figure 3.3 A PC and a switch connected via a straight-through cable

When devices are connected with a straight-through cable, a pin pair on one connector connects to the same pin pair on the other connector. This works well when connecting a PC to a switch. As shown in figure 3.3, PCs use the 1–2 pin pair to transmit data (this is often shortened to Tx), and switches use the 1–2 pin pair to receive data (often shortened to Rx). Likewise, switches use the 3–6 pin pair to transmit data, and PCs use the 3–6 pin pair to receive data.

However, what would happen if two switches were connected? Or two PCs? Or two routers? In these cases, using a straight-through cable would cause problems, as shown in figure 3.4.

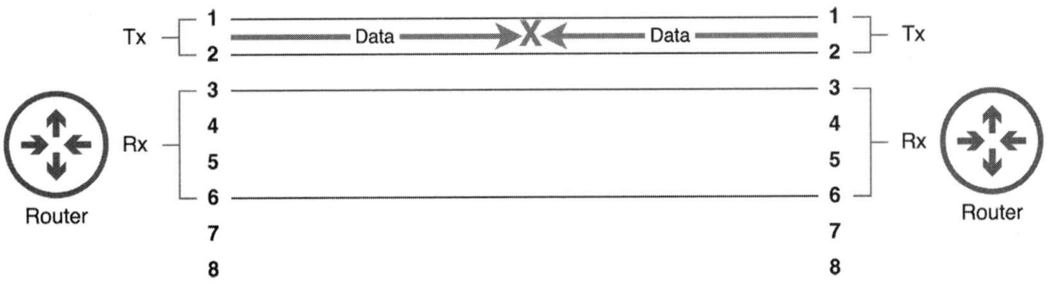

Figure 3.4 Two routers connected via a straight-through cable. Because both routers transmit data using the same pin pair, communication fails.

When two devices that transmit using the same pin pair are connected with a straight-through cable, they will not be able to communicate. The Tx pins of one device are connected to the Tx pins of the other device. For devices like this to communicate, they need a cable that is wired differently: a crossover cable.

CROSSOVER CABLES

A crossover cable connects opposite pin pairs; pins 1 and 2 on one end of the cable connect to pins 3 and 6 on the other end. This allows devices that transmit data on the same pin pair to communicate with each other. As figure 3.5 shows, devices that transmit using the same pin pair can communicate with each other when connected with a crossover cable.

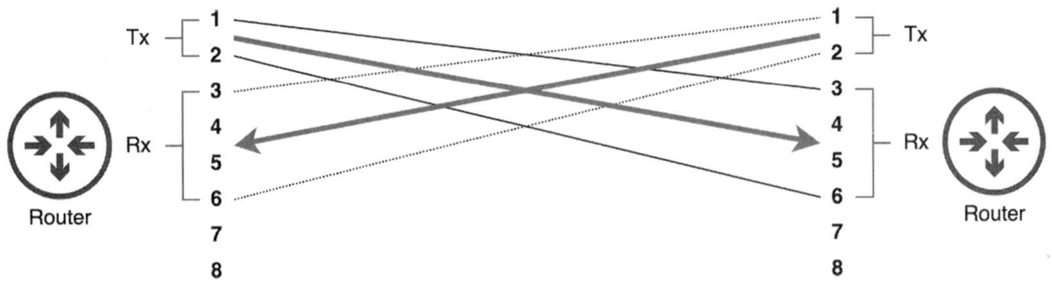

Figure 3.5 Two routers connected via a crossover cable. The Tx pin pair of one router connects to the Rx pin pair of the other router.

Table 3.3 lists some common network device types and which pins they use to transmit and receive data. To put it simply, switches transmit on pins 3 and 6 and receive on pins 1 and 2. All other devices are the opposite.

Table 3.3 Common device types and their Tx/Rx pin pairs

Device type	Transmit (Tx) pins	Receive (Rx) pins
Router	1 and 2	3 and 6
Firewall	1 and 2	3 and 6
PC/Server	1 and 2	3 and 6
Switch	3 and 6	1 and 2

NOTE Although 10BASE-T and 100BASE-T only use two wire pairs, there are still four wire pairs inside of the cable. The remaining two wire pairs are unused.

Auto MDI-X

Now that we've covered straight-through and crossover cables, I would like to share some good news: on modern networking equipment, we don't have to worry about using the correct cable type. That's because of a feature called *Auto Medium-Dependent Interface Crossover* (Auto MDI-X). Auto MDI-X allows a device to change which pins it will use to transmit and receive data depending on the device they are connected to. You should know about straight-through and crossover cables as a potential exam question, but in the field, you probably won't have to think about whether a cable is straight-through or crossover.

Figure 3.6 demonstrates this concept. The two routers are connected via a straight-through cable. Routers typically transmit data on the 1–2 pair and receive data on the 3–6 pair, but thanks to Auto MDI-X, the router on the right reverses that; it transmits data on the 3–6 pair and receives data on the 1–2 pair.

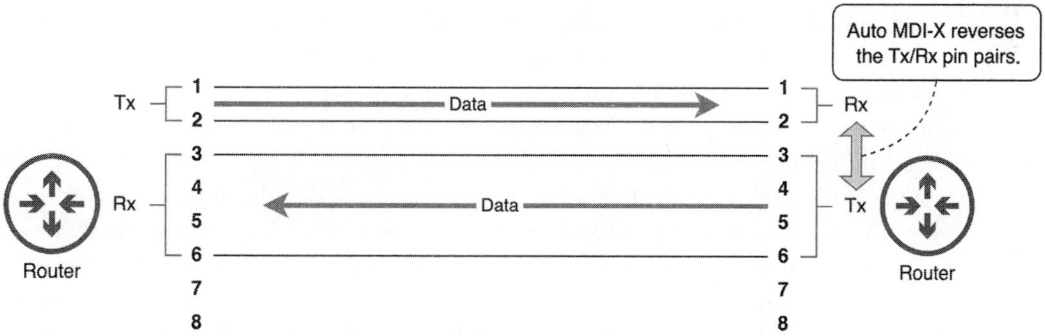

Figure 3.6 Two routers connected via a straight-through cable. The router on the right uses Auto MDI-X to adjust which pins it uses to transmit and receive data.

1000BASE-T and 10GBASE-T

1000BASE-T and 10GBASE-T take advantage of all eight wires in a cable, so a total of four wire pairs are used. The same 1–2 and 3–6 pin/wire pairs are used as in 10BASE-T and 100BASE-T. The remaining two pairs are the pair in positions 4 and 5 and the pair in positions 7 and 8. This is shown in figure 3.7.

Figure 3.7 Pin and wire pairs used on 1000BASE-T and 10GBASE-T connections. All eight wires of the cable are used.

Additionally, instead of a device using each pair of wires exclusively for transmitting or receiving data, each wire pair can be used for both purposes simultaneously.

If a crossover cable is used, the 1–2 and 3–6 pairs are crossed over as in 10BASE-T and 100BASE-T, and the new 4–5 and 7–8 are crossed over as well. However, thanks to Auto MDI-X, we no longer have to worry about selecting the proper cable type.

3.4 Fiber-optic connections

Copper UTP connections are still the most common type of connection within a LAN. Both the cables and the switch ports themselves are fairly inexpensive, and they are supported by nearly all modern devices that connect to a network. However, there is a major limitation that can make copper connections unfeasible in some cases: the maximum cable length of 100 meters. For connections between devices on the same floor of a building, 100 meters is usually more than enough, but for some connections between devices on separate floors, it might not suffice. And certainly, for connections between buildings and WAN connections, the next type of cabling is preferred: fiber-optic cabling.

Fiber-optic cables, instead of transmitting electrical signals along a copper wire, transmit light signals along a glass fiber. The glass fiber used is more flexible than you might think of when you imagine glass, but still, fiber-optic cables must be handled with care; a sharp bend in the cable can damage the glass fiber, rendering the cable unusable. Even if the glass fiber doesn't snap, bending the cable can cause light to leak out of the cable, resulting in a weakening of the signal.

3.4.1 The anatomy of a fiber-optic cable

A typical fiber-optic connection does not use a single cable but rather two: one for transmitting data and one for receiving data. These cables connect to a *Small Form-Factor Pluggable* (SFP) transceiver that is inserted into an SFP port on the device. SFP transceivers are modular and must be purchased separately from the device itself (and you'd probably be surprised at how much those little things cost).

Figure 3.8 shows a Cisco switch with a couple of SFP transceivers: one inserted into an SFP port and one on top of the switch. Notice that two cables connect to the SFP transceiver, not one. When connecting two devices with fiber-optic cables, it's important to connect the cables correctly: one device's transmitter must connect to the other device's receiver; otherwise, communication is not going to happen (similar to correctly selecting straight-through/crossover cables when connecting devices that don't support Auto MDI-X).

Figure 3.8 A Cisco switch with an SFP transceiver inserted into one of its SFP ports. An additional SFP is placed on top of the switch.

As shown in figure 3.9, there are a few layers to a fiber-optic cable. An outer jacket (4) and buffer (3) serve to protect and contain the inner components. A layer of reflective cladding (2) helps carry the light signal along the glass core (1). The core is a very thin glass fiber, although the thickness of the core depends on the type of cable.

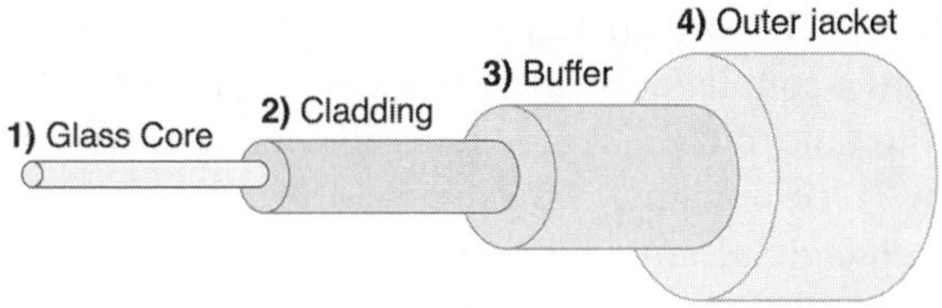

Figure 3.9 The typical structure of a fiber-optic cable. An outer jacket (4) and buffer (3) serve to protect and contain the inner components. A layer of reflective cladding (2) helps carry the light signal along the glass core (1).

All types of fiber-optic cabling can carry a signal farther than copper cabling, but even within the category of fiber-optic cabling, the maximum supported length can vary greatly. There are two main types of fiber-optic cabling: *multimode fiber* (MMF) and *single-mode fiber* (SMF). Figure 3.10 shows how light travels along MMF and SMF cables.

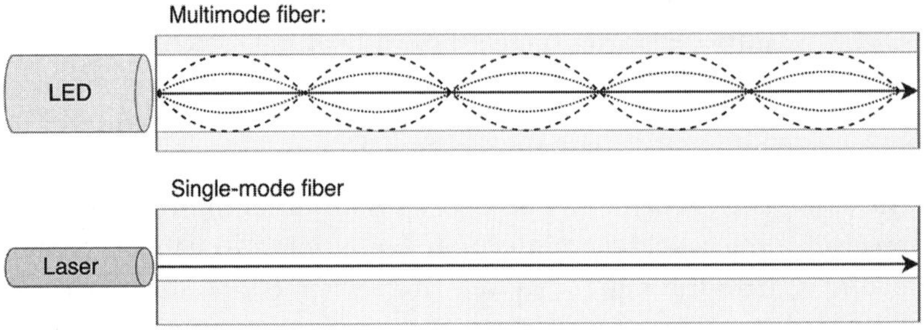

Figure 3.10 Light travels down an MMF cable at multiple angles *(modes)*, whereas light travels down SMF cables at a single angle.

MMF cables have a wider core than single-mode fiber cables. They are used in combination with LED transmitters that send light down the cable at multiple angles (*modes*), reflecting off of the cladding. MMF cables typically support maximum distances of several hundreds of meters.

SMF cables use a very narrow core in combination with laser transmitters that send light down the cable at a single angle. These laser transmitters are typically more expensive than the LED transmitters used by MMF cables. However, SMF cables also support much greater maximum distances: up to tens of kilometers.

3.4.2 *UTP vs. fiber*

Fiber-optic connections support much greater distances than copper UTP cables but at increased cost (largely due to expensive SFP transceivers). Both connection types are in common use in modern networks. UTP connections are most common for connections from switches to end hosts. In an office setting, there are generally switches on each floor, and the 100-meter maximum cable length is usually sufficient for end hosts to reach a switch on their floor. On the other hand, fiber-optic connections are more common for connections between network infrastructure—for example, connecting switches and routers that are located on separate floors or in separate buildings.

However, fiber cabling has a couple more advantages over copper UTP: one is that copper UTP cables are vulnerable to EMI. This is generally not a concern, but in environments with lots of electrical equipment, EMI can negatively affect the signals traveling along a UTP cable. A second disadvantage is that copper UTP cables can emit (*leak*) their signal outside of the cable. This leaked signal is quite weak, but it's possible that it can be detected and read, posing a security risk.

The most common considerations for whether to use copper UTP or fiber cabling are maximum distance, cost, and which connection type is supported by the devices to be connected. Most client devices (such as PCs) do not have SFP ports that can be used for fiber-optic connections, so a UTP connection is the only choice.

Summary

- Standards provide agreed-upon sets of rules for communication over networks.
- Ethernet is a family of standards defined by the Institute of Electrical and Electronics Engineers (IEEE) 802.3 working group. It defines standards for communication over physical wired connections.
- Computers compute and communicate using binary: 0s and 1s. Each binary digit is called a *bit*, and a group of 8 bits is called a *byte*.
- Network speeds are measured in bits per second using units like kilobit (1,000 bits), megabit (1,000 kilobits), gigabit (1,000 megabits), and terabit (1,000 gigabits).
- The most common connection type in Ethernet LANs uses copper unshielded twisted pair (UTP) cables. Unshielded means the wires in the cable do not have a metallic shield around them to protect against electromagnetic interference (EMI). Twisted pair means the eight wires in the cable are twisted together to form four pairs of two wires. The twisting of the wires reduces EMI between the wires of each pair.
- UTP cables use 8 position 8 contact (8P8C) connectors, also known as *Registered Jack-45* (RJ45).
- 10BASE-T and 100BASE-T connections use two of the four wire/pin pairs in a UTP cable, and 1000BASE-T and 10GBASE-T connections use all four pairs. All connection types support a maximum cable length of 100 meters.
- In 10BASE-T and 100BASE-T connections, different device types send and receive data using different pins of the connector; however, Auto MDI-X allows devices to automatically adjust which pins to use for which purpose.
- Fiber-optic cables send light signals down a glass fiber core and support much greater maximum distances than UTP cables.
- Single-mode fiber (SMF) cables support greater maximum distances (tens of kilometers) than multimode fiber (MMF) cables (hundreds of meters), but the laser-based small form factor pluggable (SFP) transceivers used by SMF connections are more expensive than the LED-based transceivers used by MMF connections.
- Fiber-optic connections are more expensive than copper UTP connections, largely due to the cost of the SFP transceivers.
- UTP connections are more common between end hosts and switches because of their lower cost and because the 100-meter maximum cable length is usually sufficient. Additionally, most client devices (such as PCs) only support UTP connections.
- Fiber-optic connections are more common between network infrastructure devices because of the increased maximum cable length. Network devices often connect to other network devices on different floors and in different buildings.

4 The TCP/IP networking model

This chapter covers

- What networking models are and why we need them
- The OSI model
- The TCP/IP model and its layers
- How each layer plays a role in moving data across a network
- Data encapsulation and de-encapsulation

In the previous chapter, we looked at Ethernet; specifically, we looked at the types of physical connections defined by the Ethernet standard. Ethernet also defines rules for how devices can communicate over those connections. However, Ethernet alone isn't sufficient for two computers to communicate over a network (e.g., for a PC to retrieve a web page from a server over the internet). Communicating over a network is a complex process, and it requires a variety of protocols, each of which performs specific functions and, when brought together, enables network communications.

In this chapter, we will look at a couple of models that define the various functions required to enable computers to communicate over a network: the *Open Systems Interconnection* (OSI) model and the *TCP/IP* model (named after two key protocols of the model: Transmission Control Protocol and Internet Protocol). TCP/IP is the model currently used by modern networks all over the world.

Neither of these models is explicitly listed as a CCNA exam topic. However, the information in this chapter is fundamental networking knowledge. We will examine the functions of various network protocols throughout the two volumes of this book, so it's important to have a framework to understand it all. That's the role of these networking models—to provide a framework to organize the various functions that make a network work.

The purpose of this chapter is to provide a high-level overview of how data travels from source to destination across a network. In the rest of this book, we will fill in the gaps regarding the exact mechanisms that make network communications possible, but first we need a framework.

4.1 Conceptual models of networking

Since the beginning of computer networking, there have been several attempts to create models that define the various functions necessary for computers to communicate with each other. Several of these models were *vendor-proprietary*, meaning they were created by a specific vendor (i.e., IBM) to be used by their products. However, the vendor-proprietary approach was not ideal; each vendor designed its own communication protocols, so enabling communication between different vendors' products was no simple task.

> **DEFINITION** A *protocol* is a set of rules defining how data should be communicated between devices in a network. Protocols can be thought of as the languages computers use to communicate; two computers using different networking protocols are like two humans speaking different languages—they won't be able to communicate.

These days we all enjoy the benefits of the alternative approach: *vendor neutral*. In a vendor-neutral model, with vendor-neutral protocols that can be used by devices of all kinds, we don't have to worry about whether an Apple MacBook will be able to access a website hosted on a Linux web server or whether a PC running Windows will be able to send an email that can be read on a smartphone running Android.

Networking models are frameworks that define the various functions needed to allow data to travel from source to destination over a network. These functions are typically divided into *layers*, with each layer describing a certain role required to enable network communications. Then, protocols can be designed to fill those roles.

Using layers allows for a modular design: at each layer of the model, there are several protocols that can fill the necessary roles of the layer. For example, in the previous chapter, we looked at some aspects of Ethernet (IEEE 802.3) and also briefly mentioned wireless LANs as defined by IEEE 802.11 (best known as Wi-Fi). Both protocols serve the same purpose: they define how data should be sent over a particular physical medium (UTP/fiber cables for Ethernet, radio waves for Wi-Fi). An email application on a computer doesn't need to care about whether a message will be sent over the network via a wired Ethernet connection or a wireless Wi-Fi connection; as long as the email application performs its role, it can expect the other layers to perform their roles as well.

There are two networking models that network professionals should be familiar with: OSI and TCP/IP. Although the TCP/IP model is the model used in modern networks, the OSI model has also had a large influence on how we think and talk about networks and is still considered core knowledge for anyone involved in networking (despite not being in use in modern networks).

4.2 The OSI reference model

The *Open Systems Interconnection reference model* is a conceptual model of networking developed by the *International Organization for Standardization* (ISO). Most people simply call it the OSI model.

> **International Organization for Standardization**
>
> The ISO publishes standards related to various aspects of technology. Looking at the name, you may wonder why it's abbreviated as ISO and not IOS. The ISO decided upon the abbreviation to have one shared abbreviation regardless of language. Rather than being an acronym for International Organization for Standardization, the organization states that ISO is derived from the Greek word *isos*, meaning "equal."

The OSI model defines seven layers, each with its own functions that contribute to the process of communicating over a network. Table 4.1 lists the seven layers of the OSI model.

Table 4.1 The seven layers of the OSI model

Layer	Name
7	Application
6	Presentation
5	Session
4	Transport
3	Network
2	Data Link
1	Physical

Because this chapter focuses on the TCP/IP model, we won't cover the role of each of the seven layers listed in table 4.1. The OSI model is a relic of the past that I don't recommend digging too deeply into unless you're interested in the history of how networks developed.

> **EXAM TIP** Although we will focus on the TCP/IP model in this chapter, the terminology of the OSI model is still widely used, so it's worth remembering the seven layers and their names. Most students use a mnemonic to help with this: for example, "Please Do Not Teach Students Pointless Acronyms," using the first letter of each layer's name from Layers 1 to 7.

4.3 The TCP/IP model

The TCP/IP model was born out of research and development funded by the US Department of Defense (DOD) Defense Advanced Research Projects Agency (DARPA). It was then called the ARPANET reference model, but it has since evolved into the *Internet Protocol Suite*, which was defined in *Request for Comments* (RFC) 1122. RFCs are documents published by the Internet Engineering Task Force (IETF) to define standard protocols for the internet. Some more common names for this model are the TCP/IP suite, TCP/IP model, or just TCP/IP. TCP and IP are two of the foundational protocols included in the model, so they are often used to refer to it.

> **RFCs and the IETF**
>
> The IETF is an organization that defines the standard protocols used by the internet. RFCs are the documents published by the IETF that define these protocols. Many of these documents are informational or experimental and sometimes humorous (e.g., check out RFC 1149 at https://datatracker.ietf.org/doc/html/rfc1149, which describes how to send network messages using birds).
>
> However, some RFCs go on to be recognized as *Internet Standards*; these are the RFCs that define the protocols that make up the TCP/IP model. For example, TCP, IP, and other well-known protocols like HTTPS (which you'll see at the beginning of the previous URL I copied) are Internet Standards.

The TCP/IP model as defined in RFC 1122 has four layers; however, network engineers typically reference a five-layer TCP/IP model. The five-layer version of the model, as indicated by the thick border in table 4.2, is what we will be using in this book. The table lists the layers of the TCP/IP model, their equivalent OSI model layers, and some example protocols that belong to each layer of the model.

Table 4.2 The TCP/IP model

OSI model	Four-layer TCP/IP model	Five-layer TCP/IP model	Example protocols
Application	Application	Application	HTTP
Presentation			HTTPS
Session			FTP
			SSH
Transport	Transport	Transport	TCP
			UDP
Network	Internet	Network	IPv4
			IPv6
Data Link	Link	Data Link	Ethernet
			802.11 (Wi-Fi)
Physical		Physical	

NOTE The similar layers of the OSI model and TCP/IP model are not entirely equivalent; although they have similarities, they are two independent models.

As table 4.2 shows, instead of the three upper layers (Application, Presentation, and Session) of the OSI model, TCP/IP uses a single layer called the Application Layer. Additionally, in the four-layer version of the TCP/IP model, the concerns of the bottom two layers of the five-layer version are addressed by a single layer called the Link Layer. However, for the purpose of the CCNA and understanding networking, the five-layer model is generally more useful, and it is the one we will refer to throughout this book.

The example protocols listed in table 4.2 are some of the protocols we will cover in this book; they are just a few of the protocols you should know for the CCNA exam. I included them in the table for reference, but we will cover how they function in the rest of this book. In this chapter, we will focus on understanding the role of each layer of the TCP/IP model.

EXAM TIP The layers of the TCP/IP model can be referred to by their names or their numbers: the Physical Layer is Layer 1, the Data Link Layer is Layer 2, the Network Layer is Layer 3, the Transport Layer is Layer 4, and the Application Layer is Layer 7. As I mentioned previously, the terminology of the OSI model is still widely used (for better or for worse!), so even when referring to the TCP/IP model, the Application Layer is typically called Layer 7 rather than Layer 5 or 4.

4.3.1 *The layers of the TCP/IP model*

Each layer of the TCP/IP model provides an essential function in enabling computers to communicate over a network. The end goal is for an application on one computer to be able to communicate with an application on another computer over a network (e.g., a PC's web browser communicating with a web server). Figure 4.1 demonstrates this process; a PC (PC1) accesses a web page hosted on a server (SRV1). As we examine each layer of the TCP/IP model in the following pages, we will see how the layers work together to enable this communication.

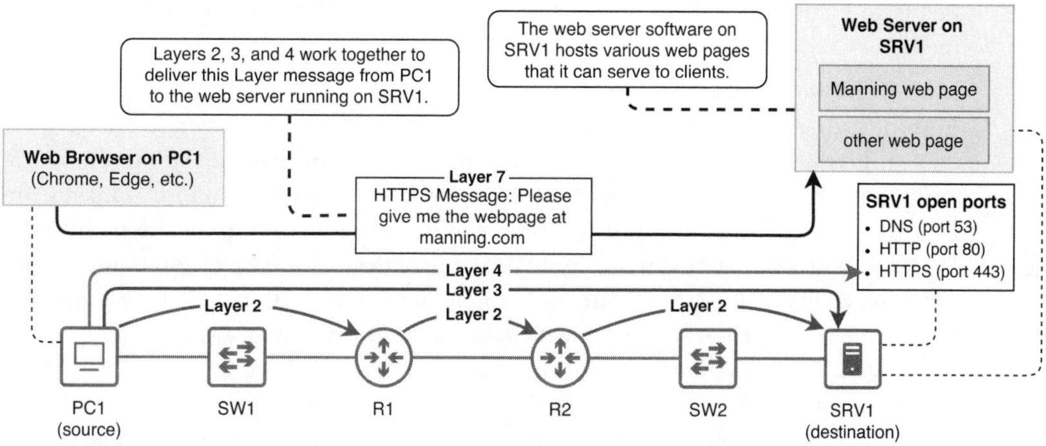

Figure 4.1 A web browser on PC1 uses a Layer 7 protocol (HTTPS) to request a web page from the web server on SRV1. Layers 2, 3, and 4 work together to deliver the message to the appropriate application on SRV1. Layer 1 is the medium over which the communication occurs.

The functions defined by each layer of the TCP/IP model include

- Physical specifications, such as cables and radio waves
- Communication between intermediate nodes in the path to the destination
- End-to-end communication from the original source node to the final destination node
- Addressing messages to a specific application on the destination node
- How an application should interface with the network

Now let's examine each layer of the TCP/IP model one by one to see how they enable network communications. The goal of this chapter is to provide a framework we can build upon in the rest of this book with details of how the different protocols of each layer fulfill their roles.

LAYER 1: THE PHYSICAL LAYER

The Physical Layer is fairly self-explanatory; it defines the physical requirements for transmitting data (a series of bits) from one node to another. Those bits could be encoded as electrical signals traveling along a copper cable, light signals on a fiber-optic cable, or radio waves in a wireless connection.

We covered this in chapter 3: IEEE 802.3 (Ethernet) and IEEE 802.11 (Wi-Fi) both define specifications at the Physical Layer. For example, Ethernet defines connector and cable types, how data should be encoded into electrical (or light) signals, and countless other minutiae about how to communicate over UTP and fiber-optic cables. Likewise, Wi-Fi defines what radio frequencies should be used for wireless LAN communication, how radio waves should be modulated to encode data, etc.

To summarize, the Physical Layer of the TCP/IP model defines the physical requirements to enable a series of bits to travel from one node to another over a physical medium.

Layer 2: The Data Link Layer

Ethernet and Wi-Fi do not only define physical specifications; they also specify how data should be addressed and sent to another node connected to the same physical medium within a LAN. The Data Link Layer's job is to prepare data for transmission over that physical medium so it can be received by the next node in the path to the final destination. That next node could be the final destination itself or the next router in the path. The journey from one node to the next in the path is called a *hop*, and the job of the Data Link Layer is to provide *hop-to-hop* delivery of messages.

Figure 4.2 demonstrates the concept of network hops. PC1 sends a message to SRV1, perhaps a request to access a file hosted on the server. For PC1's message to reach SRV1, it must make three hops through the network: from PC1 to R1, from R1 to R2, and from R2 to SRV1. The Data Link Layer's job is to forward the message from one hop to the next until the message reaches the destination host: SRV1. Notice that a message traveling through a switch does not count as a hop. We will examine why this is when we look at Ethernet LAN switching in chapter 6.

> **NOTE** PC1, R1, R2, and SRV1 are examples of *hostnames*. A hostname is a name used to identify each device in the network. The hostname of each device in figure 4.2 follows the pattern I will use throughout this book: PC*X* for PCs, SW*X* for switches, R*X* for routers, and SRV*X* for servers.

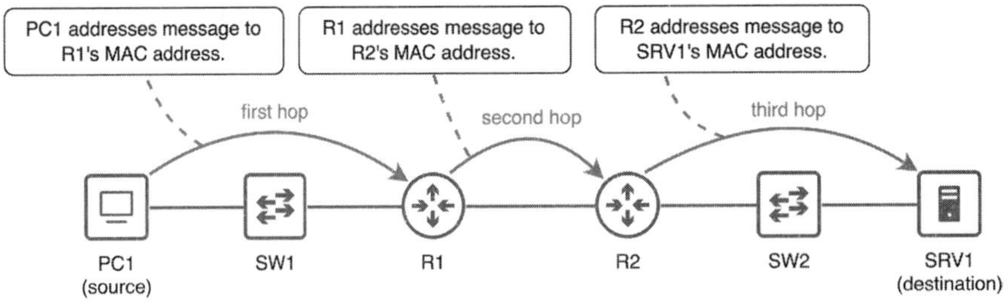

Figure 4.2 TCP/IP Layer 2. A message sent from PC1 to SRV1 takes three hops through the network: from PC1 to R1, from R1 to R2, and from R2 to SRV1. At each hop, the message is addressed to the next hop's MAC address. A message traveling through a switch does not count as a hop.

The Data Link Layer achieves this hop-to-hop delivery by using *media access control* (MAC) addresses, a kind of network address assigned to each port of a device. At each hop, the message is sent to the MAC address of the next hop. In the first hop, PC1 addresses the message to R1's MAC address. In the second hop, R1 addresses the message to R2's MAC address. In the final hop, R2 addresses the message to SRV1's MAC address.

> **NOTE** The roles of SW1 and SW2 may seem unclear in figure 4.2. As covered in chapter 2, the role of a switch is to provide many ports for end hosts to connect to the LAN. For the sake of avoiding clutter, I only show one end host connected to each switch (PC1 to SW1 and SRV1 to SW2). However, in reality, there could be 40+ end hosts connected to each of them. In chapter 6, we will examine how switches function.

Layer 3: The Network Layer

We just looked at how the Data Link Layer is used to forward a message from hop to hop until it reaches the final destination. At each hop, the message is sent to the MAC address of the next hop. However, we still need a way for the original source host to address the message to the final destination host. That is the role of the Network Layer: end-to-end delivery.

The type of address used at the Network Layer is the Internet Protocol (IP) address. Chances are you've heard of IP addresses before, although you might be unsure about how they work. We will cover IP addresses in chapter 7. Figure 4.3 shows how PC1 addresses a message to SRV1 by addressing it to SRV1's IP address. The destination IP address of the message remains the same throughout the journey, whereas the destination MAC address is different at each hop.

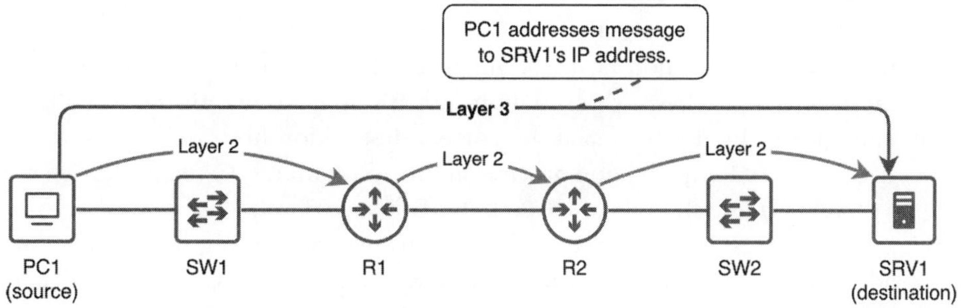

Figure 4.3 TCP/IP Layer 3. PC1 addresses a message to SRV1's IP address. Layer 3 is responsible for the end-to-end delivery of the message, whereas Layer 2 is responsible for the hop-to-hop delivery. The destination MAC address of the message changes at each hop, but the destination IP address remains the same throughout the journey.

IPv4 and IPv6

There are two versions of IP in use today: IP version 4 (IPv4) and IP version 6 (IPv6). Network engineers must be familiar with both, and both are part of the CCNA exam. IPv4 and IPv6 use different address formats. The following is an example of an IPv4 address and an IPv6 address:

- IPv4 address: 203.0.113.255
- IPv6 address: 2001:db8:1:1:2fe3:1:32a:af01

Although IPv4 has been the dominant version of IP for a long time, IPv6 is steadily gaining popularity. In recent years, IPv6's adoption has accelerated as the number of available IPv4 addresses is running out. We will cover both address types in this book.

Understanding how Layers 2 and 3 work together to deliver a message to its destination is a fundamental concept you must understand for the CCNA exam. In this chapter, I provide a high-level overview of the concepts; we will review these concepts and dig deeper in later chapters of this volume. At this point, it is enough to know the following points:

- Layer 2 uses MAC addresses to provide hop-to-hop delivery of messages.
- Layer 3 uses IP addresses to provide end-to-end delivery of messages.
- Layers 2 and 3 work together to allow a message to travel through the network to its final destination.
- The destination IP address of a message remains the same throughout the journey, whereas the destination MAC address is different at each hop.

LAYER 4: THE TRANSPORT LAYER

Layers 2 and 3 work together to deliver a message from the source host across a network to the destination host. You might think that's the end of the story because the message has reached its destination, but it's actually not all the way there. It's not enough for the data to reach the correct destination host; we need a way to address data to a specific application process on the destination host (e.g., a service running on a server). That is the role of Layer 4, the Transport Layer.

Like Layers 2 and 3, Layer 4 also uses its own addressing scheme: *port numbers*. By addressing a message to a particular port, you can send messages to a particular application process on the destination host. Computers run many different applications simultaneously, so this is a very important function. For example, a PC can simultaneously run an online game, a web browser with various tabs that each access a different website, an antivirus application that communicates with an external server for updates, and countless other applications. Port numbers allow the PC to ensure that data it receives from the network reaches the proper destination process.

> **NOTE** Layer 4 port numbers are not related to the physical ports on a device that we connect cables to (which are an aspect of Layer 1, the Physical Layer). Same name, different concept.

Figure 4.4 demonstrates this concept. Layers 2 and 3 work together to deliver PC1's message to SRV1, and Layer 4 delivers the message to the appropriate application process on SRV1. SRV1 is a server that provides a few services to clients in the network. It is a *name server* using the *Domain Name System* (DNS) to convert website names to IP addresses for clients (that's what happens when you type manning.com into a web browser). It is also a web server that uses *Hypertext Transfer Protocol* (HTTP) and *Hypertext Transfer Protocol Secure* (HTTPS) to allow clients to access the websites it hosts. DNS, HTTP, and HTTPS are Layer 7 (Application Layer) protocols, and they each accept messages using a different Layer 4 port number.

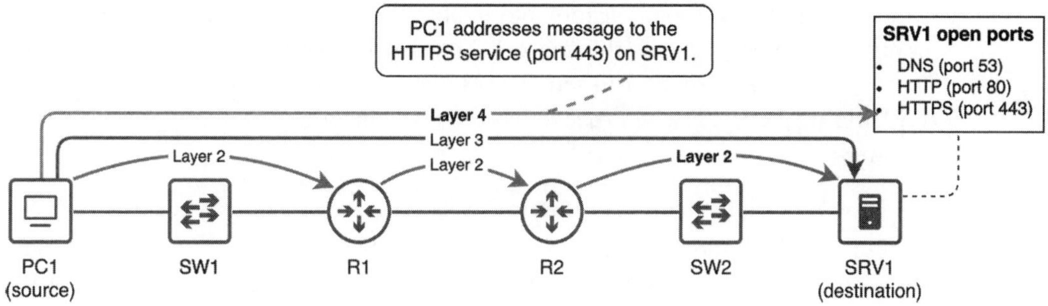

Figure 4.4 Layers 2 and 3 work together to deliver PC1's message to SRV1. At Layer 4, PC1 addresses the message to port 443, which is used by the HTTPS protocol. Three ports are open on SRV1 (53, 80, 443), meaning it will accept messages addressed to any of those ports.

> **NOTE** All three addresses—the MAC address (Layer 2), the IP address (Layer 3), and the port number (Layer 4)—are included in the same message. We will examine how this works in section 4.3.2.

TCP and UDP

The two most common Layer 4 protocols are *Transmission Control Protocol* (TCP)—the "TCP" in TCP/IP—and *User Datagram Protocol* (UDP). Both protocols allow computers to address messages to specific application services on the destination host, but there are several differences between the two.

For example, TCP implements checks to ensure that each message reaches its destination and is used by Application Layer protocols such as HTTP and HTTPS (used for accessing websites). UDP, on the other hand, takes a "send it and forget it" approach; it doesn't check to ensure that every message reaches the destination. UDP is used by *Voice over IP* (VoIP) protocols—used for phone calls—and live video streaming protocols, among others. We will cover TCP and UDP in chapter 22 of this book.

Layer 7: The Application Layer

The Application Layer is the interface between the applications running on a computer and the network. Using Layer 7 protocols, an application running on a computer can prepare a message to be sent over the network. This message could be, for example, a request from a web browser to retrieve a web page that is hosted on a web server. Layers 2, 3, and 4 are then responsible for delivering that message to the appropriate application on the destination computer.

> **NOTE** Although the TCP/IP model only has five layers (or four, in the original definition), Layer 7 is the most common term used for the Application Layer, so that is what I will use throughout this book. That is due to the influence of the OSI model, as mentioned previously.

Layer 7 protocols such as HTTPS are not user applications themselves; rather, they provide services for those applications to enable them to communicate with applications on other computers over the network. Figure 4.1 shows the complete process that enables a web browser on PC1 to send a message to request a web page from the web server running on SRV1. The process that the message goes through to reach SRV1 is as follows:

- *Layer 7*—PC1's web browser uses HTTPS to request the web page.
- *Layer 4*—PC1 addresses the message to port 443, which is used by the HTTPS protocol. This ensures that the message reaches the correct application on SRV1.
- *Layer 3*—PC1 addresses the message to the IP address of SRV1, and the destination IP address of the message remains the same as the message travels from PC1 across the network to SRV1.
- *Layer 2*—PC1 addresses the message to the next hop in the path to SRV1, which is R1. After receiving the message, R1 forwards it to the next hop (R2) by addressing the message to R2's MAC address. Finally, R2 forwards the message to the final destination (SRV1) by addressing the message to SRV1's MAC address. Unlike the destination IP address of the message, the destination MAC address is changed at each hop.

> **DEFINITION** To *forward* a message is to send it to the next node in the path to the destination, whether that is the final destination node itself or the next router in the path to the destination. In later chapters of this volume, we will examine how routers and switches make forwarding decisions to deliver messages to the correct destination.

4.3.2 Data encapsulation and de-encapsulation

In this section, we'll see how the layers of the TCP/IP model work together to allow computers to communicate with each other. By now, you should be familiar with the basic purpose of each layer of the TCP/IP model:

- *Layer 7 (Application)*—The interface between applications and the network
- *Layer 4 (Transport)*—Provides application-to-application delivery of messages
- *Layer 3 (Network)*—Provides end-to-end delivery of messages
- *Layer 2 (Data Link)*—Provides hop-to-hop delivery of messages
- *Layer 1 (Physical)*—The physical medium over which communication happens

DATA ENCAPSULATION

The process a host goes through to send data is a five-step process. It begins with the Layer 7 protocol preparing some data to be sent. In the second step, a Layer 4 protocol then adds a *header* to that data addressed to a certain port.

> **DEFINITION** A *header* is supplemental data added to the front of a message that is to be transmitted over a network. A protocol's header contains the data used by that protocol. For example, a Layer 4 protocol will include a destination port number, as well as other information.

In the third step, the message is passed to Layer 3, which adds its own header to that data. This header will be addressed to the IP address of the destination host. In the fourth step, the message will then be passed to Layer 2, which adds both a header and a trailer.

> **DEFINITION** A *trailer* is also supplemental data added to a message that is to be transmitted over a network. Whereas a *header* is added to the beginning of a message, a *trailer* is added to the end. The Ethernet trailer contains a small block of data used to check for errors in the message. For example, errors can occur during transmission as a result of electromagnetic interference.

At Layer 2, the message is addressed to the next-hop device. Finally, in the fifth step, the host will transmit the bits over the physical medium, such as a UTP cable. The process of adding headers (and trailers) to data before sending it over a network is called *encapsulation*. To summarize that process:

1. The Application Layer protocol prepares data.
2. Layer 4 encapsulates the data with a header addressed to a port number on the destination host.
3. Layer 3 encapsulates the data with a header addressed to the IP address of the destination host.

4. Layer 2 encapsulates the data with a header addressed to the MAC address of the next hop. It also encapsulates the data with a trailer, used to check for errors.
5. The host transmits the bits of data over the physical medium (e.g., encoded as electrical signals over a UTP cable).

Figure 4.5 demonstrates the five-step process of encapsulation and transmission.

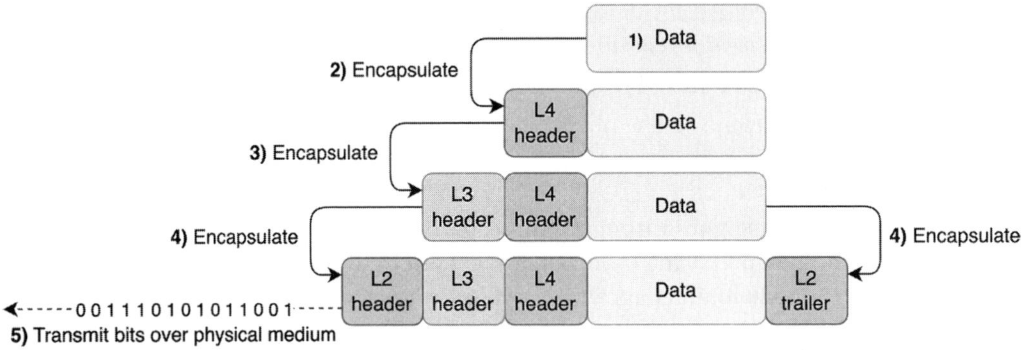

Figure 4.5 The five-step process of encapsulating and transmitting data: (1) the Application Layer protocol prepares some data, (2) Layer 4 encapsulates the data with a header, (3) Layer 3 encapsulates the data with a header, (4) Layer 2 encapsulates the data with a header and trailer, and (5) the host transmits the bits over the physical medium (i.e., a UTP cable).

NOTE The Layer 2 header is the beginning of the message; it is the first part sent. The Layer 2 trailer is the end of the message; it is the last part sent.

DATA DE-ENCAPSULATION

When the destination host receives the message, it goes through the opposite process: *de-encapsulation.* In the de-encapsulation process, the host receiving the message inspects the information in each header/trailer and then removes them until it gets to the data inside. Like encapsulating and transmitting a message, receiving and de-encapsulating a message can also be summarized into five steps, summarized as follows (also see figure 4.6):

1. The destination host receives the message.
2. It inspects the Layer 2 header and trailer, removes them, and passes the message to Layer 3.
3. It inspects the Layer 3 header, removes it, and passes the message to Layer 4.
4. It inspects the Layer 4 header, removes it, and sends the data to the appropriate application.
5. The application receives and processes the data.

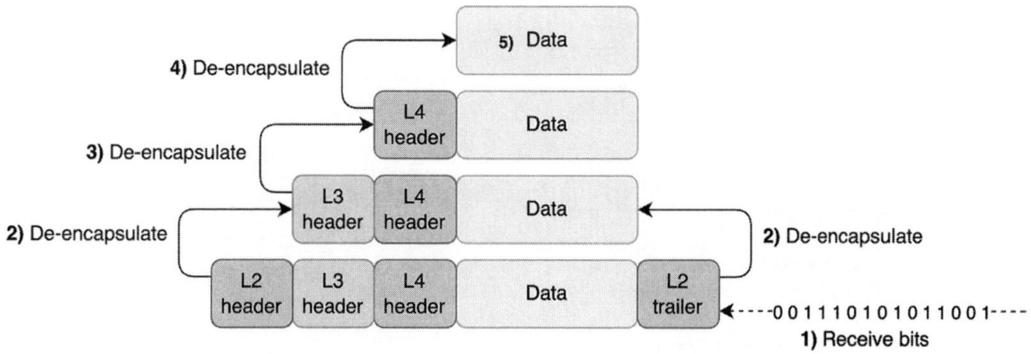

Figure 4.6 The five-step process of receiving and de-encapsulating data: (1) the destination host receives bits (the message), (2) the Layer 2 header/trailer is inspected and removed, (3) the Layer 3 header is inspected and removed, (4) the Layer 4 header is inspected and removed, and (5) the data is received and processed by the application.

Protocol data units

At each stage in the encapsulation/de-encapsulation process, there is a name given to the message:

- The combination of data and a Layer 4 header is called a *segment.*
- The combination of a segment and a Layer 3 header is called a *packet.*
- The combination of a packet and a Layer 2 header/trailer is called a *frame.*

We can also use an alternative term to describe the message at each stage—*protocol data unit* (PDU):

- A segment is a Layer 4 PDU (L4PDU).
- A packet is a Layer 3 PDU (L3PDU).
- A frame is a Layer 2 PDU (L2PDU).

The contents of each PDU (everything encapsulated by that layer's header/trailer) are called the *payload.* So, a frame's payload is a packet, a packet's payload is a segment, and a segment's payload is the application data. Figure 4.7 illustrates the different PDUs and their payloads.

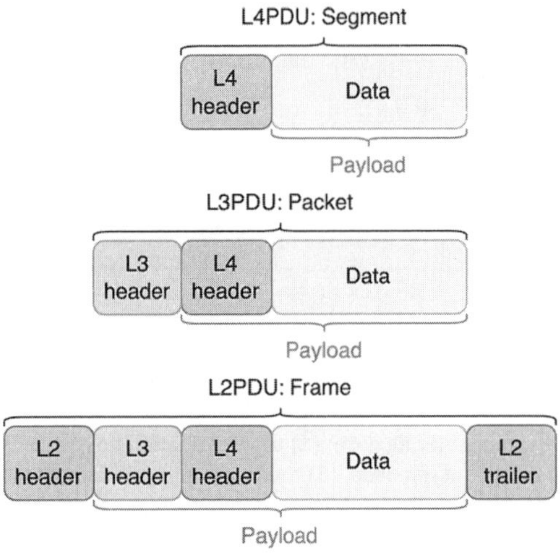

Figure 4.7 Application data encapsulated in a Layer 4 header is a segment (L4PDU); a segment encapsulated in a Layer 3 header is a packet (L3PDU); and a packet encapsulated in a Layer 2 header/trailer is a frame (L2PDU). The encapsulated contents of each PDU are that PDU's payload.

ADJACENT-LAYER AND SAME-LAYER INTERACTIONS

Within a computer, each layer of the TCP/IP model provides a service for the layer above it, called *adjacent-layer interaction.* Following is a summary of the interactions between adjacent layers of the TCP/IP model:

- Layer 4 provides a service to Layer 7 by delivering data to the appropriate application on the destination host.
- Layer 3 provides a service to Layer 4 by delivering segments to the correct destination host.
- Layer 2 provides a service to Layer 3 by delivering packets to the next hop.
- Layer 1 provides a service to Layer 2 by providing a physical medium for frames to travel over.

There is also a related concept called *same-layer interaction.* This refers to the communications between the same layer on different computers. Same-layer interactions work like this:

- Application data from one computer is sent to an application on another computer.
- When data is encapsulated with a Layer 4 header, the segment is addressed to Layer 4 of the destination host, where the information in the header will be inspected.
- When a segment is encapsulated with a Layer 3 header, the packet is addressed to Layer 3 of the destination host, where the information in the header will be inspected.

- When a packet is encapsulated with a Layer 2 header and trailer, the frame is addressed to Layer 2 of the next hop, where the information in the header and trailer will be inspected.
- Signals sent out of a physical port of one device are received by a physical port of another device.

Figure 4.8 illustrates these adjacent-layer interactions between different layers on the same computer (on Host A and on Host B), and same-layer interactions between different computers that are communicating with each other (between Host A and Host B).

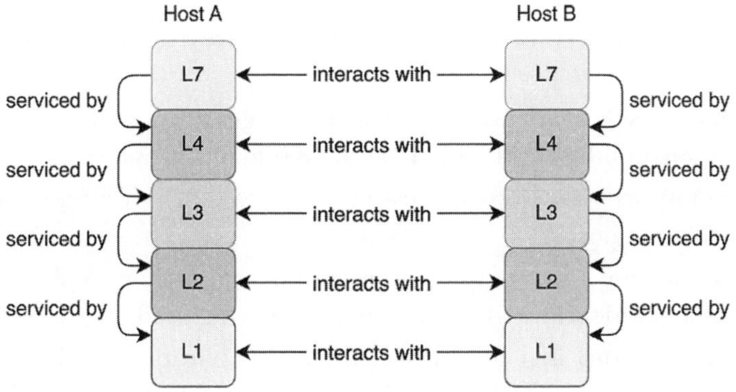

Figure 4.8 Each layer on a host provides services for the layer above it; this is called adjacent-layer interaction. When two hosts communicate, each layer on one host communicates with the same layer on the other host; this is called same-layer interaction.

Summary

- Networking models provide frameworks to define the functions necessary to enable network communications.
- Networking models are divided into layers; each layer describes a necessary function for network communications and includes multiple protocols that can fulfill the layer's role.
- The Open Systems Interconnection Reference (OSI) model is a networking model that influenced how we think and talk about networks but is not in use today.
- The OSI model has seven layers: (1) Physical, (2) Data Link, (3) Network, (4) Transport, (5) Session, (6) Presentation, and (7) Application.
- The Internet Protocol Suite (TCP/IP) model) is the networking model used in modern networks and is named after two of its key protocols: Transmission Control Protocol (TCP) and Internet Protocol (IP).
- The original TCP/IP model has four layers, but a more popular version has five: (1) Physical, (2) Data Link, (3) Network, (4) Transport, and (5) Application (called Layer 7, not Layer 5).

- Layer 1 (Physical) defines physical requirements for transmitting data, such as ports, connectors, and cables, and how data should be encoded into electrical/light signals.
- Layer 2 (Data Link) is responsible for hop-to-hop delivery of messages. A *hop* is the journey from one node in the network to the next in the path to the final destination.
- Layer 2 uses media access control (MAC) addresses to address messages to the next hop.
- Layer 3 (Network) is responsible for end-to-end delivery of messages, from the source host to the destination host.
- Layer 3 uses Internet Protocol (IP) addresses to address messages to the destination host.
- The destination MAC address of a message changes at each hop in the path to the destination, but the destination IP address remains the same.
- Layer 4 (Transport) is used to address messages to the appropriate application on the destination host.
- Layer 4's addressing scheme uses port numbers (not related to physical ports). The port number identifies the Layer 7 protocol being used.
- Layer 7 (Application) is the interface between applications and the network. Layer 7 protocols such as Hypertext Transfer Protocol Secure (HTTPS) are not applications themselves but provide services for applications to enable them to communicate over the network.
- A host *encapsulates* application data with a Layer 4 header, Layer 3 header, and Layer 2 header/trailer before being transmitted over the physical medium (cable or radio waves).
- After a message is received by a host, the host *de-encapsulates* it by inspecting and removing the Layer 2 header and trailer, inspecting and removing the Layer 3 header, inspecting and removing the Layer 4 header, and finally processing the data in the message.
- The contents encapsulated inside each *protocol data unit* (PDU) are its *payload.*
- The combination of data and a Layer 4 header is called a *segment* (L4PDU).
- The combination of a segment and a Layer 3 header is called a *packet* (L3PDU).
- The combination of a packet and a Layer 2 header/trailer is called a *frame* (L2PDU).
- Within a computer, each layer provides a service for the layer above it; this is called *adjacent-layer interaction.*
- Communication between the same layer on different computers is called *same-layer interaction.*

5 The Cisco IOS CLI

This chapter covers

- The interfaces used to configure network devices
- How to connect to the CLI of a Cisco device via the console port
- Navigating between modes of the Cisco IOS command hierarchy
- Viewing and saving a device's configuration files
- Password-protecting a Cisco IOS device

This chapter is a break from the networking theory of the previous chapter; it's time to get hands-on with Cisco routers and switches. Understanding the theory of networking is absolutely essential, but networking is also a skill that must be practiced, and that means configuring network devices.

In the CCNA exam topics list, you will find a few different verbs, such as *explain X*, *describe Y*, and *identify Z*, indicating that Cisco expects you to have a theoretical understanding of the listed concepts and how they work. However, there are also many exam topics that state *configure X* or *configure and verify Y*. For these topics, in addition to having a theoretical understanding of their concepts, you must be able to configure them on Cisco network devices and verify their operations.

As an introduction to making configuration changes to a Cisco device and saving those changes, in this chapter, we will touch on exam topic 5.3: Configure and verify device access control using local passwords. However, this chapter is not specifically aimed at one of the CCNA exam topics but rather lays a necessary foundation for all of the exam topics that require you to configure and verify various protocols.

5.1 Shells: GUI and CLI

A *shell* is a computer program that allows a user to interact with the computer. It's the interface between the computer and the user, and it's called a *shell* because it's the outer layer of the operating system. To configure a Cisco router or switch, you use a shell to give commands to the device. In this section, we will look at the two types of shells we will use in this book.

5.1.1 GUI and CLI

There are two main kinds of shells: *graphical user interface* (GUI, pronounced "G-U-I" or "gooey") and *command-line interface* (CLI). Let's examine these two types.

GRAPHICAL USER INTERFACES

A GUI allows a user to manipulate the computer via a graphical interface. Regardless of your degree of experience or inexperience with computers, I'm certain you've used a GUI before. If you have a Windows PC, the GUI is what you're interacting with when you open, close, and move windows, or when you open the Start menu to search for a program, etc. This is the *Windows shell*. If you have a smartphone, you use a GUI to interact with the phone and its apps.

Although most of the CCNA exam does not focus on GUIs, you are expected to be familiar with one GUI for the exam: the Cisco *wireless LAN controller* (WLC) GUI. We will cover wireless LANs and how to configure a WLC via the GUI in part 4 of volume 2 of this book. Figure 5.1 shows a screenshot of the GUI of a Cisco WLC.

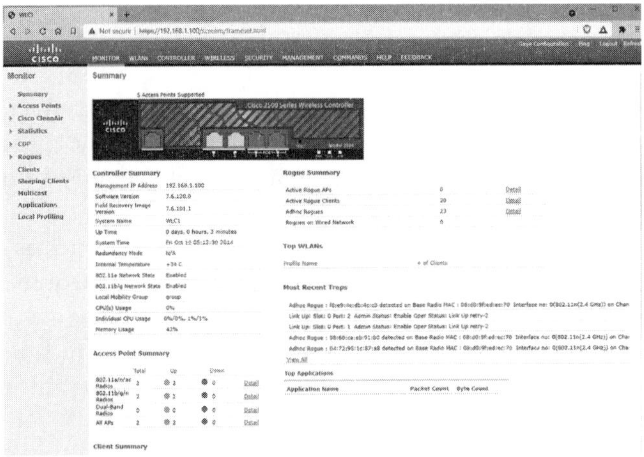

Figure 5.1 The GUI of a Cisco wireless LAN controller, accessed via a web browser

COMMAND-LINE INTERFACES

A CLI is a text-based interface that allows you to control and interact with a device by entering *commands*, which are lines of text. A famous CLI you might have seen before is the Windows *Command Prompt*, as pictured in figure 5.2. Although the vast majority of users use the GUI exclusively (or almost exclusively), the Command Prompt CLI provides an alternative way to interact with the PC.

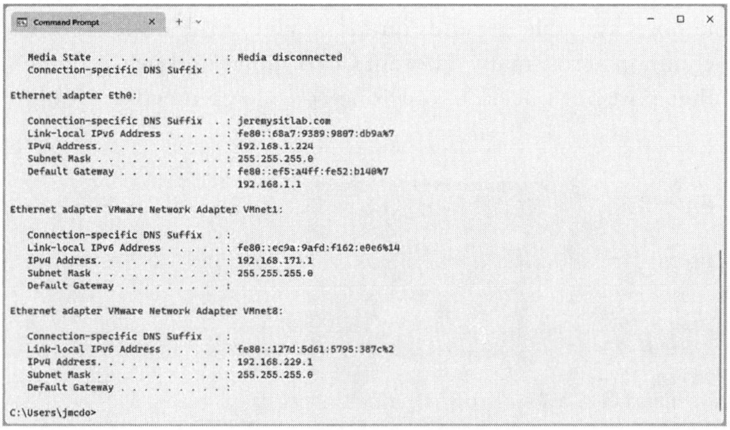

Figure 5.2 The Command Prompt CLI of a Windows PC, accessed from within the Windows shell GUI

For the CCNA exam, you must be familiar with the CLI of Cisco routers and switches running Cisco IOS. For those with no prior experience with a CLI (such as myself when I started my CCNA studies in 2018), this can seem intimidating. However, by the end of this chapter, I hope you will see that navigating around the Cisco IOS CLI isn't so complicated.

> **EXAM TIP** Throughout the two volumes of this book, I will introduce various CLI commands to configure the protocols you must know for the CCNA exam. Hands-on practice with these commands—for example, using Cisco Packet Tracer—is an essential part of preparing for the CCNA exam.

5.1.2 Accessing the CLI of a Cisco device

To configure Cisco devices, you first have to connect your computer to the device to access the CLI. There are two main methods to do so:

- Connect a PC/laptop to the *console port* of the device with a *console cable*.
- Connect to the device over the network using a protocol like *Telnet* or *Secure Shell* (SSH).

We will cover Telnet and SSH in chapter 5, volume 2. Until then, we will focus on connections via the console port of the device. The console port is a physical port that allows you to connect a computer directly to the device (as opposed to connecting via the network infrastructure). In order to do so, you must be physically near the device; a console cable is typically only a few feet in length.

> **NOTE** Console ports cannot be used to communicate over the network. They are dedicated to configuring the device via the CLI.

Figure 5.3 shows two console ports on a Cisco switch: USB Mini-B and RJ45. The exact type of console ports available depends on the model of the device, but USB Mini-B and RJ45 are common across many different Cisco router and switch models. You can connect to either port but not both; only one console connection is supported at a time.

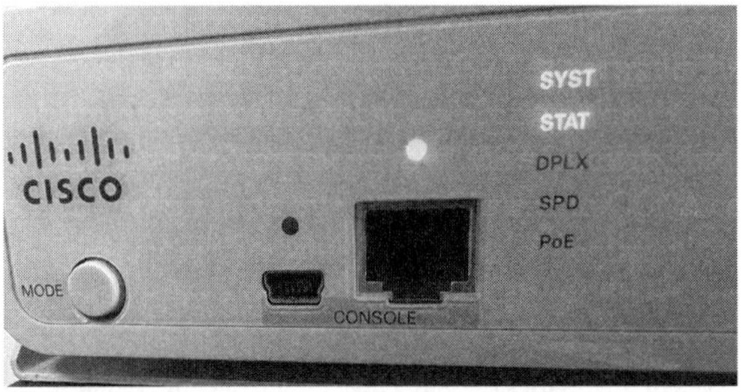

Figure 5.3 Two console ports on a Cisco switch: USB Mini-B (left) and RJ45 (right)

Console cables come in a variety of types with a variety of different connectors. The type used depends on the ports available on the device itself—the PC connecting to it. Perhaps the simplest option is to use a standard USB cable to connect your PC to the device's USB console port (make sure the cable has the correct USB connector types for your PC and the device you want to connect to).

To connect to the RJ45 console port, you must use a *rollover cable.* This is a different pattern than the *straight-through* and *crossover* cables we covered in chapter 3; rollover cables are wired as follows:

- Pin 1 to pin 8
- Pin 2 to pin 7
- Pin 3 to pin 6
- Pin 4 to pin 5
- Pin 5 to pin 4
- Pin 6 to pin 3
- Pin 7 to pin 2
- Pin 8 to pin 1

The wiring of a rollover cable is illustrated in figure 5.4.

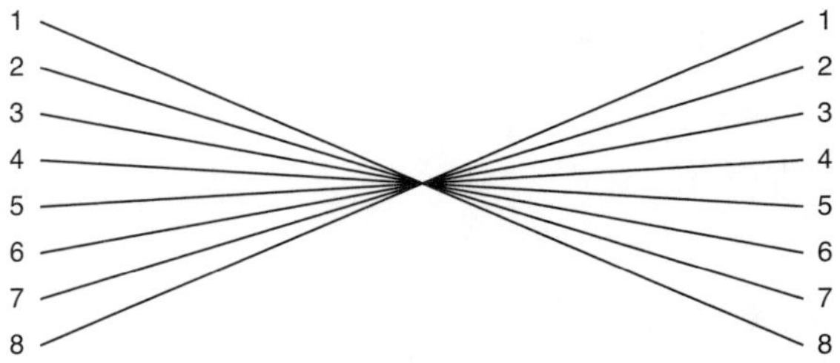

Figure 5.4 The wiring of a rollover cable, used to connect a PC to the RJ45 console port of a network device. Pin 1 on one end connects to pin 8 on the other end, pin 2 to pin 7, pin 3 to pin 6, pin 4 to pin 5, pin 5 to pin 4, pin 6 to pin 3, pin 7 to pin 2, pin 8 to pin 1.

After physically connecting your PC to the device's console port, you then need to use a type of application called a *terminal emulator* to access the CLI. A terminal emulator is a software application that replicates the functions of a *computer terminal*—an old hardware device consisting of a monitor and keyboard that was used to input data into (and receive and display data from) a computer. A popular (and free) terminal emulator on Windows is PuTTY (www.putty.org), but there are many options available for a variety of platforms.

When using a terminal emulator to connect from a PC to a device's console port, there are a few settings you will have to configure. Those are

- *Speed*—The rate at which data is sent
- *Data bits*—The number of bits of information used for each character of text sent to the device
- *Stop bits*—Sent after every character to allow the receiving device to detect the end of the character
- *Parity*—An extra bit sent with each character to be used for error detection
- *Flow control*—Provides support for circumstances where a device sends data faster than the receiver can handle

The appropriate value for each setting depends on the device you are configuring; to learn the appropriate settings for a particular device, you will have to check the manufacturer's documentation for that device. Figure 5.5 shows how to initiate a console connection to a Cisco device in PuTTY.

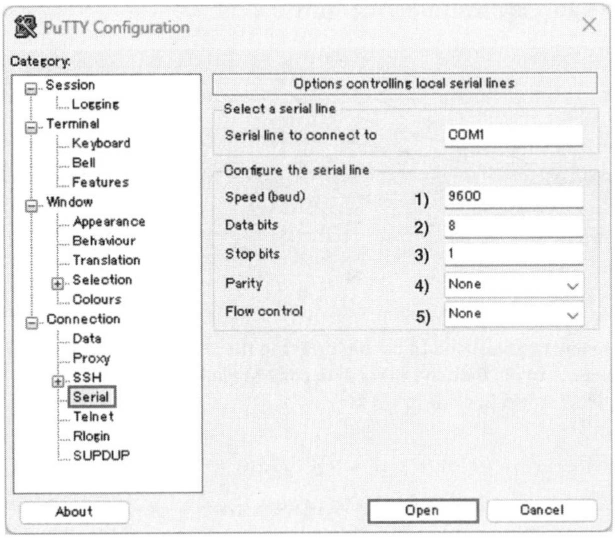

Figure 5.5 How to use PuTTY to access a Cisco device's CLI via the console port. From the Serial tab, configure the following settings, and then click Open: (1) Speed (baud): 9600 bits per second, (2) Data bits: 8, (3) Stop bits: 1, (4) Parity: None, (5) Flow control: None.

NOTE You won't be tested on how to use PuTTY or another terminal emulator to connect to a device's console port in the CCNA exam, but I am including this information just in case you have physical hardware to practice on. To get hands-on lab practice for the CCNA, I recommend Cisco Packet Tracer, in which you can simply click on a device's icon to access the CLI.

5.2 Navigating the Cisco IOS CLI

Now we will finally get hands-on in the Cisco IOS CLI, navigating through different modes and giving commands to a Cisco device. I want to emphasize once again that networking is not just theory but also a practical skill. It will be difficult to absorb this information without putting it into practice yourself, so I highly recommend following along in Packet Tracer (or the CLI of a real Cisco router or switch) as you read and trying out the different commands and shortcuts we cover.

When you first access the CLI of a new Cisco device, you are given the option to configure the device using the *system configuration dialog*, as shown in the following example:

```
        --- System Configuration Dialog ---
Would you like to enter the initial configuration dialog? [yes/no]: no
```

Type no, and press Enter to exit the dialog.

NOTE In the CLI output shown in this book, **bold** text indicates commands typed by the user. Normal text indicates the output shown by the device.

The system configuration dialog is a step-by-step configuration wizard that allows you to do a simple setup of the device without having to know Cisco IOS CLI commands. This feature is typically not used, and it's not something you need to know for the CCNA, so I recommend skipping it by typing **`no`** and pressing the Enter key (the options `[yes/no]` are shown in square brackets).

5.2.1 *The EXEC modes*

After skipping the system configuration dialog, you are shown a prompt like the following, where you can type commands and press Enter to send them to the device. The format of the prompt is the hostname (in this case, `Router`, the default hostname of Cisco routers) followed by a greater-than sign. This indicates that you are in *user EXEC mode*:

```
Router>
```

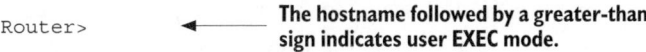

The hostname followed by a greater-than sign indicates user EXEC mode.

NOTE All of the commands we cover in this chapter apply to both Cisco routers and switches. They both run the same operating system: Cisco IOS.

User EXEC mode is the least-privileged mode in the Cisco IOS command hierarchy; it allows you to enter some basic commands to view information about the device's configuration and status. However, it does not allow you to do anything intrusive like make any changes to the device's configuration, restart the device, etc. To demonstrate a simple command that you can use in user EXEC mode, I type **`show clock`** and press Enter. The router then displays the current time of its clock:

```
Router> show clock
*02:21:03.832 UTC Fri Feb 10 2023
```

Views the time of the device's clock

EXAM TIP There are a variety of **`show`** commands that you will become familiar with throughout this book. Learning the available **`show`** commands and how to interpret their output is a major part of studying for the CCNA.

Checking the time is clearly not intrusive, so the **`show clock`** command is available in user EXEC mode. However, a more intrusive command like **`reload`**, which restarts the device, does not work in user EXEC mode, as shown in the following example. The router displays an error message instead (a percent sign indicates a message from IOS):

```
Router> reload
% Unknown command or computer name, or unable to find computer address
```

The reload command can't be used in user EXEC mode.

To access more powerful commands, you must enter the next mode in the IOS command hierarchy: *privileged EXEC mode.* To access privileged EXEC mode, use the **enable** command. From privileged EXEC mode, the **reload** command now works:

```
Router> enable
Router# reload
Proceed with reload? [confirm]
%SYS-5-RELOAD: Reload requested by console. Reload Reason: Reload Command.
```

Enters privileged EXEC mode

Uses the reload command again

Hit enter to reload the device.

A message indicates that the device will reload.

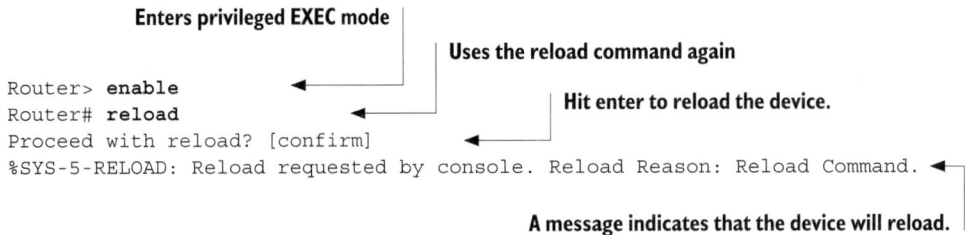

NOTE The greater-than sign (>) in the prompt changes to a hash (#) when in privileged EXEC mode.

Privileged EXEC mode gives unlimited access to the available **show** commands as well as many other commands to control various features of the device. To return to user EXEC mode from privileged EXEC mode, you can use the **disable** command. However, **disable** is rarely used because there are no commands in user EXEC mode that you can't use in privileged EXEC mode; there's rarely a need to return to user EXEC mode.

Although privileged EXEC mode is more powerful than user EXEC mode, both modes are limited in that they do not allow you to make changes to the device's configuration. The EXEC modes only allow you to view the device's status and configuration, as well as execute operational commands to perform actions like restart the device, save the configuration, move and delete files, etc.

5.2.2 Global configuration mode

To make changes to the configuration of the device, we must leave the EXEC modes and proceed to the next mode in the IOS command hierarchy: *global configuration mode.* To do so, use the **configure terminal** command from privileged EXEC mode:

```
Router# configure terminal
Enter configuration commands, one per line.  End with CNTL/Z.
Router(config)#
```

Enters global configuration mode

The prompt changes to hostname(config)# when in global configuration mode.

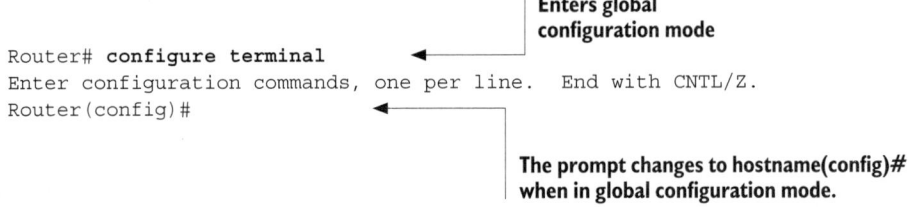

Although there are only two EXEC modes in the Cisco CLI (*user EXEC mode* and *privileged EXEC mode*), there are several configuration modes that we will examine throughout this book. In this chapter, we will only look at the first one: global configuration mode. From global configuration mode, you can configure various features like the device's hostname and passwords. From this mode, you can also access the other configuration modes that we will look at in later chapters of this book's two volumes.

One configuration that you can make from global configuration mode is to change the hostname of the device with the **`hostname`** command, as shown in the following example. Notice that after executing the command, the prompt changes from `Router` to `R1`, indicating that the hostname has changed. The command takes effect immediately. Configuring a unique hostname on each device in the network is essential to make them easy to identify. For the purpose of this book, we will use simple numerical identifiers (R1, R2, etc.). In a real enterprise network, other information, such as the device's location, is often included in the hostname (i.e., Office1_R1):

```
Router(config)# hostname R1
R1(config)#
```

Changes the device's hostname (points to `Router(config)# hostname R1`)

The prompt immediately changes to reflect the new hostname. (points to `R1(config)#`)

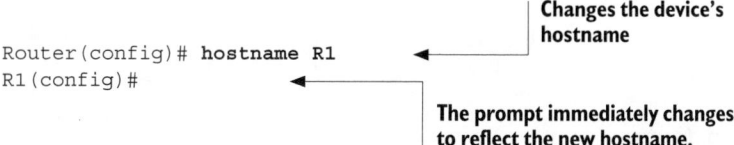

> **NOTE** If you want to undo a configuration command, you can use **`no`** in front of the command. For example, after the **`hostname R1`** command, **`no hostname R1`** would remove the command and revert the device's hostname to the default of `Router`.

To return from global configuration mode to privileged EXEC mode, there are a few options. The **`end`** command, the Ctrl-C keyboard shortcut, and the Ctrl-Z keyboard shortcut will return you to privileged EXEC mode from global configuration mode or any other configuration mode. The **`exit`** command will return you to privileged EXEC mode from global configuration mode. However, if you're in another configuration mode, it will return you to global configuration mode. Figure 5.6 shows how to navigate between user EXEC mode, privileged EXEC mode, and global configuration mode.

> **NOTE** If you use the Ctrl-Z shortcut in the middle of typing a command, the device will execute the typed command before returning to privileged EXEC mode; it's equivalent to pressing Enter and then issuing **`end`**. Be careful! Ctrl-C does not do this; it will just return you to privileged EXEC mode.

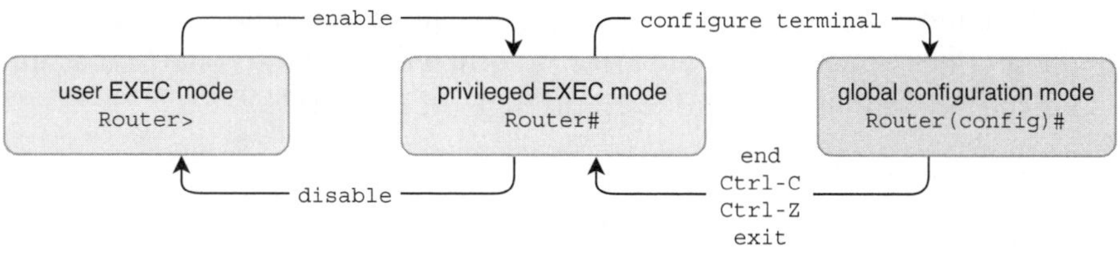

Figure 5.6 How to navigate between user EXEC mode, privileged EXEC mode, and global configuration mode in the Cisco IOS command hierarchy

Configuration modes such as global configuration mode allow you to configure the device, but EXEC mode commands like **show** do not work. However, the **do** command allows you to use EXEC mode commands from a configuration mode, so you don't have to return to privileged EXEC mode. This can speed up your workflow when you are configuring a device but also want to use **show** commands to check its status. The following example demonstrates this; the **show clock** command results in an error message, but the **do show clock** command displays the time of the device's clock:

```
R1(config)# show clock
                 ^
% Invalid input detected at '^' marker.
R1(config)# do show clock
*03:06:22.892 UTC Fri Feb 10 2023
```

Show commands don't work in global configuration mode.

Uses do to execute the command in global configuration mode

5.2.3 Keyboard shortcuts

There are several keyboard shortcuts that can help you more smoothly navigate through the CLI and enter commands. We covered two in the previous section; Ctrl-C and Ctrl-Z can be used to return to privileged EXEC mode from any configuration mode. There are many others, and we will look at a few of them next.

When typing commands in the CLI, there is a cursor indicating where the next character will be inserted when typed. By default, this will be after the previous character, as you would probably expect. You can also move the cursor, for example, to fix an error in a previously typed word. The following are some keyboard shortcuts that can be used to move the cursor and edit the current command you are typing:

- *Left arrow*—Moves the cursor left
- *Right arrow*—Moves the cursor right
- *Backspace*—Moves the cursor left and deletes the previous character
- *Ctrl-A*—Moves the cursor to the beginning of the command you are typing
- *Ctrl-E*—Moves the cursor to the end of the command you are typing
- *Ctrl-U*—Deletes all characters to the left of the cursor

You can also use the keyboard to view previously executed commands, which Cisco IOS stores in a memory buffer. This is useful if you made a mistake in a previous command and want to correct it without typing out the entire command again; you can return to the previous command, fix the error, and then execute the command again. You can use the following shortcuts to scroll through the buffer:

- *Up arrow*—Previous command
- *Down arrow*—Next command

5.2.4 Context-sensitive help

You will have to learn many different commands to prepare for the CCNA, and those commands are only a fraction of all of the available commands in Cisco IOS. For the purpose of the CCNA exam, it is important to practice and become familiar with the various commands we will look at in this book. However, Cisco IOS has a feature called *context-sensitive help* that can help you if you have forgotten a command.

VIEWING THE AVAILABLE COMMANDS

A question mark (`?`) can be used for help in the Cisco IOS CLI in a few ways:

- To list the available commands in the current EXEC or configuration mode
- To list the keywords available for a command
- To list the possible completions of a partially typed command or keyword

In the first use case, the question mark is used to list the commands available in the current mode of the CLI hierarchy, along with a brief description of each command. Note that you don't have to press Enter; the list of commands is shown immediately after typing the question mark. The first few commands available in user EXEC mode are as follows:

```
R1> ?                                   <- Uses context-sensitive help to view the available commands
Exec commands:
  <1-99>            Session number to resume
  access-enable     Create a temporary Access-List entry
  access-profile    Apply user-profile to interface
  clear             Reset functions
  connect           Open a terminal connection
. . .
```

A list of available commands is displayed.

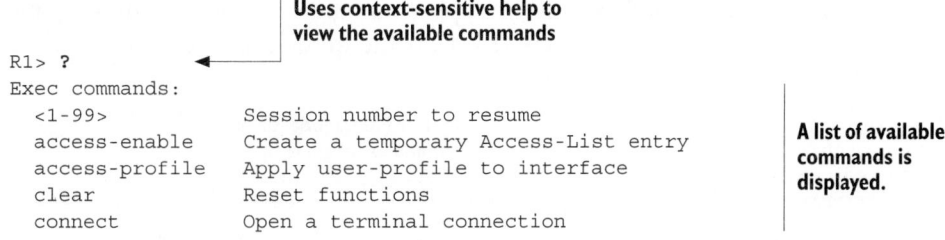

Few Cisco IOS commands are a single word; most commands include one or more *keywords*, which are further parameters typed after the initial command. The **show** command we looked at previously is an example of this; **show** on its own is not a valid command, but **show clock** is. In the second use case of the question mark, you can use it after a command to view the available keywords. The following example demonstrates this:

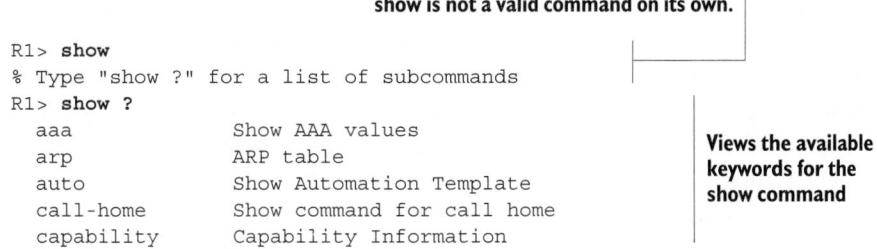

```
R1> show                                              <- show is not a valid command on its own.
% Type "show ?" for a list of subcommands
R1> show ?
  aaa              Show AAA values
  arp              ARP table
  auto             Show Automation Template
  call-home        Show command for call home
  capability       Capability Information
. . .
```

Views the available keywords for the show command

You can also use the question mark in this manner after a keyword to display any further keywords. For example, **show clock ?** lists the keyword **detail**, which can be used to view more information about the device's clock. This is shown in the following example:

```
R1> show clock ?
  detail  Display detailed information
  |       Output modifiers
  <cr>    <cr>
```

Views the available options after show clock

The other two options displayed are also worth mentioning:

- The pipe (|) can be used to filter the output of a **show** command. I will show an example of this later in this chapter.
- `<cr>` means carriage return, which refers to the Enter key. This means that you can simply press Enter to execute the command. Although a keyword (**detail**) is available, **show clock** on its own is a valid command.

The third use case for the question mark is to display the possible completions of a partially typed command or keyword. In this case, the question mark should be typed immediately after the partially typed command, without a space. For example, typing **e?** in user EXEC mode will list multiple commands that begin with **e**. Typing **en?**, on the other hand, will show that **enable** is the only command that begins with **en**, as shown in the following example:

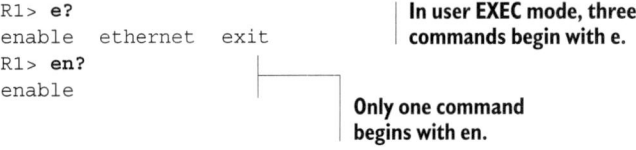

```
R1> e?
enable  ethernet  exit
R1> en?
enable
```

In user EXEC mode, three commands begin with e.

Only one command begins with en.

AUTO-COMPLETING COMMANDS

Typing various commands can be tedious when manually configuring a device. Fortunately, Cisco IOS does not require you to type full commands; it only requires you to type enough characters so that there is only one possible command that begins with those characters.

If you type enough characters so that there is only one possible command beginning with those characters and then press the Tab key, IOS will automatically complete the command for you. For example, typing **en** and then pressing Tab will automatically complete the command to **enable**. Then you can simply press Enter to execute the command. However, if you don't type enough characters and there are multiple possible commands beginning with the character(s) you have typed, the command won't work; it will simply print the character(s) again on a new line. This is shown in the following example. Note that `<Tab>` indicates where I pressed the Tab key:

```
R1> e<Tab>
R1> en<Tab>
R1> enable
R1#
```

Typing e and pressing Tab reprints e on a new line.

Typing en and pressing Tab auto-completes the command to enable.

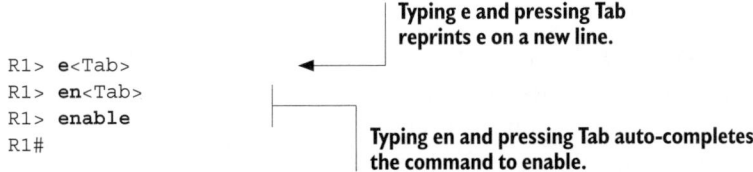

But wait, there's more: you don't even have to use Tab to complete the command. Using the previous example of the **`enable`** command, if you type **`e`** and then press Enter to execute the command, the terminal will display an error message stating that **`e`** is an ambiguous command. That is because there are multiple possible commands beginning with **`e`**. However, if you type **`en`** and press Enter, the command is accepted as **`enable`**, and you are brought to privileged EXEC mode:

```
R1> e
% Ambiguous command:  "e"
R1> en
R1#
```

Typing e and pressing Enter gives an error message.

Typing en and pressing Enter executes the enable command.

> **NOTE** Auto-completion with Tab and executing partial commands both apply to a command's keywords too. For example, **`conf t`** can be used instead of **`configure terminal`** to enter global configuration mode.

Table 5.1 summarizes these context-sensitive help features. Spend some time experimenting with them in the CLI; once you get used to them, you will probably find yourself using them quite often as you practice configuring and verifying the various IOS features you need to know for the CCNA.

Table 5.1 Cisco IOS context-sensitive help features

Command	Description
?	Lists the available commands in the current mode
command **?**	Lists the available keywords for the command
partial-command **?**	Lists the possible commands beginning with the currently typed characters
partial-command<Tab>	Automatically completes the command if there is only one option beginning with the currently typed characters
partial-command<Enter>	Executes the command if there is only one option beginning with the currently typed characters

5.3 IOS configuration files

Cisco IOS devices make use of two different text files that store the device's configurations: running-config and startup-config. The two files are each stored in different hardware memory and serve different purposes. You can view each configuration file with the **`show running-config`** and **`show startup-config`** commands.

> **NOTE** The output of **`show running-config`** and **`show startup-config`** can be quite long. When the output of a command is beyond a certain length, only partial output will be shown with a prompt that says `--More--` at the bottom. Use the Enter key to scroll through the output one line at a time or the spacebar to scroll through the output one screen at a time.

The configurations in the running-config file determine the current operations of the device. When you enter a configuration command in the CLI, you are modifying the running-config file. Changes take effect instantly; as shown previously, after the **`hostname`** command is executed, the hostname of the device changes immediately.

The running config file is stored in *random-access memory* (RAM). It is important to note that the contents of RAM are lost when the device is powered off or restarted; therefore, changes to running-config are lost in either event. To save configuration changes so they persist even if the device is powered off or restarted, the startup-config file is used.

The configurations in startup-config do not determine the current operations of the device. Rather, the startup-config is the configuration file that is loaded by the device when it boots up—for example, after being powered on or restarted. The contents of the startup-config file are copied to the running-config file in RAM when the device boots up.

The startup-config file is stored in a special type of RAM called *nonvolatile RAM* (NVRAM). The contents of NVRAM are kept even when the device is powered off or restarted, so to save changes made to the running-config file, the contents must be copied to startup-config. Otherwise, the device will have a *factory-default* configuration every time it boots up.

> **DEFINITION** *Factory-default* refers to the original state of the device as it is sent from the factory, before any configuration changes are made.

There are a few different commands (entered in privileged EXEC mode) that can be used to copy the contents of the running-config file to the startup-config file. The effect of each of these commands is the same, so it doesn't matter which one you use:

- **`write`**
- **`write memory`**
- **`copy running-config startup-config`**

NOTE A new device that has booted up for the first time won't even have a startup-config file until you use one of these commands. If no startup-config file is present, the device uses the factory-default configuration.

If you want to return a device to its factory-default configuration, you can erase startup-config and then restart the device with the **`reload`** command. Just as with saving the configuration, there are a few different commands you can use to delete startup-config:

- **`write erase`**
- **`erase nvram:`**
- **`erase startup-config`**

5.4 Password-protecting privileged EXEC mode

Privileged EXEC mode not only allows a user to execute any of the available **`show`** commands to gather information about the device's configuration and status, but it also allows the user to access global configuration mode and make configuration changes to the device. Because of this, it's always a good idea to configure a password to prevent unauthorized users from accessing privileged EXEC mode. In this section, we will look at the *enable password* and its more secure version, the *enable secret.*

5.4.1 Configuring the enable password

The enable password is a password that you must enter to access privileged EXEC mode. It's also the name of the command used to configure the password; you configure it with the **`enable password`** command in global configuration mode. After you configure the enable password, any time a user uses the **`enable`** command in user EXEC mode, the user will have to enter that password to access privileged EXEC mode.

NOTE The enable password is case-sensitive: *cisco* and *Cisco* are two different passwords.

In the following example, I configure an enable password of *ccna,* use **`exit`** to return to privileged EXEC mode, and use **`disable`** to return to user EXEC mode. When I then use **`enable`** to return to privileged EXEC mode again, I have to enter the configured enable password of *ccna* to gain access. Note that, for security purposes, passwords are not displayed as you type them in Cisco IOS:

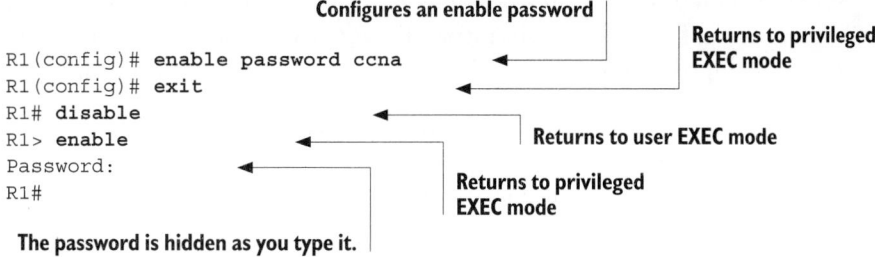

```
R1(config)# enable password ccna     <- Configures an enable password
R1(config)# exit                     <- Returns to privileged EXEC mode
R1# disable                          <- Returns to user EXEC mode
R1> enable                           <- Returns to privileged EXEC mode
Password:                            <- The password is hidden as you type it.
R1#
```

There is a major problem with the enable password: it is stored in *cleartext*, meaning the exact password (*ccna* in this case) is stored in the configuration file as is. Anyone who can see running-config can read the password, and this is a major security concern. The following example demonstrates this: I use the command **`show running-config | include enable`** to view the enable password in running-config. The command is displayed exactly as I configured it, with the password in cleartext:

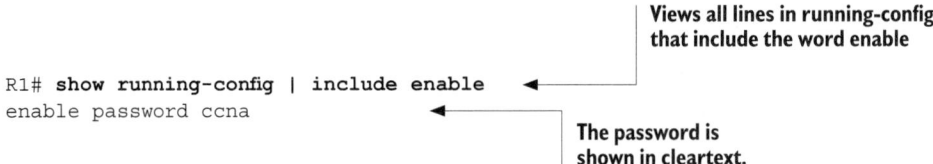

```
R1# show running-config | include enable      <-- Views all lines in running-config that include the word enable
enable password ccna                          <-- The password is shown in cleartext.
```

> **NOTE** After a **`show`** command, a pipe (|) followed by the keyword **`include`** allows you to filter output to only show lines including the specified characters (**`enable`**, in this case).

To improve the security of **`enable password`**, you can use the **`service password-encryption`** command in global configuration mode. This encrypts all current passwords configured on the device, as well as passwords you configure in the future. The following example demonstrates this: after issuing the command and viewing running-config again, the original password is not shown. Instead, the password is stored as *ciphertext* (encrypted text):

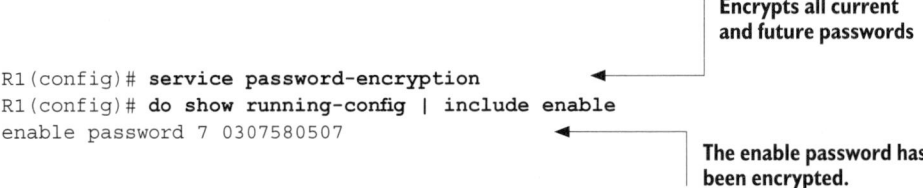

```
R1(config)# service password-encryption       <-- Encrypts all current and future passwords
R1(config)# do show running-config | include enable
enable password 7 0307580507                  <-- The enable password has been encrypted.
```

> **NOTE** The `7` before the ciphertext string `0307580507` indicates the encryption type.

The **`service password-encryption`** command encrypts passwords using *type 7* encryption. It is a very weak form of encryption that is easily reversed with free tools available on the internet (a Google search for "cisco type 7 decrypt" will give many results). Although it does prevent someone from looking over your shoulder to read the password as you look at running-config, it does not provide sufficient protection. To provide improved security, you should use the enable secret instead.

> **NOTE** If you use the **`no service password-encryption`** command to undo the encryption, currently encrypted passwords will not be decrypted. Future passwords, however, will not be encrypted.

The enable password is an example of a *legacy* feature—something that has been replaced with a newer feature (the enable secret) but is still supported in Cisco IOS. The differences between the enable password and the enable secret are a potential exam question, but when configuring network devices, you should always use the enable secret.

5.4.2 Configuring the enable secret

The *enable secret* is a more secure password that can be configured to protect access to privileged EXEC mode. It stores the password as a *hash*, rather than encrypted ciphertext. *Hashing* can be thought of as one-way encryption; it can't be reversed. The enable secret can be configured with the **enable secret** command in global configuration mode. In the following example, I configure an enable secret and view it in running-config:

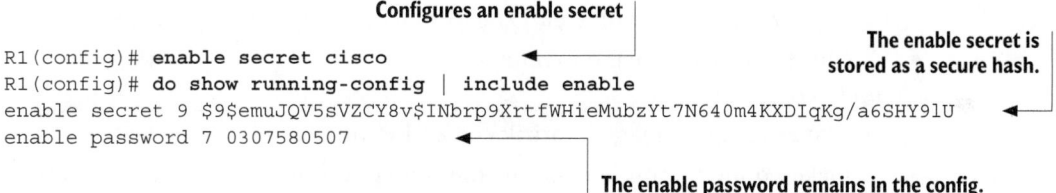

```
R1(config)# enable secret cisco                          <-- Configures an enable secret
R1(config)# do show running-config | include enable
enable secret 9 $9$emuJQV5sVZCY8v$INbrp9XrtfWHieMubzYt7N640m4KXDIqKg/a6SHY9lU   <-- The enable secret is stored as a secure hash.
enable password 7 0307580507                             <-- The enable password remains in the config.
```

NOTE Notice that the enable password remains in the configuration. If both the enable password and enable secret are configured, only the enable secret can be used. The **enable password** command remains in the configuration but cannot be used to access privileged EXEC mode.

The **enable secret** command hashes the specified password using the default hashing algorithm of the device. There are a few different hashing algorithms that can be used to hash the password, and the hashing algorithms available vary depending on the IOS version of the device. On the platform I am using for this demonstration, the algorithm type is *scrypt* (pronounced *S-crypt*), also known as *type 9* (as indicated by the `9` before the hash in the previous example's output). On many older devices, the default algorithm is *Message Digest 5* (MD5), also known as *type 5*. Type 5 is not as secure as type 9, so type 9 should be used when possible. In chapter 11, volume 2, we will examine the different hashing algorithms supported by Cisco IOS and how to configure secrets using specific hashing algorithms.

Summary

- A *shell* is a computer program that allows a user to interact with the computer. A *graphical user interface* (GUI) is a shell with a graphical interface, and a *command-line interface* (CLI) is a shell with a text-based interface.
- For the CCNA exam, you must be able to use the Cisco IOS CLI to configure the protocols and features listed in the exam topics list.

- The CLI of a network device can be accessed by connecting a PC to the device's *console port* with a console (crossover) cable or by connecting over the network infrastructure using *Telnet* or *Secure Shell* (SSH).
- After physically connecting a PC to the device's console port, a *terminal emulator* application (such as PuTTY) is required to access the CLI.
- To give commands to a network device, you type commands in the CLI and press Enter.
- After connecting to a device's CLI, you will be in *user EXEC mode*, which only allows you to view basic information about the device but not perform anything intrusive. The format of the prompt is `hostname>`.
- To access more powerful commands, use the **`enable`** command to access *privileged EXEC mode*, which provides unlimited access to EXEC mode commands. For example, you can view information about the device, restart it, save the configuration, move and delete files, etc. The format of the prompt is `hostname#`.
- Use the **`disable`** command to return to user EXEC mode from privileged EXEC mode.
- Use the **`reload`** command in privileged EXEC mode to restart the device.
- To make configuration changes to the device, use the **`configure terminal`** command in privileged EXEC mode to access *global configuration mode*. The prompt is `hostname(config)#`.
- Global configuration mode allows you to make configuration changes to the device. It also allows you to access other configuration modes for specific features.
- To change the hostname of the device, use the **`hostname`** command in global configuration mode.
- To undo a command, use **`no`** in front of the command. For example, **`no hostname R1`**.
- Use the **`end`** command, the **`exit`** command, or the Ctrl-C/Ctrl-Z shortcuts to return to privileged EXEC mode from global configuration mode.
- When in a configuration mode, you can use **`do`** in front of a command to execute EXEC mode commands.
- Keyboard shortcuts can be used to move the cursor and scroll through previously executed commands.
- *Context-sensitive help* can be used for guidance within the CLI. It can list available commands and possible completions for partially written words.
- Cisco IOS devices use two configuration files: the *running-config* file and the *startup-config* file.
- The running-config file is stored in RAM and determines the current operations of the device. Configuration commands change running-config and immediately take effect. The running-config file is lost when the device is powered off or restarted.

- The startup-config file is stored in *nonvolatile RAM* (NVRAM) and does not determine the current operations of the device. The contents of startup-config are copied to running-config when the device boots up.
- To save the running-config file to the startup-config file, use **`write`**, **`write memory`**, or **`copy running-config startup-config`** in privileged EXEC mode.
- To return the device to the factory-default configuration, delete startup-config with **`write erase`**, **`erase nvram:`**, or **`erase startup-config`**, and restart the device with **`reload`**.
- Privileged EXEC mode can be password-protected with an *enable password* or *enable secret.* If both the **`enable password`** and **`enable secret`** commands are configured, only the enable secret can be used to access privileged EXEC mode.
- The enable password can be configured with the **`enable password`** command in global configuration mode. It is stored in the configuration as cleartext by default but can be encrypted with the **`service password-encryption`** command (type 7).
- The enable password remains in Cisco IOS as a legacy feature, but on modern devices, the enable secret should be used instead.
- The enable secret can be configured with the **`enable secret`** command in global configuration mode. It is stored in the configuration as a *hash,* using one of multiple hashing algorithms. The hashing algorithms available vary depending on the IOS version.
- *Message Digest 5* (MD5) is type 5 encryption, and *scrypt* is *type 9. scrypt* is more secure and should be used instead of MD5 if supported by the device.

6 Ethernet LAN switching

This chapter covers

- The definition of a LAN
- The contents of the Ethernet header and trailer
- How switches learn the MAC addresses of devices in the network
- How switches forward frames to the appropriate destination
- How network hosts use ARP to learn the MAC address of other hosts
- The ping utility

In this chapter, we will cover Ethernet LAN switching, which is the process switches use to forward frames to their proper destinations within a LAN. A frame is a Layer 2 PDU, including the Layer 2 header, trailer, and payload; we covered PDUs in chapter 4. When a network host sends a frame out of its port, it is the switch's role to make sure the frame reaches its proper destination.

This chapter covers material from domain 1.0 of the CCNA exam topics: Network Fundamentals. Specifically, we will cover the following topics:

- 1.13 Describe switching concepts
  - 1.13a MAC learning and aging
  - 1.13b Frame switching
  - 1.13c Frame flooding
  - 1.13d MAC address table

It is often said that switches are Layer 2 devices or that they operate at Layer 2. The reason for this is that switches use information in the Layer 2 header (the Ethernet header) to make forwarding decisions. This is in contrast to routers, which use information in the Layer 3 header (the IP header) to make forwarding decisions. We will cover how routers forward network traffic between LANs in part 2 of this book, but for now, we will focus on how switches forward traffic within a LAN.

6.1 Local area networks

In chapter 2, I defined a local area network (LAN) as a group of interconnected devices in a limited area, such as an office, and stated that the role of a switch is to connect devices within a LAN. The precise definition of a LAN can vary depending on the context, but for the purpose of this lesson, how the devices are connected is more significant than the actual physical distance between them. Figure 6.1 demonstrates this concept.

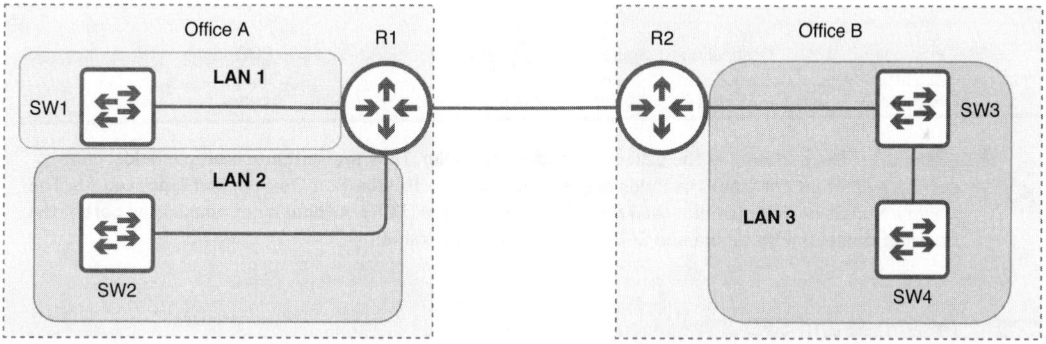

Figure 6.1 Two offices with two switches in each office. In Office A each switch is a separate LAN because the switches are connected via a router. In Office B both switches are in the same LAN because they are directly connected to each other.

There are two offices in the diagram, so you might say there are two LANs, which would not be incorrect if defining a LAN only by physical location. However, in Office A, the two switches are not directly connected to each other; each is connected to a different port on R1, and the purpose of a router is to provide connectivity *between* LANs. So, each switch in Office A can be considered its own LAN. For end hosts connected to SW1 to communicate with end hosts connected to SW2, their messages must pass through R1 because it separates the two LANs.

In Office B, however, SW3 and SW4 are directly connected to each other. End hosts connected to one switch can communicate with end hosts connected to the other switch without the messages having to pass through a router. SW3, SW4, and all of the end hosts connected to them are in a single LAN.

Another term for a LAN is a *Layer 2 domain*—a portion of a network where frames are switched, and hosts connected to the switch(es) can communicate with each other without the use of a router. Keep this definition in mind throughout this chapter; we will examine how switches forward frames within a Layer 2 domain.

6.2 The Ethernet header and trailer

Switches make forwarding decisions using information in the Ethernet header, so to understand switching, it's important to understand the contents of that header (and trailer). Figure 6.2 shows the structure of an Ethernet frame. Note that the *Preamble* and *Start Frame Delimiter* (SFD) are included in the diagram but are not considered part of an Ethernet frame. We will examine why shortly.

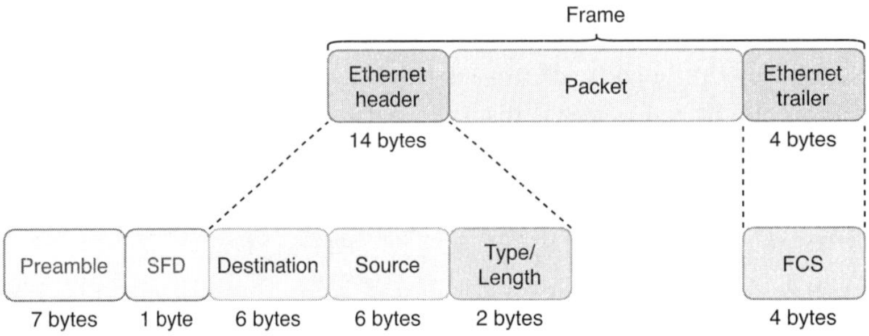

Figure 6.2 The contents of the Ethernet header and trailer. They are split into multiple fields, each serving a different purpose. The fields of the header are the Destination, Source, and Type/Length. The trailer consists of a single field: the Frame Check Sequence (FCS). Although not considered part of the Ethernet frame, the Preamble and SFD are sent with each frame.

6.2.1 Preamble and SFD

The Preamble and SFD are sent with each Ethernet frame to allow the receiving device to synchronize its *receiver clock* and prepare to receive the incoming frame. This *clock* has nothing to do with the date and time but rather with how the receiving device interprets the incoming electrical signals—the receiving device needs to determine the precise length of 1 bit.

The device sending an Ethernet frame facilitates this by sending the Preamble and SFD. The Preamble is 7 bytes (56 bits—remember that 1 byte is 8 bits) in length and is simply a series of alternating 1s and 0s like this: 10101010. Then, the SFD is 1 byte in length and signals that the Preamble is done and the frame is going to start. The bit pattern of the SFD is 10101011.

The reason the Preamble and SFD are not considered part of the Ethernet frame, although they are sent with each frame, is that they are purely a function of Layer 1, the Physical Layer. They do not contain information that influences what the receiving device decides to do with the frame. As mentioned in previous chapters, Ethernet includes specifications at both Layers 1 and 2, but the Layer 1 aspects of Ethernet are not considered part of a frame, which is a Layer 2 concept.

6.2.2 Destination and source

The Destination and Source fields are perhaps the most significant of the Ethernet header and trailer; the Destination field is the destination MAC address of the frame, and the Source field is the source MAC address of the frame.

DEFINITION A *media access control* (MAC) address is a type of address used by Layer 2 protocols such as Ethernet and Wi-Fi. MAC addresses are 6 bytes (48 bits) in length and are typically written as a series of 12 hexadecimal characters. They are assigned by the device's manufacturer and should be globally unique.

Layer 2 provides hop-to-hop delivery of messages, and MAC addresses enable that. At Layer 3, the message is addressed to the IP address of the final destination host, but at Layer 2, the message is addressed to the MAC address of the next hop. Within a LAN, it is a switch's job to look at the destination MAC address of the frame and forward it to the appropriate destination. The source MAC address field is also important because it helps the switch learn which port each host is connected to (more about that shortly).

As indicated in figure 6.2, each of these fields is 6 bytes (48 bits) in length because 6 bytes is the length of a MAC address. However, when we represent MAC addresses, we typically don't write them out in binary; a long string of 1s and 0s isn't very human-readable or easy to remember. Instead, we write MAC addresses in *hexadecimal*.

The hexadecimal number system

The number system we typically use in our daily lives is the *decimal* number system, which uses 10 digits to represent all values: 0, 1, 2, 3, 4, 5, 6, 7, 8, 9. Hexadecimal is a number system that uses 16 digits; it uses the same 10 digits in the decimal system and borrows 6 letters from the alphabet: A, B, C, D, E, and F.

Because more digits are available, hexadecimal can express large values in fewer characters. In decimal, to express the value after 9, we have to add another character—it becomes 10, a 1 and a 0. Hexadecimal can express that same value in a single character: A. The efficiency of hexadecimal over decimal becomes more significant as the values become greater. Table 6.1 lists some decimal numbers and their equivalent hexadecimal numbers.

Table 6.1 Decimal numbers and their hexadecimal equivalents

Dec.	Hex.		Dec.	Hex.		Dec.	Hex.		Dec.	Hex.
0	0		8	8		16	10		24	18
1	1		9	9		17	11		25	19
2	2		10	A		18	12		26	1A
3	3		11	B		19	13		27	1B
4	4		12	C		20	14		28	1C
5	5		13	D		21	15		29	1D
6	6		14	E		22	16		30	1E
7	7		15	F		23	17		31	1F

NOTE You can use a prefix to indicate whether a number is a decimal or hexadecimal number: *0d* for decimal and *0x* for hexadecimal. This can be useful in networking because we use multiple systems: binary, decimal, and hexadecimal. Ten in decimal is 10, but 10 in hexadecimal is equal to 16 in decimal. To clearly differentiate between the two, you can write *0d10* or *0x10.*

In part 5 of this book (IPv6), we will practice converting between decimal, hexadecimal, and binary. For now, that is not necessary; it is enough to understand that MAC addresses are typically written in hexadecimal.

CHARACTERISTICS OF MAC ADDRESSES

We have already covered two characteristics of MAC addresses: they are 6 bytes in length and are usually written in hexadecimal. By writing them in hexadecimal, we can express the address in fewer characters; MAC addresses are written as 12 hexadecimal characters rather than 48 bits (1s and 0s). The details regarding how those 12 characters are notated can vary. The following is a single MAC address written using three different notational conventions. Of course, because this is a CCNA book, I will follow Cisco's convention for writing MAC addresses, but it's worth knowing that they can be written in other ways. For comparison, I have also included the address written in binary—I'm sure you'll agree that the hexadecimal representations are easier to read:

- 0cf5.a452.b101 (used by Cisco IOS)
- 0C-F5-A4-52-B1-01 (used by Windows)
- 0c:f5:a4:52:b1:01 (used by macOS)
- 000011001111010110100100010100101011000100000001 (binary)

Unlike IP addresses (which we'll cover in chapter 7), MAC addresses are not assigned by the network admin or engineer configuring the device. Instead, each port of a network device has a MAC address that is assigned to it by the manufacturer. For this reason, another name for a MAC address is a *burned-in address* (BIA): it is "burned into" the physical port. A MAC address is globally unique—it should not be shared by a port on any other device in the world.

NOTE It is possible to override a manufacturer-assigned MAC address with manual configuration, but it is extremely rare to do so.

To ensure that MAC addresses remain globally unique, the first half of each MAC address (the first 3 bytes) is an *organizationally unique identifier* (OUI) assigned to the manufacturer by the IEEE. Then, the manufacturer is free to use the second half to assign unique MAC addresses to each device they manufacture. For example, the MAC addresses of the first three ports of the Cisco switch in my home network are

- 0cf5.a452.b101
- 0cf5.a452.b102
- 0cf5.a452.b103

0cf5.a4 is Cisco's OUI (actually, Cisco has many OUIs), and the second half is a unique identifier for each port on the switch. As you probably noticed, those three MAC addresses are quite similar—only the final digit is different. That's because MAC addresses on the same device are typically assigned sequentially.

Let's summarize MAC addresses before moving on:

- MAC addresses are 6-byte (48-bit) addresses assigned to ports by the device's manufacturer. Another name for a MAC address is *burned-in address* (BIA).
- MAC addresses are globally unique.
- The first 3 bytes are an organizationally unique identifier (OUI), assigned to the manufacturer by the IEEE.
- The last 3 bytes are unique to the port itself.
- MAC addresses are written as 12 hexadecimal characters.

6.2.3 Type/Length

The Type/Length field is a 2-byte field that can be used either to indicate the *type* of the encapsulated packet (e.g., an IP version 4 packet or an IP version 6 packet) or to indicate the length of the encapsulated packet (in bytes). There are historical reasons why this field can be used for two purposes, but both uses are now officially part of the Ethernet standard. These days, in almost all cases, this field is used to indicate the type of the encapsulated packet: instead of this field indicating length, the end of the frame is indicated by a special signal after the frame.

NOTE The original IEEE 802.3 standard used the Type/Length field exclusively to indicate the length of the encapsulated packet, and an additional header was used to indicate the type of encapsulated protocol: the *Logical Link Control* (LLC) header, sometimes with an additional *Subnetwork Access Protocol* (SNAP) extension to that header. However, this is beyond the scope of the CCNA exam.

A value of 1500 (decimal) or less in this field means that it indicates the *length* of the encapsulated packet in bytes. For example, if the value is 1500, it means the encapsulated packet is 1500 bytes in length.

A value of 1536 or greater in this field indicates the *type* of the encapsulated packet, which is usually IP version 4 (IPv4) or IP version 6 (IPv6). When used to indicate the type of the encapsulated packet, this field is called the *EtherType* field. For reference, here are the values in this field for IPv4 and IPv6, both of which are significant topics on the CCNA exam (usually hexadecimal notation is used; I'm including the decimal numbers for comparison):

- IPv4: 0x0800 (0d2048)
- IPv6: 0x86DD (0d34525)

NOTE Values between 1500 and 1536 should not be used in this field.

6.2.4 *Frame Check Sequence*

The *Frame Check Sequence* (FCS) is the only field of the Ethernet trailer. It is 4 bytes in length and is used to detect corrupted data in the frame. Before a device sends a frame, it uses an algorithm to calculate a *checksum*, a small block of data that is appended to the end of the frame as the FCS field.

Then, when the frame's destination host receives the frame, it calculates its own checksum for the frame (with the same algorithm) and compares it to the one calculated by the sender. If the two checksums are the same, the receiver can safely assume that the data has not been corrupted in transit. However, if the checksums calculated by the sender and receiver are different, the receiver will discard the frame—the data has been corrupted in transit (perhaps because of electromagnetic interference).

FCS is the name of the field, but the name for this kind of checksum is *cyclic redundancy check* (CRC). The term *cyclic* refers to the kind of algorithm used to calculate the checksum. *Redundancy* means that the field is *redundant*—it expands the size of the message but doesn't add any additional information. *Check* is self-explanatory—it is used to check if the frame traveled from source to destination without the data being corrupted.

6.3 *Frame switching*

Now that we have looked at the information in the Ethernet header and trailer, let's see how switches use the Source and Destination fields to build a *MAC address table* and forward frames to the appropriate destination(s) within a LAN.

6.3.1 *MAC address learning*

When a switch has to make a decision about how to forward a frame, it looks up the frame's destination MAC address in its MAC address table, which is a list of the MAC addresses in the LAN and which port each is connected to. We will examine the frame-forwarding process in section 6.3.2, but first, how does a switch build its MAC address table?

NOTE Another name for a MAC address table is *CAM table*, named after the kind of memory the table is stored in (*content addressable memory*).

This is the role of the Source field of the Ethernet header. When a switch receives a frame on one of its ports, it examines the Source field and creates an entry for that MAC address in its MAC address table, associating that MAC address with the port the frame was received on. This entry says "To reach this MAC address, forward the frame out of this port." This makes sense: if a switch receives a frame from MAC address X on port Y, the switch knows it can reach the host with MAC address X out of port Y. This process is called *MAC address learning*. Figure 6.3 shows a simple network with two switches, each with two PCs connected. By examining the Source field of frames that arrive on its ports, each switch has built a MAC address table that tells it which port each MAC address is connected to (directly or via another switch).

DEFINITION MAC addresses learned by a switch in this manner are known as *dynamic* MAC addresses—they are automatically (*dynamically*) learned. This is in contrast to *static* MAC addresses, which are manually (*statically*) configured, although that is quite rare. A switch will remove a dynamic MAC address from its MAC address table after 5 minutes of inactivity (if it doesn't receive a frame from that MAC address for 5 minutes); this is called *MAC aging*.

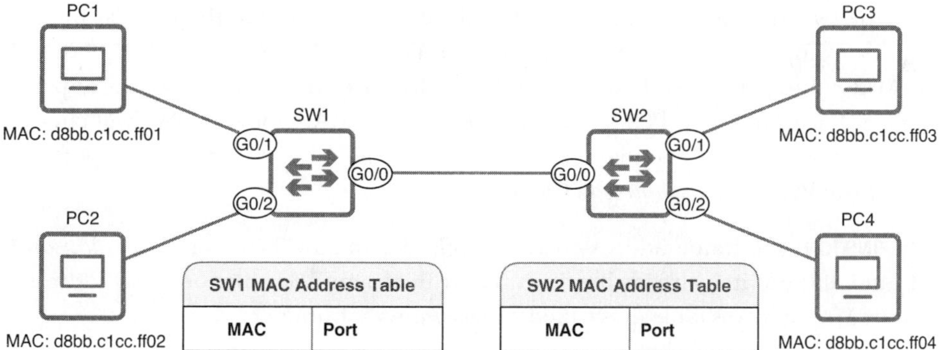

SW1 MAC Address Table

MAC	Port
d8bb.c1cc.ff01	G0/1
d8bb.c1cc.ff02	G0/2
d8bb.c1cc.ff03	G0/0
d8bb.c1cc.ff04	G0/0

SW2 MAC Address Table

MAC	Port
d8bb.c1cc.ff01	G0/0
d8bb.c1cc.ff02	G0/0
d8bb.c1cc.ff03	G0/1
d8bb.c1cc.ff04	G0/2

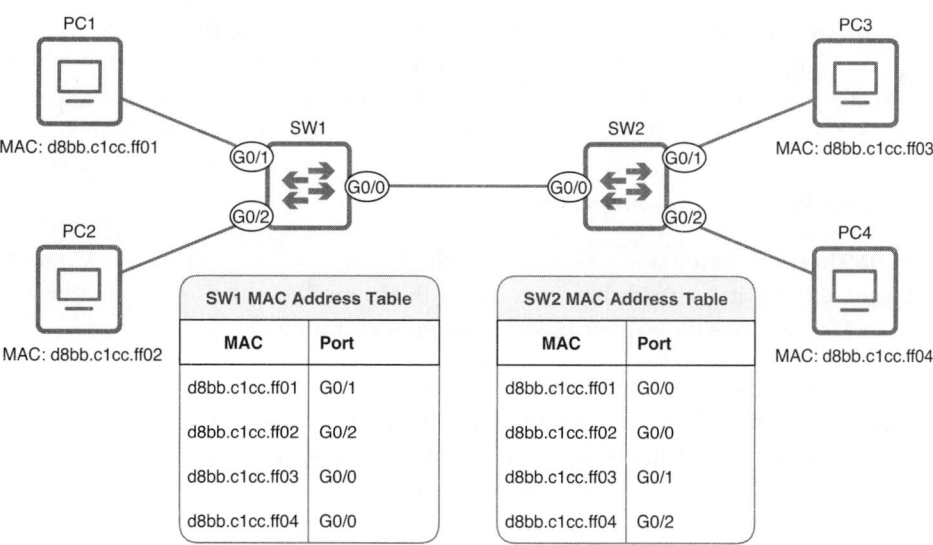

Figure 6.3 A network with two switches, each with two PCs connected. SW1 and SW2 have learned the MAC address of each PC by examining the Source field of frames received on their ports as the PCs communicate with each other. SW1 knows it can reach PC1 via its G0/1 port, PC2 via its G0/2 port, and PC3/PC4 via its G0/0 port. SW2 knows it can reach PC1/PC2 via its G0/0 port, PC3 via its G0/1 port, and PC4 via its G0/2 port.

Figure 6.3 shows the state of the network after the switches have learned the MAC addresses of the devices in the LAN. However, we are missing a few pieces of the puzzle, such as how switches forward traffic before they have built their MAC address tables and how the PCs learn each others' MAC addresses.

Port names on Cisco devices

Ports on Cisco devices have a name indicating their maximum supported speed (Ethernet = 10 Mbps, FastEthernet = 100 Mbps, GigabitEthernet = 1 Gbps, TenGigabitEthernet = 10 Gbps), followed by one to three numbers. How many numbers are used depends on the model of the device.

In this book, I will use a two-number system (X/Y), where the first number is the *slot* on the device, and the second number is the port number within that slot. A *slot* is a group of ports on a network device. In many cases, the ports in a slot are modular, meaning you can insert *modules* with different kinds of ports depending on your needs. Additionally, I will shorten the names to use the first letter only: E = Ethernet, F = FastEthernet, G = GigabitEthernet, T = TenGigabitEthernet.

Furthermore, port numbers on physical Cisco switches start from 1 (G0/1, G0/2, G0/3, etc). However, for most examples in this book, I will use virtual devices running in Cisco's emulation software CML (Cisco Modeling Labs), in which port numbers start from 0 (G0/0, G0/1, G0/2, etc).

6.3.2 Frame flooding and forwarding

Once the switches have learned the MAC address of each host in the LAN, as in figure 6.3, forwarding traffic is simple: when a switch receives a frame, it looks up the destination MAC address in its MAC address table and forwards the frame out of the appropriate port. For example, if PC1 sends a frame to PC2's MAC address, SW1 will check its MAC address table and see that it should forward the frame out of its G0/2 port. This frame from PC1 is a *known unicast* frame.

DEFINITION A frame addressed to a single destination host is called a *unicast* frame. If the switch already has an entry for the frame's destination MAC address in its MAC address table, it is called a *known unicast* frame.

The action a switch takes upon receiving a known unicast frame is to forward it out of the appropriate port. Now let's examine what happens when a switch receives a unicast frame and doesn't have an entry for the frame's destination MAC address in its MAC address table—an *unknown unicast* frame. Figure 6.4 shows what happens when PC1 sends a message to PC3, and both switches have an empty MAC address table.

DEFINITION An *unknown unicast frame* is a frame addressed to a single destination host, but the switch doesn't have an entry for the frame's destination MAC address in its MAC address table.

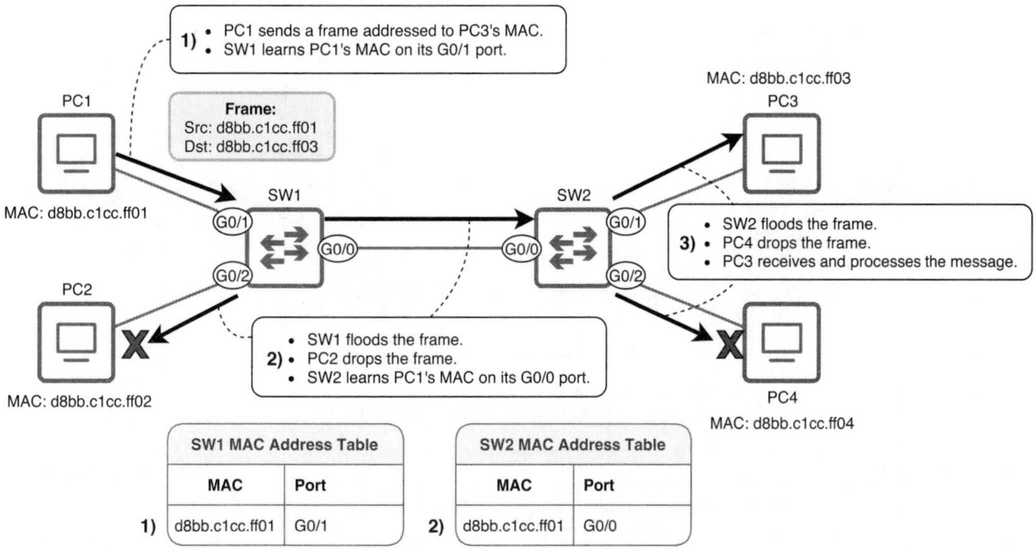

Figure 6.4 PC1 sends a unicast frame to PC3, but neither SW1 nor SW2 have an entry for the destination MAC address in their MAC address table. (1) PC1 sends the frame, and SW1 learns PC1's MAC address. (2) SW1 floods the frame. SW2 learns PC1's MAC address. PC2 drops the frame. (3) SW2 floods the frame. PC4 drops the frame. PC3 receives and processes it.

PC1 sends a unicast frame addressed to PC3's MAC address. SW1 uses the Source of the frame to learn PC1's MAC address, and then it *floods* the frame—it sends the frame out of every port except the one it was received on (G0/1). SW1 doesn't have an entry for the PC3's MAC address in its MAC address table, so by flooding the frame, it hopes the frame will be able to reach PC3, and then it will later be able to learn PC3's MAC address when PC3 sends a reply.

DEFINITION To *flood* a frame is to send it out of all ports, except the port the frame was received on. Switches take this action on receiving an unknown unicast frame.

When SW1 floods the frame, both PC2 and SW2 receive it. Because the destination MAC address of the frame is not PC2's, it drops the frame. SW2, on the other hand, will treat the frame just like SW1 did; it will learn PC1's MAC address and then flood the frame out of its G0/1 and G0/2 ports.

When SW2 floods the frame, both PC3 and PC4 receive it. Like PC2, PC4 will drop the frame because the destination MAC address is not its own. However, PC3 sees that the frame is destined for its own MAC address, so PC3 will receive and process the message. Figure 6.5 shows what then happens when PC3 sends a reply back to PC1.

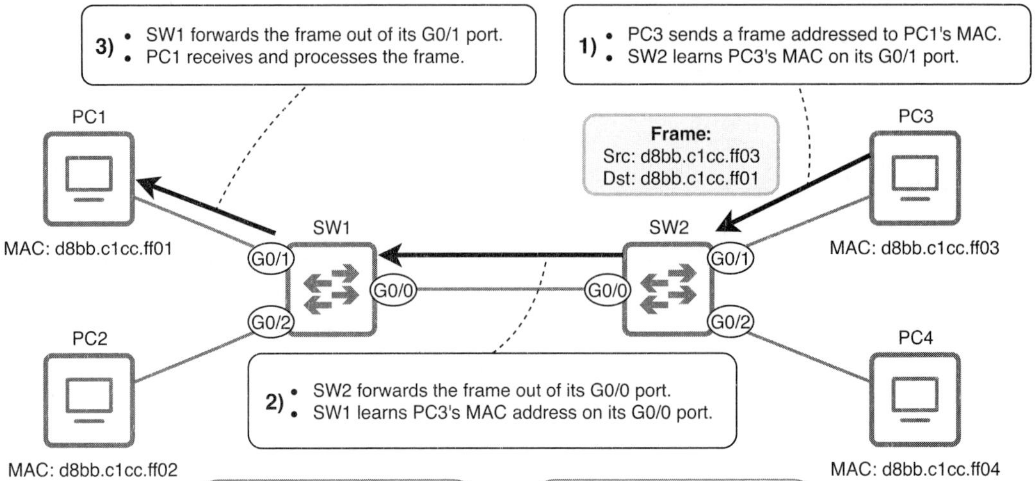

SW1 MAC Address Table

	MAC	Port
	d8bb.c1cc.ff01	G0/1
2)	d8bb.c1cc.ff03	G0/0

SW2 MAC Address Table

	MAC	Port
	d8bb.c1cc.ff01	G0/0
1)	d8bb.c1cc.ff03	G0/1

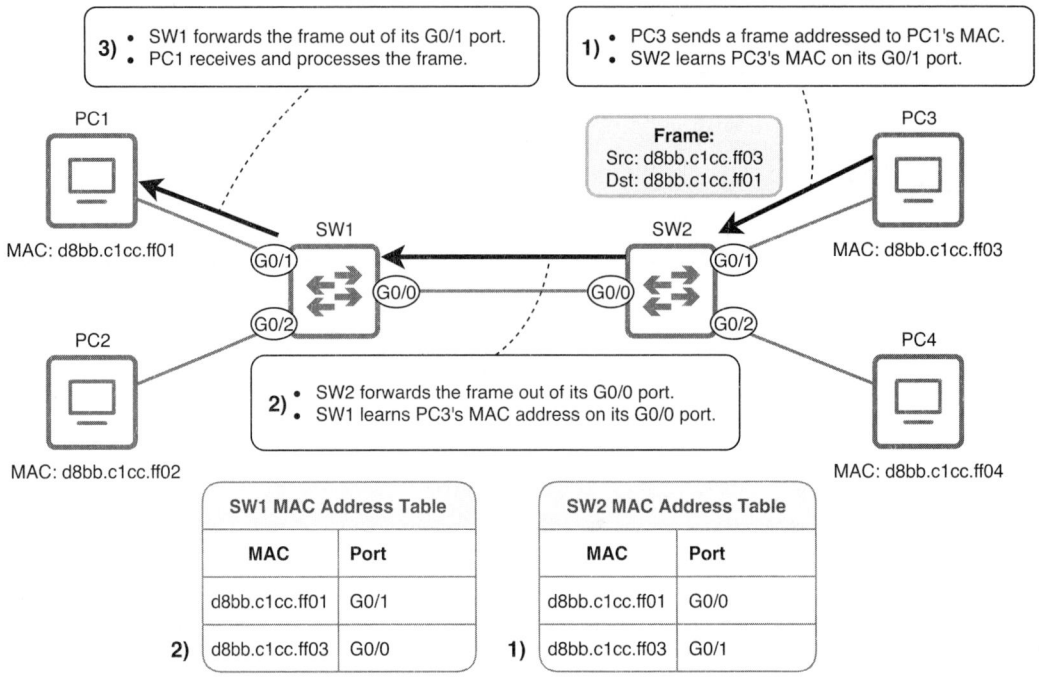

Figure 6.5 PC3 replies to PC1's message. (1) PC3 sends the frame, and SW2 learns PC3's MAC address. (2) SW2 forwards the frame out of its G0/0 port, and SW1 learns PC3's MAC address. (3) SW1 forwards the frame out of its G0/1 port, and PC1 receives and processes it.

PC3's reply to PC1 is also a unicast frame, but this time both SW1 and SW2 have an entry for the frame's destination (PC1's MAC address) in their MAC address tables, so rather than flooding the frame, each switch simply forwards it out of the port specified by the entry in its MAC address table. First, PC3 sends the frame, and SW2 learns PC3's MAC address on its G0/1 port. SW2 then forwards the frame out of its G0/0 port, and SW1 learns PC3's MAC address on its G0/0 port. Finally, SW1 forwards the frame out of its G0/1 port, and PC1 receives and processes the message. Remember what action a switch takes for each kind of unicast frame:

- *Known unicast frame (forward)*—The switch will send the frame out of the port specified by the MAC address's entry in the MAC address table.
- *Unknown unicast frame (flood)*—The switch will send the frame out of all ports except the one it was received on.

NOTE A switch is *transparent* to its connected hosts; PC1 and PC3 address their messages directly to each other, not to SW1 or SW2, exactly as they would if they were directly connected with a single cable. This is why a message passing through a switch is not considered a hop (as stated in chapter 4). Also, switches do not modify the frames they switch in any way; they simply forward or flood them as appropriate.

6.3.3 The MAC address table in Cisco IOS

The command to view a Cisco switch's MAC address table is **show mac address-table** (in user EXEC or privileged EXEC mode). As the following example shows, there are a few more columns than just the MAC address and port. The `Type` column indicates whether the MAC address was dynamically learned (`DYNAMIC`) or statically configured (`STATIC`). The `Vlan` column indicates which *virtual LAN* (VLAN) each MAC address was learned in. We will cover VLANs in chapter 12. For now, just note that all of the MAC addresses are in VLAN 1 by default:

```
SW1# show mac address-table
          Mac Address Table
-------------------------------------------

Vlan    Mac Address       Type        Ports
----    -----------       --------    -----
   1    5254.0017.7cd2    DYNAMIC     Gi0/0
   1    d8bb.c1cc.ff01    DYNAMIC     Gi0/1
   1    d8bb.c1cc.ff02    DYNAMIC     Gi0/2
   1    d8bb.c1cc.ff03    DYNAMIC     Gi0/0
   1    d8bb.c1cc.ff04    DYNAMIC     Gi0/0
```

Views SW1's MAC address table

A list of MAC addresses and the port each was learned on

NOTE Cisco abbreviates GigabitEthernet ports as "GiX/X," not "GX/X."

Above the MAC addresses of PC1, PC2, PC3, and PC4 in the previous example, there is an additional MAC address in SW1's MAC address table (`5254.0017.7cd2`). This is the MAC address of SW2's G0/0 port. Although the MAC addresses of a switch's ports don't play a role when it is forwarding traffic between hosts, switches periodically exchange messages with each other and learn each other's MAC addresses in the process. We will cover some of these messages exchanged among switches in this book.

Although you can usually leave a switch to learn MAC addresses by itself and clear them as needed (after 5 minutes of inactivity), you can manually clear dynamic MAC addresses from a switch's MAC address table with the **clear mac address-table dynamic** command. The following example shows this; I clear SW1's MAC address table and then view it again, but it is empty:

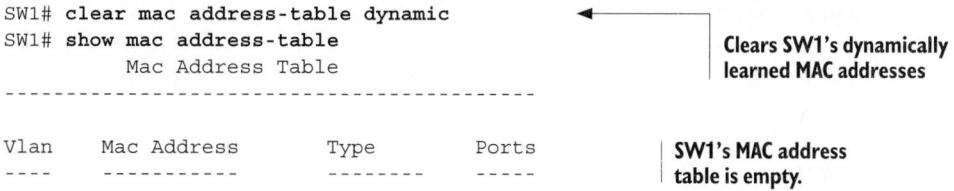

```
SW1# clear mac address-table dynamic
SW1# show mac address-table
          Mac Address Table
-------------------------------------------

Vlan    Mac Address       Type        Ports
----    -----------       --------    -----
```

Clears SW1's dynamically learned MAC addresses

SW1's MAC address table is empty.

You can also specify a specific address to remove from the MAC address table or tell the switch to remove all MAC addresses learned on a specific port. To clear a specific dynamic MAC address from the table, you can use the **`clear mac address-table dynamic address`** *`mac-address`* command. To clear all dynamic MAC addresses learned on a specific interface, use the **`clear mac address-table dynamic interface`** *`interface-name`* command.

However, as stated previously, you usually will not have to manually interfere with a switch's MAC address learning and aging processes. Note that this command uses the term *interface* instead of *port*. As you will see when we cover more configurations, this is true of most commands within Cisco IOS.

> **NOTE** When I use bold and italics in a command, the bolded words indicate the command and its keywords that you must type. The italicized words indicate *arguments* for which you must provide a value. For example, in **`clear mac address-table dynamic address`** *`mac-address`*, you must type **`clear mac address-table dynamic address`** and then specify the *`mac-address`* to clear.

6.4 Address Resolution Protocol

Now we have looked at how switches forward frames and learn the MAC addresses of devices in their LAN. Next we will take a step back to fill in another piece of the puzzle—how the PCs know each other's MAC address. For PC1 and PC3 to send messages to each other, they first need to learn each other's MAC address. To do so, they use *Address Resolution Protocol* (ARP).

ARP allows a host to learn the MAC address of another host in the LAN. ARP involves two messages: an *ARP request* (used to ask another host what its MAC address is) and an *ARP reply* (used to inform another host of this host's MAC address). The ARP request message is sent in a new kind of frame: not unicast but *broadcast*. The ARP reply is a unicast frame sent to the MAC address of the host that sent the ARP request.

> **DEFINITION** A *broadcast frame* is a frame addressed to the *broadcast MAC address*: ffff.ffff.ffff. A switch will flood broadcast frames, like unknown unicast frames. Broadcast frames are used by hosts to send messages to all other hosts in the LAN.

If an ARP request is broadcast (addressed to all other hosts in the LAN), how does the sender specify which host's MAC address it wants to learn? It does so by specifying the *IP address* of the host it wants to know the MAC address of. Figure 6.6 demonstrates this. PC1 wants to send a message to PC3 but doesn't know PC3's MAC address. So, PC1 uses ARP to learn PC3's MAC address.

> **NOTE** The IP addresses of PC1, PC2, PC3, and PC4 are shown in figure 6.6, but it's not necessary to understand the structure of IP addresses yet. We will cover IP addresses in the next chapter.

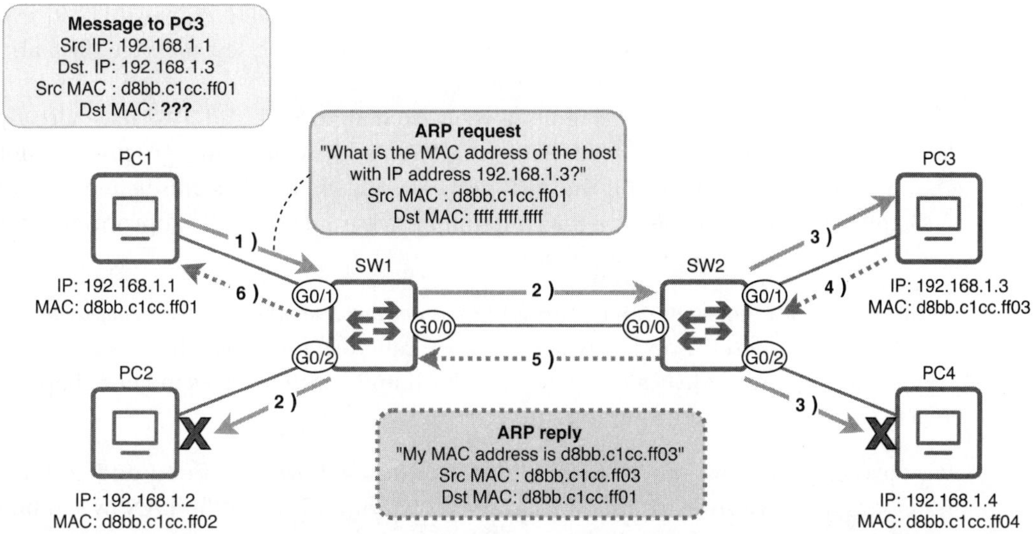

Figure 6.6 An ARP request and reply exchange between PC1 and PC3. PC1 wants to send a message to PC3 but does not know PC3's MAC address, so PC1 uses ARP to learn PC3's MAC address.

Here's the process shown in figure 6.6:

1. PC1 sends an ARP request addressed to the broadcast MAC (ffff.ffff.ffff).
2. SW1 floods the frame. PC2 sees the ARP request is not for its own IP address, so it drops the message.
3. SW2 floods the frame. PC4 sees the ARP request is not for its own IP address, so it drops the message. PC3 sees the ARP request is for its own IP address.
4. PC3 sends an ARP reply to PC1.
5. SW2 forwards the ARP reply out of its G0/0 port.
6. SW1 forwards the ARP reply out of its G0/1 port. PC1 now knows PC3's MAC address, so it will be able to send the original message to PC3.

NOTE The group of devices that will receive a broadcast frame sent by one of the group's members are in the same *broadcast domain.* A broadcast domain can be thought of as equivalent to a LAN or Layer 2 domain. All of the devices in figure 6.6 are in the same broadcast domain because they receive each other's broadcast frames.

After the ARP exchange is complete, PC1 knows PC3's MAC address; it will store PC3's MAC address in its ARP table, which is a list of IP addresses and their associated MAC addresses. ARP can be thought of as the bridge between Layers 2 and 3 of the TCP/IP model. ARP is used to map a known Layer 3 address (IP address) to an unknown Layer 2 address (MAC address).

Now PC1 will be able to send its message in a frame addressed to PC3's MAC address. It is also worth mentioning that upon receiving PC1's ARP request message, PC3 also stores PC1's MAC address in its own ARP table.

Note that, thanks to the ARP request–reply exchange, SW1 and SW2 have already learned PC1 and PC3's MAC addresses (the MAC address learning process was not shown in figure 6.6 to focus on the ARP process). So, when PC1 sends its message to PC3, the switches won't flood it—they will simply forward it out of the appropriate port because it is a known unicast message.

> **NOTE** Unicast messages can be thought of as *one-to-one* and broadcast as *one-to-all.* Additionally, there is another type of message called *multicast,* which is *one-to-multiple* (but not necessarily all). We will touch on multicast messages in later chapters of this volume and volume 2.

We have covered how switches learn MAC addresses, how they flood and forward frames, and how hosts learn the MAC address of another host in the LAN by sending an ARP request to that host's IP address, but there is still one more part to the puzzle. How does a host know the IP address of the host it wants to send a message to? The answer is, "It depends." We will cover some possibilities in this book—for example, the *Domain Name System* (DNS), which is used to convert hostnames (i.e., manning.com) into IP addresses. As another option, the user of the device could manually specify the IP address to send a message to, such as when using *ping* to test connectivity.

> **NOTE** A device doesn't have to use ARP every time it sends a message. After it has used ARP to learn another device's MAC address, it stores that information in its ARP table for future use.

6.5 Ping

Ping is a software utility that tests the reachability of hosts over a network. It's not directly connected to the topic of Ethernet switching, but it is a tool I'll be referencing throughout the book, and it also serves to fill the final piece of the puzzle in this chapter—how a source host knows the IP address of the destination host it wants to send a message to.

To send a ping message to another host on the network, the command is **`ping`** *`ip-address`* (this is true for Cisco IOS, Windows, Linux, macOS, etc.). The IP address of the destination host is specified directly in the command, so that's how the source host knows the IP address of the destination host.

Ping is a component of the *Internet Control Message Protocol* (ICMP), which plays a supporting role for the *Internet Protocol* (IP). In your networking career (or career in nearly any other area of IT), you'll certainly use ping very frequently as a simple way to test whether two hosts can reach each other over the network; it is a very common diagnostic and troubleshooting tool. Like ARP, ping consists of two messages: an *ICMP echo request* and an *ICMP echo reply*. However, unlike ARP, both messages used by ping are unicast.

Ping can also be used to measure the *round-trip time* (RTT) between two hosts—the time it takes a message to travel from one host to another and back. The following example shows a ping from a Cisco router (R1) to another host on its local network. In Cisco IOS, a single **ping** command sends five ICMP echo requests. As highlighted, the output lists the minimum, average, and maximum RTT for those five requests:

```
PC1# ping 10.0.0.12
Type escape sequence to abort.
Sending 5, 100-byte ICMP Echos to 10.0.0.12, timeout is 2 seconds:
!!!!!
Success rate is 100 percent (5/5), round-trip min/avg/max = 3/3/4 ms
```

Sends five ICMP echo requests (pings) to the specified IP address

Each exclamation mark indicates a successful ping.

The five exclamation marks (`!!!!!`) in the output indicate successful pings—ICMP echo requests that received an ICMP echo reply. If any of the requests do not receive a reply, a period (`.`) is displayed instead. For example, if the first request did not receive a reply, the output would be `.!!!!`.

Summary

- A *local area network* (LAN) can be defined as a portion of a network where hosts can communicate with each other without the use of a router. This is also called a *Layer 2 domain.*
- The Ethernet header has three fields: Destination, Source, and Type/Length. The Ethernet trailer has one field: the Frame Check Sequence (FCS).
- Although they are not considered part of the Ethernet frame, the Preamble and Start Frame Delimiter (SFD) are sent with each frame.
- The Preamble is a 7-byte series of alternating binary 1s and 0s. The SFD is a single byte in length and uses the bit pattern 10101011 to indicate the end of the Preamble and the beginning of the frame.
- The Destination and Source fields are each 6 bytes in length and contain the MAC address of the frame's sender (Source) and its intended receiver (Destination). MAC addresses are assigned by the manufacturer and should be globally unique.
- MAC addresses are usually written in hexadecimal, a number system that uses 16 characters: 0, 1, 2, 3, 4, 5, 6, 7, 8, 9, A, B, C, D, E, and F. When written in hexadecimal, MAC addresses are 12 characters in length.
- The first half of a MAC address is the *organizationally unique identifier* (OUI), which is assigned to the device's manufacturer by the IEEE. The second half of the MAC address can be used freely by the manufacturer to assign a unique MAC address to each port of the devices it manufactures.
- The Type/Length field either indicates the *type* of the encapsulated packet (i.e., IPv4 or IPv6) or the *length* of the encapsulated packet in bytes. If the value is 1500

or less, it indicates the length of the packet. If the value is 1536 or greater, it indicates the type (in this case, the name is *EtherType*).

- The FCS field uses a *cyclic redundancy check* (CRC) to allow the receiving host to check for errors in the frame that might have occurred in transit.
- A switch makes decisions about how to forward frames by looking up each frame's destination MAC address in the switch's MAC address table.
- A switch builds its MAC address table by looking at the source MAC address field of frames it receives and creating an entry in the MAC address table, associating the MAC address with the port the frame was received on. This is called *MAC address learning*.
- MAC addresses learned like this are called *dynamic MAC addresses*.
- If a switch doesn't receive a frame from a dynamic MAC address for 5 minutes, it will remove the entry from the MAC address table. This is called *MAC address aging*.
- A frame addressed to a single host is called a *unicast* frame. If the switch already has an entry for the frame's destination MAC in its MAC address table, it is a *known unicast* frame, and the switch will forward it out of the appropriate port. If the switch does not have an entry for the frame's destination MAC in its MAC address table, it is an *unknown unicast* frame, and the switch will *flood* the frame, sending it out of all ports (except the one it was received on).
- The **`show mac address-table`** command allows you to view the MAC address table of a Cisco switch. Dynamic MAC addresses can be cleared with **`clear mac address-table dynamic`**, **`clear mac address-table dynamic address`** *`mac-address`*, or **`clear mac address-table dynamic interface`** *`interface-name`*.
- Address Resolution Protocol (ARP) allows a host to learn the MAC address of another host in the network. It uses two messages: an *ARP request* and an *ARP reply*.
- The ARP request is sent to the broadcast MAC address (ffff.ffff.ffff), so it is flooded by switches. The ARP reply is a unicast message.
- A *broadcast domain* is a group of devices that receive broadcast messages from each other. Devices connected to the same switch (or different switches, but the switches are connected) are in the same broadcast domain.
- The ARP table is used to store IP address-to-MAC address mappings, so an ARP request doesn't have to be sent before every single packet.
- Ping is a utility that tests connectivity between two network hosts. It is a component of the Internet Control Message Protocol (ICMP) and is a common diagnostic and troubleshooting tool. To send a ping, use the **`ping`** *`ip-address`* command.
- Ping uses two messages: an *ICMP echo request* and an *ICMP echo reply*. Both are unicast messages.

7 IPv4 addressing

This chapter covers

- The fields of the IPv4 header
- The binary number system
- How to convert between decimal and binary
- The structure of IPv4 addresses
- How to configure IPv4 addresses on Cisco routers

In chapter 6, we focused on Layer 2 of the TCP/IP model: how switches use information in the Ethernet header to make forwarding decisions. In this chapter, we will move up a layer to Layer 3 and look at the contents of the *Internet Protocol version 4* (IPv4) header, focusing on IPv4 addressing.

We are now in the realm of routers, rather than switches. Whereas switches use information in the Layer 2 header to decide how to forward messages to their proper destinations, routers use information in the Layer 3 header to make their forwarding decisions. In this chapter, we won't yet focus on exactly how routers make those forwarding decisions; we will leave that for part 2 of this book. Instead, we will first focus on the contents of the IPv4 header and the addresses used in that header.

The specific exam topic we will cover is topic 1.6: Configure and verify IPv4 addressing and subnetting. However, IPv4 addressing is not only relevant to exam topic 1.6; it is a fundamental topic that is essential to understanding nearly any other CCNA exam topic. Also note that we will cover *subnetting*, the second half of topic 1.6, in part 2 of this book.

Given the name *IPv4*, you may wonder what happened to previous versions. The history and characteristics of IPv0, v1, v2, and v3, although important steps in the evolution toward IPv4, are not necessary to know for the CCNA exam, so we will not cover them. It is IPv4, officially defined in RFC 791 (simply titled "Internet Protocol") that is the foundation of modern networks such as the internet.

NOTE In addition to IPv4, IPv6 is another major exam topic that has its own part in this volume. IPv6 was introduced in 1995 to replace IPv4, but its adoption has been slow. Although IPv6 adoption is accelerating as the available IPv4 address pool runs out, it seems that for the foreseeable future, network engineers will have to be familiar with both IPv4 and IPv6.

7.1 The IPv4 header

Before looking at the details of IPv4 addressing, it's helpful to understand the header that contains those addresses. However, the IPv4 header doesn't just contain IPv4 addresses; it contains a variety of fields, each serving a different role in enabling the end-to-end delivery of packets (the role of Layer 3).

The IPv4 header is more complex than the Ethernet header, as you'll probably notice when looking at figure 7.1. In total, there are 14 fields (although the Options field is optional), whereas the Ethernet header and trailer only have 4 (6 if you include the Preamble and SFD).

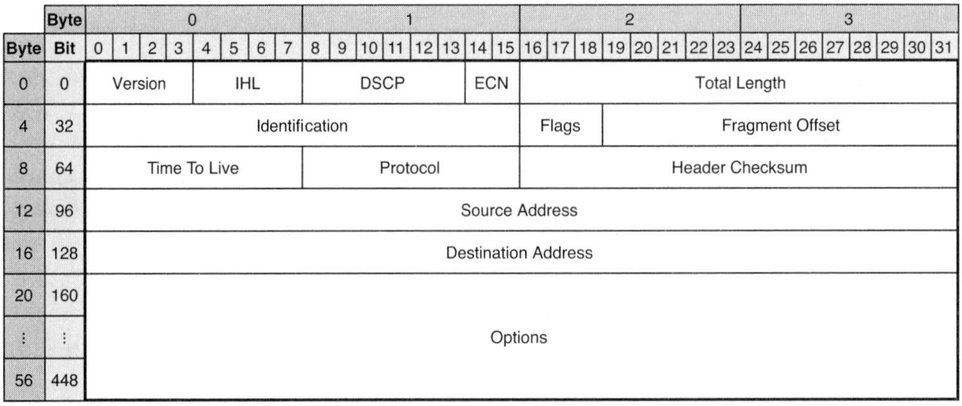

Figure 7.1 The format of the IPv4 header. The header is typically 20 bytes in size (the minimum size) but can be up to 60 bytes if the Options field is used.

Before we examine the purpose of each field of the header, I want to clarify how to read figure 7.1. The fields of the header are contained within the thick border and should be read from left to right, top to bottom; the first bit of the header is in the top-left position, and the last bit is in the bottom-right position. The numbers along the top indicate that each row is 4 bytes (32 bits) in length. The numbers on the left of each row indicate the starting byte/bit number of that row. For example, the second row starts at byte 4 (the fifth byte), which is bit 32 (the thirty-third bit).

NOTE In networking, you'll have to get used to counting from 0. For example, the range from 0 to 31 includes 32 bits in total: bit 0 is the first bit, bit 1 is the second bit, etc. Likewise, byte 0 is the first byte, byte 1 is the second byte, byte 2 is the third byte, byte 3 is the fourth byte, etc.

As stated, the Options field is optional (and variable in size), so the length of the IPv4 header is variable. Without the Options field, the header is 20 bytes in length, from the first bit of the Version field to the last bit of the Destination Address field. With the Options field at its maximum size (40 bytes), the IPv4 header is 60 bytes in length. However, the Options field is rarely used and is beyond the scope of the CCNA exam.

EXAM TIP For the purpose of the CCNA exam, don't worry about memorizing the length and position of each field of the IPv4 header. Questions on the CCNA exam are more substantial than trivia like "What's the length of field X?" For the purpose of this chapter, it's sufficient to have a basic understanding of the purpose of each field. This chapter focuses on the IPv4 addresses in the Source Address and Destination Address fields, and in the rest of this book, we will look at other fields in greater detail as required.

7.1.1 The Version field

The first field of the IPv4 header is the *Version* field. It is 4 bits in length. As I mentioned previously, there are two versions of IP used in modern networks: IPv4 and IPv6. The purpose of this field is simple: to indicate which version of IP is being used. In modern networks, you can expect to find one of two values in this field:

- A value of 0b0100 (0d4) indicates IPv4.
- A value of 0b0110 (0d6) indicates IPv6.

NOTE As mentioned in chapter 6, the prefix *0b* indicates a binary number, and the prefix *0d* indicates a decimal number. We will look at how to convert between the two number systems later in this chapter.

7.1.2 The IHL field

The second field is the *Internet Header Length* (IHL) field, which is 4 bits in length. This field is used to indicate the length of the IPv4 header. The reason this field is necessary is because the IP header is variable in length, depending on whether the Options field is present or not (and the Options field itself is variable in length too).

The IHL field indicates the length of the IPv4 header in 4-byte increments. For example, if the value of this field is 5, it means the header is 20 bytes in length (the minimum length of the IPv4 header).

> **NOTE** A value less than 5 should not be used in this field because the IPv4 header cannot be less than 20 bytes in length.

Any value greater than 5 in the IHL field indicates that the Options field is present in the header. The maximum value of the IHL field is 15, indicating that the header is 60 bytes in length (the maximum length of the IPv4 header). In that case, the Options field is 40 bytes in length, and the rest of the header is 20 bytes.

7.1.3 The DSCP and ECN fields

The next two fields are *Differentiated Services Code Point* (DSCP), which is 6 bits in length, and *Explicit Congestion Notification* (ECN), which is 2 bits in length. This byte of the IPv4 header used to be called the *Type of Service* field and still is sometimes, but DSCP + ECN is the current definition.

These fields are used for *Quality of Service* (QoS), which is a network feature used to prioritize specific types of network traffic over other types. A common use case for QoS is to prioritize delay-sensitive network traffic—network traffic for which it is very important to reach the destination as soon as possible, without delay. One example of this is voice and video traffic; I think most of us know how frustrating it can be to have a Zoom call (or a call using any similar application) with poor quality. QoS helps ensure that this traffic is forwarded with as little delay as possible.

> **NOTE** QoS is another CCNA exam topic, and we will cover it in chapter 10 of volume 2 of this book.

7.1.4 The Total Length field

The *Total Length* field is a 16-bit field that indicates the total length of the packet—the IPv4 header and its payload. Don't confuse this with the IHL field, which indicates the length of the IPv4 header alone. Figure 7.2 illustrates the difference between the IHL and Total Length fields.

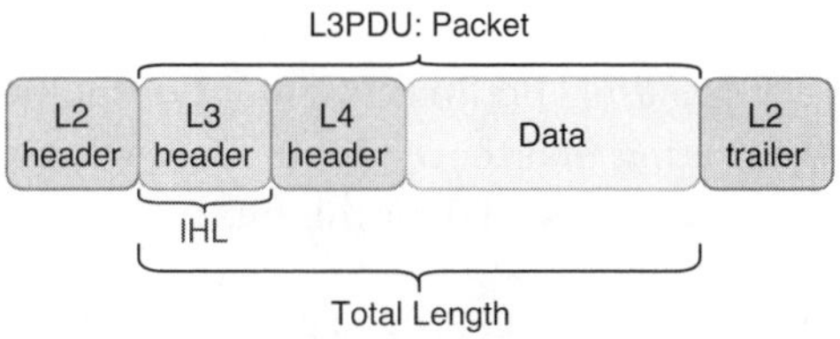

Figure 7.2 The difference between the IHL and Total Length fields. The IHL field indicates the length of the IPv4 header (Layer 3 header), whereas the Total Length field indicates the length of the entire packet. The Layer 2 header and trailer are shown to emphasize that a packet will always be encapsulated in a frame before being sent; a packet alone is not ready to be sent over the physical medium.

Another difference between the IHL and Total Length fields is that the value of the Total Length field indicates the length of the packet in bytes, rather than 4-byte increments. For example, a value of 100 in the Total Length field means the packet is 100 bytes in length, and a value of 1,000 in the Total Length field means the packet is 1,000 bytes in length.

7.1.5 The Identification, Flags, and Fragment Offset fields

The *Identification*, *Flags*, and *Fragment Offset* fields, 32 bits in total, are used together to support packet *fragmentation*—when a packet is broken up into multiple smaller packets called *fragments*. IPv4 uses a concept called *maximum transmission unit* (MTU) to indicate the maximum size a packet should be, and any packet larger than the MTU will be fragmented. Then, the final destination host of the packet reassembles the fragments to restore the original packet.

The typical MTU is 1,500 bytes, and this should be supported on all modern devices. However, if for some reason a router in the packet's path to the destination has a lower MTU, it will fragment the packet. Another possibility is that a host sends packets larger than the standard 1,500-byte size (sometimes packet sizes up to 9,000 bytes are used). If a router in the path to the destination doesn't support those larger packets, it will fragment them. Let's briefly examine the role of each of these three fields.

IDENTIFICATION FIELD

This field is 16 bits in length and is used to identify which original packet a fragment belongs to. When a packet is fragmented, all of its fragments must have the same value in this field.

FLAGS FIELD

This field is 3 bits in length and is used to control and identify fragments. The 3 bits of this field (bit 0, bit 1, and bit 2) are defined as follows:

- *Bit 0: Reserved*—This bit's use hasn't been defined, so it is always set to 0.
- *Bit 1: Don't Fragment (DF) bit*—If this bit is set to 1, it means the packet should not be fragmented. In that case, if the packet's size is greater than the MTU, it will be discarded.

- *Bit 2: More Fragments (MF) bit*—If this bit is set to 1, it means there are more fragments remaining—this one isn't the last. The final fragment of the packet will have a value of 0 in this field (indicating that there are no more fragments). An unfragmented packet will always have a value of 0 for this bit.

FRAGMENT OFFSET FIELD

This field is 13 bits in length and is used to indicate the position of the fragment within the original packet. This allows fragmented packets to be reassembled even if the fragments arrive out of order. This is rare, but if there are multiple paths to a destination, different fragments might take different paths, in which case they may arrive at the destination out of order.

7.1.6 The TTL field

The *Time To Live* (TTL) field is an 8-bit field. When a host sends a packet, it will set an initial value in this field (a common value is 64), and then each router that forwards the packet will decrease the value in this field by 1. If the value reaches 0, the router will drop the packet.

The reason for this mechanism is to prevent packets from *looping* around the network infinitely. A *loop* is when a message travels around the network without being able to find its destination. For example, if there are three routers (R1, R2, and R3), a looping packet might be passed from R1 to R2, from R2 to R3, from R3 to R1, from R1 to R2, from R2 to R3, etc. in a loop. Figure 7.3 shows an example of a looped packet being dropped thanks to the TTL field.

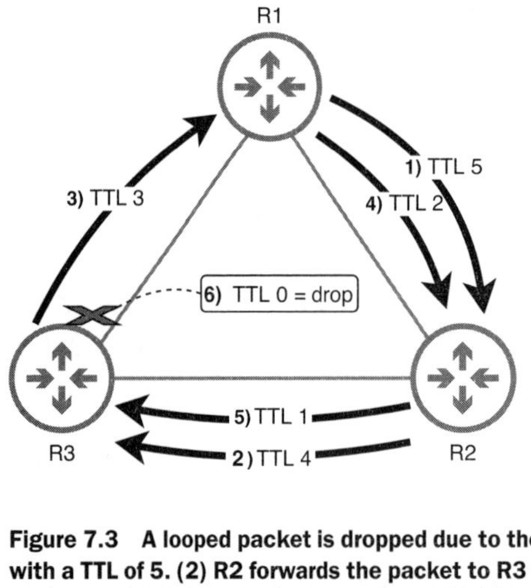

Figure 7.3 A looped packet is dropped due to the TTL mechanism. (1) R1 forwards the packet to R2 with a TTL of 5. (2) R2 forwards the packet to R3 with a TTL of 4. (3) R3 forwards the packet to R1 with a TTL of 3. (4) R1 forwards the packet to R2 with a TTL of 2. (5) R2 forwards the packet to R3 with a TTL of 1. (6) R3 wants to forward the packet to R1 but drops the packet because it must decrement the TTL to 0.

Loops should not occur in a properly configured network, but mistakes can happen. The TTL field prevents packets from looping indefinitely; once the packet's TTL reaches 0, it will be dropped.

7.1.7 The Protocol field

The *Protocol* field is 8 bits in length and is used to indicate what kind of message is encapsulated inside of the packet. This is similar to the Ethernet header's *EtherType* field, which indicates the type of message encapsulated in the frame (for example, an IPv4 packet or an IPv6 packet).

In the previous chapter, we covered the ping utility, which is a component of ICMP. If a packet contains an ICMP message, that is indicated with a value of 1 in this field. The following are the Protocol field values of some protocols we will cover in this book:

- *1*—ICMP
- *6*—Transmission Control Protocol (TCP)
- *17*—User Datagram Protocol (UDP)
- *89*—Open Shortest Path First (OSPF)

7.1.8 The Header Checksum field

The *Header Checksum* field is 16 bits in length and is used to check for errors in the IPv4 header. The mechanism is similar to the FCS in the Ethernet trailer. However, a major difference is that the Header Checksum field only checks for errors in the IPv4 header, not in the entire packet. On the other hand, the Ethernet FCS field doesn't just check for errors in the Ethernet header; it checks for errors in the entire frame.

7.1.9 The Source Address and Destination Address fields

These two fields contain the IP address of the host sending the packet (*Source Address* field) and the intended recipient of the packet (*Destination Address* field). Each of these fields is 32 bits in length—the length of an IPv4 address. We will cover the structure of IPv4 addresses in detail later in this chapter.

7.1.10 The Options field

The final field of the IPv4 header is the *Options* field. As mentioned previously, this field is optional and variable in length—from 0 bytes (if not used) to 40 bytes in length; this is the reason the IPv4 header requires a field to indicate the length of the header itself. This field is rarely used, and its use cases are beyond the scope of the CCNA exam.

7.2 The binary number system

To understand IPv4 addresses, you have to understand the binary number system, as well as how to convert between binary and decimal numbers. And to understand how binary numbers work, let's first review how decimal numbers work. We're all familiar with decimal numbers because we use them in our daily lives, but many of us don't think about how the decimal number system actually works.

7.2.1 *Decimal*

The decimal number system uses 10 digits: 0, 1, 2, 3, 4, 5, 6, 7, 8, and 9. All values are expressed using those 10 digits. For this reason, the decimal number system is also called *base 10*. Values from 0 to 9 can be expressed with a single digit, but to express greater values, we have to use more digits. For example, the number after 0d9 is 0d10—a 1 in the tens position and a 0 in the ones position.

After counting up to 0d99 (9 in the tens position and 9 in the ones position), we have to add a third digit; the number after 0d99 is 0d100—a 1 in the hundreds position and a 0 in both the tens and ones positions. Because decimal uses 10 digits, the value of each additional position increases tenfold as you add more digits: 1, then 10, then 100, then 1,000, etc. That's why, in the number 1,009 (for example), the 1 on the left has a greater value than the 9 on the right, even though on its own, the number 9 has a greater value than the number 1.

7.2.2 *Binary*

Counting in the binary system follows the same process but with only two digits: 0 and 1. For this reason, the binary number system is also called *base 2*. Only the values 0 and 1 can be expressed with a single digit; to express greater values, we have to add more digits.

The value after 0b1 is 0b10—a 1 in the twos position and a 0 in the ones position; this is equivalent to 0d2. After 0b10 is 0b11 (equivalent to 0d3), and then once again, both positions have reached their maximum value, so a third digit is needed. This results in 0b100 (equivalent to 0d4). Whereas the value of each decimal position increases 10-fold, the value of each binary position doubles because binary uses two digits. Figure 7.4 shows an eight-digit binary number with the value of each position above each bit (binary digit).

128	64	32	16	8	4	2	1
1	0	1	0	1	1	0	1

Figure 7.4 An 8-bit (1-byte) number with the value of each bit written above. The decimal equivalent of 0b10101101 is 0d173. This can be calculated by adding the value of each bit that is set to 1.

> **NOTE** The rightmost digit of a binary number is called the *least-significant bit*, because it has the least value. The leftmost digit is called the *most-significant bit*, because it has the greatest value.

Table 7.1 lists some decimal numbers and their binary equivalents. With only two digits available, binary numbers quickly grow in size (the value after 0b11111 would be 0b100000). That is why, although computers use binary numbers,, we convert those binary values to other number systems (decimal and hexadecimal) to make them more human-readable.

Table 7.1 Decimal numbers and their binary equivalents

Dec.	Bin.	Dec.	Bin.	Dec.	Bin.	Dec.	Bin.
0	0	8	1000	16	10000	24	11000
1	1	9	1001	17	10001	25	11001
2	10	10	1010	18	10010	26	11010
3	11	11	1011	19	10011	27	11011
4	100	12	1100	20	10100	28	11100
5	101	13	1101	21	10101	29	11101
6	110	14	1110	22	10110	30	11110
7	111	15	1111	23	10111	31	11111

Although IPv4 addresses are 32 bits in length, the good news is that you only have to be able to convert between binary and decimal for numbers up to 8 bits in length. That is because IPv4 addresses are divided into four groups of 8 bits, making them more manageable.

CONVERTING BINARY NUMBERS TO DECIMAL

Converting binary numbers to decimal is a simple process—just add up the values of the bits that are set to 1. Figure 7.5 demonstrates this process.

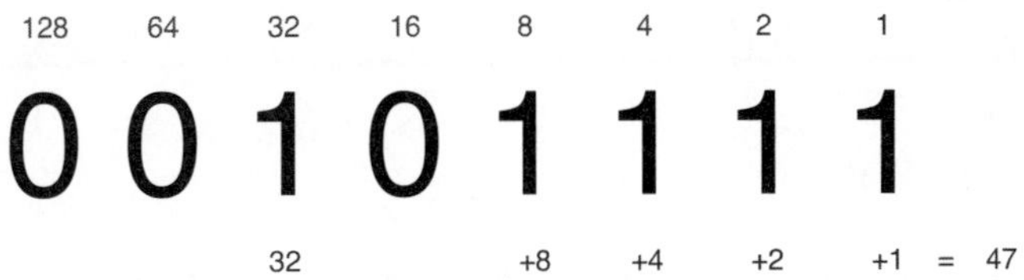

Figure 7.5 The binary number 00101111 is equal to 47 in decimal. To calculate this, add the value of each bit that is set to 1: 32 + 8 + 4 + 2 + 1 = 47.

I highly recommend spending some time practicing this. To do so, write some random 8-bit numbers (11011010, 01011100, 11101110, etc.), and practice converting them to decimal. With some practice, you should be able to convert from binary to decimal in your head, without writing down the value of each bit. To check your answers, you can do a quick internet search for "binary to decimal converter"; there are plenty of free tools available.

> **NOTE** The minimum value of an 8-bit number (with all bits set to 0) is 0d0. The maximum value of an 8-bit number (with all bits set to 1) is 0d255. Therefore, 8 bits provide 256 possible values: from 0d0 (0b00000000) to 0d255 (0b11111111).

CONVERTING DECIMAL NUMBERS TO BINARY

Converting from decimal to binary takes a few more steps. There are a few methods to do this, but figure 7.6 demonstrates the process I use. First, attempt to subtract the value of the most significant bit (128) from the decimal number. If the result is a positive number, note the remainder, and write a 1 in that bit position. If the subtraction would result in a negative value, do not subtract; just write a 0 in that bit position. Then, subtract the value of the second-most significant bit (64) from the remainder of the previous subtraction (or the original number, if you couldn't subtract 128 from the number), and repeat the process until you reach 0. Figure 7.6 shows how this works:

1. Subtracting 128 from 206 gives a remainder of 78. Write a 1 in the 128 position.
2. Subtracting 64 from 78 gives a remainder of 14. Write a 1 in the 64 position.
3. 32 cannot be subtracted from 14. Write a 0 in the 32 position.
4. 16 cannot be subtracted from 14. Write a 0 in the 16 position.
5. Subtracting 8 from 14 gives a remainder of 6. Write a 1 in the 8 position.
6. Subtracting 4 from 6 gives a remainder of 2. Write a 1 in the 4 position.
7. Subtracting 2 from 2 gives a remainder of 0. Write a 1 in the 2 position.
8. We have reached 0, so write a 1 in the remaining position.

We now have the answer: 0d206 is equivalent to 0b11001110.

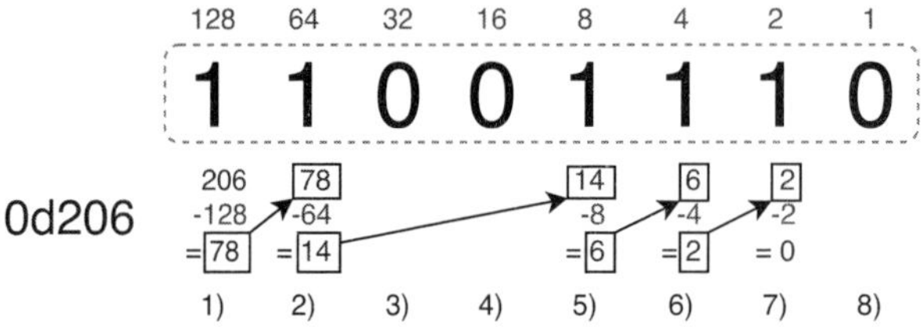

Figure 7.6 The process of converting a decimal number (206) to a binary number (11001110) by subtracting each bit's decimal value

Instead of using subtraction, you can convert from decimal to binary using addition if you prefer. Begin with a running total of 0, and progressively add the values of each bit, starting from the leftmost (most significant) bit, without exceeding the value of the decimal number you're converting. Here are the steps for converting the decimal number 206 to binary:

1. 0 + 128 = 128. Write a 1 in the 128 position.
2. 128 + 64 = 192. Write a 1 in the 64 position.
3. 192 + 32 = 224, which is greater than 206. Write a 0 in the 32 position.
4. 192 + 16 = 208, which is greater than 206. Write a 0 in the 16 position.
5. 192 + 8 = 200. Write a 1 in the 8 position.
6. 200 + 4 = 204. Write a 1 in the 4 position.

7. 204 + 2 = 206. Write a 1 in the 2 position.
8. We have reached the original value (206). Write a 0 in the remaining position.

Like converting from binary to decimal, this process becomes much easier with practice, and eventually you should be able to do it in your head. To practice, write some random numbers from 0 to 255 (56, 127, 201, 199, etc.), and try converting them into binary.

For additional practice with converting between decimal and binary (in both directions), you can try the Binary Game on Cisco Learning Network: https://learningnetwork.cisco.com/s/binary-game. Try it a few times each day; as you practice and improve, your scores in the Binary Game should increase, and you'll find yourself able to do the necessary calculations in your head.

EXAM TIP Being able to quickly convert between decimal and binary is a big help on the CCNA exam, especially when it comes to *subnetting* (the topic of chapter 11). The CCNA exam has a 2-hour time limit—don't unnecessarily spend time doing binary-to-decimal and decimal-to-binary conversions. A bit of practice with Cisco's Binary Game goes a long way.

Exam applications

Binary is a fundamental topic with applications to various CCNA exam topics. In addition to IPv4 addressing (the topic of this chapter), the following are some other topics that require you to be proficient with binary, including converting between binary and decimal:

- *IPv4 subnetting*—*Subnetting* is the process of dividing networks into smaller networks and is the second half of exam topic 1.6: Configure and verify IPv4 addressing and subnetting. To subnet IPv4 networks, you need to be able to convert IPv4 addresses from decimal to binary and vice versa. We will cover subnetting in chapter 11 of this book.
- *IPv6 addressing*—This is exam topic 1.8: Configure and verify IPv6 addressing and prefix. To understand IPv6 addresses, you need to be able to convert between binary, decimal, and hexadecimal (because IPv6 addresses are usually written in hexadecimal). We will cover IPv6 in part 5 of this book.
- *IPv4 and IPv6 routing*—This includes nearly all of domain 3.0 of the CCNA exam topics (IP Connectivity) and is 25% of the entire CCNA exam. For example, to know how a router will forward a packet, you must identify the *most specific matching route*—the route with the most bits that match the packet's destination IP address. To do that, you must understand binary numbers. We will cover the concept of the most specific matching route in chapter 9 and other topics in domain 3.0 in parts 4 and 5 of this volume.

  Access Control Lists (ACLs)—ACLs are exam topic 5.6: Configure and verify access control lists. ACLs are used to permit or deny specific network traffic, and they do that by comparing bits in the configured ACL to the bits of a packet's source and/or destination IP addresses. To configure appropriate ACLs, you must understand the binary system. We will cover ACLs in part 6 of this book.

7.3 IPv4 addressing

An IPv4 address is a 32-bit number that identifies a host at Layer 3 of the TCP/IP Model. IP addresses (whether IPv4 or IPv6) are used to address a message to its final intended recipient, unlike MAC addresses, which are used to address a message to the next hop. Whereas switches are said to be Layer 2 devices, routers are said to be *Layer 3 devices* or to *operate at Layer 3* because they make forwarding decisions based on the destination IP address of messages (located in the Layer 3 header).

NOTE In this chapter, we will look at how to configure IPv4 addresses on routers, but we will cover how routers forward packets in part 2 of this book.

7.3.1 The structure of an IPv4 address

IPv4 addresses are 32 bits in length, but a 32-bit string of 1s and 0s isn't very human-readable or easy to remember. To make them easier to read, IPv4 addresses are represented using decimal numbers instead of binary. To simplify it even further, we first split the 32-bit IPv4 address into four groups of 8 bits called *octets*, separated by a period, and then convert each of the octets to decimal; this is called *dotted decimal notation*. This is why, for the purpose of the CCNA, you only need to be able to convert between binary and decimal for numbers of up to 8 bits. Figure 7.7 shows an IPv4 address written in dotted decimal as well as in binary.

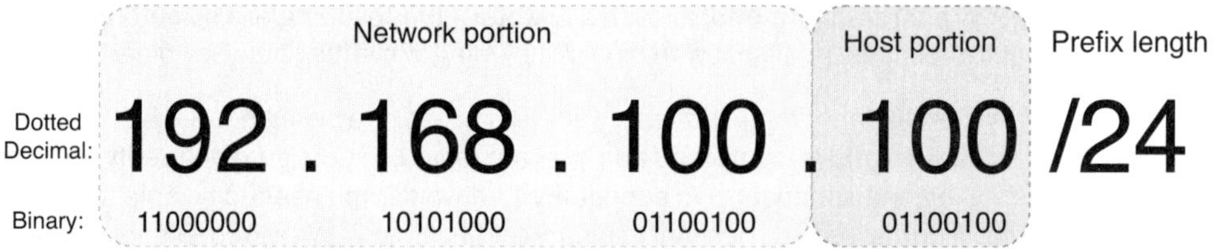

Figure 7.7 An IPv4 address written in both dotted decimal and binary. The 32-bit address is split into four octets consisting of 8 bits each. The address is divided into two parts: the *network portion* and the *host portion.* The *prefix length* indicates the size of the network portion in bits, and the remainder is the host portion.

> **Octet and byte**
>
> You may wonder what the difference is between an octet and a byte, both of which I have defined as a group of 8 bits. An octet always means 8 bits. However, a byte isn't necessarily 8 bits; a byte is the minimum unit of data that a computer can read from or write to at one time. This is almost always 8 bits, but in the past, there have been computers that use 6-, 7-, and 9-bit bytes. Therefore, the term *octet* is sometimes used instead to refer to a group of 8 bits. In the context of IPv4 addresses, octet is preferred.

PREFIX LENGTH

The size of the network portion of an IP address can be indicated with a *prefix length* in the format /X, where X is the number of bits in the network portion. In figure 7.7, the IPv4 address is followed by /24, indicating that the network portion of the address is 24 bits in length. From that, we can infer that the remaining 8 bits are the host portion.

> **NOTE** The *network portion* of an IPv4 address is often called the *prefix* or *network prefix.*

All hosts in the same LAN as the host with IPv4 address 192.168.100.100 will share the same network portion; the first three octets of their IPv4 addresses will be the same (192.168.100). However, each host will have a unique host portion; the final octet will be unique. Some possible addresses of other hosts in the LAN could be 192.168.100.1, 192.168.100.178, 192.168.100.234, etc.

Figure 7.8 shows two networks: LAN 1 and LAN 2. Notice that the IP address of each host in LAN 1 begins with 192.168.1, and the IP address of each host in LAN 2 begins with 192.168.2. The router (R1) serves to connect the two LANs; its G0/0 interface has IP address 192.168.1.1/24, and its G0/1 interface has IP address 192.168.2.1/24. Hosts in the separate LANs can communicate with each other via R1. Notice that the switches do not have IP addresses—this is because switches are not Layer 3 aware. Switches operate at Layer 2 of the TCP/IP model and do not get involved with Layer 3.

> **NOTE** When talking about routers, the term *interface* is typically used instead of *port.*

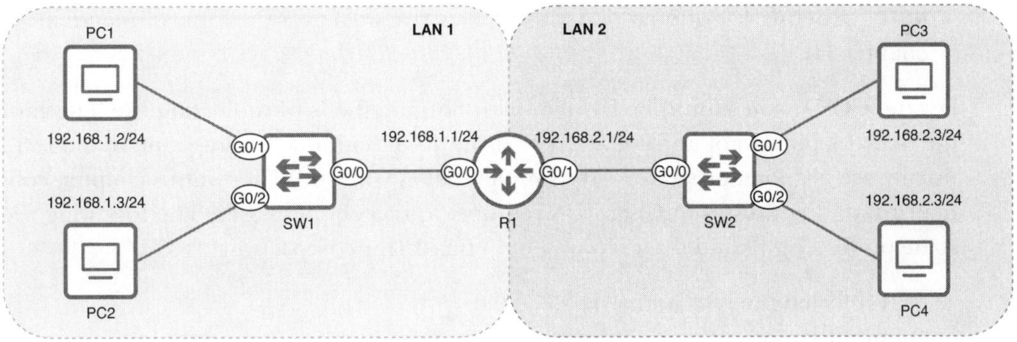

Figure 7.8 Two networks (LAN 1 and LAN 2) connected via a router (R1). IP addresses of hosts in each LAN share the same network portion: 192.168.1 in LAN 1 and 192.168.2 in LAN 2.

> **NOTE** The exact meaning of the term *network* can vary. You could say figure 7.8 depicts a network consisting of two LANs. However, in the context of IP addresses and prefix lengths, you can think of a network as being synonymous with a LAN—a group of devices that can communicate directly with each other, without the use of a router.

NETMASKS

Instead of indicating the prefix length with /X, another common method is to use a *netmask*—another string of 32 bits that is paired with an IP address to indicate which bits of the IP address are the network portion and which are the host portion. A bit in the netmask that is set to 1 means the bit in the same position of the IP address is part of the network portion; a bit in the netmask that is set to 0 means the bit in the same position of the IP address is part of the host portion.

Like IPv4 addresses, netmasks are usually written in dotted decimal notation. Figure 7.9 shows an IPv4 address (172.16.20.21) with a netmask (255.255.0.0). The first 16 bits of the netmask are 1, meaning the first 16 bits of the IPv4 address are the network portion.

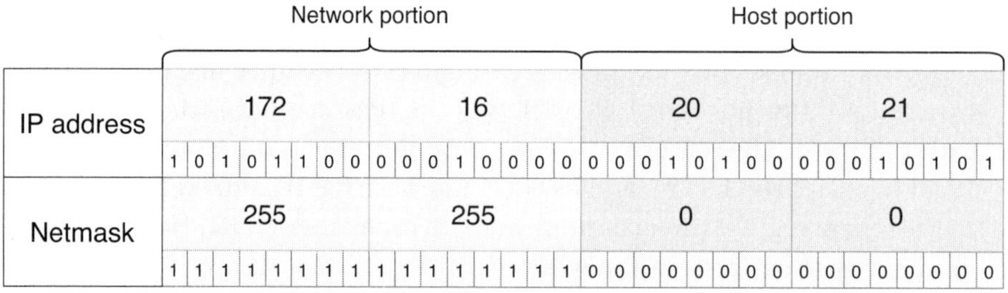

Network portion
Host portion
IP address
172
16
20
21
1 0 1 0 1 1 0 0 0 0 0 1 0 0 0 0 0 0 0 1 0 1 0 0 0 0 0 1 0 1 0 1
Netmask
255
255
0
0
1 1 1 1 1 1 1 1 1 1 1 1 1 1 1 1 0 0 0 0 0 0 0 0 0 0 0 0 0 0 0 0

Figure 7.9 An IPv4 address (top) and its netmask (bottom). The first 16 bits of the netmask are set to 1, indicating that the first 16 bits of the IPv4 address are the network portion. This is equivalent to a /16 prefix length.

> **NOTE** A netmask is often called a *subnet mask*; we will cover the topic of *subnets* in chapter 11.

For the CCNA, you should be familiar with both methods of indicating the length of the network portion of an IPv4 address: using /X notation and using a netmask. I will usually use /X notation because it's simpler, but as you'll see later in this chapter, configuring IPv4 addresses in Cisco IOS requires you to use netmasks. The following are some prefix lengths and their equivalent netmasks for comparison:

- Prefix length: /8 = netmask: 255.0.0.0
- Prefix length: /16 = netmask: 255.255.0.0
- Prefix length: /24 = netmask: 255.255.255.0

> **NOTE** A netmask is always a series of 1s followed by a series of 0s; this is because IPv4 addresses are always structured to have the network portion on the left (the most significant bits) and the host portion on the right (the least significant bits). Netmasks like 0.0.0.255 or 255.0.255.0 are not possible.

7.3.2 Configuring IPv4 addresses on a router

Unlike MAC addresses, which are assigned to a device by its manufacturer, IP addresses must be assigned by the engineer or admin configuring the device. Let's look at how to configure IP addresses on a Cisco router.

NOTE End hosts like PCs usually receive their IP addresses automatically using *Dynamic Host Configuration Protocol* (DHCP), the topic of chapter 4 of volume 2. However, the IP addresses of network infrastructure devices like routers are usually manually configured.

Figure 7.10 zooms in on R1 from figure 7.8 and shows how to configure IP addresses on and enable R1's G0/0 and G0/1 interfaces. In the rest of this section, we will analyze these configurations and use `show` commands to verify the status of R1's interfaces before and after configuration. Here are the basic steps:

1. From user EXEC mode, move to privileged EXEC mode and then global configuration mode.
2. Access interface configuration mode for the G0/0 interface, configure an IP address and netmask, and enable the interface.
3. Access interface configuration mode for the G0/1 interface, configure an IP address and netmask, and enable the interface.

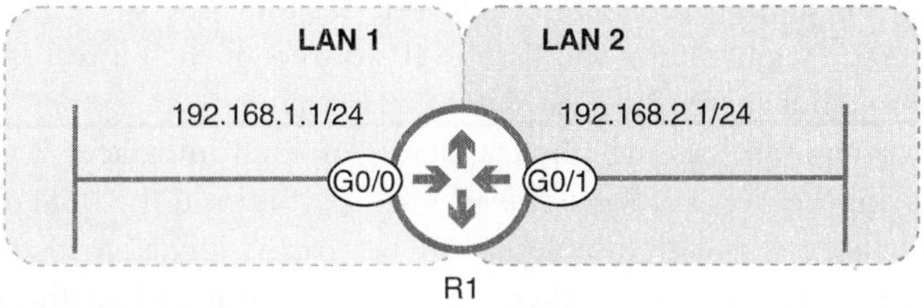


```
1) R1> enable
   R1# configure terminal
2) R1(config)# interface g0/0
   R1(config-if)# ip address 192.168.1.1 255.255.255.0
   R1(config-if)# no shutdown
3) R1(config-if)# interface g0/1
   R1(config-if)# ip address 192.168.2.1 255.255.255.0
   R1(config-if)# no shutdown
```

Figure 7.10 How to configure IP addresses and enable router interfaces. R1 is connected to two LANs: 192.168.1.1/24 (G0/0) and 192.168.2.1/24 (G0/1).

NOTE The switches and PCs present in figure 7.8 have been replaced with perpendicular lines at the end of the connections in figure 7.10. This is a common technique in network diagrams to indicate that a LAN is connected to an interface, but its details are not important to the diagram. Figure 7.10 focuses on R1, so there is no need to show the switches and PCs.

PREVERIFICATION

Let's confirm the default state of R1's interfaces before we configure them—before configuring a device, it's best to confirm the device's current state. A convenient command to view a router's interfaces is **`show ip interface brief`**, executed in user EXEC or privileged EXEC mode. You will be using this command a lot! The following example shows the output of the command on R1 before configuring its interfaces:

```
R1# show ip interface brief                        <-- Views information about R1's interfaces
Interface              IP-Address    OK? Method Status                  Protocol
GigabitEthernet0/0     unassigned    YES unset  administratively down   down
GigabitEthernet0/1     unassigned    YES unset  administratively down   down
GigabitEthernet0/2     unassigned    YES unset  administratively down   down
GigabitEthernet0/3     unassigned    YES unset  administratively down   down
```

R1's four interfaces are listed.

The `Interface` column lists R1's interfaces—it has four, and we will configure two of them. The `IP-Address` column will list the IP address of each interface after we have configured them, but currently it just states `unassigned`.

The `Status` column lists the physical status of each interface. If the interface is connected to another device, the status will be up; if it isn't, the `Status` will be `down`, and if the interface is manually disabled, it will be `administratively down` (regardless of whether it is connected to another device). As shown earlier, the default state is `administratively down`—Cisco router interfaces are disabled by default and must be manually enabled.

The `Protocol` column indicates whether the Layer 2 protocol of the interface is functioning properly. For an Ethernet interface, this is fairly simple—if the `Status` column says up, the `Protocol` should be up as well. If the `Status` column says `down` or `administratively down`, the `Protocol` should be `down`.

CONFIGURATION

To configure a device's interfaces, we must use a new mode in the hierarchy of the IOS CLI: *interface configuration mode*. To access interface configuration mode, use the **`interface`** *`interface-name`* command from the global configuration mode. The following example demonstrates this:

```
R1# configure terminal                                    ← Accesses global configuration mode
Enter configuration commands, one per line.  End with CNTL/Z.
R1(config)# interface gigabitethernet0/0                  ← Accesses interface configuration mode for G0/0
R1(config-if)#                                            ← The prompt changes to R1(config-if)#.
```

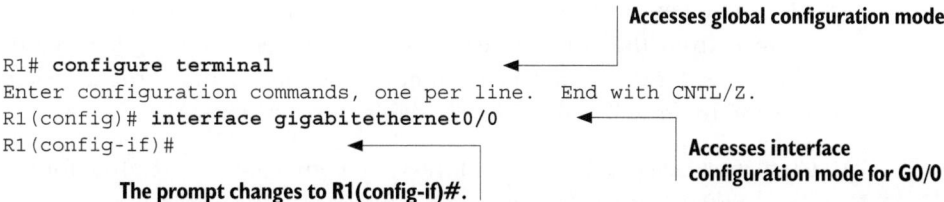

Notice that the prompt changes from `R1(config)#` to `R1(config-if)#`, indicating interface configuration mode. The name of the interface you are configuring isn't shown in the prompt, so before doing any configurations, I recommend double-checking that you used the correct interface name after the **`interface`** command.

> **NOTE** Instead of using the **`interface gigabitethernet0/0`** command to enter interface configuration mode for the G0/0 interface, you can use **`interface g0/0`**—there is no need to type out the full interface name.

The command to configure an interface's IP address is **`ip address`** *`ip-address netmask`*; as I mentioned previously, you need to know netmasks when configuring IP addresses in Cisco IOS. In the following example, I configure the IP address of R1's G0/0 interface. The netmask is 255.255.255.0 because the prefix length is /24—the first 24 bits of the netmask are set to 1, and the last 8 are set to 0:

```
R1(config-if)# ip address 192.168.1.1 255.255.255.0      ← Configures the 192.168.1.1 IP address with a /24 netmask
```

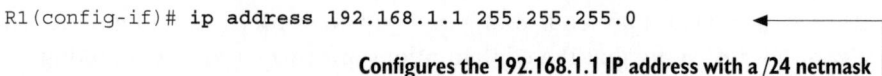

However, G0/0 still isn't ready to forward traffic; the interface is still disabled. To change that, you must use the **`no shutdown`** command, as shown in the following example. After issuing the command, two messages are displayed, indicating that the interface is up and running. The first message indicates that the interface is physically operational (the `Status` column of **`show ip interface brief`**), and the second message indicates that the Layer 2 protocol is operational (the `Protocol` column of **`show ip interface brief`**):

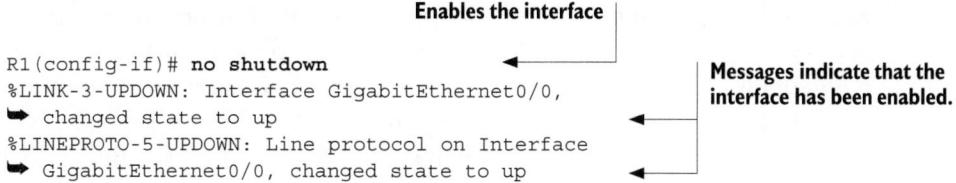

```
R1(config-if)# no shutdown                                ← Enables the interface
%LINK-3-UPDOWN: Interface GigabitEthernet0/0,
➥ changed state to up                                    ← Messages indicate that the interface has been enabled.
%LINEPROTO-5-UPDOWN: Line protocol on Interface
➥ GigabitEthernet0/0, changed state to up                ←
```

NOTE As mentioned in chapter 5, **`no`** can be used in front of a command to remove it from the configuration. Router interfaces are disabled by default because they have the **`shutdown`** command applied to them; the **`no shutdown`** command removes it and therefore enables the interface.

R1's G0/0 interface now has an IP address and is enabled—it's ready to forward traffic. Next let's configure the G0/1 interface, as in the following example:

```
R1(config-if)# interface g0/1
R1(config-if)# ip address 192.168.2.1 255.255.255.0
R1(config-if)# no shutdown
%LINK-3-UPDOWN: Interface GigabitEthernet0/1, changed state to up
%LINEPROTO-5-UPDOWN: Line protocol on Interface GigabitEthernet0/1, changed state to up
```

Enters interface configuration mode for G0/1

Configures G0/1's IP address and enables it

NOTE To access interface configuration mode for another interface, you don't have to return to global configuration mode; you can do it directly from interface configuration mode. Note that there is no indication that I switched from configuring G0/0 to G0/1—again, always double-check that you used the correct interface name after the **`interface`** command.

FINAL VERIFICATION

R1's G0/0 and G0/1 are both configured and enabled. After configuration, it's always a good idea to verify that the configurations are correct. In the following example, I once again used the **`show ip interface brief`** command to verify:

```
R1# show ip interface brief
Interface            IP-Address     OK? Method Status                Protocol
GigabitEthernet0/0   192.168.1.1    YES manual up                    up
GigabitEthernet0/1   192.168.2.1    YES manual up                    up
GigabitEthernet0/2   unassigned     YES unset  administratively down down
GigabitEthernet0/3   unassigned     YES unset  administratively down down
```

G0/0 and G0/1 each have an IP address and are up/up.

Notice that G0/0 and G0/1 both have the correct IP addresses and are up in both the `Status` and `Protocol` columns. However, **`show ip interface brief`** doesn't display the netmask. To double-check that the netmask is correct, you can use the **`show ip interface`** `[interface-name]` command, as in the following example. Notice that, although you must use a netmask when configuring IP addresses, the prefix length is displayed as /X in the output of this command. This command shows a lot of output, so I am only including the first few lines of each interface:

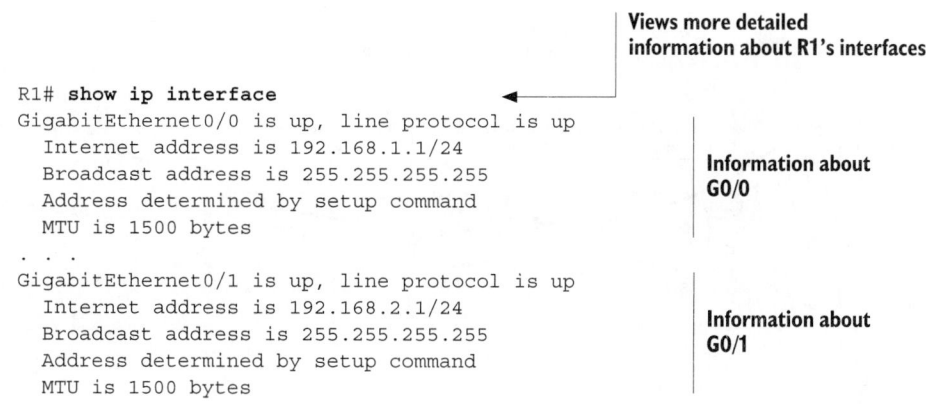

```
R1# show ip interface                              <- Views more detailed information about R1's interfaces
GigabitEthernet0/0 is up, line protocol is up
  Internet address is 192.168.1.1/24                  Information about G0/0
  Broadcast address is 255.255.255.255
  Address determined by setup command
  MTU is 1500 bytes
. . .
GigabitEthernet0/1 is up, line protocol is up
  Internet address is 192.168.2.1/24                  Information about G0/1
  Broadcast address is 255.255.255.255
  Address determined by setup command
  MTU is 1500 bytes
. . .
```

> **NOTE** When stating the format of a command, keywords and arguments in square brackets are optional. The **`show ip interface`** command is valid on its own and shows information for all interfaces; however, **`show ip interface g0/0`** limits the output to only the stated interface.

In addition to the prefix length, there are two more things I would like to point out about the previous output, related to other topics covered in this chapter: first, the line `Broadcast address is 255.255.255.255` indicates the IP address that will be used to send a message to all hosts in the local network: 255.255.255.255. This is a specially reserved IP address for broadcast packets. If R1 wants to send a message to all hosts in LAN 1, it will send a packet addressed to 255.255.255.255 out of its G0/0 interface (encapsulated in a frame addressed to the MAC address ffff.ffff.ffff).

Second, the final line of the included output states `MTU is 1500 bytes`. As mentioned when we looked at the IPv4 header, this means that if R1 has to forward a frame larger than 1,500 bytes out of either of its interfaces, it must fragment the packet first.

> **NOTE** After verifying that the configurations are correct, it's always a good idea to save the configuration with one of the commands covered in chapter 5: **`write`**, **`write memory`**, or **`copy running-config startup-config`**.

R1 is now ready to forward traffic between LAN 1 and LAN 2. Figure 7.11 shows how PC1 can send a packet to PC3 via R1; PC1 sends the packet in a frame addressed to the MAC address of R1's G0/0 interface, and then R1 forwards the packet in a frame addressed to the MAC address of PC3. Remember that Layer 3 provides end-to-end delivery, and Layer 2 provides hop-to-hop delivery. Although not shown in the diagram, before PC1 can encapsulate the packet in a frame, it must use ARP to learn R1 G0/0's MAC address. Likewise, R1 must use ARP to learn PC3's MAC address.

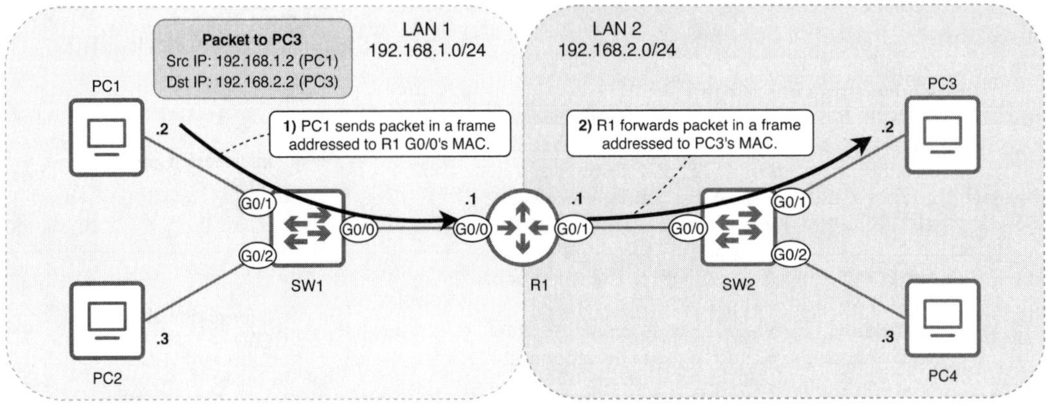

Figure 7.11 PC1 sends a packet to PC3 via R1. The packet is addressed to PC3's IP address. (1) PC1 sends the packet in a frame addressed to the MAC address of R1's G0/0 interface. (2) R1 forwards the packet in a frame addressed to the MAC address of PC3. For R1 to serve its purpose of connecting the two networks together, it must have an appropriate IP address on each of its interfaces, which we configured in this section.

> **NOTE** Figure 7.11 indicates the IP address of each host differently than in previous diagrams. The *network address* (covered in section 7.3.3) is written next to each LAN's name, and only the host portion of each host's IP address is written next to the host. This is a common technique to reduce the amount of text in a diagram. PC1 and PC3 both have .2 written next to them, but their IP addresses are not the same; the network portion of PC1's IP address is 192.168.1, and PC3's is 192.168.2. The same logic applies for PC2 and PC4.

For a router to forward packets to *remote* networks (that aren't directly connected to the router itself), additional configurations are required; we will cover those configurations in later chapters of this volume. However, in the example network shown in figure 7.11, LAN 1 and LAN 2 are both directly connected to R1—no more configurations are needed. PC1 and PC2 in LAN 1 can now communicate with PC3 and PC4 in LAN 2 via R1.

7.3.3 Attributes of an IPv4 network

Each IPv4 network has a few attributes you should be able to identify: the network address, broadcast address, maximum number of hosts, first usable address, and last usable address of the network.

NETWORK ADDRESS

The *network address* is the first address of any network, and it is used to identify the network; it cannot be assigned to a host. An IPv4 address is a network address if all bits of its host portion are set to 0. Figure 7.12 shows an example of a network address: 192.168.100.0/24.

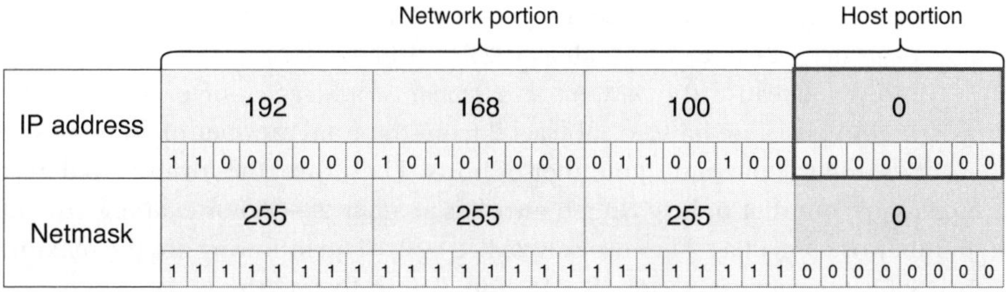

Network portion
Host portion
IP address
192
168
100
0
1 1 0 0 0 0 0 0 1 0 1 0 1 0 0 0 0 1 1 0 0 1 0 0 0 0 0 0 0 0 0 0
Netmask
255
255
255
0
1 1 1 1 1 1 1 1 1 1 1 1 1 1 1 1 1 1 1 1 1 1 1 1 0 0 0 0 0 0 0 0

Figure 7.12 192.168.100.0 is a network address, as indicated by the host portion of 00000000. This address is used to identify the 192.168.100.0/24 network as a whole and cannot be assigned to a host. 192.168.100.100 (used in figure 7.7) is a host address in the 192.168.100.0/24 network.

Broadcast address

The *broadcast address* is the last address of any network, and like the network address, it can't be assigned to a host. The broadcast address can be used to address a message to all hosts in the local network. An IPv4 address is a broadcast address if all bits of its host portion are set to 1. Figure 7.13 shows the broadcast address of the 192.168.100.0/24 network.

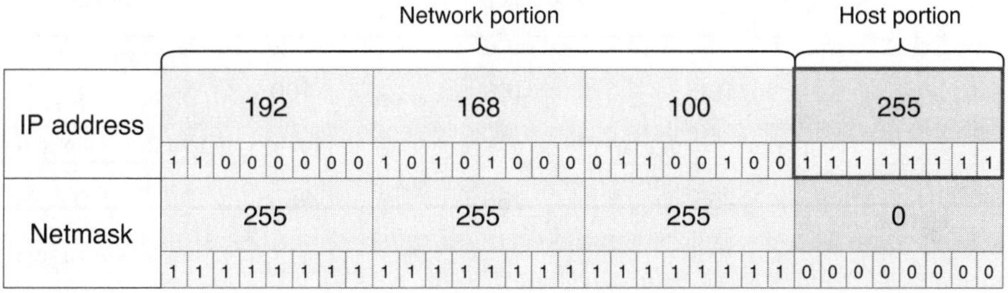

Network portion
Host portion
IP address
192
168
100
255
1 1 0 0 0 0 0 0 1 0 1 0 1 0 0 0 0 1 1 0 0 1 0 0 1 1 1 1 1 1 1 1
Netmask
255
255
255
0
1 1 1 1 1 1 1 1 1 1 1 1 1 1 1 1 1 1 1 1 1 1 1 1 0 0 0 0 0 0 0 0

Figure 7.13 192.168.100.255 is a broadcast address, as indicated by the host portion of 11111111. This address can be used to address a message to all hosts in the 192.168.100.0/24 network.

> **NOTE** To send a message to all devices on the local network, hosts will usually address messages to 255.255.255.255, rather than the broadcast address of their local network. 255.255.255.255 is a specially reserved broadcast address. However, the broadcast address 192.168.100.255 can be used by hosts in other networks to send a message to all hosts in the 192.168.100.0/24 network.

Maximum number of hosts

The *maximum number of hosts* in a network is the number of IP addresses available to assign to hosts connected to the network. To calculate the total number of IP addresses in a network, the formula is 2^y, where y is the number of host bits. For example, with a

/24 prefix length, there are eight host bits; 2^8 is equal to 256, so there are 256 total IP addresses in a /24 network (such as 192.168.100.0/24).

However, because the *network* and *broadcast* addresses of each network can't be assigned to hosts, we have to subtract 2 from the total number of addresses in the network to find the maximum number of hosts. Therefore, the formula to determine the maximum number of hosts in a network is actually $2^y - 2$. For example, the maximum number of hosts of a /24 network is 254 ($2^8 - 2$). The following are the maximum number of hosts in networks with /8, /16, and /24 prefix lengths:

- /8: $2^{24} - 2 = 16,777,214$ hosts
- /16: $2^{16} - 2 = 65,534$ hosts
- /24: $2^8 - 2 = 254$ hosts

FIRST AND LAST USABLE ADDRESSES

The *first usable address* of a network is the first IP address that can be assigned to a host; in other words, it's the first IP address after the network address. It is simple to calculate—just add one to the network address (change the least significant bit to 1). Figure 7.14 shows the first usable address of the 192.168.100.0/24 network.

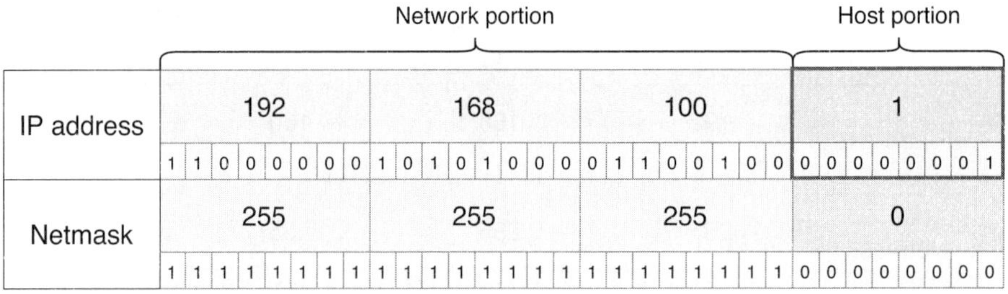

Figure 7.14 192.168.100.1 is the first usable address of the 192.168.100.0/24 network. It is the first address after the network address.

> **NOTE** The first usable address of a network is often assigned to that network's router. For example, in the previous section, we assigned IP addresses 192.168.1.1 and 192.168.2.1 to R1s interfaces—the first usable addresses of their respective networks.

The *last usable address* of a network is the last IP address that can be assigned to a host; it's the last IP address before the broadcast address. This address is also simple to find—subtract 1 from the broadcast address (change the least significant bit to 0). Figure 7.15 shows the last usable address of the 192.168.100.0/24 network.

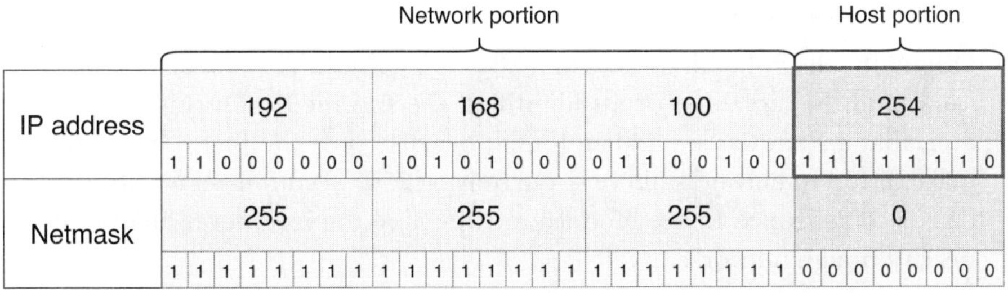

Figure 7.15 192.168.100.254 is the last usable address of the 192.168.100.0/24 network. It is the last address before the broadcast address.

If you know the first and last usable addresses, you know the range of usable addresses: from the first usable address to the last usable address. For example, the range of usable addresses in the 192.168.100.0/24 network is from 192.168.100.1 to 192.168.100.254: 254 addresses in total.

Exam scenario

On the CCNA exam, you may be asked questions that require you to identify one or more of these attributes of a network. The following is an example question:

Q: PC1's IP address is 172.20.20.127/16. What is the usable address range of the network PC1 belongs to?

- A 172.20.20.1–172.20.20.254
- B 172.20.20.0–172.20.20.255
- C 172.20.0.1–172.20.255.254
- D 172.20.0.0–172.20.255.255

To find the usable address range of a network, you need to know the first and last usable addresses of the network. This is fairly simple when using a prefix length of /8, /16, or /24; the division between the network portion and host portion is between octets (in this case, between the second and third octets, because the prefix length is /16).

To find the first usable address, simply change the octet(s) of the host portion to 0 (this is the network address), and then add 1 to the last octet: PC1's address is 172.20.20.127, the network address is 172.20.0.0, and the first usable address is 172.20.0.1.

To find the last usable address, change the octet(s) of the host portion to 255 (this is the broadcast address), and then subtract 1 from the last octet: PC1's address is 172.20.20.127, the broadcast address is 172.20.255.255, and the last usable address is 172.20.255.254. Now you know the usable address range: from 172.20.0.1 to 172.20.255.254. Therefore, the answer to this question is C.

This process will become more challenging when we cover *subnetting* in chapter 11 of this book. When subnetting, we use prefix lengths that do not fit neatly between octets of an IP address, such as /19, /23, /28, etc. In that case, it is important to be proficient at converting between decimal and binary so you can identify the network and host bits, convert the host bits to 0 or 1 as necessary, convert them back to decimal, etc.

7.3.4 IPv4 address classes

Originally, all IPv4 addresses used a /8 prefix length; the first octet identified the network, and the last three octets identified the specific host within that network. However, that system was soon abandoned; because only the first 8 bits could be used to make different networks, there could only be 256 (2^8) different networks (LANs): from 0.x.x.x to 255.x.x.x. In the modern world where the internet is ubiquitous, that is not nearly enough networks.

NOTE The formula to calculate the number of available networks is 2^x, where *x* is the number of bits in the network portion.

To improve that system and allow for more networks of various sizes, IPv4 addresses were organized into five classes: class A, class B, class C, class D, and class E. Table 7.2 lists the five IPv4 address classes and some information about them.

Table 7.2 IPv4 address classes

Class	First octet bit pattern	First octet decimal range	Prefix length	Note
A	0xxxxxxx	0–127	/8	Address range: 0.0.0.0–127.255.255.255
B	10xxxxxx	128–191	/16	Address range: 128.0.0.0–191.255.255.255
C	110xxxxx	192–223	/24	Address range: 192.0.0.0 to 223.255.255.255
D	1110xxxx	224–239		Reserved for multicast addresses
E	1111xxxx	240–255		Reserved for experimental purposes

The class of an IPv4 address is determined by the first 1 to 4 bits of the address; class A addresses begin with 0, class B addresses begin with 10, class C addresses begin with 110, class D addresses begin with 1110, and class E addresses begin with 1111. Classes A, B, and C are the ranges from which hosts are assigned IPv4 addresses. For example, the IP addresses we configured on R1 in this chapter are from the class C range. Classes D and E are reserved for particular purposes; we won't cover them in this book, except for a few mentions of multicast IP addresses (class D).

NOTE Some addresses in each class are reserved for special purposes and can't be assigned to hosts. For example, class A addresses with a first octet of *0* or *127* are reserved.

Classes A, B, and C each use a specific prefix length: class A addresses use a /8 prefix length (netmask 255.0.0.0), class B addresses use a /16 prefix length (netmask 255.255.0.0), and class C addresses use a /24 prefix length (netmask 255.255.255.0). Because an IPv4 address is always 32 bits in length, if the network portion is larger, the host portion is smaller (and vice versa). This gives some characteristics to each class:

- Few class A networks exist (128), but each class A network contains many addresses (16,777,216).
- Class B networks are a middle ground. There are 16,384 class B networks, each containing 65,536 addresses.
- Many class C networks exist (2,097,152), but each class C network contains relatively few addresses (256).

Figure 7.16 represents these characteristics visually. A larger network portion means a smaller host portion and vice versa. There is a tradeoff between the two.

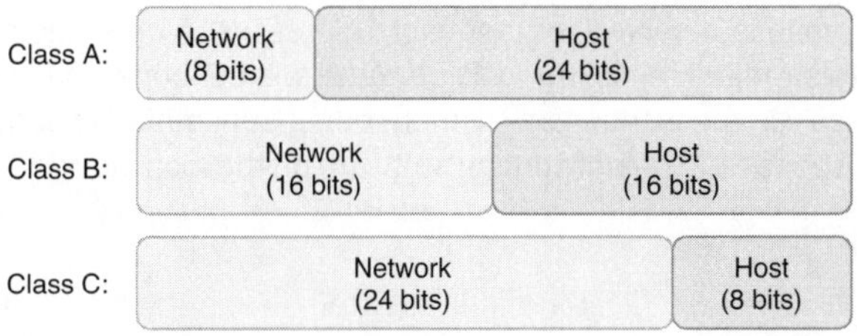

Figure 7.16 The network portion and host portion sizes of class A, class B, and class C IPv4 addresses

Class A networks were intended for very large organizations such as Internet Service Providers and the United States Department of Defense (DoD); the vast majority of organizations don't need anywhere near 16,777,216 IP addresses. Class B networks were intended for medium- to large-sized businesses, and class C for small- to medium-sized businesses.

Table 7.3 summarizes the characteristics of classes A, B, and C. You don't have to memorize the number of networks and addresses per network for each address class; just understand that a smaller network portion means fewer networks with more hosts in each network, and a larger network portion means more networks with fewer hosts in each network.

Table 7.3 Characteristics of classes A, B, and C

Class	First octet	Size of network portion	Size of host portion	Number of networks	Addresses per network
A	0xxxxxxx	8 bits	24 bits	128 (2^7)	16,777,216 (2^{24})
B	10xxxxxx	16 bits	16 bits	16,384 (2^{14})	65,536 (2^{16})
C	110xxxxx	24 bits	8 bits	2,097,152 (2^{21})	256 (2^8)

NOTE The reason why there are only 2^7 class A networks, even though the network portion is 8 bits in length, is that the first bit is fixed as 0—only 7 bits are available to change and make different networks. The same reasoning applies for why there are 2^{14} class B networks (not 2^{16}) and 2^{21} class C networks (not 2^{24}).

Networks that follow the class A, B, and C rules are called *classful networks*. Although important to study and understand even today, this system is now obsolete and has been replaced with *classless networking*, a system in which prefix lengths are not restricted by class. We will cover this in chapter 11 when we look at *subnetting*.

Reserved addresses

Within each address class, there are several ranges of IP addresses that are reserved and cannot be assigned to hosts. Here are two examples:

- 0.0.0.0/8: Any IP address that begins with the first octet 0 is reserved.
- 127.0.0.0/8: This range is reserved for *loopback addresses*. A message sent to any IP address in this range (i.e., `ping 127.0.0.1`) will be looped back to the local host—the device you are working on—without being transmitted over the network. This can be used to test the networking software on the local device.

Summary

- The IPv4 header is 20 to 60 bytes in length and contains 14 fields.
- The *Version* field indicates the version of IP (IPv4 or IPv6).
- The *Internet Header Length* (IHL) field indicates the length of the header in 4-byte increments.
- The *Differentiated Services Code Point* (DSCP) and *Explicit Congestion Notification* (ECN) fields are used to prioritize certain kinds of traffic. This is called *Quality of Service* (QoS).
- The *Total Length* field indicates the length of the entire packet in bytes.
- The *Identification*, *Flags*, and *Fragment Offset* fields support packet fragmentation. If a packet is larger than an interface's *Maximum Transmission Unit* (MTU), the router will divide the packet into multiple smaller packets called *fragments*. The standard MTU is 1500 bytes.
- The *Time To Live* (TTL) field is used to prevent packets from looping indefinitely around the network. Each time a router forwards a packet, its TTL is decremented by 1, and if it reaches 0, the packet is dropped.
- The *Protocol* field indicates the type of message encapsulated inside of the packet, such as ICMP, TCP, UDP, or OSPF.
- The *Header Checksum* field is used to check for errors in the IPv4 header.
- The *Source Address* field contains the IPv4 address of the host that sent the packet.
- The *Destination Address* field contains the IPv4 address of the packet's intended recipient.
- The *Options* field is optional and variable in length—from 0 bytes (if not used) to a maximum of 40 bytes in length. This field is rarely used.

- The decimal number system uses 10 digits: 0, 1, 2, 3, 4, 5, 6, 7, 8, and 9. It is also called *base 10.* The value of each digit position increases tenfold: 1, 10, 100, 1000, etc.
- The binary number system uses two digits: 0 and 1. It is also called *base 2.* The value of each digit position increases twofold: 1, 2, 4, 8, 16, 32, 64, 128, etc.
- An 8-bit binary number provides 256 possible values: from 0d0 (00000000) to 0d255 (11111111).
- For the CCNA exam, you must be able to convert between binary and decimal for numbers of up to 8 bits in length. You can practice at https://learningnetwork.cisco.com/s/binary-game.
- An IPv4 address is a 32-bit number that identifies a host at Layer 3. It is divided into four groups of 8 bits called *octets* and written in *dotted decimal notation.*
- IPv4 addresses are divided into two parts: the *network portion* and the *host portion.* All hosts within a LAN will have the same network portion but a unique host portion.
- The size of the network portion can be indicated with a *prefix length* in the format /X, where X is the number of bits in the network portion. Any bits that are not part of the network portion are part of the host portion.
- The size of the network portion can also be indicated with a *netmask* (also called a *subnet mask*). A netmask is a string of 32 bits that is paired with an IP address to indicate which bits of the IP address are the network portion and which are the host portion.
- A 1 in the netmask means the bit in the same position as the IP address is part of the network portion. A 0 in the netmask means the bit in the same position as the IP address is part of the host portion.
- The **`show ip interface brief`** command lists a router's interface and information about their IP addresses and status.
- The **`show ip interface`** `[`*`interface-name`*`]` command shows more detail about each interface.
- Router interfaces are disabled by default and must be enabled with the **`no shutdown`** command.
- Interface configuration mode can be accessed with the **`interface`** *`interface-name`* command from global configuration mode.
- An interface's IPv4 address can be configured with the **`ip address`** *`ip-address netmask`* command in interface configuration mode.
- The network address of a network is the first address of the network, with a host portion of all 0s. It is used to identify the network and cannot be assigned to a host.
- The broadcast address of a network is the last address of the network, with a host portion of all 1s. It can be used to send a message to all hosts in the network.

However, to send a message to all hosts on the local network, the address 255.255.255.255 is usually used.

- The maximum number of hosts of a network is the number of IP addresses that can be assigned to hosts. The formula is $2^y - 2$, where y is the number of bits in the host portion. Two is subtracted for the network and broadcast addresses.
- The *first usable address* of a network is the first address that can be assigned to a host. The *last usable address* is the last address that can be assigned to a host.
- IPv4 addresses can be organized into five classes: A, B, C, D, and E. Class D is reserved for multicast addresses, and Class E is reserved for experimental purposes. Addresses from classes A, B, and C are assigned to network hosts.
- Class A addresses have a first octet of 0–127 and use a /8 prefix length. Class B addresses have a first octet of 128–191 and use a /16 prefix length. Class C addresses have a first octet of 192–223 and use a /24 prefix length.
- Networks that follow class A, B, and C rules are called classful networks. This system is now obsolete and has been replaced with classless networking, which is more flexible.

8 Router and switch interfaces

This chapter covers

- How to configure interfaces and verify their status
- Interface speed and duplex settings
- Using autonegotiation to automatically determine an interface's speed and duplex
- Errors that can occur when sending and receiving messages over a network

In chapter 7, we looked at how to configure IP addresses on and enable router interfaces. In this chapter, we will dig deeper into the topic of interfaces and how they operate. Whereas the previous chapter covered how to configure IP addresses on interfaces (a Layer 3 concept), this chapter will focus primarily on Layer 1 concepts, such as how to configure the speed at which an interface can send and receive data. Specifically, we will cover the following CCNA exam topics:

- 1.3.b Connections (Ethernet shared media and point-to-point)
- 1.4 Identify interface and cable issues (collisions, errors, mismatch duplex, and/or speed)

In previous chapters, I have used the terms *port* and *interface.* The exact definitions of these terms depend on who you ask; some say a port is a Layer 2 entity that forwards frames within a LAN (switches have ports), and an interface is a Layer 3 entity that forwards packets between LANs (routers have interfaces). Another definition is that a port is the physical connector on a device that you plug a cable into, and an interface is the representation of that port within the software (hence, most Cisco IOS commands use the term `interface` rather than `port`).

In reality, these terms are often used interchangeably—even Cisco's documentation isn't consistent regarding these terms. In this book, I will generally use the term *port* to refer to a physical connector on a device and *interface* when talking about configurations, except in situations where one term is generally accepted as the standard over the other (in which case I will point that out).

8.1 Configuring interfaces

In this section, we will look at how to configure three aspects of an interface: description, speed, and duplex. Figure 8.1 shows how to configure these settings on Cisco routers and switches running Cisco IOS.

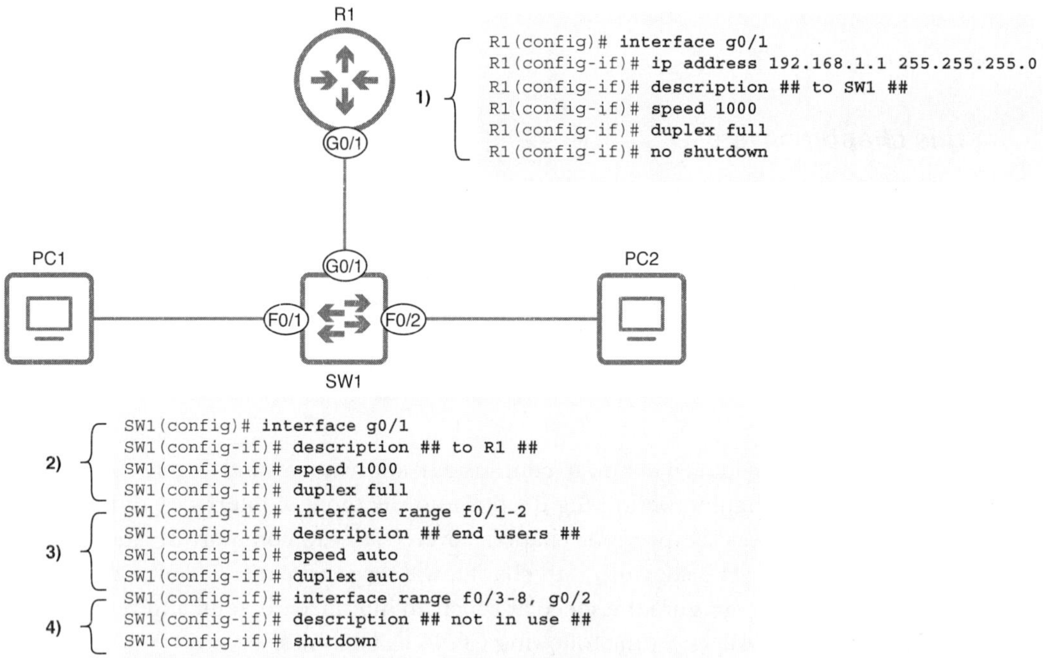

Figure 8.1 Interface configurations on R1 and SW1: (1) configuring R1's G0/1 interface with an IP address, description, and manual speed and duplex settings; (2) configuring SW1's G0/1 interface with a description, and manual speed and duplex settings; (3) configuring SW1's connections to end-user devices (PCs) using autonegotiation; (4) disabling SW1's unused interfaces.

Before we examine the configurations in figure 8.1 in detail, there are a couple of things worth mentioning that illustrate some differences between routers and switches. First, notice that I configured an IP address on R1's G0/1 interface but not on SW1's interfaces; this is because switch interfaces don't need IP addresses to perform their role of forwarding frames within a LAN. Switches are not Layer 3 aware; they only use Layer 2 information (MAC addresses) to decide how to forward frames.

The second point is that I used **`no shutdown`** on R1's G0/1 interface to enable it but not on SW1's G0/1, F0/1, or F0/2 interfaces. That is because, unlike router interfaces, which are disabled by default, switch interfaces are enabled by default.

> **EXAM TIP** In figure 8.1, I used **`shutdown`** to disable SW1's unused ports. This is considered a security best practice.

Switch interfaces are enabled by default to allow switches to operate in a plug-and-play manner; this means that to use the switch, you simply need to connect devices to it—no configuration is required. However, although a switch does not require configuration to perform its most basic function of forwarding frames, most enterprise networks will require configurations on switches to use more advanced features (which we will cover in both volumes of this book).

> **NOTE** A switch that is designed to be used in a plug-and-play manner is called an *unmanaged switch*. Unmanaged switches are inexpensive and are sometimes used in very small networks. The CCNA focuses on *managed switches*, which allow you to configure more advanced features.

8.1.1 Interface descriptions

An interface description is a simple string of text that you can configure to describe or name an interface. A common use is to indicate what device is connected to the interface. The command to configure an interface's description is **`description`** *`description`*, where *`description`* is a string of text such as "connected to R1's G0/1 interface." The following example shows how I configured the descriptions of SW1's F0/1 and F0/2 interfaces. F0/1 and F0/2 are connected to end-user devices (PCs), so I configured their descriptions as `## end users ##`:

```
SW1# configure terminal
SW1(config)# interface range f0/1-2              ← Configures F0/1 and F0/2 simultaneously
SW1(config-if)# description ## end users ##      ← Applies a description to both interfaces
```

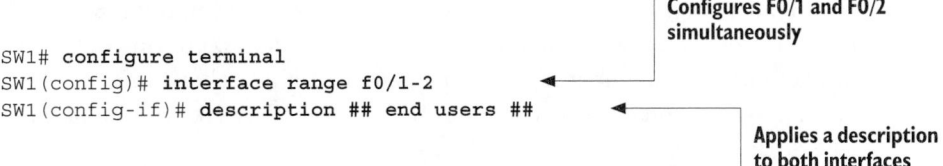

> **NOTE** The two hash symbols (##) at the beginning and end of the description are not necessary. I use them in my interface descriptions to help them stand out when viewing them in the CLI.

Notice that I used the **`interface range f0/1-2`** command to configure SW1's F0/1 and F0/2 interfaces at the same time; **`interface range`** can be a big timesaver when configuring multiple interfaces! The command to configure a range of interfaces is **`interface range`** *`type slot/port-port`*. Let me explain each of those arguments in the command:

- `type` means Ethernet, FastEthernet, GigabitEthernet, etc.
- `slot` is the first number in the interface name.
- `port` is the second number in the interface name.

> **NOTE** Another example from figure 8.1 is **`interface range f0/3-8, g0/2`**. This configures F0/3, F0/4, F0/5, F0/6, F0/7, F0/8, and G0/2. To include interfaces of a different type in the same **`interface range`** command, you must separate the interface names with a comma.

Interface descriptions are optional, but I highly recommend configuring them; interface descriptions that are consistently configured and updated as needed make it much easier to identify the purpose of each interface when viewing the configurations at a later date.

To view interface descriptions on a router or switch, you can use the **`show interfaces description`** command. The following example shows the output of that command after configuring SW1's interface descriptions (some output is omitted for the sake of space). Note that the command also lists the Layer 1 status (`Status`) and Layer 2 status (`Protocol`) of each interface:

```
SW1# show interfaces description          <-- Views a list of interfaces and their descriptions
Interface    Status         Protocol    Description
Fa0/1        up             up          ## end users ##        <-- Interface status and descriptions are shown.
Fa0/2        up             up          ## end users ##
Fa0/3        down           down        ## not in use ##
. . .
Gi0/1        up             up          ## to R1 ##
Gi0/2        down           down        ## not in use ##
```

Another command that can be used to view interface descriptions is **`show interfaces status`**. However, this command only works on switches, not on routers. We will use this command in the next few sections as well, as it also shows information about the interface speed and duplex. The following example shows the output of this command (the descriptions are displayed in the `Name` column):

```
SW1# show interfaces status
Port      Name               Status       Vlan       Duplex  Speed Type
Fa0/1     ## end users ##    connected    1          a-full  a-100 10/100BaseTX
Fa0/2     ## end users ##    connected    1          a-full  a-100 10/100BaseTX
Fa0/3     ## not in use ##   notconnect   1            auto   auto 10/100BaseTX
. . .
Gi0/1     ## to R1 ##        connected    1          a-full a-1000 10/100/1000BaseTX
Gi0/2     ## not in use ##   notconnect   1            auto   auto 10/100/1000BaseTX
```

8.1.2 Interface speed

An interface's speed is the maximum rate at which it can send and receive traffic, measured in bits per second. Most interfaces support multiple speeds—for example, most FastEthernet interfaces support speeds of both 10 and 100 Mbps—in which case they can be called *10/100 interfaces*. Likewise, most GigabitEthernet interfaces support speeds of 10, 100, and 1,000 Mbps (1 Gbps) and are therefore called *10/100/1000 interfaces*. Ideally, an interface will operate at its maximum speed, but if connected to a device that only supports slower speeds, it's important that an interface can match the speed of the other device.

The speed at which an interface operates can be manually configured or automatically determined by the device using a process called *autonegotiation*, in which the connected devices communicate with each other to determine at what speed they should operate. Cisco IOS devices use autonegotiation by default, and in most cases, you can leave autonegotiation enabled. However, there are cases where you should manually configure an interface's speed, such as when the neighboring device does not use autonegotiation. The command to manually configure an interface's speed is **speed** {*speed* | **auto**}, where *speed* is specified in megabits per second.

> **NOTE** When writing the syntax of a command, options in curly braces are a mandatory choice. In the **speed** command, you must either specify the *speed* value or use **auto** to enable autonegotiation.

In the following example, I use context-sensitive help to show the available options when configuring the speed of SW1's G0/1 interface: **10**, **100**, **1000**, and **auto**. I then manually configure the speed at 1 Gbps (1,000 Mbps) and use **show running-config interface g0/1** to verify the interface's configuration:

```
SW1(config)# interface g0/1
SW1(config-if)# speed ?
  10    Force 10 Mbps operation
  100   Force 100 Mbps operation
  1000  Force 1000 Mbps operation
  auto  Enable AUTO speed configuration
SW1(config-if)# speed 1000
```

The available keywords for the speed command

Manually configures a speed of 1,000 Mbps

```
SW1(config-if)# do show running-config interface g0/1     <-- Views G0/1's settings
. . .                                                          in the running-config
interface GigabitEthernet0/1
 description ## to R1 ##
 speed 1000
End
```

NOTE You can use the **show running-config interface** *interface-name* command to view the active configurations for a specific interface. To view the active configurations for all interfaces, use **show running-config | section interface**.

In the next example, I configure **speed auto** on SW1's F0/1 and F0/2 interfaces and then view F0/1's configuration. However, **speed auto** is not shown because it is the default setting. To avoid clutter in a device's configuration files, many default settings are hidden:

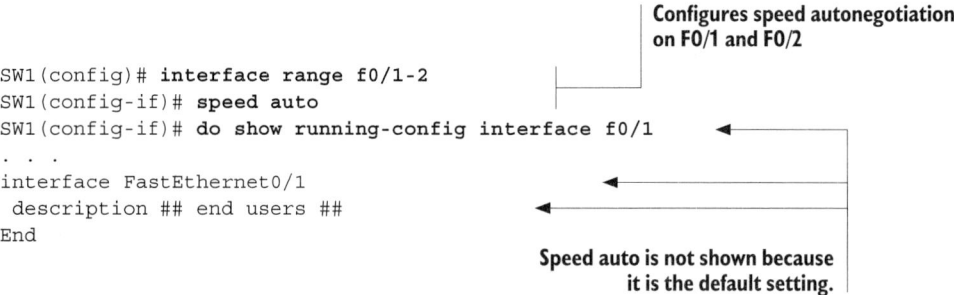

```
                                                Configures speed autonegotiation
                                                on F0/1 and F0/2
SW1(config)# interface range f0/1-2
SW1(config-if)# speed auto
SW1(config-if)# do show running-config interface f0/1
. . .
interface FastEthernet0/1
 description ## end users ##
End
                                                Speed auto is not shown because
                                                it is the default setting.
```

NOTE In figure 8.1 and the previous example, I configured **speed auto**, but because that is the default setting, it is not actually necessary to issue that command.

8.1.3 Interface duplex

An interface's *duplex* setting refers to whether it is able to send and receive data at the same time or not. There are two types of duplex:

- *Half duplex*—The interface can send and receive data but not at the same time.
- *Full duplex*—The interface can send and receive data at the same time.

NOTE The opposite of duplex is *simplex*, which is one-way communication. The communication from a keyboard to a computer is an example of simplex communication; the keyboard sends data to the computer, but the computer does not send data to the keyboard.

An example of half-duplex communication is an IEEE 802.11 wireless LAN (Wi-Fi). Because devices connected to a wireless LAN share the same physical medium (radio frequency), devices must wait their turn to communicate; they cannot send and receive data at the same time. We will focus on wireless LANs in part 4 of volume 2 of this book, but for now we will focus on wired LANs using Ethernet.

An example of full-duplex communication is a wired Ethernet LAN using a switch (or switches). Devices connected to a switch are able to send and receive traffic at the same time, which allows much greater performance compared to half duplex. However, devices connected to a wired LAN weren't always able to operate in full duplex. Before switches, devices called *hubs* were used to connect devices in a LAN, and devices connected to a hub had to operate in half-duplex mode (these days, hubs are almost never used).

ETHERNET HUBS

To understand duplex, let's examine one of the precursors to the Ethernet switch: the Ethernet hub. The basic role of a hub is the same as a switch: to connect hosts in a LAN. Switches use Layer 2 information (MAC addresses) to forward frames to the appropriate destination (or flood them as necessary). Hubs, on the other hand, aren't Layer 2 aware; when bits of data are received on one port, they simply repeat those bits out of all other ports. This means that all devices in the LAN receive every frame sent in the LAN; each device then examines the destination MAC address of the frame to determine whether it should keep or discard the frame. Hubs are considered Layer 1 devices; they receive and repeat electrical signals but don't examine those signals to make forwarding decisions.

A major downside of hubs is that they do not have memory to store frames before flooding them. Therefore, if two devices connected to a hub attempt to send frames at the same time, the hub will attempt to flood both frames at the same time, resulting in a garbled mess rather than two coherent messages; this is called a collision, and all devices connected to a hub are said to be in the same *collision domain*. Only one device in a collision domain can send traffic at a time without causing collisions. Thus, devices connected to a hub must operate in half duplex, not full duplex.

COLLISION DOMAINS

A *collision* occurs when two messages are sent simultaneously over a shared medium and then collide, resulting in an incoherent signal—like if two people talk at the same time, making you unable to understand either of them. A *collision domain* is a network segment in which simultaneous transmission will result in collisions. As mentioned previously, all hosts connected to a hub are in the same collision domain; this means that only one can transmit at a time. While one host is transmitting, the others can only receive data—they have to wait their turn to transmit. Figure 8.2 shows what happens when two hosts connected to a hub attempt to transmit at the same time.

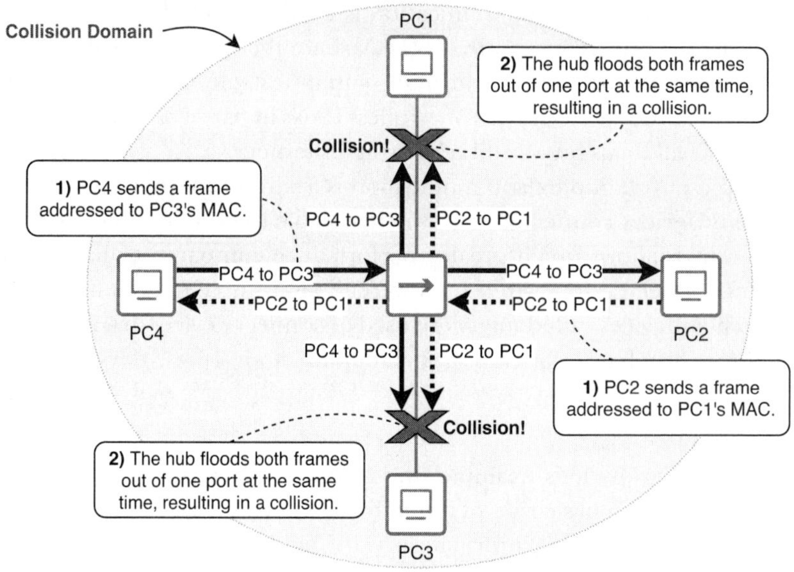

Figure 8.2 Four PCs are connected to a hub, and two attempt to transmit at the same time, resulting in collisions. All four PCs are in the same collision domain. (1) PC2 sends a frame addressed to PC1's MAC address, and PC4 sends a frame addressed to PC3's MAC address. (2) The hub attempts to flood both frames at the same time, resulting in collisions. Neither PC1 nor PC3 receive their respective frames intact.

Unlike hosts connected to a hub, each host connected to a switch is in its own collision domain; switches are able to store frames in memory and forward (or flood) them one after the other, avoiding collisions. This means that hosts connected to a switch can operate in full-duplex mode; all devices in the LAN can send and receive traffic at the same time, with no worry of messages colliding.

> **NOTE** Exam topic 1.3.b states, "Connections (Ethernet shared media and point-to-point)." All devices connected to a hub are connected to a *shared medium*; each device has to share the medium and wait its turn to transmit. Connections to a switch are considered Ethernet *point-to-point* connections—connections between only two devices: the switch and its connected device. Devices connected to a switch do not have to share the medium—they do not have to wait their turn to transmit.

Collisions should not occur in a switched LAN; if collisions occur, it is an indicator of a problem in the network (we will cover some possible problems in section 8.3). Figure 8.3 shows how a switch is able to flood frames one after the other without causing collisions.

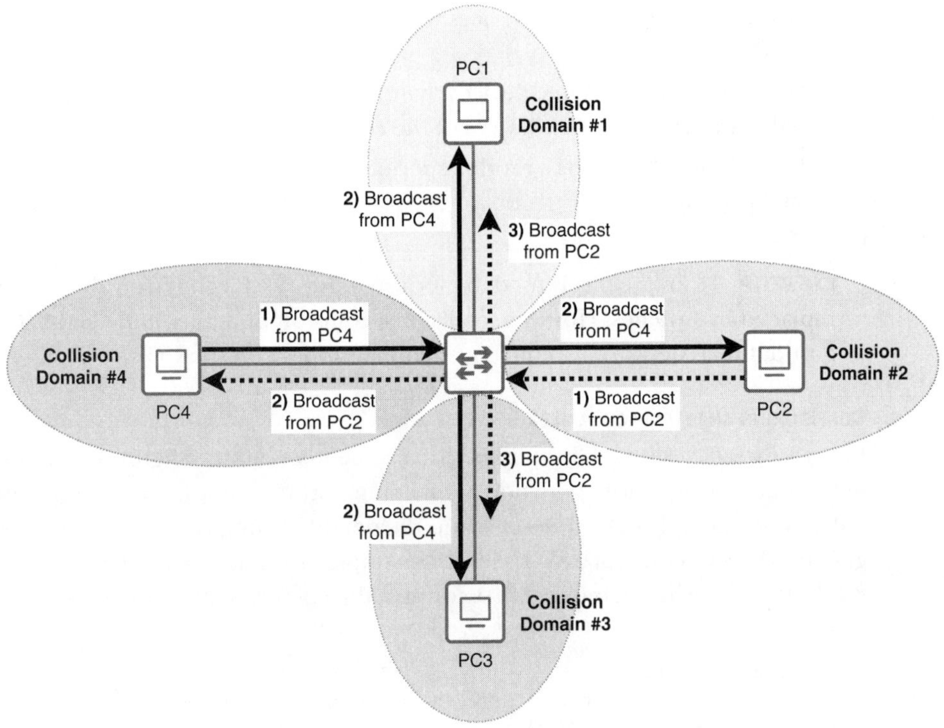

Figure 8.3 Four PCs are connected to a switch, each in its own collision domain. (1) PC2 and PC4 each send a broadcast frame at the same time. (2) The switch floods the frames, but it does not flood PC2's frame to PC1 or PC3; it buffers the frame in memory. (3) The switch floods PC2's frame to PC1 and PC3 after it has finished flooding PC4's frame.

CARRIER-SENSE MULTIPLE ACCESS WITH COLLISION DETECTION

To facilitate communications over a shared medium (a LAN using a hub), devices use a method called *carrier-sense multiple access with collision detection* (CSMA/CD). Let's examine each part of that title:

- *Carrier-sense* means that devices will attempt to sense whether the medium is in use (by "listening" for electrical signals) before transmitting a message.
- *Multiple access* means that a shared medium is used (i.e., accessed by multiple devices).
- *Collision detection* means that if a collision occurs, devices connected to the medium will detect it (and send a signal to notify other devices of the collision).

CSMA/CD helps devices connected to a hub avoid collisions and deal with collisions when they inevitably happen; interfaces operating in half-duplex mode must use CSMA/CD. The CSMA/CD process is as follows:

1 Before sending a frame, devices wait until they detect that other devices are not sending.
2 When a collision occurs, devices that detect the collision will send a jamming signal to inform the other devices of the collision.
3 Each device then waits a random period of time before sending frames again.
4 The process repeats.

EXAM TIP Hubs are rarely used in modern networks, having been almost entirely replaced by switches. However, collisions, collision domains, and CSMA/CD are foundational networking concepts that may appear on the CCNA exam.

CONFIGURING AN INTERFACE DUPLEX

Like an interface's speed, its duplex can also be manually configured or automatically determined using autonegotiation. The command to configure an interface's duplex is **`duplex {auto | full | half}`**, and the default setting is **`auto`** (which uses autonegotiation). Let's configure SW1's interface duplex settings, as in the example in figure 8.1. In the following example, I first confirm the current status with **`show interfaces status`**:

```
SW1# show interfaces status
Port      Name              Status      Vlan  Duplex  Speed Type
Fa0/1     ## end users ##   connected   1     a-full  a-100 10/100BaseTX
Fa0/2     ## end users ##   connected   1     a-full  a-100 10/100BaseTX
Fa0/3     ## not in use ## notconnect  1     auto    auto 10/100BaseTX
. . .
Gi0/1     ## to R1 ##       connected   1     a-full   1000 10/100/1000BaseTX
Gi0/2     ## not in use ## notconnect  1     auto    auto 10/100/1000BaseTX
```

The prefix a- indicates autonegotiation.

Note that the current duplex state for SW1's active interfaces (F0/1, F0/2, and G0/1) is `a-full`. This means that they are operating in full duplex, which was decided using autonegotiation. Interfaces that are not active (i.e., not connected to another device) are `auto`, meaning autonegotiation is enabled, but SW1 hasn't decided if those interfaces will operate in half or full duplex (because they aren't connected to another device yet).

NOTE In the `Speed` column of the previous example, F0/1 and F0/2 show `a-100`, meaning autonegotiation was used to decide on a speed of 100 Mbps. G0/1 simply displays `1000`, because I manually configured a speed of 1,000 Mbps.

Next, let's configure the duplex of SW1's interfaces according to figure 8.1. In the following example, I do so and then confirm with **`show interfaces status`**:

```
SW1# configure terminal
SW1(config)# interface g0/1
SW1(config-if)# duplex full
```

Manually configures G0/1's duplex

Uses duplex autonegotiation (default) on F0/1 and F0/2

F0/1 and F0/2 use speed and duplex autonegotiation (the default settings).

```
SW1(config-if)# interface range f0/1-2
SW1(config-if)# duplex auto
SW1(config-if)# do show interfaces status
Port      Name               Status       Vlan  Duplex  Speed Type
Fa0/1     ## end users ##    connected    1     a-full  a-100 10/100BaseTX
Fa0/2     ## end users ##    connected    1     a-full  a-100 10/100BaseTX
Fa0/3     ## not in use ## notconnect 1         auto   auto 10/100BaseTX
. . .
Gi0/1     ## to R1 ##        connected    1     full   1000 10/100/1000BaseTX
Gi0/2     ## not in use ## notconnect 1         auto   auto 10/100/1000BaseTX
```

G0/1's duplex and speed are manually set to full/1000.

Notice that G0/1's duplex has changed from `a-full` to `full`; this means the interface was manually configured to operate in full duplex. The output for F0/1 and F0/2, however, does not change. As with **`speed auto`**, **`duplex auto`** is the default setting, so it is not necessary to issue the command to enable autonegotiation—I include it in the example to demonstrate that.

> **NOTE** Although duplex is an important concept to understand, in modern wired networks, you can expect all devices to operate in full duplex; there's no reason to use half duplex. However, wireless LANs operate in half duplex, so we will return to the topic of half duplex when we cover wireless LANs in part 4 of volume 2 of this book.

8.2 Autonegotiation

In section 8.1, we learned that autonegotiation can be used to automatically determine the speed and duplex at which an interface operates without manual configuration. In most cases, you can leave autonegotiation enabled without any issues, although some engineers prefer to manually configure speed and duplex for connections between network infrastructure devices (such as between routers and switches). The reason for this is that manually configuring the speed and duplex settings means that there is one less thing to potentially not work properly (autonegotiation) and cause problems. However, manual configuration does include the potential for human error, and it is extremely rare for autonegotiation to malfunction, so this is not a hard-and-fast rule.

In either case, it is best to leave autonegotiation enabled for connections to end devices such as PCs. Different end devices might support different speeds, and manually configuring speed settings for each PC (or other end device) in a network is often not feasible.

In the autonegotiation process, each device advertises its capabilities to its neighbor, and the two agree upon the best operational mode supported by both neighbors. Table 8.1 lists some operational modes in order of priority—greater speeds are prioritized over lesser speeds, and full duplex is prioritized over half duplex (as you would probably expect).

Table 8.1 Operational modes

Priority	Operational mode
1	10 Gbps, full duplex
2	1 Gbps, full duplex
3	100 Mbps, full duplex
4	100 Mbps, half duplex
5	10 Mbps, full duplex
6	10 Mbps, half duplex

NOTE Table 8.1 only includes full duplex for 10 and 1 Gbps. 1 Gbps/half duplex is possible, but devices that support it are very rare; you can't configure that combination on a Cisco device, for example. Speeds of 10 Gbps or greater do not support half duplex, only full duplex.

Figure 8.4 shows an example of autonegotiation between a router and a switch. After each device advertises its capabilities, it chooses the best mode shared by both devices (100 Mbps, full duplex).

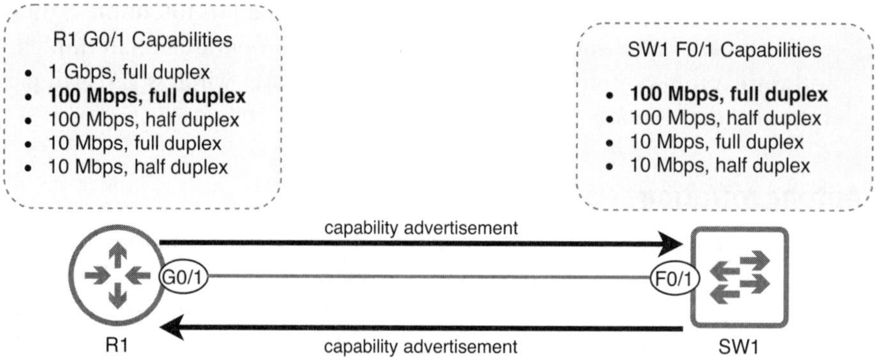

Figure 8.4 A router and a switch advertise their speed and duplex capabilities to each other. The best option supported by both R1 and SW1 is 100 Mbps/full duplex, as highlighted in bold. Although R1 G0/1 is capable of 1 Gbps/full duplex, it will operate at 100 Mbps/full duplex to match SW1 F0/1.

Figure 8.4 demonstrates what happens when both devices are using autonegotiation, but what if speed and duplex are manually configured on one end of the connection and autonegotiation is used on the other end? In such a situation, the device with autonegotiation enabled will behave as follows:

- *Speed*—Tries to sense the speed at which the other device is operating. If that fails, uses the slowest supported speed (i.e., 10 Mbps on a 10/100/1000 interface).
- *Duplex*—If the speed is 10 or 100 Mbps, uses half duplex. If the speed is 1,000 Mbps or greater, uses full duplex.

These behaviors can result in some problems, and figure 8.5 demonstrates one of those problems. R1 G0/1 is using autonegotiation, but SW1 F0/1's speed and duplex are manually configured. R1 is able to sense the speed at which SW1 F0/1 is operating (100 Mbps) and match its speed. However, following the previously stated rules, R1 G0/1 operates in half duplex, not full duplex. This creates a *duplex mismatch.* If R1 fails to sense SW1's operating speed, R1 G0/1 will operate at 10 Mbps, resulting in a *speed mismatch.* We will cover speed and duplex mismatches in section 8.3.

```
R1(config)# interface g0/1
R1(config-if)# speed auto
R1(config-if)# duplex auto
```

```
SW1(config)# interface f0/1
SW1(config-if)# speed 100
SW1(config-if)# duplex full
```

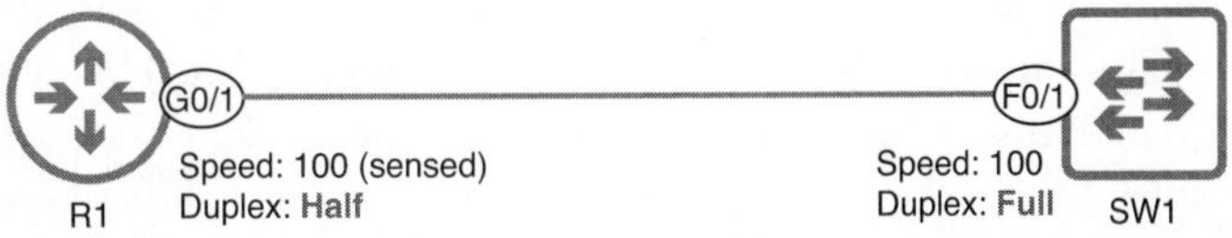

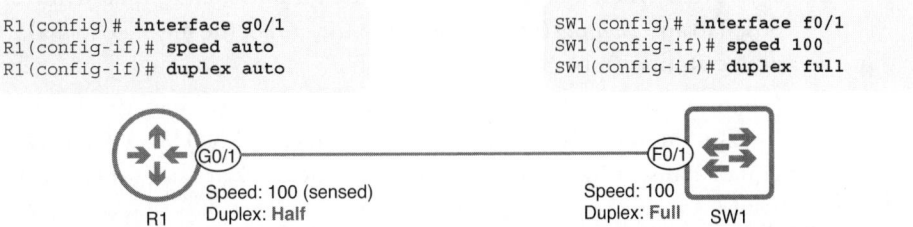

Figure 8.5 A router and switch are connected, but only the router is using autonegotiation. R1 senses SW1's speed (100 Mbps) and matches its speed to SW1. However, because R1 G0/1 is operating at 100 Mbps, it operates in half duplex. This creates a duplex mismatch between R1 G0/1 (half duplex) and SW1 F0/1 (full duplex).

> **EXAM TIP** An autonegotiation-enabled device's behavior when connected to a device with manually configured speed and duplex settings is a potential exam question. Be aware of how the autonegotiation-enabled device will select its operational speed and duplex, as well as the possible negative results (speed or duplex mismatch).

8.3 Interface errors

Cisco IOS devices maintain various counters to keep track of errors encountered when sending or receiving messages (such as when messages collide). When a device encounters errors while sending or receiving messages on an interface, it increments the relevant counter(s). You can view these counters in the output of **show interfaces**, as shown in the following example:

```
SW1# show interfaces f0/1
. . .
     164850273 packets input, 138587749740 bytes, 0 no buffer
     Received 606 broadcasts (0 multicasts)
     0 runts, 0 giants, 0 throttles
     0 input errors, 0 CRC, 0 frame, 0 overrun, 0 ignored
     0 watchdog, 0 multicast, 0 pause input
     0 input packets with dribble condition detected
     165209751 packets output, 180164587250 bytes, 0 underruns
     0 output errors, 0 collisions, 0 interface resets
```

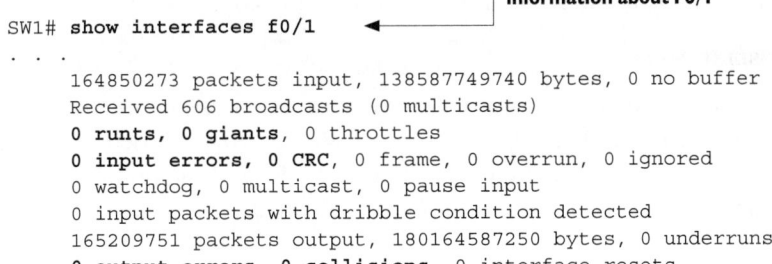

Views detailed information about F0/1

Various errors and statistics are listed at the bottom of the output.

```
0 unknown protocol drops
0 babbles, 0 late collision, 0 deferred
0 lost carrier, 0 no carrier, 0 pause output
0 output buffer failures, 0 output buffers swapped out
```

Various errors and statistics are listed at the bottom of the output.

I have highlighted some errors in the output that you should be able to identify for the CCNA. Let's take a look at what each error type means:

- *Runts* are frames received that are smaller than the minimum frame size, which is 64 bytes. When a device wants to send a frame smaller than 64 bytes, it is supposed to add *padding* (bytes of all 0s) to the end of the message to make it 64 bytes in size. Runts can be caused by collisions.
- *Giants* are frames received with a payload greater than the interface's MTU (maximum transmission unit), which is typically 1,500 bytes. Giants are usually a sign of a misconfiguration; devices in the network are not using consistent MTU values.
- *Input errors* is a counter that includes all errors for received frames.
- *CRC* (Cyclic Redundancy Check) counts frames that failed the FCS (Frame Check Sequence) check in the Ethernet trailer. This could be the result of electromagnetic interference (EMI) causing data corruption.
- *Output errors* is a counter that includes all errors for transmitted frames.
- *Collisions* is a counter for all collisions that happen when the device is transmitting a frame. If the device is connected to a hub, collisions are expected. In a switched LAN, this counter should remain at 0.
- *Late collision* is a counter for collisions that happen after the 64th byte of the frame has been transmitted. This counter is significant because, due to the timing of CSMA/CD, collisions should only occur within the first 64 bytes of a frame's transmission. If a collision occurs after that, it often indicates that one of the devices is not using CSMA/CD to check the medium before transmitting (probably due to a duplex mismatch).

As indicated in their descriptions, some of these errors are expected as a result of collisions and are therefore normal occurrences in LANs using hubs. Others are a sign of a problem in the network, such as a misconfiguration or hardware malfunction. In addition to these errors, for the CCNA exam, you must also be familiar with speed mismatches and duplex mismatches and the consequences of each.

8.3.1 Speed mismatches

Speed mismatches—when two connected interfaces attempt to communicate at different speeds—are a fairly simple problem. They are almost always caused by a misconfiguration (e.g., one interface configured with **`speed 100`** and the other configured with **`speed 1000`**). The result of a speed mismatch is that both interfaces will be in a down/

down state (referring to the `Status` and `Protocol` columns in the output of **`show ip interface brief`**). The two devices will not be able to communicate with each other. Figure 8.6 demonstrates this.

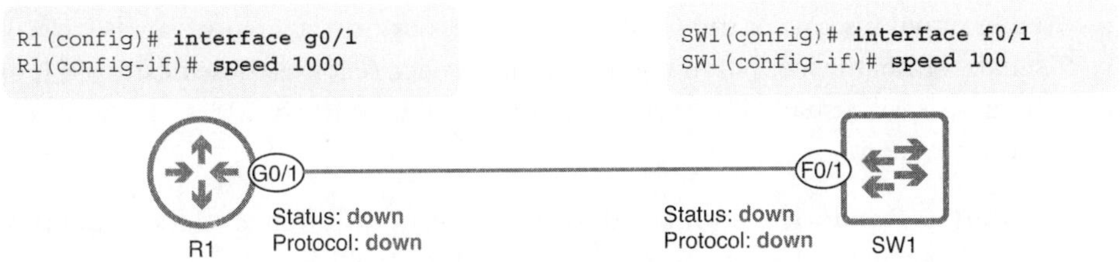

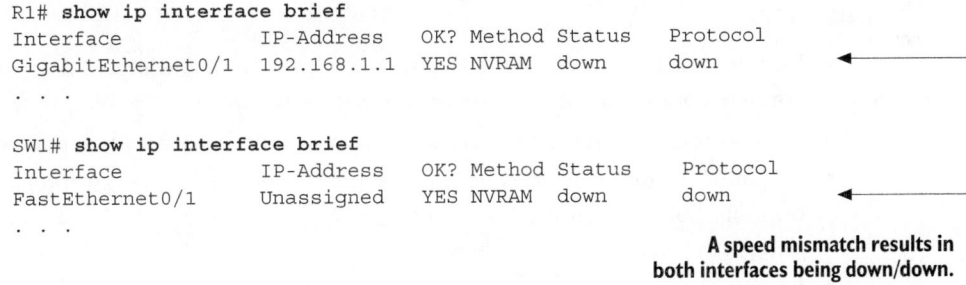

Figure 8.6 A speed mismatch between a router and a switch. Because of the speed mismatch, their interfaces are in a down/down state; R1 and SW1 cannot communicate.

The following examples show the output of **`show ip interface brief`** for both R1 and SW1 after configuring mismatching speeds on each:

```
R1# show ip interface brief
Interface             IP-Address    OK? Method Status    Protocol
GigabitEthernet0/1    192.168.1.1   YES NVRAM  down      down
. . .

SW1# show ip interface brief
Interface             IP-Address    OK? Method Status     Protocol
FastEthernet0/1       Unassigned    YES NVRAM  down       down
. . .
```

A speed mismatch results in both interfaces being down/down.

Speed mismatches are a risk when manually configuring interface speeds; there is always a chance for human error. However, if you're careful, they shouldn't occur.

> **EXAM TIP** For the CCNA exam, remember the result of a speed mismatch: both interfaces will be in a down/down state. The interfaces will not be operational.

8.3.2 Duplex mismatches

Duplex mismatches—when two connected interfaces are operating at different duplex settings—can be a bit harder to identify than speed mismatches. Even with a duplex mismatch, both interfaces will be operational—they will be in an up/up state and able to forward network traffic. A duplex mismatch can occur when each end of the connection is configured with a different duplex setting (**`duplex full`** and **`duplex half`**) or when one end is using autonegotiation and the other isn't (as we saw in figure 8.5).

The effect of a duplex mismatch is that the performance of the link will be greatly reduced; the device operating in half duplex will have to wait for the other device to stop transmitting before it can transmit any data. If the full-duplex device transmits a frame while the half-duplex device is also transmitting a frame, the half-duplex device will interpret that as a collision (although a collision hasn't actually occurred). In the output of **show interfaces**, you can expect to see incrementing `collisions` and `late collision` counters on the half-duplex device.

When the half-duplex device thinks it has detected a collision, it will send a jamming signal (as part of the CSMA/CD process), destroying any frames currently being sent by either device. When the full-duplex device receives these destroyed (corrupted) frames, it will usually increase the `Runts` and/or `CRC` counters on the interface that received them.

NOTE Two devices connected with UTP or fiber Ethernet cables can both send and receive traffic at the same time without collisions occurring. If there is a duplex mismatch, the half-duplex device may detect false collisions when the full-duplex device transmits, but a collision hasn't actually physically occurred. Actual collisions should only occur in a wired LAN when connecting multiple hosts with a hub, which is extremely rare in modern networks.

Summary

- Router interfaces are disabled by default (they have the **shutdown** command applied), but switch interfaces are enabled by default.
- It is considered best practice to disable unused switch ports with **shutdown**.
- An interface description is a string of text used to describe an interface. It is optional (but recommended) and can be configured with the **description** *description* command in interface configuration mode.
- You can use the **interface range** command to configure multiple interfaces at once.
- You can use **show interfaces description** to view a list of interfaces along with their status and description.
- You can use **show interfaces status** (on switches only) to view a list of interfaces and other information, like their description, status, duplex, and speed.
- An interface's speed is the maximum rate at which it can send and receive traffic. Most interfaces support multiple speeds, such as 10/100 or 10/100/1000.
- An interface's speed can be configured with **speed** {*speed* | **auto**}, where *speed* is specified in Mbps. The default setting is **speed auto**, which uses autonegotiation to determine the interface's operating speed.
- You can use **show running-config interface** *interface-name* to view the active configurations for a specific interface or **show running-config | section interface** to view the active configurations for all interfaces.
- To avoid clutter, default configurations often do not appear in the running-config (or startup-config). For example, the **speed auto** command is not shown.
- An interface's duplex setting determines whether it is able to send and receive data at the same time. An interface operating in half duplex can send and receive

data but not at the same time. An interface operating in full duplex can send and receive data at the same time.

- The opposite of duplex is simplex, which is one-way communication.
- Wireless LANs operate in half duplex. Wired LANs using switches operate in full duplex, but wired LANs using hubs operate in half duplex.
- Hubs are Layer 1 devices that simply repeat signals received on an interface out of all other interfaces; all devices in the LAN receive every frame sent in the LAN. They are legacy hardware, rarely (if ever) used in modern networks.
- Hubs do not have memory to store frames before flooding them. If a hub receives two frames at once, it will attempt to flood both at once, resulting in a *collision.*
- A collision domain is a network segment in which simultaneous transmissions will result in collisions. Only one host in a collision domain can transmit at a time.
- All hosts connected to a hub are in the same collision domain, but all hosts connected to a switch are in their own collision domain (and therefore don't have to worry about collisions).
- Devices operating in half duplex use carrier-sense multiple access with collision detection (CSMA/CD) to detect and deal with collisions.
- An interface's duplex can be configured with **`duplex`** {**`auto`** | **`full`** | **`half`**}. The default is **`duplex auto`**.
- Autonegotiation allows devices to automatically determine what speed and duplex settings an interface should use. The two devices advertise their capabilities to each other and select the best mode supported by both devices.
- If only one device is using autonegotiation, it will try to sense the speed of the other device. If that fails, it will use the slowest supported speed. If the speed is 10 or 100 Mbps, it will use half duplex. If the speed is 1000 Mbps or greater, it will use full duplex.
- Cisco IOS uses various counters to keep track of errors encountered when sending and receiving messages. They can be viewed in the output of **`show interfaces`**. Some examples are runts, giants, CRC, collisions, and late collisions.
- A speed mismatch occurs when two connected interfaces attempt to communicate at different speeds. This will result in both interfaces being down/down; the interfaces will not be operational.
- Speed mismatches are usually caused by a misconfiguration.
- A duplex mismatch occurs when two connected interfaces operate at different duplex settings: half and full. The interfaces will be operational, but performance will be greatly reduced.
- Duplex mismatches can be caused by one side being configured as full duplex and the other as half duplex. They can also be caused by one side using autonegotiation and the other not.

Part 2

Routing fundamentals and subnetting

Having covered the fundamentals of computer networking and how devices communicate within a LAN in part 1, it's time to expand our horizon to cover *routing*—how routers forward packets between networks. We will begin in chapter 9 by covering the fundamentals of routing, including how MAC addresses and IP addresses are used together to allow a message to traverse multiple network hops and how to configure static routes on a Cisco router, giving it precise instructions about how to forward messages across the network.

Chapter 10 is unique in this book. Rather than introducing new concepts, it ties the key concepts we have covered so far together, examining how a packet travels from a source host to a destination host step by step. A solid understanding of the various processes involved in a packet's journey from A to B is critical, so this is not a chapter that you should skip over!

Finally, chapter 11 covers a topic that is a common source of frustration for many CCNA students: subnetting. Subnetting is the process of dividing networks into sub-networks (subnets) of various sizes, allowing networks to break free from the strict and inflexible address classes that we covered in chapter 7. My approach to subnetting emphasizes a step-by-step approach with a focus on understanding the underlying binary, and with a bit of effort and practice, you'll master this critical skill. The goal of part 2 is to expand your knowledge beyond the confines of a single LAN, equipping you with both the theoretical understanding and the practical skills needed to build a network that allows hosts in separate LANs to communicate.

9 Routing fundamentals

This chapter covers

- How end hosts send IP packets to local and remote destinations
- The routing process
- Reading and interpreting a router's routing table
- Configuring static routes on a router
- Using default routes to provide internet connectivity

In this chapter, we will cover routing—the process by which routers forward IP packets between networks. Specifically, we will cover elements of the following CCNA exam topics:

- 3.1 Interpret the components of a routing table
- 3.2 Determine how a router makes a forwarding decision by default
- 3.3 Configure and verify IPv4 and IPv6 static routing

The term *routing* can actually refer to two different processes: the process by which routers build their *routing table* (a database of known destinations and how to forward packets toward them) and the process of actually forwarding packets. In this chapter, we will cover both aspects of routing, and we will build upon this foundation in future chapters of this volume and volume 2.

9.1 How end hosts send packets

Before we examine the details of how routers forward IP packets, let's take a look at the end hosts that send those packets to each other. After a host prepares a packet to send to another host, it must encapsulate that packet in a frame; even though we are focusing on routing, a Layer 3 process, do not forget about Layer 2! Packets are never sent over the cable (or radio waves) without being encapsulated in a frame.

The destination MAC address of the frame depends on the destination IP address of the packet. If the packet is destined for a host in the same network as the sender, the destination MAC address will be that of the destination host; in this case, there is no need for a router. Figure 9.1 demonstrates this process when PC1 sends a packet to PC2. The destination IP and MAC addresses are both PC2s; there is no need for R1 to route the packet because the source and destination are in the same network (the 192.168.1.0/24 network).

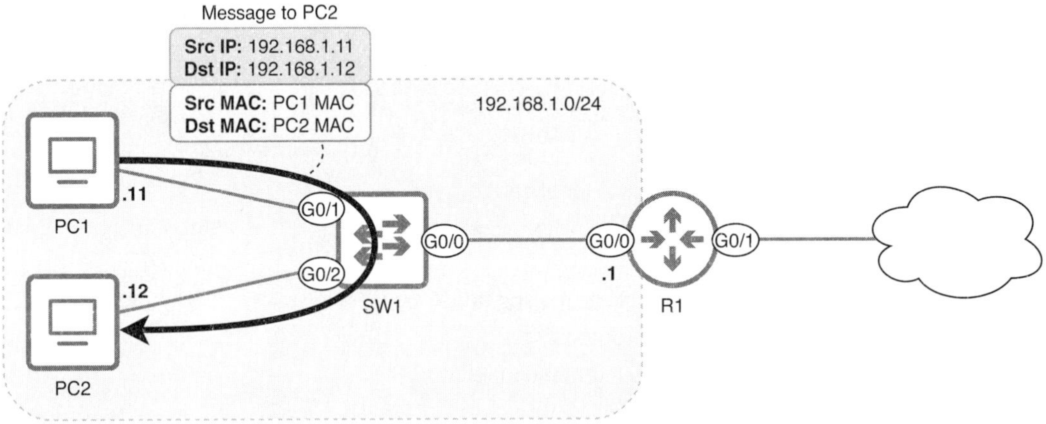

Figure 9.1 PC1 (192.168.1.11) sends a packet to PC2 (192.168.1.12). Because PC1 and PC2 are both in the same network (192.168.1.0/24), PC1 encapsulates the packet in a frame addressed to PC2's MAC address. PC1 does not need to send the packet to R1 for routing. This diagram assumes PC1 already knows PC2's MAC address; if not, PC1 will first send an ARP request to learn PC2's MAC address.

> **NOTE** A cloud icon, as shown in figure 9.1, is often used to represent the internet. However, that is not always its purpose. A cloud icon can be used to summarize elements that are not relevant to the diagram. The cloud in figure 9.1 indicates that R1 connects to another network, the details of which aren't relevant to the diagram. That other network could be the internet, or it could be another part of the same enterprise's network.

On the other hand, if an end host like a PC wants to send a packet to a destination outside of its local network, it must send the packet to its *default gateway*—the router that provides connectivity to other networks. In figure 9.2, R1 is the default gateway of the 192.168.1.0/24 network. For PC1 and PC2 to send packets to destinations outside of 192.168.1.0/24, they must encapsulate the packet in a frame addressed to the MAC address of R1's G0/0 interface. Figure 9.2 demonstrates how PC1 sends a packet to PC3: it encapsulates the packet in a frame, which is addressed to the MAC address of R1's G0/0 interface. R1 then forwards the packet out of its G0/1 interface, encapsulated in a new frame addressed to PC3's MAC address.

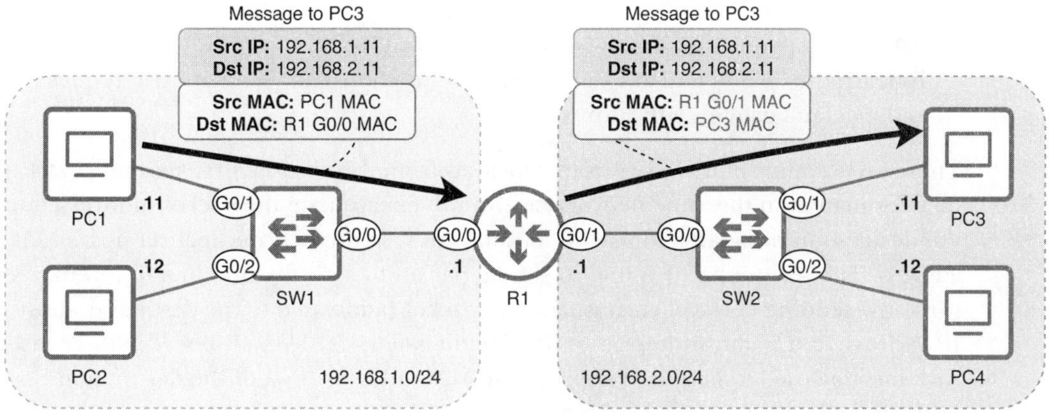

Figure 9.2 PC1 (192.168.1.11) sends a packet to PC3 (192.168.2.11). Because PC1 and PC3 are in separate networks, PC1 sends the packet in a frame addressed to its default gateway's MAC address—that of R1's G0/0 interface. R1 then forwards the packet out of its G0/1 interface, encapsulated in a new frame addressed to PC3's MAC address. This diagram assumes PC1 already knows R1 G0/0's MAC address; if not, PC1 will send an ARP request to learn it. Likewise, R1 must also learn PC3's MAC address.

> **NOTE** The default gateway's IP address is usually the first usable address of the network. For example, in the 192.168.1.0/24 network, it's 192.168.1.1, and in the 192.168.2.0/24 network, it's 192.168.2.1. That doesn't have to be the case, but it's common practice, and I will follow that practice in this book. The IP addresses of the PCs, on the other hand, are arbitrary. In this chapter's examples, the PCs' IP addresses end in .11 and .12, but there is no particular significance to those addresses.

How does PC1 know what its default gateway is? An end host can learn the IP address of its default gateway in a couple of ways. One way is manual configuration, in which an admin manually specifies the default gateway on each device. However, this is very rare for user devices like PCs; they usually use the second method—*Dynamic Host Configuration Protocol* (DHCP)—to automatically learn information like their default gateway's IP address, as well as their own IP address (DHCP is covered in chapter 4 of volume 2 of this book). On a Windows device, you can use the `ipconfig` command in the Command Prompt application to view information like the device's IP address, netmask (called the *subnet mask* in the command's output), and default gateway. The following example shows the output of this command on PC1:

```
C:\Users\jmcdo> ipconfig                          ◄── Views the PC's network
. . .                                                 interface settings
Ethernet adapter Local Area Connection:
   Connection-specific DNS Suffix  . :
   IPv4 Address. . . . . . . . . . . : 192.168.1.11    The PC's IP address,
   Subnet Mask . . . . . . . . . . . : 255.255.255.0   netmask, and default
   Default Gateway . . . . . . . . . : 192.168.1.1     gateway are shown.
. . .
```

NOTE A host's default gateway is configured as an IP address, not a MAC address. To learn the default gateway's MAC address, the host must send an ARP request to the default gateway's IP address.

There are a couple of main points to take away from this section: first, to send a packet to a destination in the same network, a host will encapsulate the packet (addressed to the destination host's IP address) in a frame addressed to the destination host's MAC address. The second point is that to send a packet to a destination in a different network, the sending host will encapsulate the packet (addressed to the destination host's IP address) in a frame addressed to the default gateway's MAC address. In either case, ARP must be used to learn the appropriate MAC address (that of the destination host or the default gateway).

9.2 The basics of routing

In section 9.1, we saw how a host sends packets to destinations outside of its local network; it sends each packet in a frame addressed to the MAC address of the default gateway. Now we'll examine how the default gateway—which is a router—performs its role of forwarding packets between networks, which is called routing. Figure 9.3 gives a high-level overview of how R1 forwards a packet from PC1 to PC3.

NOTE R1's routing table in figure 9.3 is simplified—we will examine R1's complete routing table in section 9.2.1.

When a router receives a frame destined for its own MAC address, it will de-encapsulate the frame to examine the packet inside (if the destination is not its own MAC address, it will discard the frame). If the destination IP address of the packet is its own IP address, it will continue to de-encapsulate the message—it is a message for the router itself.

However, if the destination IP address of the packet is not its own IP address, the router will attempt to route the packet to forward it toward the packet's destination. It does that by looking up the packet's destination IP address in its routing table to find a suitable route. If a suitable route is found, it will forward the packet according to that route. If not, it will discard the packet.

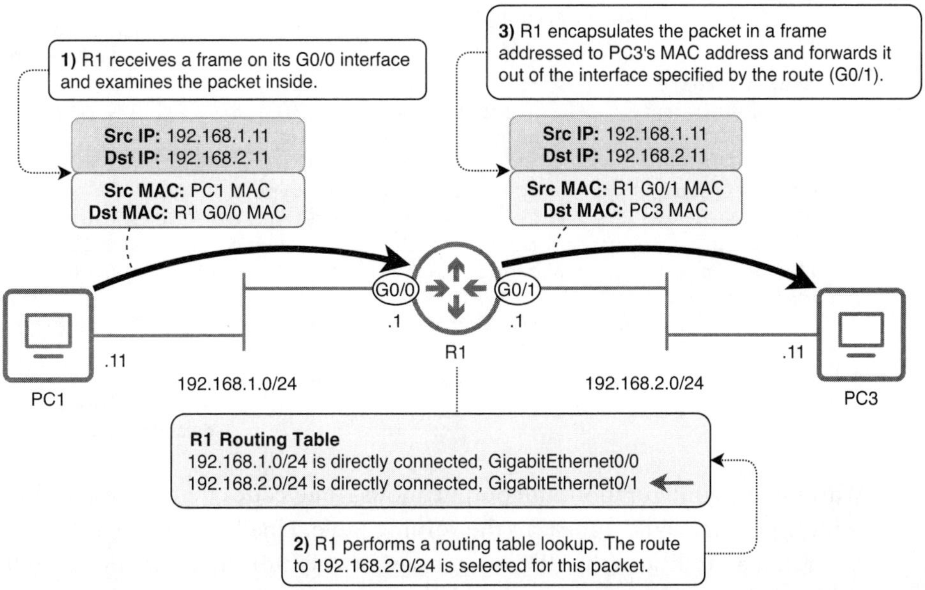

Figure 9.3 R1 receives a packet from PC1 and forwards it to PC3. (1) R1 receives a frame on its G0/0 interface. The frame is addressed to R1's own MAC address, so it examines the packet inside. (2) R1 looks up the packet's destination IP address in its routing table. 192.168.2.11 is in the 192.168.2.0/24 network, so it selects that route to forward the packet. (3) R1 encapsulates the packet in a new frame destined for PC3's MAC address and forwards it out of the interface specified by the route (G0/1).

9.2.1 *The routing table*

A router's routing table is a database of destinations known by the router. It can be thought of as a set of instructions:

- To send a packet to destination X, forward the packet to next hop Y.
- Or, if the destination is in a directly connected network, forward the packet directly to the destination.
- Or, if the destination is the router's own IP address, continue to de-encapsulate the message (don't forward the packet).

The example we saw in figure 9.3 is an example of the second kind of instruction; the destination of the packet (PC3, 192.168.2.11) is in a network directly connected to R1 (192.168.2.0/24), so R1 forwards the packet directly to the destination (by encapsulating it in a frame addressed to PC3).

Unlike switches, which can build their MAC address table automatically without any configuration, a router's routing table will be empty by default—it will not be able to forward packets. The following example shows R1's routing table before any configuration—the command to view the routing table is `show ip route`:

```
       R1# show ip route                         ◄── Views R1's routing table
Codes: L - local, C - connected, S - static, R - RIP, M - mobile, B - BGP
       D - EIGRP, EX - EIGRP external, O - OSPF, IA - OSPF inter area
       N1 - OSPF NSSA external type 1, N2 - OSPF NSSA external type 2
       E1 - OSPF external type 1, E2 - OSPF external type 2
       i - IS-IS, su - IS-IS summary, L1 - IS-IS level-1, L2 - IS-IS level-2
       ia - IS-IS inter area, * - candidate default, U - per-user static route
       o - ODR, P - periodic downloaded static route, H - NHRP, l - LISP
       a - application route
       + - replicated route, % - next hop override, p - overrides from PfR
                                                   ── Various codes identifying
                                                      different route types

       Gateway of last resort is not set           ◄── R1 doesn't have a
                                                       default route.
```

Without any configuration, the output shows some codes that represent the different route types that could appear in the routing table. Finally, `Gateway of last resort is not set` indicates that R1 doesn't have a default route, something we'll cover in section 9.4.

Let's configure R1 and see how the output of **`show ip route`** changes. First, we won't actually configure any routes; rather, let's configure R1's IP addresses and enable its interfaces, as in the following example:

```
R1# configure terminal
R1(config)# interface g0/0
R1(config-if)# ip address 192.168.1.1 255.255.255.0     Configures and
R1(config-if)# no shutdown                              enables G0/0
R1(config-if)# interface g0/1
R1(config-if)# ip address 192.168.2.1 255.255.255.0
R1(config-if)# no shutdown
                                                        Configures and enables G0/1
```

R1's interfaces are now configured according to the previous diagrams: 192.168.1.1/24 on G0/0 and 192.168.2.1/24 on G0/1. Now let's examine R1's routing table again and see what has changed (omitting some of the codes to save space):

```
R1# show ip route
Codes: L - local, C - connected, S - static, R - RIP, M - mobile, B - BGP
. . .
Gateway of last resort is not set
      192.168.1.0/24 is variably subnetted, 2 subnets, 2 masks
C        192.168.1.0/24 is directly connected, GigabitEthernet0/0    Two routes
L        192.168.1.1/32 is directly connected, GigabitEthernet0/0    for G0/0
      192.168.2.0/24 is variably subnetted, 2 subnets, 2 masks
C        192.168.2.0/24 is directly connected, GigabitEthernet0/1    Two routes
L        192.168.2.1/32 is directly connected, GigabitEthernet0/1    for G0/1
```

Just by configuring IP addresses on and enabling R1's two interfaces, R1 has inserted four routes into its routing table: two connected routes (indicated by code `C`) and two local routes (indicated by code `L`).

NOTE The line `192.168.1.0/24 is variably subnetted, 2 subnets, 2 masks` is not a route. This statement means that in the routing table, there are two routes to subnets that fit within the 192.168.1.0/24 class C network, with two different netmasks (/24 and /32). The same applies for the similar line about 192.168.2.0/24. We will cover subnets in chapter 11.

CONNECTED ROUTES

A *connected route* is a route to the network an interface is connected to. One connected route is automatically added to the routing table for each interface that has an IP address and is in an up/up state (you can check the interface's state with **`show ip interface brief`**). For example, R1's G0/0 interface has IP address 192.168.1.1/24, so it automatically adds a route to the 192.168.1.0/24 network into its routing table.

NOTE 192.168.1.0/24 is the network address, with all bits of the host portion set to 0. This can be determined by simply changing the final octet from 1 to 0 since the netmask on the interface is /24.

A connected route will state that the network is directly connected, and it will also state which interface it is connected to. To view only the connected routes in R1's routing table, in the following example, I filter the output using the pipe (|) followed by **`include C`** to display only lines that include `C`:

A connected route to G0/0's network

```
R1# show ip route | include C
Codes: L - local, C - connected, S - static, R - RIP, M - mobile, B - BGP
C        192.168.1.0/24 is directly connected, GigabitEthernet0/0
C        192.168.2.0/24 is directly connected, GigabitEthernet0/1
```

A connected route to G0/1's network

With these routes in its routing table, R1 knows that to forward a packet to a host with an IP address in the 192.168.1.0/24 or 192.168.2.0/24 networks, it should send the packet out of the interface specified in the route in a frame addressed directly to the destination host. We saw this in figure 9.3; the destination IP address of the packet was 192.168.2.11 (PC3), so R1 forwarded the packet out of the G0/1 interface in a frame addressed to PC3's MAC address.

Figure 9.4 shows how the route to 192.168.1.0/24 includes all IP addresses from 192.168.1.0 through 192.168.1.255. The network portion of the route's address is fixed, but the host portion can be any 8-bit number.

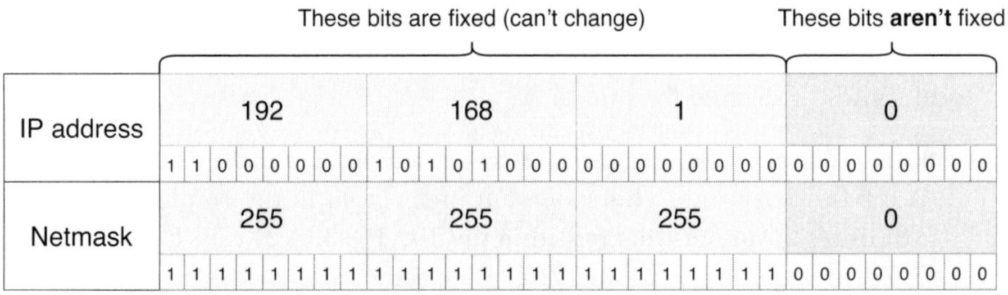
These bits are fixed (can't change)
These bits **aren't** fixed
IP address
192
168
1
0
1 1 0 0 0 0 0 0 1 0 1 0 1 0 0 0 0 0 0 0 0 0 0 1 0 0 0 0 0 0 0 0
Netmask
255
255
255
0
1 1 1 1 1 1 1 1 1 1 1 1 1 1 1 1 1 1 1 1 1 1 1 1 0 0 0 0 0 0 0 0

Figure 9.4 The IP address and prefix length (written as a netmask) of the route to 192.168.1.0/24. Due to the /24 prefix length, the first three octets are fixed (the bits can't change). However, the last octet can be any 8-bit number: .1, .11, .100, .179, etc. This means that any packet with a destination IP address beginning with 192.168.1 can be forwarded using this route.

> **EXAM TIP** A route to more than one destination IP address is called a *network route*; it's a route to a network, rather than a route to a single destination IP address. A connected route is an example of a network route. The term *network route* is explicitly mentioned in exam topic 3.3.b, so remember that definition.

LOCAL ROUTES

A *local route* is a route to the exact IP address configured on the router's interface. Like connected routes, one local route is automatically added to the routing table for each interface that has an IP address and is in an up/up state. In the following example, I use **`show ip route | include L`** to view only R1's local routes. Note that like connected routes, local routes also state `X is directly connected`, followed by the interface:

A local route to G0/0's IP address

```
R1# show ip route | include L
Codes: L - local, C - connected, S - static, R - RIP, M - mobile, B - BGP
. . .
L        192.168.1.1/32 is directly connected, GigabitEthernet0/0
L        192.168.2.1/32 is directly connected, GigabitEthernet0/1
```

A local route to G0/1's IP address

To specify the exact IP address of the interface, a local route uses a /32 prefix length; all bits of the netmask are set to 1. This is the case regardless of the netmask configured on the interface. For example, even though R1's interfaces both have /24 prefix lengths, their local routes are /32. The reason for this is that a local route specifies only a single IP address. As stated previously, a route to 192.168.1.0/24 includes all IP addresses from 192.168.1.0 through 192.168.1.255; because the prefix length is /24, the final octet can be any number from 0 to 255. On the other hand, a route to

192.168.1.1/32 includes only 192.168.1.1, due to its /32 prefix length; all bits are considered part of the network portion and cannot be changed. Figure 9.5 shows the IP address of R1 G0/0 with a /32 prefix length (written as a netmask).

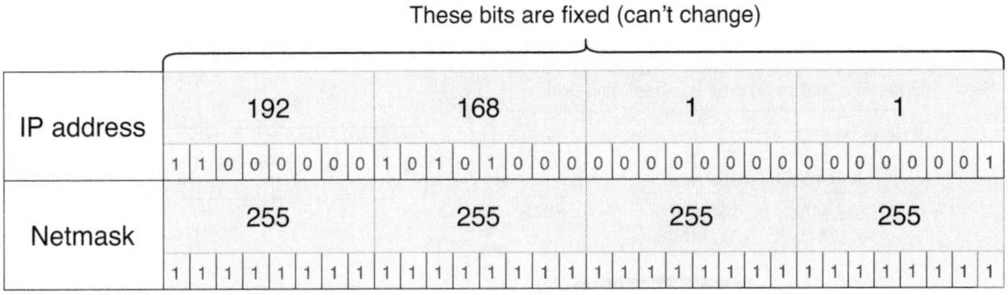
These bits are fixed (can't change)
IP address
192
168
1
1
1 1 0 0 0 0 0 0 1 0 1 0 1 0 0 0 0 0 0 0 0 0 0 1 0 0 0 0 0 0 0 1
Netmask
255
255
255
255
1 1 1 1 1 1 1 1 1 1 1 1 1 1 1 1 1 1 1 1 1 1 1 1 1 1 1 1 1 1 1 1

Figure 9.5 The IP address of R1's G0/0 interface and a /32 prefix length written as a netmask in dotted decimal and binary. With a prefix length of /32, the route only includes a single IP address (192.168.1.1, in this case). A packet destined for 192.168.1.2, for example, cannot use this route.

A local route tells the router that packets destined for the IP address specified in the route are for the router itself; it should continue to de-encapsulate the message and examine its contents. In this case, the router does not forward the packet; it just receives the packet for itself. The local route is necessary to distinguish the router's own IP address from other IP addresses in the connected network. If R1 only had a connected route to 192.168.1.0/24 but no local route, it would forward packets destined for 192.168.1.1 out of its G0/0 interface, rather than receiving the packets for itself.

> **EXAM TIP** A route to a single destination IP address (with a /32 prefix length) is called a *host route*; it's a route to a single host. A local route is an example of a host route. This is in contrast to a network route, which we covered earlier; a network route is any route with a prefix length shorter than /32. The term *host route* is explicitly mentioned in exam topic 3.3.c, so remember that definition.

9.2.2 Route selection

When a router forwards a packet, it has to decide which route in its routing table it will use to forward the packet, and this is called *route selection.* To determine how to forward a particular packet, the router will select the *most specific matching route.* Let's define that term:

- *Matching route*—The packet's destination IP address is part of the network specified in the route. If not, the packet can't be forwarded using this route.
- *Most specific*—The route with the longest prefix length.

Let's use an example to clarify that concept. Figure 9.6 shows the route selection process when R1 receives a packet addressed to 192.168.1.1. The packet's destination IP address matches two routes in R1's routing table, so it selects the more specific of the two.

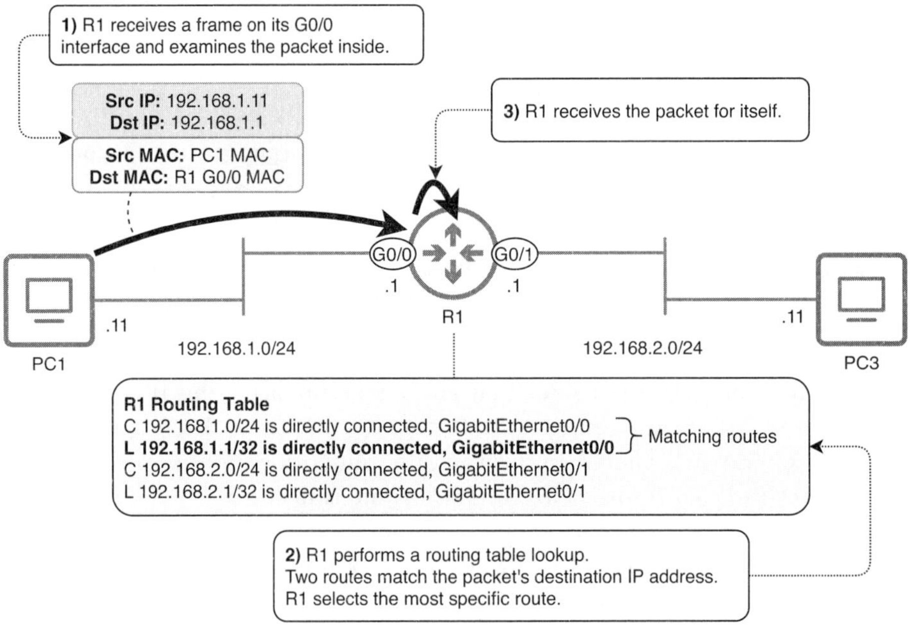

Figure 9.6 R1 receives a packet and selects the best route for that packet. (1) R1 receives a frame on its G0/0 interface. The destination MAC is its own, so it de-encapsulates it and examines the packet inside. (2) The packet's destination IP address is 192.168.1.1. R1 performs a routing table lookup and finds that two routes match the packet's destination IP address: the connected route to 192.168.1.0/24 and the local route to 192.168.1.1/32. R1 selects the most specific route: 192.168.1.1/32. (3) Because R1 selects a local route, it receives the packet for itself; it does not forward the packet.

A route with a /24 prefix length includes 256 different IP addresses. For example, 192.168.1.0/24 includes 192.168.1.0 through 192.168.1.255. On the other hand, a route with a /32 prefix length includes only a single IP address, so a /32 route is more specific than a /24 route. In fact, a /32 route is the most specific route possible; if a packet's destination IP address matches a /32 route, that route will always be selected for that packet, regardless of how many other matching routes there are.

> **EXAM TIP** Be aware of this major difference between Layer 3 forwarding done by routers and Layer 2 forwarding done by switches: when a router looks up a packet's destination IP address in its routing table, it looks for the most specific

matching route. On the other hand, when a switch looks up a frame's destination MAC address in its MAC address table, it looks for an exact match; partial matches don't count.

What happens if there aren't any routes in the routing table that match a packet's destination IP address? In that case, the router will drop the packet; it won't flood it out of all ports like switches do with unknown unicast frames. A switch sometimes floods frames, but a router never floods packets; it forwards the packet, receives the packet for itself, or drops the packet. Table 9.1 summarizes the actions a router can take on a packet.

Table 9.1 Actions a router can take on a packet

Matching conditions	Router's action
The packet's destination IP address matches one or more nonlocal routes.	Forward the packet according to the most specific matching route
The packet's destination IP address matches a local route.	Receive the packet for itself
The packet's destination IP address does not match any routes.	Drop the packet

9.3 Static routing

The packet forwarding process outlined in section 9.2 is called routing, but the term *routing* is also used to refer to the processes routers use to learn routes. In addition to the connected and local routes a router automatically inserts into its routing table, there are two main methods by which routers can learn routes:

- *Dynamic routing*—Routers use *dynamic routing protocols* (i.e., OSPF) to share information with each other and build their routing tables.
- *Static routing*—An engineer/admin manually configures routes on the router.

Connected routes allow the router to forward packets to destinations in networks directly connected to the router, and local routes allow the router to receive packets destined for its own IP addresses. However, to forward packets toward destinations that are not in directly connected networks, the router must learn of those destinations using one of the aforementioned methods (we will cover dynamic routing in chapters 17 and 18).

When forwarding a packet toward a destination that is not directly connected to the router, it must encapsulate the packet in a frame addressed to the MAC address of the *next hop*, which is the next router in the path to the destination. Figure 9.7 demonstrates this process.

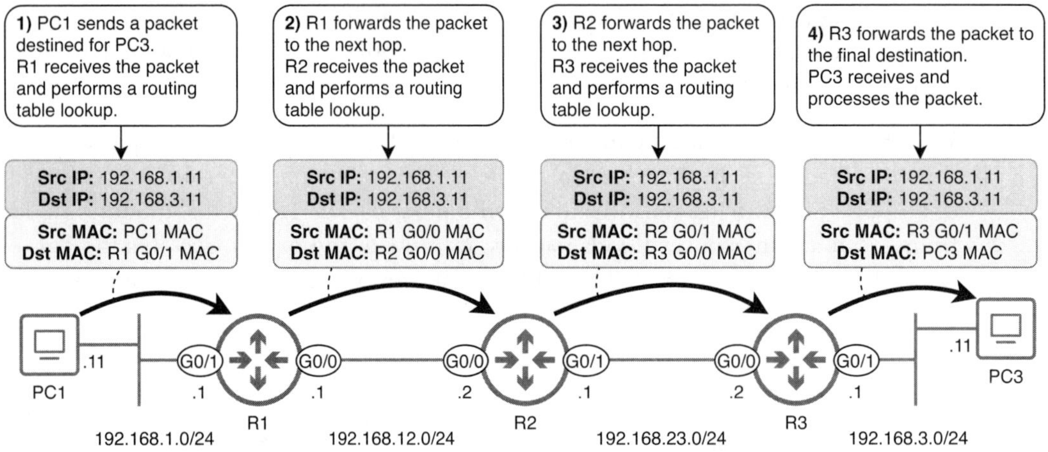

Figure 9.7 PC1 sends a packet to PC3 via R1, R2, and R3. (1) PC1 sends the packet in a frame to R1 G0/1. R1 receives it and performs a routing table lookup. (2) R1 forwards the packet in a frame to R2 G0/0. R2 receives it and performs a routing table lookup. (3) R2 forwards the packet in a frame to R3 G0/0's MAC. R3 receives the packet and performs a routing table lookup. (4) R3 forwards the packet in a frame to PC3, which receives and processes it.

Figure 9.7 shows how routers forward packets toward remote (not directly connected) destinations. However, routers have no such routes in their routing tables by default; those routes must be manually configured. Without configuring any static routes, if R1 receives a packet from PC1 destined for 192.168.3.11, R1 won't find any matching routes when it performs the routing table lookup; it will have no choice but to drop the packet. Table 9.2 lists the networks that each router in figure 9.7 is aware of without configuring static routes.

Table 9.2 Each router's known and unknown networks

Router	Known networks	Unknown networks
R1	192.168.1.0/24 192.168.12.0/24	192.168.3.0/24 192.168.23.0/24
R2	192.168.12.0/24 192.168.23.0/24	192.168.1.0/24 192.168.3.0/24
R3	192.168.3.0/24 192.168.23.0/24	192.168.1.0/24 192.168.12.0/24

Given the goal of enabling two-way communication between PC1 and PC3, which routes do we have to configure? Looking at table 9.2, you might assume that we have to configure six routes, so that each router knows about all networks within the greater network.

However, to forward packets between two hosts, each router only needs routes to the networks of the communicating hosts (PC1 and PC3). R1, for example, doesn't need to know about the network between R2 and R3 (192.168.23.0/24); R1 only needs to know that to forward a packet toward a destination in 192.168.3.0/24, it should forward the packet to R2. Figure 9.8 demonstrates this concept; if we configure a route to 192.168.3.0/24 on R1, with R2's IP address specified as the next hop, R1 will be able to forward the packet to R2. It doesn't need to know the details of the path the packet will take after R2; it just needs to know that R2 is the next hop.

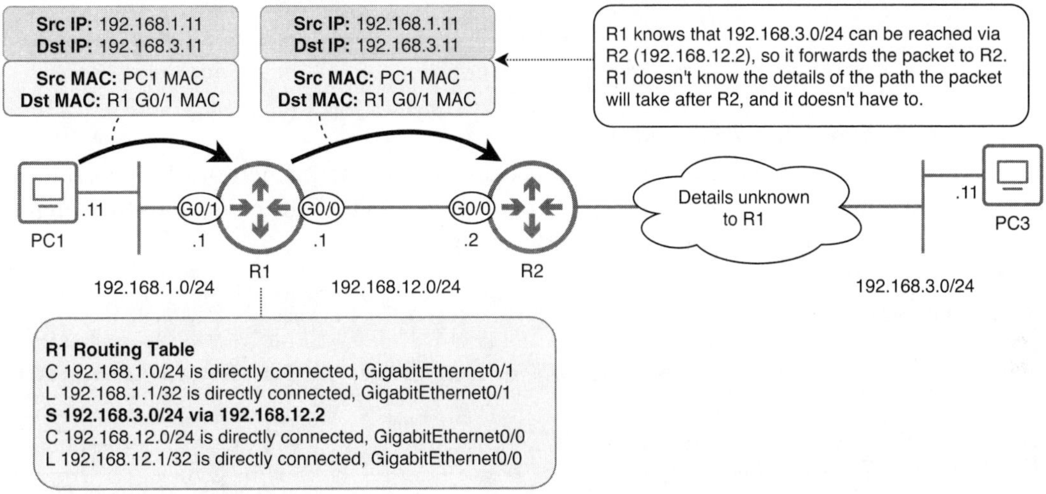

Figure 9.8 R1 forwards a packet destined for 192.168.3.11 (PC3). R1 has a static route to 192.168.3.0/24 via 192.168.12.2 (R2). R1 knows that to forward a packet toward the 192.168.3.0/24 network, it should forward the packet to R2. R1 doesn't know the details of the path the packet will take after R2, and it doesn't have to.

To summarize, each router needs a route to 192.168.3.0/24 so that it can forward packets from PC1 to PC3 and a route to 192.168.1.0/24 so that it can forward packets from PC3 to PC1. R1 already has a connected route to 192.168.1.0/24, and R3 already has a connected route to 192.168.3.0/24. Table 9.3 lists the static routes that we must configure to enable two-way communication between PC1 and PC3.

Table 9.3 Routes required to enable communication between PC1 and PC3

Router	Required routes	Next hop
R1	192.168.3.0/24	192.168.12.2 (R2 G0/0)
R2	192.168.1.0/24	192.168.12.1 (R1 G0/0)
	192.168.3.0/24	192.168.23.2 (R3 G0/0)
R3	192.168.1.0/24	192.168.23.1 (R2 G0/1)

NOTE In this example, we are talking about the routes required to enable two-way communication between PC1 and PC3. Although not necessary for that purpose, there is nothing wrong with configuring a route to 192.168.23.0/24 on R1 and a route to 192.168.12.0/24 on R3.

9.3.1 Configuring static routes

The command to configure a static route is, from global configuration mode, `ip route`. However, there are a few different options regarding the arguments you provide with the command:

- **`ip route`** *`destination-network netmask next-hop`*
- **`ip route`** *`destination-network netmask exit-interface`*
- **`ip route`** *`destination-network netmask exit-interface next-hop`*

STATIC ROUTES SPECIFYING THE NEXT HOP

A static route can be configured by specifying the destination network address, the netmask, and the IP address of the next hop. Figure 9.9 shows the commands to configure each of the necessary routes on R1, R2, and R3.

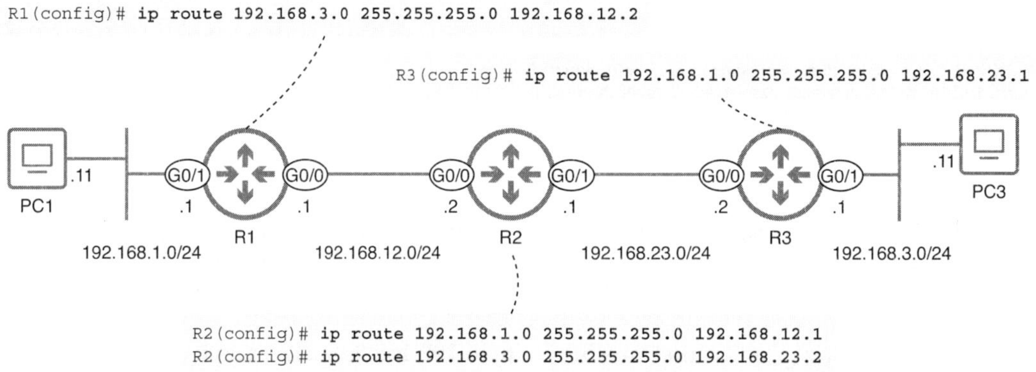

Figure 9.9 Configuring static routes on R1, R2, and R3 to enable two-way communication between PC1 and PC3. The routes specify the next-hop IP address. R1 requires a route to 192.168.3.0/24, R2 requires routes to 192.168.1.0/24 and 192.168.3.0/24, and R3 requires a route to 192.168.1.0/24.

A static route that specifies only the next-hop IP address is called a *recursive static route.* The reason for the name *recursive* is that the route necessitates multiple lookups in the routing table to forward a packet:

- A lookup to find the IP address of the next hop
- A lookup to find which interface the next hop is connected to

To demonstrate that, let's look at R1's routing table in the following example. When R1 receives a packet destined for 192.168.3.11, it finds that the most specific matching route (actually, the only matching route) is the static route:

```
R1# show ip route
Codes: L - local, C - connected, S - static, R - RIP, M - mobile, B - BGP
. . .
      192.168.1.0/24 is variably subnetted, 2 subnets, 2 masks
```

```
                                        Matches the packet's destination (192.168.3.11)
C        192.168.1.0/24 is directly connected, GigabitEthernet0/1
L        192.168.1.1/32 is directly connected, GigabitEthernet0/1
S     192.168.3.0/24 [1/0] via 192.168.12.2                     <--
      192.168.12.0/24 is variably subnetted, 2 subnets, 2 masks
C        192.168.12.0/24 is directly connected, GigabitEthernet0/0   <--
L        192.168.12.1/32 is directly connected, GigabitEthernet0/0
                                        Matches the next-hop IP address (192.168.12.2)
```

NOTE The `[1/0]` in the static route indicates the *administrative distance* (AD) and *metric* of the route, respectively. AD and metric will be covered in chapter 17; they are not relevant to this chapter.

The static route states `S 192.168.3.0/24 [1/0] via 192.168.12.2` (note the code `S` for static), but that information alone doesn't tell R1 which interface to forward the packet out of. To learn that, it then performs a second lookup for the next-hop IP address: 192.168.12.2. The most specific (and only) matching route for 192.168.12.2 is the connected route to 192.168.12.0/24, which specifies the G0/0 interface. Now, after two lookups, R1 knows the next-hop IP address and the interface to forward the packet out of.

NOTE R1 knows the next-hop IP address, but the information R1 really needs is the next-hop MAC address. To learn that, it must send an ARP request to the next-hop IP address.

STATIC ROUTES SPECIFYING THE EXIT INTERFACE

Rather than specifying the next-hop IP address of the route, you can specify the *exit interface*—the interface the router should forward packets out of. The following example shows the same static routes as we saw in figure 9.9 but configured using the exit interface:

- `R1(config)#` **`ip route 192.168.3.0 255.255.255.0 g0/0`**
- `R2(config)#` **`ip route 192.168.1.0 255.255.255.0 g0/0`**
- `R2(config)#` **`ip route 192.168.3.0 255.255.255.0 g0/1`**
- `R3(config)#` **`ip route 192.168.1.0 255.255.255.0 g0/0`**

A static route that specifies only the exit interface is called a *directly connected static route*. The reason for this is that the route will appear as a directly connected network in the routing table. The following example shows the route to 192.168.3.0/24 in R1's routing table:

```
R1# show ip route
Codes: L - local, C - connected, S - static, R - RIP, M - mobile, B - BGP
. . .
S     192.168.3.0/24 is directly connected, GigabitEthernet0/0     <--
. . .
                              The static route appears as "directly connected."
```

There is a downside to this kind of static route: because R1 thinks that the 192.168.3.0/24 network is directly connected to its G0/0 interface, it will try to send packets in frames addressed directly to PC3, rather than in frames addressed to the next hop.

This means that R1 won't send an ARP request to learn the next-hop MAC address; instead, it will send an ARP request to learn PC3's MAC address. The problem is that this ARP request won't reach PC3—it will only reach R2 (broadcast messages don't go beyond their local network). However, R2 can use a feature called *proxy ARP* to reply on behalf of PC3, telling R1 to send the packet to R2 G0/0's MAC address. This is demonstrated in figure 9.10.

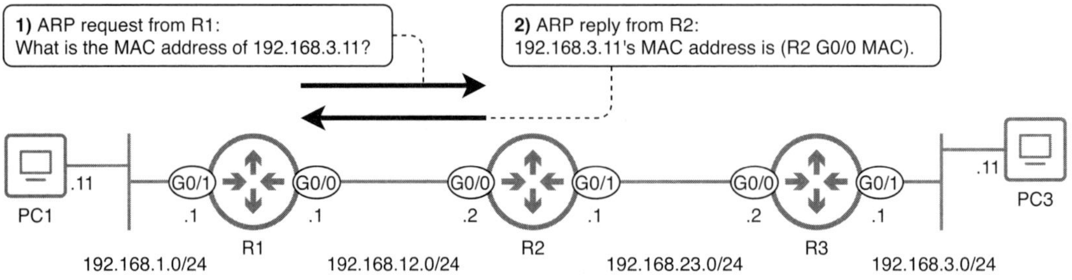

Figure 9.10 A proxy ARP exchange between R1 and R2. (1) R1 sends an ARP request to learn PC3's MAC address. (2) 192.168.3.11 isn't R2's IP address, but R2 has a route to 192.168.3.0/24 in its routing table, so R2 uses proxy ARP to reply on behalf of PC3.

> **NOTE** A router will only use proxy ARP to reply to an ARP request if it has a route to the destination in its routing table. Otherwise, it will ignore the request.

The following example shows R1's ARP table (you can view it with the `show arp` command). Notice that the same MAC address (`Hardware Addr`) is listed for both 192.168.12.2 and 192.168.3.11—the MAC address of R2's G0/0 interface:

```
R1# show arp
Protocol  Address          Age (min)  Hardware Addr   Type   Interface
. . .
Internet  192.168.3.11             0  5254.0003.e684  ARPA   GigabitEthernet0/0
. . .
Internet  192.168.12.2             0  5254.0003.e684  ARPA   GigabitEthernet0/0
```

R2 G0/0's MAC address is listed for both IP addresses.

The reliance on proxy ARP is a downside to directly connected static routes for two reasons. First, although proxy ARP is enabled on Cisco routers by default, in some cases, it might be disabled (e.g., if R2 is not a Cisco router). If proxy ARP is disabled on R2, it won't reply to R1's ARP request, and R1 won't be able to forward the packet to PC3.

The second downside is that R1 will need to make a separate ARP entry for every host in 192.168.3.0/24. It thinks each host in 192.168.3.0/24 is directly connected, so it will try to learn each host's MAC address; that could waste memory on R1 if there are a lot of hosts in the network. On the other hand, if the next-hop IP address is specified instead of the exit interface, R1 will only need one ARP entry to forward packets to 192.168.3.0/24: an ARP entry for the next hop.

> **NOTE** Although we are focusing on R1 as an example, the same applies for R2, which will think that the 192.168.1.0/24 and 192.168.3.0/24 networks are directly connected, as well as for R3, which will think that the 192.168.1.0/24 network is directly connected.

You should know the definition of and be able to configure directly connected static routes, but because of the downsides of relying on proxy ARP, I recommend that you do not use them in a real network. Rather, use recursive static routes or the next option: fully specified static routes.

Static routes specifying both the exit interface and next hop

The third option when configuring a static route is to specify both the exit interface and the next hop, which is called a *fully specified static route.* The following are the same four static routes, this time configured as fully specified static routes:

- `R1(config)# ip route 192.168.3.0 255.255.255.0 g0/0 192.168.12.2`
- `R2(config)# ip route 192.168.1.0 255.255.255.0 g0/0 192.168.12.1`
- `R2(config)# ip route 192.168.3.0 255.255.255.0 g0/1 192.168.23.2`
- `R3(config)# ip route 192.168.1.0 255.255.255.0 g0/0 192.168.23.1`

The benefit of this kind of static route is that the router knows both the next-hop IP address and which interface to forward the packet out of; there is no need to do a recursive lookup or to rely on proxy ARP. The following example shows how a fully specified route appears in the routing table:

```
R1# show ip route
Codes: L - local, C - connected, S - static, R - RIP, M - mobile, B - BGP
. . .
S      192.168.3.0/24 [1/0] via 192.168.12.2, GigabitEthernet0/0
. . .
```

The route indicates both the next hop and the exit interface.

This type of static route may seem the best of the three, but in reality, you can use either recursive or fully specified static routes without a noticeable difference in performance. Directly connected static routes, however, should generally be avoided.

9.3.2 Configuring a default route

A *default route* is a route to the least-specific destination possible: 0.0.0.0/0. This route matches all possible IP addresses, from 0.0.0.0 through 255.255.255.255. Because it is the least-specific route possible, the default route will only be selected if there aren't any more specific routes in the router's routing table.

A default route is often used to provide a route to the internet. There are over 1 million routes in the global internet routing table, which is far more than most routers can handle. Fortunately, there's no need for a router to know about any specific destination networks over the internet; if the router has a default route to the internet, it can use that route to forward packets toward the internet, and then the Internet Service Provider (ISP) infrastructure will take care of forwarding the packets to the proper destination.

More specific routes can be used for destinations in the internal corporate network, and then all other traffic (that doesn't match any other routes) will be routed using the default route. Figure 9.11 shows an example of this: R1 has specific routes to 192.168.2.0/24 and 192.168.3.0/24 and then a default route to the internet; packets with destinations that don't match 192.168.2.0/24 or 192.168.3.0/24 (or R1's connected and local routes) will be forwarded using the default route.

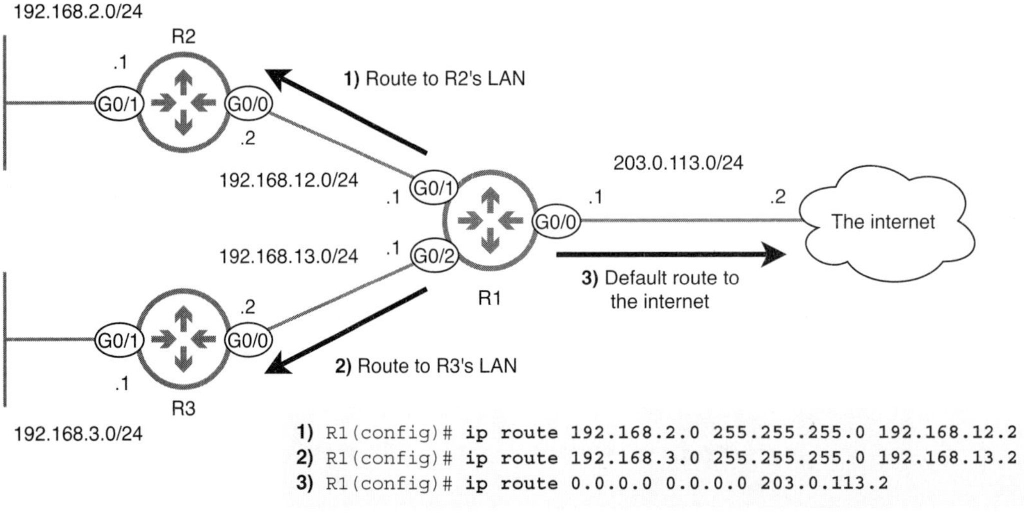

Figure 9.11 R1 has two routes to specific destination networks and one default route to the internet. (1) A route to 192.168.2.0/24, with R2 G0/0 as the next hop. (2) A route to 192.168.3.0/24, with R3 G0/0 as the next hop. (3) A default route, with the ISP's IP address (203.0.113.2) as the next hop.

To configure a default route, specify a destination network of `0.0.0.0` and a netmask of `0.0.0.0` in the `ip route` command; that results in 0.0.0.0/0, which includes all possible IP addresses. If a router does not have a default route configured, you will see the statement `Gateway of last resort is not set` above the routes in the routing table, as shown in the following example. This means the router does not have a default route:

```
R1# show ip route
Codes: L - local, C - connected, S - static, R - RIP, M - mobile, B - BGP
. . .
Gateway of last resort is not set          ◄── R1 doesn't have a default route.
. . .
```

NOTE *Gateway of last resort* is another term for the default gateway. The default route on a router is like a PC's default gateway; it's used to forward traffic to destinations outside of the router's known networks.

After configuring the static routes shown in figure 9.11, the output changes. In the following example, I use the **`show ip route static`** command to view only R1's static routes. Note that the ISP's IP address (`203.0.113.2`) is now listed as the gateway of last resort:

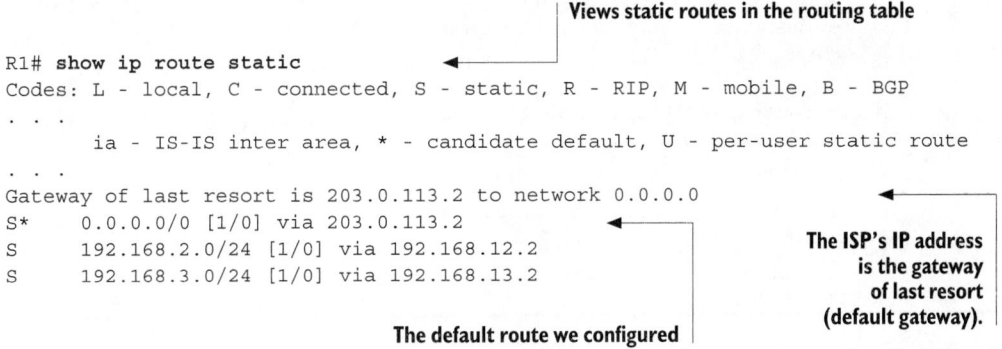

```
R1# show ip route static                   ◄── Views static routes in the routing table
Codes: L - local, C - connected, S - static, R - RIP, M - mobile, B - BGP
. . .
       ia - IS-IS inter area, * - candidate default, U - per-user static route
. . .
Gateway of last resort is 203.0.113.2 to network 0.0.0.0   ◄── The ISP's IP address is the gateway of last resort (default gateway).
S*     0.0.0.0/0 [1/0] via 203.0.113.2     ◄── The default route we configured
S      192.168.2.0/24 [1/0] via 192.168.12.2
S      192.168.3.0/24 [1/0] via 192.168.13.2
```

NOTE Earlier in this chapter, I stated that a router will drop packets that don't match any routes in its routing table. However, if the router has a default route, that situation won't occur; the default route matches all IP addresses. If a packet doesn't match a more specific route, the router will forward it via the default route, rather than dropping the packet.

Exam scenarios

Routing is a key topic of the CCNA exam. Here are a few examples of how your knowledge of routing fundamentals might be tested on the CCNA exam:

1 (multiple choice, multiple answers)
You issue the command **`ip route 10.0.0.0 255.0.0.0 192.0.2.1`**. Which of the following statements are true about the route created by the command? (select two)

(continued)

- **A** It is a network route.
- **B** It is a host route.
- **C** It is a recursive route.
- **D** It is a directly connected route.
- **E** It is a fully specified route.

This question requires you to distinguish between different route types. Network and host routes are classifications based on the route's destination (a network of IP addresses or a single IP address). Recursive, directly connected, and fully specified routes are classifications based on how the route's next hop is specified (next-hop IP address, exit interface, or both). In this case, (A) is correct because the route's destination is 10.0.0.0/8—a network, not a single IP address. And (C) is correct because the route specifies only the next-hop IP address, making it a recursive route.

2 (drag and drop)

Your knowledge of route types could also be tested with a drag-and-drop question like this: drag and drop the routes on the left to the correct route types on the right.

(A) **ip route 192.168.1.0 255.255.255.0 GigabitEthernet0/1**	Recursive
(B) **ip route 0.0.0.0 0.0.0.0 203.0.113.120**	Directly connected
(C) **ip route 172.20.0.0 255.255.0.0 GigabitEthernet0/1 192.168.2.1**	Fully specified
(D) **ip route 192.0.2.0 255.255.255.0 172.16.25.209**	

In this case, (A) is a directly connected route because it specifies only the exit interface, (B) and (D) are recursive routes because they specify only the next-hop IP address, and C) is a fully specified route because it specifies both.

3 (lab simulation)

A lab simulation on the CCNA exam could provide you with a network diagram and ask you to configure static routes to enable hosts in different networks to communicate with each other. Remember the basic syntax of the ip route command to configure static routes. If the question expects you to configure a certain type of static route (recursive, directly connected, or fully specified), it should state so; Cisco exams can be difficult, but they aren't unfair.

Summary

- The term *routing* can refer to the process of forwarding packets between networks and the process of building a routing table.
- Hosts in the same network can send packets to each other without the use of a router. However, to send packets to destinations outside of the local network, a router is required.

- The router a host will send packets destined for external networks to is called the *default gateway*. The host will send the packets in frames addressed to the default gateway's MAC address.
- A host's default gateway can be manually configured or automatically learned via DHCP.
- You can use the **`ipconfig`** command in the Windows Command Prompt to see information such as the PC's IP address, netmask, and default gateway.
- The routing table is the router's database of known destinations. It is a set of instructions about what action to take on packets. The routing table can be viewed with **`show ip route`**.
- For each interface that has an IP address and is in an up/up state, the router will automatically add two routes to its routing table: a connected route and a local route.
- A connected route is a route to the network that an interface is connected to. Connected routes are indicated by code `C` in the routing table. If a router receives a packet destined for a host in a directly connected network, it will forward the packet directly to the destination host (in a frame addressed to the host's MAC address).
- A *local route* is a route to the exact IP address configured on the interface. Local routes use a /32 prefix length to specify a single IP address. If a router receives a packet destined for the IP address of a local route, it means the packet is destined for the router itself; the router will receive the packet for itself—it will not forward it.
- A route to more than one destination IP address (any route with a prefix length shorter than /32) is called a *network route*. A connected route is an example of a network route.
- A route to a single destination IP address (a route with a /32 prefix length) is called a *host route*. A local route is an example of a host route.
- The process of deciding which route is appropriate for forwarding a packet is called *route selection*. To determine how to forward a particular packet, the router will select the *most specific matching route*—the matching route with the longest prefix length.
- A /32 route is the most specific route possible; it specifies only one IP address. A /0 route (default route) is the least specific route possible; it specifies every possible IP address.
- Whereas Layer 3 forwarding involves looking in the routing table for the most specific matching route, Layer 2 forwarding involves looking for an exact match in the MAC address table; partial matches don't count.
- If there aren't any routes that match a packet's destination IP address, the router will drop the packet.

- To route packets to destinations that aren't directly connected to the router, the router needs to learn routes to those destinations either via *dynamic routing* (using a protocol such as OSPF) or *static routing* (in which routes are manually configured on the router).
- To forward a packet toward a remote destination, the router will encapsulate the packet in a frame destined for the MAC address of the *next hop*—the next router in the path to the destination.
- For a router to forward packets between two hosts, the router needs routes to each host's network; it doesn't need routes to every network in the path between each destination.
- The command to configure a static route is **`ip route`** *`destination-network netmask`* {*`next-hop`* | *`exit-interface`* | *`exit-interface next-hop`*}.
- A static route that specifies only the next hop is called a *recursive static route*; it requires multiple lookups in the routing table to forward a packet: one to find the next-hop IP address and one to find which interface the next hop is connected to.
- A static route that specifies only the exit interface is called a *directly connected static route* because it causes the router to treat the network as a directly connected network.
- Directly connected static routes require proxy ARP to function. Proxy ARP allows a router to reply to ARP requests on behalf of other hosts. Proxy ARP is enabled on Cisco routers by default but might not be enabled on other vendors' routers.
- A static route that specifies both the exit interface and the next hop is called a *fully specified static route.*
- A *default route* is a route to 0.0.0.0/0. Because it is the least specific route possible, it will only be used to forward packets that don't match any other routes in the routing table.
- If a router has a default route, it won't drop packets that don't match other routes; instead, it will forward those packets using the default route.
- The default route is often used to provide a route to the internet; it is not feasible for a router to learn specific routes to each possible destination over the internet.

10 The life of a packet

This chapter covers

- A review of the processes involved in delivering a packet from source to destination
- How switches forward frames
- Address Resolution Protocol
- How routers forward packets

The concepts we have covered so far—the TCP/IP model, frame switching, ARP, IPv4 addresses, routing, etc.—are fundamental concepts we will build upon in the rest of this book's two volumes. In this chapter, we will review many of those concepts and see the role each plays in delivering a packet from the sending host to the packet's intended destination.

This chapter is unique among the others in this book in that it does not cover new information; everything in this chapter has been covered in previous chapters. Instead of introducing new concepts, the goal of this chapter is to take the most important concepts from previous chapters and tie them all together into one coherent whole.

Figure 10.1 shows the network we will use for this chapter; we used the same when looking at routing in chapter 9. Figure 10.1 also summarizes the different processes involved in delivering a packet from PC1 to PC3: ARP, switching, routing, etc. We will review these processes throughout this chapter.

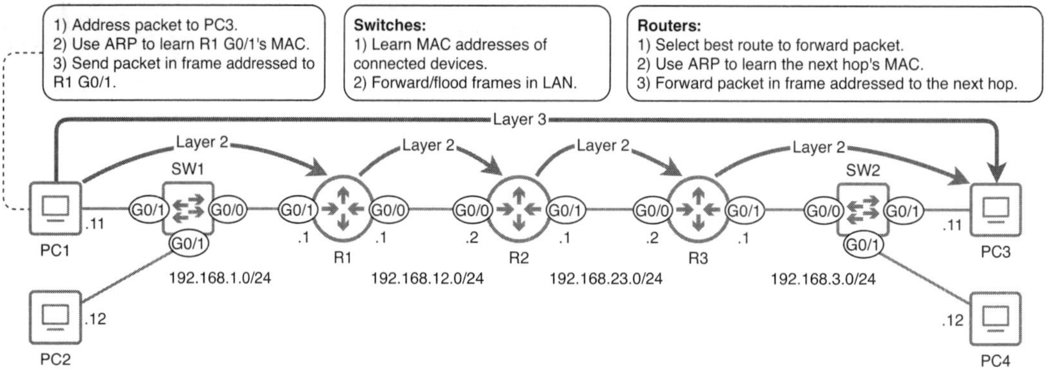

Figure 10.1 A summary of actions taken by each device when PC1 sends a packet to PC3. PC1 prepares a packet addressed to PC3, uses ARP to learn the default gateway's MAC address (R1 G0/1), and sends the packet in a frame to that MAC address. The switches learn the MAC addresses of connected devices and forward/flood frames as appropriate. The routers select the best route to forward the packet, use ARP to learn the next hop's MAC address, and forward the packet in a frame addressed to that MAC address.

NOTE The arrows in figure 10.1 are a reminder that, at Layer 3, the packet is addressed to PC3 (IP address 192.168.3.11) throughout the whole journey. However, at Layer 2, the packet is encapsulated in a new frame at each hop, and each frame is addressed to the next hop (until R3 finally addresses its frame to PC3).

10.1 The life of a packet from PC1 to PC3

Figure 10.1 provides an outline of the different processes involved in delivering a packet from PC1 to PC3. Now let's examine the process step by step to see how the different components we've covered in the book so far come together to enable communications over the network.

10.1.1 PC1 to R1

In our scenario, PC1 wants to send a packet to PC3. The type of packet is not significant for this example, so let's assume it's an ICMP echo request message sent by issuing the **`ping 192.168.3.11`** command on PC1.

PC1's IP address is 192.168.1.11, and it has a /24 prefix length (netmask 255.255.255.0), so it knows that its local network includes IP addresses 192.168.1.0 (the network address) through 192.168.1.255 (the broadcast address). Therefore, it knows that PC3 (192.168.3.11) is not in its local network. This means that PC1 must send the packet to its default gateway in a frame addressed to the default gateway's MAC address (rather than the MAC address of PC3 itself).

PC1 knows that its default gateway's IP address is 192.168.1.1 (most likely learned via DHCP, which we will cover in chapter 4 of volume 2), but the information it actually needs is the MAC address of the default gateway; it needs to send the packet (destined for PC3) in a frame addressed to R1 G0/1's MAC address. To learn R1 G0/1's MAC address, it will use ARP. Figure 10.2 outlines the ARP exchange between PC1 and R1.

NOTE ARP isn't used to learn the MAC address of the packet's destination (PC3), but the MAC address of the default gateway (R1 G0/1). Because PC1 and PC3 are in separate LANs, they do not need to know each other's MAC address.

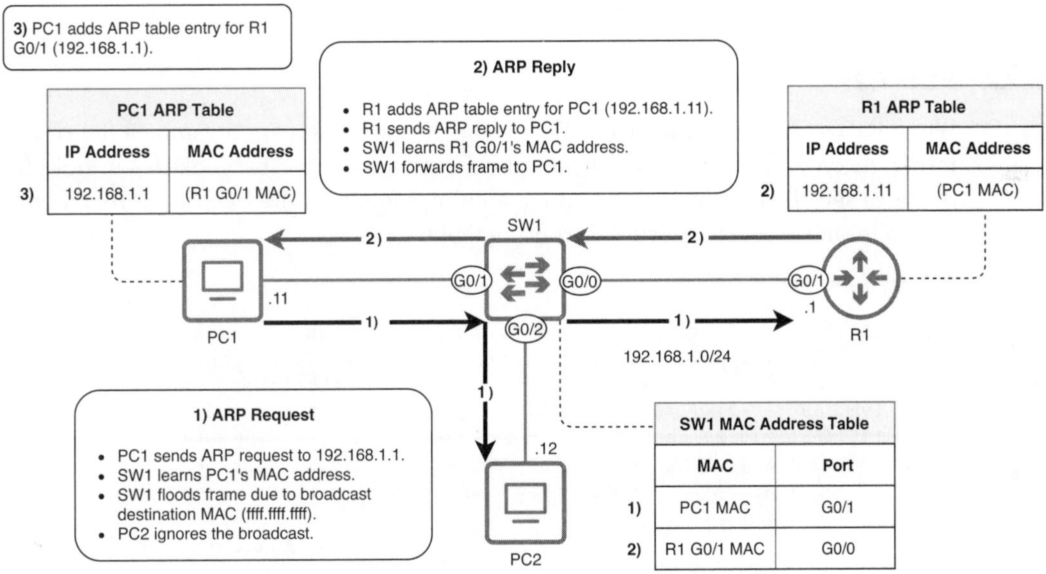

Figure 10.2 PC1 uses ARP to learn R1 G0/1's MAC address. (1) PC1 sends an ARP request to 192.168.1.1. SW1 learns PC1's MAC address and floods the frame due to the destination MAC address of ffff.ffff.ffff. (2) After receiving the ARP request, R1 adds an ARP table entry associating IP address 192.168.1.11 with PC1's MAC address. R1 then sends an ARP reply to PC1. SW1 learns R1 G0/1's MAC address and forwards the frame to PC1. (3) After receiving the ARP reply, PC1 adds an ARP table entry associating IP address 192.168.1.1 with R1 G0/1's MAC address.

NOTE To reduce clutter, figure 10.2 only briefly mentions PC2. Upon receiving the ARP request from PC1 (which was flooded by SW1), PC2 simply drops the message—the ARP request is not addressed to PC2's own IP address, so PC2 ignores it.

After the ARP exchange, PC1 now knows the MAC address of its default gateway (in the process, R1 also learns PC1's MAC address and creates an ARP entry). PC1 can now encapsulate the packet to PC3 in a frame addressed to R1's G0/1 interface. In the following section, we'll see what actions R1 takes upon receiving the frame (and the packet inside the frame) from PC1.

SW1's role is to learn the MAC addresses of connected devices and then forward or flood frames as necessary. It will flood broadcast frames (i.e., PC1's ARP request) and unknown unicast frames. It will forward known unicast frames (i.e., R1's ARP reply).

> **EXAM TIP** Know the difference between a switch's MAC address table and an end host or router's ARP table. A MAC address table maps MAC addresses to switch ports and is used to allow a switch to forward frames out of the correct port. An ARP table maps IP addresses to MAC addresses and is used to allow a router or end host to encapsulate packets in frames with the proper destination MAC address.

10.1.2 R1 to R2

When R1 receives the frame from PC1, it de-encapsulates it and examines the packet inside. As covered in chapter 9, it then performs a routing table lookup—it looks for the most specific matching route (the matching route with the longest prefix length). The following example shows R1's routing table:

```
R1# show ip route
. . .
      192.168.1.0/24 is variably subnetted, 2 subnets, 2 masks
C        192.168.1.0/24 is directly connected, GigabitEthernet0/1
L        192.168.1.1/32 is directly connected, GigabitEthernet0/1
S     192.168.3.0/24 [1/0] via 192.168.12.2, GigabitEthernet0/0     <--
      192.168.12.0/24 is variably subnetted, 2 subnets, 2 masks
C        192.168.12.0/24 is directly connected, GigabitEthernet0/0
L        192.168.12.1/32 is directly connected, GigabitEthernet0/0
```

The most specific matching route

The most specific matching route is the static route to 192.168.3.0/24 via next hop 192.168.12.2 (actually, it's the only matching route). However, just like how PC1 knew the IP address of its default gateway but not the MAC address (and therefore had to use ARP to learn the MAC address), R1 knows the IP address of the next hop but not its MAC address (and therefore has to use ARP).

R1 sends an ARP request to learn the MAC address of 192.168.12.2 (R2 G0/0), and R2 sends an ARP reply. In the process, they both learn each other's MAC addresses and create entries in their ARP tables. R1 is now ready to encapsulate the packet in a frame addressed to R2 G0/0's MAC address and forward it out of the G0/0 interface. Figure 10.3 outlines the process up to this point.

> **NOTE** The ARP request sent from R1 to R2 is addressed to the broadcast MAC address (ffff.ffff.ffff). However, R2 is the only device that receives the message—there is no switch to flood the frame in the LAN between R1 and R2.

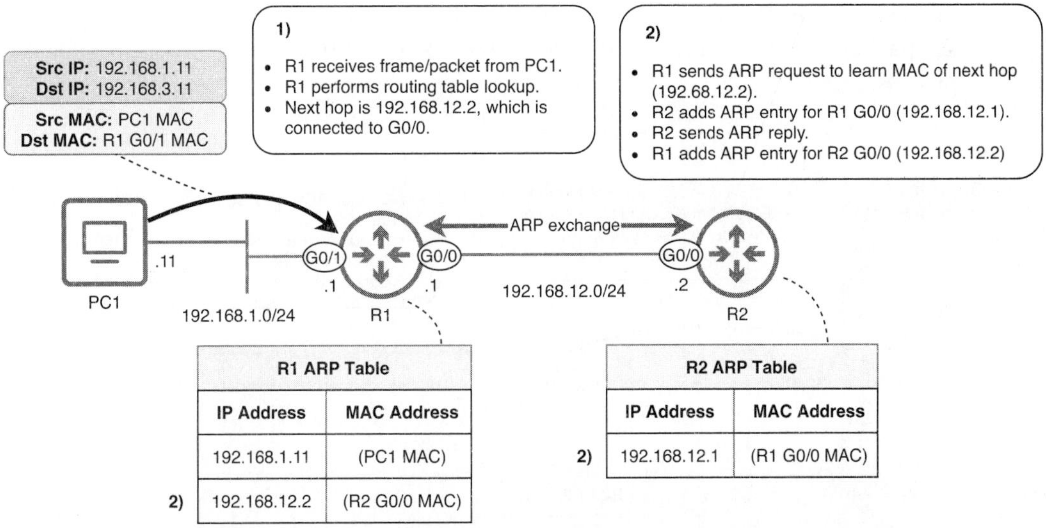

Figure 10.3 R1 receives PC1's message, performs a routing table lookup, and uses ARP to learn the MAC address of the next hop. (1) R1 receives the frame/packet and performs a routing table lookup. The most specific matching route is to 192.168.3.0/24, next hop 192.168.12.2. (2) R1 uses ARP to learn the MAC address of 192.168.12.2 (R2 G0/0). R1 and R2 both add entries to their ARP tables. R1 is now ready to forward the packet to the next hop.

NOTE I have simplified the ARP exchange in figure 10.3, but remember that it consists of an ARP request from R1 to R2 and then an ARP reply from R2 to R1.

10.1.3 R2 to R3

When R2 receives the frame from R1, it de-encapsulates it and examines the packet inside. The process it then goes through is identical to the process R1 went through previously. First, it performs a routing table lookup to find the most specific matching route. The following example shows R2's routing table:

```
R2# show ip route                                    The most specific matching route
. . .
S      192.168.1.0/24 [1/0] via 192.168.12.1, GigabitEthernet0/0
S      192.168.3.0/24 [1/0] via 192.168.23.2, GigabitEthernet0/1   <--
       192.168.12.0/24 is variably subnetted, 2 subnets, 2 masks
C         192.168.12.0/24 is directly connected, GigabitEthernet0/0
L         192.168.12.2/32 is directly connected, GigabitEthernet0/0
       192.168.23.0/24 is variably subnetted, 2 subnets, 2 masks
C         192.168.23.0/24 is directly connected, GigabitEthernet0/1
L         192.168.23.1/32 is directly connected, GigabitEthernet0/1
```

The only route that matches destination 192.168.3.11 is the static route to 192.168.3.0/24, via next hop 192.168.23.2 (R3's G0/0 interface). To learn the MAC address of the next hop, R2 sends an ARP request, and R3 sends an ARP reply. In the process, R2 and R3 create entries in their ARP tables, and R2 is now ready to forward the packet in a frame addressed to R3 G0/0's MAC address. Figure 10.4 outlines this process.

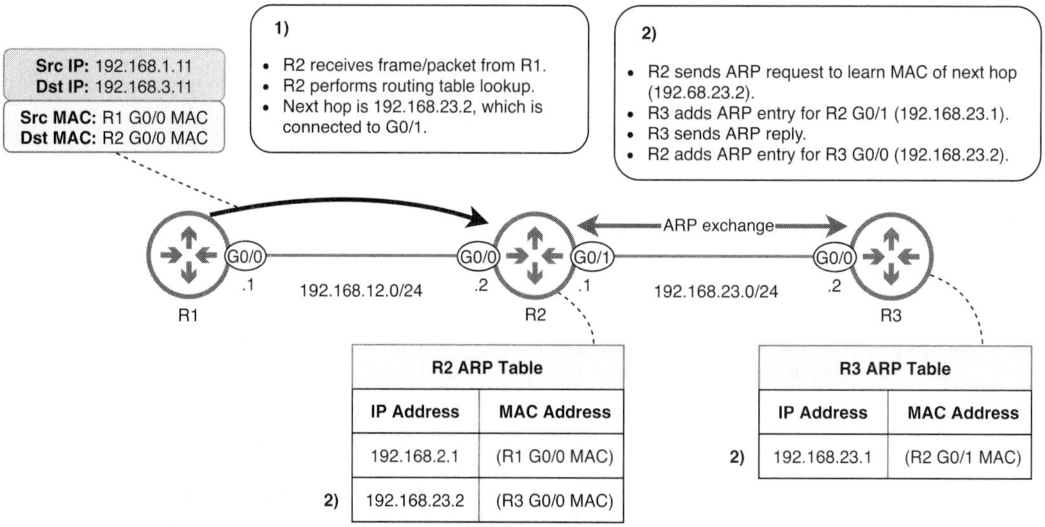

Figure 10.4 R2 receives the frame from R1, performs a routing table lookup and uses ARP to learn the MAC address of the next hop. (1) R2 receives the frame/packet and performs a routing table lookup. The most specific matching route is to 192.168.3.0/24, next hop 192.168.23.2. (2) R2 uses ARP to learn the MAC address of 192.168.23.2 (R3 G0/0). R2 and R3 both add entries to their ARP tables. R2 is now ready to forward the packet to the next hop.

10.1.4 R3 to PC3

After R2 forwards the message and it reaches R3, the packet is now at the final router before the destination. R3 goes through the same process as R1 and R2 did previously; it performs a routing table lookup to find the most specific matching route. The following example shows R3's routing table:

```
R3# show ip route
. . .
S      192.168.1.0/24 [1/0] via 192.168.23.1, GigabitEthernet0/0
       192.168.3.0/24 is variably subnetted, 2 subnets, 2 masks
C         192.168.3.0/24 is directly connected, GigabitEthernet0/1
L         192.168.3.1/32 is directly connected, GigabitEthernet0/1
       192.168.23.0/24 is variably subnetted, 2 subnets, 2 masks
C         192.168.23.0/24 is directly connected, GigabitEthernet0/0
L         192.168.23.2/32 is directly connected, GigabitEthernet0/0
```

The most specific matching route (annotation pointing to the 192.168.3.0/24 connected route)

The only matching route is the route to 192.168.3.0/24, which is a connected route. Because the packet's destination is in a directly connected network, R3 will encapsulate the packet in a frame addressed to the destination host's MAC address—the MAC address of PC3. To do that, it must use ARP.

SW2 floods the ARP request message to both PC3 and PC4; PC4 ignores it, but PC3 sends an ARP reply back to R3. In that process, SW2 learns the MAC addresses of R3 G0/1 and PC3. R3 and PC3 also learn each other's MAC addresses and add entries to their ARP tables. Figure 10.5 demonstrates this process.

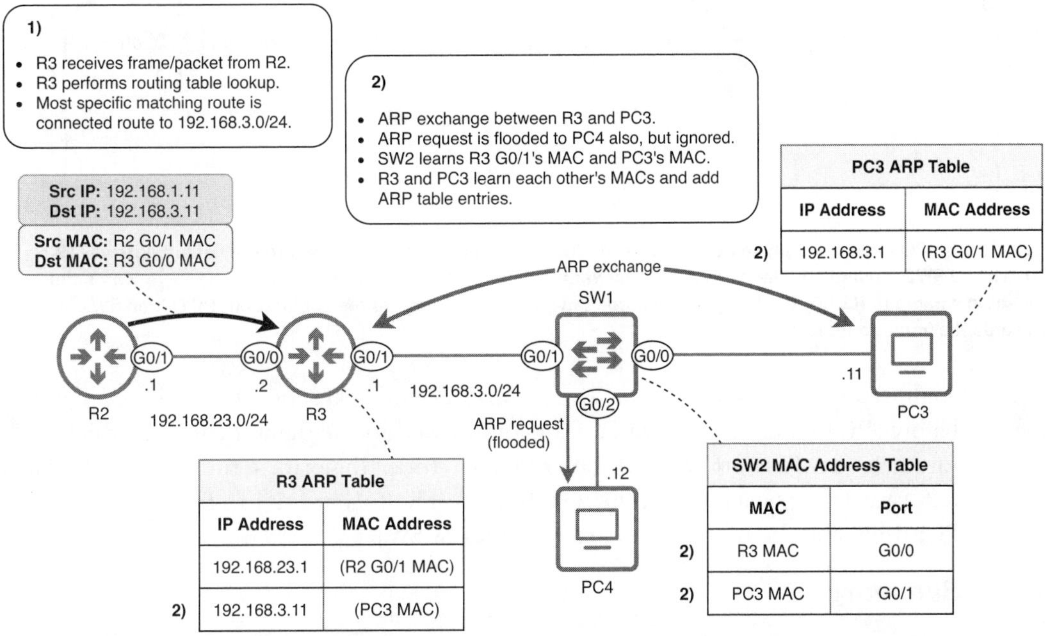

Figure 10.5 R3 receives the frame from R2, performs a routing table lookup and uses ARP to learn the MAC address of the next hop. (1) R3 receives the frame/packet and performs a routing table lookup. The most specific matching route is the connected route to 192.168.3.0/24. (2) R3 uses ARP to learn the MAC address of 192.168.3.11 (PC3). SW2 learns the MAC addresses of R3 G0/1 and PC3. R3 and PC3 both add entries to their ARP tables. R3 is now ready to forward the packet to the destination.

R3 is now able to forward the packet in a frame addressed to PC3's MAC address. The packet has reached its final destination! Upon receipt of the packet, PC3 will process it as appropriate. Earlier I stated that PC1's message was an ICMP echo request message. In that case, PC3 will send an ICMP echo reply message back to PC1.

10.2 The life of a packet from PC3 to PC1

The processes involved in delivering PC3's response to PC1 are similar, but there are two major differences: the switches have already learned the necessary MAC addresses, and the PCs and routers already have the necessary ARP table entries. This simplifies the process a bit—because the devices already have the necessary information in their tables, there is no need for the switches to learn MAC addresses or the PCs and routers to use ARP. Figure 10.6 outlines how PC3's packet is delivered to PC1, addressed to and from different MAC addresses at each hop.

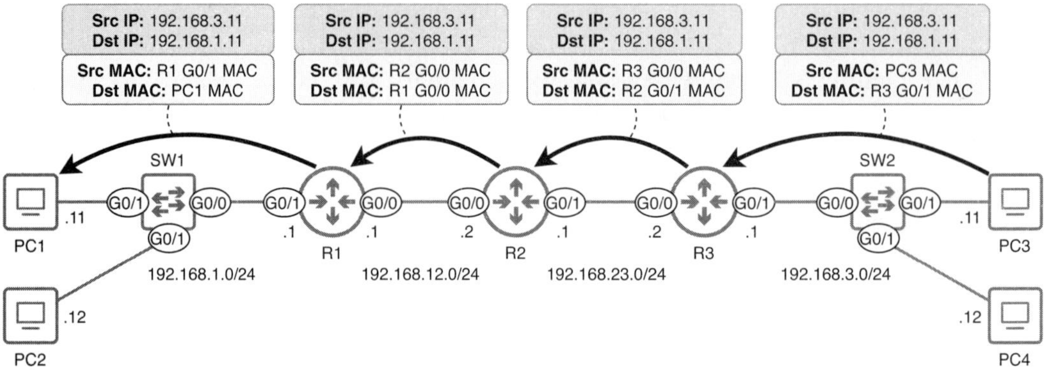

Figure 10.6 PC3 sends a reply to PC1. PC3 sends the packet in a frame addressed to the default gateway (R3 G0/1), and SW2 forwards the frame to R3. R3 forwards the packet in a frame to R2 G0/1, and R2 forwards the packet in a frame to R1 G0/0. Finally, R1 forwards the packet in a frame to the destination (PC1), and SW1 forwards the frame to PC1.

Aside from the lack of MAC address learning and ARP, the process is the same as before. PC3 sends its packet in a frame addressed to the default gateway, which SW2 forwards out of the proper port. The routers in the path perform routing table lookups to forward the packet toward the next hop until R1 forwards it in a frame addressed to PC1 itself, and the frame is forwarded to PC1 by SW1.

Summary

- To send packets to remote destinations, an end host (such as a PC) will send the packet to its default gateway (router). To do so, it will encapsulate the packet in a frame addressed to the default gateway's MAC address. It uses ARP to learn the default gateway's MAC address.
- ARP involves two messages: ARP request (broadcast) and ARP reply (unicast).
- When a device receives an ARP request, it doesn't just send an ARP reply; it also makes an entry in its own ARP table, mapping the IP address of the host that sent the request to that host's MAC address.
- Switches learn MAC addresses and forward or flood frames as appropriate. They do not modify the frames they forward; their operations are transparent to the devices connected to them.
- A switch will flood broadcast and unknown unicast frames. It will forward known unicast frames.
- When a router receives a frame addressed to its own MAC address, it will de-encapsulate it and examine the packet inside. It then performs a routing table lookup to determine how to forward the packet (or drop the packet or receive it for itself).
- A router will forward a packet according to the most specific matching route: the matching route with the longest prefix length.

- To forward a packet to the next hop in the path, a router will forward the packet in a frame addressed to the next hop's MAC address. It uses ARP to learn the next hop's MAC address.
- To forward a packet to the packet's destination host, a router will forward the packet in a frame addressed to the destination host's MAC address, using ARP to learn the MAC address.

11 Subnetting IPv4 networks

This chapter covers

- What subnetting is and why it's necessary
- How to borrow bits from the host portion of a network to expand the network portion and create subnets
- How to identify the five attributes of a subnet
- How to divide a network into subnets of equal and variable sizes

In chapter 7, we covered IPv4 address classes, focusing on classes A, B, and C—the three classes of addresses which can be assigned to hosts. Each class is defined by the first bit(s) of the address, and the prefix length of addresses in each range is also defined:

- Class A addresses begin with 0b0 and use a /8 prefix length.
- Class B addresses begin with 0b10 and use a /16 prefix length.
- Class C addresses begin with 0b110 and use a /24 prefix length.

This addressing architecture, called *classful addressing*, was defined in the original *Internal Protocol* standard in 1981 (RFC 791). However, with the rapid growth of the internet, classful addressing soon proved to be too rigid, resulting in inefficient use of addresses; the pool of available IPv4 addresses was drying up. Subnetting, which involves dividing a larger network up into smaller networks, is one answer to this problem and is a fundamental skill for network engineers. Subnetting is the second half of CCNA exam topic 1.6: Configure and verify IPv4 addressing and subnetting.

Before we get started, I want to emphasize that subnetting is a skill, and it requires practice to become proficient. Just reading this chapter alone won't make you good at subnetting; you need to spend some time actually doing it. However, if you read through this chapter carefully and do the recommended practice, you'll be a confident "subnetter" in no time.

11.1 What is subnetting?

The problem with classful addressing is that it doesn't allow us to create networks of appropriate sizes. The smallest network size—a class C network—contains 254 usable addresses (2^8-2 for the network and broadcast addresses). That is far more addresses than necessary for a home network or many small offices. Assigning a class C network to a small office with only a few dozen devices would result in over 200 IP addresses left unused.

However, a class C network is too small for most enterprise networks, meaning that a class B network would be required. A class B network contains 65,534 ($2^{16}-2$) usable addresses, far more than even a very large network requires, resulting in thousands of wasted addresses. And a class A network contains 16,777,214 usable addresses, a ludicrous number of addresses for a single network. These classful rules were designed for simplicity, not efficiency, but with the internet's exploding popularity, a better solution was needed.

To support the fast-growing internet and use the available IPv4 address space more efficiently, a new system was introduced in 1993: *Classless Inter-Domain Routing* (*CIDR*, pronounced like "cider"). CIDR throws out the rules of classful addressing and replaces them with a more flexible system. With CIDR, prefix lengths don't have to be /8, /16, or /24. Instead, the boundary between the network portion and host portion of an IP address can be in the middle of an octet, resulting in prefix lengths like /23, /26, /28, etc.

> **NOTE** The method of notating an address's prefix length with /X is also known as *CIDR notation* because it was introduced with CIDR. Before CIDR notation, the prefix length was always indicated with a netmask, such as 255.255.255.0. Another term for netmask is *subnet mask*; I will use the latter term in this chapter because we are focusing on subnetting, but the terms are interchangeable.

With CIDR, an enterprise can be assigned an address block that can be divided into networks of appropriate size, called *subnets* (*subdivided networks*). The process of dividing an address block into subnets is called *subnetting*.

NOTE An *address block* is a range of IP addresses. It can be used to refer to a network before it has been subnetted. For example, 192.168.1.0/24 is an address block (including IP addresses 192.168.1.0 through 192.168.1.255), which can be divided into multiple smaller networks (subnets).

Figure 11.1 demonstrates how a /24 address block can be divided into subnets. The 192.168.1.0/24 address range allows for a single subnet with a /24 prefix length, including all addresses from 192.168.1.0 through 192.168.1.255. Dividing the /24 address block in half gives two /25 subnets, each containing 128 addresses. Or it can be divided into four /26 subnets, each containing 64 addresses. For each bit by which you extend the prefix length, the number of possible subnets doubles, but the number of addresses in each subnet halves.

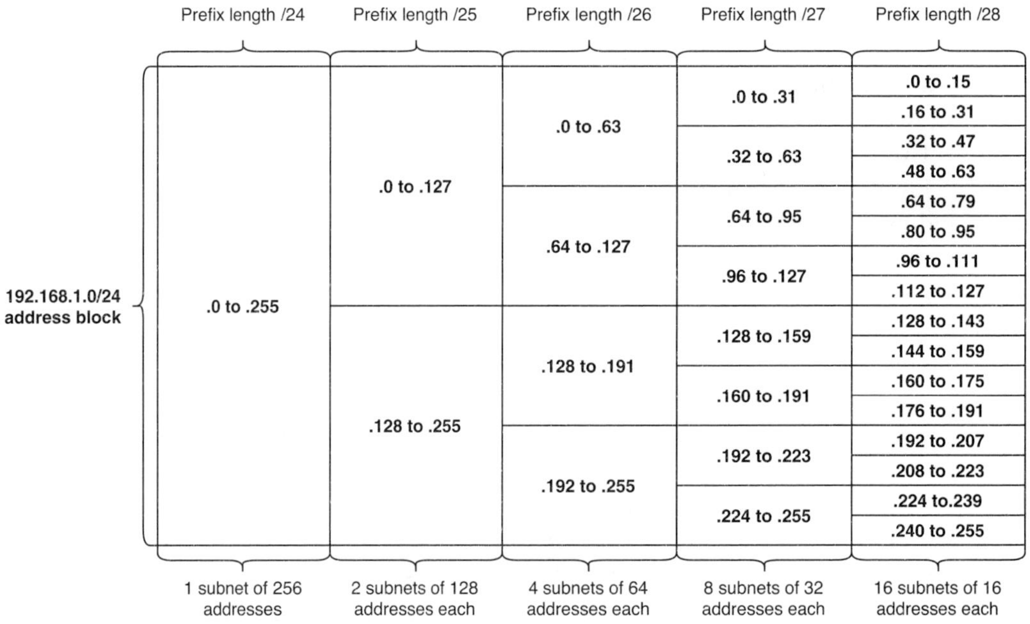

Figure 11.1 The 192.168.1.0/24 address block (network) divided into smaller subnets. With a /24 prefix length, it is one subnet of 256 addresses. Using a /25 prefix length allows the block to be divided into two subnets of 128 addresses each. /26 allows for 4 subnets of 64 addresses each. /27 allows for 8 subnets of 32 addresses each. /28 allows for 16 subnets of 16 addresses each.

NOTE Figure 11.1 only shows prefix lengths of up to /28, but longer prefix lengths follow the same pattern: increasing the length of the prefix length by 1 bit doubles the number of possible subnets, but halves the number of addresses contained in each subnet.

11.2 FLSM subnetting

Subnetting is the process of dividing an address block into smaller subnets. That process can be done in a couple of different ways: *Fixed-Length Subnet Masking* (FLSM) divides the block into subnets of equal sizes. On the other hand, *Variable-Length Subnet Masking* (VLSM) divides the block into subnets of varying sizes depending on how many addresses are actually needed in the subnet.

In the real world, VLSM is what you'll be using; it allows you to more efficiently use a block of addresses since you can make each subnet only as large as it needs to be—this wastes fewer addresses. However, FLSM serves as a useful stepping stone when learning how to subnet, and you should know it for the CCNA exam, so in this section, we will focus on FLSM.

11.2.1 Subnetting /24 address blocks

First, we will look at how to subnet address blocks with a prefix length of /24 or greater. The reason for this is that it allows us to focus only on the final octet of the address, simplifying the process a bit.

The network portion of an address block cannot be changed; if you are given the 192.168.1.0/24 address block, you can't assign 192.168.2.1 (or any other IP address not included in the 192.168.1.0/24 range) to a host. However, the host portion is fair game—you can use the last 8 bits to make various IP addresses to assign to hosts. This is the key to subnetting; to make subnets, you "borrow" bits from the host portion and add them to the network portion. You are then free to change the binary value of those borrowed bits between 0 and 1 to make different subnets. Figure 11.2 demonstrates how 1 bit can be borrowed from the host portion of 192.168.1.0/24 to make two different subnets: 192.168.1.0/25 and 192.168.1.128/25.

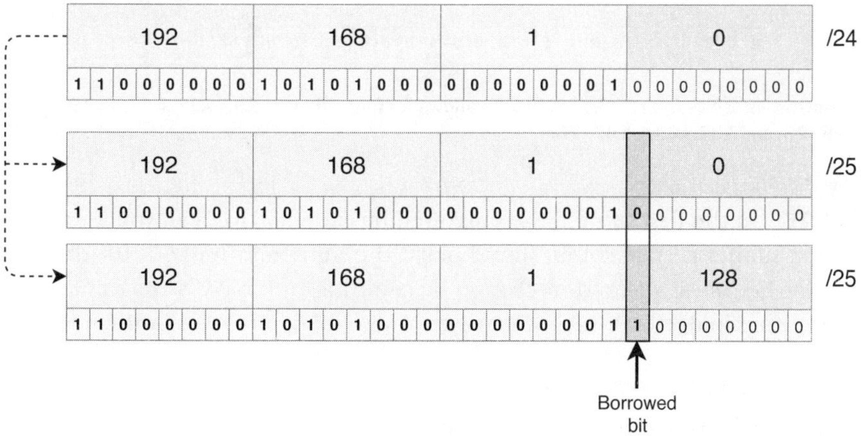

Figure 11.2 Borrowing 1 bit from the host portion of 192.168.1.0/24 allows us to create two subnets: 192.168.1.0/25 and 192.168.1.128/25. The borrowed bit was part of the host portion of the original address block, but it is part of the network portion of each subnet (as indicated by the /25 prefix length).

> **NOTE** In previous examples, the network address always ended in .0. However, when subnetting, because the boundary between the network portion and host portion can lie in the middle of an octet, the network address does not necessarily end in .0. 192.168.1.0 is the network address of the 192.168.1.0/25 subnet, and 192.168.1.128 is the network address of the 192.168.1.128/25 subnet.

With the borrowed bit set to 0, we get the first subnet: 192.168.1.0/25. If we change the borrowed bit to 1, we get the second subnet: 192.168.1.128/25. That's how subnets are made: by changing the binary value of the borrowed bit(s).

Borrowing a single bit from the host portion allows us to make two subnets, so how many subnets can we make if we borrow 2 bits? We covered this in section 11.1: each bit added to the prefix length (each bit borrowed from the host portion) doubles the number of subnets. The formula is 2^x, where *x* is the number of borrowed bits, and therefore borrowing 2 bits allows us to make 4 (2^2) subnets. Figure 11.3 shows the four subnets that can be made by borrowing 2 bits from the host portion of the 192.168.1.0/24 block.

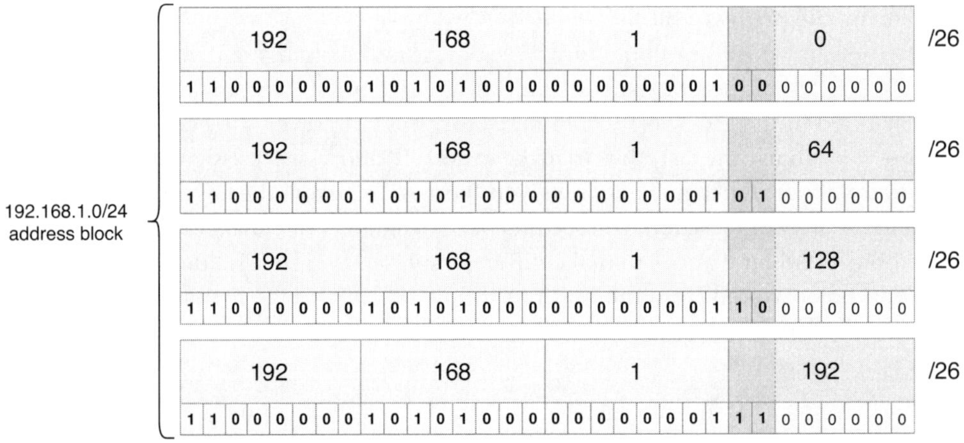

Figure 11.3 Borrowing 2 bits from 192.168.1.0/24 allows for four subnets: 192.168.1.0/26, 192.168.1.64/26, 192.168.1.128/26, and 192.168.1.192/26.

> **NOTE** In the first subnet, the borrowed bits are 00. How can you know what the next subnet is? Just count up in binary: the number after 00 is 01, then 10, and then 11. As we covered in chapter 7, counting in binary is the same process as counting in decimal, except there are only two digits to work with: 0 and 1.

CALCULATING THE FIVE ATTRIBUTES OF A /24+ SUBNET

In chapter 7, we covered five attributes of an IPv4 network: network address, broadcast address, first usable address, last usable address, and maximum number of hosts. Those same attributes apply when dividing networks into subnets. Here's a quick review of each attribute:

- *Network address*—The first address of a subnet, with a host portion of all 0s.
- *Broadcast address*—The last address of a subnet, with a host portion of all 1s.
- *First usable address*—The first address in the subnet that can be assigned to a host. It can be calculated by adding 1 to the network address (changing the last bit to 1).
- *Last usable address*—The last address in the subnet that can be assigned to a host. It can be calculated by subtracting 1 from the broadcast address (changing the last bit to 0).
- *Maximum number of hosts*—The number of IP addresses available to assign to hosts. The formula is $2^y - 2$, where y is the number of bits in the host portion. 2 is subtracted because the network and broadcast addresses cannot be assigned to hosts.

Figure 11.4 shows the five attributes of one of the subnets from figure 11.3: the 192.168.1.64/26 subnet. The calculations are the same as we covered in chapter 7—just keep in mind that the borrowed bits are now part of the network portion. Because the prefix length in this example is /26, only the last 6 bits are the host portion.

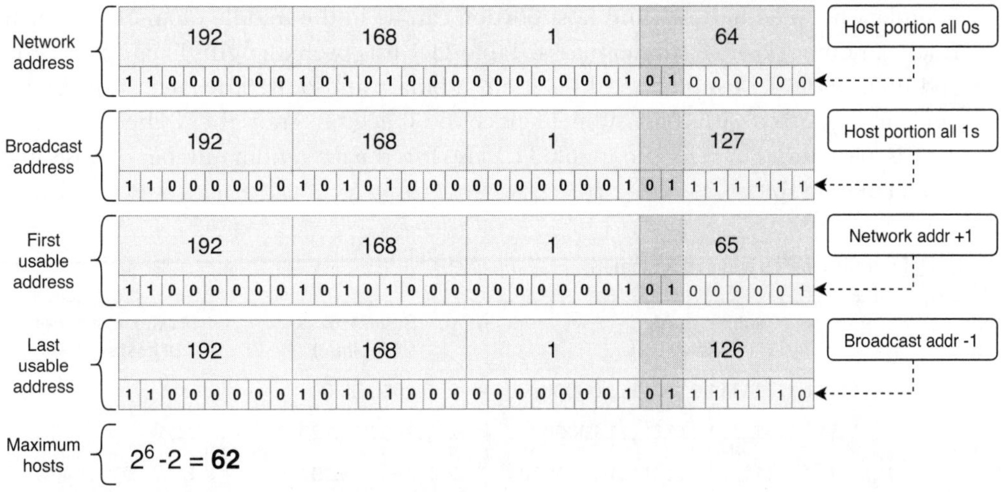

Figure 11.4 The five attributes of the 192.168.1.64/26 subnet. The first 26 bits are the network portion, and the final 6 bits are the host portion. The network address is 192.168.1.64 (host portion all 0s). The broadcast address is 192.168.1.127 (host portion all 1s). The first usable address is 192.168.1.65 (network address + 1). The last usable address is 192.168.1.126 (broadcast address – 1). The maximum number of hosts in the subnet is 62 (26 – 2).

A common subnetting problem is something like this: "PC1 has IP address 172.16.20.27/28. What is the network address of the subnet it belongs to?" To solve a question like this, you can follow these three steps:

1. Write the address in binary: 10101100.00010000.00010100.00011011
2. Change the host portion to all 0s: 10101100.00010000.00010100.00010000
3. Convert back to dotted decimal: 172.16.20.16. That's the answer!

EXAM TIP You should be able to identify any of the five attributes of a particular subnet, not just the network address. Such problems could appear on the CCNA exam as standalone questions or as part of more complex questions.

/24+ SUBNET MASKS

Ideally, we would be able to just write prefix lengths in CIDR notation, without having to worry about subnet masks. However, because you have to use subnet masks when configuring IP addresses and static routes in Cisco IOS, they are necessary to learn.

To review, a subnet mask is a series of 32 bits that indicates which bits in an IP address are part of the network portion and which are part of the host portion. A bit set to 1 in the subnet mask means that the bit in the same position of the IP address is part of the network portion, and a bit set to 0 in the subnet mask means that the bit in the same position of the IP address is part of the host portion. And because an IP address consists of the network portion followed by the host portion, a subnet mask is a series of 1s followed by a series of 0s (unless it is all 0s, as in /0, or all 1s, as in /32).

When only dealing with /8, /16, and /24 prefix lengths, subnet masks are simple: 255.0.0.0, 255.255.0.0, or 255.255.255.0, respectively. When using CIDR, however, the boundary between network and host portion can lie in the middle of an octet, which results in other possible subnet masks. Table 11.1 lists prefix lengths from /24 to /32 and their equivalent subnet masks written in binary and dotted decimal. You should familiarize yourself with these subnet masks; you'll need to know them when configuring Cisco routers. For reference, table 11.1 also lists the maximum number of hosts in a subnet of each size.

Table 11.1 /24+ prefix lengths and subnet masks

Prefix length	Subnet mask (binary)	Subnet mask (decimal)	Maximum number of hosts (2^y-2)
/24	11111111.11111111.11111111.00000000	255.255.255.0	254
/25	11111111.11111111.11111111.10000000	255.255.255.128	126
/26	11111111.11111111.11111111.11000000	255.255.255.192	62
/27	11111111.11111111.11111111.11100000	255.255.255.224	30
/28	11111111.11111111.11111111.11110000	255.255.255.240	14
/29	11111111.11111111.11111111.11111000	255.255.255.248	6
/30	11111111.11111111.11111111.11111100	255.255.255.252	2
/31	11111111.11111111.11111111.11111110	255.255.255.254	2 (see the following)
/32	11111111.11111111.11111111.11111111	255.255.255.255	1 (see the following)

Prefix lengths of /31 and /32 are special cases when it comes to calculating the maximum number of hosts in a subnet. A /31 prefix length, for example, leaves a single host bit. If we use the formula $2^y - 2$ to calculate the maximum number of hosts in the subnet, the result is 0; a single host bit only allows for two addresses, and those are taken by the network and broadcast addresses, resulting in no usable addresses. For this reason, /31 prefix lengths were unused for a long time.

However, for the purpose of further preserving the IPv4 address space, an exception to the normal rules was made for /31 prefix lengths: they can be used for *point-to-point* links—connections between two routers, which only require two IP addresses. In this case, the subnet does not have a network address or broadcast address. Before this exception was made, point-to-point links used /30 prefix lengths, leaving two host bits and therefore two usable addresses ($2^2 - 2 = 2$). This works fine, and /30 prefix lengths are still commonly used for point-to-point links today, but /31 prefix lengths are more efficient; they only consume two IP addresses, rather than four.

NOTE Although /31 subnets are more efficient, /30 subnets are still the more common choice since /31 technically breaks the network/broadcast address rule.

Figure 11.5 demonstrates a point-to-point link between two routers, providing two options for the subnet used for the connection: 203.0.113.0/30 can be used, which consumes a total of four addresses. Or 203.0.113.0/31 can be used, which consumes only two addresses.

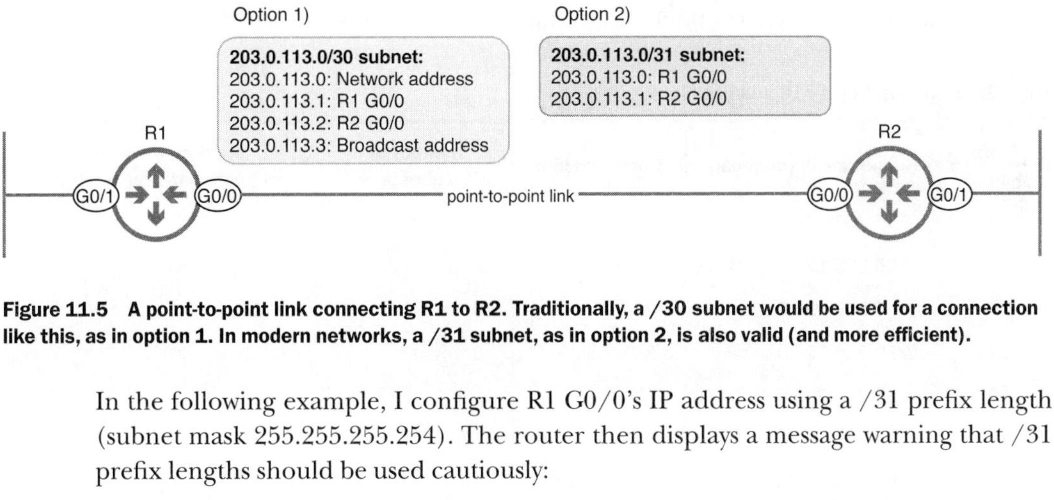

Figure 11.5 A point-to-point link connecting R1 to R2. Traditionally, a /30 subnet would be used for a connection like this, as in option 1. In modern networks, a /31 subnet, as in option 2, is also valid (and more efficient).

In the following example, I configure R1 G0/0's IP address using a /31 prefix length (subnet mask 255.255.255.254). The router then displays a message warning that /31 prefix lengths should be used cautiously:

```
R1(config-if)# ip address 203.0.113.0 255.255.255.254      ← Configures a /31 prefix length
% Warning: use /31 mask on non point-to-point interface cautiously      ← A warning message is displayed.
```

NOTE A /32 subnet mask can be used to specify a single IP address in a route, as covered in chapter 9. However, a /32 subnet mask is rarely configured on an interface (although we will cover an exception in chapter 18, on OSPF).

11.2.2 Subnetting /16 address blocks

Subnetting an address block with a prefix length shorter than /24 can seem intimidating at first; you can no longer focus only on the final octet of the address. However, let me assure you that the process of subnetting does not change at all:

- The number of subnets you can make is still 2^x, where x is the number of borrowed bits.
- The maximum number of hosts per subnet is still $2^y - 2$, where y is the number of host bits.
- The subnet's network address is still the address with a host portion of all 0s.

I think you get the idea! The only difference is that converting between decimal and binary takes a little more care. Because there's no need to introduce any new concepts, in this section, I'll demonstrate how the previous concepts apply to address blocks with a /16+ prefix length. Table 11.2 summarizes some ways a /16 address block can be subnetted. As before, each borrowed bit doubles the amount of subnets that can be made but halves the total number of addresses per subnet (table 11.2 displays the maximum number of hosts per subnet, rather than the total number of addresses).

Table 11.2 Subnetting a /16 address block

Prefix length	Subnet mask (decimal)	Borrowed bits	Number of subnets	Maximum number of hosts per subnet (2^y-2)
/16	255.255.0.0	0	1	65,534
/17	255.255.128.0	1	2	32,766
/18	255.255.192.0	2	4	16,382
/19	255.255.224.0	3	8	8190
/20	255.255.240.0	4	16	4094
/21	255.255.248.0	5	32	2046
/22	255.255.252.0	6	64	1022
/23	255.255.254.0	7	128	510
/24	255.255.255.0	8	256	254
/25	255.255.255.128	9	512	126

NOTE Table 11.2 only shows prefix lengths up to /25, but /16 address blocks can be subnetted up to /32 as well.

In figure 11.3, we saw how borrowing two bits from the 192.168.1.0/24 address block allows for four subnets to be made. Figure 11.6 demonstrates the same, but this time using the 192.168.0.0/16 address block.

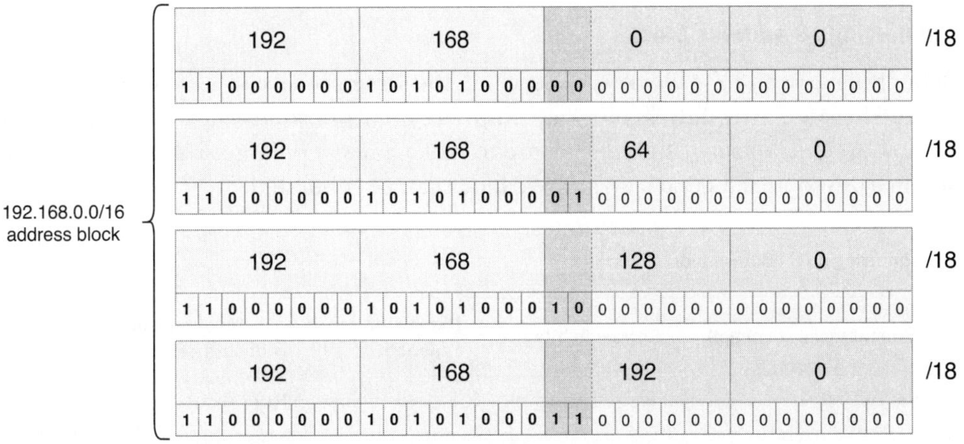

Figure 11.6 Borrowing two bits from 192.168.0.0/16 allows for four subnets: 192.168.0.0/18, 192.168.64.0/18, 192.168.128.0/18, and 192.168.192.0/18.

Calculating the five attributes is the same process as before. Figure 11.7 takes one of the subnets from figure 11.6 (192.168.128.0/18) and shows the five attributes of that subnet.

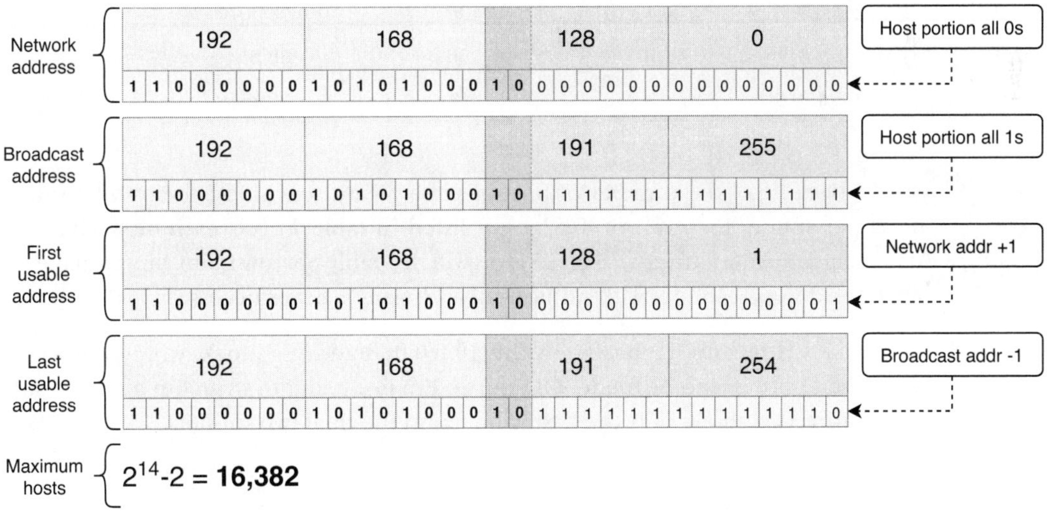

Figure 11.7 The five attributes of the 192.168.128.0/18 subnet. The first 18 bits are the network portion, and the final 14 bits are the host portion. The network address is 192.168.128.0 (host portion all 0s). The broadcast address is 192.168.191.255 (host portion all 1s). The first usable address is 192.168.128.1 (network address + 1). The last usable address is 192.168.191.254 (broadcast address – 1). The maximum number of hosts in the subnet is 16,382 (214 – 2).

NOTE /18 is a very large subnet size, containing 16,382 host addresses per subnet. You will probably never configure a /18 subnet on an interface, but for the CCNA exam, you should be able to create subnets of any size.

11.2.3 Subnetting /8 address blocks

Subnetting a /8 address block is, once again, the same process we have seen up to this point. However, a /8 address block means there are 24 host bits—lots of bits to either borrow and make lots of subnets, or use to make a few very large subnets. Table 11.3 summarizes some ways that a /8 address block can be subnetted.

Table 11.3 Subnetting a /8 address block

Prefix length	Subnet mask (decimal)	Borrowed bits	Number of subnets	Maximum number of hosts per subnet (2^y-2)
/8	255.0.0.0	0	1	16,777,214
/9	255.128.0.0.0	1	2	8,388,606
/10	255.192.0.0	2	4	4,194,302
/11	255.224.0.0	3	8	2,097,150
/12	255.240.0.0	4	16	1,048,574
/13	255.248.0.0	5	32	524,286
/14	255.252.0.0	6	64	262,142
/15	255.254.0.0	7	128	131,070
/16	255.255.0.0	8	256	65,534
/17	255.255.128.0	9	512	32,766

NOTE Because of the number of host bits in a /8 address block, the number of hosts per subnet for each prefix length listed in table 11.3 is extremely large. When actually subnetting a /8 block, you will probably borrow many bits to make smaller subnets; a subnet with millions of addresses is never necessary.

In figure 11.8, I borrow 12 bits from the 10.0.0.0/8 address block, which allows for 4,096 separate subnets to be made. Of course, I'm not going to write out all 4,096 subnets, so figure 11.8 shows only the first subnet and the final two subnets.

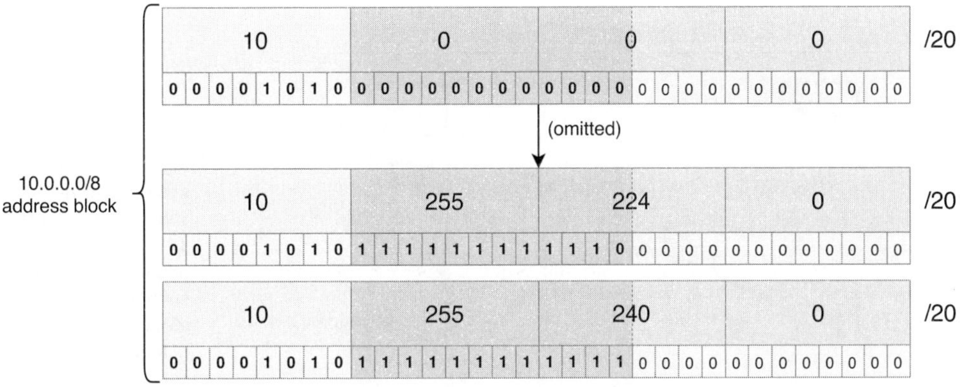

Figure 11.8 Borrowing 12 bits from 10.0.0.0/8 allows for 4,096 subnets. 10.0.0.0/20 is the first subnet, and 10.255.224.0/20 and 10.255.240.0/20 are the final two.

> **NOTE** Figure 11.8 differs from the previous examples in that the borrowed bits cross between octets (all of the second octet and the first four bits of the third octet). This doesn't change anything about how subnetting works! Keep in mind that the octet divisions only exist to make addresses more human-readable; to a computer, an IP address is just a series of 32 bits—no octet divisions.

Calculating the five attributes of a subnet doesn't change, regardless of the size of the original address block or how many bits you borrow, so we won't go through a third example here. For some additional practice, I recommend taking one of the subnets shown in figure 11.8 and calculating the five attributes: network address, broadcast address, first usable address, last usable address, and maximum number of hosts.

11.2.4 FLSM scenarios

As mentioned at the beginning of this chapter, subnetting is a skill that takes practice to become proficient. At the end of this chapter, I will give some recommendations for free websites where you can find subnetting practice questions. Before that, let's go through a couple of scenarios that resemble what you might find on those websites (and on the CCNA exam itself).

Figure 11.9 provides a practice scenario in which we will use FLSM to divide the 172.25.190.0/23 address block into four subnets of equal size, calculate the maximum number of hosts in each subnet, and configure the first usable address of each subnet on R1's interfaces.

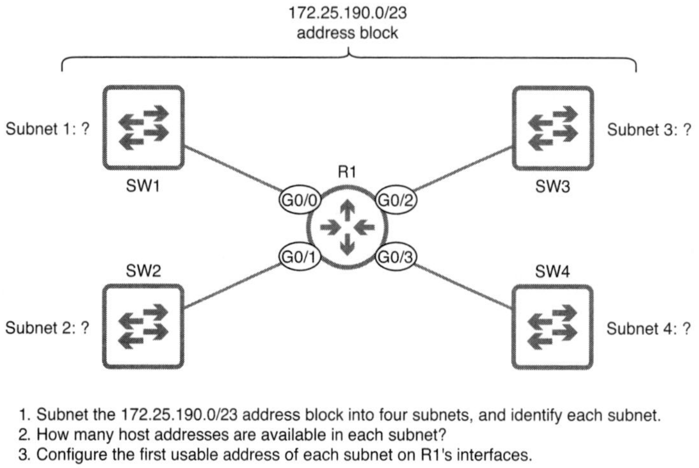

Figure 11.9 An FSLM scenario in which you must subnet the 172.25.190.0/23 address block into four subnets of equal size, identify the number of host addresses per subnet, and configure the first usable address of each subnet on R1's interfaces

NOTE The example in figure 11.9 is the first time we are beginning with an address block that is not /8, /16, or /24, but the subnetting process remains the same.

To begin, let's identify the four subnets. How many bits do we need to borrow to divide an address block into four subnets? As we've seen in a couple of previous examples, we need to borrow 2 bits to make four subnets because $2^2 = 4$. Then, we can just count up with those 2 borrowed bits to create four subnets. Figure 11.10 shows the four subnets that can be created by borrowing 2 bits from the 172.25.190.0/23 address block. Because we borrow 2 bits from the host portion, each subnet's prefix length is /25 (/23 + 2).

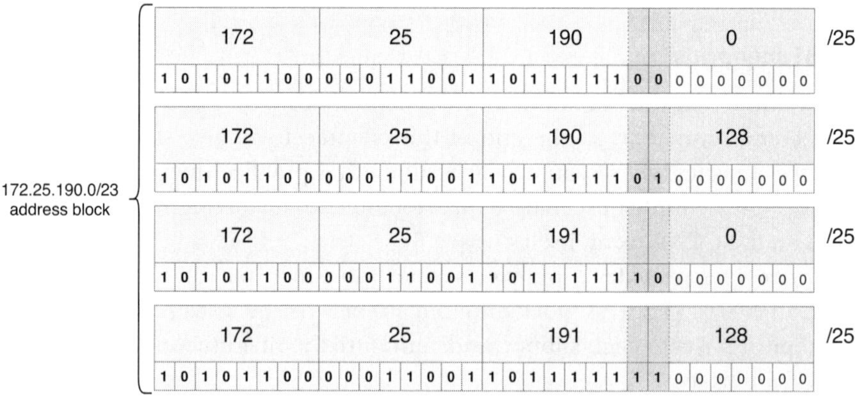

Figure 11.10 The subnets that can be created by subnetting 172.25.190.0/23 into four equal parts: 172.25.190.0/25, 172.25.190.128/25, 172.25.191.0/25, and 172.25.191.128/25. Borrowing 2 bits from the host portion of the /23 address block results in four /25 subnets.

We have now solved the first part of the scenario: identifying the four subnets. The second part asks how many host addresses are available in each subnet. To solve this, just use the same formula as always: $2^y - 2$ (y being the number of host bits). The original address block was /23, meaning there were 9 host bits. However, after borrowing 2 host bits to make subnets, 7 host bits remain. Therefore, there are 126 ($2^7 - 2$) host addresses available in each subnet.

The final part of the scenario says to configure the first usable address of each subnet on R1's interfaces. The first usable address can be calculated with the usual method: add 1 to the network address of each subnet. In the following example, I configure R1's interfaces with the first usable address of each subnet:

```
R1(config)# interface g0/0
R1(config-if)# ip address 172.25.190.1 255.255.255.128
R1(config-if)# interface g0/1
R1(config-if)# ip address 172.25.190.129 255.255.255.128
R1(config-if)# interface g0/2
R1(config-if)# ip address 172.25.191.1 255.255.255.128
R1(config-if)# interface g0/3
R1(config-if)# ip address 172.25.191.129 255.255.255.128
```

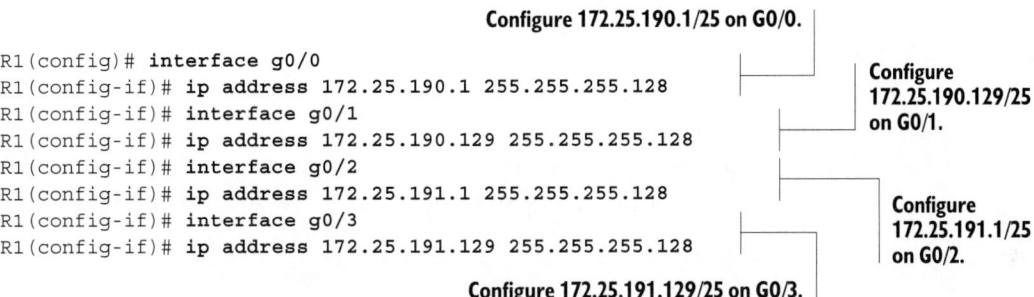

Configure 172.25.190.1/25 on G0/0.

Configure 172.25.190.129/25 on G0/1.

Configure 172.25.191.1/25 on G0/2.

Configure 172.25.191.129/25 on G0/3.

We have now solved the scenario! Let's walk through one more scenario, this time text only: you have been given the 10.224.0.0/11 address block. You must create 2,000 subnets, which will be assigned to various offices and departments within a large company. What prefix length must you use to create a sufficient number of subnets? How many host addresses are in each subnet?

To solve this scenario, we first have to determine how many bits we must borrow to create 2,000 subnets. If you have learned your powers of 2, this shouldn't be too difficult: 1 bit gives 2 subnets, 2 bits gives 4 subnets, 3 bits gives 8 subnets, and so on, and then 11 bits gives 2,048 subnets. That's 48 more than we need in the scenario, but borrowing 10 bits would give only 1,024 subnets (not enough), so 11 bits is our answer. Borrowing 11 bits from the host portion results in a /22 prefix length, which is the answer to the first part of the scenario. Figure 11.11 demonstrates this and shows the first subnet and the last (2,048th) subnet.

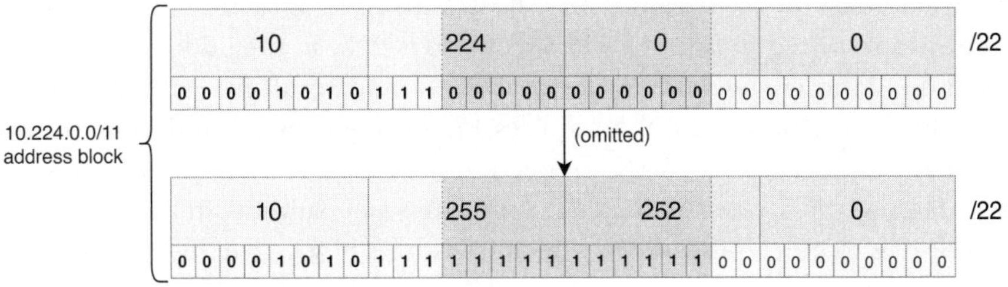

Figure 11.11 Borrowing 11 bits from the host portion of the 10.224.0.0/11 address block allows for 2,048 subnets. The first subnet is 10.224.0.0/22 (all borrowed bits set to 0), and the last (2048th) subnet is 10.255.252.0/22 (all borrowed bits set to 1).

A /22 prefix length means that 10 host bits remain, so now we can calculate the number of host addresses in each subnet: 1022 ($2^{10} - 2$). And now we have solved the scenario!

NOTE Because the number of subnets increases by a power of 2 for each borrowed bit, you often won't be able to create exactly the number of subnets needed; you'll probably end up with some extra subnets, which is not a bad thing—they can be used to accommodate network expansions in the future. Likewise, you often won't be able to create subnets of exactly the size you need; you'll usually have some extra addresses in each subnet.

11.3 VLSM subnetting

Variable-Length Subnet Masking (VLSM) allows us to subnet an address block even more efficiently than FLSM by creating subnets of varying sizes. Although FLSM is a helpful introduction to subnetting, when actually subnetting networks in the real world, chances are you'll be doing VLSM. Figure 11.12 shows the scenario I will use to demonstrate VLSM.

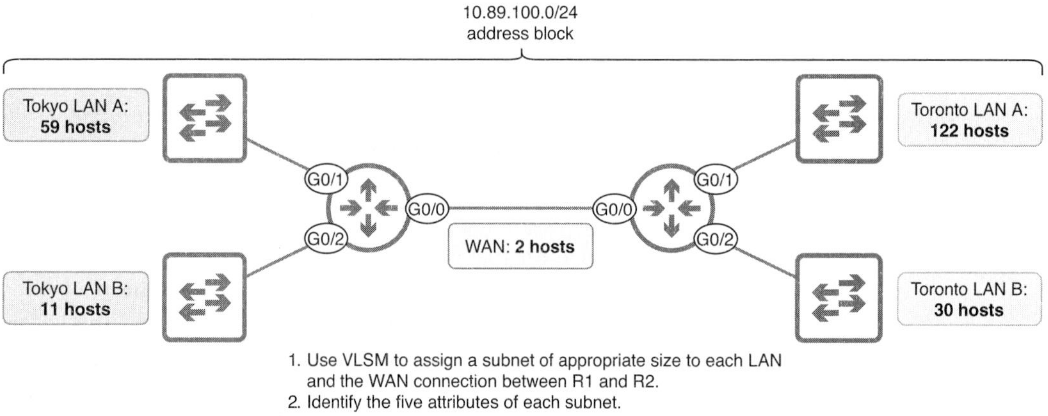

Figure 11.12 A VLSM scenario in which you must assign subnets from the 10.89.100.0/24 address block to each LAN and the WAN connection and identify the five attributes of each subnet

A /24 address block includes 254 host addresses, and the total number of host addresses required in figure 11.12's scenario is 226, so the address space is sufficient. Using FLSM to create subnets of equal size would result in some subnets having too few addresses (Toronto LAN A requires 122 host addresses) and some subnets having too many addresses (the WAN connection only requires 2 host addresses, for R1 and R2). However, if we use VLSM, we can make some subnets smaller and some larger, allowing us to efficiently use the available address block. The high-level VLSM process is as follows:

1 Assign the largest subnet at the start of the address block.

2 Assign the second-largest subnet after it.

3 Repeat the process until all subnets have been assigned.

The five subnets in figure 11.12, in order from largest to smallest, are Toronto LAN A (122 hosts), Tokyo LAN A (59 hosts), Toronto LAN B (30 hosts), Tokyo LAN B (11 hosts), and the WAN connection (2 hosts)—so let's start by assigning Toronto LAN A.

> **NOTE** Router IP addresses are included in the "host" counts; any device with an IP address can be considered a host. The term *end host* is usually used to refer to PCs, servers, etc. to distinguish them from network infrastructure devices like routers.

Figure 11.13 visually represents the five subnets that will result from this process: one /25 subnet (128 addresses), one /26 subnet (64 addresses), one /27 subnet (32 addresses), one /28 subnet (16 addresses), and one /30 subnet (4 addresses). In the following sections, we'll walk through how to perform VLSM subnetting and create these five subnets.

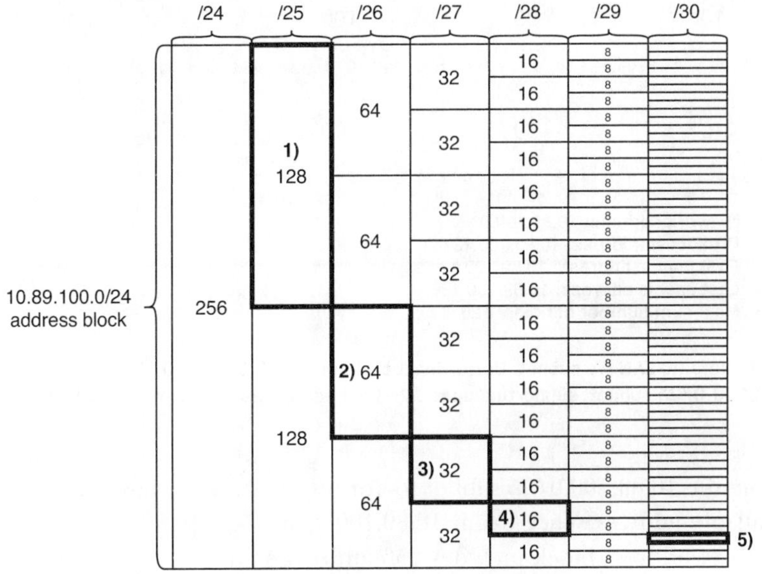

1. **Toronto LAN A:** 10.89.100.0/25 (.0 to .127)
2. **Tokyo LAN A:** 10.89.100.128/26 (.128 to .191)
3. **Toronto LAN B:** 10.89.100.192/27 (.192 to .223)
4. **Tokyo LAN B:** 10.89.100.224/28 (.224 to .239)
5. **WAN:** 10.89.100.240/30 (.240 to .243)

Remaining: 10.89.100.244 - 10.89.100.255

Figure 11.13 The 10.89.100.0/24 address block, divided into five subnets of varying sizes. (1) Toronto LAN A is 10.89.100.0/25, containing 128 addresses. (2) Tokyo LAN A is 10.89.100.128/26, containing 64 addresses. (3) Toronto LAN B is 10.89.100.192/27, containing 32 addresses. (4) Tokyo LAN B is 10.89.100.224/28, containing 16 addresses. (5) The WAN connection is 10.89.100.240/30, containing 4 addresses. After subnetting, 12 addresses remain unused: 10.89.100.244 through 10.89.100.255.

NOTE For practical reasons, figure 11.13 doesn't show the number of addresses in /30 subnets (4 addresses each) and doesn't include columns for /31 subnets (2 addresses each) and /32 subnets (1 address each).

11.3.1 Assigning Toronto LAN A's subnet

Toronto LAN A requires 122 host addresses, so the question is, what is the minimum number of host bits required to provide at least 122 host addresses? Referring to the formula we use to calculate the maximum number of host bits in a subnet ($2^y - 2$), what is the minimum *y* value that would serve our purpose? The answer is 7 because $2^7 - 2 = 126$, only a few more addresses than we need. Six host bits would give us only 62 host addresses ($2^6 - 2$)—not enough for the 122 hosts in Toronto LAN A. To leave 7 host bits, we have to borrow 1 bit from the /24 address block. Figure 11.14 shows the resulting subnet when we borrow a single host bit from the 10.89.100.0/24 address block: 10.89.100.0/25—Toronto LAN A's subnet! Figure 11.14 also lists the five attributes of the subnet.

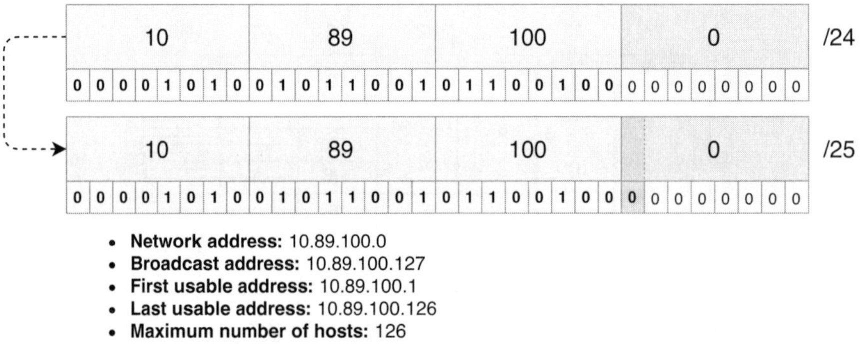

Figure 11.14 Toronto LAN A's subnet. Borrowing 1 bit from the 10.89.100.0/24 address block results in the 10.89.100.0/25 subnet, supporting up to 126 host addresses—enough for the 122 hosts in the LAN.

By assigning the 10.89.100.0/25 subnet to Toronto LAN A, we have already used half of the available address space: from 10.89.100.0 through 10.89.100.127. The entire 10.89.100.0/24 address block includes 256 addresses, and a single /25 subnet takes up 128 of those addresses (keep in mind that only 126 of those 128 addresses can be assigned to hosts). We will assign the rest of the subnets from the remaining range of addresses: 10.89.100.128 through 10.89.100.255.

11.3.2 Assigning Tokyo LAN A's subnet

After assigning Toronto LAN A's subnet and identifying its five attributes, we can easily identify one more piece of information: Tokyo LAN A's network address. The last address (not the last *usable* address) in Toronto LAN A is 10.89.100.127—the broadcast address. Without knowing any other information about Tokyo LAN A, we can identify its first IP address (the first address immediately after Toronto LAN A's broadcast address), which is 10.89.100.128. This is Tokyo LAN A's network address because the first IP address of a subnet is the network address.

Now that we know Tokyo LAN A's network address we just need to figure out how many host bits are needed (which determines the prefix length), and then we can calculate the other attributes. Tokyo LAN A requires enough addresses for 59 hosts, so 6 host bits are required, giving 62 ($2^6 - 2$) usable addresses—a /26 prefix length. Therefore, the subnet we should assign to Tokyo LAN A is 10.89.100.128/26. Figure 11.15 shows the subnet and its five attributes.

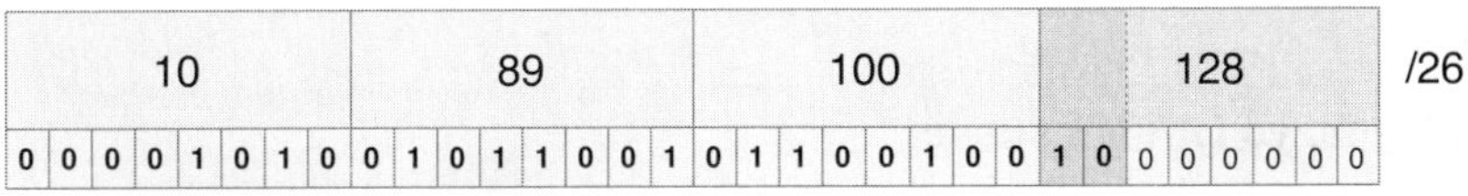

- **Network address:** 10.89.100.128
- **Broadcast address:** 10.89.100.191
- **First usable address:** 10.89.100.129
- **Last usable address:** 10.89.100.190
- **Maximum number of hosts:** 62

Figure 11.15 Tokyo LAN A's subnet. The network address is 10.89.100.128—the first address after Toronto LAN A. A /26 prefix length is used to allow for up to 62 host addresses—enough for the 59 hosts in the LAN.

We have now assigned three-quarters of the 10.89.100.0/24 address block: a /25 subnet (one-half) and a /26 subnet (one-quarter). The remaining range of addresses is 10.89.100.192 through 10.89.100.255, and we will assign the remaining three subnets from that range.

11.3.3 Assigning Toronto LAN B's subnet

The IP address immediately after Tokyo LAN A's final address (its broadcast address) is 10.89.100.192, and that is Toronto LAN B's network address. What about its prefix length? Toronto LAN B requires IP addresses for at least 30 hosts, meaning 5 host bits are required, which gives exactly 30 ($2^5 - 2$) host addresses. Therefore, Toronto LAN B's subnet should use a /27 prefix length, resulting in subnet 10.89.100.192/27. Figure 11.16 shows the subnet and its five attributes.

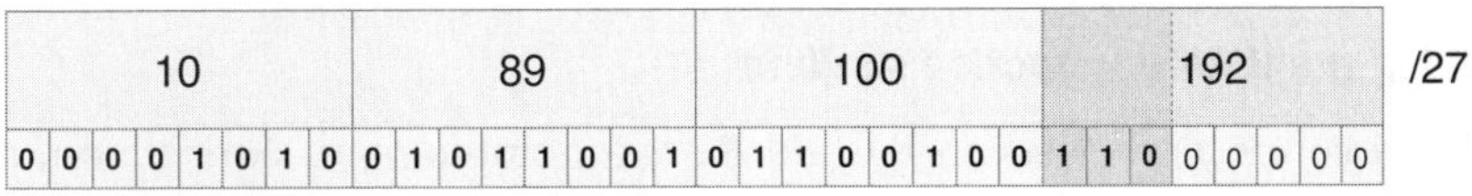

- **Network address:** 10.89.100.192
- **Broadcast address:** 10.89.100.223
- **First usable address:** 10.89.100.193
- **Last usable address:** 10.89.100.222
- **Maximum number of hosts:** 30

Figure 11.16 Toronto LAN B's subnet. The network address is 10.89.100.192—the first address after Tokyo LAN A. A /27 prefix length is used to allow for up to 30 host addresses—exactly the amount needed.

> **NOTE** In a real-world situation, you should leave a bit of room in each subnet to allow for future growth; you may need to add more hosts to the subnet at some point. However, when doing subnetting scenarios like this (and on the CCNA exam), just use the most efficient prefix length, leaving as few unused addresses in the subnet as possible.

We have now assigned seven-eighths of the 10.89.100.0/24 address block: a /25 subnet (one-half), a /26 subnet (one-quarter), and a /27 subnet (one-eighth). The remaining range of addresses is 10.89.100.224 through 10.89.100.255, and we will use that range to assign the remaining subnets: Tokyo LAN B and the WAN connection between R1 and R2.

11.3.4 Assigning Tokyo LAN B's subnet

We can use the same process to assign Tokyo LAN B's subnet. Its network address is the first address after the previous LAN's (Toronto LAN B's) broadcast address, so Tokyo LAN B's network address is 10.89.100.224. Tokyo LAN B is a small LAN, requiring only 11 host addresses. Therefore, only 4 host bits are required, allowing for up to 14 (2^4 – 2) host addresses, so Tokyo LAN B's subnet is 10.89.100.224/28. Figure 11.17 shows the subnet and its five attributes.

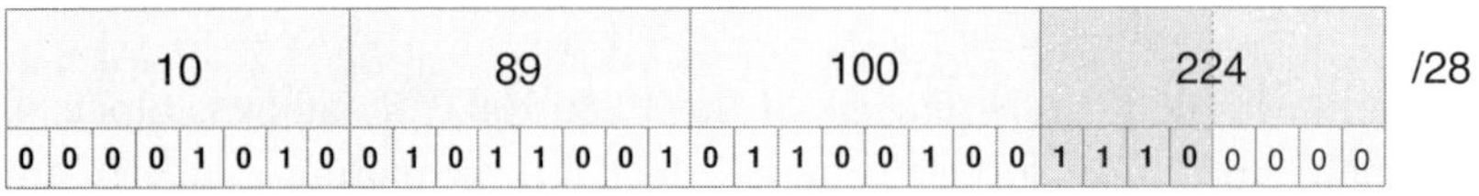

- **Network address:** 10.89.100.224
- **Broadcast address:** 10.89.100.239
- **First usable address:** 10.89.100.225
- **Last usable address:** 10.89.100.238
- **Maximum number of hosts:** 14

Figure 11.17 Tokyo LAN B's subnet. The network address is 10.89.100.224—the first address after Toronto LAN B. A /28 prefix length is used to allow for up to 14 host addresses—sufficient for the 11 hosts in the LAN.

Only one-sixteenth of the 10.89.100.0/24 address block remains—addresses 10.89.100.240 through 10.89.100.255. Fortunately, that is more than enough addresses for the final subnet: the WAN connection between R1 and R2.

11.3.5 Assigning the WAN connection's subnet

The WAN connection between R1 and R2 is a point-to-point connection, requiring only two host addresses. The network address is 10.89.100.240 (the first address after Tokyo LAN B's broadcast address), but what should the prefix length be? As we covered in section 11.2.1, there are two options: a /30 prefix length (two usable addresses, four addresses in total) or a /31 prefix length (two usable addresses, without network and broadcast addresses). Either prefix length is a valid choice, but for this example, I'll use a /30 prefix length, so the WAN connection's subnet is 10.89.100.240/30. Figure 11.18 shows the subnet and its five attributes.

10	89	100	240	/30
0 0 0 0 1 0 1 0	0 1 0 1 1 0 0 1	0 1 1 0 0 1 0 0	1 1 1 1 0 0 0 0	

- **Network address:** 10.89.100.240
- **Broadcast address:** 10.89.100.243
- **First usable address:** 10.89.100.241
- **Last usable address:** 10.89.100.242
- **Maximum number of hosts:** 2

Figure 11.18 The WAN connection's subnet. The network address is 10.89.100.240—the first address after Tokyo LAN B. A /30 prefix length is used to allow for two host addresses—one for R1, and one for R2.

> **NOTE** When I visually represented these five subnets in figure 11.13, I selected a /30 prefix length for the WAN connection's subnet. The main reason for that choice was a practical one; the boxes to represent /31 subnets in the diagram would be too small. For consistency's sake, I used a /30 prefix length here, but keep in mind that a /31 prefix length is valid too and is actually superior in that it consumes fewer addresses.

And now we are done! We have assigned all five subnets, with only a few IP addresses to spare (10.89.100.244 through 10.89.100.255); these addresses are free to be used as needed in the future as this hypothetical enterprise expands. With FLSM, this would not have been possible, but VLSM gives us the flexibility to create subnets of varying sizes.

Exam scenarios

Being comfortable with subnetting is a key element of CCNA exam success. Here are a couple of examples of how your knowledge of subnetting might be tested on the CCNA exam:

1 (multiple choice, multiple answers)
Which of the following prefix length to subnet mask pairs are correct? (Select two.)

- A /25 = 255.255.255.192
- B /15 = 255.252.0.0
- C /29 = 255.255.255.248
- D /27 = 255.255.255.240
- E /18 = 255.255.192.0
- F /10 = 255.224.0.0

Subnet masks are necessary for configuring IP addresses and static routes in Cisco IOS, so it's important that you are able to identify the correct subnet mask for a given prefix length. Fortunately, subnet masks are fairly simple—a series of binary 1s followed by a series of binary 0s. In this case, (C) is the first correct option; /29 is equivalent to 255.255.255.248 (29 binary 1s followed by 3 binary 0s, written in dotted decimal). (E) is the second correct option; /18 is equivalent to 255.255.192.0. As I've said previously, being comfortable converting between binary and dotted decimal is key!

(continued)

2 (drag and drop)
Drag each subnet on the left to its appropriate usable host address range on the right. There are more usable address ranges provided than subnets, so not all address ranges will be used.

(A) 10.23.24.128/25	10.23.24.65 - 10.23.24.79
(B) 10.23.24.128/27	10.23.24.65 - 10.23.24.78
(C) 10.23.24.64/26	10.23.24.65 - 10.23.24.126
(D) 10.23.24.64/28	10.23.24.129 - 10.23.24.254
	10.23.24.129 - 10.23.24.190
	10.23.24.129 - 10.23.24.158

Identifying a subnet's usable address range requires identifying the subnet's first and last usable addresses; they identify the start and end of the usable address range. In this question, (A)'s usable address range is 10.23.24.129 to 10.23.24.254, (B)'s usable address range is 10.23.24.129 to 10.23.24.158, (C)'s usable address range is 10.23.24.65 to 10.23.24.126, and (D)'s usable address range is 10.23.24.65 to 10.23.24.78. To solve this question, just focus on the final octet of each address; the first three octets are the same in all of them.

11.4 Additional subnetting practice

To become proficient at subnetting, you need to practice. Fortunately, there are some free websites that generate subnetting problems you can solve. One example is https://www.subnetting.net/, but you can find others with a quick Google search. I recommend spending a bit of time each day practicing subnetting for at least a week or two or until you feel confident solving questions on the practice sites.

Before sending you off to try out practice questions, I want to mention two points. First, some practice questions you encounter may not explicitly state the size of the address block you must subnet. Here's an example: "What is the maximum number of valid subnets and usable hosts per subnet that you can get from the network 172.26.0.0 255.255.252.0?" In such cases, assume the original address block is a classful network. In this example, the IP address is 172.26.0.0, which is a class B address (because it starts with 0b10), so you can assume that the address block is /16 (172.26.0.0/16).

The second point is that some questions will ask about *wildcard masks*, which are similar to subnet masks, but not actually related to the topic of subnetting. We will cover wildcard masks in chapter 17 (Dynamic Routing), as well as chapters 23 and 24 (Access Control Lists). For now, you can skip any questions on a practice website that mention wildcard masks.

The "magic number" method

Some instructors teach shortcuts that can help you solve subnetting scenarios without having to think about the underlying binary; one famous example is called the "magic number" method. I do not agree with these methods for CCNA candidates because I think they only serve as a crutch, helping you to solve subnetting problems without understanding how subnetting actually works. It may seem cumbersome to always be thinking about binary, but with practice, it will become effortless. And you'll become better not just at subnetting but at all of the other necessary skills that require proficiency with binary (I listed some in chapter 7).

Summary

- *Classless Inter-Domain Routing* (CIDR) replaced classful addressing, allowing prefix lengths outside of the traditional /8, /16, and /24.
- With CIDR, an address block can be divided into smaller networks called *subnets*. This process is called *subnetting*.
- *Fixed-Length Subnet Masking* (FLSM) subnetting divides an address block into subnets of equal size.
- *Variable-Length Subnet Masking* (VLSM) subnetting divides an address block into subnets of varying size.
- To subnet an address block, you "borrow" bits from the host portion of the address block and add them to the network portion. Whereas the network portion of the original address block cannot be changed, the borrowed bits can be changed to make different subnets.
- Each additional borrowed bit doubles the number of subnets that can be made: 1 borrowed bit = 2 subnets, 2 borrowed bits = 4 subnets, 3 borrowed bits = 8 subnets, etc. However, each additional borrowed bit halves the number of addresses in each subnet because there are fewer bits in the host portion.
- The five attributes of an IPv4 network are calculated in the same manner for subnets: the network address is the first address of a subnet (host portion of all 0s), the broadcast address is the last address of a subnet (host portion of all 1s), the first usable address is the first address after the network address, the last usable address is the last address before the broadcast address, and the maximum number of hosts is $2^y - 2$, where y is the number of host bits.
- For point-to-point links (connections between two routers), either a /30 or a /31 prefix length can be used. /30 consumes four addresses (network address, broadcast address, and two host addresses), whereas /31 consumes only two addresses (two host addresses, without a network or broadcast address).
- To subnet an address block using VLSM, assign the largest subnet at the start of the address block, assign the second-largest subnet after it, and repeat the process until all subnets have been assigned.

- The network address of the next subnet is the address immediately after the broadcast address of the current subnet.
- In a real-world situation, you should leave some room in each subnet for future growth. When doing subnetting scenarios for practice (or for the CCNA exam), be as efficient as possible (leave as few unused addresses as possible).

Part 3

Layer 2 concepts

In part 3, we will build upon your foundational understanding of how switches provide connectivity within a LAN. You have already grasped the basics of MAC address learning and aging, frame forwarding and flooding, and other key operations of switches. Now, let's delve deeper into several advanced features that optimize and secure LANs. We'll start in chapter 12 by exploring virtual LANs (VLANs), which allow us to divide a single physical switch into multiple virtual switches, dividing the LAN into multiple separate segments and enhancing its security and efficiency.

In chapter 13, we will continue on the topic of VLANs, covering two auxiliary protocols that streamline the configuration and management of VLANs on Cisco switches: Dynamic Trunking Protocol (DTP) and VLAN Trunking Protocol (VTP). We will then shift our attention to Spanning Tree Protocol (STP) in chapter 14 and Rapid Spanning Tree Protocol (RSTP) in chapter 15. These protocols are vital for preventing broadcast storms—broadcast frames that infinitely loop around the switches in the LAN, clogging up the LAN and preventing hosts in the LAN from communicating.

Finally, we will conclude part 3 by examining EtherChannel in chapter 16. EtherChannel allows multiple physical connections between two switches to form a single logical connection, increasing the available bandwidth in the LAN. By the end of part 3, you will understand these concepts both theoretically and practically and be able to implement them on Cisco switches; this is essential both for CCNA exam success and for any network professional who wants to design, implement, and troubleshoot modern LANs effectively.

12 VLANs

This chapter covers

- How to divide a switch into multiple virtual switches with VLANs
- How to configure trunk ports to carry traffic in multiple VLANs
- Routing between VLANs with a router or multilayer switch

In chapter 11, we covered subnetting, which allows us to divide a network into smaller subnets. This is an example of network *segmentation*—the division of a network into smaller parts. Virtual LANs (VLANs, pronounced "V-LANs"), the topic of this chapter, can be likened to subnets in that they also allow us to divide up a network into smaller parts. With VLANs, we can divide a LAN (a broadcast domain) into smaller LANs, called VLANs. Whereas subnets allow us to segment the network at Layer 3, VLANs allow us to segment the network at Layer 2. In this chapter, we will cover three CCNA exam topics, all related to the topics of switches and VLANs:

- 1.1.b Layer 2 and Layer 3 switches
- 2.1 Configure and verify VLANs (normal range) spanning multiple switches
- 2.2 Configure and verify interswitch connectivity

12.1 Why we need VLANs

To understand a technology, it's important to understand why that technology exists—to understand the problem it solves. To demonstrate the role VLANs play in segmenting networks, let's examine a network without segmentation, a network with Layer 3 segmentation, and a network with both Layer 3 and Layer 2 segmentation.

12.1.1 Layer 3 segmentation with subnets

Figure 12.1 depicts an office LAN consisting of three different departments: engineering, HR, and sales. All hosts belong to the 172.16.1.0/24 network, enabling them to communicate directly without using the router as an intermediary.

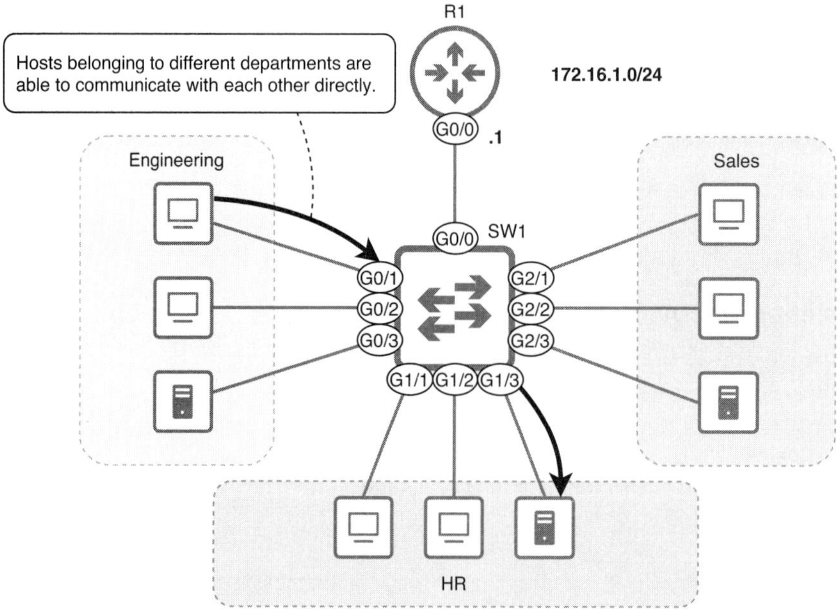

Figure 12.1 An unsegmented LAN. All hosts are in the 172.16.1.0/24 network, and VLANs are not used to segment the LAN at Layer 2. Hosts belonging to different departments can communicate with each other directly (by sending their packets in frames addressed directly to each other).

From an information security standpoint, this is not suitable for modern networks. Instead of having all hosts within a single large network, we should use subnetting to segment the network at Layer 3, with each department assigned its own subnet. Figure 12.2 demonstrates how hosts in different departments communicate after the network has been divided into separate subnets.

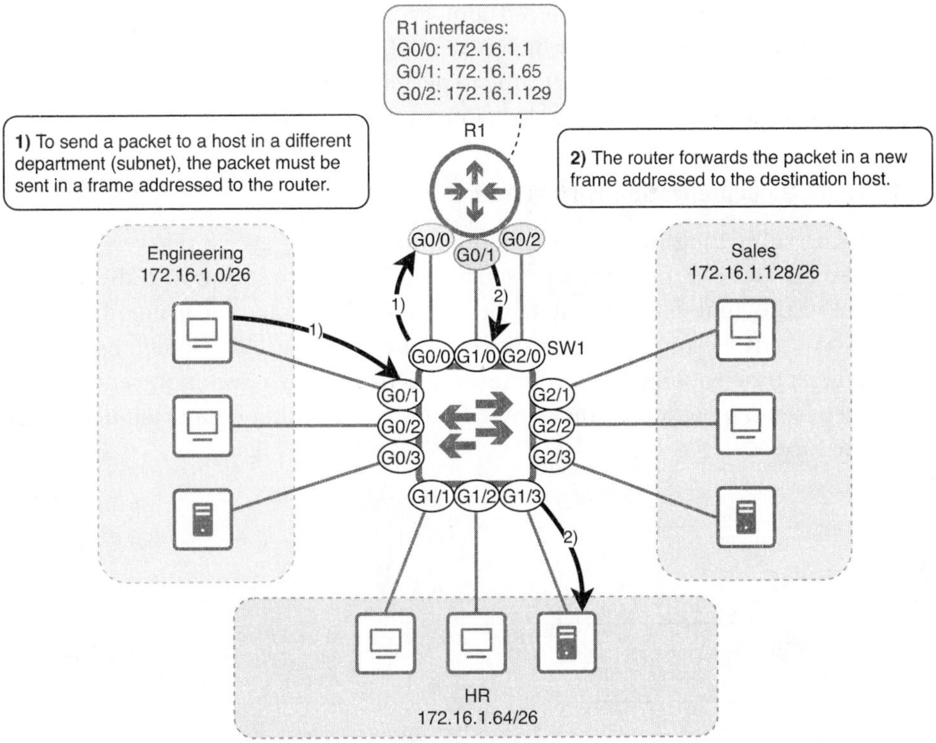

Figure 12.2 A LAN segmented into three subnets. The engineering department uses subnet 172.16.1.0/26, the HR department uses subnet 172.16.1.64/26, and the sales department uses subnet 172.16.1.128/26. R1 has one interface in each subnet. Communication between hosts in different departments must go through R1.

NOTE In an ideal network, hosts in each subnet would have their own switch to connect to. However, in reality, switches are usually shared, as in figure 12.2; hosts in 172.16.1.0/26, 172.16.1.64/26, and 172.16.1.128/26 all connect to SW1. Network infrastructure is a cost, so reducing the necessary amount of hardware is desirable.

You might be wondering how segmenting the LAN into separate subnets enhances security. By requiring traffic between departments to pass through the router, you can control which traffic is permitted and which is not; security policies can be implemented on the router to control traffic. Figure 12.2 depicts a PC in the engineering department accessing a server used by the HR department; this is an example of traffic you might want to restrict. You could choose to block all hosts outside the HR department from accessing the server or only allow specific types of communication with the server.

NOTE In this chapter, we will not cover how to use a router to control which traffic is permitted and which is denied. For now, we will segment the network but will not specify which traffic to permit or deny. We will cover *access control lists* (one method to control traffic) in part 6 of this book.

12.1.2 Layer 2 segmentation with VLANs

Using subnetting, we have segmented the LAN at Layer 3. However, switches aren't Layer 3 aware. From SW1's perspective, all hosts are still part of the same LAN; they are in the same broadcast domain. A broadcast frame sent from any host connected to SW1 will be received by all other connected hosts (the same applies to unknown unicast frames). Figure 12.3 demonstrates this: when a host in the engineering department sends a broadcast frame, SW1 floods it to all other connected hosts, regardless of the subnet.

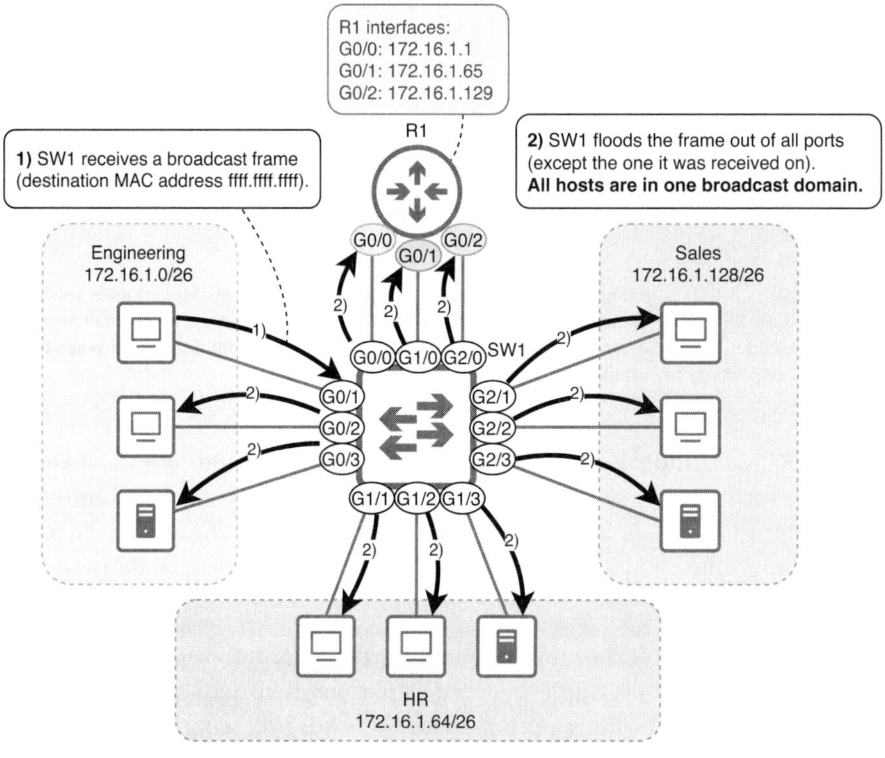

Figure 12.3 Although hosts are divided into three subnets, at Layer 2, they are still part of the same broadcast domain (LAN). (1) SW1 receives a broadcast frame from a host in the engineering department. (2) SW1 floods the frame out of all ports, except the one it was received on. The LAN has been segmented at Layer 3, but not at Layer 2.

NOTE One definition of a LAN is "a group of interconnected devices in a limited area," but as covered in chapter 6, a more nuanced definition considers how the devices are connected and how network traffic is forwarded between them, rather than just their physical location. For this chapter, a LAN is the same thing as a broadcast domain—the group of devices that will receive a broadcast frame sent by any other member of the group.

From a security perspective, this is still not suitable—traffic from hosts in one subnet can reach hosts in other subnets. Furthermore, all hosts being in the same broadcast domain can have negative effects on network performance; the unnecessary flooding of frames out of all ports can cause or worsen network congestion. To solve these issues, we should segment the network at Layer 2, and we can use VLANs to do so.

VLANs allow us to divide a single physical switch into multiple virtual switches, thereby dividing the broadcast domain into multiple broadcast domains. Figure 12.4 demonstrates this concept, illustrating how SW1 is divided into multiple virtual switches. By assigning each of SW1's ports to a specific VLAN, SW1 is divided into three virtual switches: one for VLAN 10, one for VLAN 20, and one for VLAN 30. These VLAN numbers are arbitrary; I selected VLANs 10, 20, and 30 for this example, but any numbers within the valid range can be used (more on that in section 12.2.1).

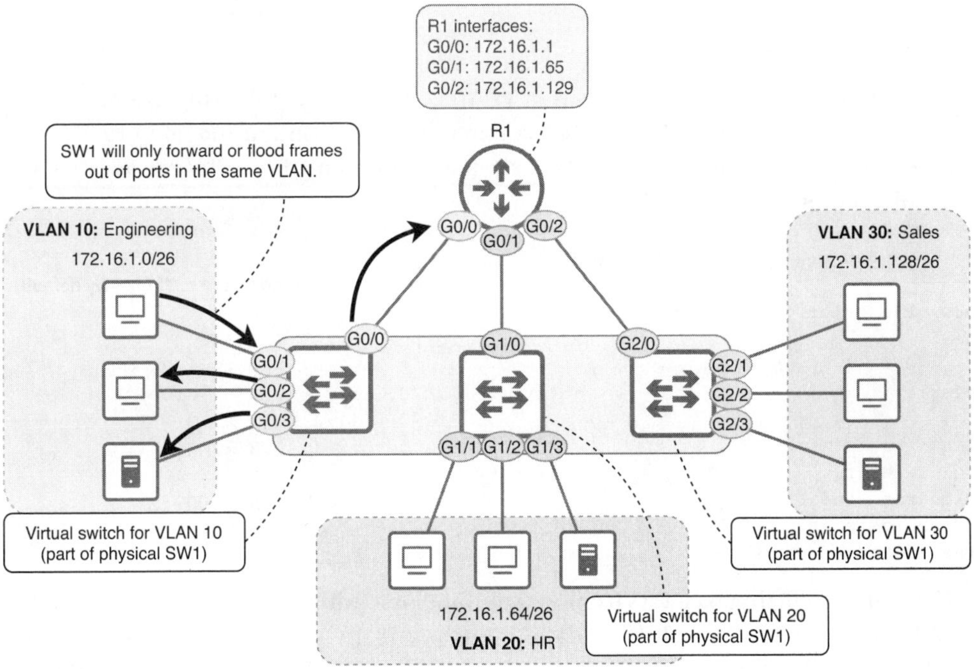

Figure 12.4 By assigning SW1's interfaces to three separate VLANs, SW1 is divided into three virtual switches, each a separate broadcast domain. G0/0, G0/1, G0/2, and G0/3 are part of VLAN 10. G1/0, G1/1, G1/2, and G1/3 are part of VLAN 20. G2/0, G2/1, G2/2, and G2/3 are part of VLAN 30. SW1 will not forward or flood a frame out of ports in a different VLAN than the port the frame was received on.

NOTE The physical network in figure 12.4 is the same as we saw in figure 12.3; the only difference is that SW1's ports are now in three separate VLANs. I have shown SW1 as three separate virtual switches to illustrate how VLANs work. Network diagrams are usually not represented in this manner; in a typical network diagram, VLANs are labeled, but only the physical switch is shown.

We have now successfully segmented the LAN at both Layer 3 (with subnets) and Layer 2 (with VLANs). SW1 will not forward or flood frames between VLANs—hosts in separate VLANs can only communicate with each other through R1. As a general rule, there should be a one-to-one relationship between subnets and VLANs, as shown in figure 12.4—one subnet per VLAN. If you continue your studies beyond the CCNA, you will find cases where there are multiple subnets associated with a single VLAN, but for the CCNA, you can assume that they are one-to-one.

12.2 Configuring VLANs and access ports

Up to this point in the book, we haven't done much configuration of switches. That's because a switch can fulfill its basic role of forwarding frames without any particular configuration; it builds its MAC address table automatically by examining the source MAC address of frames it receives and then can forward frames between hosts in a LAN. However, to use VLANs, we must configure them on the switch's ports.

12.2.1 Creating and naming VLANs

First, let's examine the default status of VLANs on SW1. The following example shows the output of the **show vlan brief** command before configuring any VLANs. This command shows the list of VLANs that exist on the switch (the *VLAN database*), as well as which ports are in each VLAN:

Views SWI's VLAN database

All ports are in VLAN 1 by default.

```
SW1# show vlan brief
VLAN Name                             Status    Ports
---- -------------------------------- --------- -------------------------------
1    default                          active    Gi0/0, Gi0/1, Gi0/2, Gi0/3
                                                Gi1/0, Gi1/1, Gi1/2, Gi1/3
                                                Gi2/0, Gi2/1, Gi2/2, Gi2/3
1002 fddi-default                     act/unsup
1003 token-ring-default               act/unsup
1004 fddinet-default                  act/unsup
1005 trnet-default                    act/unsup
```

VLANs 1002–1005 also exist by default.

There are two main takeaways from that output. First, without any configuration, all of SW1's ports are in VLAN 1. VLAN 1 is the *default VLAN*—the VLAN that all ports are in by default. We can also confirm this by looking at the switch's MAC address table; all MAC addresses are learned in VLAN 1, as shown in the leftmost column of the following example:

```
SW1# show mac address-table
          Mac Address Table
-------------------------------------------
Vlan    Mac Address       Type        Ports
----    -----------       --------    -----
   1    5254.0000.04c5    DYNAMIC     Gi2/0
   1    5254.000e.a694    DYNAMIC     Gi2/1
   1    5254.000f.d41a    DYNAMIC     Gi1/0
   1    5254.0011.fbcf    DYNAMIC     Gi0/1
. . .
```

SW1 learned all MAC addresses in VLAN 1.

The second takeaway from the output of **`show vlan brief`** is that VLANs 1002, 1003, 1004, and 1005 also exist on the switch by default. These VLANs are reserved for use by *FDDI* and *Token Ring*—two legacy Data Link Layer technologies. FDDI and Token Ring are no longer used in modern networks, but even in modern versions of Cisco IOS, these four VLANs are reserved for backward compatibility—they cannot be deleted or used for Ethernet VLANs.

> **NOTE** There are 4096 VLANs in total (from 0 through 4095), but VLANs 0 and 4095 are reserved for special purposes beyond the scope of the CCNA exam. With VLANs 1002–1005 being reserved for FDDI and Token Ring, the range of usable VLANs is 1 to 1001 and 1006 to 4094 (4,090 VLANs in total). That means that a single LAN (broadcast domain) can be divided into a maximum of 4,090 VLANs—far more VLANs than most LANs will ever need.

To configure a VLAN, use the **`vlan`** *`vlan-id`* command from global configuration mode (*`vlan-id`* is a number). That will take you to VLAN configuration mode, from which you can also configure the VLAN's name with the **`name`** *`vlan-name`* command. In the following example, I create and name VLANs 10, 20, and 30 on SW1 and then confirm with **`show vlan brief`** (leaving VLANs 1002–1005 out of the output to save space):

```
SW1(config)# vlan 10
SW1(config-vlan)# name Engineering
SW1(config-vlan)# vlan 20
SW1(config-vlan)# name HR
SW1(config-vlan)# vlan 30
SW1(config-vlan)# name Sales
SW1(config-vlan)# end
SW1# show vlan brief
VLAN Name                             Status    Ports
---- -------------------------------- --------- -------------------------------
1    default                          active    Gi0/0, Gi0/1, Gi0/2, Gi0/3
                                                Gi1/0, Gi1/1, Gi1/2, Gi1/3
                                                Gi2/0, Gi2/1, Gi2/2, Gi2/3

10   Engineering                      active
20   HR                               active
30   Sales                            active
. . .
```

Creates and names VLAN 10

Creates and names VLAN 20

Creates and names VLAN 30

VLANs 10, 20, and 30 are in SW1's VLAN database.

> **NOTE** Naming a VLAN is optional. If you don't configure a name, the default name is *VLANxxxx*, where *xxxx* is the VLAN ID in four digits (i.e., *VLAN0010* for VLAN 10).

In the previous example, the status of each VLAN is `active`. However, you can temporarily disable a VLAN by using the **`shutdown`** command in VLAN configuration mode. In the following example, I disable VLAN 10 on SW1 and confirm with **`show vlan brief`**. Notice that the status changes to `act/lshut` (active/locally shutdown):

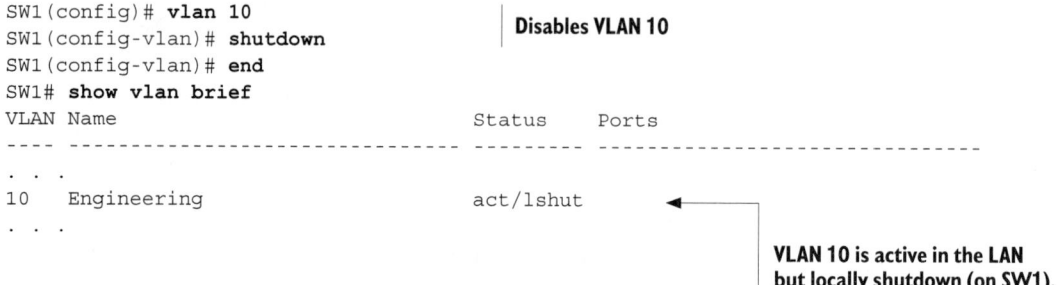

```
SW1(config)# vlan 10                          | Disables VLAN 10
SW1(config-vlan)# shutdown                    |
SW1(config-vlan)# end
SW1# show vlan brief
VLAN Name                             Status    Ports
---- -------------------------------- --------- -------------------------------
. . .
10   Engineering                      act/lshut   <--
. . .                                                VLAN 10 is active in the LAN
                                                     but locally shutdown (on SW1).
```

> **NOTE** If you want to delete a VLAN entirely, you can negate the command you used to create it by adding **`no`** in front of it, such as **`no vlan 10`**.

12.2.2 Assigning ports to VLANs

Now that we have created VLANs 10, 20, and 30 on SW1, let's assign SW1's ports to the appropriate VLANs. There are two steps to do so:

1. Configure SW1's ports in access mode.
2. Configure the access mode VLAN of the ports.

An *access port* is a switch port that belongs to a single VLAN, as opposed to a *trunk port*, which carries traffic in multiple VLANs (we will cover trunk ports in section 12.3). By default, Cisco switch ports use a protocol called *Dynamic Trunking Protocol* (DTP) to automatically determine whether each port should operate in access mode or trunk mode. We will cover DTP in chapter 13, but for now, just know that it is best practice to manually configure access or trunk mode, rather than letting DTP automatically determine interfaces' status.

You can manually configure a switch port to operate in access mode with the **`switchport mode access`** command in interface configuration mode. Then, use the **`switchport access vlan`** *`vlan-id`* command to configure which VLAN the port belongs to. In the following example, I configure SW1's G0/0, G0/1, G0/2, and G0/3 interfaces as access ports in VLAN 10, its G1/0, G1/1, G1/2, and G1/3 interfaces as access ports in VLAN 20, and its G2/0, G2/1, G2/2, and G2/3 ports as access ports in VLAN 30:

```
SW1(config)# interface range g0/0-3
SW1(config-if-range)# switchport mode access
SW1(config-if-range)# switchport access vlan 10
SW1(config-if-range)# interface range g1/0-3
SW1(config-if-range)# switchport mode access
SW1(config-if-range)# switchport access vlan 20
SW1(config-if-range)# interface range g2/0-3
SW1(config-if-range)# switchport mode access
SW1(config-if-range)# switchport access vlan 30
```

Configures G0/0–3 as access ports in VLAN 10

Configures G1/0–3 as access ports in VLAN 20

Configures G2/0–3 as access ports in VLAN 30

> **NOTE** If you use the **`switchport access vlan`** command to assign a port to a VLAN that doesn't exist yet on the switch, the switch will automatically create the VLAN. This means that it's not necessary to create VLANs with the **`vlan`** command before assigning ports to VLANs (although it's necessary if you want to use the **`name`** command to name the VLANs).

We have now finished configuring SW1! It will forward and flood frames between hosts in each VLAN but not between VLANs—each VLAN is a separate broadcast domain. Keep in mind that VLANs are configured on the switch ports; although it's common to say that an end host is *in VLAN X*, that host is not actually aware of what VLAN it is in—VLANs are a concept used by switches, not typical end hosts like PCs.

> **NOTE** There are exceptions where end hosts are VLAN aware; we will look at an example when we cover virtual machines in chapter 17 of volume 2.

12.3 Connecting switches with trunk ports

Access ports are assigned to a single VLAN, and only forward and flood traffic between ports in the same VLAN. Trunk ports, on the other hand, are not assigned to a single VLAN; rather, they can forward traffic in multiple VLANs. Figure 12.5 shows a situation in which a trunk port should be used: the LAN consists of two switches (SW1 and SW2), and hosts in VLANs 10, 20, and 30 are connected to each switch. For hosts in each VLAN to be able to communicate with each other, the link between SW1 and SW2 must be able to carry traffic in multiple VLANs; to enable that, frames sent between SW1 and SW2 are *tagged* to indicate which VLAN each frame belongs to.

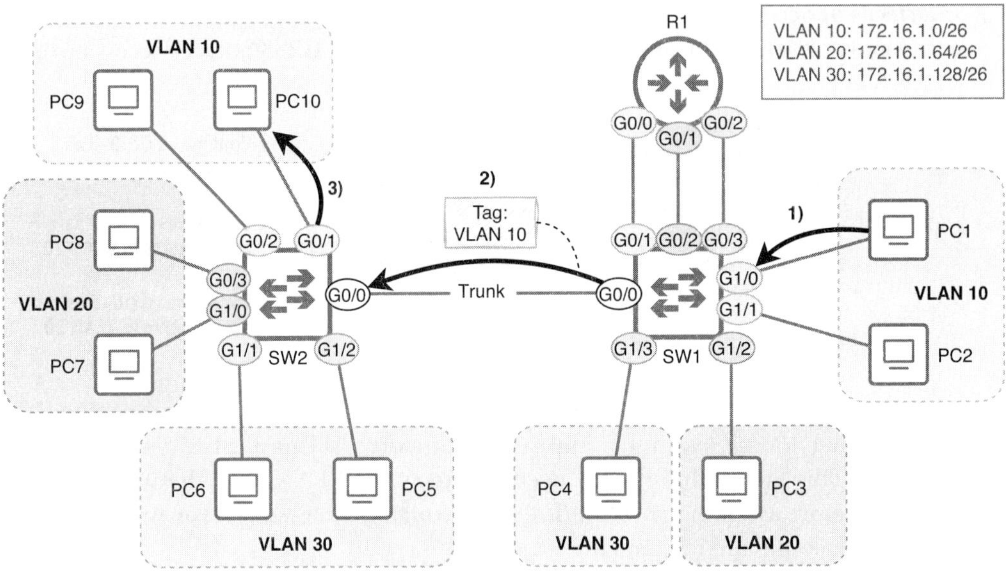

Figure 12.5 SW1 and SW2 are connected by a trunk link, which can carry traffic in multiple VLANs. SW1 and SW2 are two physical switches, each consisting of three virtual switches—one for each VLAN. (1) PC1 (connected to SW1) sends a frame addressed to PC10's MAC. (2) SW1 forwards the frame out of its G0/0 port, which is in trunk mode. It adds a tag to the frame, indicating that the frame is in VLAN 10. (3) SW2 forwards the frame out of its G0/1 port (untagged).

> **NOTE** Instead of connecting SW1 and SW2 with a single trunk link, another option is to use a separate access link between the switches for each VLAN (one for VLAN 10, one for VLAN 20, and one for VLAN 30). Although this could work in small networks with few VLANs, this does not scale to networks with many VLANs; a trunk link is a better option.

That's how trunk ports work: the switch forwarding a frame adds a tag before sending it out of the trunk port. For that reason, another name for a trunk port is a *tagged port.* The switch receiving the frame then checks the tag and assigns the frame to the VLAN specified by the tag. If the frame's destination is in a different VLAN than the one specified by the tag, the switch won't be able to forward the frame to its proper destination; remember, hosts in different VLANs can't communicate directly with each other.

Likewise, another name for an access port is an *untagged port*; frames forwarded by an access port are not tagged to indicate the VLAN, and frames received by an access port are assigned to the VLAN specified in the **`switchport access vlan`** command. Because access ports are associated with only one VLAN, a tag is not necessary to identify which VLAN frames that are sent and received by the port belong to.

> **NOTE** Access ports are typically used to connect to end hosts, such as PCs. Trunk ports are typically used to connect to other switches (and sometimes routers, as we'll see in section 12.4).

12.3.1 The IEEE 802.1Q tag

The protocol used to tag frames forwarded out of trunk ports is *IEEE 802.1Q* (typically pronounced "dot one Q"). The 802.1Q tag is 4 bytes in length and is added in between the Source and EtherType fields of the Ethernet header. Figure 12.6 shows the position of the 802.1Q tag within a frame, as well as the fields of the tag.

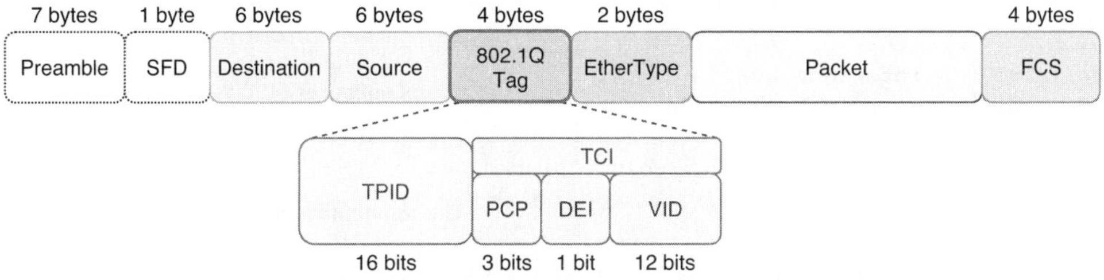

Figure 12.6 The 802.1Q tag's position in an Ethernet frame and the field of the tag. The fields are TPID (Tag Protocol Identifier) and TCI (Tag Control Information). TCI contains three subfields: PCP (Priority Code Point), DEI (Drop Eligible Indicator), and VID (VLAN Identifier).

The *Tag Protocol Identifier* (TPID) field is 16 bits in length and always contains the value 0x8100. When a frame is 802.1Q tagged, the TPID field is in the position the EtherType field would normally be. When the switch sees the value 0x8100 here, it knows the frame is tagged using 802.1Q; that's the purpose of the TPID field.

The second half of the 802.1Q is the *Tag Control Information* (TCI), which contains three subfields: PCP, DEI, and VID. The *Priority Code Point* (PCP) field is 3 bits in length and can be used to mark frames as higher or lower in priority; this is used for *Quality of Service* (QoS), a topic we will cover in chapter 10 of volume 2. The *Drop Eligible Indicator* (DEI) field is a single bit in length and is also used for QoS; it can be used to indicate frames that can be dropped if the network is congested.

The *VLAN Identifier* (VID) field is perhaps the most important; it's the field that indicates which VLAN the frame is in. It is 12 bits in length, and that's why there are 4,096 VLANs in total ($2^{12} = 4096$).

Cisco Inter-Switch Link

Before IEEE 802.1Q, Cisco developed a protocol called *Inter-Switch Link* (ISL) to tag frames over trunk links. As a Cisco-proprietary protocol, ISL can only be used by Cisco switches. Whereas 802.1Q adds a 4-byte tag to the Ethernet header, ISL encapsulates the Ethernet frame with a 26-byte header and 4-byte trailer, containing an FCS (separate from the Ethernet trailer's FCS).

ISL is now considered deprecated and is not supported on new Cisco switches. However, you may still encounter Cisco switches that support both 802.1Q and ISL; in such cases, an extra command is required when configuring trunk ports, as we will cover in section 12.3.2. Although you don't have to know ISL itself for the CCNA exam, you should understand how it affects trunk configuration on switches that support it (by requiring an extra command).

12.3.2 Configuring trunk ports

To demonstrate the configuration of trunk ports, let's configure SW1's G0/0 port as we saw in figure 12.5—a trunk link capable of carrying traffic in VLANs 10, 20, and 30. Although I will only demonstrate SW1's side of the link, if you're trying this out yourself, make sure that SW2's G0/0 port is configured to match (with the same commands as on SW1). In the following example, I attempt to configure SW1 G0/0 as a trunk, but the command is rejected.

```
SW1(config)# interface g0/0
SW1(config-if)# switchport mode trunk
Command rejected: An interface whose trunk encapsulation
➥is "Auto" can not be configured to "trunk" mode.
```

Configures G0/0 as a trunk port

The command is rejected.

The reason the command is rejected is that SW1 supports both 802.1Q and ISL. By default, ports on a switch that supports both 802.1Q and ISL will use DTP (mentioned earlier in section 12.2.2) to automatically determine which of the two protocols to use for the trunk. However, to manually configure the port in trunk mode, you must also manually configure the encapsulation protocol (802.1Q or ISL); you can't manually configure trunk mode, but you can allow DTP to automatically determine whether to use 802.1Q or ISL. The command to configure which protocol to use is **`switchport trunk encapsulation {dot1q | isl}`**. In the following example, I configure G0/0 to use 802.1Q, and then I can successfully configure G0/0 as a trunk port:

```
SW1(config-if)# switchport trunk encapsulation dot1q
SW1(config-if)# switchport mode trunk
SW1(config-if)#
```

Manually configures 802.1Q encapsulation

The command works this time.

> **NOTE** If a switch only supports 802.1Q (not ISL), it is not necessary to use the **`switchport trunk encapsulation`** command before **`switchport mode trunk`**; in fact, the switch won't even support the **`switchport trunk encapsulation`** command.

After configuring a port as a trunk, it will no longer appear in the output of **`show vlan brief`**. The example below demonstrates this; G0/0 is not present in the output. Note that I configured SW1's access ports in their appropriate VLANs, according to figure 12.5:

```
SW1# show vlan brief
VLAN Name                             Status    Ports
---- -------------------------------- --------- -------------------------------
1    default                          active    Gi2/0, Gi2/1, Gi2/2, Gi2/3
10   Engineering                      active    Gi0/1, Gi1/0, Gi1/1
20   HR                               active    Gi0/2, Gi1/2
30   Sales                            active    Gi0/3, Gi1/3
```

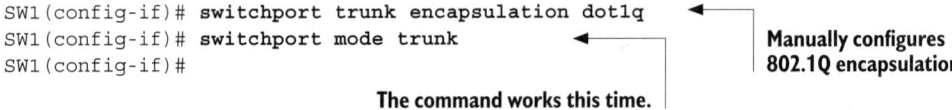

G0/1, G1/0, and G1/1 are access ports in VLAN 10.

G0/2 and G1/2 are access ports in VLAN 20.

G0/3 and G1/3 are access ports in VLAN 30.

To verify trunk ports, you can use the command **show interfaces trunk**, as shown in the following example. The output is divided into four parts, but we will focus on the first three:

```
SW1# show interfaces trunk
Port        Mode         Encapsulation  Status       Native vlan
Gi0/0       on           802.1q         trunking     1

Port        Vlans allowed on trunk
Gi0/0       1-4094

Port        Vlans allowed and active in management domain
Gi0/0       1,10,20,30
. . .
```

Views SW1's trunk ports

G0/0 is a trunk port.

All VLANs (1–4094) are allowed on G0/0.

VLANs 1, 10, 20, and 30 are allowed and active.

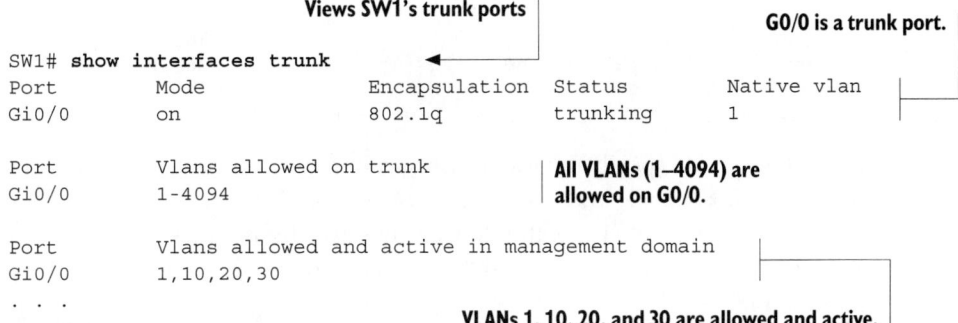

The first section (the top two lines) lists each trunk port and some basic information. The value of `on` in the `Mode` column means that G0/0 is manually configured as a trunk (with the **switchport mode trunk** command). The encapsulation column is self-explanatory; the value is `802.1q` because I configured the **switchport trunk encapsulation dot1q** command earlier. The `Status` column says `trunking`; this is expected because I manually configured G0/0 in trunk mode. The final column is `Native vlan`; the native VLAN is an important topic to understand for the CCNA, and we will cover it in this section.

The second part of the output lists the VLANs allowed on each trunk port (`Vlans allowed on trunk`). As indicated by `1-4094`, all VLANs are allowed on a trunk port by default; this means that traffic in all VLANs can be forwarded and received by the port.

However, the following part lists the VLANs that are allowed and exist on the switch (`Vlans allowed and active in management domain`). VLAN 1 exists by default, and I created VLANs 10, 20, and 30, so those four are listed here. If a VLAN does not exist on a switch, it cannot forward traffic in that VLAN; therefore, although all VLANs are allowed on the trunk, SW1 can only forward traffic in VLANs 1, 10, 20, and 30.

NOTE The *management domain* referred to in the line `Vlans allowed and active in management domain` is a reference to the *VLAN Trunking Protocol* (VTP) domain. VTP is one of the topics of chapter 13, so I won't mention it any further in this chapter.

Modifying the list of allowed VLANs

Although all VLANs are allowed on a trunk port by default, it is considered best practice to allow only the necessary VLANs. This can help to limit the size of broadcast domains; if a VLAN isn't allowed on a trunk, broadcast (and unknown unicast) frames in that VLAN won't be flooded out of the interface. The command to configure the list of VLANs allowed on the trunk is **switchport trunk allowed vlan**, and then there are several possible keywords and arguments, as shown in the following example:

Configures the VLANs allowed on the trunk

```
SW1(config-if)# switchport trunk allowed vlan
  WORD    VLAN IDs of the allowed VLANs when this port is
  ➥ in trunking mode
  add     add VLANs to the current list
  all     all VLANs
  except  all VLANs except the following
  none    no VLANs
  remove  remove VLANs from the current list
```

The available keywords and arguments

WORD allows you to specify the list of VLANs allowed on the trunk as an argument, such as **switchport trunk allowed vlan 10,20,30**; this will allow only VLANs 10, 20, and 30 on the trunk. This is the desired state for the network we saw in figure 12.5, which uses only VLANs 10, 20, and 30. I demonstrate this configuration in the following example:

Allows VLANs 10, 20, and 30

```
SW1(config-if)# switchport trunk allowed vlan 10,20,30
SW1(config-if)# do show interfaces trunk
. . .
Port        Vlans allowed on trunk
Gi0/0       10,20,30
. . .
```

Only VLANs 10, 20, and 30 are allowed on G0/0.

The other options are keywords, and for the CCNA exam, it's important to understand how each keyword functions. **add** and **remove** are used to modify the current list of allowed VLANs. In the following example, I add VLAN 1 and remove VLAN 30 from the list of allowed VLANs; the list of allowed VLANs then changes to 1, 10, and 20:

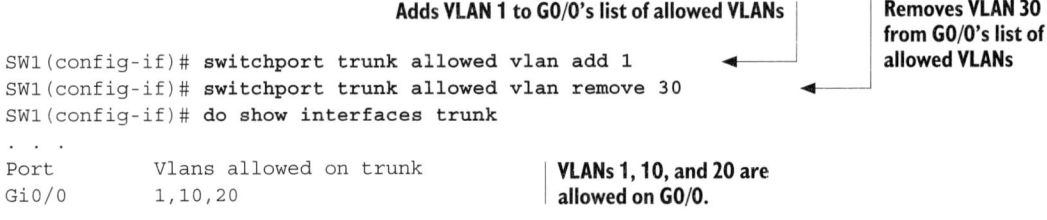

Adds VLAN 1 to G0/0's list of allowed VLANs

Removes VLAN 30 from G0/0's list of allowed VLANs

```
SW1(config-if)# switchport trunk allowed vlan add 1
SW1(config-if)# switchport trunk allowed vlan remove 30
SW1(config-if)# do show interfaces trunk
. . .
Port        Vlans allowed on trunk
Gi0/0       1,10,20
. . .
```

VLANs 1, 10, and 20 are allowed on G0/0.

The **all** and **none** keywords are self-explanatory; **all** allows all VLANs (the default setting), and **none** allows no VLANs, preventing the port from forwarding or receiving any traffic. In the following example, I demonstrate both keywords:

```
SW1(config-if)# switchport trunk allowed vlan all
SW1(config-if)# do show interfaces trunk
. . .
Port        Vlans allowed on trunk
Gi0/0       1-4094
. . .
SW1(config-if)# switchport trunk allowed vlan none
SW1(config-if)# do show interfaces trunk
. . .
Port        Vlans allowed on trunk
Gi0/0       none
. . .
```

Allows all VLANs on G0/0

All VLANs are allowed on G0/0.

Allows no VLANs on G0/0

No VLANs are allowed on G0/0.

The final keyword is **except**, which allows all VLANs except the VLAN(s) you specify as an argument. In the following example, I return the list of allowed VLANs to the desired state (allowing only VLANs 10, 20, and 30) by using the **except** keyword and specifying all VLANs except 10, 20, and 30 (a bit unconventional, but this is just a demonstration!):

```
SW1(config-if)# switchport trunk allowed vlan except
➥ 1-9,11-19,21-29,31-4094
SW1(config-if)# do show interfaces trunk
. . .
Port        Vlans allowed on trunk
Gi0/0       10,20,30
. . .
```

Allows all VLANs on G0/0 except 1–9, 11–19, 21–29, and 31–4094

Only VLANs 10, 20, and 30 are allowed on G0/0.

> **Don't forget add!**
>
> A common rookie mistake (and the subject of many networking memes—yes, such a thing exists!) is to forget the **add** keyword when modifying the list of allowed VLANs on a trunk. For example, if you want to add VLAN 40 to the list of allowed VLANs, but you use the command **switchport trunk allowed vlan 40**, you haven't added VLAN 40 to the list of allowed VLANs; you have replaced the list of allowed VLANs with only VLAN 40!
>
> It's a simple mistake, but the results can be disastrous: blocking all communications over the trunk except for hosts in a single VLAN. This is a potential "trick question" on the exam, so make sure you are aware of the difference between specifying the list of allowed VLANs (**switchport trunk allowed vlan** *vlans*) and adding to the list of allowed VLANs (**switchport trunk allowed vlan add** *vlans*).

THE NATIVE VLAN

As mentioned in section 12.2, access ports (untagged ports) send and receive frames without 802.1Q tags. Trunk ports (tagged ports), on the other hand, send and receive frames with 802.1Q tags to indicate which VLAN each frame belongs to, but what happens if a switch receives an untagged frame on a trunk port? The native VLAN is the answer to that question.

The *native VLAN* is the VLAN that untagged traffic received on a trunk port is assigned to. Furthermore, any traffic in the native VLAN forwarded by a trunk port is forwarded without a tag. By default, the native VLAN is VLAN 1, as shown in the output of **show interfaces trunk**:

```
SW1# show interfaces trunk
Port        Mode             Encapsulation  Status        Native vlan
Gi0/0       on               802.1q         trunking      1
. . .
```

VLAN 1 is the native VLAN by default.

EXAM TIP The default VLAN and the native VLAN are often confused. The default VLAN is the VLAN that access ports are assigned to by default: VLAN 1 (this cannot be changed). The native VLAN is the VLAN that untagged frames are assigned to when received on a trunk port, and frames in the native VLAN are forwarded untagged over that port. The native VLAN is also VLAN 1 by default, but this can be changed per port.

To configure the native VLAN of a trunk port, use the **`switchport trunk native vlan`** *`vlan-id`* command. In the following example, I configure VLAN 30 as the native VLAN on SW1's G0/0 interface and then confirm with **`show interfaces trunk`**:

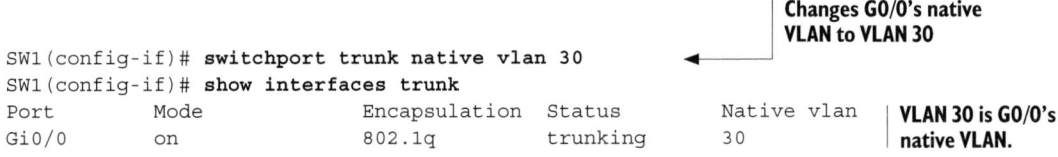

```
SW1(config-if)# switchport trunk native vlan 30
SW1(config-if)# show interfaces trunk
Port          Mode              Encapsulation  Status          Native vlan
Gi0/0         on                802.1q         trunking        30
. . .
```

Changes G0/0's native VLAN to VLAN 30

VLAN 30 is G0/0's native VLAN.

Figure 12.7 shows how traffic in the native VLAN is forwarded over a trunk link. The frame from PC1 to PC10 (both in VLAN 10) is tagged when SW1 forwards it to SW2. The frame from PC4 to PC5 (both in VLAN 30), however, is not tagged when SW1 forwards it to SW2; VLAN 30 is the native VLAN on SW1's G0/0 port. Likewise, VLAN 30 is the native VLAN on SW2's G0/0 port, so when the frame is received by SW2, SW2 assigns the frame to VLAN 30 and forwards it to the destination (which is also in VLAN 30).

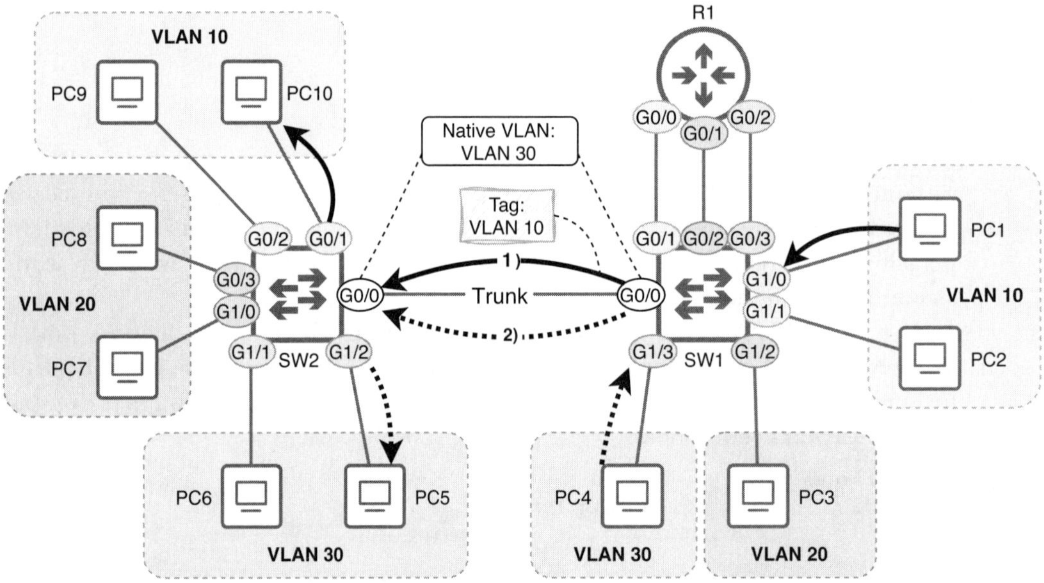

Figure 12.7 Frames forwarded over a trunk link in the native VLAN and a non-native VLAN. (1) PC1's frame to PC10 is tagged over the trunk link because VLAN 10 is not the native VLAN. (2) PC4's frame to PC5 is untagged over the trunk link because VLAN 30 is the native VLAN.

NOTE The native VLAN is configured per port. If a switch has multiple trunk ports, it is possible to configure a different native VLAN on each port.

Native VLAN mismatch

Because the native VLAN is configured on each switch's ports, it is possible to configure a different native VLAN on each end of a link. However, this is a misconfiguration and should not be done. Make sure the native VLAN matches on both ends of the link! Figure 12.8 shows one example of what can happen when there is a native VLAN mismatch.

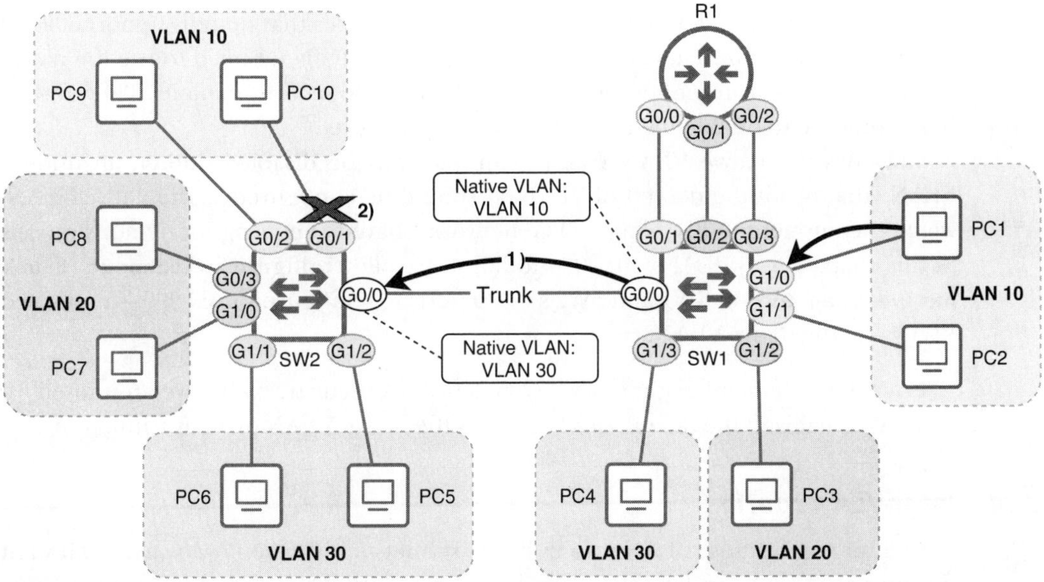

Figure 12.8 A native VLAN mismatch resulting in frames not reaching their destination. SW1 G0/0's native VLAN is VLAN 10, and SW2 G0/0's is VLAN 30. (1) PC1's frame to PC10 is untagged over the trunk link because VLAN 10 is SW1 G0/0's native VLAN. (2) When SW2 receives the frame, it assigns the frame to VLAN 30 (SW2 G0/0's native VLAN) and therefore cannot forward the frame to its destination (in VLAN 10).

SW1 G0/0's native VLAN is 10, but SW2 G0/0's native VLAN is 30. When PC1 sends a frame to PC10, SW1 forwards the frame untagged to SW2. However, when SW2 receives the untagged frame, it assigns the frame to VLAN 30 (SW2 G0/0's native VLAN). Because the frame's destination is connected to SW2's G0/1 (an access port in VLAN 10), SW2 cannot forward the frame to its proper destination. When traffic crosses from one VLAN to another like this, it is called *VLAN hopping*.

NOTE Cisco switches typically run *Per-VLAN Spanning Tree Plus* (PVST+) or *Rapid Per-VLAN Spanning Tree Plus* (Rapid-PVST+). If there is a native VLAN mismatch, these protocols will prevent traffic from being forwarded over the trunk in the mismatched VLANs and display a message indicating so. We will cover PVST+ and Rapid-PVST+ in chapters 14 and 15, respectively. *Cisco Discovery Protocol* (CDP) can also detect native VLAN mismatches but will not block traffic in the mismatched VLANs; it will only display messages indicating the mismatch. We will cover CDP in chapter 1 of volume 2.

DISABLING THE NATIVE VLAN

The native VLAN was developed to accommodate devices that do not support 802.1Q tagging, such as hubs. However, these days, there is usually no need to use the native VLAN, and its use can render the network vulnerable to security exploits. Therefore, it is best practice to disable the native VLAN on trunk ports.

However, the native VLAN feature can't actually be disabled; rather, an unused VLAN (that is not the default of VLAN 1) should be configured as the native VLAN, which is equivalent to disabling it. The network I have been using for demonstrations in this chapter uses VLANs 10, 20, and 30, so I could configure **`switchport trunk native vlan 999`** on SW1 and SW2's G0/0 ports to configure VLAN 999—an unused VLAN—as the native VLAN.

EXAM TIP Remember that as a best practice for security: configure an unused VLAN (that isn't the default of VLAN 1) as the native VLAN on your trunk ports.

12.4 Inter-VLAN routing

Even after segmenting a LAN into multiple subnets and VLANs, we usually still want the subnets/VLANs to be able to communicate with each other (and external networks). Although routing is a Layer 3 concept and VLANs are a Layer 2 concept, the term *inter-VLAN routing* is used to refer to routing between subnets in a LAN that is segmented using VLANs.

Up to this point, all of the diagrams in this chapter (aside from figure 12.1, which only depicted one subnet) have shown three links between R1 and SW1—one per subnet/VLAN. This is one option for inter-VLAN routing; the router interfaces are configured as normal, and the switch ports are configured as access ports. Figure 12.9 shows how PC3 (in VLAN 20) can communicate with PC10 (in VLAN 10) in this case.

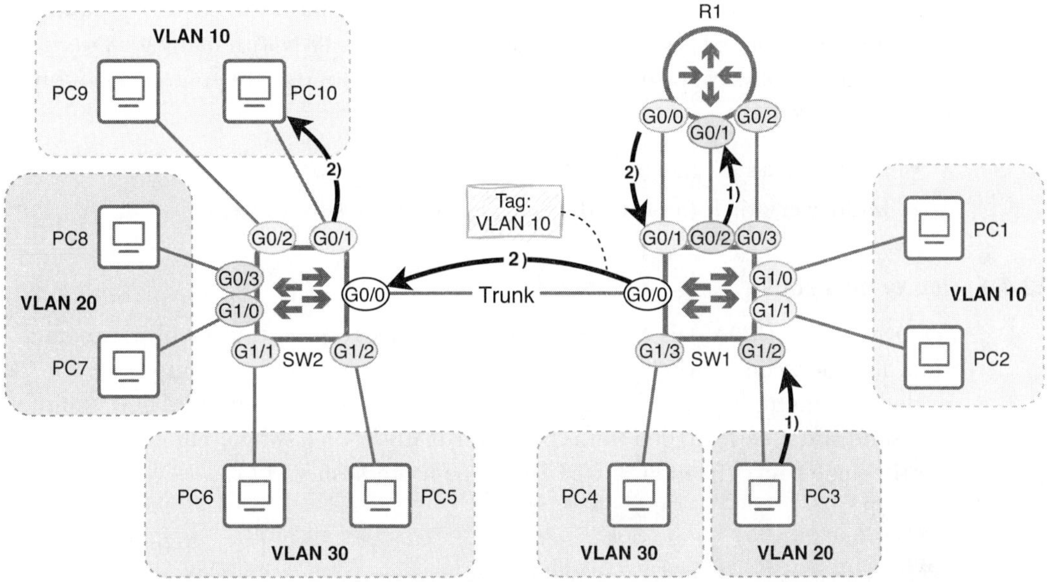

Figure 12.9 PC3 (in VLAN 20) sends a packet to PC10 (in VLAN 10). (1) PC3 sends the packet in a frame addressed to its default gateway (R1 G0/1). SW2 forwards it out of its G0/2 port (untagged). (2) R1 routes the packet, forwarding it out of G0/0 in a new frame addressed to PC10. The frame is forwarded to PC10 by SW1 and SW2. It is tagged only when crossing the trunk link from SW1 G0/0 to SW2 G0/0.

The following examples show how R1 and SW1 can be configured to enable inter-VLAN routing in this manner:

```
R1(config)# interface g0/0
R1(config-if)# ip address 172.16.1.1 255.255.255.192
R1(config-if)# no shutdown
R1(config-if)# interface g0/1
R1(config-if)# ip address 172.16.1.65 255.255.255.192
R1(config-if)# no shutdown
R1(config-if)# interface g0/2
R1(config-if)# ip address 172.16.1.129 255.255.255.192
R1(config-if)# no shutdown
```

- **Configures and enables R1 G0/0 (VLAN 10's default gateway)**
- **Configures and enables R1 G0/1 (VLAN 20's default gateway)**
- **Configures and enables R1 G0/2 (VLAN 30's default gateway)**

```
SW1(config)# interface g0/1
SW1(config-if)# switchport mode access
SW1(config-if)# switchport access vlan 10
SW1(config-if)# interface g0/2
SW1(config-if)# switchport mode access
SW1(config-if)# switchport access vlan 20
SW1(config-if)# interface g0/3
SW1(config-if)# switchport mode access
SW1(config-if)# switchport access vlan 30
```

- **Configures and enables SW1 G0/1 (VLAN 10)**
- **Configures and enables SW1 G0/2 (VLAN 20)**
- **Configures and enables SW1 G0/3 (VLAN 30)**

However, this method of inter-VLAN routing is not common for the same reason it's not common to connect switches using access ports: in a LAN with many VLANs, you'll soon run out of physical ports on your devices. Instead, one of the following options is usually preferred:

- Router on a stick (a trunk link between the switch and router)
- Multilayer switch (a switch that can also route packets)

12.4.1 Router on a stick

Router on a stick (ROAS) is a method of inter-VLAN routing that involves creating a trunk link between a switch and a router; a single physical router interface can be divided into multiple virtual *subinterfaces*, each with its own IP address. These subinterfaces send and receive tagged frames, like a trunk port on a switch. Figure 12.10 shows how the same packet from PC3 to PC10 can be routed using ROAS.

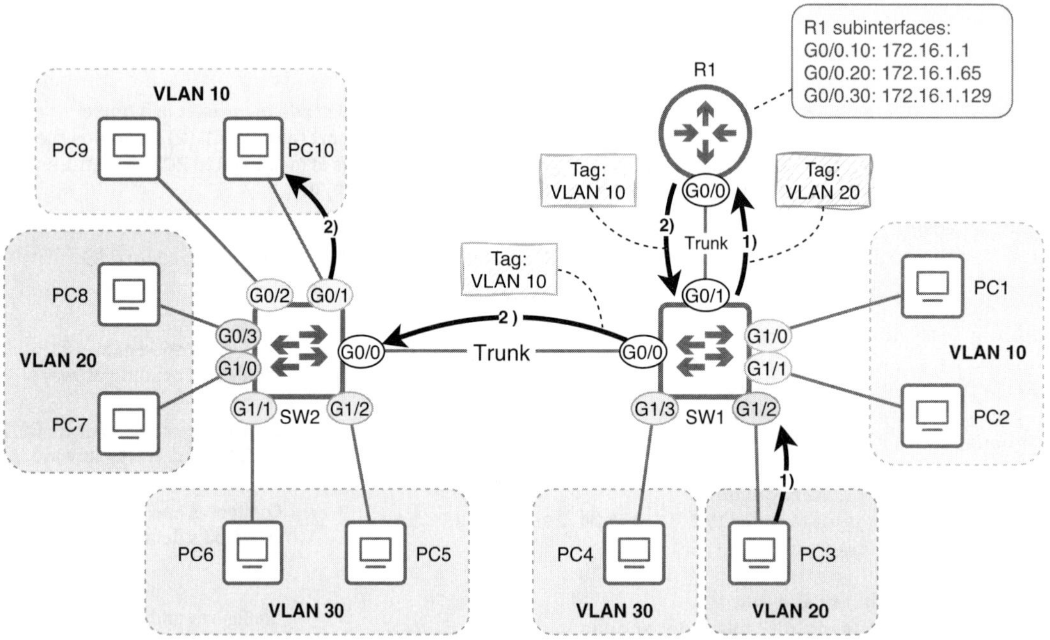

Figure 12.10 PC3 (in VLAN 20) sends a packet to PC10 (in VLAN 10), and the packet is routed using the router on a stick method. R1's G0/0 interface has three subinterfaces: G0/0.10 (VLAN 10, 172.16.1.1), G0/0.20 (VLAN 20, 172.16.1.65), and G0/0.30 (VLAN 30, 172.16.1.129). PC3's frame to R1 is tagged in VLAN 20 over the trunk link from SW1 G0/1 and R1 G0/0. R1's frame to PC10 is tagged in VLAN 10 over the trunk link from R1 G0/0 to SW1 G0/1, and the trunk link from SW1 G0/0 to SW2 G0/0.

NOTE A router's physical interface and virtual subinterfaces all share the same MAC address. When a frame arrives on the physical interface, the router knows which subinterface the frame is destined for based on the frame's VLAN tag rather than based on the frame's destination MAC address.

CONFIGURING ROAS

Let's see how to configure ROAS as shown in figure 12.10. SW1's side of the connection is a trunk port, just like we configured in section 12.3. In the following example, I configure SW1 G0/1 as a trunk port, allow only the necessary VLANs, and change the native VLAN to an unused VLAN:

```
SW1(config)# interface g0/1
SW1(config-if)# switchport trunk encapsulation dot1q
SW1(config-if)# switchport mode trunk
SW1(config-if)# switchport trunk allowed vlan 10,20,30
SW1(config-if)# switchport trunk native vlan 999
```

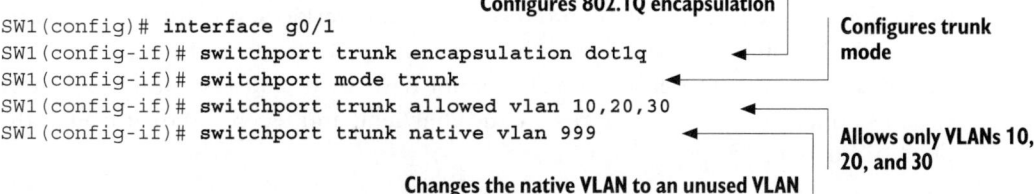

Configures 802.1Q encapsulation

Configures trunk mode

Allows only VLANs 10, 20, and 30

Changes the native VLAN to an unused VLAN

NOTE As mentioned previously, switches that only support 802.1Q (and not ISL) don't require the **`switchport trunk encapsulation`** command before the **`switchport mode trunk`** command.

Next up is R1's configuration; here we'll use some new commands. To configure a subinterface, use the **`interface`** command and follow the interface name with a period and a number that identifies the subinterface, such as **`interface g0/0.10`**; this will bring you to subinterface configuration mode. In the following example, I enable R1's G0/0 interface and then enter subinterface configuration mode for the G0/0.10 subinterface. Notice that the prompt changes to `R1(config-subif)#`:

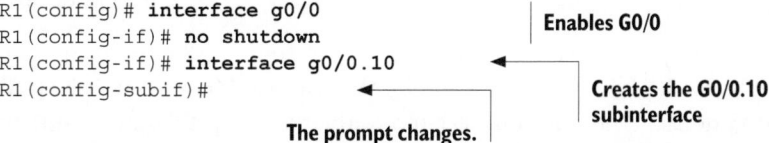

```
R1(config)# interface g0/0
R1(config-if)# no shutdown
R1(config-if)# interface g0/0.10
R1(config-subif)#
```

Enables G0/0

Creates the G0/0.10 subinterface

The prompt changes.

NOTE The G0/0 interface itself does not need any additional configurations; just make sure you enable it with **`no shutdown`**.

Once in subinterface configuration mode, there are two things to configure on the subinterface: the VLAN associated with the subinterface and the IP address. To configure the VLAN ID, use the **`encapsulation dot1q`** *`vlan-id`* command. In the following example, I configure the VLAN ID and IP address of R1's G0/0.10 subinterface:

```
R1(config-subif)# encapsulation dot1q 10
R1(config-subif)# ip address 172.16.1.1 255.255.255.192
```

Configures VLAN 10 on G0/0.10

Configures G0/0.10's IP address

After these configurations, any frames R1 receives on its G0/0 interface that are tagged with VLAN 10 will be sent to the G0/0.10 subinterface, and any frames sent by the G0/0.10 subinterface will be tagged with VLAN 10.

> **NOTE** The number used to identify the subinterface (the `.10` in `G0/0.10`) does not have to match the VLAN ID; the number has no significance beyond identifying the subinterface. It's the **`encapsulation dot1q`** command that tells the router which VLAN to associate with this subinterface. However, I recommend you match these two numbers; there's no reason not to.

In the following example, I configure two more subinterfaces: one for VLAN 20 and one for VLAN 30. I then confirm with the **`show ip interface brief`** command. Notice that the G0/0 interface itself does not have an IP address; rather, the three virtual subinterfaces have IP addresses, and they send and receive traffic through the physical G0/0 interface:

```
R1(config-subif)# interface g0/0.20
R1(config-subif)# encapsulation dot1q 20
R1(config-subif)# ip address 172.16.1.65 255.255.255.192
R1(config-subif)# interface g0/0.30
R1(config-subif)# encapsulation dot1q 30
R1(config-subif)# ip address 172.16.1.129 255.255.255.192
R1(config-subif)# do show ip interface brief
Interface              IP-Address      OK? Method Status                Protocol
GigabitEthernet0/0     unassigned      YES manual up                    up
GigabitEthernet0/0.10  172.16.1.1      YES manual up                    up
GigabitEthernet0/0.20  172.16.1.65     YES manual up                    up
GigabitEthernet0/0.30  172.16.1.129    YES manual up                    up
. . .
```

Configures the G0/0.20 subinterface

Configures the G0/0.30 subinterface

G0/0's three subinterfaces

The physical G0/0 interface

The ROAS configuration is now complete; R1 can route traffic between the three subnets/VLANs in the LAN, using the single physical trunk connection with SW1. Note that I didn't do any configurations related to the native VLAN on R1's side of the connection; if not using the native VLAN, there is no need to do any particular configurations on the router.

CONFIGURING THE NATIVE VLAN WITH ROAS

If you decide to use the native VLAN over the ROAS trunk, there are two methods to configure the router's side of the connection:

- Use the **`encapsulation dot1q`** *`vlan-id`* **`native`** command on the appropriate subinterface.
- Configure the IP address for the native VLAN on the physical interface, not a subinterface.

Let's try both. In the following example, I show the ROAS configuration once again, this time configuring VLAN 10 as the native VLAN by adding the **`native`** keyword to the **encapsulation dot1q** command. Aside from that, the configurations are identical to the previous examples:

```
R1(config)# interface g0/0
R1(config-if)# no shutdown                                   Enables G0/0
R1(config-if)# interface g0/0.10
R1(config-subif)# encapsulation dot1q 10 native              Configures the G0/0.10
R1(config-subif)# ip address 172.16.1.1 255.255.255.192      subinterface and specifies
                                                             VLAN 10 as the native VLAN
R1(config-subif)# interface g0/0.20
R1(config-subif)# encapsulation dot1q 20                     Configures the G0/0.20
R1(config-subif)# ip address 172.16.1.65 255.255.255.192     subinterface
R1(config-subif)# interface g0/0.30
R1(config-subif)# encapsulation dot1q 30                     Configures the G0/0.30
R1(config-subif)# ip address 172.16.1.129 255.255.255.192    subinterface
```

In the following example, I use the second method of configuring the native VLAN on the router. I don't configure a subinterface for VLAN 10, but rather configure the native VLAN's IP address on the G0/0 interface itself; the **encapsulation dot1q** command is not necessary for VLAN 10 in this case, although it's still needed on the subinterfaces of the non-native VLANs (VLANs 20 and 30):

```
R1(config)# interface g0/0
R1(config-if)# no shutdown                                   Configures the native VLAN's IP
R1(config-if)# ip address 172.16.1.1 255.255.255.192         address directly on G0/0
R1(config-if)# interface g0/0.20
R1(config-subif)# encapsulation dot1q 20                     Configures the G0/0.20
R1(config-subif)# ip address 172.16.1.65 255.255.255.192     subinterface
R1(config-subif)# interface g0/0.30
R1(config-subif)# encapsulation dot1q 30                     Configures the G0/0.30
R1(config-subif)# ip address 172.16.1.129 255.255.255.192    subinterface
```

> **NOTE** Whichever method you use to configure the native VLAN on the router, make sure the native VLAN matches on the switch.

12.4.2 Multilayer switching

The third option for inter-VLAN routing, and perhaps the most popular (although ROAS is common as well), is to use a multilayer switch. A *multilayer switch* (also called a *Layer 3 switch*) is a switch that is also capable of routing packets; it's a switch with a router built in.

> **NOTE:** A standard switch that only forwards frames can be called a Layer 2 switch. However, nowadays, almost all switches have some degree of Layer 3 capabilities, so the difference between a multilayer switch and a Layer 2 switch is often determined by how you use the switch rather than the switch itself.

INTER-VLAN ROUTING VIA SVIS

Multilayer switches perform inter-VLAN routing using virtual interfaces called *switch virtual interfaces* (SVIs). Each SVI is an interface on the multilayer switch's built-in router, and hosts in each VLAN use the IP address of their VLAN's SVI as their default gateway.

Figure 12.11 shows the internal logic of how SW1 (now a multilayer switch) routes a packet from PC1 to PC5. PC1 sends the packet in a frame addressed to SW1's VLAN 10 SVI—each SVI has a unique MAC address. SW1's internal router routes the packet via the VLAN 30 SVI and forwards it out of the G0/0 trunk port in a frame (tagged in VLAN 30) addressed to PC5's MAC, and SW2 forwards the frame to PC5 (untagged).

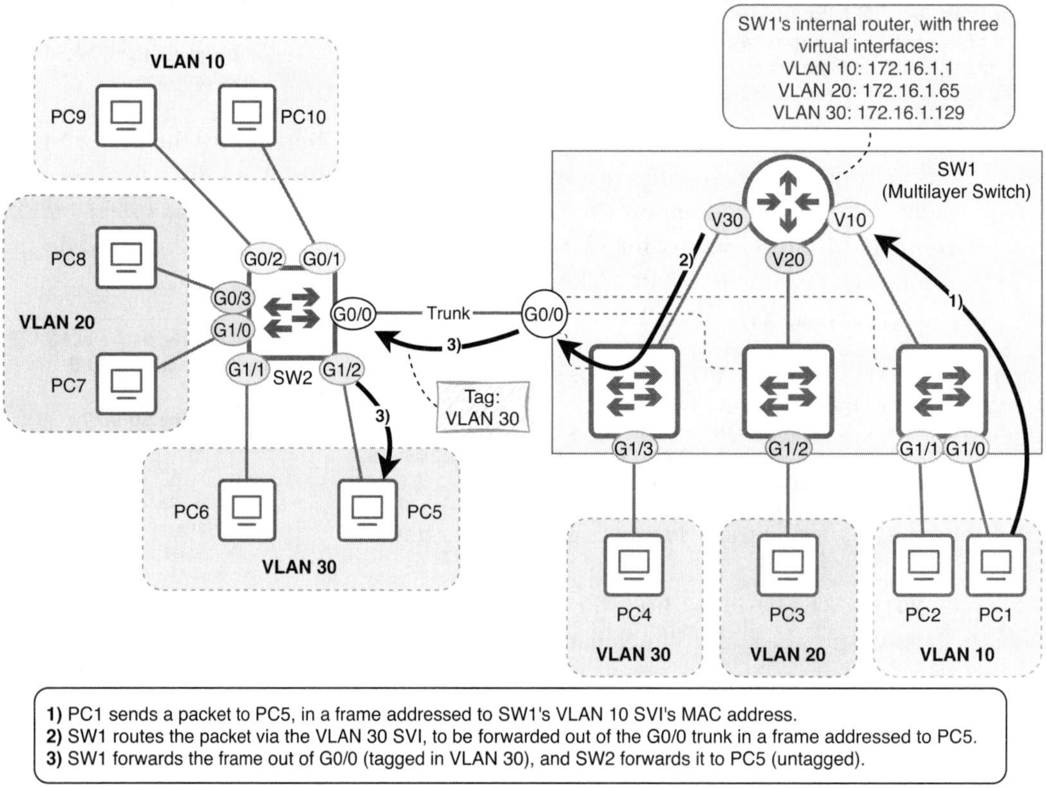

Figure 12.11 SW1, a multilayer switch, routes a packet from PC1 to PC5. SW1 has three SVIs: VLAN 10 (172.16.1.1), VLAN 20 (172.16.1.65), and VLAN 30 (172.16.1.129), allowing SW1 to route packets internally, without relying on an external router.

> **NOTE** R1 is no longer present in the figure 12.11 diagram; if we configure SVIs on SW1, there is no need to rely on an external router for inter-VLAN routing.

The first step to configure SW1, as in figure 12.11, is to enable IP routing with the command `ip routing` in global configuration mode. Without this command, the switch won't be able to forward packets between subnets/VLANs.

After enabling IP routing, the next step is to configure SW1's SVIs. The command to configure an SVI is **interface vlan** *vlan-id*; then, just configure an IP address on the SVI like a router interface. Unlike when configuring a router subinterface (in which the subinterface identifier is not significant), the *vlan-id* specified in the **interface vlan** command is significant; it's what specifies which VLAN the SVI is associated with. In the following example, I enable IP routing and then configure SW1's SVIs for VLAN 10, VLAN 20, and VLAN 30, with the IP addresses configured on R1 in previous examples:

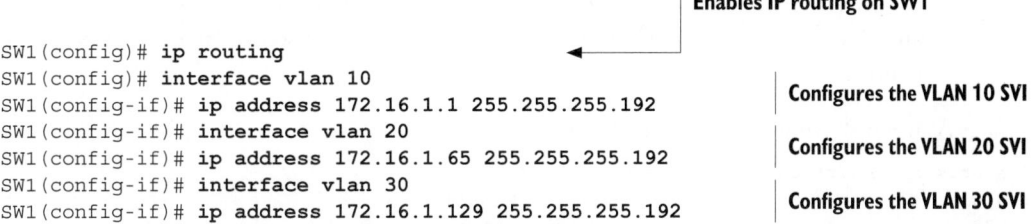

```
SW1(config)# ip routing                                  <- Enables IP routing on SW1
SW1(config)# interface vlan 10
SW1(config-if)# ip address 172.16.1.1 255.255.255.192      Configures the VLAN 10 SVI
SW1(config-if)# interface vlan 20
SW1(config-if)# ip address 172.16.1.65 255.255.255.192     Configures the VLAN 20 SVI
SW1(config-if)# interface vlan 30
SW1(config-if)# ip address 172.16.1.129 255.255.255.192    Configures the VLAN 30 SVI
```

NOTE On some switches, SVIs may be administratively disabled by default. In that case, use **no shutdown** to enable each SVI.

SW1 is now ready to route packets in the LAN; like a router, SW1 inserts connected and local routes into its routing table for each SVI, so there is no need to configure static routes. In the following example, I check SW1's routing table with **show ip route**:

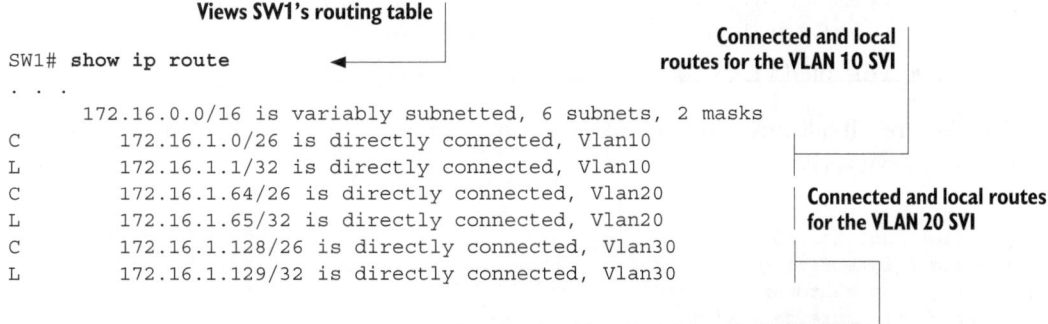

```
SW1# show ip route                                       <- Views SW1's routing table
. . .
      172.16.0.0/16 is variably subnetted, 6 subnets, 2 masks
C        172.16.1.0/26 is directly connected, Vlan10      Connected and local
L        172.16.1.1/32 is directly connected, Vlan10      routes for the VLAN 10 SVI
C        172.16.1.64/26 is directly connected, Vlan20     Connected and local routes
L        172.16.1.65/32 is directly connected, Vlan20     for the VLAN 20 SVI
C        172.16.1.128/26 is directly connected, Vlan30    Connected and local routes
L        172.16.1.129/32 is directly connected, Vlan30    for the VLAN 30 SVI
```

For an SVI to function, it must be in an up/up state (referring to the `Status` and `Protocol` columns in the output of **show ip interface brief**), just like a physical interface. For an SVI to be in an up/up state, there are four requirements; refer to this list if you need to troubleshoot an SVI that won't reach an up/up state:

1. The VLAN associated with the SVI must exist on the switch (i.e., created with the **vlan** *vlan-id* command).
2. The switch must have at least one of the following:
   A. An access port associated with the VLAN (using the **switchport access vlan** command) in an up/up state.

   B A trunk port that allows the VLAN (using the **`switchport trunk allowed vlan`** command) in an up/up state.
3 The VLAN must be enabled (must not have the **`shutdown`** command applied).
4 The SVI must be enabled (must not have the **`shutdown`** command applied).

EXAM TIP Make sure you understand the difference between a VLAN and an SVI. A *VLAN* is a Layer 2 concept—a virtual broadcast domain that divides up a switch. An *SVI* is a virtual Layer 3 interface that is associated with a VLAN. To create a VLAN, use the **`vlan`** command. To create an SVI, use the **`interface vlan`** command.

As the following example shows, SW1's SVIs are currently in an up/up state:

```
SW1# show ip interface brief | include Vlan
Vlan10                 172.16.1.1      YES manual up                    up
Vlan20                 172.16.1.65     YES manual up                    up
Vlan30                 172.16.1.129    YES manual up                    up
```

SW1's SVIs are up/up.

To demonstrate the requirements, in the following example, I violated one requirement for each of the VLAN 10, VLAN 20, and VLAN 30 SVIs:

- I deleted VLAN 10 from SW1 (requirement 1).
- I disabled SW1's G1/3 port (an access port in VLAN 30) and removed VLAN 30 from G0/0's list of allowed VLANs (requirement 2).
- I disabled VLAN 20 with **`shutdown`** (requirement 3).

As a result, all three SVIs move to an up/down state; they will no longer be able to route packets:

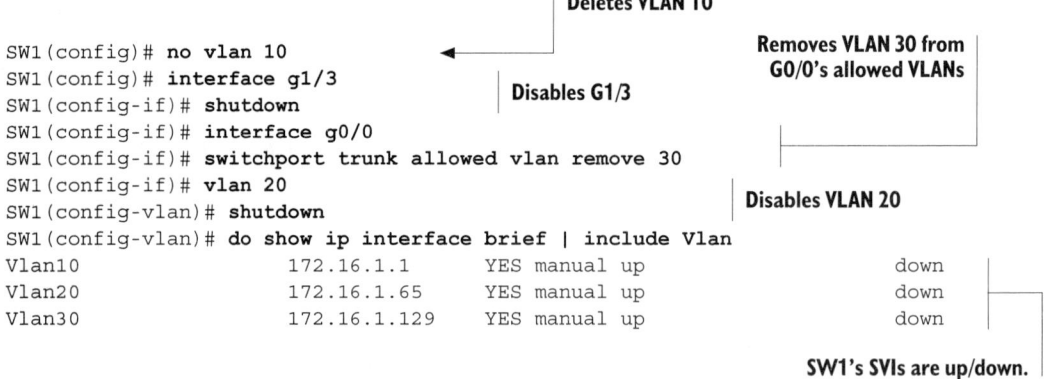

```
SW1(config)# no vlan 10                              <- Deletes VLAN 10
SW1(config)# interface g1/3                          <- Disables G1/3
SW1(config-if)# shutdown
SW1(config-if)# interface g0/0                       <- Removes VLAN 30 from G0/0's allowed VLANs
SW1(config-if)# switchport trunk allowed vlan remove 30
SW1(config-if)# vlan 20                              <- Disables VLAN 20
SW1(config-vlan)# shutdown
SW1(config-vlan)# do show ip interface brief | include Vlan
Vlan10                 172.16.1.1      YES manual up                    down
Vlan20                 172.16.1.65     YES manual up                    down
Vlan30                 172.16.1.129    YES manual up                    down
```

SW1's SVIs are up/down.

USING ROUTED PORTS FOR EXTERNAL CONNECTIVITY

Routing within a LAN is important, but it's also essential for hosts in the LAN to be able to reach external networks, such as the internet or another LAN in the corporate network. To provide external connectivity, it's common to use a routed port on a multilayer switch. A *routed port* is a physical port on a multilayer switch that has been configured to function like a router's interface. Figure 12.12 shows how SW1's G0/1 port can be used as a routed port, providing connectivity to external networks via R1.

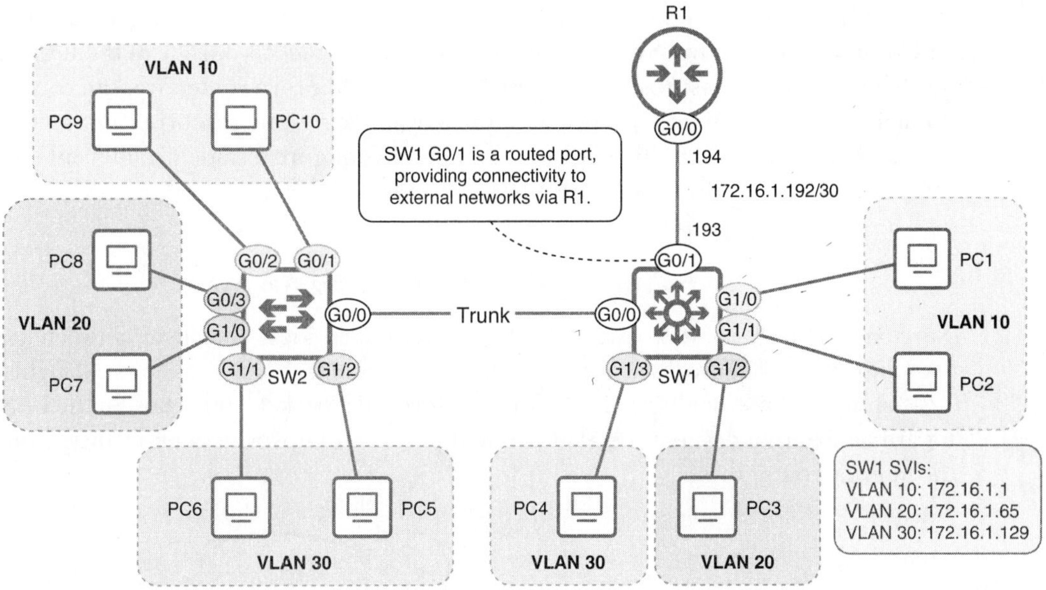

Figure 12.12 SW1, a multilayer switch, uses a routed port (G0/1) to provide connectivity to external networks (via R1, in this case). Like a router interface, SW1 G0/1 is configured with an IP address: 172.16.1.193.

NOTE SW1's icon in figure 12.12 is a new one. Network diagrams typically use an icon like this to represent multilayer switches, differentiating them from Layer 2 switches.

To configure a routed port, use the **no switchport** command in interface configuration mode; then, you can configure an IP address just like on a router's interface. In the following example, I configure SW1 G0/1 as a routed port with an IP address and then check SW1's routing table:

```
SW1(config)# interface g0/1
SW1(config-if)# no switchport
SW1(config-if)# ip address 172.16.1.193 255.255.255.252
SW1(config-if)# do show ip route
. . .
      172.16.0.0/16 is variably subnetted, 8 subnets, 3 masks
C        172.16.1.0/26 is directly connected, Vlan10
L        172.16.1.1/32 is directly connected, Vlan10
C        172.16.1.64/26 is directly connected, Vlan20
L        172.16.1.65/32 is directly connected, Vlan20
C        172.16.1.128/26 is directly connected, Vlan30
L        172.16.1.129/32 is directly connected, Vlan30
```

Makes G0/1 a routed port

Configures G0/1's IP address

```
C        172.16.1.192/30 is directly connected, GigabitEthernet0/1
L        172.16.1.193/32 is directly connected, GigabitEthernet0/1
```

Connected and local routes for G0/1

SW1 G0/1 is now a routed port with an IP address, and SW1 has added connected and local routes for it, but SW1 still isn't able to forward packets outside of the LAN; it needs a route (or routes) to external destinations. Just like on a router, you can configure static routes on a multilayer switch or use a dynamic routing protocol (the topic of part 4 of this volume). In the following example, I configure a static default route on SW1, using R1's IP address as the next hop:

```
SW1(config)# ip route 0.0.0.0 0.0.0.0 172.16.1.194
```

SW1's default route (using R1 as the next hop)

Now that SW1 has a route to external networks, it can provide connectivity between the LAN and external networks, as well as between the subnets/VLANs in the LAN. Figure 12.13 shows the internal logic of how SW1 can forward a packet from a host in the LAN toward an external destination; SW1's routed port (G0/1) provides connectivity from the internal router to R1.

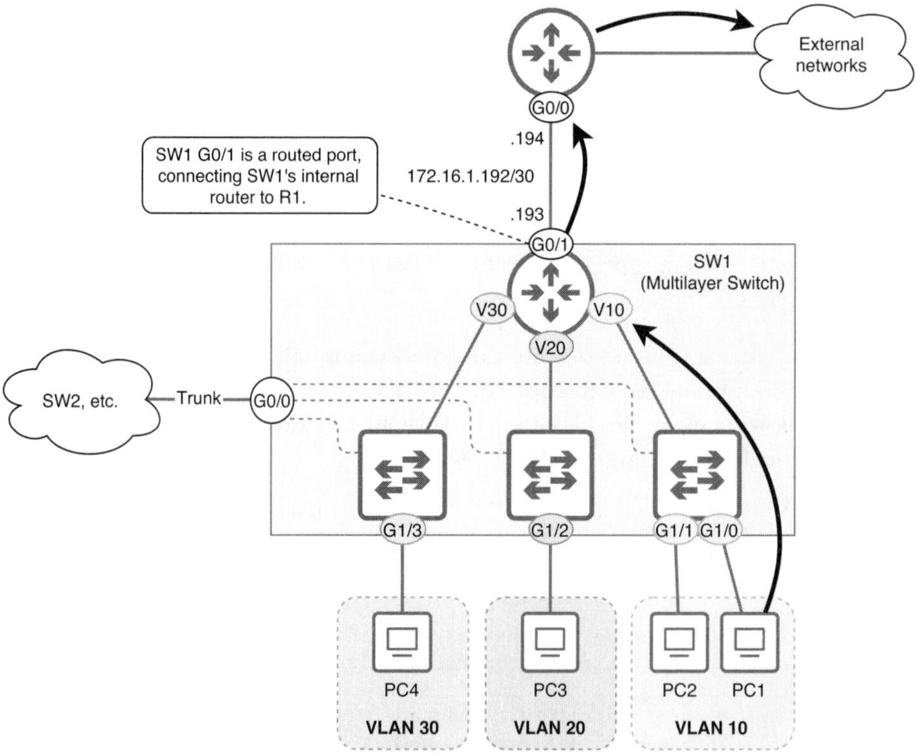

Figure 12.13 A host in the LAN sends a packet to an external destination, routed by SW1. G0/1 is a routed port, connecting SW1's internal router to R1.

Exam scenarios

VLANs are one of the major topics of the CCNA exam, so you can expect at least a few VLAN-related questions on the CCNA exam. The following are a few questions demonstrating how your understanding of VLANs might be tested on the CCNA exam:

1 (multiple choice, multiple answers)
Examine the following configuration of SW1's G0/0 interface:

```
interface GigabitEthernet0/0
 switchport access vlan 5
 switchport trunk native vlan 10
 switchport mode trunk
```

Which of the following statements are true? (select two)

- A SW1 G0/0 is a trunk port.
- B SW1 G0/0 is an access port.
- C SW1 will assign untagged frames received on G0/0 to VLAN 5.
- D SW1 will assign untagged frames received on G0/0 to VLAN 10.

The challenging part of this question is that G0/0 has configurations related both to access ports and trunk ports. The **`switchport access vlan 5`** command implies that SW1 will assign untagged frames received on G0/0 to VLAN 5. However, the **`switchport trunk native vlan 10`** command implies that SW1 will assign them to VLAN 10. The key to this question is that the **`switchport mode`** command specifies **`trunk`**, so G0/0 is operating as a trunk port (and A is one of the correct answers). Therefore, the **`switchport access vlan 5`** command will not affect G0/0; it is only significant if G0/0 is operating as an access port. So, the second correct answer is D; SW1 will assign untagged frames received on G0/0 to VLAN 10 (the native VLAN).

2 (drag and drop)
On the left are four statements about the native VLAN and the default VLAN. Drag the statements to the default VLAN or native VLAN on the right. Each statement can only be used once.

(A) Related to access ports	Default VLAN
(B) Related to trunk ports	
(C) VLAN 1 by default, and can be changed	Native VLAN
(D) VLAN 1 by default, and cannot be changed	

The correct answers are A/D for the default VLAN and B/C for the native VLAN. As mentioned in the note in section 12.3.2, the default VLAN and native VLAN are often confused, so make sure you can differentiate between the two for the exam.

3 (lab simulation)

A lab simulation might provide you with a network diagram and ask you to configure access ports and trunk ports as appropriate. Remember the basic configurations of each:

(continued)

- *Access ports*—**switchport mode access**, **switchport access vlan** *vlan-id*
- *Trunk ports*—**switchport trunk encapsulation dot1q** (if needed), **switchport mode trunk**, **switchport trunk allowed vlan** *vlans*

Summary

- *Network segmentation* is the process of dividing a network into smaller parts and provides network security and performance benefits. Subnets can be used to segment a network at Layer 3, and *virtual LANs* (VLANs) can be used to segment a network at Layer 2.
- VLANs divide a broadcast domain (LAN) into multiple broadcast domains by dividing a physical switch into multiple virtual switches. Frames sent by a host in one VLAN cannot be forwarded/flooded to hosts in another VLAN.
- Although there can be multiple subnets per VLAN, for the CCNA exam, you can assume a one-to-one relationship (one subnet per VLAN).
- Use the **show vlan brief** command to view the VLANs that exist on the switch and which ports are in each VLAN.
- VLANs 1 and 1002–1005 exist by default and cannot be deleted. VLAN 1 is the *default VLAN*—the VLAN that all ports are in by default. VLANS 1002–1005 are reserved for use by *FDDI* and *Token Ring*—two legacy Data Link Layer technologies.
- Use the **vlan** *vlan-id* command to create a VLAN, and then the **name** *vlan-name* command to give the VLAN an optional name (the default name is *VLANxxxx*). You can use the **shutdown** command to temporarily disable the VLAN or **no vlan** *vlan-id* to delete the VLAN.
- An *access port* is a switch port that sends and receives traffic in a single VLAN. Access ports are also called *untagged ports* because they send and receive frames without VLAN tags.
- Use the **switchport mode access** command to configure a port in access mode. Then, use the **switchport access vlan** *vlan-id* command to configure which VLAN the port belongs to. If you assign a port to a VLAN that doesn't exist yet on the switch, the switch will automatically create the VLAN.
- A *trunk port* is a switch port that sends and receives traffic in multiple VLANs. Trunk ports differentiate between VLANs by adding a VLAN tag to each frame using the *IEEE 802.1Q* protocol.
- The 802.1Q tag is 4 bytes in length and is added between the Source and EtherType fields of the Ethernet header. The main fields of the 802.1Q tag are TPID and TCI.

- The *Tag Protocol Identifier* (TPID) field always contains the value 0x8100; it is used to identify 802.1Q-tagged frames.
- The *Tag Control Information* (TCI) field consists of three subfields: *Priority Code Point* (PCP) and *Drop Eligible Indicator* (DEI) are used for *Quality of Service* (QoS). The *VLAN Identifier* (VID) field is used to indicate which VLAN the frame is in. The VID field is 12 bits in length, and for that reason, there are 4,096 (2^{12}) VLANs in total.
- To configure a trunk port, use the **`switchport mode trunk`** command. If the switch supports both 802.1Q and ISL, you must use the **`switchport trunk encapsulation dot1q`** command first; if the switch only supports 802.1Q, this command is not needed.
- Use the **`show interfaces trunk`** command to verify trunk ports, including information such as which VLANs are allowed on each trunk port.
- By default, all VLANs are allowed on a trunk port, meaning it can forward and receive frames in all VLANs.
- Use the **`switchport trunk allowed vlan`** command to specify the VLANs allowed on a trunk. You can specify the list of VLANs or use the keywords **`add`**, **`all`**, **`except`**, **`none`**, or **`remove`**.
- The *native VLAN* is the VLAN that is untagged on a trunk port. Untagged frames received on a trunk port are assigned to the native VLAN, and frames in the native VLAN are forwarded untagged. The native VLAN of a trunk port is VLAN 1 by default.
- The native VLAN can be configured with the **`switchport trunk native vlan`** *`vlan-id`* command. The command is configured per port, so each port on a switch can have a different native VLAN, but make sure the native VLAN matches on both sides of a trunk connection.
- It is recommended that you configure an unused VLAN (that is not the default of VLAN 1) as the native VLAN, which is equivalent to disabling it.
- *Inter-VLAN routing* is the process of routing between subnets in a LAN that is segmented using VLANs. Inter-VLAN routing can be performed by an external router or by a *multilayer switch* (a switch that has routing capabilities).
- A router can perform inter-VLAN routing by using a separate interface per subnet/VLAN or by *router on a stick* (ROAS), in which a trunk link connects the router and switch.
- ROAS uses virtual subinterfaces. To configure a subinterface, use the **`interface`** command and add a period and a number to identify the subinterface to the end of the interface name (i.e., **`interface g0/0.10`**). The subinterface identifier does not have to match the VLAN ID.
- Configure a subinterface's VLAN with the **`encapsulation dot1q`** *`vlan-id`* command. Then, configure an IP address in the same manner as on a router.

- If using the native VLAN over the ROAS trunk, use the **encapsulation dot1q** *vlan-id* **native** command on the native VLAN's subinterface. Or, configure the native VLAN's IP address on the physical interface (the **encapsulation dot1q** command is not necessary on the physical interface).
- A multilayer switch can also be called a *Layer 3 switch* (in contrast to a standard *Layer 2 switch*). A multilayer switch uses *switch virtual interfaces* (SVIs) to perform inter-VLAN routing. Each SVI is associated with a VLAN and can be configured with the **interface vlan** *vlan-id* command.
- Use the **ip routing** command on a multilayer switch to allow the switch to route packets.
- A physical port on a multilayer switch can be configured as a *routed port*, which functions like a router interface. Use the **no switchport** command to convert a switch port to a routed port, and then configure an IP address on it.
- To forward packets to external destinations, multilayer switches need routes, just like routers—either static routes or routes learned via a dynamic routing protocol (such as OSPF).

13 Dynamic Trunking Protocol and VLAN Trunking Protocol

This chapter covers

- Switch port administrative and operational modes
- How switches use Dynamic Trunking Protocol to determine a port's operational mode
- How to use VLAN Trunking Protocol to automate VLAN administration

In this chapter, we will look at two protocols related to VLANs, the topic of the previous chapter. Dynamic Trunking Protocol (DTP) and VLAN Trunking Protocol (VTP) are both auxiliary protocols designed to streamline VLAN configuration and management on Cisco switches. As in chapter 12, in this chapter, we will cover the following two exam topics:

- 2.1 Configure and verify VLANs (normal range) spanning multiple switches
- 2.2 Configure and verify interswitch connectivity

Before Cisco's major overhaul of the CCNA exam topics in 2020, both DTP and VTP were listed as exam topics. Their removal in 2020 led some to believe that DTP and VTP would not be covered on the CCNA exam, but this is a misunderstanding; although the exam topics list no longer explicitly names DTP and VTP, they both play important roles in the configuration of VLANs and interswitch connectivity on Cisco switches, and you are expected to know them for the CCNA exam.

13.1 Dynamic Trunking Protocol

Dynamic Trunking Protocol (DTP) is a Cisco-proprietary protocol that allows Cisco switches to automatically determine the operational mode of their ports. A port's *operational mode* is the mode the port operates in (access or trunk), as opposed to the *administrative mode,* which is the port's configured mode (using the **`switchport mode`** command). If a switchport is manually configured as an access port or trunk port, the port's administrative and operational modes will be identical:

- A port configured with **`switchport mode access`** (administrative mode) will always operate as an access port (operational mode).
- A port configured with **`switchport mode trunk`** (administrative mode) will always operate as a trunk port (operational mode).

When using DTP, neighboring switches send each other DTP messages, informing each other of their port's administrative mode. Depending on the combination of administrative modes of the connected ports, the switches decide the appropriate operational mode for their ports.

NOTE Only switches use DTP; to make a switch port connected to a router operate as a trunk port (when using router on a stick), you must manually configure trunk mode on the port.

DTP was developed to streamline the deployment of switches by requiring less manual configuration of port modes, but it was found to be a security vulnerability (more on that later in this chapter), so today it is generally considered best practice to disable DTP on switch ports. However, DTP is active on Cisco switches by default, so it's important to understand how it works, even if only to know how to disable it.

NOTE As a Cisco-proprietary protocol, DTP only works on Cisco switches. If you want your Cisco switch to have a trunk connection with a switch from another vendor, you must manually configure trunk mode with **`switchport mode trunk`**.

13.1.1 DTP negotiation

In chapter 12, we manually configured access and trunk ports. However, there are two other options for the **`switchport mode`** command: **`switchport mode dynamic auto`** and **`switchport mode dynamic desirable`**. Rather than explicitly specifying which mode the port should operate in, these administrative modes tell the switch to use DTP to determine the port's operational mode. By default, a port in one of these modes will operate as an access port, but if the connected switches both agree, a trunk link will be formed.

Figure 13.1 shows two Cisco switches connected by their G0/0 ports, each with an administrative mode of **`dynamic auto`**. The result is an access link; the switches agree that they will not form a trunk. This process of exchanging DTP messages and agreeing upon an operational mode is called *DTP negotiation.*

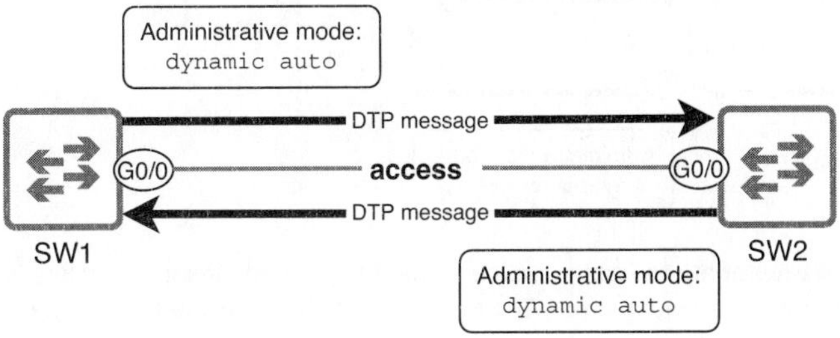

Figure 13.1 Two connected switches negotiate their ports' operational mode by sending DTP messages. Both ports use the default administrative mode of `dynamic auto`, resulting in an access link; SW1 G0/0 and SW2 G0/0 operate as access ports.

> **NOTE** **`dynamic auto`** is the default administrative mode for all Cisco switch ports, so by default, two Cisco switches that are connected will not form a trunk; the connection will remain in access mode.

To view a port's administrative and operational modes, use the **`show interfaces`** *`interface-name`* **`switchport`** command, as in the following example. Note that the operational mode is `static access`; this means it is an access port that is assigned to a specific VLAN (the VLAN specified in the **`switchport access vlan`** command, or the default of VLAN 1). There are also *dynamic access* ports, in which the switch decides the port's VLAN based on the connected device, but dynamic access ports are beyond the scope of the CCNA:

```
SW1# show interfaces g0/0 switchport
Name: Gig0/0
Switchport: Enabled
Administrative Mode: dynamic auto
Operational Mode: static access
. . .
```

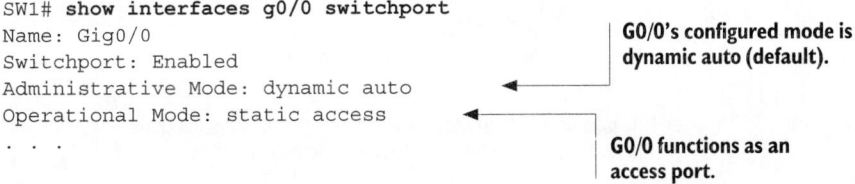

G0/0's configured mode is dynamic auto (default).

G0/0 functions as an access port.

Although a port with administrative mode **`dynamic auto`** uses DTP to negotiate its operational mode, it does not actively try to form a trunk link with its neighbor; that's why two connected ports in **`dynamic auto`** mode do not form a trunk, as we saw in figure 13.1.

If we change the administrative mode of SW1 G0/0 to **`dynamic desirable`**, the result is different; a port in **`dynamic desirable`** mode actively attempts to form a trunk. Figure 13.2 shows the result: a trunk link between SW1 and SW2.

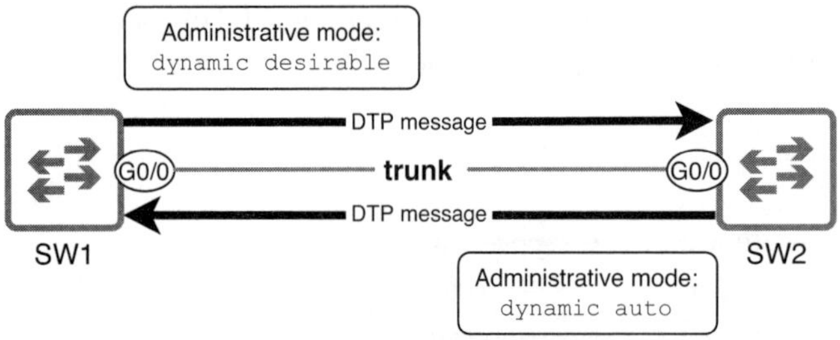

Figure 13.2 SW1 and SW2 negotiate to form a trunk link. SW1 G0/0's administrative mode is `dynamic desirable`, and SW2 G0/0's is `dynamic auto`. The result is an operational mode of `trunk`.

As shown in the following example, SW1 G0/0's operational mode is now `trunk`:

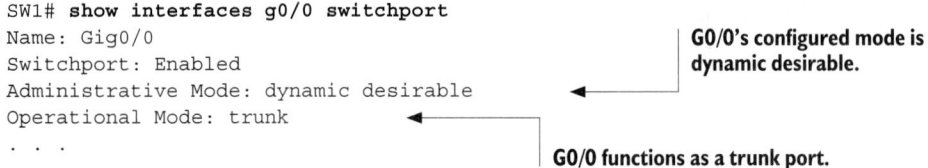

```
SW1# show interfaces g0/0 switchport
Name: Gig0/0
Switchport: Enabled
Administrative Mode: dynamic desirable
Operational Mode: trunk
. . .
```


Table 13.1 lists the four administrative modes that can be configured with the **`switchport mode`** command and gives a brief description of each.

Table 13.1 Switch port administrative modes

Mode	Description	Port sends DTP messages?
`access`	Manually configures an access port. Operational mode will always be access.	No
`trunk`	Manually configures a trunk port. Operational mode will always be trunk.	Yes
`dynamic auto`	The port uses DTP to negotiate its operational mode but does not actively try to form a trunk with its neighbor. Will form a trunk if connected to a port in trunk or dynamic desirable mode.	Yes
`dynamic desirable`	The port uses DTP to negotiate its operational mode and actively tries to form a trunk with its neighbor. Will form a trunk if connected to a port in trunk, dynamic auto, or dynamic desirable mode.	Yes

NOTE Although administrative mode **`trunk`** manually configures a trunk port, the port will still send DTP messages; the purpose is to ensure that the neighboring port also operates in trunk mode (if the neighbor is in **`dynamic auto`** or **`dynamic desirable`** mode).

For the CCNA exam, it's important to understand the resulting operational mode of each combination of administrative modes; table 13.2 shows the results of each combination. Note that `access` + `trunk` is not a valid combination; either the switches will detect the mismatch and block the link, or the traffic that passes through the link will be limited to only the trunk port's native VLAN and the access port's VLAN (because both are untagged). Either way, don't use this combination!

Table 13.2 Switch port administrative modes

Administrative modes	access	trunk	dynamic desirable	dynamic auto
Access	access	invalid	access	access
Trunk	invalid	trunk	trunk	trunk
Dynamic desirable	access	trunk	trunk	trunk
Dynamic auto	access	trunk	trunk	access

EXAM TIP Make sure that you can identify the operational mode that results from each combination of administrative modes; it's a potential exam question.

Trunk encapsulation negotiation

In addition to negotiating a port's operational mode, DTP can also negotiate which protocol a port uses to tag frames if it becomes a trunk: 802.1Q or ISL. Of course, this only applies to switches that support both 802.1Q and ISL. As I mentioned in chapter 12, modern Cisco switches only support 802.1Q, so I wouldn't expect any questions related to ISL on the CCNA exam.

If a switch supports both protocols, its default setting is `switchport trunk encapsulation negotiate`. If both switches are using `negotiate`, the result will be ISL. If one side specifies a protocol (`dot1q` or `isl`), the side using `negotiate` will agree to use the same encapsulation. An encapsulation mismatch (`dot1q` on one side, `isl` on the other) is a misconfiguration. If you encounter a switch that supports both 802.1Q and ISL, you should manually configure 802.1Q with `switchport trunk encapsulation dot1q`, as we covered in chapter 12.

13.1.2 *Disabling DTP*

As I mentioned previously, DTP was developed to streamline the deployment of switches by allowing them to automatically determine the operational status of the ports. However, it is also a security vulnerability; an attacker can take advantage of DTP to form a trunk link with a switch, gaining access to all VLANs in the LAN.

In the default administrative mode of `dynamic auto`, a switch port connected to an end host will operate in access mode; end hosts don't use DTP, so they can't negotiate a trunk. This means that the end host will have access only to a single VLAN, and communication between that VLAN and other VLANs can be controlled by configuring security policies on the router.

However, if a malicious user uses something like *Yersinia* (a hacking tool) to send DTP messages out of their PC, they can negotiate to form a trunk link with the switch port, giving them access to all VLANs in the LAN, presenting a security threat. Figure 13.3 depicts an attacker who has used DTP to negotiate a trunk with a switch.

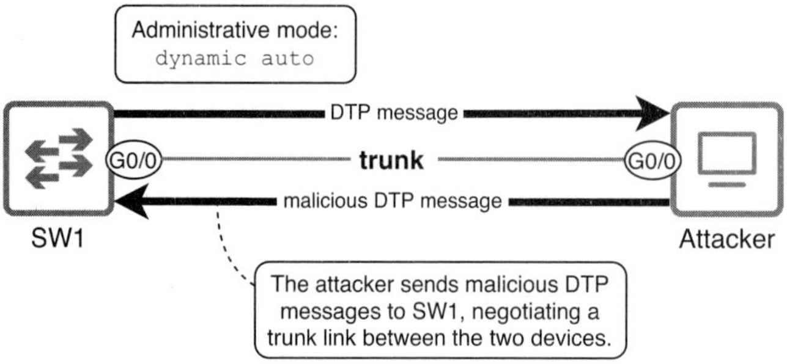

Figure 13.3 An attacker sends malicious DTP messages to SW1 to form a trunk. This gives the attacker access to all VLANs in the LAN, presenting a security threat.

Because of the security implications and to reduce the amount of unnecessary traffic (DTP messages) being sent in the LAN, it is recommended that you disable DTP. There are two ways to do this:

- Manually configure the port as an access port with **`switchport mode access`**.
- Explicitly disable DTP with **`switchport nonegotiate`**.

In the following example, I use **`show interfaces g0/0 switchport`**. The output states `Negotiation of Trunking: On`; this means the port is sending DTP messages. I then configure G0/0 as an access port and check again; notice that trunk negotiation is now `Off`:

```
SW1# show interfaces g0/0 switchport
Name: Gi0/0
Switchport: Enabled
Administrative Mode: dynamic auto          <-- G0/0's administrative mode is dynamic auto.
Operational Mode: static access
. . .
Negotiation of Trunking: On                <-- DTP is enabled.
. . .
SW1# configure terminal
SW1(config)# interface g0/0                    | Configures G0/0 as
SW1(config-if)# switchport mode access         | an access port
SW1(config-if)# do show interfaces g0/0 switchport
Name: Gi0/0
Switchport: Enabled
```

```
Administrative Mode: static access
Operational Mode: static access
. . .
Negotiation of Trunking: Off              <------ DTP is disabled.
. . .
```

As demonstrated in the previous example, manually configuring access mode disables DTP on the port; it won't send DTP messages. However, the second method can be used to ensure that the port never sends DTP messages, regardless of its current mode (access or trunk). In the following example, I configure G0/0 as a trunk port and confirm that negotiation is `On`. I then use **`switchport nonegotiate`** to disable DTP and confirm again:

```
SW1(config)# interface g0/0                          | Configures G0/0 as
SW1(config-if)# switchport mode trunk                | a trunk port
SW1(config-if)# do show interfaces g0/0 switchport
Name: Gi0/0
Switchport: Enabled
Administrative Mode: trunk
Operational Mode: trunk
. . .
Negotiation of Trunking: On              <------ DTP is enabled.
. . .
SW1(config-if)# switchport nonegotiate          <------ Disables DTP
SW1(config-if)# do show interfaces g0/0 switchport
Name: Gi0/0
Switchport: Enabled
Administrative Mode: trunk
Operational Mode: trunk
. . .
Negotiation of Trunking: Off              <------ DTP is disabled.
. . .
```

Even if you manually configure a port in access mode, it is recommended that you also use **`switchport nonegotiate`** to ensure that DTP messages are never sent, even if you later configure the port in trunk mode.

> **EXAM TIP** Remember that as a security best practice, use **`switchport nonegotiate`** to disable DTP on switch ports.

13.2 VLAN Trunking Protocol

VLAN Trunking Protocol (VTP) is another Cisco-proprietary protocol that plays a role in VLAN configuration on Cisco switches. VTP allows switches to automatically synchronize their *VLAN database*, the file that stores information about the VLANs that exist on the switch. Using VTP, switches in a LAN send each other messages with information about the VLANs in their VLAN database, and the switches synchronize their database according to the latest version of the database.

NOTE The VLAN database is stored in a file called *vlan.dat* in flash memory; use the **dir flash:** or **show flash:** commands to view the contents of flash memory. You can use **show vlan brief** to view the contents of the VLAN database (as we covered in chapter 12).

Figure 13.4 demonstrates why it's important for switches in a LAN to have the same VLANs in their VLAN database; PC1 sends a frame to PC2, but SW2 drops the frame because VLAN 4 isn't in SW2's VLAN database.

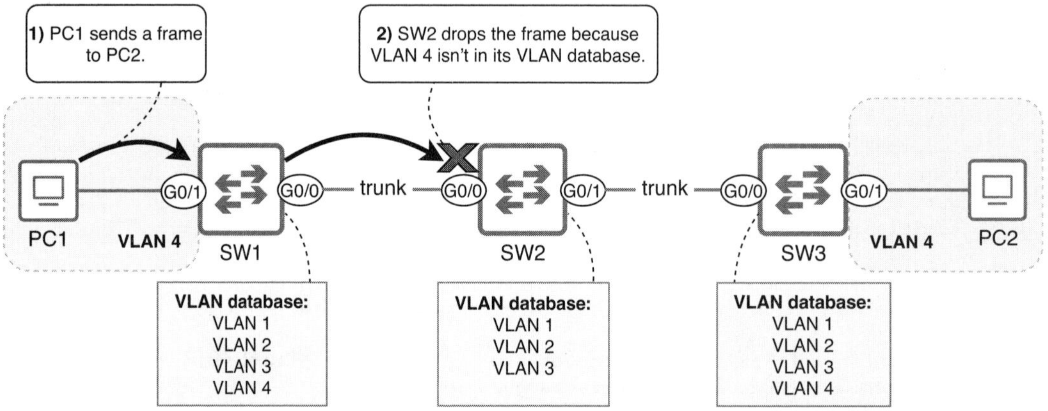

Figure 13.4 A missing VLAN on SW2 prevents PC1 from communicating with PC2. 1) PC1 sends a frame to PC2. 2) SW2 drops the frame because VLAN 4 isn't in its VLAN database.

VTP can ensure that all VLANs exist on all switches in the LAN. In a small LAN like figure 13.4, VTP might not seem necessary; manually creating VLAN 4 on SW2 wouldn't be such a hassle. However, in a large LAN with dozens of switches, VTP can both save time and reduce human error by propagating VLAN changes without requiring manual configuration on every single switch.

NOTE Like DTP, VTP is a Cisco-proprietary protocol that only runs on Cisco switches; it cannot be used to synchronize VLANs with another vendor's switches.

13.2.1 VTP synchronization

Figure 13.5 shows how VLANs created on SW1 can be propagated to SW2 and SW3 using VTP. Starting with only VLAN 1, I created VLANs 2, 3, and 4 on SW1. This causes SW1 to increment the VTP *revision number*—a number that keeps track of the latest version of the VLAN database. The revision number starts at 0 and is updated each time there is a change to the VLAN database, such as a VLAN being created, deleted, or renamed. This causes SW1 to send VTP messages to SW2 and SW3, informing them of the updates to the VLAN database. SW2 and SW3 then update their VLAN databases to match SW1.

NOTE VLANs 1002 to 1005 also exist by default on Cisco switches and cannot be removed. I won't mention them in this chapter because they are reserved for legacy technologies (Token Ring and FDDI) that are not used in modern networks, as mentioned in chapter 12.

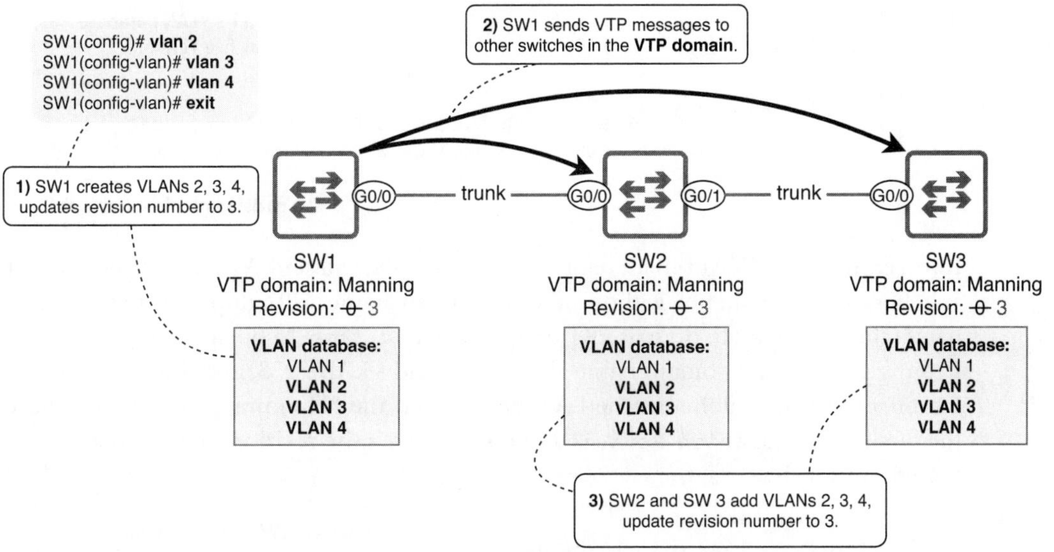

Figure 13.5 VLANs created on SW1 are propagated to other switches in the VTP domain "Manning." (1) SW1 creates VLANs 2, 3, and 4, updating its revision number to 3 (incrementing by 1 each time it creates a VLAN). (2) SW1 sends VTP messages to other switches in the VTP domain. (3) SW2 and SW3 add VLANs 2, 3, and 4 to their VLAN databases, updating their revision number to match SW1's.

NOTE VTP messages are only sent out of trunk ports, not access ports.

Figure 13.5 also introduced the concept of the *VTP domain*—the group of switches in a LAN that all share the same VTP domain name. By default, switches do not have a VTP domain name; in this state, VTP is not active. You can configure VLANs on the device, but it will not send VTP messages to other switches in the LAN. The following example shows the output of **`show vtp status`**—a useful command to view the current state of VTP on the switch—before configuring VTP or any VLANs on SW1. We will cover the relevant fields of this output throughout the rest of this chapter.

NOTE A switch that does not have a VTP domain name is said to be in domain *NULL*.

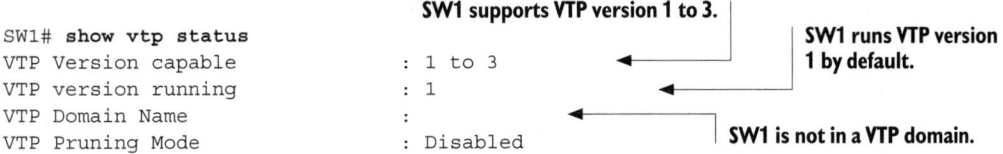

```
SW1# show vtp status
VTP Version capable             : 1 to 3
VTP version running             : 1
VTP Domain Name                 :
VTP Pruning Mode                : Disabled
```

SW1 supports VTP version 1 to 3.

SW1 runs VTP version 1 by default.

SW1 is not in a VTP domain.

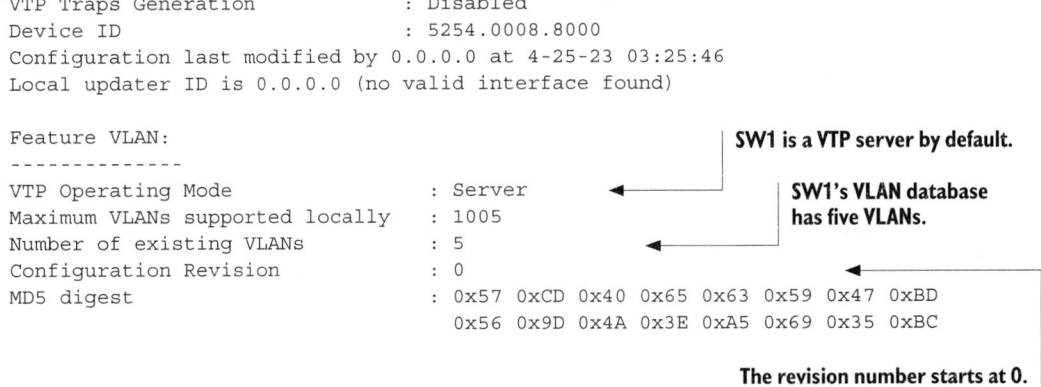

```
VTP Traps Generation              : Disabled
Device ID                         : 5254.0008.8000
Configuration last modified by 0.0.0.0 at 4-25-23 03:25:46
Local updater ID is 0.0.0.0 (no valid interface found)

Feature VLAN:
--------------
VTP Operating Mode                  : Server
Maximum VLANs supported locally     : 1005
Number of existing VLANs            : 5
Configuration Revision              : 0
MD5 digest                          : 0x57 0xCD 0x40 0x65 0x63 0x59 0x47 0xBD
                                      0x56 0x9D 0x4A 0x3E 0xA5 0x69 0x35 0xBC
```

SW1 is a VTP server by default. (VTP Operating Mode)

SW1's VLAN database has five VLANs. (Number of existing VLANs)

The revision number starts at 0. (Configuration Revision)

If you configure a VTP domain name on one switch, it will send VTP messages to other switches, and all switches without a VTP domain name will adopt the new domain name; the command to do so is **`vtp domain`** *`domain-name`*. In the following examples, I configure the VTP domain name "Manning" and VLANs 2, 3, and 4 on SW1. Then, I confirm that all switches in the LAN have joined the "Manning" domain and share the same `Configuration Revision` number—this is the revision number that I mentioned previously:

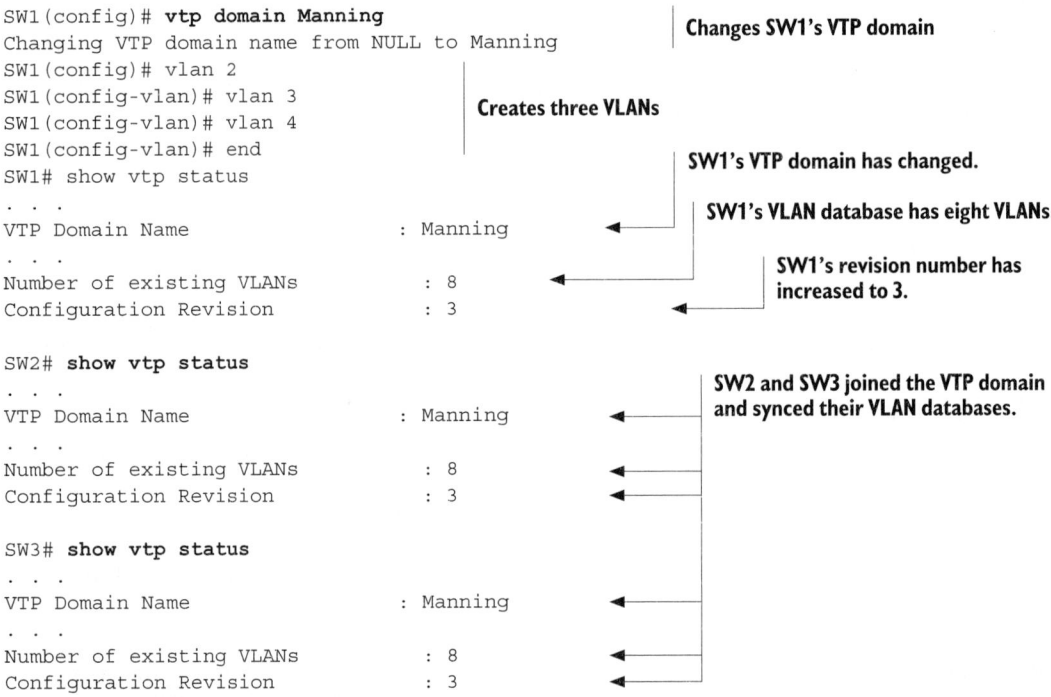

```
SW1(config)# vtp domain Manning
Changing VTP domain name from NULL to Manning
SW1(config)# vlan 2
SW1(config-vlan)# vlan 3
SW1(config-vlan)# vlan 4
SW1(config-vlan)# end
SW1# show vtp status
. . .
VTP Domain Name                   : Manning
. . .
Number of existing VLANs            : 8
Configuration Revision              : 3

SW2# show vtp status
. . .
VTP Domain Name                   : Manning
. . .
Number of existing VLANs            : 8
Configuration Revision              : 3

SW3# show vtp status
. . .
VTP Domain Name                   : Manning
. . .
Number of existing VLANs            : 8
Configuration Revision              : 3
```

Changes SW1's VTP domain (vtp domain Manning)

Creates three VLANs (vlan 2, vlan 3, vlan 4)

SW1's VTP domain has changed.

SW1's VLAN database has eight VLANs.

SW1's revision number has increased to 3.

SW2 and SW3 joined the VTP domain and synced their VLAN databases.

Because the revision number is used to keep track of the latest version of the VLAN database, switches will only synchronize their VLAN database if they receive a VTP message from a switch with a higher revision number, not a lower one; a VTP message with a lower (or equal) revision number is considered old information.

13.2.2 VTP modes

A Cisco switch can operate in one of four VTP modes: server, client, transparent, and off, each mode with its own characteristics. The VTP mode can be configured with the **`vtp mode`** *`mode`* command. Switches in server mode and client mode actively participate in VTP and synchronize their VLAN databases to match each other, whereas switches in transparent mode and off mode do not. Table 13.3 summarizes each mode.

Table 13.3 VTP modes

Mode	Description
Server	This is the default mode. The switch can create/modify/delete VLANs. It will advertise changes to its VLAN database and synchronize its VLAN database upon receiving an advertisement with a higher revision number.
Client	The switch cannot create/modify/delete VLANs but otherwise behaves the same as a server.
Transparent	The switch can create/modify/delete VLANs, but it will not advertise changes to its own VLAN database and will not synchronize its VLAN database with others. The switch does not directly participate in the VTP domain, but it will forward VTP messages between switches in the same domain.
Off	The switch can create/modify/delete VLANs, but it will not advertise changes to its own VLAN database and will not synchronize its VLAN database with others. The switch does not participate in VTP at all.

Switches are in VTP *server* mode by default. In this mode, a switch can create, modify (ie. rename), and delete VLANs, and those changes will be advertised to other switches in the domain. A VTP server will also synchronize its own VLAN database if it receives a VTP message with a higher revision number.

VTP *client* mode is similar to server mode, except for one difference: the switch cannot create/modify/delete VLANs. I demonstrate this in the following example by configuring SW3 VTP client mode and then attempting to create VLAN 5:

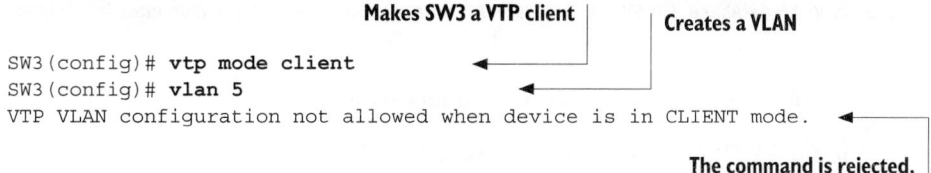

```
SW3(config)# vtp mode client          <- Makes SW3 a VTP client
SW3(config)# vlan 5                   <- Creates a VLAN
VTP VLAN configuration not allowed when device is in CLIENT mode.   <- The command is rejected.
```

NOTE Cisco recommends that all switches in the domain be in server mode if they have sufficient memory resources. Any modern switch should have sufficient resources to store VLAN information, so you can safely leave all switches in VTP server mode.

In a VTP domain, in most cases, all switches will be in server (or client) mode; they are the modes that take advantage of VTP's VLAN database synchronization. *Transparent* mode prevents the switch from synchronizing its VLAN database with other switches. You can create, modify, and delete VLANs on the switch, but it will not advertise those changes to other switches. However, the switch will forward VTP messages between switches in the same domain. Transparent mode should be used in cases where a switch needs to be managed independently from other switches, without interrupting VTP's operation on the rest of the switches in the LAN. Figure 13.6 demonstrates how VTP transparent mode works; SW2 has a VLAN database separate from SW1 and SW3 but forwards SW1's VTP messages to SW3.

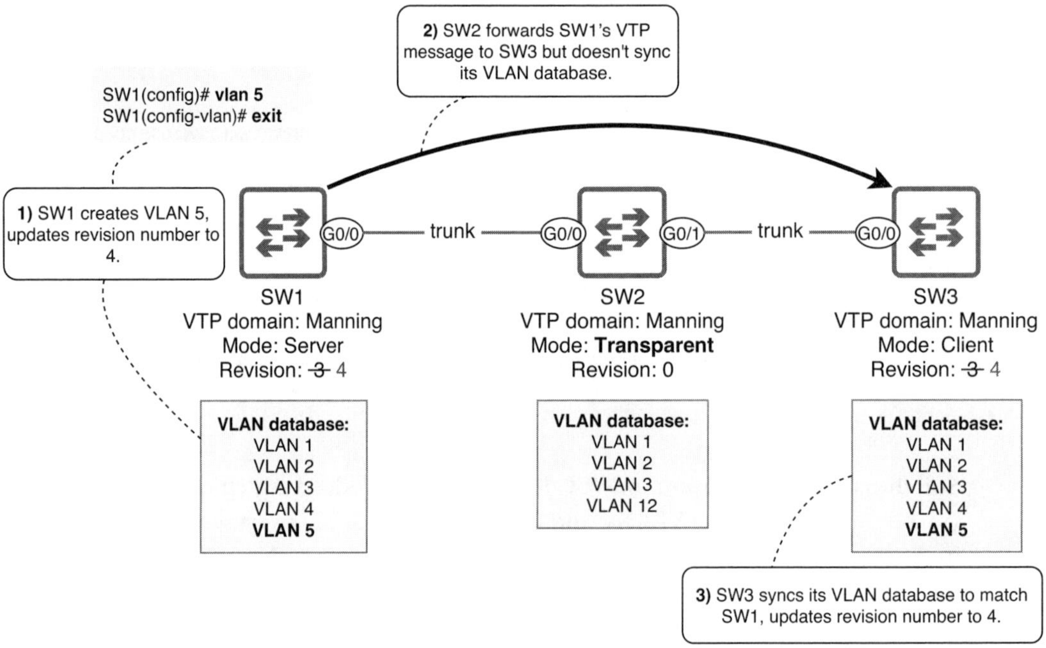

Figure 13.6 SW2, in transparent mode, forwards VTP messages but does not synchronize its VLAN database. (1) SW1 creates VLAN 5 and updates its revision number. (2) SW2 forwards SW1's VTP messages to SW3 but doesn't synchronize its VLAN database. (3) SW3 syncs its VLAN database to match SW1 and updates its revision number.

> **NOTE** A switch in VTP transparent mode will always have revision number 0.

The final VTP mode is *off*, which disables VTP on the switch. Like transparent mode, the switch won't synchronize its VLAN database with other switches, but it also won't forward VTP messages between switches using VTP. If VTP is not being used in the LAN, you should configure `vtp mode off` to disable VTP on all switches.

13.2.3 VTP versions

You may have noticed the following lines when I showed the complete output of **show vtp status** in section 13.2.1:

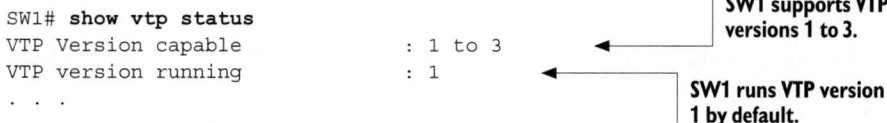

```
SW1# show vtp status
VTP Version capable                : 1 to 3
VTP version running                : 1
. . .
```

SW1 supports VTP versions 1 to 3.

SW1 runs VTP version 1 by default.

There are three different versions of VTP available, and version 1 is the default. You can configure the VTP version with the **vtp version** *version* command. Versions 1 and 2 are very similar; one difference is that version 2 supports *Token Ring*, which is not relevant to modern networks, so there isn't much reason to use version 2 over version 1.

Version 3, on the other hand, brings various improvements over the previous two versions and should always be preferred if using VTP. Let's look at a few of those improvements that are relevant to the CCNA. We already covered one of the improvements: off mode. Before version 3, VTP only had three modes: server, client, and transparent. There was no way to actually disable VTP on a switch; the closest thing was to configure all switches in transparent mode.

> **NOTE** Although off mode was added in VTP version 3, switches that support version 3 can use off mode even if they are running version 1 or 2.

Now let's cover two other significant changes brought by VTP version 3: the primary server and extended-range VLAN support.

The primary server

In VTP version 3, only one switch in the VTP domain can create, modify, and delete VLANs: the *primary server*. Other VTP servers (now called *secondary servers*) are no different than VTP clients, except that you can make a secondary server become the primary server with the command **vtp primary** in privileged EXEC mode.

> **NOTE** Although most VTP commands are global config mode commands, the **vtp primary** command is a privileged EXEC mode command.

In the following example, I enable VTP version 3 on SW1 and attempt to create VLAN 6, which fails. I then use the **vtp primary** command to make SW1 the primary server, and I am then able to create VLAN 6:

```
SW1(config)# vtp version 3
SW1(config)# vlan 6
VTP VLAN configuration not allowed when device is not
➥the primary server for vlan database.
SW1(config)# do vtp primary
This system is becoming primary server for feature vlan
No conflicting VTP3 devices found.
Do you want to continue? [confirm]
```

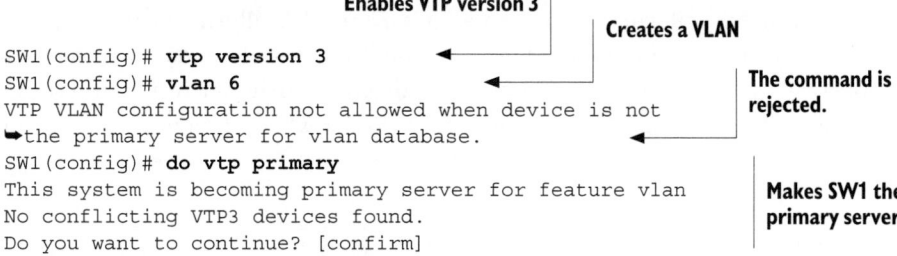

Enables VTP version 3

Creates a VLAN

The command is rejected.

Makes SW1 the primary server

```
SW1(config)# vlan 6
SW1(config-vlan)# exit
```

SW1 can now create VLANs.

> **NOTE** In this example, I executed the **vtp primary** command in global config mode by adding **do** in front of the command. The **vtp primary** command on its own does not work in global config mode; it's a privileged EXEC mode command.

Only one switch in the domain can be the primary server; if you use the **vtp primary** command on a second switch, the first one will revert to being a secondary server. The reason for allowing only one switch in the domain to create, modify, and delete VLANs is to avoid the problem of a newly-connected switch overwriting the VLAN database for the domain—a problem we'll cover in section 13.2.4.

EXTENDED-RANGE VLANS

In old versions of Cisco IOS, only VLANs 1 to 1005 were available for use; these are called the *normal-range VLANs*. In those versions of IOS, VLANs 1006 to 4094 were reserved for internal use by applications on the switch; a user could not create them or assign ports to those VLANs. In a later version of IOS, VLANs 1006 to 4094 were made available and called the *extended-range VLANs*; these days, all Cisco switches support both the normal- and extended-range VLANs.

Even after extended-range VLANs were made available for use, VTP versions 1 and 2 only supported normal-range VLANs. The only way to create extended-range VLANs on switches before VTP version 3 was to configure the switch in transparent mode, rendering it unable to participate in the VTP domain.

VTP version 3 brought the ability to create and propagate extended-range VLANs; the primary server can create extended-range VLANs and propagate them to other switches in the VTP domain.

13.2.4 Is VTP dangerous?

VTP doesn't have a very good reputation—and for good reason: it has caused a lot of network outages over the years. First, let's look at why VTP has a bad reputation, and then we'll see how version 3 fixes the problems with VTP.

The danger of VTP is the potential for a newly connected switch to overwrite the VLAN database of all switches in the domain. Because switches using VTP synchronize their VLAN database to the switch with the highest revision number, if the newly connected switch has a higher revision number (and is in the same domain), all switches in the domain will synchronize to match it. Figure 13.7 illustrates how this can happen: SW4, with a revision number of 50, is connected to a VTP domain with a revision number of 5, causing the other switches to synchronize with it. As a result, hosts in VLANs 10, 20, and 30 will lose network connectivity; those VLANs no longer exist in the network!

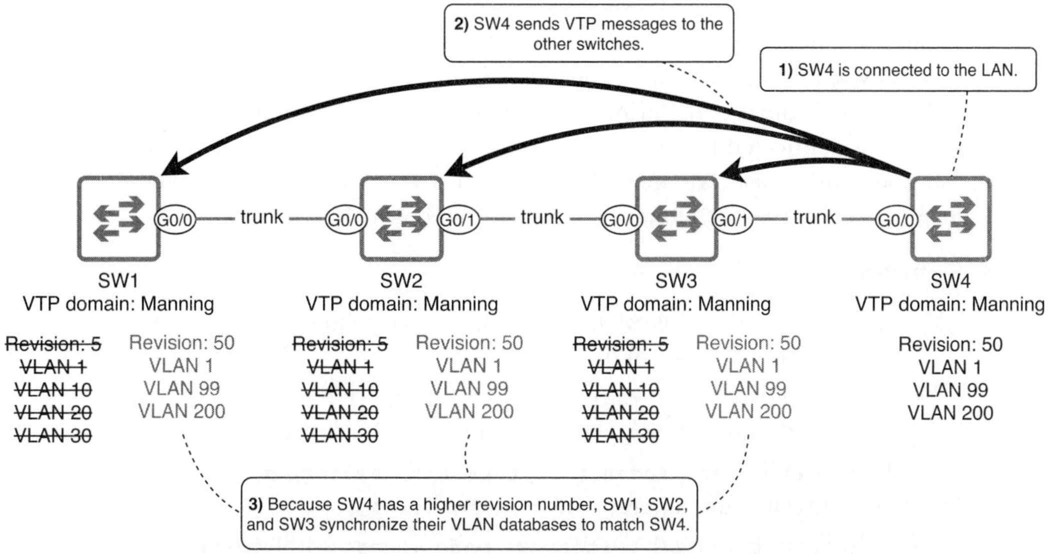

Figure 13.7 SW4 is connected to the network and overwrites the VLAN databases of SW1, SW2, and SW3. (1) SW4 is connected to the LAN. (2) SW4 sends VTP messages to the other switches. (3) Because SW4 has a higher revision number (50 vs. 5), SW1, SW2, and SW3 synchronize their VLAN databases to match SW4. Hosts in VLANs 10, 20, and 30 will be unable to communicate over the network because their VLANs no longer exist.

> **NOTE** You may be wondering, how could a newly added switch have a high revision number in the first place? One possibility is that it was used as a *lab switch* for testing and verifying before being added to the corporate network.

This is a very careless mistake, and standardized procedures for adding new devices to the network would prevent it from happening; one recommended procedure is to reset the VTP revision number of a switch to 0 before connecting it to the network. There are three methods for doing so:

- Change the VTP domain name to a different one and then back to the original name.
- Change the VTP mode to transparent and then back to server or client (only works in versions 1 and 2).
- Change the VTP mode to off and then back to server or client (only works in versions 1 and 2).

> **EXAM TIP** Remember these three methods for resetting the revision number.

Resetting the revision number to 0 eliminates the risk of a newly added switch overwriting the VLAN database of switches in the network. However, it's an unfortunate truth that many corporations have few, if any, standardized procedures for such things, and in any case, people can get careless. As a result, many people have been burned by VTP, giving it a bad reputation.

However, the primary server mechanism in version 3 eliminates this risk; switches will only synchronize to the primary server, so even if a new switch with a higher revision number is connected to the LAN, switches in the LAN won't synchronize to it. When using version 3, there's no need to be afraid of VTP, and it can be a great tool for automating some of the workflows of configuring a network.

Summary

- *Dynamic Trunking Protocol* (DTP) allows Cisco switches to automatically determine the operational mode of their ports.
- A port's *administrative mode* is how it is configured with the **`switchport mode`** command, and its *operational mode* is the mode it operates in (access or trunk).
- Use the **`show interfaces`** *`interface-name`* **`switchport`** command to view the administrative and operational modes of a port.
- A port configured with **`switchport mode access`** will always operate as an access port, and a port configured with **`switchport mode trunk`** will always operate as a trunk port.
- **`switchport mode dynamic auto`** and **`switchport mode dynamic desirable`** configure the port to use DTP to determine its operational mode.
- **`dynamic auto`** mode does not actively try to form a trunk with its neighbor but will form a trunk if the neighbor's mode is **`trunk`** or **`dynamic desirable`**.
- **`dynamic desirable`** mode actively tries to form a trunk with its neighbor and will form a trunk if the neighbor's mode is **`trunk`**, **`dynamic auto`**, or **`dynamic desirable`**.
- DTP is considered a security vulnerability and should be disabled. It is considered best practice to manually configure each port's mode and disable DTP with **`switchport nonegotiate`** on each port.
- *VLAN Trunking Protocol* (VTP) allows Cisco switches to synchronize their VLAN database—the file that stores information about VLANs on the switch (vlan.dat).
- The VTP *revision number* is used to keep track of the latest version of the VLAN database. Each time a change is made, the revision number is incremented by 1. A switch will synchronize to match a higher revision number but not a lower (or equal) one.
- The *VTP domain* is the group of switches in a LAN that share the same VTP domain name; a switch will only synchronize with another switch in the same domain.
- By default, a switch has no domain name; it is said to be in domain *NULL*. In this state, the switch can create/modify/delete VLANs, but it won't send VTP messages to other switches.

- You can configure a switch's VTP domain name with the **`vtp domain`** *`domain-name`* command.
- Use the **`show vtp status`** command to view the current state of VTP on the switch.
- A switch can operate in one of four VTP modes: server, client, transparent, and off. Use the **`vtp mode`** *`mode`* command to configure the mode (server is the default).
- A switch in VTP server mode can create/modify/delete VLANs. It will advertise changes to its VLAN database and synchronize its VLAN database upon receiving an advertisement with a higher revision number.
- A switch in VTP client mode cannot create/modify/delete VLANs but otherwise behaves the same as a server.
- A switch in VTP transparent mode can create/modify/delete VLANs but operates independently from other switches in the VTP domain. It will forward VTP messages between switches in the VTP domain but will not send its own VTP messages or synchronize its VLAN database with other switches.
- A switch in VTP off mode can create/modify/delete VLANs but does not participate in VTP at all.
- There are three versions of VTP: 1, 2, and 3. Versions 1 and 2 are very similar, but version 3 brought many improvements.
- VTP version 3 introduced off mode; before, VTP couldn't be disabled. The closest thing was to configure all switches in VTP transparent mode.
- In VTP version 3, only one switch in the domain can create, modify, and delete VLANs: the primary server. Switches in the domain will only synchronize with the primary server. Other servers are called *secondary servers*; they function the same as VTP clients.
- Use the **`vtp primary`** command (in privileged EXEC mode) on a VTP server to make it the primary server. There can only be one; if you configure **`vtp primary`** on a second server, the first one will revert to being a secondary server.
- VTP version 3 is the only version that supports *extended-range* VLANs (VLANs 1006 to 4094). Versions 1 and 2 only support *normal-range* VLANs (VLANs 1 to 1005).
- One risk of VTP is that a newly connected switch with a higher revision number can overwrite the VLAN database of all switches in the LAN. Version 3 solves this problem because switches will only synchronize with the primary server.
- To reset a switch's VTP revision number to 0, you can change the domain name to a different one and then back to the original. Alternatively, you can change the mode to transparent or off and then back to server or client, but this only works in versions 1 and 2.

14 Spanning Tree Protocol

This chapter covers

- How Layer 2 loops lead to broadcast storms
- How Spanning Tree Protocol detects and prevents Layer 2 loops
- The various STP port roles, states, and timers
- Using PortFast to accelerate STP convergence

This chapter is about *Spanning Tree Protocol* (STP), a protocol that runs on all Cisco switches by default and solves a significant problem in LANs: Layer 2 loops that result in frames looping around the network indefinitely. STP is mentioned in exam topic 2.5: Identify basic operations of Rapid PVST+ Spanning Tree Protocol. Exam topic 2.5 specifically refers to the *rapid* version of the protocol, the topic of chapter 15. However, to understand Rapid STP, we first have to cover the original protocol, and that's what we'll do in this chapter.

14.1 The need for STP

In chapter 7 (IPv4 addressing), we briefly covered the fields of the IPv4 header; one of those is the *Time-to-Live* (TTL) field, which is decremented each time a router forwards a packet. When the value in the TTL field reaches 0, the packet is dropped, preventing packets from looping around the network indefinitely as the result of a misconfiguration; this is called a *routing loop* or *Layer 3 loop*.

The Ethernet header has no such field; if a loop occurs between switches—a Layer 2 loop—there is no mechanism in place to prevent frames from looping around the LAN indefinitely. If there are too many frames looping around the LAN, the switches can be overwhelmed, resulting in a loss of service for all hosts in the LAN.

So, how do Layer 2 loops occur? Whereas Layer 3 loops are the result of a misconfiguration somewhere in the network, Layer 2 loops are inevitable in a LAN where there are multiple paths between any two nodes in the LAN, as a result of the flooding of *BUM traffic* (broadcast, unknown unicast, and multicast) frames.

NOTE I will mention multicast traffic a few times throughout this book's two volumes. For now, just know that multicast frames are flooded by switches by default.

Having multiple paths between hosts is an example of *redundancy* and is a desirable thing in a network. Redundancy means having additional network devices and connections beyond the minimum necessary for communication. By having redundant devices and connections, network service isn't lost if one device or connection fails—there is no *single point of failure*.

However, without something like STP to prevent loops, frames will loop indefinitely in a LAN with redundant connections, as demonstrated in figure 14.1. Any one of the connections between switches in the figure could be removed (e.g., the connection between SW2 and SW3), and the PCs would still be able to communicate with each other; this is an example of redundancy.

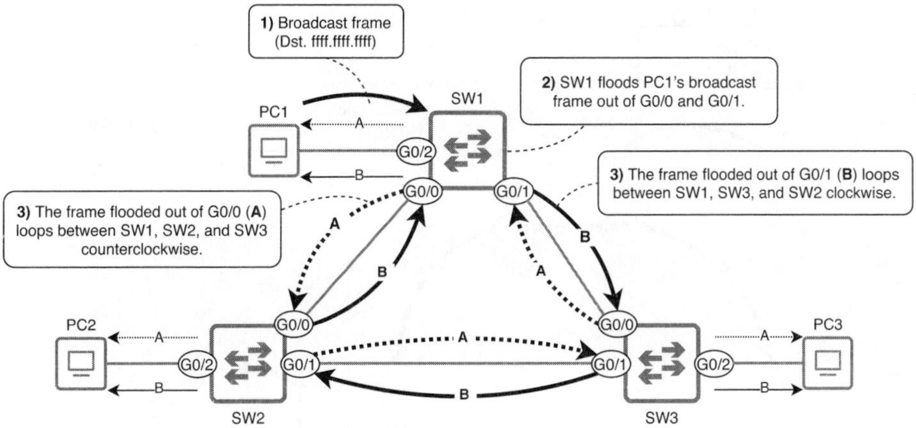

Figure 14.1 PC1 sends a broadcast frame, and SW1 floods it. When SW2 and SW3 receive their copies of the frame, they flood it too, resulting in two loops: counterclockwise (A) and clockwise (B). These frames will loop indefinitely between SW1, SW2, and SW3.

NOTE As the arrows pointing toward the PCs in figure 14.1 indicate, SW1, SW2, and SW3 will also flood the looping frames toward connected end hosts, potentially overwhelming them by requiring the hosts to process the looping frames repeatedly.

There are two main problems caused by Layer 2 loops. First, if enough looping frames accumulate in the network, the result is a *broadcast storm*, consuming so many network resources (CPU resources on the devices or bandwidth of the links) that the network is rendered unusable. PCs and other end hosts connected to the switches also receive the same frames repeatedly, which could overwhelm their available resources too.

The second problem is *MAC address flapping*—when a switch learns the same MAC address repeatedly on separate ports. Using the example in figure 14.1, when SW1 first receives PC1's broadcast frame, it learns PC1's MAC address on the G0/2 port. However, when looped Frame A arrives back on G0/1, it learns PC1's MAC address on that port, and the same applies when looped Frame B arrives back on G0/0. SW1 will constantly update the entry for PC1's MAC address in its MAC address table between multiple ports, resulting in PC1 being unable to receive frames; SW1 doesn't know which port PC1 is actually connected to.

A Layer 2 loop can bring down a LAN in a matter of seconds (depending on the amount of BUM traffic), so it's absolutely essential to avoid Layer 2 loops. That's the role of STP.

14.2 How STP works

STP can be summarized in one sentence: it prevents Layer 2 loops by blocking redundant connections, leaving only a single active path between any two nodes in a LAN. Figure 14.2 shows an example: the link between SW2 and SW3 is disabled, preventing a Layer 2 loop from occurring.

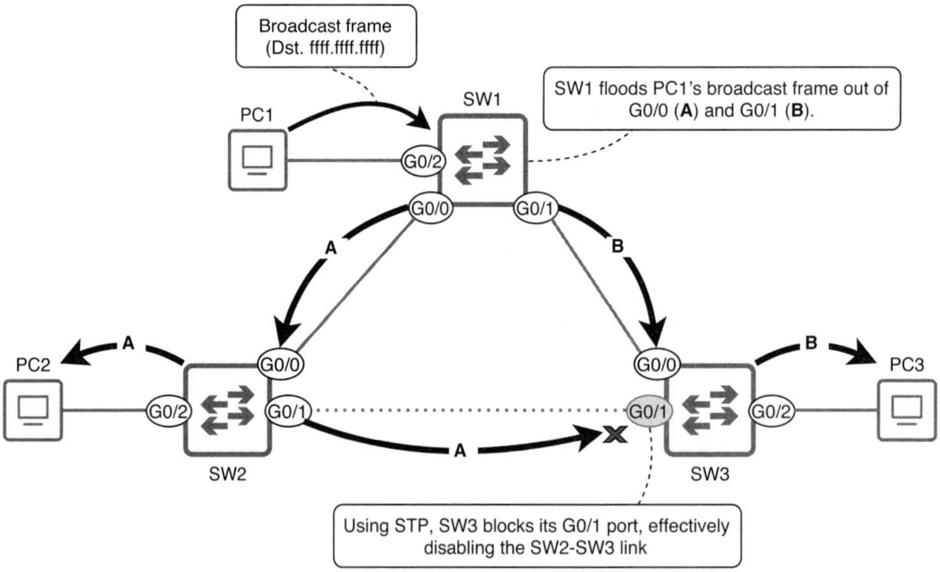

Figure 14.2 PC1 sends a broadcast frame, and SW1 floods it. Using STP, SW3 blocks its G0/1 port, effectively disabling the SW2-SW3 connection; this prevents a Layer 2 loop from occurring.

Although the physical topology in figure 14.2 is the same as in figure 14.1, thanks to STP there is no longer a Layer 2 loop. SW3's G0/1 port is now in the *blocking* state; it does not forward frames and does not process received frames (except for STP-related messages). All other ports are in the *forwarding state*; they can forward and receive frames as normal. The SW2 G0/1 to SW3 G0/1 link is unused but is available to take over if there is a problem on another link.

> **NOTE** The term *topology* refers to how devices are arranged and connected in a network. In figure 14.2, SW1, SW2, and SW3 are physically connected in a *ring topology*, forming a circle. The term *STP topology* can be used to refer to the logical arrangement of switches and their connections as a result of STP—some actively carrying network traffic, and some blocked by STP to prevent Layer 2 loops.

Whereas figures 14.1 and 14.2 only showed three switches, figure 14.3 shows a LAN with many more switches connected in a *mesh*—a network topology in which each node is connected to each other node (*full mesh*) or as many other nodes as possible but not all (*partial mesh*). In a network like this, there are countless Layer 2 loops. However, with STP, the switches will automatically put ports in the blocking state to create a loop-free topology. Although network traffic does not pass over the disabled links, they are available to take over if one of the active links fails.

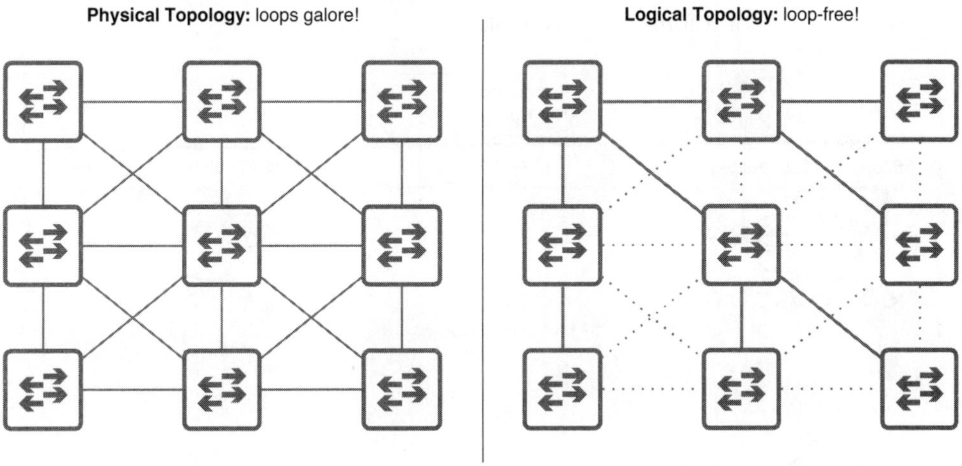

Figure 14.3 STP creates a loop-free topology in a meshed LAN. In the physical topology (left), there are countless ways that frames could loop around the network. However, STP creates a logical topology (right) that is loop-free.

> ### What's a spanning tree?
>
> A *spanning tree* is a concept in the mathematical field of *graph theory*. In graph theory, a *graph* is a structure that models relationships between objects (also called *nodes*). A *tree* is a subgraph in which any two nodes are connected by exactly one path, and *spanning* means that the tree includes all nodes; the tree spans across all nodes.

(continued)

Let's compare that to a network using STP. Each switch running STP is a node in the graph, with various physical connections between them (the physical topology in figure 14.3). STP disables some of the connections, leaving only one active path between any two nodes; this is the subgraph—the spanning tree (the logical topology in figure 14.3).

14.3 The STP algorithm

The process STP uses to create a loop-free topology is called the *STP algorithm*. There are three main steps in the algorithm:

1. Root bridge election
2. Root port selection
3. Designated port selection

Figure 14.4 shows an example of a LAN after STP created a loop-free topology. In this section, we will examine this LAN and go through the STP algorithm step by step. Note that I designed this LAN to demonstrate various aspects of the STP algorithm rather than to represent a realistic LAN topology; we will cover LAN architecture best practices in chapter 15 of volume 2 of this book.

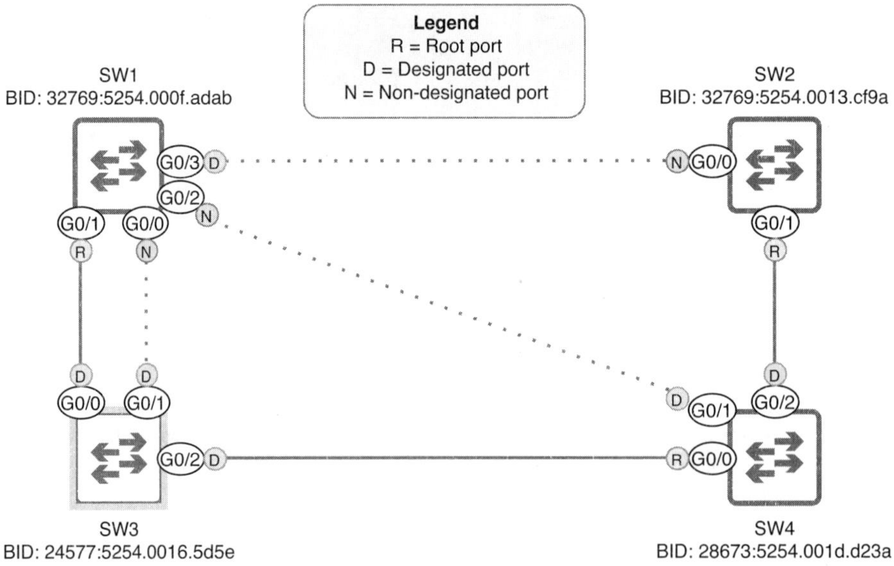

Figure 14.4 A LAN after STP has created a loop-free topology. SW3 is the root bridge, and each other switch has one root port leading to SW3. The remaining ports are either designated or non-designated ports; non-designated ports are blocked, disabling their connections.

14.3.1 Root bridge election

The first step in the STP algorithm is to elect a single switch as the root bridge for the LAN. The *root bridge* is the central point of reference for the STP topology, and in later steps, all other switches ensure that they have exactly one active path to reach the root bridge.

> **NOTE** STP was developed for use with Ethernet *bridges*, which were predecessors to switches. As a result, STP uses the term *bridge* rather than *switch*. Although modern networks use switches instead of bridges, the original terminology (such as *root bridge*) persists. In the context of STP, *bridge* and *switch* can be considered synonymous.

The root bridge election is carried out by switches sharing STP *Bridge Protocol Data Unit* (BPDU) messages with each other. Actually, the information shared in BPDUs is used to make all of the decisions in the STP algorithm, not just the root bridge election. BPDUs are sent every 2 seconds and contain various pieces of STP-related information; the two pieces of information relevant to the root bridge election are the switch's own *bridge identifier* (BID)—a number that uniquely identifies the switch in the LAN—and the BID of the switch it believes to be the root bridge.

When a switch first boots up, it does not yet know the root bridge of the LAN, so it declares itself to be the root bridge. Figure 14.5 demonstrates this: the four switches have all booted up at the same time, and each switch sends BPDUs declaring itself to be the root bridge (the `My BID` and `Root BID` fields match).

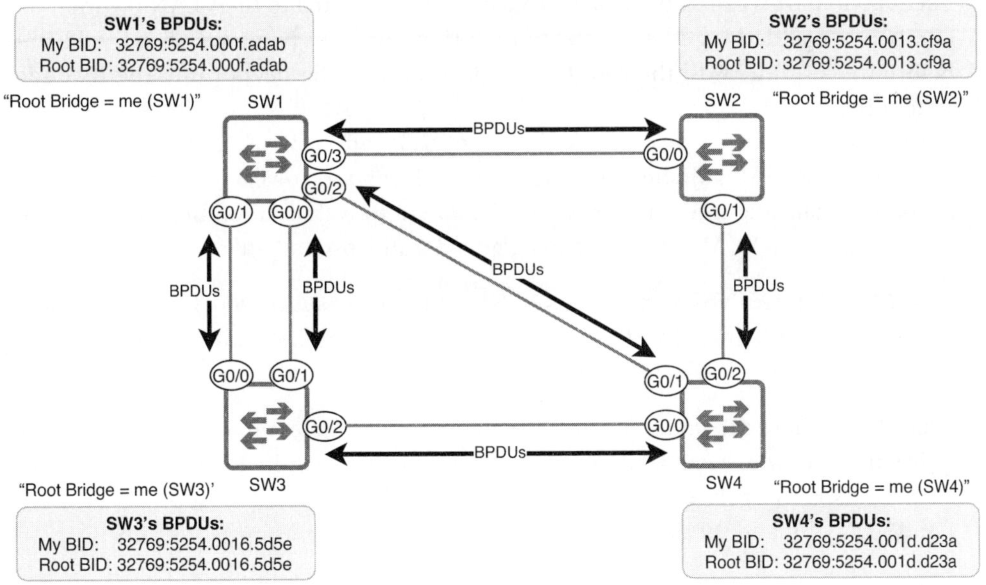

Figure 14.5 SW1, SW2, SW3, and SW4 boot up simultaneously, each switch declaring itself the root bridge. The switches send BPDUs out of their ports, containing information such as the switch's own BID and the BID of the switch it believes to be the root bridge (itself, in this case).

THE BID

The switch that sends the superior BPDU will be elected the root bridge of the LAN. The *superior BPDU* is the BPDU that has superior parameters according to the STP algorithm. When it comes to electing the root bridge, that means the BPDU with the numerically lowest `My BID` field. Before we determine which of the four switches has the lowest BID, let's examine the structure of the BID, as shown in figure 14.6. The BID is a 64-bit number that consists of a 16-bit bridge priority and a 48-bit MAC address.

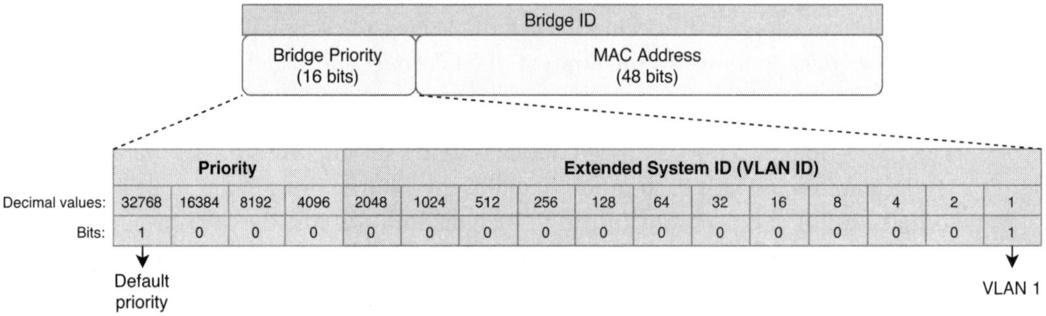

Figure 14.6 The contents of the STP BID. It is divided into two parts: a 16-bit bridge priority and a 48-bit MAC address. The bridge priority consists of two further parts: a configurable priority value (default 32768) and the Extended System ID, which is equal to the VLAN ID in Cisco's implementation of STP.

The *bridge priority* itself consists of two parts, the first being a configurable priority value. By default, the most significant bit is set to 1, which is equivalent to 0d32768. The second part is called the *Extended System ID* and is equal to the VLAN ID; these two numbers are added together to create the bridge priority (e.g., 32,768 + 1 = 32,769). Before we continue with the root bridge election, let's dig deeper into the Extended System ID.

Cisco switches run a proprietary version of STP called *Per-VLAN Spanning Tree Plus* (PVST+). In PVST+, switches run a separate STP *instance* for each VLAN; they create a separate spanning tree for each VLAN. The benefit is that different links can be disabled in different VLANs, resulting in balanced traffic over all links.

> **NOTE** Before PVST+, there was PVST, which only supported ISL encapsulation over trunk links. PVST+ supports both ISL and 802.1Q, and modern Cisco switches all run PVST+, not PVST.

If all VLANs share the same STP instance, blocked links go completely unused until an active link fails, which can lead to congestion on the active links. Figure 14.7 shows how a separate spanning tree can be made for each VLAN. The LAN has two VLANs (VLAN 1 and VLAN 2), and the switches have disabled different links in each VLAN.

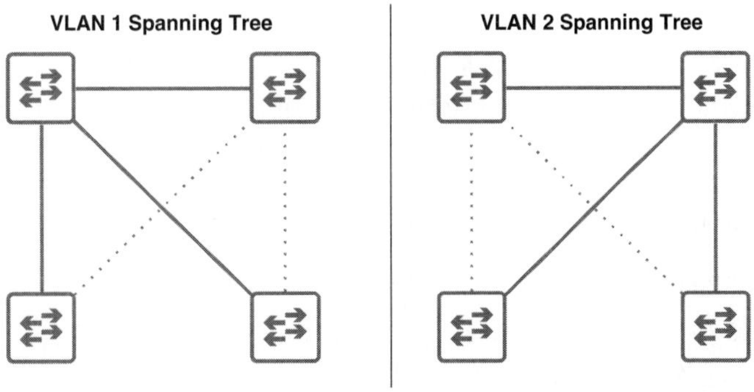

Figure 14.7 Switches in a LAN create separate spanning trees for VLANs 1 and 2 by disabling different links in each VLAN (as indicated by the dotted lines). Traffic in VLAN 1 will use different links than traffic in VLAN 2, avoiding network congestion.

Because the VLAN ID becomes part of the BID, the switch will have a unique bridge priority for each STP instance (for each VLAN running STP). For example, with the default priority of 32768, the total bridge priority will be 32769 (32,768 + 1) in VLAN 1 and 32770 (32,768 + 2) in VLAN 2.

> **NOTE** For the rest of this chapter, we will focus on a single-VLAN topology. I would not expect any questions about creating a unique spanning tree for each VLAN on the CCNA exam.

Why include the VLAN ID in the bridge priority?

The STP standard (IEEE 802.1D) specifies that each switch must have a unique BID. This is achieved by combining the bridge priority with the switch's MAC address. Even if all switches in the LAN have the same bridge priority, MAC addresses are unique, so the result is a unique BID for each switch.

However, Cisco switches running PVST+ run a separate STP instance for each VLAN. As we covered in chapter 12, each VLAN is like a separate virtual switch, so to comply with the standard, each STP instance running on the switch must have a unique BID. That's the role of the Extended System ID, which is set to the VLAN ID of the STP instance. By adding the VLAN ID to the priority value, each STP instance will have a unique bridge priority and, therefore, a unique BID.

For example, if a switch running two STP instances (VLAN 1 and VLAN 2) has the default priority value of 32768 and a MAC address 5254.000f.adab, the resulting BID would be 32769:5254.000f.adab for VLAN 1 and 32770:5254.000f.adab for VLAN 2. Note that the bridge priority is written in decimal, whereas the MAC address is written in hexadecimal (as usual), and the two are often separated by a colon, as in 32769:5254.000f.adab.

COMPARING BIDS

Now that we've covered the bridge priority (priority + VLAN ID), what is the MAC address that forms the second part of the BID? It's not the MAC of any of the switch's ports; rather, it's a separate MAC address that identifies the switch as a whole. In this section, we'll compare BIDs and see how the MAC address is used as a tiebreaker. The following are the BIDs of the four switches we saw in figure 14.5:

- SW1: 32769:5254.000f.adab
- SW2: 32769:5254.0013.cf9a
- SW3: 32769:5254.0016.5d5e
- SW4: 32769:5254.001d.d23a

Which of these BIDs is numerically lower and, therefore, superior? To compare them, first compare the bridge priorities. In this case, all four switches have the same bridge priority of 32769, so we must compare the MAC addresses to break the tie.

> **NOTE** Although we divide the BID into multiple parts, remember that it is just a 64-bit number. The bits written on the left (those that make up the bridge priority) are the most significant, which is why you should compare them first when determining which BID is numerically lower.

When comparing MAC addresses, remember that they are just numbers written in a hexadecimal format, and comparing them is the same process you go through when comparing decimal numbers. For example, when comparing the decimal numbers 1999 and 9111, how do you know the second number is greater when it has only one 9, whereas the first number has three? The reason is the 9 in 9111 is the most significant digit; the single 9 in 9111 has a greater value (9,000) than all of the other digits in 1999 combined. Just by seeing that the most significant digit of 9111 is greater than that of 1999, you can declare that 9111 is the greater of the two—no need to compare the other three digits.

The same applies when finding the greater (or lesser, in this case) of two or more MAC addresses: compare the most significant digits first. The first six digits of all four MAC addresses (the OUI) are the same: 5254.00. Then, the following digit is 1 for SW2, SW3, and SW4, but 0 for SW1, and therefore SW1 has the lowest BID of the four—it is the root bridge! We can confirm this with the **`show spanning-tree`** command on SW1, as in the following example:

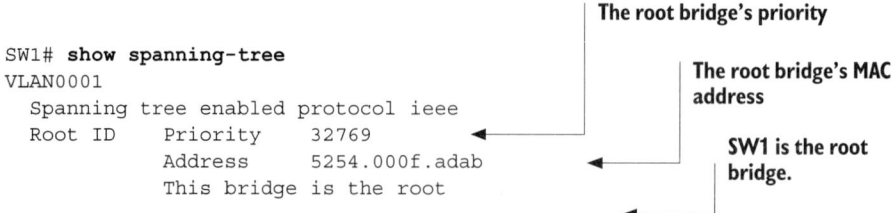

```
SW1# show spanning-tree
VLAN0001
  Spanning tree enabled protocol ieee
  Root ID    Priority    32769                ◄── The root bridge's priority
             Address     5254.000f.adab       ◄── The root bridge's MAC address
             This bridge is the root          ◄── SW1 is the root bridge.
. . .
```

```
  Bridge ID  Priority    32769  (priority 32768 sys-id-ext 1)
             Address     5254.000f.adab
. . .
```

This switch's priority (same as previously because it is the root)

This switch's MAC address (same as previously because it is the root)

CONFIGURING THE BRIDGE PRIORITY

As we just confirmed, SW1 is the root bridge for the LAN because it has the lowest MAC address. However, it is possible to configure the bridge priority to change which switch becomes the root bridge. This is often desirable because of the role of the root bridge; it serves as the central reference point for the spanning tree, and the other switches will ensure that their most efficient path to reach the root bridge is enabled. If a switch is connected to the router that end hosts use to access external networks, it's a good choice to be the root bridge; there should be an efficient path to reach the router without frames having to pass through too many switches.

Following the example we saw in figure 14.4, let's configure SW3 as the root bridge and lower SW4's priority so it functions as a *secondary root bridge*—the bridge that will take over as the root if the root bridge malfunctions (because it has the lowest BID of the remaining switches). The command to configure a switch's root priority is **spanning-tree vlan** *vlan-id* **priority** *priority-value*. In the following example, I attempt to set SW3's priority to 20000, but an error message is displayed:

```
SW3(config)# spanning-tree vlan 1 priority 20000
% Bridge Priority must be in increments of 4096.
% Allowed values are:
  0     4096  8192  12288 16384 20480 24576 28672
  32768 36864 40960 45056 49152 53248 57344 61440
```

Configures SW3's STP priority

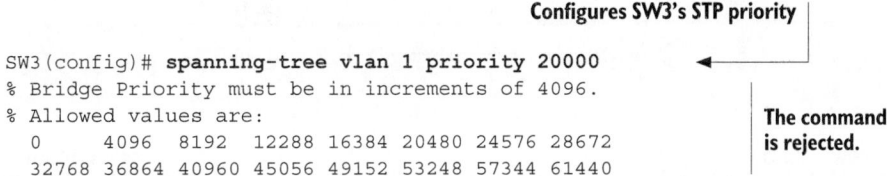

The command is rejected.

As the error message states, the priority can only be configured in increments of 4096. The reason is that although the bridge priority field as a whole is 16 bits in length, only the four most significant bits make up the configurable priority value: the bits with values of 0d32768, 0d16384, 0d8192, and 0d4096. The lesser 12 bits are fixed as the VLAN ID (VLAN 1 in our examples here). That's why the bridge priority must be configured in increments of 4096: it's the value of the least significant bit that we can change. In the following example, I configure SW3's priority as 24576 and SW4's priority as 28672 and then confirm with **show spanning-tree** on SW4:

```
SW3(config)# spanning-tree vlan 1 priority 24576

SW4(config)# spanning-tree vlan 1 priority 28672
SW4(config)# do show spanning-tree
VLAN0001
  Spanning tree enabled protocol ieee
  Root ID    Priority    24577
```

The priority configured on SW3 (+1 for VLAN ID)

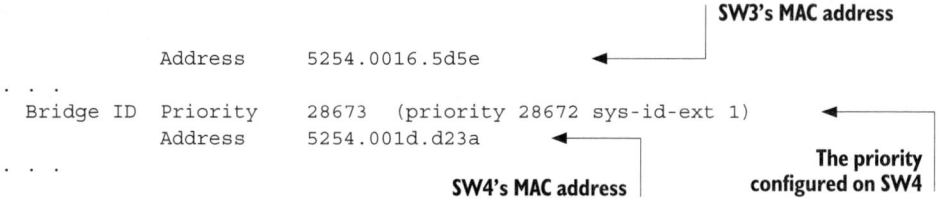

```
              Address     5254.0016.5d5e
. . .
  Bridge ID  Priority    28673  (priority 28672 sys-id-ext 1)
              Address     5254.001d.d23a
. . .
```

SW3's MAC address

SW4's MAC address

The priority configured on SW4

Figure 14.8 shows the result after configuring the bridge priorities of SW3 and SW4. All four switches agree that SW3 is the root bridge. SW4 has a lower BID than SW1 and SW2, but it is not the root bridge yet; that would only happen if SW3 malfunctions and a new root bridge election is held.

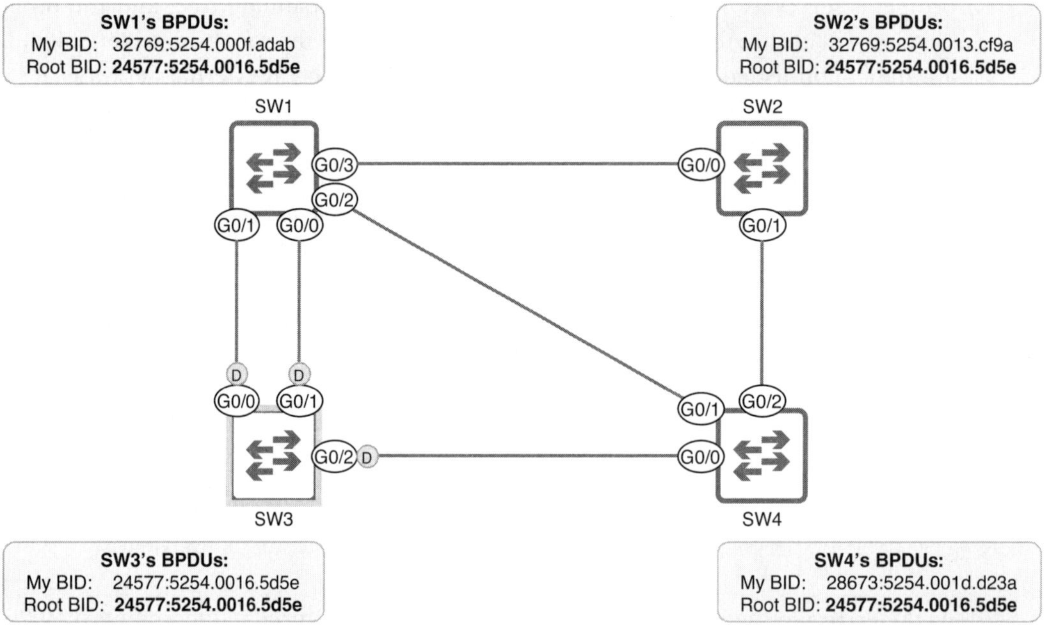

Figure 14.8 After configuring SW3's priority to 24576 (+1 for VLAN 1), all four switches agree that SW3 is the root bridge because it has the lowest BID. All ports on the root bridge are designated ports (indicated by D). If SW3 malfunctions and a new election is held, SW4 will become the new root bridge because it has the second-lowest BID.

> **NOTE** All ports on the root bridge are designated ports, meaning they are in the forwarding state (not the blocking state). We will examine designated ports further in section 14.3.3.

There is one more method to configure the bridge priority that you should know for the CCNA exam: the **`spanning-tree vlan`** *`vlan-id`* **`root`** {**`primary`** | **`secondary`**} command. The **`secondary`** keyword is simple: it sets the priority to 28672 (one increment of 4096 under the default of 32768). The **primary** keyword, on the other hand, works like this:

- Set the priority to 24576 (two increments of 4096 under the default).
- Or, if 24576 isn't sufficient to make the switch become the root bridge (i.e., the current root bridge's priority is 24576), set the priority to the highest multiple of 4096 that will make the switch the root bridge.

These commands will serve their purpose if all other switches in the LAN have the default priority of 32768; the switch configured with the **primary** keyword will be the root bridge, and the switch configured with the **secondary** keyword will be next in line if the root bridge fails.

However, using these commands is not recommended. There are a couple of reasons: first, there's no guarantee that configuring this command with the **secondary** keyword will make the switch the next in line to become the root bridge if the current root bridge fails; another non-root switch could have a priority value lower than 28672. Likewise, there are situations where this command with the **primary** keyword will fail: it cannot set the switch's priority to 0. The following example shows what happens when the current root bridge (SW1) has a priority of 4096, and you use this command with the **primary** keyword on another switch (SW2):

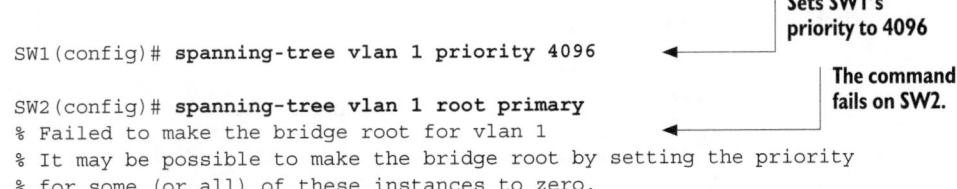

```
SW1(config)# spanning-tree vlan 1 priority 4096        <-- Sets SW1's priority to 4096

SW2(config)# spanning-tree vlan 1 root primary
% Failed to make the bridge root for vlan 1            <-- The command fails on SW2.
% It may be possible to make the bridge root by setting the priority
% for some (or all) of these instances to zero.
```

EXAM TIP The best way to ensure that a switch will be the root bridge is to use the **spanning-tree vlan** *vlan-id* **priority 0** command. Then, the only way to usurp the root is to use the same command on another switch that has a lower MAC address (and, therefore, a lower BID). Remember this point for the exam!

14.3.2 Root port selection

After electing the root bridge, each non-root switch will select one of its ports as its *root port*—the port with the best path to the root bridge. The switch calculates this based on information in the BPDUs it receives from its neighbors. The root port is selected using a few parameters: the root cost (which measures the port's proximity to the root bridge), the neighbor's BID, and the neighbor's port ID, in that order of priority:

1. Lowest root cost
2. Lowest neighbor BID
3. Lowest neighbor port ID

A port's *root cost* is a value that indicates how efficient the path to the root bridge is via that port; a lower value is better. Each port has a given cost value associated with it, as shown in table 14.1.

Table 14.1 STP port cost values

Speed	Cost
10 Mbps	100
100 Mbps	19
1 Gbps	4
10 Gbps	2

A port's root cost is the total cost of the ports leading toward the root bridge (not just the cost of the individual port), and the port with the lowest root cost will become the root port. If there are multiple ports on the switch with the same root cost, the port connected to the neighbor with the lowest BID will become the root port. If two or more ports have the same root cost and are connected to the same neighbor, the port connected to the port on the neighbor switch with the lowest port ID will become the root port. Figure 14.9 shows which port each non-root switch selects as its root port and how it comes to that decision. In the rest of this section, we will go through each switch's decision step by step.

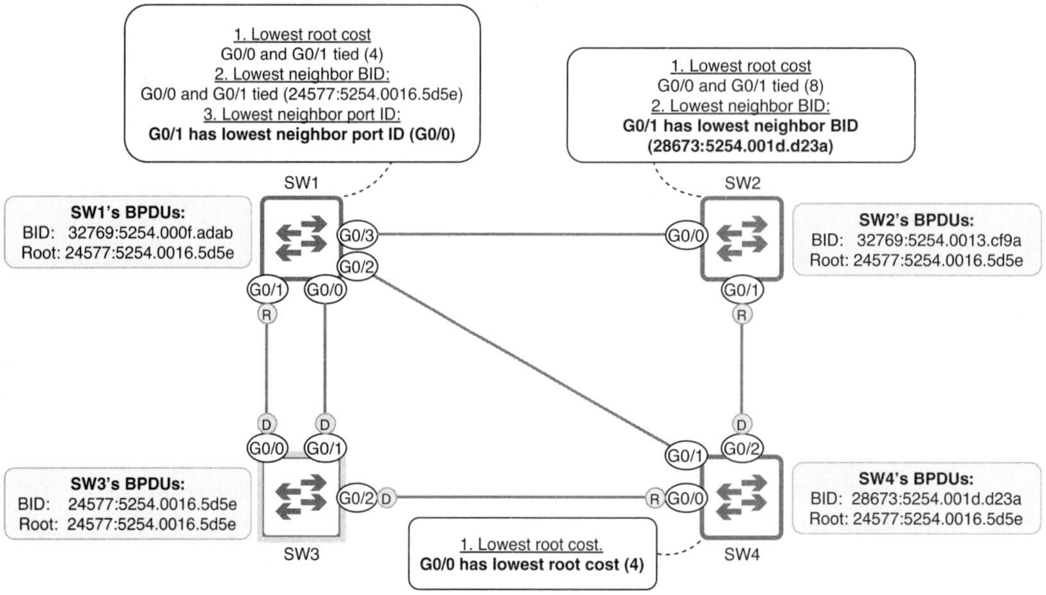

Figure 14.9 Non-root switches each select one root port. SW4 selects G0/0 because it has the lowest root cost of its ports. SW2 G0/0 and G0/1 have the same root cost, so SW2 selects G0/1 because it has the lowest neighbor BID. SW1 G0/0 and G0/1 have the same root cost and neighbor BID, so SW1 selects G0/1 because it has the lowest neighbor port ID.

LOWEST ROOT COST

As I've mentioned a couple of times already, the decisions that make up the STP algorithm are all based on information in the BPDUs passed among the switches. Once the root bridge has been decided, it is the only switch that generates new BPDUs; other switches receive those BPDUs and forward them to their neighbors, updating some information in the BPDUs. One of the pieces of information in a BPDU is the root cost. The BPDUs sent by the root bridge all have a cost of 0 (the root bridge's cost to reach itself is 0). When non-root switches forward those BPDUs, they add the cost of the port they received the BPDUs on.

Figure 14.10 demonstrates how switches advertise their root cost to each other and each switch's logic in selecting its root port. Only SW4 is able to do so at this step. SW3 (the root bridge) sends BPDUs with a root cost of 0. When SW1 and SW4 forward those BPDUs, they add the cost of the ports on which they received those BPDUs; in this case, all ports are GigabitEthernet ports, so they have a cost of 4. When SW2 forwards the BPDUs it receives from SW1 and SW4, it adds its own ports' cost (4) to the cost of the BPDUs it received (4); it advertises a cost of 8.

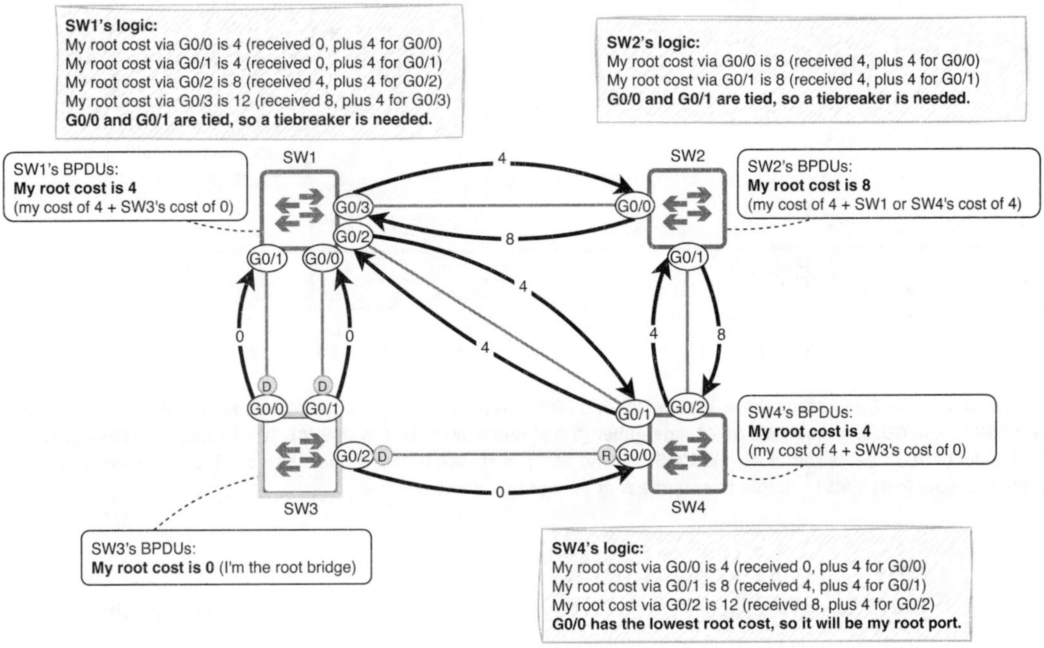

Figure 14.10 Switches advertise their root cost to each other in BPDUs. SW3 (the root bridge) advertises a root cost of 0, SW1 and SW4 advertise a root cost of 4, and SW2 advertises a root cost of 8. SW4 selects G0/0 as its root port because it has the lowest root cost of its three ports. SW1 and SW2 are unable to select a root port based on root cost alone; a tiebreaker is needed.

Although SW4 is able to determine its root port based only on root cost, SW1 and SW2 cannot; SW1 has a root cost of 4 via both its G0/0 and G0/1 ports, and SW2 has a root cost of 8 via both its G0/0 and G0/1 ports. For SW1 and SW2 to select their root ports, they must proceed to the next step in the selection process: the lowest neighbor BID.

LOWEST NEIGHBOR BRIDGE ID

When a switch sends BPDUs, one of the pieces of information it includes is its own BID. This can then be used by the receiving switch as a tiebreaker when deciding its root port. The port connected to the neighbor with the lowest BID will become the switch's root port. Figure 14.11 shows how SW1 and SW2 compare their neighbors' BIDs to decide their root ports; SW2 is able to select G0/1, but SW1 is not yet able to select a root port.

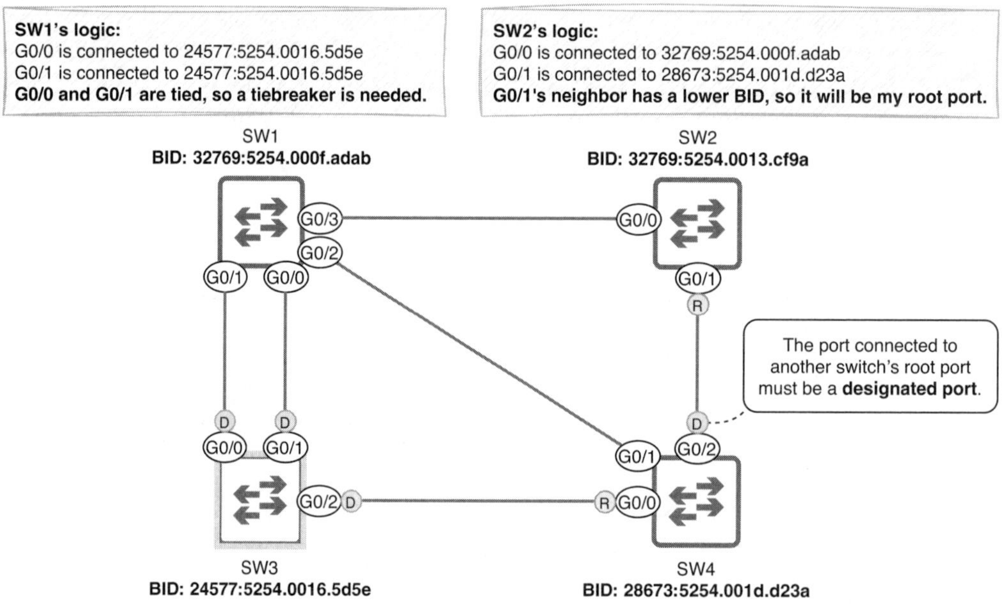
SW1's logic:
G0/0 is connected to 24577:5254.0016.5d5e
G0/1 is connected to 24577:5254.0016.5d5e
G0/0 and G0/1 are tied, so a tiebreaker is needed.
SW2's logic:
G0/0 is connected to 32769:5254.000f.adab
G0/1 is connected to 28673:5254.001d.d23a
G0/1's neighbor has a lower BID, so it will be my root port.
SW1
BID: 32769:5254.000f.adab
SW2
BID: 32769:5254.0013.cf9a
G0/3
G0/2
G0/1
G0/0
G0/0
G0/1
R
The port connected to another switch's root port must be a designated port.
D
D
G0/0
G0/1
D
G0/1
G0/2
G0/2
D
R
G0/0
SW3
BID: 24577:5254.0016.5d5e
SW4
BID: 28673:5254.001d.d23a

Figure 14.11 SW1 compares the neighbor BID of its G0/0 and G0/1 ports, and SW2 compares the neighbor BID of its G0/0 and G0/1 ports. SW2 G0/1's neighbor (SW4) has a lower BID than SW2 G0/0's neighbor (SW1), so SW2 selects G0/1 as its root port. SW1's G0/0 and G0/1 ports are both connected to SW3, so they both have the same neighbor BID; SW1 is unable to select a root port at this point.

> **NOTE** The port connected to another switch's root port must be a designated port (forwarding). The root port provides the switch's single path to the root bridge, so its neighbor must not block the link.

LOWEST NEIGHBOR PORT ID

Another piece of information included in an STP BPDU is the port ID of the port that sent the BPDU. This is used as the final tiebreaker when selecting the root port. It's worth emphasizing that when using the port ID as a tiebreaker, it's the neighbor's port IDs that count—not the local switch's port ID. When deciding SW1's root port, we have to compare the port IDs of SW3's ports that are connected to SW1.

The *port ID* is a unique identifier for each port of the switch; like the BID, it consists of a configurable priority value (128 by default) and a sequential number (1 for the first port, 2 for the second port, etc). In the following example, I use **`show spanning-tree`** on SW3 to check the IDs of its G0/0 and G0/1 ports (in the `Prio.Nbr` column):

```
SW3# show spanning-tree
. . .
Interface           Role Sts Cost      Prio.Nbr Type
------------------- ---- --- --------- -------- --------------------------------
Gi0/0               Desg FWD 4         128.1    P2p
Gi0/1               Desg FWD 4         128.2    P2p
Gi0/2               Desg FWD 4         128.3    P2p
```

SW3 G0/0's port ID is 128.1.

SW3 G0/1's port ID is 128.2.

> **NOTE** To influence root port selection, you can configure a port's priority value (the first part of the port ID) with the **`spanning-tree vlan`** *`vlan-id`* **`port-priority`** *`priority-value`* in interface config mode. However, I would not expect any questions about this on the CCNA exam. Generally, you can just compare the ports' names to decide which has a lower port ID. G0/0 is lower than G0/1 (0 is lower than 1), so it has a lower port ID.

Figure 14.12 shows how SW1 selects its root port. SW1 G0/0 is connected to SW3 G0/1 (port ID 128.2), and SW1 G0/1 is connected to SW3 G0/0 (port ID 128.1). Because the neighbor port ID of G0/1 is lower, SW1 selects G0/1 as its root port.

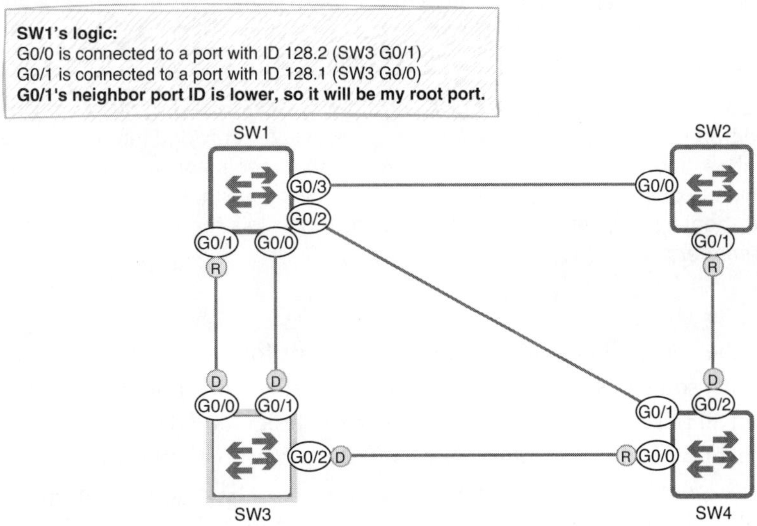

Figure 14.12 SW1 compares the neighbor port IDs of its G0/0 and G0/1 ports. G0/1 is connected to a lower port ID (SW3 G0/0, port ID 128.1) than G0/0 (SW3 G0/1, port ID 128.2), so G0/1 selects G0/1 as its root port.

EXAM TIP Remember that you're comparing the neighbor's port IDs, not the local switch's port IDs; that's a potential trick question on the exam!

14.3.3 Designated port selection

Now that each non-root switch has selected a root port, the final step is to select designated ports. Whereas a root port is a port in the forwarding state that points toward the root bridge, a *designated port* is a port in the forwarding state that points away from the root bridge. That's why every port on the root bridge is a designated port—they all point away from the root bridge.

There must be exactly one designated port for each segment in the LAN. The exact meaning of the term *segment* can vary, but in this case, a segment is a link between switches. Designated ports are selected using the following parameters (in order of priority):

1. The port on the switch with the lowest root cost becomes designated.
2. The port on the switch with the lowest BID becomes designated.

What is a segment?

A segment is a division of a network, the extent of which depends on the context. A *Layer 1 segment* can be defined as an electrical connection between devices and is equivalent to a collision domain; this is the meaning of *segment* as used in this chapter. Two connected switches are another example of a Layer-1 segment. Another example is a group of devices connected to an Ethernet hub; an electrical signal sent by one device is received by all other devices connected to the hub.

A *Layer 2 segment* is equivalent to a LAN or broadcast domain—a group of devices that can send frames directly to each other. If a physical LAN is divided into multiple VLANs, each VLAN is its own Layer 2 segment. A *Layer 3 segment* is equivalent to a subnet. As I mentioned in chapter 12 (VLANs), Layer 2 and Layer 3 segments usually have a one-to-one relationship (one subnet per VLAN), but it is possible for a single VLAN to include multiple subnets.

In electing the root bridge and selecting a root port for each switch, we were already able to identify some designated ports in the LAN: all ports on the root bridge are designated, and all ports connected to a root port are designated. For each remaining segment, there must be one designated port, and the other ports must be non-designated. *Non-designated* ports are in the blocking state; this is how STP prevents loops.

First, SW1 G0/0 is connected to SW3 G0/1 (a designated port) and is, therefore, a non-designated port; there can only be one designated port per segment. That leaves two segments remaining: the SW1 G0/2 to SW4 G0/1 link and the SW1 G0/3 to SW2

G0/0 link. Figure 14.13 shows which ports will be designated and non-designated, and how those decisions were made. In the rest of this section, we will go through the process step by step.

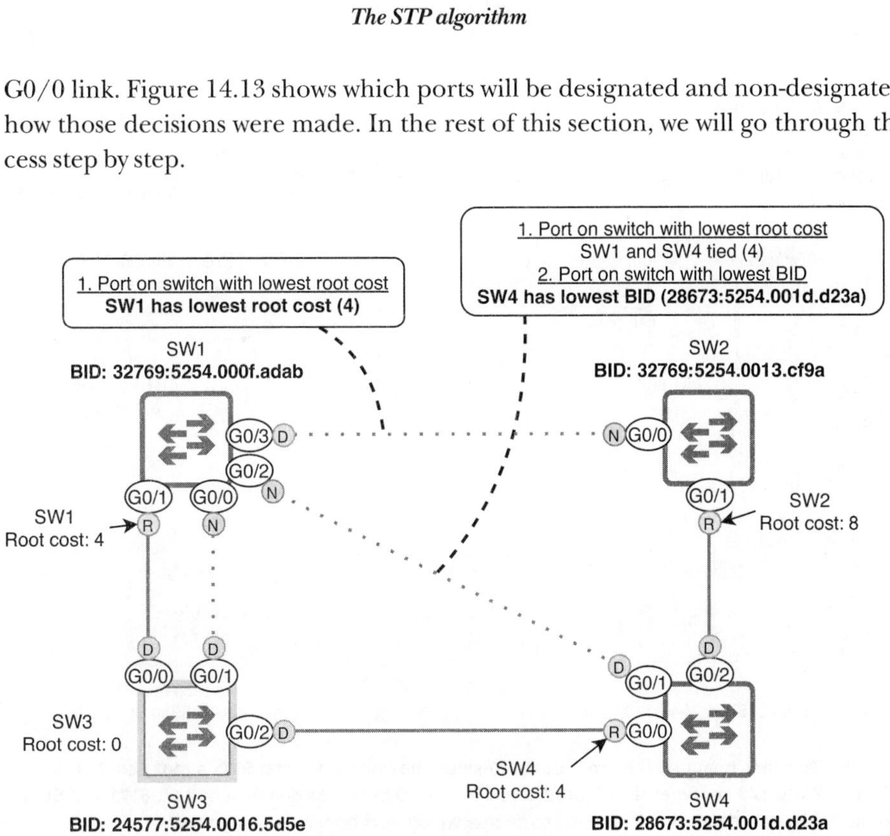

Figure 14.13 Each segment must have exactly one designated port. All ports on the root bridge are designated, and so are all ports connected to a root port. One designated port is selected on each remaining segment, and the remaining ports are non-designated.

PORT ON THE SWITCH WITH LOWEST ROOT COST

The first parameter used to decide which side of the remaining links becomes designated is root cost: the port on the switch with the lowest root cost becomes designated, and the other port becomes non-designated. Pay attention to the wording: it's "the port *on the switch with* the lowest root cost becomes designated," not "the port with the lowest root cost becomes designated." We are comparing the root cost of each switch via its root port, not the cost of each port whose role is being decided.

Figure 14.14 shows how the switches compare their root costs to decide which port becomes designated. SW1's root cost (4) is lower than SW2's root cost (8), so SW1's port becomes designated, and SW2's becomes non-designated. SW1 and SW4 have the same root cost (4) and, therefore, will have to use a tiebreaker to decide which port becomes designated.

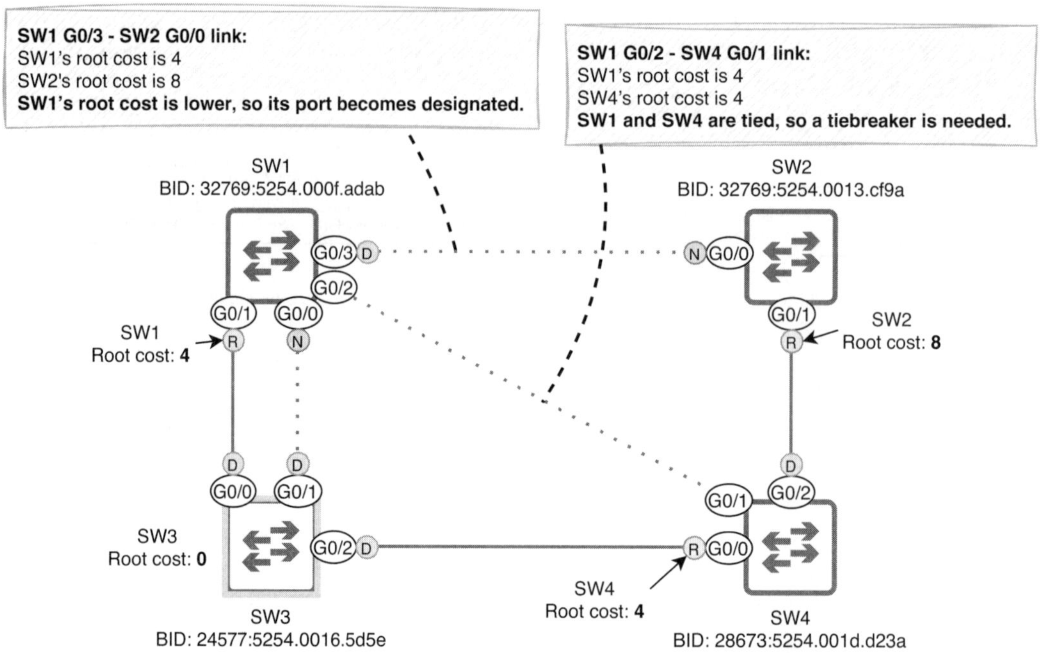

Figure 14.14 Switches compare their root costs to select designated ports. SW1's root cost (4) is lower than SW2's (8), so SW1 G0/3 becomes designated, and SW2 G0/0 becomes non-designated. SW1 and SW4 have the same root cost (4), so a tiebreaker is needed to decide which port becomes designated.

PORT ON SWITCH WITH LOWEST BRIDGE ID

As a tiebreaker to decide which port becomes designated, the switches will compare their BIDs; the port on the switch with the lowest BID will become designated, and the port on the other switch will become non-designated. Figure 14.15 shows how SW1 and SW4 compare BIDs to decide which switch's port becomes designated; SW4's BID is lower than SW1's, so SW4 G0/1 becomes designated, and SW1 G0/2 becomes non-designated.

All port roles have now been decided: root, designated, and non-designated. Note that BPDUs are only sent out of designated ports. When a switch first boots up, it believes it is the root bridge, so all of its ports are designated; the switch sends BPDUs out of all its ports. However, if it then becomes a non-root switch and some of its ports transition to other roles (root or non-designated), the switch does not send BPDUs out of those ports. BPDUs originate from the root bridge and are forwarded throughout the LAN via designated ports only. To summarize this section, here is a summary of the STP algorithm:

1 Root bridge election (one per LAN)
   - Lowest BID
2 Root port selection (one per switch, excluding root bridge)

   - Lowest root cost
   - Lowest neighbor BID
   - Lowest neighbor port ID
3. Designated port selection (one per segment)
   - Port on the switch with the lowest root cost
   - Port on the switch with the lowest BID

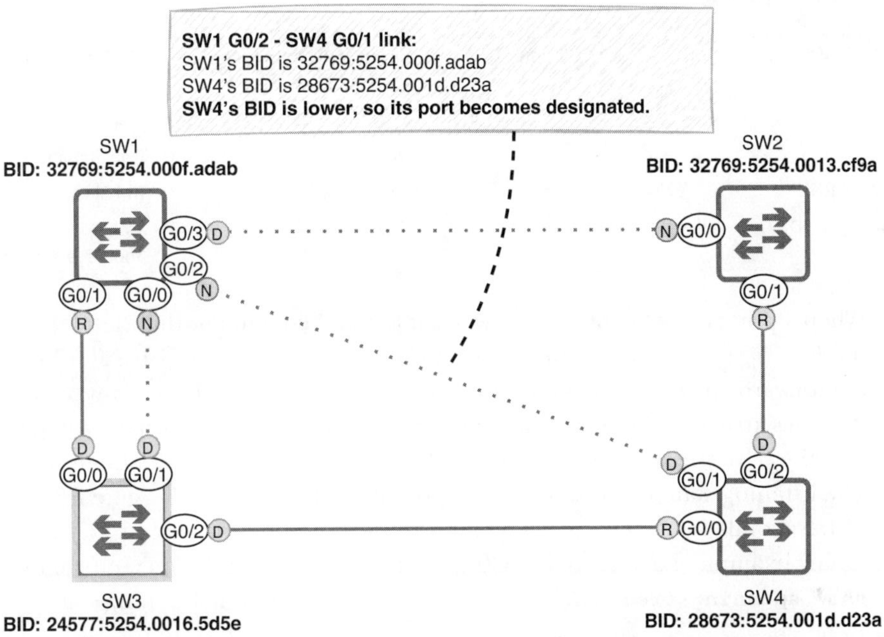

Figure 14.15 Switches compare their BIDs as a tiebreaker when selecting designated ports. SW4's BID (28673:5254.001d.d23a) is lower than SW1's BID (32769:5254.000f.adab), so SW4 G0/1 becomes designated, and SW1 G0/2 becomes non-designated.

14.4 STP port states and timers

In section 14.3, we covered root, designated, and non-designated ports; these are the STP *port roles*. In addition to the three roles, there are multiple *port states*. I already mentioned two of them: the forwarding state and the blocking state.

In the forwarding state, the port is active and can forward and receive frames. In a stable LAN, root and designated ports should be in the forwarding state. In the blocking state, the port is disabled and cannot forward or receive frames; non-designated ports should be in the blocking state. However, there are some other transitional states that a port goes through in preparation to forward frames, as well as some timers that govern how long the port spends in each state.

14.4.1 STP port states

There are four main STP port states: blocking, listening, learning, and forwarding. You might also hear of a fifth state: *disabled*. This refers to a port that isn't operational—for example, if it is disabled with the **shutdown** command or isn't connected to another device; STP isn't active on such a port, so it's usually not included as an STP port state. Table 14.2 summarizes the four main states that we will examine in this section.

Table 14.2 STP port states

State	Forward frames?	Learn MAC addresses?	Stable or transitional?
Blocking (BLK)	No	No	Stable (non-designated)
Listening (LIS)	No	No	Transitional
Learning (LRN)	No	Yes	Transitional
Forwarding (FWD)	Yes	Yes	Stable (root, designated)

When a port is first enabled (e.g., when it is connected to another device), it will enter the *listening* state. In this state, the port can only send and receive STP BPDUs; it does not forward any regular data frames, and the switch does not learn any MAC addresses if frames arrive on the port. The point of this state is to decide what's going to happen with the port; the switch decides if it will be a root, designated, or non-designated port. The listening state is transitional; the port should remain in the state for a maximum of 15 seconds (we'll see why 15 seconds is the maximum in section 14.4.2). In the following example, I disable SW2's G0/1 port, reenable it, and then confirm its state with **show spanning-tree**; LIS in the Sts column indicates the listening state:

```
SW2(config)# interface g0/1
SW2(config-if)# shutdown
SW2(config-if)# no shutdown
SW2(config-if)# do show spanning-tree
. . .
Interface           Role Sts Cost      Prio.Nbr Type
------------------- ---- --- --------- -------- --------------------------------
Gi0/0               Altn BLK 4         128.1    P2p
Gi0/1               Root LIS 4         128.2    P2p
```

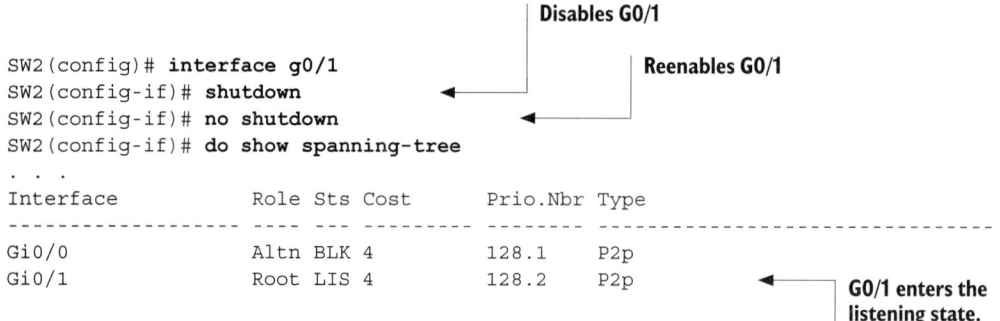

Disables G0/1 (→ shutdown)

Reenables G0/1 (→ no shutdown)

G0/1 enters the listening state. (→ Gi0/1 line)

NOTE In the previous output, G0/0's role is Altn, meaning *alternate*; this is equivalent to the non-designated role. Alternate is a port role introduced in Rapid STP, which we'll cover in chapter 15; the terminology is now used even with a switch running standard STP.

If the port becomes a non-designated port, it will immediately transition to the *blocking* state. In this state, the port is effectively disabled; it does not forward frames. Its only job is to listen for BPDUs and react if there is a change in the network. Note that its status will still be `up/up` in the output of **`show ip interface brief`**; the port is still operational and ready to transition to the listening state if there is a change in the network. However, in the output of **`show spanning-tree`**, its status will be `BLK` (as in the previous output).

If it is decided in the listening state that the port will be a root or designated port, after 15 seconds, it will transition to the *learning* state. This state is similar to the listening state, with one difference: it will start learning MAC addresses when it receives frames. The purpose of this state is to prepare the port to start forwarding traffic; like the listening state, it is transitional.

NOTE A port in the learning state continues listening for BPDUs. If it senses a change in the network and changes its role to become a non-designated port, it will immediately transition to the blocking state.

After being in the learning state for 15 seconds, a root or designated port will finally transition to the *forwarding* state—a fully operational switch port capable of forwarding traffic. Figure 14.16 shows how a port transitions between the four states.

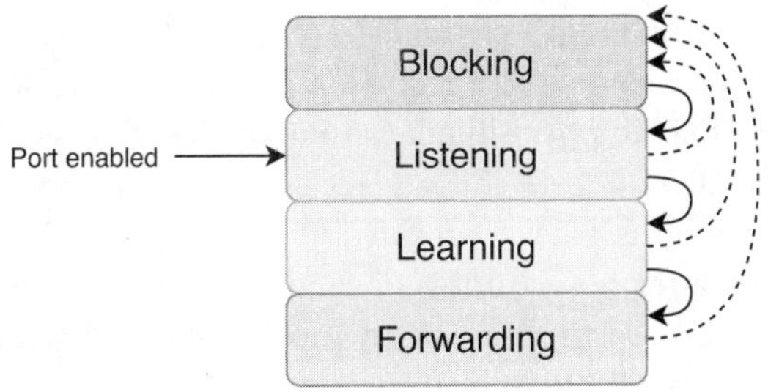

Figure 14.16 How a switch port transitions through the STP port states. A newly enabled port begins in the listening state and then either transitions to the blocking or learning state and then the forwarding state. A port in any state can transition immediately to blocking, but for a port to transition to the forwarding state, it must transition through the listening and learning states.

Once all switches in the network have decided their ports' roles and all ports are in a blocking or forwarding state, the STP has *converged*; the LAN is stable. If there are changes to the network (e.g., ports failing, ports being disabled, new switches being added, etc.), the switches will use STP to recalculate the topology, and the network will reconverge in a new, stable topology.

14.4.2 STP timers

There are three timers that govern how STP operates, as summarized in table 14.3.

Table 14.3 STP timers

Timer	Purpose	Duration
Hello	How often BPDUs are sent	2 seconds
Forward delay	The length of the listening and learning states	15 seconds (per state)
Max age	How long a switch will wait to change the STP topology after ceasing to receive BPDUs on a port	20 seconds

The *hello* timer is simple: it determines how often BPDUs are sent. By default, it is 2 seconds, meaning BPDUs are sent every 2 seconds. The hello timer of the root bridge dictates how often BPDUs are sent in the LAN; all BPDUs originate from the root bridge and are then forwarded by the other switches out of their designated ports. This applies to the other timers too; the timers of the root bridge are used by all switches in the LAN.

NOTE The hello timer (and the other timers) can be modified, but it is rare to do so, and it is beyond the scope of the CCNA exam.

The *forward delay* timer determines the length of the listening and learning states. By default, it is 15 seconds; the listening state is 15 seconds, and the learning state is 15 seconds. This means that a newly enabled port will take a total of 30 seconds before it is able to forward frames (except BPDUs).

In a LAN with redundant connections, it's very important that loops don't occur—a loop can bring down a LAN in a matter of seconds—so each switch port spends a certain amount of time in each state before transitioning to another state. This allows the switch to be absolutely sure it won't cause a loop by transitioning a port to the forwarding state.

The final timer is the *max age* timer; it determines how long a switch will wait to change the STP topology after ceasing to receive BPDUs on a port. By default, the max age timer is 20 seconds; with the default hello timer of 2 seconds, it means a port can miss 10 BPDUs before the switch decides it should recalculate the STP topology (i.e., elect a new root bridge, recalculate port roles, etc.).

This means it can take STP up to 50 seconds to move a blocking port into the forwarding state: 20 seconds for the max age timer, 15 seconds for the listening state, and 15 seconds for the learning state. Figure 14.17 shows an example of how this can cause a problem: a hardware failure (perhaps on SW3's G0/0 port) causes SW1 to stop receiving BPDUs on G0/1, but it takes 50 seconds before SW1 G0/0 can take over as the root port and start forwarding traffic.

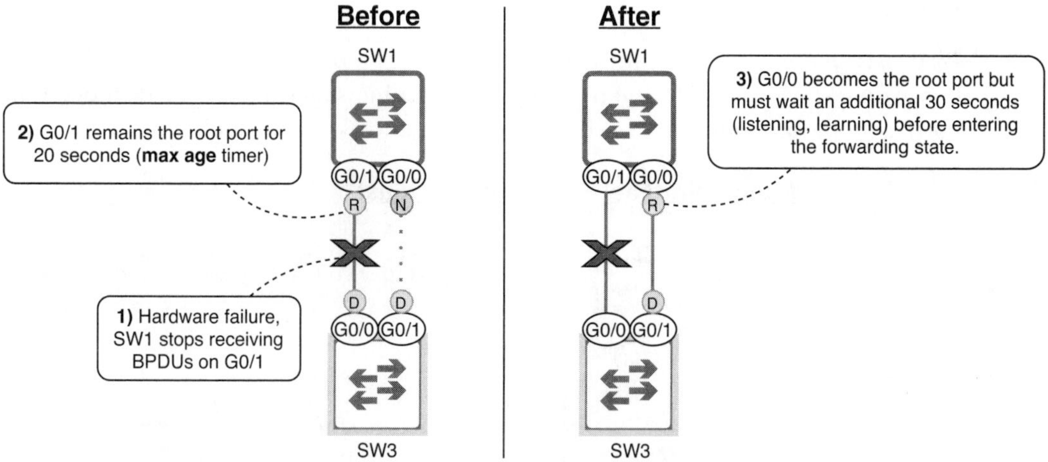

Figure 14.17 STP's timers cause SW1 to be unable to forward traffic for 50 seconds. (1) A hardware failure prevents SW1 from receiving BPDUs on G0/1. (2) G0/1 remains the root port for 20 seconds. (3) G0/0 becomes the new root port but must wait an additional 30 seconds before entering a forwarding state.

NOTE If the hardware failure causes SW1's G0/1 port to become totally non-operational (down/down state), SW1 will react immediately—no need to wait for the max age timer. However, SW1's new root port (G0/0) will still have to transition through the listening and learning states, resulting in 30 seconds of downtime.

Although STP's timers can be slow, it's for a good reason: to make sure a port doesn't start forwarding prematurely and cause a Layer 2 loop. However, there are several features that improve STP's speed, and we'll cover one in section 14.5, which discusses PortFast and the related BPDU Guard. Furthermore, in chapter 15, we'll cover Rapid STP, an evolution of STP that greatly reduces the amount of time required for STP convergence.

14.5 PortFast and BPDU Guard

Cisco switches include a suite of optional STP features (sometimes called the *STP toolkit*) that can speed up STP's convergence and improve stability. For the CCNA exam, you need to know a few of these optional STP features. In this section, we'll cover two: PortFast and BPDU Guard.

So far, we have focused on connections between switches, but STP is active on all switch ports—not just those connected to other switches. Switch ports connected to devices that do not use STP (such as PCs) will always be designated ports; there is no risk of a Layer 2 loop. However, due to STP's timer-based operation, it will take 30 seconds after connecting a device before the device can actually access the network—before the switch port enters the forwarding state. This can be frustrating for users who aren't aware of STP, and it is an inconvenience in any case.

14.5.1 PortFast

PortFast is an optional STP feature that allows a switch port to move immediately to the forwarding state, bypassing the listening and learning states. Figure 14.18 shows how PortFast allows a connected device to access the network immediately.

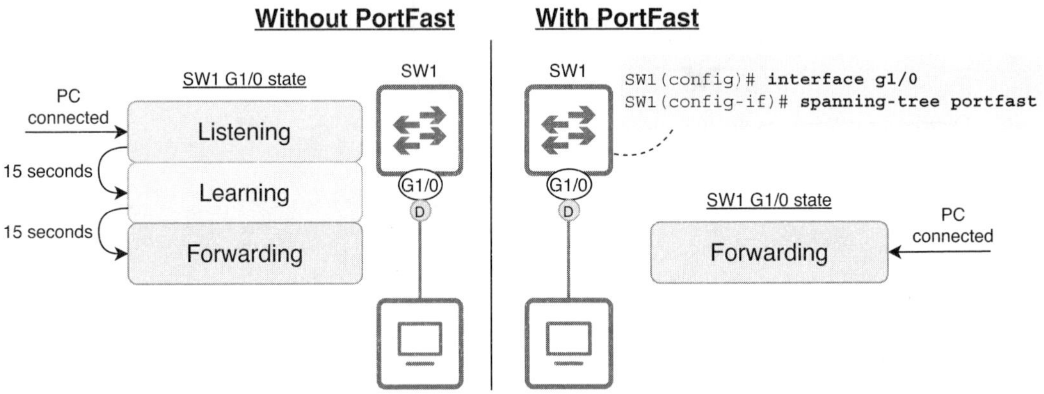

Figure 14.18 PortFast allows a switch port to immediately move to the forwarding state. Without PortFast, when an end host is connected to a switch port, it must wait 30 seconds before it can access the network. With PortFast, the end host can access the network immediately, bypassing the listening and learning states.

To enable PortFast on a specific port, use the **spanning-tree portfast** command in interface config mode. Another option is to use the **spanning-tree portfast default** command in global config mode to enable PortFast on all access ports (not trunk ports). As the following example shows, the switch displays a lengthy warning after configuring PortFast:

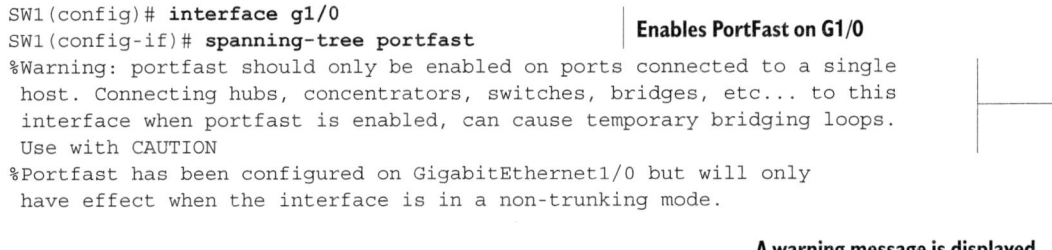

```
SW1(config)# interface g1/0
SW1(config-if)# spanning-tree portfast
%Warning: portfast should only be enabled on ports connected to a single
 host. Connecting hubs, concentrators, switches, bridges, etc... to this
 interface when portfast is enabled, can cause temporary bridging loops.
 Use with CAUTION
%Portfast has been configured on GigabitEthernet1/0 but will only
 have effect when the interface is in a non-trunking mode.
```

Enables PortFast on G1/0

A warning message is displayed.

Because PortFast puts switch ports in the forwarding state immediately, bypassing the listening and learning states, it is important that you enable it only on ports intended for end hosts. Do not connect switches to PortFast-enabled ports; otherwise, Layer 2 loops can occur, as stated in the warning message in the previous example.

14.5.2 BPDU Guard

BPDU Guard is another optional STP feature that disables a switch port if it receives a BPDU; it should be enabled on all PortFast-enabled ports. Remember, PortFast-enabled ports should only connect to end hosts, which do not send BPDUs. If a user carelessly connects another switch to a port meant for end hosts, BPDU Guard disables the port and prevents the newly connected switch from affecting the STP topology (e.g., by becoming the new root bridge).

To enable BPDU Guard on a port, use the **`spanning-tree bpduguard enable`** command in interface config mode. Another option is to use the **`spanning-tree portfast bpduguard default`** command in global config mode; this automatically enables BPDU Guard on all PortFast-enabled ports. In the following example, I enable PortFast and BPDU Guard on a switch port:

```
SW4(config)# interface g0/0
SW4(config-if)# spanning-tree portfast            | Enables PortFast
SW4(config-if)# spanning-tree bpduguard enable    <-- Enables BPDU Guard
```

The port I enabled PortFast and BPDU Guard on in the example is connected to another switch, so we can see BPDU Guard in action—don't do this in a real network! If a switch port with BPDU Guard enabled receives a BPDU from another switch, it enters an *error-disabled* state. The following example shows the error messages displayed when BPDU Guard disables a port:

```
%SPANTREE-2-BLOCK_BPDUGUARD: Received BPDU on port Gi0/0
➥with BPDU Guard enabled. Disabling port.
%PM-4-ERR_DISABLE: bpduguard error detected on Gi0/0,
➥putting Gi0/0 in err-disable state
```

An error-disabled port is nonoperational; its status will be down/down in the output of **`show ip interface brief`**. This is an example of the STP disabled state I mentioned in section 14.4. To reenable an error-disabled port, first solve the problem that caused the error (disconnect the switch from the PortFast/BPDU Guard-enabled port), and then use the **`shutdown`** and **`no shutdown`** commands on the port to reset it.

> **EXAM TIP** Remember these best practices: only enable PortFast on ports meant for end hosts, and enable BPDU Guard on all PortFast-enabled ports. It is possible to use only PortFast or only BPDU Guard, but best practice is to use both features together.

Summary

- The Ethernet header does not have a mechanism to drop looping frames, so they will loop indefinitely.
- If enough looping frames accumulate, a *broadcast storm* can occur, using up so many network resources that the network becomes unusable.
- *Redundancy* is the practice of having additional network devices and connections beyond the minimum necessary for communication to eliminate single points of failure.

- Layer 2 loops occur as a result of the flooding of *BUM traffic*—broadcast, unknown unicast, and multicast frames—in a LAN with redundant connections.
- *Spanning Tree Protocol* (STP) prevents Layer 2 loops in a LAN by blocking redundant connections, leaving only one active path to each destination in the LAN.
- The process STP uses to create a loop-free topology is called the *STP algorithm.* It consists of three main steps: (1) root bridge election, (2) root port selection, and (3) designated port selection.
- All of the decisions in the algorithm are made by switches sharing STP *Bridge Protocol Data Unit* (BPDU) messages, which are sent every 2 seconds.
- The *root bridge* is the central point of reference for the STP topology. All switches in the LAN will ensure they have exactly one active path to the root bridge.
- The switch with the lowest *bridge ID* (BID) becomes the root bridge. The BID is a 64-bit number that uniquely identifies the switch. It consists of a 16-bit *bridge priority* and a 48-bit MAC address.
- The bridge priority consists of a configurable priority value (default 32768) and the *Extended System ID,* which is the VLAN ID.
- Cisco's implementation of STP is called *Per-VLAN Spanning Tree Plus* (PVST+), which creates a separate spanning tree for each VLAN.
- When a switch boots up, it announces itself as the root bridge and sends BPDUs out of all ports. If it receives BPDUs from a switch with a lower BID, it will accept that switch as the root bridge.
- Use the **`show spanning-tree`** command to view information about the root bridge's BID, the local switch's BID, and the local switch's ports.
- Use the **`spanning-tree vlan`** *`vlan-id`* **`priority`** *`priority-value`* command to configure the switch's priority for the specified VLAN (in increments of 4096).
- You can also use **`spanning-tree vlan`** *`vlan-id`* **`root`** {**`primary`** | **`secondary`**} to configure the priority. The **`secondary`** keyword sets the priority to 28672, and the **`primary`** keyword sets the priority to 24576, or the highest multiple of 4096 that will make the switch the root bridge (but it won't set the priority to 0).
- After electing the root bridge, all non-root switches will select exactly one *root port,* which provides the switch's single active path to the root bridge.
- The root port is selected using the following parameters in order of priority: (1) lowest root cost, (2) lowest neighbor BID, and (3) lowest neighbor port ID.
- A port's *root cost* indicates how efficient the path to the root bridge is via that port.
- When the root bridge sends BPDUs, they have a root cost of 0. When a non-root switch forwards BPDUs, it adds the cost of the port it received the BPDU on.
- The STP port cost values are 10 Mbps = 100, 100 Mbps = 19, 1 Gbps = 4, and 10 Gbps = 2.
- If a switch has the same root cost via two or more ports, the port connected to the neighbor with the lowest BID becomes the root port. If two or more of those

ports are connected to the same neighbor, the port connected to the neighbor's port with the lowest port ID becomes the root port.

- The *port ID* is a unique identifier for each port of the switch. It consists of a priority value (128 by default) and a sequential number.
- Each segment (link) must have exactly one designated port. All ports on the root bridge are designated, and the port connected to a root port must be designated.
- The remaining links then select one designated port, and the rest of the ports will be *non-designated* (blocking).
- Designated ports are selected with the following parameters in order of priority: (1) the port on the switch with the lowest root cost and (2) the port on the switch with the lowest BID.
- The four STP *port states* are blocking, listening, learning, and forwarding. There is also the *disabled* state, which refers to a nonoperational port.
- A newly enabled port will enter the *listening* state, where the switch decides its role.
- If the port becomes non-designated, it will immediately move to the *blocking* state, in which it is effectively disabled (this is how STP prevents loops).
- If the port becomes root or designated, it will move to the *learning* state, in which it starts to learn MAC addresses to build the MAC address table. Then, it will move to the *forwarding* state, where it can finally forward frames.
- The *hello* timer determines how often BPDUs are sent. It is 2 seconds by default.
- The *forward delay* timer determines the length of the listening and learning states. It is 15 seconds (per state) by default.
- The *max age* timer determines how long a switch will wait to change the STP topology after ceasing to receive BPDUs on a port.
- The timers on the root bridge dictate the timers that will be used on all switches in the LAN.
- It can take up to 50 seconds (max age timer + listening state + learning state) for a port to start forwarding after a change in the network.
- It can take 30 seconds for a newly enabled port to start forwarding frames.
- *PortFast* is an optional feature that can be configured on ports connected to end hosts to allow them to move directly to the forwarding state (no listening/learning).
- Use the **`spanning-tree portfast`** command in interface config mode to enable PortFast on a specific port or the **`spanning-tree portfast default`** command in global config mode to enable PortFast on all access ports.
- BPDU Guard should be configured on PortFast-enabled ports to disable them in case another switch is connected to the port.
- Use the **`spanning-tree bpduguard enable`** command in interface config mode to enable BPDU Guard on a specific port or the **`spanning-tree portfast`**

bpduguard default command in global config mode to enable it on all Port-Fast-enabled ports.

- If a BPDU Guard–enabled port receives a BPDU, the port will enter an *error-disabled* state, rendering it nonoperational. To reenable the port, disconnect the switch that caused the error and use **shutdown** and **no shutdown** on the port.

15 Rapid Spanning Tree Protocol

This chapter covers

- The standard and Cisco-proprietary versions of Spanning Tree Protocol
- A comparison of the port costs, states, and roles of STP and Rapid STP
- How RSTP-enabled switches react to topology changes
- How RSTP link types affect convergence
- Optional STP features Root Guard, Loop Guard, and BPDU Filter

In this chapter, we will continue to look at Spanning Tree Protocol (STP). There's a reason STP is enabled by default on almost any vendor's switches: Layer 2 loops are disastrous for a LAN. However, there are some downsides to the original STP as defined by IEEE 802.1D, the main one being speed; it can take up to 50 seconds to converge and reach a new, stable state after a change in the LAN. When STP was first released, 50 seconds was an acceptable time frame, but expectations have changed by now.

The answer to the increased demand for speed in modern LANs is *Rapid Spanning Tree Protocol* (RSTP), the topic of this chapter. The good news is that since we covered the original STP in chapter 14, you're already 80% of the way to understanding RSTP (from the perspective of the CCNA—there is more nuance when you dig deeper). In this chapter, we will continue from the previous chapter and finish covering exam topic 2.5: Identify basic operations of Rapid PVST+ Spanning Tree Protocol.

15.1 Spanning Tree Protocol versions

Before we look at the specifics of RSTP, let's briefly look at some of the different versions of STP, including industry-standard and Cisco-proprietary versions. In chapter 14, I mentioned two versions of STP: the protocol standardized in IEEE 802.1D and Cisco's PVST+. Cisco switches run PVST+, but the information in chapter 14 applies to both versions; the only difference is that PVST+ creates a separate spanning tree for each VLAN. This allows each VLAN to have a separate root bridge and a distinct topology of active and disabled links.

Likewise, RSTP was first standardized in IEEE 802.1w, and Cisco then developed *Rapid Per-VLAN Spanning Tree Plus* (Rapid PVST+), which runs on Cisco switches. The difference between 802.1w and Rapid PVST+ is the same as the difference between 802.1D and PVST+: whereas 802.1w creates a single spanning tree in the LAN, Rapid PVST+ creates a separate spanning tree for each VLAN, allowing traffic in different VLANs to use different links.

Modern Cisco switches can run both PVST+ and Rapid PVST+, but which version runs by default depends on the switch model and IOS version. To check which version is running on a switch, use the **`show spanning-tree`** command as in the following example; the line `Spanning tree enabled protocol ieee` indicates that PVST+ is running:

```
SW1# show spanning-tree
VLAN0001
  Spanning tree enabled protocol ieee          <---- PVST+ is running.
. . .
```

To configure which version of STP the switch should use, use the **`spanning-tree mode`** {**`pvst`** | **`rapid-pvst`**} command in global config mode. In the following example, I configure the switch to use Rapid PVST+ and then confirm with **`show spanning-tree`**; the line `Spanning tree enabled protocol rstp` indicates that Rapid PVST+ is running:

```
SW1(config)# spanning-tree mode rapid-pvst     <---- Enables Rapid PVST+
SW1(config)# do show spanning-tree
VLAN0001
  Spanning tree enabled protocol rstp          <---- Rapid PVST+ is running.
. . .
```

NOTE The keyword used to enable each mode is different from how it appears in the output of **`show spanning-tree`**. PVST+ is configured with **`spanning-tree mode pvst`** but appears as `Spanning tree enabled protocol ieee`. Rapid PVST+ is configured with **`spanning-tree mode rapid-pvst`** but appears as

`Spanning tree enabled protocol rstp`. Keep in mind that Cisco switches do not run the IEEE-standard versions of STP and RSTP—they run PVST+ and Rapid PVST+.

Although the ability to create a unique spanning tree for each VLAN is a benefit of PVST+ and Rapid PVST+ over their standard counterparts, there is a downside: in a LAN with many VLANs, a switch runs a separate STP instance and sends unique Bridge Protocol Data Units (BPDUs) for each VLAN. If there are 100 VLANs, each switch runs 100 STP instances and sends 100 BPDUs out of each designated port every 2 seconds. This taxes switch CPU and memory resources and can negatively affect network performance and stability.

Additionally, having many STP instances increases the complexity of managing the switches; configuring, monitoring, and troubleshooting 100 instances of STP can be unnecessarily complex. The reality is that in a LAN with 100 VLANs, there likely isn't a need for 100 unique spanning trees; you'll probably assign one switch as the root bridge for 50 of the VLANs and another switch as the root bridge for the remaining 50 VLANs, resulting in only two unique spanning trees.

In such a LAN, *Multiple Spanning Tree Protocol* (MSTP) might be preferred. With MSTP, you can group multiple VLANs into a single instance. For example, in a LAN with 100 VLANs, you might create two MSTP instances and group 50 VLANs in one instance and 50 VLANs in the other. This allows you to avoid congestion by balancing traffic over separate links, without using up resources by running 100 STP instances. And MSTP uses RSTP's mechanics for quick convergence—no 50-second waits like in 802.1D. Figure 15.1 shows how MSTP groups multiple VLANs into each instance.

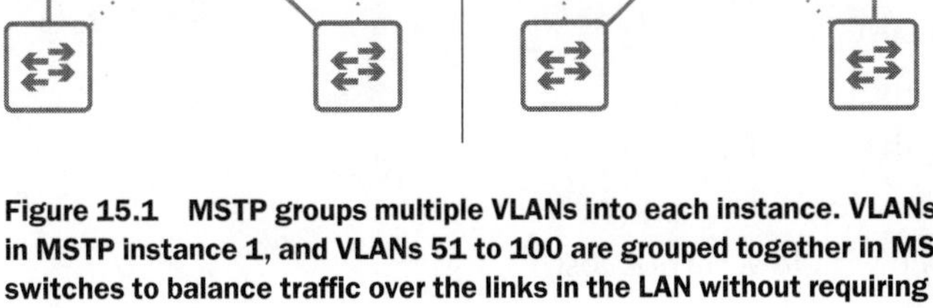

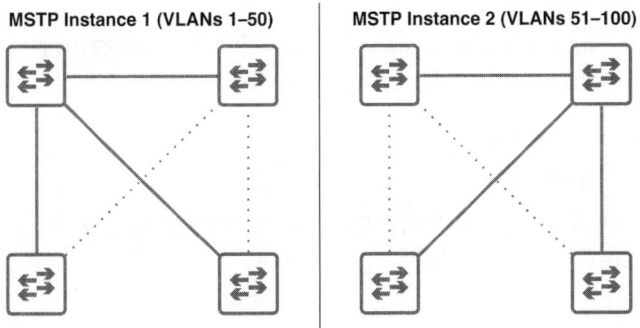

Figure 15.1 MSTP groups multiple VLANs into each instance. VLANs 1 to 50 are grouped together in MSTP instance 1, and VLANs 51 to 100 are grouped together in MSTP instance 2. This allows the switches to balance traffic over the links in the LAN without requiring a separate STP instance for each VLAN.

The details of MSTP are beyond the scope of the CCNA exam, so a basic understanding of its benefit (grouping multiple VLANs per instance) is sufficient. Table 15.1 summarizes the different versions of STP you should be aware of for the CCNA.

Table 15.1 STP versions

Version	Standard or Cisco-proprietary	Description
STP	Standard (802.1D)	The original standard. Creates only a single spanning tree.
PVST+	Cisco-proprietary	Cisco's upgrade to 802.1D. Creates a separate spanning tree for each VLAN.
RSTP	Standard (802.1w)	Much faster convergence than 802.1D. Creates only a single spanning tree.
Rapid PVST+	Cisco-proprietary	Cisco's upgrade to 802.1w. Creates a separate spanning tree for each VLAN.
MSTP	Standard (802.1s)	Uses RSTP mechanics for fast convergence. Groups multiple VLANs into each spanning tree instance.

15.2 STP and RSTP comparison

As the word "rapid" in the name suggests, the fundamental difference between STP and RSTP is speed. Whereas 802.1D's STP is a timer-based protocol in which a port can take up to 50 seconds to begin forwarding, 802.1w's RSTP uses a synchronization mechanism in which RSTP-enabled switches communicate with each other to bring ports immediately to the forwarding state, without waiting for timers to count down.

> **EXAM TIP** The details of RSTP's sync mechanism are beyond the scope of the CCNA exam. Instead, focus on learning the RSTP port costs, states, roles, and link types covered in this chapter.

Although we will cover the various differences between STP and RSTP, keep in mind that the algorithm for calculating the topology is identical:

- Root bridge election (one per LAN)
  - Lowest bridge ID (BID)
- Root port selection (one per switch, excluding root bridge)
  - Lowest root cost
  - Lowest neighbor BID
  - Lowest neighbor port ID
- Designated port selection (one per segment)
  - Port on switch with lowest root cost
  - Port on switch with lowest BID

In STP, the remaining ports will all be nondesignated. In RSTP, they will be one of two roles: alternate or backup (we will cover them in section 15.2.3). Figure 15.2 shows the same LAN we looked at in chapter 14, this time using RSTP. The only difference is that the nondesignated ports are now alternate ports.

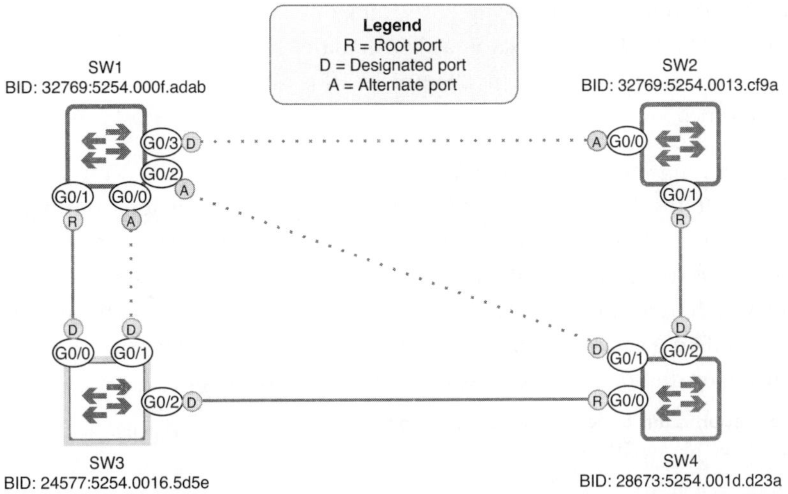

Figure 15.2 A LAN after RSTP has created a loop-free topology. The only difference in the topology between STP and RSTP is that the nondesignated ports are now called alternate ports.

NOTE A technical detail that could come up on the exam is how STP and RSTP handle BPDUs. In STP, the root bridge sends BPDUs every 2 seconds, and the other switches forward them out of their designated ports. In RSTP, all switches send BPDUs out of their designated ports every two seconds, whether they received a BPDU from the root bridge or not.

15.2.1 Port costs

STP defines port costs for speeds of up to 10 Gbps (with a cost of 2). RSTP, on the other hand, introduces a new set of port costs to accommodate ports of greater speeds—up to 10 Tbps. The original STP port costs are now called the *short* costs, and the new RSTP port costs are called the *long* costs. Table 15.2 lists the short and long costs of ports of various speeds.

Table 15.2 Short and long port costs

Speed	Short cost	Long cost
10 Mbps	100	2,000,000
100 Mbps	19	200,000
1 Gbps	4	20,000
10 Gbps	2	2,000
100 Gbps	-	200
1 Tbps	-	20
10 Tbps	-	2

EXAM TIP To remember the long costs, pick one as a point of reference (such as 10 Gbps = 2,000). Then you can easily calculate the long costs of ports of other speeds: increasing the speed by a factor of 10 reduces the cost by a factor of 10 and vice versa.

Although the long method of calculating port costs was introduced in RSTP, keep in mind that switches don't necessarily use it by default, even when running RSTP—it depends on the switch model and software version. To view which method (short or long) a switch is using, use the **`show spanning-tree pathcost method`** command, and to modify which method the switch uses to calculate port costs, use the **`spanning-tree pathcost method`** {**`short`** | **`long`**} command in global config mode. As you can see in the following example, my switch uses the short costs by default:

```
SW1# show spanning-tree pathcost method
Spanning tree default pathcost method used is short
```

The default method is short.

15.2.2 Port states

Whereas STP has four main states (blocking, listening, learning, forwarding), RSTP combines the first two states into a single state called *discarding*. Table 15.3 compares the STP and RSTP port states.

Table 15.3 STP and RSTP port states

STP port state	RSTP port state
Blocking	Discarding
Listening	
Learning	Learning
Forwarding	Forwarding

When an RSTP port is first enabled, it will enter the discarding state. If it is decided that the port will be an alternate or backup port (more on that in section 15.2.3), it will remain in the discarding state, blocking traffic to prevent Layer 2 loops. However, if the port becomes a root or designated port, it will proceed to the forwarding state in one of two ways, as shown in figure 15.3.

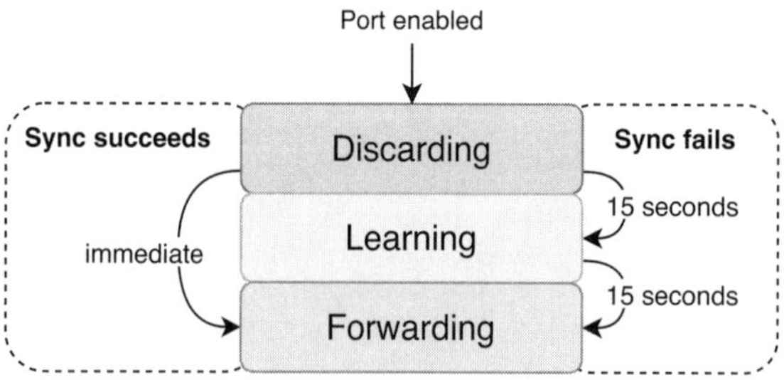

Figure 15.3 An RSTP port can transition to the forwarding state in one of two ways. If the RSTP sync mechanism succeeds, the port immediately transitions to the forwarding state. If the RSTP sync mechanism fails, the port transitions from discarding to learning to forwarding, like a regular STP port.

If the RSTP sync mechanism succeeds, the port immediately transitions to the forwarding state—no need to wait for any timers. This is expected if the port is connected to another RSTP-enabled switch. However, the sync mechanism will not work in all situations—for example, if the port is connected to a device that doesn't use RSTP, such as a router, a PC, or even a switch that is using STP instead of RSTP. In that case, the port will remain in the discarding state for 15 seconds (the duration of the forward delay timer), then transition to the learning state for another 15 seconds, and then finally transition to the forwarding state—this is like a regular STP port transitioning through the listening and learning states before forwarding.

> **NOTE** RSTP and STP are compatible. However, a port on an RSTP-enabled switch that is connected to a port on an STP-enabled switch will not be able to take advantage of RSTP's sync mechanism. The port on the RSTP-enabled switch will operate like a regular STP port.

These days, you can safely expect that all switches will support RSTP, so you should only expect the timer-based transition to the forwarding state on ports connected to a host like a PC. However, as we covered in chapter 14, PortFast can be configured on such ports to allow them to start forwarding frames immediately—we will cover PortFast again in section 15.3.

15.2.3 Port roles

The three port roles of STP are root, designated, and nondesignated; we covered these in chapter 14. In RSTP, the root and designated roles remain unchanged. A root port is a forwarding port that points toward the root bridge; it provides the switch's only active path to reach the root bridge. A designated port is a forwarding port that points away from the root bridge, and all segments must have exactly one designated port. However, the nondesignated port role has been replaced by two distinct roles: alternate and backup. Like nondesignated ports, alternate and backup ports block traffic to prevent Layer 2 loops.

ALTERNATE ROLE

An RSTP *alternate port* can be thought of as an alternative for the switch's root port; it provides an alternative path toward the root bridge and is ready to take over (by transitioning to the forwarding state) if the root port fails. The rule for becoming an alternate port is as follows: any port that is not a root or designated port is an alternate port if the switch is not the designated bridge for that segment.

> **NOTE** *Designated bridge* is a new term; it is the switch that has the designated port for a particular segment. This term applies to both STP and RSTP.

In almost all cases, a port that is neither a root port nor a designated port will be an alternate port. Figure 15.4 explains why each of the alternate ports in the LAN is in that state.

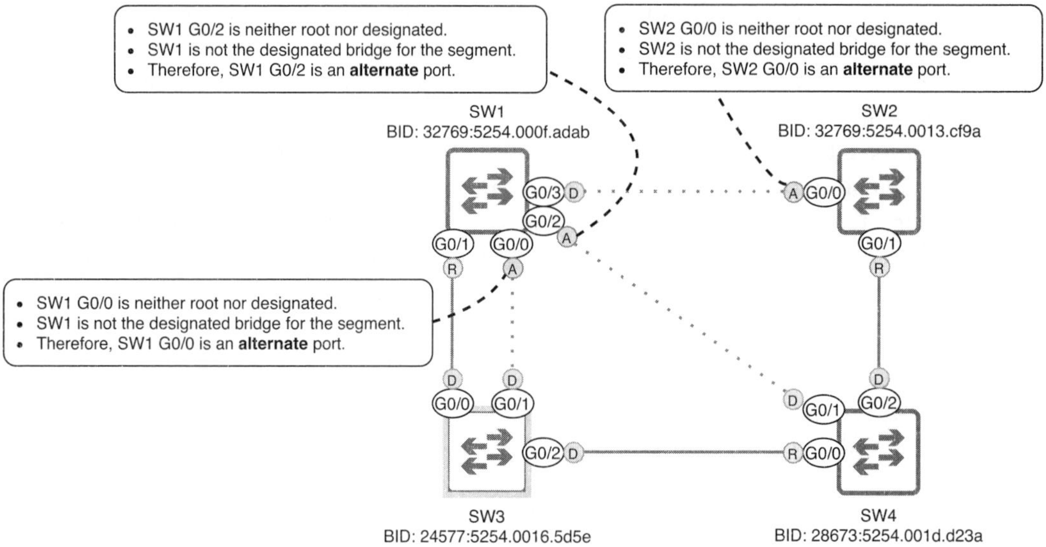

• SW1 G0/2 is neither root nor designated.
• SW1 is not the designated bridge for the segment.
• Therefore, SW1 G0/2 is an **alternate** port.
• SW2 G0/0 is neither root nor designated.
• SW2 is not the designated bridge for the segment.
• Therefore, SW2 G0/0 is an **alternate** port.
SW1
BID: 32769:5254.000f.adab
SW2
BID: 32769:5254.0013.cf9a
G0/3 D
G0/2
A
G0/1
G0/0
R
A
A G0/0
G0/1
R
• SW1 G0/0 is neither root nor designated.
• SW1 is not the designated bridge for the segment.
• Therefore, SW1 G0/0 is an **alternate** port.
D
G0/0
D
G0/1
D G0/1
D G0/2
G0/2 D
R G0/0
SW3
BID: 24577:5254.0016.5d5e
SW4
BID: 28673:5254.001d.d23a

Figure 15.4 A port will become an alternate port if it is neither root nor designated and if the switch is not the designated bridge for the segment. In almost all cases, a port that is neither root nor designated will be an alternate port.

NOTE A simple way to define an alternate port is as a port in the discarding state that is connected to a designated port on another switch.

BACKUP ROLE

An RSTP *backup port* provides a backup path to the same segment as a designated port on the same switch. This will only occur if two ports on the same switch are connected to the same segment (collision domain)—for example, with a hub. You will most likely never use a hub in a modern network, so I wouldn't expect to encounter a backup port "in the wild." However, backup ports are worth covering, even if just for the possibility of a question about them on the exam.

The rule for becoming a backup port is as follows: any port that is not a root or designated port is a backup port if the switch is the designated bridge for that segment. In figure 15.5, I have added a hub between SW1 and SW3 (and removed SW2 and SW4 from the diagram), connecting their four ports to the same segment. SW1 G0/1 becomes an alternate port (because SW1 isn't the designated bridge for the segment), but SW3 G0/1 becomes a backup port (because SW3 is the designated bridge for the segment).

NOTE We can simplify this rule too: a backup port is a port in the discarding state that is connected to a designated port on the same switch (via a hub). In figure 15.5, SW3 G0/1 is connected to SW3 G0/0 (a designated port) via a hub.

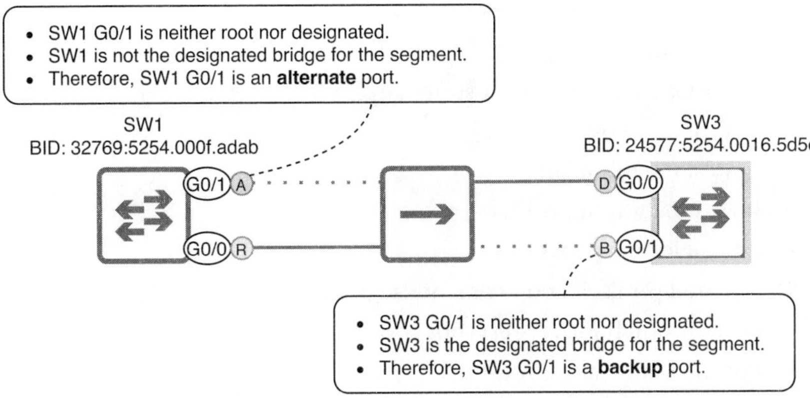

• SW1 G0/1 is neither root nor designated.
• SW1 is not the designated bridge for the segment.
• Therefore, SW1 G0/1 is an **alternate** port.
SW1
BID: 32769:5254.000f.adab
SW3
BID: 24577:5254.0016.5d5e
G0/1 A
G0/0 R
D G0/0
B G0/1
• SW3 G0/1 is neither root nor designated.
• SW3 is the designated bridge for the segment.
• Therefore, SW3 G0/1 is a **backup** port.

Figure 15.5 SW1 and SW3 both have multiple ports connected to the same segment. SW1 G0/1 becomes an alternate port because SW1 is not the designated bridge for the segment. SW3 G0/1 becomes a backup (B) port because SW3 is the designated bridge for the segment.

In the following example, I use the **`show spanning-tree`** command on SW1 and SW3 to confirm their port roles; `Altn` stands for alternate, and `Back` stands for backup. Note that the `Sts` column states `BLK` in each case; even though the blocking state was renamed to discarding in RSTP, this command retains the "blocking" terminology:

```
SW1# show spanning-tree
. . .
Interface           Role Sts Cost      Prio.Nbr Type
------------------- ---- --- --------- -------- --------------------------------
Gi0/0               Root FWD 4         128.1    Shr
Gi0/1               Altn BLK 4         128.2    Shr

SW3# show spanning-tree
. . .
Interface           Role Sts Cost      Prio.Nbr Type
------------------- ---- --- --------- -------- --------------------------------
Gi0/0               Desg FWD 4         128.1    Shr
Gi0/1               Back BLK 4         128.2    Shr
```

SW1 G0/0 is a root port.
SW1 G0/1 is an alternate port.
SW3 G0/0 is a designated port.
SW3 G0/1 is a backup port.

Why does SW1 G0/0 become a root port instead of SW1 G0/1, and why does SW3 G0/0 become a designated port instead of SW3 G0/1? When multiple ports on the same switch are connected to the same segment, there is an additional tiebreaker for the root/designated port selection steps of the STP algorithm: the port with the lowest port ID on the local switch becomes root/designated. SW1 G0/0 has a lower port ID than SW1 G0/1, so G0/0 becomes a root port, and G0/1 becomes an alternate port. Likewise, SW3 G0/0 has a lower port ID than SW3 G0/1, so G0/0 becomes a designated port, and G0/1 becomes a backup port. With these tiebreakers added, the STP algorithm is as follows:

- Root bridge election (one per LAN)
  - Lowest BID
- Root port selection (one per switch, excluding root bridge)
  - Lowest root cost
  - Lowest neighbor BID
  - Lowest neighbor port ID
  - Lowest local port ID
- Designated port selection (one per segment)
  - Port on switch with lowest root cost
  - Port on switch with lowest BID
  - Lowest local port ID

NOTE These tiebreakers apply to STP too. If SW1 and SW3 were running STP rather than RSTP, their alternate/backup ports would both be nondesignated ports; there is no such distinction of roles in STP.

In chapter 14, I mentioned that every port on the root bridge should be designated. This is almost always true, but as we just saw, if multiple ports on the root bridge are connected to the same segment, only one can be designated; the "one designated port per segment" rule wins out. So rather than "every port on the root bridge should be designated," a more accurate rule is "the root bridge is the designated bridge for every segment." However, because you will rarely (if ever) encounter a LAN using hubs, you'll most often hear that every port on the root bridge should be designated.

15.2.4 RSTP topology changes

In chapter 14, we covered an example in which a switch's nondesignated port took 50 seconds to move to a forwarding state after a change in the topology (due to a hardware failure). Although the details of the topology change processes of STP and RSTP are beyond the scope of the CCNA exam, let's take a brief look at one way that RSTP speeds up the process. Figure 15.6 shows the same example from chapter 14, this time using RSTP.

Whereas an STP-enabled switch waits 20 seconds (the max age timer) after ceasing to receive BPDUs on a port to react and initiate the topology change process, RSTP only waits until a port misses three BPDUs (6 seconds by default) to react. Then, as in figure 15.6, the next-best port can sync with its neighbor and immediately move to the forwarding state; a 50-second process has been shortened to just over 6 seconds.

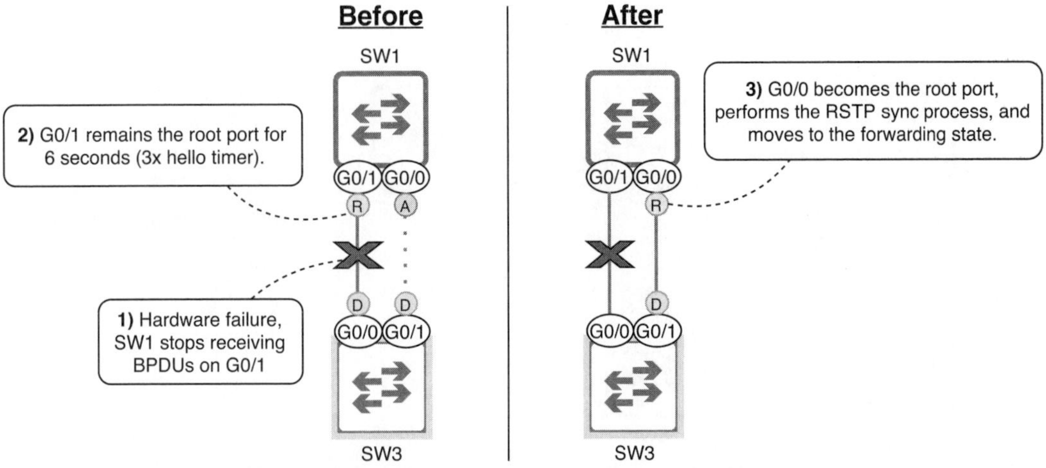

Figure 15.6 RSTP speeds up convergence after a topology change like this from 50 seconds to just over 6 seconds. (1) Due to a hardware failure, SW1 stops receiving BPDUs on G0/1 (without the port going down). (2) G0/1 remains the root port for 6 seconds (3× the hello timer of 2 seconds). (3) G0/0 becomes the root port and, after performing the RSTP sync process, immediately moves to the forwarding state.

NOTE If the hardware failure caused SW1's G0/1 port to go down (enter a disabled state), the process would be even faster; there would be no need to wait 6 seconds. In that case, SW1 G0/0 will immediately initiate the sync process, bringing the total downtime to less than 1 second.

15.3 RSTP link types

Another aspect of RSTP is the concept of *link types*. These types influence how ports transition through the RSTP port states and react to network changes. RSTP defines three link types:

- *Point-to-point*—Full-duplex ports that can use the RSTP sync mechanism to immediately transition to the forwarding state.
- *Shared*—Half-duplex ports that cannot use the RSTP sync mechanism. They must transition through the states like standard STP ports.
- *Edge*—Ports connected to end hosts that can use PortFast to immediately transition to the forwarding state.

Figure 15.7 illustrates these three link types on three switches.

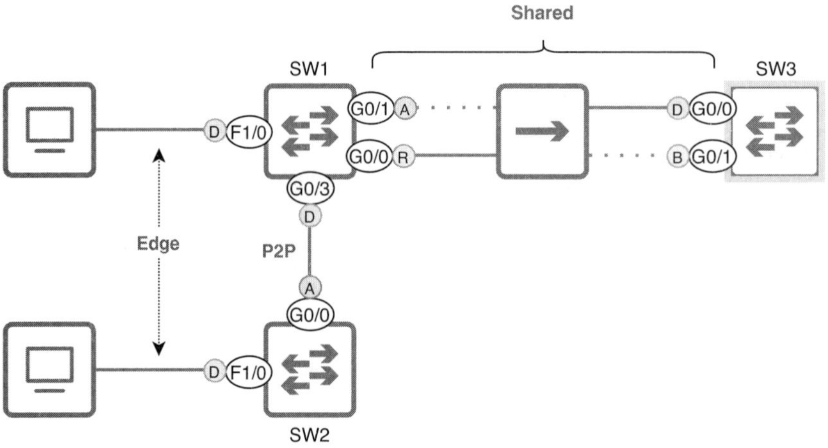

Figure 15.7 RSTP differentiates between three link types: point-to-point, shared, and edge. A full-duplex link is considered a point-to-point link. A half-duplex link is considered a shared link. A link between a switch and an end host that uses PortFast is considered an edge link.

An RSTP *point-to-point* link is a link that operates in full duplex, meaning that the connected ports (i.e. SW1 G0/3 and SW2 G0/0) operate in full duplex. These are the only links that can take advantage of RSTP's sync mechanism to rapidly transition ports to the forwarding state. Although full-duplex ports will automatically use the point-to-point link type, you can also manually configure it with the **`spanning-tree link-type point-to-point`** command in interface config mode.

An RSTP *shared* link is a link that operates in half duplex. In figure 15.7, SW1 and SW3 are connected via a hub, and devices connected to a hub must operate in half-duplex; therefore, the link is an RSTP shared link. Ports connected to a shared link cannot use RSTP's sync mechanism; in effect, they operate like regular STP links, taking 30 seconds to move to the forwarding state. Half-duplex ports will automatically use the shared link type, but if necessary, the **`spanning-tree link-type shared`** command can be used to manually configure it.

> **NOTE** Like the backup port role, you probably won't encounter the shared link type in a real network.

Finally, there is the *edge* link type. These are ports that connect to end hosts: SW1 F1/0 and SW2 F1/0. These ports don't need to use the RSTP sync mechanism; there is no risk of a Layer 2 loop, so they can immediately transition to the forwarding state. Does a port connected to an end host immediately transitioning to the forwarding state sound familiar?

On Cisco switches, the edge link type must be manually configured by enabling PortFast on the appropriate ports (with the **`spanning-tree portfast`** command, as we covered in chapter 14)—not the **`spanning-tree link-type`** command like point-to-point and shared links. Note that this is the only link type that can't be automatically determined by the switch based on the port's duplex mode; you must manually configure it.

NOTE A port that is connected to an end host but hasn't been configured with the **`spanning-tree portfast`** command won't immediately transition to the forwarding state—it will have to wait 30 seconds like a regular STP port.

One more characteristic of edge ports is that RSTP doesn't consider any activity on them (such as moving to the forwarding or discarding states) a topology change and doesn't notify its neighbors of the activity. Because edge ports connect to end hosts (not switches), and therefore pose no risk of causing Layer 2 loops, there's no need to notify other switches of activity on those ports; they don't affect the rest of the RSTP topology.

Topology changes

STP and RSTP each have defined processes for reacting to changes in the topology, allowing switches to adapt to the new topology with minimal disruptions; the details of these processes are beyond the scope of the CCNA exam. STP triggers its topology change process in the following situations:

- When any port transitions to the forwarding state
- When a port in the learning state or forwarding state transitions to the blocking state or disabled state

Switches using RSTP, on the other hand, only trigger the topology change process when a port with a non-edge link type (point-to-point or shared) transitions to the forwarding state; they don't trigger the process when an edge port transitions to the forwarding state or when any port transitions to the discarding state.

EXAM TIP The details of STP/RSTP topology changes are beyond the scope of the CCNA exam, but remember this characteristic of RSTP edge ports: they don't trigger the topology change process when moving to the forwarding state.

You can view the type of link of each port with the **`show spanning-tree`** command. The final column on the right lists the link types: point-to-point (`P2p`), shared (`Shr`), and edge (`Edge`). In the following example, I use the command on SW1:

```
SW1# show spanning-tree
. . .
Interface           Role Sts Cost      Prio.Nbr Type
------------------- ---- --- --------- -------- --------------------------------
Gi0/0               Root FWD 4         128.1    Shr
Gi0/1               Altn BLK 4         128.2    Shr
Gi0/3               Desg FWD 4         128.4    P2p
Fa1/0               Desg FWD 19        128.9    P2p Edge
```

Shr indicates a shared link.

P2p indicates a point-to-point link.

P2p Edge indicates a point-to-point edge link (a full-duplex link using PortFast).

NOTE F1/0's type is listed as `P2p Edge`. In Cisco IOS, an edge port will appear as `P2p Edge` if it operates in full duplex or `Shr Edge` if it operates in half duplex.

In a modern network that uses only switches (not hubs), links between two switches should have the point-to-point type, and links between a switch and an end host should have the edge link type (more specifically, the point-to-point edge).

15.4 Root Guard, Loop Guard, and BPDU Filter

In chapter 14, we covered two optional STP features: PortFast and BPDU Guard. While these are the two most common features in the so-called STP toolkit, the CCNA exam expects you to know a few more tools that expand STP's (or RSTP's) functionality. In this section, we will discuss Root Guard, Loop Guard, and BPDU Filter.

NOTE All of these optional STP features—PortFast, BPDU Guard, Root Guard, Loop Guard, and BPDU Filter—work in both STP and RSTP.

15.4.1 Root Guard

Root Guard is a feature that enhances the stability of the STP topology by preventing external switches from becoming the root bridge. A common scenario where Root Guard is useful is when a LAN of switches is controlled by two different entities, such as a service provider and a customer (who connects to the service provider's network). The service provider can use Root Guard to ensure that one of its switches remains the root bridge, maintaining a consistent STP topology even if a customer connects a switch with a lower bridge ID. Figure 15.8 illustrates this scenario.

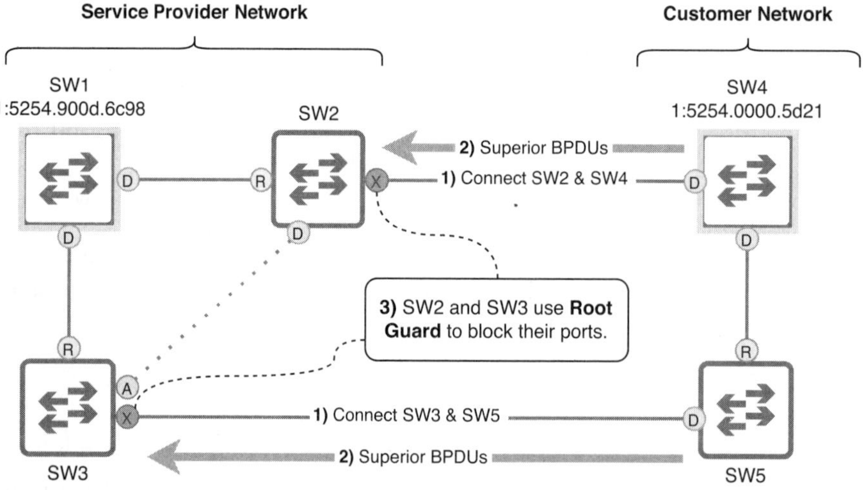

Figure 15.8 Root Guard prevents a newly connected customer network from affecting the service provider's STP topology. (1) The customer's SW4 and SW5 are connected to the service provider's SW2 and SW3. (2) SW4's bridge ID is lower than SW1's, so the BPDUs sent by SW4 and SW5 are superior to SW1's BPDUs. (3) SW2 and SW3 use Root Guard to block their ports that receive the superior BPDUs.

When a Root Guard-enabled port receives a superior BPDU, the port will enter the *root-inconsistent* state; in effect, this disables the port, preventing the switch from accepting the superior BPDU. In this state, the customer is unable to access the service provider's network. To fix this problem, the customer needs to configure a higher bridge ID on SW4, making the BPDUs it sends inferior to those of SW1. Once the superior BPDUs are no longer received, SW2's and SW3's ports automatically recover and return to their normal state.

The following example shows how to enable Root Guard on a port with the **spanning-tree guard root** command and the error message that appears when Root Guard blocks the port.

```
SW2(config)# interface g0/2
SW2(config-if)# spanning-tree guard root
*May 18 01:13:20.478: %SPANTREE-2-ROOTGUARD_BLOCK: Root guard blocking
port GigabitEthernet0/2 on VLAN0001.
SW2(config-if)# do show spanning-tree
. . .
Interface           Role Sts Cost      Prio.Nbr Type
------------------- ---- --- --------- -------- -------------------------
Gi0/0               Root FWD 4         128.1    P2p
Gi0/1               Altn BLK 4         128.2    P2p
Gi0/2               Desg BKN*4         128.3    P2p *ROOT_Inc
```

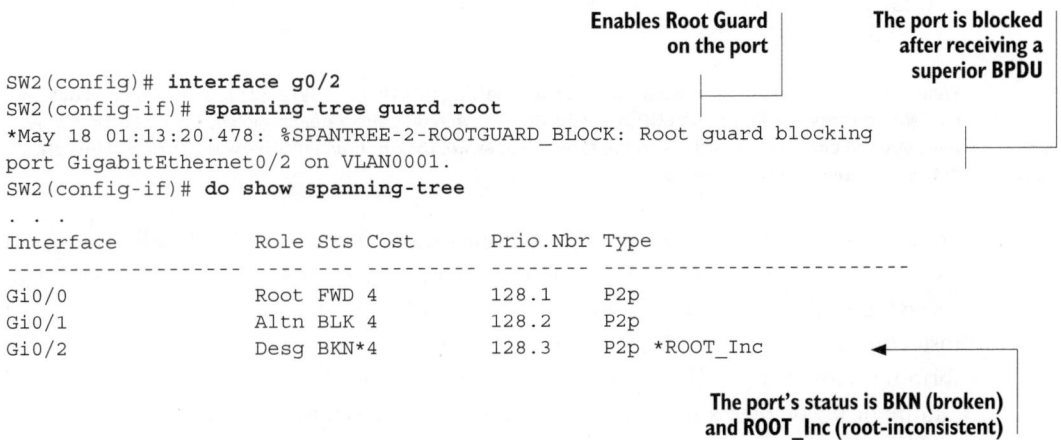

Enables Root Guard on the port

The port is blocked after receiving a superior BPDU

The port's status is BKN (broken) and ROOT_Inc (root-inconsistent)

By using Root Guard, you can ensure that your network's STP topology remains stable and consistent, preventing external or misconfigured devices from disrupting the network.

15.4.2 Loop Guard

Loop Guard, as the name implies, guards against Layer 2 loops in the LAN. The entire point of STP is to prevent loops, but Loop Guard provides an additional layer of protection against a switch port erroneously transitioning from the discarding state (the blocking state in classic STP) to the forwarding state. This can happen when the discarding port stops receiving BPDUs, causing the switch to believe that the port can move to the forwarding state without causing a loop. Figure 15.9 shows how this can cause a loop.

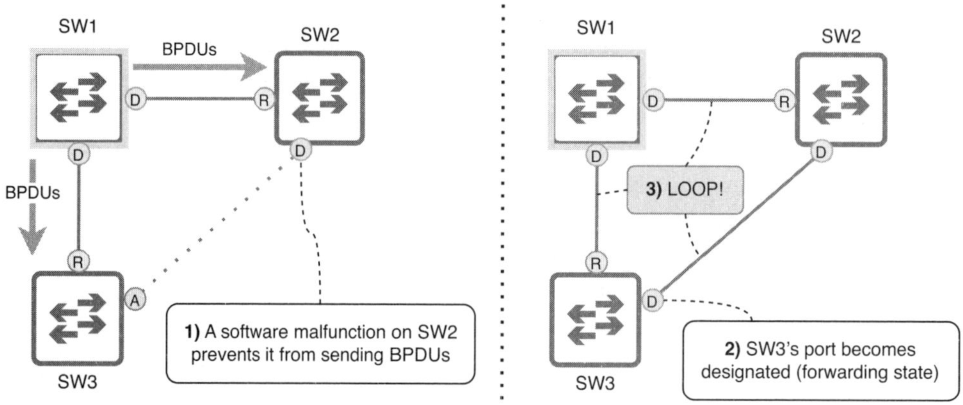

Figure 15.9 A loop is caused when SW3 stops receiving BPDUs from SW2. (1) A software malfunction on SW2 prevents it from sending BPDUs. (2) After the max age timer counts down, SW3's port becomes a designated port and transitions to the forwarding state. (3) All three links between the switches are active, resulting in a Layer 2 loop.

To avoid such a problem, you can configure Loop Guard on SW3's alternate port using the **spanning-tree guard loop** command. If a Loop Guard-enabled port stops receiving BPDUs, the port will move into the *loop-inconsistent* state, disabling the port instead of allowing it to transition to the forwarding state; this prevents a loop from forming. However, if SW2 recovers and starts sending BPDUs again, SW3's port will automatically recover and transition back to its normal state (discarding).

The following example shows how to enable Loop Guard and the error message that appears when Loop Guard blocks the port to prevent a loop.

Enables Loop Guard on the port

The port is blocked after ceasing to receive BPDUs

```
SW2(config)# interface g0/1
SW2(config-if)# spanning-tree guard loop
*May 18 01:29:31.261: %SPANTREE-2-LOOPGUARD_BLOCK: Loop guard blocking
port GigabitEthernet0/1 on VLAN0001.
SW2(config-if)# do show spanning-tree
. . .
Interface           Role Sts Cost      Prio.Nbr Type
------------------- ---- --- --------- -------- ------------------------
Gi0/0               Root FWD 4         128.1    P2p
Gi0/1               Desg BKN*4         128.2    P2p *LOOP_Inc
```

The port's status is BKN (broken) and LOOP_Inc (loop-inconsistent)

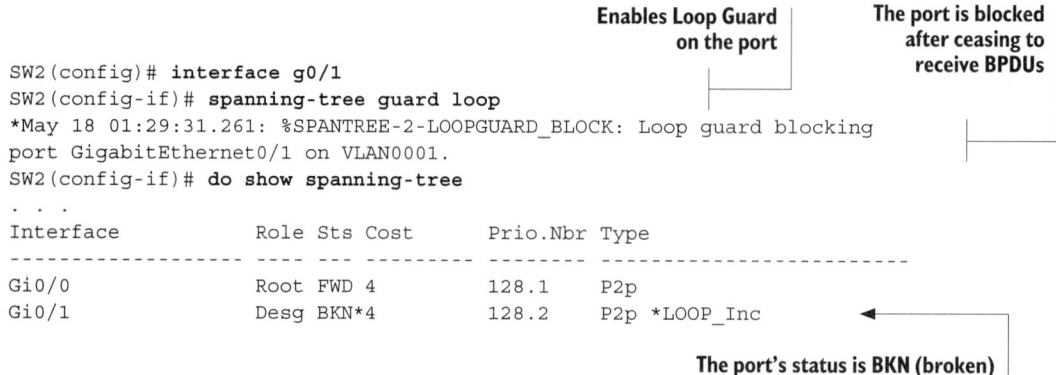

With Loop Guard, you can provide an additional safeguard against potential network loops, ensuring the stability and reliability of the LAN. A Layer 2 loop can bring down any LAN, so avoiding them is critical.

NOTE Root Guard and Loop Guard are mutually exclusive; you can't enable both of them on the same port simultaneously. This is because they serve different roles: Root Guard takes action based on receiving superior BPDUs, while Loop Guard takes action based on not receiving BPDUs.

15.4.3 BPDU Filter

BPDU Filter is a feature that can be used to prevent BPDUs from being sent or received on specific ports. This can be desirable on ports where STP isn't necessary, such as those connected to end hosts, since there is no risk of causing a loop. BPDU Filter can be enabled in two ways, with different behaviors depending on how you activate it:

- Enabling BPDU Filter on a specific port
  - Use **`spanning-tree bpdufilter enable`** in interface config mode.
  - This enables BPDU Filter on the specific port.
  - The port will not send BPDUs and will ignore any BPDUs it receives.
  - This effectively disables STP on the port.
- Enable BPDU Filter globally for all PortFast-enabled ports
  - Use **`spanning-tree portfast bpdufilter default`** in global config mode.
  - This enables BPDU Filter on all PortFast-enabled ports (RSTP edge ports).
  - The port will not send BPDUs.
  - If the port receives a BPDU, PortFast and BPDU Filter will be disabled. The port will then operate as a normal STP or RSTP port.

Of the optional STP features that we have covered in this chapter and the previous one—PortFast, BPDU Guard, Root Guard, Loop Guard, and BPDU Filter—BPDU Filter has the fewest use cases; I recommend avoiding it in general. Especially when enabled in interface config mode, BPDU Filter poses the risk of causing a Layer 2 loop if the port is connected to another switch; STP is effectively disabled on the BPDU Filter-enabled port, so it won't move to the discarding state even if there is a loop in the LAN. Enabling BPDU Filter carelessly is a great way to bring down a network—use with extreme caution!

Summary

- STP, standardized by IEEE 802.1D, was modified by Cisco to make PVST+. Likewise, RSTP, standardized by IEEE 802.1w, was modified by Cisco to make Rapid PVST+. PVST+ and Rapid PVST+ both run separate spanning tree instances for each VLAN.
- Whether a switch runs PVST+ or Rapid PVST+ by default depends on the switch model and IOS version.

- The running version of STP can be confirmed with **`show spanning-tree`**. The output `Spanning tree enabled protocol ieee` means PVST+, and `Spanning tree enabled protocol rstp` means Rapid PVST+.
- You can configure a switch to use PVST+ or Rapid PVST+ with the **`spanning -tree mode`** {**`pvst`** | **`rapid-pvst`**} command in global config mode.
- *Multiple Spanning Tree Protocol* (MSTP), standardized by 802.1s, allows multiple VLANs to be grouped together in each instance.
- The fundamental difference between STP and RSTP is speed. Rather than relying on timers, RSTP-enabled switches can use a sync mechanism to rapidly transition their ports to the forwarding state.
- The algorithm used to decide the root bridge, root ports, and designated ports in RSTP is identical to that of STP.
- Whereas STP switches only forward BPDUs from the root bridge out of their designated ports, RSTP switches send BPDUs out of their designated ports every 2 seconds, even if they didn't receive a BPDU from the root bridge.
- The original STP port costs are called the *short* costs. RSTP introduced the *long* method of calculating port costs to accommodate ports of greater speeds.
- With the long method, 10 Mbps = 2,000,000, and a 10-fold speed increase decreases the cost 10-fold (with a top speed of 10 Tbps, which has a cost of 2).
- A switch may use the short or long method of calculating costs by default, depending on the switch model and IOS version. Use the **`show spanning-tree pathcost method`** command to confirm.
- Use the **`spanning-tree pathcost method`** {**`short`** | **`long`**} command in global config mode to configure which cost-calculation method a switch will use.
- RSTP uses three port states: discarding, learning, and forwarding. The STP disabled, blocking, and listening states were combined into the RSTP discarding state.
- When an RSTP port is first enabled, it will enter the discarding state. Alternate and backup ports will remain in that state. Root and designated ports will transition to the forwarding state.
- If the RSTP sync mechanism succeeds, the port will transition immediately to the forwarding state. If the sync mechanism fails, it will spend 15 seconds each in the discarding and learning states before reaching the forwarding state.
- RSTP uses four port roles: root, designated, alternate, and backup. The alternate and backup roles are equivalent to the STP nondesignated role.
- An alternate port provides an alternate path toward the root bridge. Any port that is not a root or designated port is an alternate port if the switch is not the designated bridge for the segment.

- A backup port provides a backup path to the same segment as a designated port on the same switch. This will only occur if two ports on the same switch are connected to the same segment with a hub, which is extremely rare in modern networks.
- Any port that is not a root or designated port is a backup port if the switch is the designated bridge for the segment.
- If multiple ports on the same switch are connected to the same segment, the lowest local port ID is used as a tiebreaker for the root port and designated port selection processes.
- Whereas an STP-enabled switch waits 20 seconds (the max age timer) after ceasing to receive BPDUs on a port to react, RSTP only waits until a port misses three BPDUs (6 seconds).
- In some cases, RSTP can shorten the STP reconvergence process after a topology change to less than 1 second.
- RSTP differentiates between three link types: point-to-point, shared, and edge.
- A *point-to-point* link is a link that operates in full duplex. Ports with this link type can use the RSTP sync mechanism to rapidly transition to the forwarding state. Full-duplex ports will automatically use this link type.
- A *shared* link is a link that operates in half duplex. Ports with this link type cannot use the RSTP sync mechanism. Half-duplex ports will automatically use this link type.
- An *edge* link is a point-to-point link that connects to an end host and is configured to use PortFast. Ports with the edge link type can immediately transition to the forwarding state without using the RSTP sync mechanism.
- To manually configure the point-to-point/shared link types, use the **`spanning-tree link-type`** {**`point-to-point`** | **`shared`**} command in interface config mode. To configure the edge link type, use the **`spanning-tree portfast`** command in interface config mode.
- *Root Guard* enhances the stability of the STP topology by preventing external switches from becoming the root bridge. If a Root Guard-enabled port receives a superior BPDU, the port will enter the *root-inconsistent* state; in effect, this disables the port until it stops receiving superior BPDUs.
- Use **`spanning-tree guard root`** in interface config mode to enable Root Guard.
- *Loop Guard* guards against Layer 2 loops in a LAN by preventing a switch port from erroneously transitioning to the forwarding state. If a Loop Guard-enabled port stops receiving BPDUs, it will transition to the *loop-inconsistent* state. This disables the port until it starts receiving BPDUs again.
- Use **`spanning-tree guard loop`** in interface config mode to enable Loop Guard.
- *BPDU Filter* can be used to prevent BPDUs from being sent or received on specific ports.

- Use **`spanning-tree bpdufilter enable`** in interface config mode to enable BPDU Filter on a specific port. The port will not send BPDUs and will ignore any BPDUs it receives, effectively disabling STP on the port.
- Use **`spanning-tree portfast bpdufilter default`** in global config mode to enable BPDU Filter on all PortFast-enabled ports. The port will not send BPDUs, but if it receives a BPDU, PortFast and BPDU Filter will be disabled. The port will then operate as a normal STP or RSTP port.

16 EtherChannel

This chapter covers

- How EtherChannel combines redundant links into a single logical link
- Static and dynamic EtherChannel configuration
- How traffic is load-balanced over the physical links of an EtherChannel
- Using Layer 3 EtherChannel to provide redundant Layer 3 connections

In the previous two chapters on STP, we emphasized the essential role of STP in preventing Layer 2 loops in a LAN with redundant connections. However, the downside of STP is that all redundant links are disabled; they provide essential redundancy in a LAN but will only be used to forward traffic if an active link fails.

In this chapter, we will cover EtherChannel, a technology that helps to overcome this limitation by allowing multiple physical links to be combined into a single logical link. As a result, STP and frame-forwarding logic will treat the group of links as a single unit, allowing the whole group of links to remain active without causing Layer 2 loops. This not only maximizes usage of the available bandwidth but also improves network resilience and simplifies management—advantages that we'll delve into in this chapter. EtherChannel is CCNA exam topic 2.4: Configure and verify (Layer 2/Layer 3) EtherChannel (LACP).

16.1 How EtherChannel works

To see how EtherChannel works and why it's useful, think of the following situation. Two switches, SW1 and SW2, are connected by their G0/0 ports. However, the link is congested; there is a lot of traffic in the LAN. The link between SW1 and SW2 is a bottleneck that is negatively affecting networking performance, and users are complaining.

To remedy the problem, you add a second link between SW1 and SW2, connecting their G0/1 ports. However, users still complain about poor network performance. This time, you add a further two links between SW1 and SW2, resulting in a total of four links between the switches. Having quadrupled the bandwidth between SW1 and SW2 (from a single 1 Gbps connection to four), surely the issue has been fixed, right? Nope, the LAN is just as congested as ever.

> **NOTE** *Bandwidth* is the total number of bits that can be transferred over a connection per second—four 1 Gbps links means 4 Gbps of bandwidth. In section 16.3, we will differentiate between bandwidth and speed—two similar but different concepts.

So, what's the culprit? It's our friend from the previous two chapters: Spanning Tree Protocol. Figure 16.1 shows why the network performance won't improve, no matter how many new links you add between the two switches. STP blocks all redundant links to avoid Layer 2 loops, leaving only a single link active.

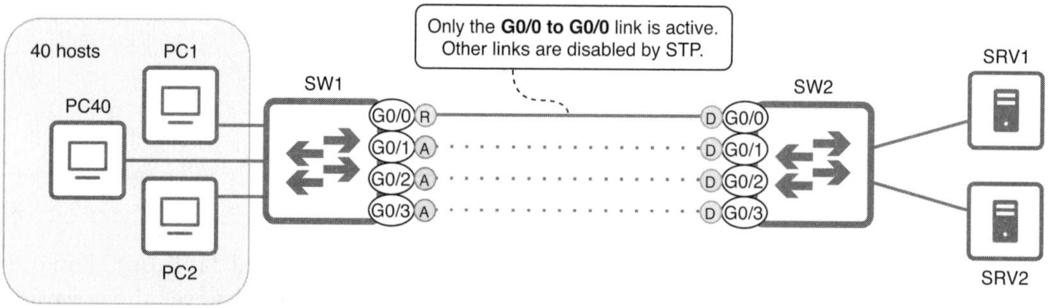

Figure 16.1 Clients connected to SW1 experience poor network performance when accessing the servers connected to SW2, but adding additional links between the switches doesn't remedy the issue. This is because STP blocks redundant links, leaving only a single active link.

Having additional links between SW1 and SW2 adds redundancy but doesn't solve the problem of congestion between the switches. The real solution to the problem is *EtherChannel*, which combines multiple physical links into a single logical link, meaning they can all remain active without causing Layer 2 loops. Figure 16.2 shows how EtherChannel combines the four 1 Gbps physical links into a single logical link with 4 Gbps of bandwidth.

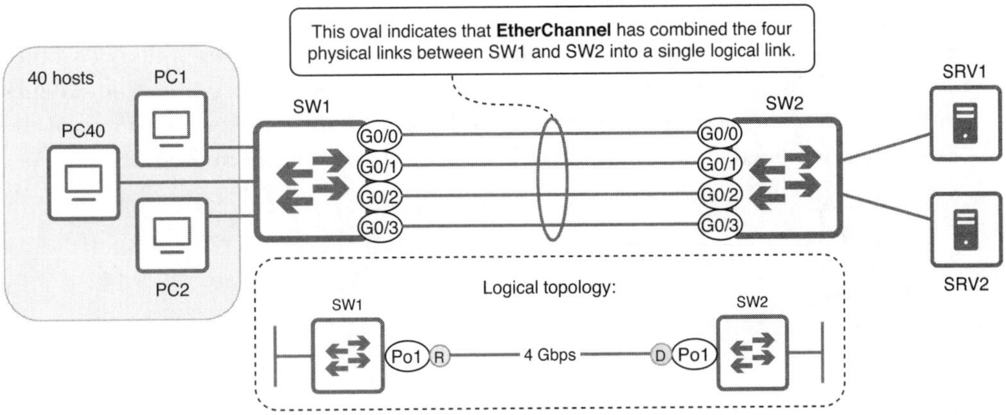

Figure 16.2 EtherChannel combines the four 1 Gbps links between SW1 and SW2 into a logical 4 Gbps link. Frame-switching and STP logic treat the four links as one. SW1's logical Po1 (`Port-channel1`) interface is an STP root port connected to SW2's logical Po1 interface, which is an STP designated port.

> **NOTE** The logical interfaces created by EtherChannel are called *port channels* in Cisco IOS; this term is often used interchangeably with EtherChannel. For consistency, I will use the term *EtherChannel* except when referring to CLI commands that use the term **`port-channel`**.

Frames forwarded between SW1 and SW2 will be distributed over the four physical links that make up the EtherChannel; this is called *load balancing* or *load distribution*, and we will cover how EtherChannel does it in section 16.3. Because the four links are treated as one logical entity, a Layer 2 loop is not created even though all ports can forward frames. Figure 16.3 shows how a broadcast frame sent by a PC reaches all hosts in the LAN but does not result in a Layer 2 loop; BUM frames received on a port that is a member of an EtherChannel will not be flooded out of other ports in the same EtherChannel.

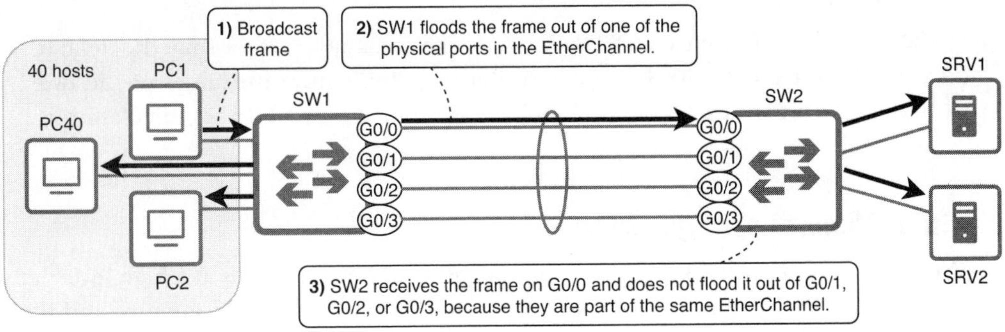

Figure 16.3 (1) PC1 send a broadcast frame and (2) SW1 floods it over the EtherChannel, sending the frame out of one of the EtherChannel's member ports. (3) SW2 receives the frame on G0/0 and floods it to SRV1 and SRV2 but does not flood the frame back to SW1 because G0/1, G0/2, and G0/3 are part of the same EtherChannel as G0/0.

It is important to note that EtherChannel does not entirely remove the need for STP in a LAN. With only two switches, all links can remain active, but in the context of a larger LAN, some links may need to be disabled. Figure 16.4 shows an example. The switches in the LAN are connected by various two-link EtherChannels. However, some of the EtherChannels need to be blocked by STP to avoid Layer 2 loops in the LAN.

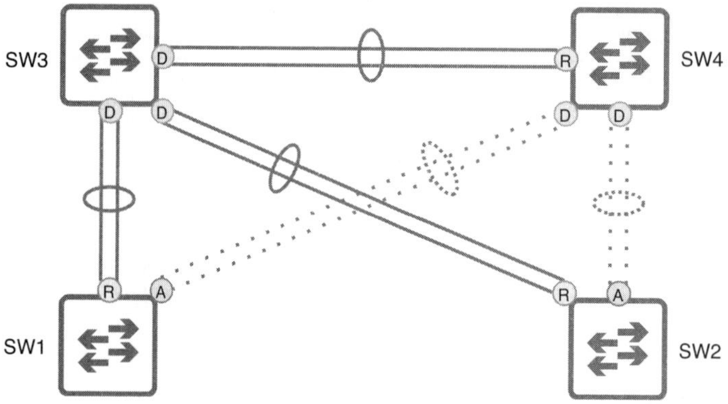

Figure 16.4 Four switches connected by EtherChannels, some blocked by STP. Without EtherChannel, only 3 of the 10 physical links would be active. With EtherChannel, 6 of the 10 physical links (three 2-link) EtherChannels are active.

Because all ports in an EtherChannel are treated as one logical port by STP, the output of `show spanning-tree` will only show the port channel interfaces, not the physical ports. I demonstrate this in the following example:

```
SW1# show spanning-tree
Interface           Role Sts Cost      Prio.Nbr Type
------------------- ---- --- --------- -------- --------------------------------
Po1                 Root FWD 3         128.65   P2p
Po2                 Altn BLK 3         128.66   P2p
```

The logical Po1 and Po2 interfaces are displayed instead of their physical member ports.

NOTE Po1 and Po2 have an STP cost of 3 in the example, rather than the default cost of 4 for a GigabitEthernet port. Because the bandwidth values of the two member ports of each port channel are combined, the STP cost calculation is affected.

16.2 EtherChannel configuration

Now that we've covered EtherChannel's purpose and how it works at a high level, let's see how to configure it on Cisco switches. There are two ways to configure an EtherChannel: configuring a *dynamic EtherChannel* causes the switches to use a protocol to negotiate with each other to form an EtherChannel, and *static EtherChannel* forces the switch to form an EtherChannel with the specified ports, without any negotiation with the neighboring device.

NOTE Dynamic and static EtherChannel configuration can be likened to dynamic and static trunk port configuration; switch ports using DTP negotiate with each other to form a trunk (dynamic), whereas manually configured trunk ports operate in trunk mode without any negotiation (static).

16.2.1 Dynamic EtherChannel

A dynamic EtherChannel configuration involves enabling a protocol on a set of switch ports. The switches will use the protocol to send messages to each other to negotiate whether to form an EtherChannel; this negotiation process involves comparing configuration parameters to make sure they match. Incorrectly configured EtherChannels can result in loops in the LAN, so it is highly recommended that you use dynamic EtherChannel instead of the other option: static EtherChannel (the topic of section 16.2.2).

Cisco switches support two dynamic EtherChannel negotiation protocols: the Cisco-proprietary *Port Aggregation Protocol* (PAgP) and the IEEE standard *Link Aggregation Control Protocol* (LACP), first defined in IEEE 802.3ad. The biggest difference between the two is that PAgP only runs on Cisco switches, whereas LACP can run on any vendor's switches.

EXAM TIP Remember the key difference between PAgP and LACP; if an exam question mentions forming an EtherChannel with a non-Cisco switch, you must use LACP.

PAgP configuration

Cisco's PAgP allows up to eight physical links to be combined into a single EtherChannel. Figure 16.5 shows a two-link EtherChannel between SW1 and SW2; you should be familiar with the **`desirable`** and **`auto`** keywords from configuring trunks with DTP. Additionally, **`switchport mode trunk`** is configured on each logical port channel interface to make the new EtherChannel a trunk link.

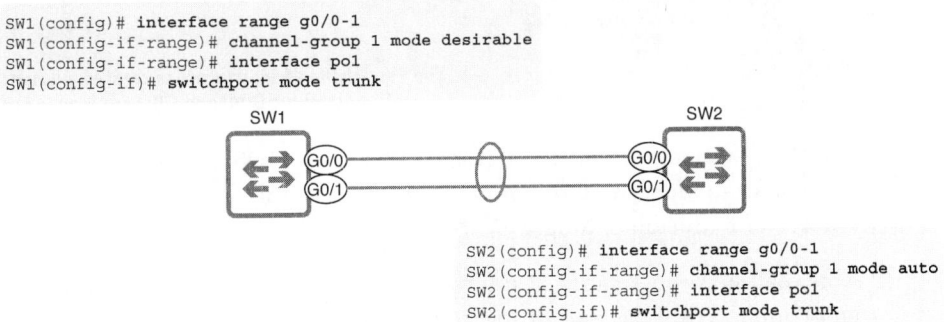

```
SW1(config)# interface range g0/0-1
SW1(config-if-range)# channel-group 1 mode desirable
SW1(config-if-range)# interface po1
SW1(config-if)# switchport mode trunk
```

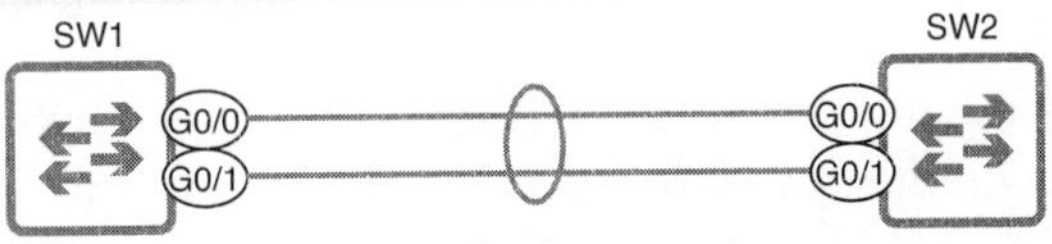


```
SW2(config)# interface range g0/0-1
SW2(config-if-range)# channel-group 1 mode auto
SW2(config-if-range)# interface po1
SW2(config-if)# switchport mode trunk
```

Figure 16.5 An EtherChannel is formed between SW1 and SW2 using PAgP. SW1's G0/0 and G0/1 ports are configured in PAgP `desirable` mode, and SW2's G0/0 and G0/1 ports are configured in PAgP `auto` mode. `switchport mode trunk` is applied to each switch's port channel interface to make the EtherChannel a trunk.

To configure an EtherChannel using PAgP, use the **channel-group** *group-number* **mode** {**desirable** | **auto**} command on the member ports. The *group-number* value is used to identify the EtherChannel on the switch; a single switch can have multiple EtherChannels, and this number identifies which ports belong to which EtherChannel. Like in DTP trunk formation, the combination of **desirable** and **auto** modes on the two ends of the connection determines whether the switches will form an EtherChannel:

- **desirable + desirable** = yes
- **desirable + auto** = yes
- **auto + auto** = no

NOTE If the switches don't form an EtherChannel, the two links will function independently—one active and one blocked by STP.

Ports in **desirable** mode will actively attempt to form an EtherChannel with the neighboring switch by sending PAgP messages. Ports in **auto** mode won't actively attempt to form an EtherChannel but will respond upon receiving PAgP messages from a **desirable**-mode neighbor and agree to form an EtherChannel.

In the following example, I configure **desirable** mode on SW1's G0/0 and G0/1 ports, as we saw in figure 16.5. After assigning both ports to channel group 1, the logical interface `Port-channel1` is automatically created, as shown in the output of **show ip interface brief**; using this logical interface, the physical G0/0 and G0/1 ports are treated as one entity by Cisco IOS:

```
SW1(config)# interface range g0/0-1
SW1(config-if-range)# channel-group 1 mode desirable
SW1(config-if-range)# do show ip interface brief
Interface           IP-Address   OK? Method  Status                 Protocol
GigabitEthernet0/0  unassigned   YES  unset  up                     up
GigabitEthernet0/1  unassigned   YES  unset  up                     up
GigabitEthernet0/2  unassigned   YES  unset  administratively down  down
GigabitEthernet0/3  unassigned   YES  unset  administratively down  down
Port-channel1       unassigned   YES  unset  down                   down
```

The Port-channel1 interface was created automatically after assigning G0/0 and G0/1 to channel group 1.

NOTE Get used to the different terms: some IOS commands use the term **channel-group**, some use **port-channel**, and some use **etherchannel**. They all refer to the same thing.

Note that the `Port-channel1` interface is in a down/down state; this is because I haven't configured SW2's end of the connection yet. You can confirm the status of any EtherChannels on a switch with the **show etherchannel summary** command, as in the following example:

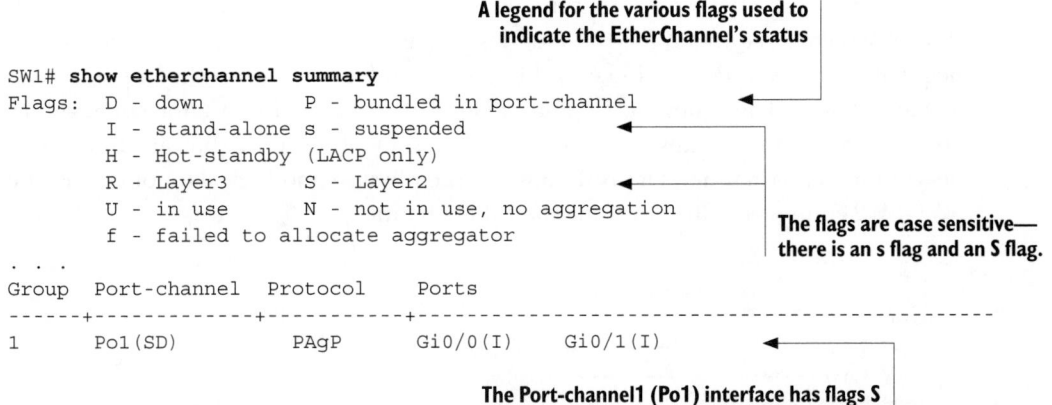

A legend for the various flags used to indicate the EtherChannel's status

```
SW1# show etherchannel summary
Flags:  D - down        P - bundled in port-channel
        I - stand-alone s - suspended
        H - Hot-standby (LACP only)
        R - Layer3      S - Layer2
        U - in use      N - not in use, no aggregation
        f - failed to allocate aggregator
. . .
Group  Port-channel  Protocol    Ports
------+-------------+-----------+-----------------------------------------------
1      Po1(SD)         PAgP      Gi0/0(I)     Gi0/1(I)
```

The flags are case sensitive—there is an s flag and an S flag.

The Port-channel1 (Po1) interface has flags S and D; the G0/0 and G0/1 ports have flag I.

A variety of flags are used to indicate the status of the EtherChannel; they are indicated in brackets next to the port channel interface and each member port. SW1's Po1 interface has the `S` and `D` flags; as indicated in the legend at the top of the output, `S` indicates a Layer 2 EtherChannel (think `S` for "switch port"). Just like regular switch ports, port channel interfaces can also be configured to operate like router interfaces with the **`no switchport`** command. We will cover that in section 16.4; for now, let's focus on Layer 2 EtherChannels. The Po1 interface also has the `D` flag, meaning `down`; in this case, it's because SW2's end hasn't been configured yet.

The G0/0 and G0/1 ports that form the EtherChannel both have the `I` flag, meaning `stand-alone` (think `I` for "independent"); although I configured them to be part of `Port-channel1`, PAgP didn't succeed in negotiating with SW2. As a result, G0/0 and G0/1 both operate as regular standalone switch ports. To complete the EtherChannel, let's configure SW2's side of the connection in **`auto`** mode, as we saw in figure 16.5. In the following example, I configure SW2's G0/0 and G0/1 ports and confirm with **`show etherchannel summary`**:

```
SW2(config)# interface range g0/0-1
SW2(config-if-range)# channel-group 1 mode auto
SW2(config-if-range)# do show etherchannel summary
Flags:  D - down        P - bundled in port-channel
. . .
        R - Layer3      S - Layer2
        U - in use      N - not in use, no aggregation
. . .
Group  Port-channel  Protocol    Ports
------+-------------+-----------+-----------------------------------------------
1      Po1(SU)         PAgP      Gi0/0(P)     Gi0/1(P)
```

Configures SW2 G0/0 and G0/1 in `auto` mode

G0/0 and G0/1 have formed an EtherChannel.

NOTE I configured **`channel-group 1`** on both SW1 and SW2, but the group number doesn't have to match on the two switches; the group number is only significant to the local switch.

After configuring SW2, notice that the flags are different from those we saw on SW1. Po1's `D` has changed to a `U` for `in use`; this means the EtherChannel was successfully negotiated and is working—I like to think of it as `U` for "up," since the opposite state is `D` for "down." The `I` next to G0/0 and G0/1 also changed to a `P` for `bundled in port-channel`; this means they are no longer standalone ports but are now members of the EtherChannel. Figure 16.6 shows the physical and logical topologies of the SW1–SW2 connection after forming the EtherChannel.

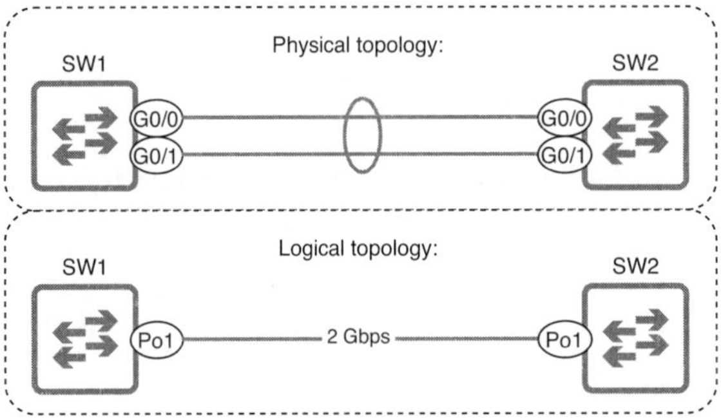

Figure 16.6 The physical and logical topologies of the SW1–SW2 connection. Physically, SW1 and SW2 are connected by two 1 Gbps links. Logically, they are connected by a single 2 Gbps link via their Po1 interfaces.

Now that the EtherChannel has been formed, we can configure each switch's port channel interface as necessary. For example, because this is a connection between switches, it probably should be a trunk link; in most cases, connections between switches need to carry traffic in multiple VLANs. In the following example, I configure SW1's Po1 interface in trunk mode and confirm with **`show interfaces trunk`**:

```
SW1(config)# interface po1
SW1(config-if)# switchport mode trunk
```

Configures port-channel1 as a trunk

Configurations made to the port channel interface will be automatically inherited by its member ports. In the following example, I use **`show running-config`** on SW1 to check the configurations of its ports; G0/0 and G0/1 have both inherited the **`switchport mode trunk`** command:

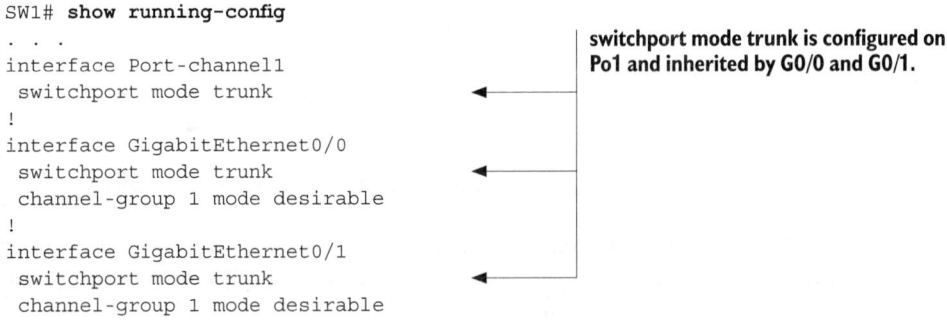

```
SW1# show running-config
. . .
interface Port-channel1
 switchport mode trunk
!
interface GigabitEthernet0/0
 switchport mode trunk
 channel-group 1 mode desirable
!
interface GigabitEthernet0/1
 switchport mode trunk
 channel-group 1 mode desirable
. . .
```

switchport mode trunk is configured on Po1 and inherited by G0/0 and G0/1.

Although G0/0 and G0/1 have inherited the **`switchport mode trunk`** command, only Po1 appears in the output of **`show interfaces trunk`**, as shown in the following example. This is because when part of an EtherChannel, physical ports are no longer viewed as independent logical entities by IOS; they are combined to form the logical port channel interface:

```
SW1# show interfaces trunk
Port        Mode             Encapsulation  Status        Native vlan
Po1         on               802.1q         trunking      1
. . .
```

The output only shows Po1, not G0/0 or G0/1.

Inheritance goes both ways; if you use the **`switchport mode trunk`** command on G0/0 and G0/1, the configuration will be inherited by Po1. In the following example, I demonstrate that on SW2:

```
SW2(config)# interface range g0/0-1
SW2(config-if-range)# switchport mode trunk
SW2(config-if-range)# do show running-config
. . .
interface Port-channel1
 switchport mode trunk
!
interface GigabitEthernet0/0
 switchport mode trunk
 channel-group 1 mode desirable
!
interface GigabitEthernet0/1
 switchport mode trunk
 channel-group 1 mode desirable
. . .
```

`switchport mode trunk` is configured on G0/0 and G0/1 and inherited by Po1.

Order of configuration

Because inheritance goes both ways, there is some flexibility to the order in which you configure EtherChannels. Assigning ports to an EtherChannel (with the **`channel-group`** command) can come before or after configuring port settings (like **`switchport mode trunk`**), and those port settings can be configured on either the member ports or the port channel interface.

However, after the EtherChannel has been created and is active in the network, it is recommended that you make configuration changes (for example, modifying the allowed VLANs) on the port channel interface, rather than the member ports. This helps ensure configuration consistency across all member ports, which is necessary for a functioning EtherChannel. Additionally, configuration changes made to the member ports, rather than the port channel interface, can cause the EtherChannel to *flap*—to briefly go down before coming up again—interrupting traffic in the LAN for a few seconds.

Although **`show etherchannel summary`** is the command you'll be using most often to verify the status of a switch's EtherChannels, another command to familiarize yourself with is **`show pagp neighbor`**, as in the following example:

The A flag is used to indicate that the neighbor port is in auto mode.

```
SW2# show pagp neighbor
Flags:  S - Device is sending Slow hello.  C - Device is in Consistent state.
        A - Device is in Auto mode.        P - Device learns on physical port.
Channel group 1 neighbors
         Partner   Partner            Partner          Partner Group
Port     Name      Device ID          Port        Age  Flags   Cap.
Gi0/0    SW1       5254.0015.8000     Gi0/0       6s   SC      10001
Gi0/1    SW1       5254.0015.8000     Gi0/1       6s   SC      10001
```

SW1 G0/0 and G0/1 do not have the A flag, so we can identify that they are not in auto mode—they must be in desirable mode.

This command displays information about the switch's PAgP-enabled neighbors; because I used the command on SW2, it shows information about SW1. Notice that the `A` flag, which stands for **`auto`** mode, does not appear under the `Partner Flags` column. This means that SW1's ports are not in **`auto`** mode; they must be in **`desirable`** mode.

> **EXAM TIP** Interpreting the output of **`show`** commands like **`show pagp neighbor`** is a major part of the CCNA exam. Although many such commands also contain information beyond the scope of the CCNA, make sure you can identify the key pieces of information.

LINK AGGREGATION CONTROL PROTOCOL

Having covered how to configure an EtherChannel using PAgP, you now know 90% of what you need to know to configure an EtherChannel using LACP. There are only a couple of practical differences that you should know for the CCNA exam. Figure 16.7 shows an LACP EtherChannel connecting two switches. Notice that the configuration is nearly identical to the PAgP EtherChannel we looked at previously.

```
SW1(config)# interface range g0/0-1
SW1(config-if-range)# channel-group 1 mode active
SW1(config-if-range)# interface po1
SW1(config-if)# switchport mode trunk
```

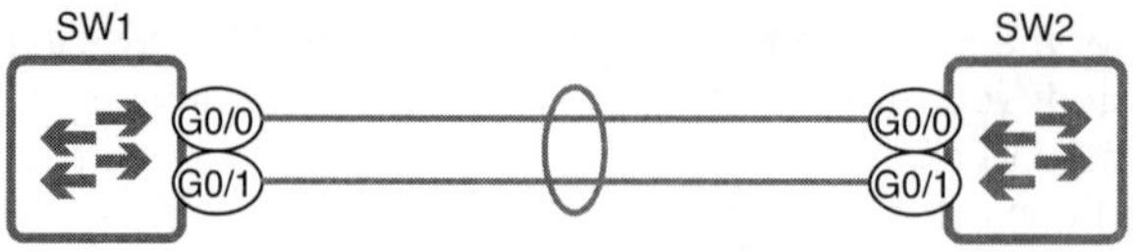


```
SW2(config)# interface range g0/0-1
SW2(config-if-range)# channel-group 1 mode passive
SW2(config-if-range)# interface po1
SW2(config-if)# switchport mode trunk
```

Figure 16.7 An EtherChannel is formed between SW1 and SW2 using LACP. SW1's G0/0 and G0/1 ports are configured in LACP `active` mode, and SW2's G0/0 and G0/1 ports are configured in LACP `passive` mode. `switchport mode trunk` is applied to each switch's port channel interface to make the EtherChannel a trunk.

The most relevant difference is the keywords used with the **`channel-group`** command when configuring an LACP EtherChannel; **`active`** and **`passive`** instead of PAgP's **`desirable`** and **`auto`**. The following LACP mode combinations will result in an EtherChannel:

- **`active`** + **`active`** = yes
- **`active`** + **`passive`** = yes
- **`passive`** + **`passive`** = no

LACP's **`active`** mode is equivalent to PAgP's **`desirable`** mode; ports in **`active`** mode will actively attempt to form an EtherChannel with the neighboring switch by sending LACP messages. Likewise, LACP's **`passive`** mode is equivalent to PAgP's **`auto`** mode; ports in **`passive`** mode won't actively attempt to form an EtherChannel but will respond if connected to a neighbor using **`active`** mode.

> **NOTE** The LACP and PAgP modes cannot be used together. For example, **`active`** (LACP) + **`desirable`** (PAgP) will not result in a valid EtherChannel. Protocols are like languages: the devices have to use the same language to communicate successfully.

A second difference between LACP and PAgP is that LACP supports up to 16 links in a single EtherChannel, whereas PAgP only supports 8. However, although LACP supports up to 16 links in an EtherChannel, only up to 8 links can be used at once; the remaining links will be inactive, waiting to take over if an active link fails.

In the following example, I configure an EtherChannel between SW1 and SW2 using LACP and enable trunk mode, as we saw in figure 16.7. Aside from the use of the **`active`** and **`passive`** keywords, the configurations are identical to the PAgP configurations we did previously:

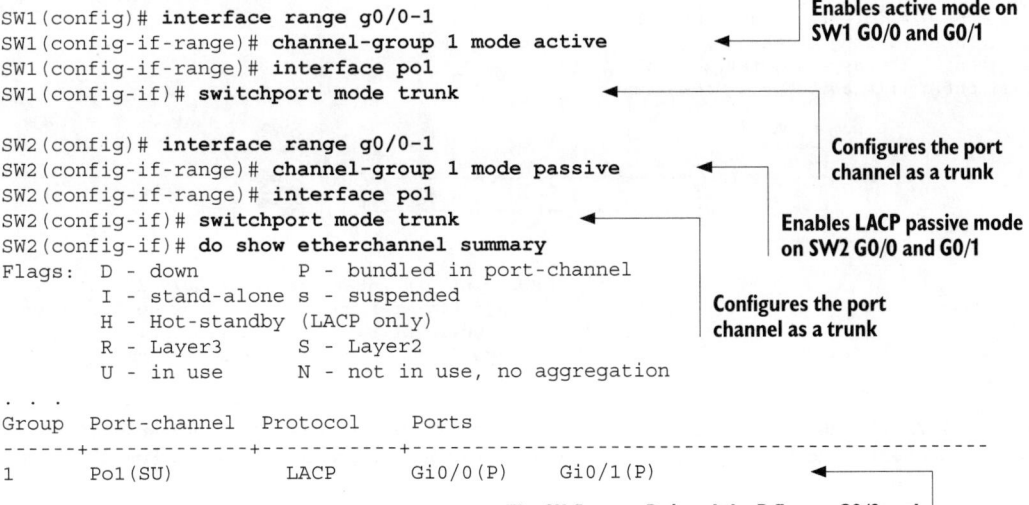

```
SW1(config)# interface range g0/0-1
SW1(config-if-range)# channel-group 1 mode active
SW1(config-if-range)# interface po1
SW1(config-if)# switchport mode trunk

SW2(config)# interface range g0/0-1
SW2(config-if-range)# channel-group 1 mode passive
SW2(config-if-range)# interface po1
SW2(config-if)# switchport mode trunk
SW2(config-if)# do show etherchannel summary
Flags:  D - down        P - bundled in port-channel
        I - stand-alone s - suspended
        H - Hot-standby (LACP only)
        R - Layer3      S - Layer2
        U - in use      N - not in use, no aggregation
. . .
Group  Port-channel  Protocol    Ports
------+-------------+-----------+-----------------------------------------------
1      Po1(SU)         LACP      Gi0/0(P)    Gi0/1(P)
```

Annotations:
- Enables active mode on SW1 G0/0 and G0/1 (channel-group 1 mode active)
- Configures the port channel as a trunk (SW1 switchport mode trunk)
- Enables LACP passive mode on SW2 G0/0 and G0/1 (channel-group 1 mode passive)
- Configures the port channel as a trunk (SW2 switchport mode trunk)
- The SU flags on Po1 and the P flag on G0/0 and G0/1 indicate an operational Layer 2 EtherChannel.

In addition to **`show etherchannel summary`**, we can verify the status of an LACP EtherChannel with the **`show lacp neighbor`** command. In the following example, I use the command on SW1, and the output shows information about SW1's neighbor (SW2):

Flag A means the neighbor port is in active mode, and flag P means the neighbor port is in passive mode.

```
SW1# show lacp neighbor
Flags:  S - Device is requesting Slow LACPDUs
        F - Device is requesting Fast LACPDUs
        A - Device is in Active mode       P - Device is in Passive mode
Channel group 1 neighbors
Partner's information:
                LACP port                       Admin  Oper   Port    Port
Port    Flags  Priority  Dev ID          Age    key    Key    Number  State
Gi0/0   SP     32768     5254.0004.8000  10s    0x0    0x1    0x1     0x3C
Gi0/1   SP     32768     5254.0004.8000   6s    0x0    0x1    0x2     0x3C
```

SW2's ports have the P flag, so they are in passive mode (as we configured).

EXAM TIP Some exam questions might expect you to read between the lines. The previous output indicates that SW1's neighbor is using **`passive`** mode, so we can deduce that SW1 must be using **`active`** mode; if both switches were using **`passive`** mode, the EtherChannel would not form.

16.2.2 Static EtherChannel

Another option for configuring EtherChannels is to not use any negotiation protocol at all; this is called a static EtherChannel. Figure 16.8 shows a static EtherChannel between SW1 and SW2, with the relevant configurations.

```
SW1(config)# interface range g0/0-1
SW1(config-if-range)# channel-group 1 mode on
SW1(config-if-range)# interface po1
SW1(config-if)# switchport mode trunk
```

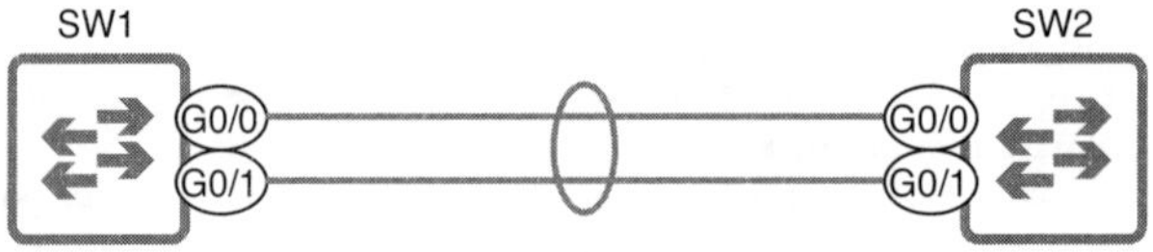


```
SW2(config)# interface range g0/0-1
SW2(config-if-range)# channel-group 1 mode on
SW2(config-if-range)# interface po1
SW2(config-if)# switchport mode trunk
```

Figure 16.8 A static EtherChannel is formed between SW1 and SW2. Both switches' ports are configured in `on` mode. `switchport mode trunk` is applied to each switch's port channel interface to make the EtherChannel a trunk.

Whereas PAgP and LACP each have two separate modes, static EtherChannels use a single mode called `on`; for a static EtherChannel to work, both sides of the connection must be in `on` mode. When using `on` mode, neither switch sends any messages to negotiate the formation of an EtherChannel; the configured ports will form an EtherChannel regardless of the state of the neighboring device.

For this reason, it is highly recommended that you use PAgP or LACP instead of manual EtherChannels; the dynamic protocols will check to make sure the neighboring device's configurations are appropriate before forming an EtherChannel. In the worst-case scenario, an improperly configured EtherChannel can result in Layer 2 loops, which are disastrous for the LAN.

NOTE There are cases in which you have to use a static EtherChannel, such as when connecting a switch to a *wireless LAN controller* (WLC). We will cover WLCs in part 4 of volume 2 of this book.

Just as an EtherChannel will not form between a switch using PAgP and a switch using LACP, a static EtherChannel will not work if connected to a switch using PAgP or LACP. Table 16.1 shows which combinations of modes will result in an operational EtherChannel.

Table 16.1 EtherChannel mode combinations

Modes	Desirable	Auto	Active	Passive	On
Desirable	Yes	Yes	No	No	No
Auto	Yes	No	No	No	No
Active	No	No	Yes	Yes	No
Passive	No	No	Yes	No	No
On	No	No	No	No	Yes

16.2.3 Physical port configurations

When configuring EtherChannels, it's very important that various port settings match, both among the ports on the same switch and between neighboring switches. Following are some of the settings that must match among the ports of an EtherChannel:

- Speed
- Duplex
- Operational mode (access or trunk)
- Allowed VLANs and native VLAN (when in trunk mode)
- Access VLAN (when in access mode)

Rather than memorizing a list of settings that must match between an EtherChannel's ports, just ensure that all ports in the same EtherChannel are configured identically. Figure 16.9 shows what can happen when a port's settings don't match the other ports in the EtherChannel.

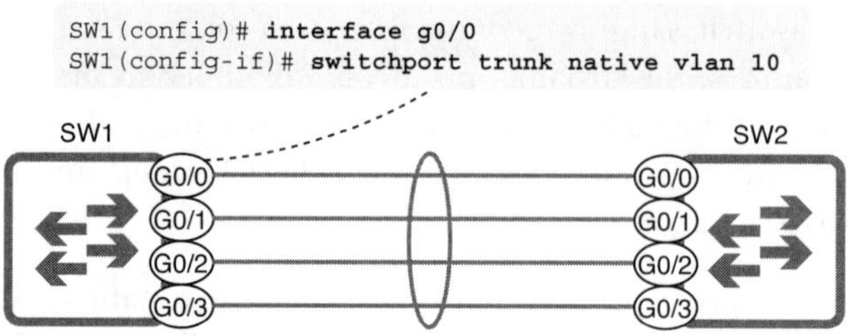

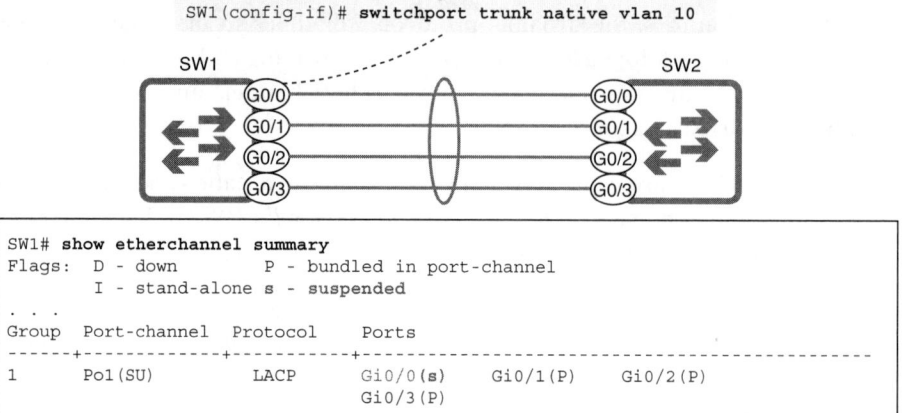

```
SW1# show etherchannel summary
Flags:  D - down        P - bundled in port-channel
        I - stand-alone s - suspended
. . .
Group  Port-channel  Protocol    Ports
------+-------------+-----------+-----------------------------------------------
1      Po1(SU)         LACP      Gi0/0(s)    Gi0/1(P)    Gi0/2(P)
                                 Gi0/3(P)
```

Figure 16.9 Changing the native VLAN of G0/0 causes it to be placed in a `suspended` state; it is disabled until its settings match the other ports in the EtherChannel.

NOTE Settings that don't have a direct effect on the port's operation, like a description configured with the **`description`** command, don't have to match.

Changing the native VLAN of SW1 G0/0 but not the other ports in the EtherChannel causes it to be suspended; it is unable to participate in the EtherChannel or forward frames at all until its settings match the other ports in the EtherChannel. In the following example, I restore SW1 G0/0's native VLAN to the default of 1 and check the EtherChannel's status; it is once again an active member of the EtherChannel:

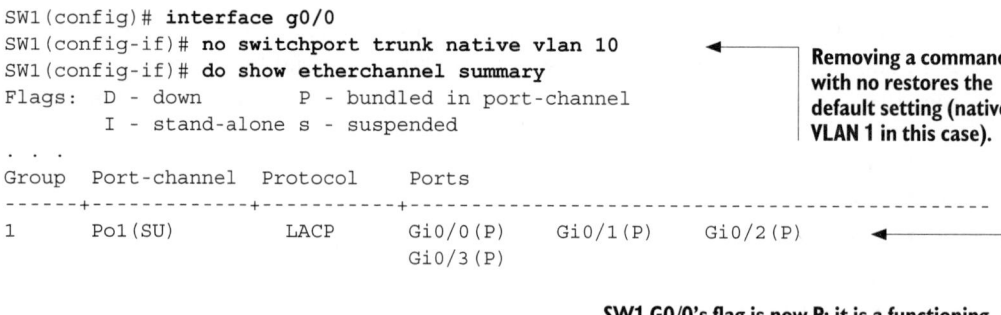

```
SW1(config)# interface g0/0
SW1(config-if)# no switchport trunk native vlan 10
SW1(config-if)# do show etherchannel summary
Flags:  D - down        P - bundled in port-channel
        I - stand-alone s - suspended
. . .
Group  Port-channel  Protocol    Ports
------+-------------+-----------+-----------------------------------------------
1      Po1(SU)         LACP      Gi0/0(P)    Gi0/1(P)    Gi0/2(P)
                                 Gi0/3(P)
```

Removing a command with no restores the default setting (native VLAN 1 in this case).

SW1 G0/0's flag is now P; it is a functioning member of the EtherChannel again.

16.3 EtherChannel load balancing

After a switch's frame-forwarding logic has determined that a frame should be forwarded out of an EtherChannel, there is an additional check on the frame: the EtherChannel load-balancing logic examines the frame and uses certain parameters to determine which physical port the frame will be forwarded out of. Figure 16.10 demonstrates this concept.

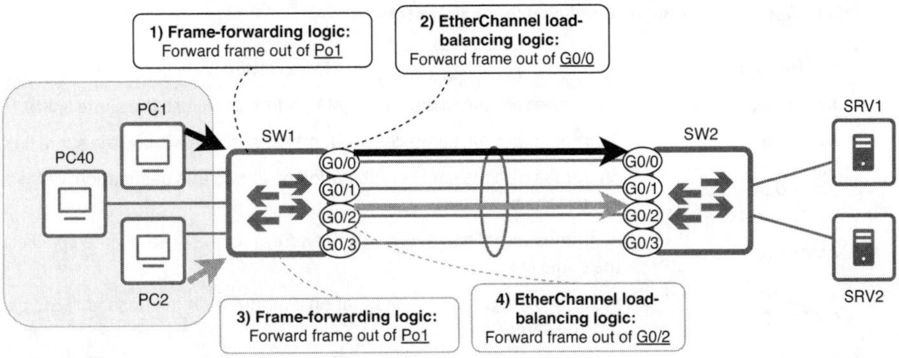

Figure 16.10 SW1's frame-forwarding logic determines that both frames will be forwarded out of Po1. However, the EtherChannel load-balancing logic determines that PC1's frame will be forwarded out of G0/0, and PC2's frame will be forwarded out of G0/2.

Frames forwarded over an EtherChannel are load-balanced over the EtherChannel's physical links by flow. A *flow* is a communication between two nodes; for example, if PC1 communicates with SRV1, all messages from PC1 to SRV1 are one flow, and all messages from SRV1 to PC1 are another flow. All messages in the same flow will be forwarded over the same physical link in the EtherChannel. Figure 16.11 shows an example; all messages from PC1 to SRV1 use the G0/0–G0/0 link, all messages from SRV1 to PC1 use the G0/1–G0/1 link, all messages from PC2 to SRV2 use the G0/2–G0/2 link, and all messages from SRV2 to PC2 use the G0/3–G0/3 link.

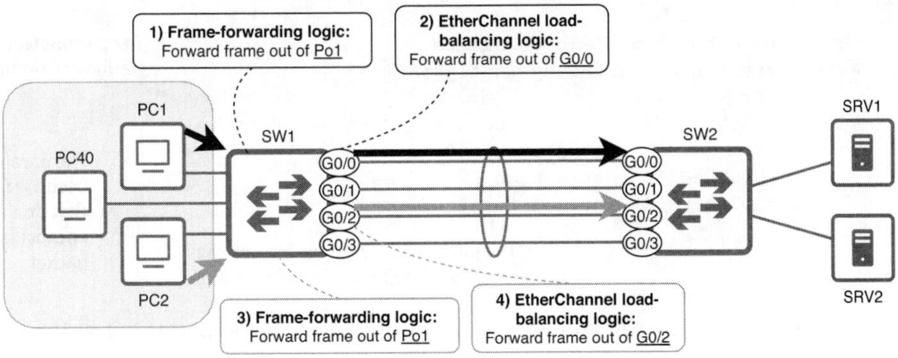

Figure 16.11 Messages forwarded over an EtherChannel are load-balanced based on flow. In this example, messages from PC1 to SRV1 use the G0/0–G0/0 link, messages from SRV1 to PC1 use the G0/1–G0/1 link, messages from PC2 to SRV2 use the G0/2–G0/2 link, and messages from SRV2 to PC2 use the G0/3–G0/3 link.

Keep in mind that figure 16.11 is just an example; EtherChannel load balancing won't always use all links of the EtherChannel equally. Fortunately, you can modify which parameter(s) the load-balancing logic takes into consideration with the **`port-channel load-balance`** *`parameters`* command in global config mode. Table 16.2 lists some possible parameters and their meanings.

Table 16.2 EtherChannel load-balancing parameters

Parameter	Description
`src-mac`	All frames with the same source MAC address will use the same link.
`dst-mac`	All frames with the same destination MAC address will use the same link.
`src-dst-mac`	All frames with the same combination of source and destination MAC addresses will use the same link.
`src-ip`	All frames with the same source IP address (in the encapsulated packet) will use the same link.
`dst-ip`	All frames with the same destination IP address (in the encapsulated packet) will use the same link.
`src-dst-ip`	All frames with the same combination of source and destination IP addresses (in the encapsulated packet) will use the same link.

NOTE The default EtherChannel load-balancing setting varies depending on the switch model and IOS version. On the switches I'm using for this chapter, the default setting is **`src-dst-ip`**. Some switches support additional parameters, too.

To check which parameters are used by the switch, use the **`show etherchannel load-balance`** command, as in the following example. Note the statement `Non-IP: Source XOR Destination MAC address`; this means that, for frames that don't encapsulate IP packets, the switch will use the source and destination MAC addresses instead. If there is no IP packet inside, there are no IP addresses to examine:

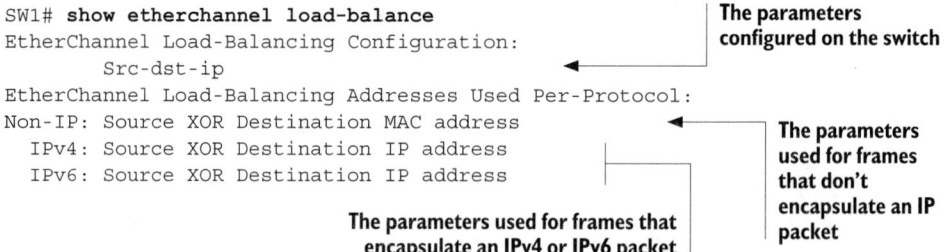

```
SW1# show etherchannel load-balance
EtherChannel Load-Balancing Configuration:
        Src-dst-ip
EtherChannel Load-Balancing Addresses Used Per-Protocol:
Non-IP: Source XOR Destination MAC address
  IPv4: Source XOR Destination IP address
  IPv6: Source XOR Destination IP address
```

The parameters configured on the switch

The parameters used for frames that don't encapsulate an IP packet

The parameters used for frames that encapsulate an IPv4 or IPv6 packet

NOTE Although the configuration command is **`port-channel load-balance`**, the **`show`** command is **`show etherchannel load-balance`**—one of the great mysteries of Cisco IOS.

If it is determined that traffic isn't being evenly balanced over the links of an EtherChannel, changing the load-balancing parameters might help. For example, load balancing based only on the destination MAC address will cause all frames destined for the default gateway to use the same link, possibly causing congestion on that link. However, such determinations are beyond the scope of the CCNA; a general understanding of how EtherChannel load balancing works is sufficient.

Lanes on a highway

EtherChannel can be compared to adding more lanes to a highway. Just as adding more lanes to a highway increases its total capacity, adding more links to an EtherChannel increases its total bandwidth—the total number of bits that can be transmitted over it per second. An EtherChannel's bandwidth is the total bandwidth of its member links.

However, adding more lanes to a highway doesn't increase the speed of each individual car; the speed limit remains the same. Likewise, adding more links to an EtherChannel doesn't increase the speed of each individual link; if an EtherChannel has four 1 Gbps links, the maximum speed of any particular communication over the EtherChannel is still 1 Gbps.

With that said, adding more lanes to a highway can reduce congestion and, thus, indirectly increase a car's speed by allowing it to drive at the speed limit without slowing down or stopping. Similarly, EtherChannel can reduce network congestion and thus increase the speed and efficiency of each communication flow.

In this context, the term *bandwidth* refers to the total capacity of a connection, and *speed* refers to the maximum transfer rate of a particular communication.

16.4 Layer 3 EtherChannel

Up to this point, we have covered *Layer 2 EtherChannels*—EtherChannels consisting of switch ports that switch frames rather than routed ports that route packets. However, we can also configure *Layer 3 EtherChannels* consisting of routed ports. Remember, on multilayer switches, you can use the `no switchport` command on a port to make it a routed port capable of forwarding packets like a router.

NOTE Some router models also support Layer 3 EtherChannels, but we will focus on configuring Layer 3 EtherChannels on multilayer switches. EtherChannel is most commonly used on switches rather than routers.

Because routed ports don't pose a risk of causing Layer 2 loops and, therefore, won't be disabled by STP, the benefits of Layer 3 EtherChannels are fewer than those of Layer 2 EtherChannels. However, they provide a simple way to load-balance packets over multiple links and can be easier to manage than multiple independent Layer 3 links; configuring IP addressing and routing for one logical interface is simpler than doing so for multiple independent interfaces.

Figure 16.12 shows a situation where you might want to use a Layer 3 EtherChannel: two LANs are connected via multilayer switches. Each LAN has a Layer 2 switch connected to a multilayer switch via a Layer 2 EtherChannel, and the two multilayer switches are connected via a Layer 3 EtherChannel.

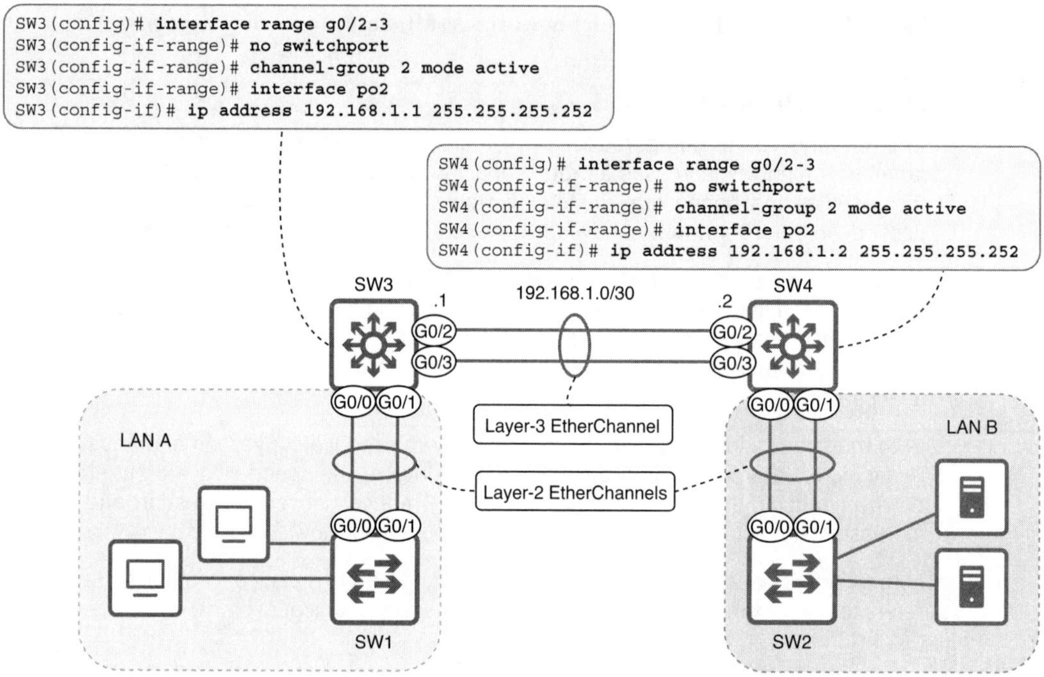

Figure 16.12 Two LANs connected via multilayer switches using Layer 3 EtherChannel. Additionally, the Layer 2 switch in each LAN uses Layer 2 EtherChannel to connect to the LAN's multilayer switch. The Layer 3 EtherChannel configuration is depicted.

Like Layer 2 EtherChannels, Layer 3 EtherChannels can be configured dynamically using PAgP, LACP, or statically with `on` mode. The only additions are the `no switchport` command to make routed ports and an IP address configured on the port channel interface. The following example shows the configuration of SW3's Layer 3 EtherChannel, as we saw in figure 16.12 using LACP as the negotiation protocol. Note that I use group 2 for this EtherChannel because group 1 is used by the Layer 2 EtherChannel connecting SW3 to SW1:

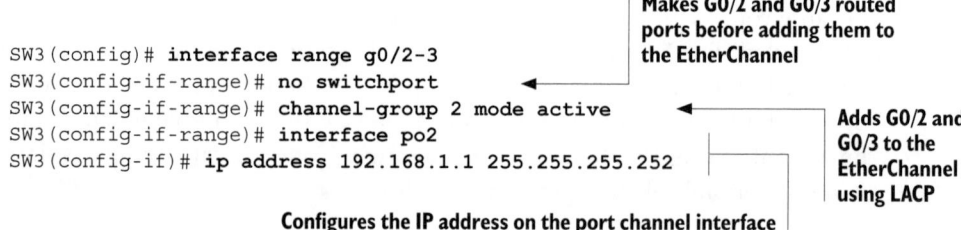

```
SW3(config)# interface range g0/2-3
SW3(config-if-range)# no switchport
SW3(config-if-range)# channel-group 2 mode active
SW3(config-if-range)# interface po2
SW3(config-if)# ip address 192.168.1.1 255.255.255.252
```

Makes G0/2 and G0/3 routed ports before adding them to the EtherChannel

Adds G0/2 and G0/3 to the EtherChannel using LACP

Configures the IP address on the port channel interface

NOTE Make sure to configure the IP address on the port channel interface, not any of the member ports.

In the following example, I configure SW4's end of the connection and confirm the EtherChannel's status. Note that whereas Po1 (a Layer 2 EtherChannel connected to SW2) has the flags `SU`, Po2 has the flags `RU`. `R` indicates a Layer 3 EtherChannel; think `R` for "routed port":

```
SW4(config)# interface range g0/2-3
SW4(config-if-range)# no switchport
SW4(config-if-range)# channel-group 2 mode active
SW4(config-if-range)# interface po2
SW4(config-if)# ip address 192.168.1.1 255.255.255.252
SW4(config-if-range)# do show etherchannel summary
Flags:  D - down        P - bundled in port-channel
        I - stand-alone s - suspended
        H - Hot-standby (LACP only)
        R - Layer3      S - Layer2
. . .
Group  Port-channel  Protocol    Ports
------+-------------+-----------+-----------------------------------------------
1      Po1(SU)         LACP      Gi0/0(P)     Gi0/1(P)
2      Po2(RU)         LACP      Gi0/2(P)     Gi0/3(P)
```

Flag R indicates a Layer 3 EtherChannel.

Po2 is a Layer 3 EtherChannel.

Summary

- EtherChannel combines multiple physical links into a single logical link. This allows multiple links between two switches to all remain in the STP forwarding state without causing Layer 2 loops.
- BUM frames received on a port that is a member of an EtherChannel will not be flooded out of other ports in the same EtherChannel.
- EtherChannel does not entirely remove the need for STP. In the context of a larger LAN, some EtherChannels may need to be disabled by STP.
- There are two main ways to configure EtherChannels: dynamic and static.
- Dynamic EtherChannels use one of two protocols—PAgP or LACP—to negotiate an EtherChannel between two neighboring switches.
- Port Aggregation Protocol (PAgP) is a Cisco-proprietary EtherChannel negotiation protocol that uses two modes: **`desirable`** and **`auto`**.
- Link Aggregation Control Protocol (LACP) is a standard EtherChannel negotiation protocol standardized by IEEE 802.3ad. It uses two modes: **`active`** and **`passive`**.
- **`desirable`** mode in PAgP actively tries to form an EtherChannel. **`auto`** mode does not actively try to form an EtherChannel but will form an EtherChannel with a neighbor in **`desirable`** mode.

- You can configure PAgP on a port with the **channel-group** *group-number* **mode** {**desirable** | **auto**} command in interface config mode. The *group-number* identifies which EtherChannel the port is a member of and is locally significant.
- After assigning a port to an EtherChannel, a logical port channel interface is automatically created. You should configure the relevant settings on the port channel interface (i.e., access or trunk mode).
- Use the **show etherchannel summary** command to check the status of EtherChannels on the switch.
- Commands configured on the port channel interface are inherited by the member ports, and vice versa. However, it is recommended that you configure port settings on the port channel interface to ensure consistency.
- Use the **show pagp neighbor** command to view information about the switch's neighbors using PAgP.
- Whereas PAgP supports EtherChannels of up to 8 links, LACP supports up to 16 links. However, only up to 8 links can be used at once; the others will act as standby links, ready to take over if an active link fails.
- **active** mode in LACP is equivalent to PAgP's **desirable** mode, and **passive** mode is equivalent to PAgP's **auto** mode. Otherwise, EtherChannel configuration and verification are identical to PAgP.
- You can configure LACP on a port with the **channel-group** *group-number* **mode** {**active** | **passive**} command in interface config mode.
- Use the **show lacp neighbor** command to view information about the switch's neighbors using LACP.
- Static EtherChannels do not use a protocol to negotiate EtherChannel formation. Ports are configured to statically form an EtherChannel without negotiating with the neighboring switch.
- Use the **channel-group** *group-number* **mode on** command to configure a port as a member of a static EtherChannel.
- An EtherChannel will not form between switch ports using a different negotiation protocol (PAgP or LACP) or between switch ports using a negotiation protocol and switch ports configured with **mode on**.
- The settings of an EtherChannel's member ports must match. For example, speed, duplex, operational mode (access or trunk), allowed VLANs, native VLAN, and access VLAN settings must match.
- If a switch's frame-switching logic determines that a frame should be forwarded or flooded out of an EtherChannel, an additional check determines which physical port the frame should be sent out of.
- Frames forwarded over an EtherChannel are load-balanced by flow. A *flow* is a communication between two nodes.

- The parameters a switch uses to identify flows can be configured with the **port-channel load-balance** *parameters* command in global config mode. Example parameters are **src-dst-mac** and **src-dst-ip**.
- Use the **show etherchannel load-balance** command to check which parameters the switch is using to identify flows for EtherChannel load balancing.
- EtherChannels are like highways: adding more links increases the EtherChannel's total capacity (bandwidth) but doesn't increase the maximum speed of any communication over the EtherChannel.
- An EtherChannel consisting of switch ports (that switch frames) is a Layer 2 EtherChannel. An EtherChannel consisting of routed ports (the route packets) is a Layer 3 EtherChannel.
- To configure a Layer 3 EtherChannel, use the **no switchport** command on the member ports before using the **channel-group** command. Then, configure an IP address on the port channel interface (not the individual member ports).

Part 4

Dynamic routing and first hop redundancy protocols

After focusing on Layer 2 concepts in part 3, part 4 is a return to Layer 3. In chapter 9, we covered static routes, which involve manually configuring routes on each router as necessary. That manual approach is simply not feasible in larger networks, and chapter 17 introduces a more scalable approach: dynamic routing. Dynamic routing protocols enable routers to communicate with each other and share routing information automatically, without the need to manually configure each router's routing table. Then, chapter 18 focuses on Open Shortest Path First (OSPF), one of the most commonly used dynamic routing protocols, and a major topic on the CCNA exam.

Chapter 19 moves away from the topic of dynamic routing to a different kind of protocol available on Cisco routers: first hop redundancy protocols (FHRPs). FHRPs enable multiple routers to team up to provide a resilient default gateway for hosts in a LAN; if a hardware failure or a similar issue affects one router, the other router is ready to take over and ensure that hosts in the LAN maintain continuous connectivity. FHRPs are a key tool in modern networks, which are expected to be reliably available on a 24/7 basis.

Part 4 is pivotal, as it dives into the more sophisticated aspects of routing and reliability. As always, the focus is on not just the theoretical knowledge of these important concepts but also the practical application on Cisco routers, both of which are essential for CCNA exam success. These are key CCNA exam topics for a good reason; dynamic routing protocols and FHRPs are used by enterprises of all sizes, and modern network professionals must be proficient at implementing them.

17 Dynamic routing

This chapter covers

- The advantages of dynamic routing over static routing
- The types of dynamic routing protocols
- How a router decides which routes to enter in its routing table
- Activating dynamic routing protocols with the network command

After focusing on Layer 2 concepts for the previous several chapters, in this chapter, we return to the topic of routing—how routers forward packets between networks. In chapter 9, we learned about static routing, in which an administrator manually configures routes to build a router's routing table. When using dynamic routing, the topic of this chapter, routers communicate with each other and build their routing tables automatically. Although static routing has its uses, dynamic routing provides several advantages that we will examine in this chapter. We will cover elements of the following exam topics:

- 3.1 Interpret the components of routing table
- 3.2 Determine how a router makes a forwarding decision by default

- 3.3 Configure and verify IPv4 and IPv6 static routing
- 3.4 Configure and verify OSPFv2

17.1 Dynamic routing vs. static routing

Dynamic routing is a process by which routers share information about the network with each other, allowing them to build their routing tables without the need for an administrator to manually configure each route. They do this using a *routing protocol*—a protocol that defines how routers communicate with each other to share routing information and how they use that information to build their routing tables. We will cover the different kinds of routing protocols in section 17.2.

Figure 17.1 shows an example of how routing protocols work. R1, R2, and R3 use a routing protocol to exchange messages, informing each other of their known networks. Each router will use this information to build its routing table, without requiring an administrator to manually configure the routes.

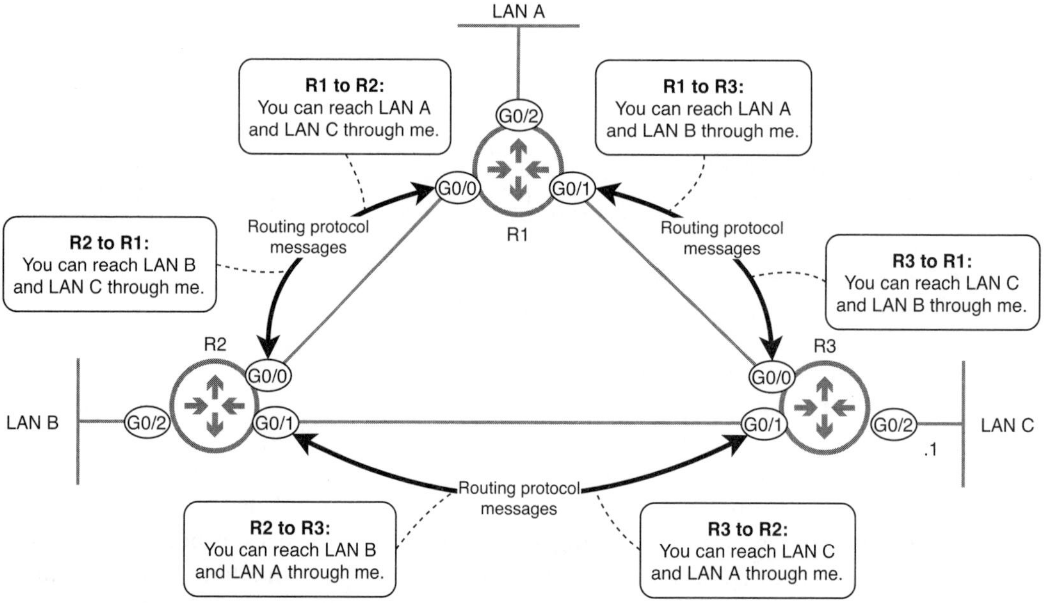

Figure 17.1 R1, R2, and R3 use a routing protocol to share routing information with each other. Each router will use this information to build its routing table.

> **NOTE** Sharing of routing information is also called *advertisement*. R1, R2, and R3 advertise their known networks to each other.

Dynamic routing provides several advantages over static routing, such as adaptability and scalability. Let's take a closer look at those two advantages.

17.1.1 Adaptability

Static routes, as the name implies, are static and unchanging; they are incapable of reacting to changes in the network. If a route becomes invalid due to a hardware failure on one of the routers in the path, the static route won't adjust automatically to find an alternate path. Figure 17.2 shows an example: the R2–R3 link goes down due to a hardware failure. This causes R3 to remove its route to 192.168.30.0/24 from its routing table; it can no longer reach the next-hop IP address. R1, however, is unaware of the link's failure. As a result, R1 keeps its route to 192.168.30.0/24 via R2 in its routing table, even though it is no longer a valid route to reach the destination.

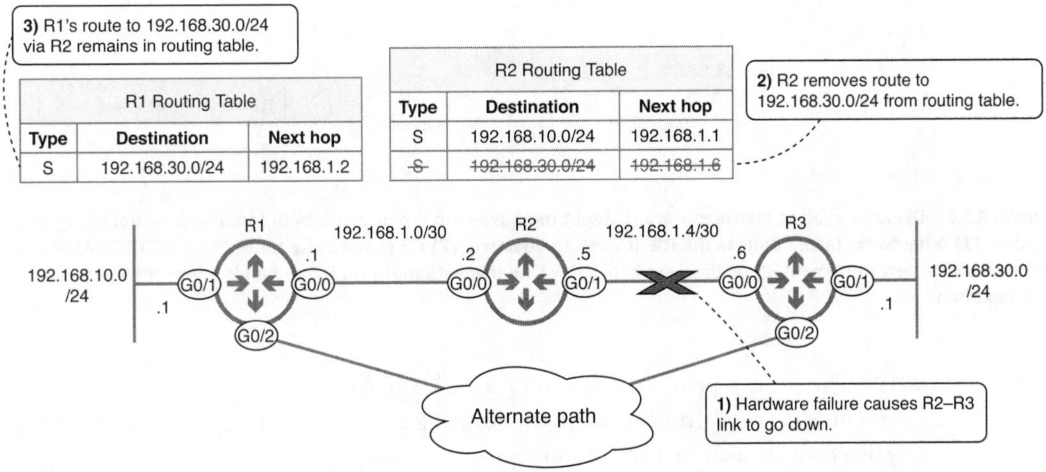

Figure 17.2 The static route on R1 is unable to adapt to a change in the network. (1) A hardware failure causes the R2–R3 link to go down. (2) R2 removes its route to 192.168.30.0/24 because it can no longer reach the next hop. (3) R1, unaware of the hardware failure, leaves its route to 192.168.30.0/24 via R2 in its routing table, despite the existence of an alternate path.

> **NOTE** If a router cannot reach a route's next-hop IP address, it will remove the route from the routing table. This applies to all kinds of routes and is why R2 removes its static route to 192.168.30.0/24 when the R2–R3 link fails.

Because R1's route to 192.168.30.0/24 via R2 remains in its routing table, it will continue to forward packets destined for hosts in the 192.168.30.0/24 network to R2. R2 then has no choice but to drop the packets because it has no route to 192.168.30.0/24 in its routing table. Figure 17.3 shows how dynamic routing fixes this; it allows R1 to automatically adapt to the network change, inserting a new route to the destination into its routing table.

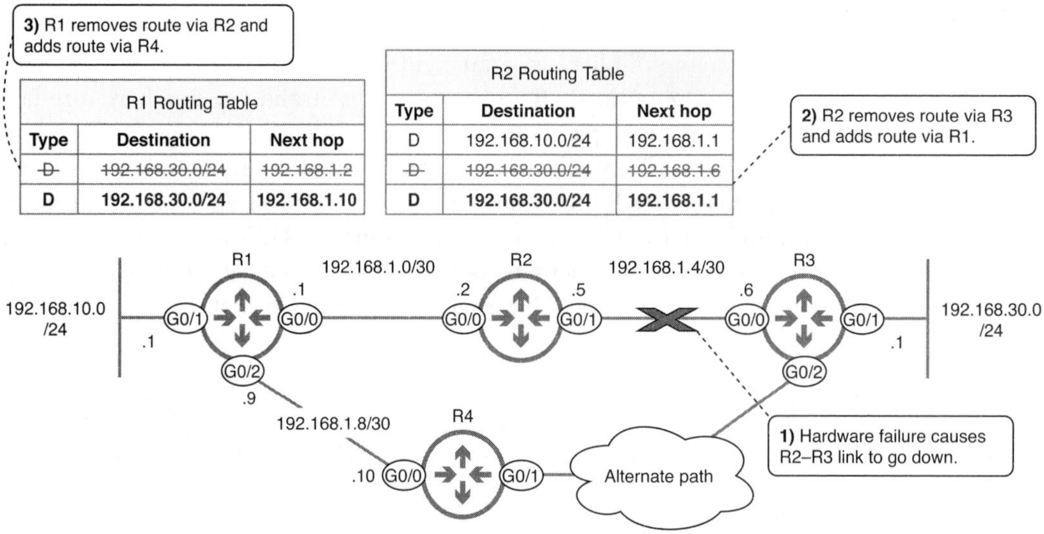

Figure 17.3 Dynamic routing allows routers to adapt to changes in the network by automatically calculating new routes. (1) A hardware failure causes the R2–R3 link to go down. (2) R2 removes its route to 192.168.30.0/24 via R3 and adds a new route with R1 as the next hop. (3) R1 removes its route via R2 and adds a new route with R4 as the next hop.

NOTE The route type of D in figure 17.3 indicates a route learned via the routing protocol Enhanced Interior Gateway Routing Protocol (EIGRP), which we will briefly cover in section 17.2. *D* stands for Diffusing Update Algorithm (DUAL), the specific algorithm EIGRP uses to calculate routes.

In a matter of seconds after the failure, all routers in the network will be aware of the change and have new routes in their routing tables. And once the failed link is restored (perhaps a faulty cable is replaced), the routers will once again adapt to that change, returning their routing tables to their previous state. The adaptability of dynamic routing improves the *resilience* of the network; it is able to automatically recover from failures with minimal downtime. This is not possible in a network that exclusively uses static routing.

17.1.2 Scalability

Another major advantage of dynamic routing is *scalability*. While static routing may be practical for small networks, it becomes increasingly complex and unmanageable as the network grows. On the other hand, dynamic routing protocols easily scale to support very large and complex networks. Figure 17.4 shows a network of six routers, each connected to a LAN containing various subnets. Additionally, two routers have connections to an ISP. This is a fairly simple network, but even in a network of this size, manually configuring static routes to every destination on each router is not very practical. A simpler option is to enable a routing protocol on each router and let them share the routing information themselves.

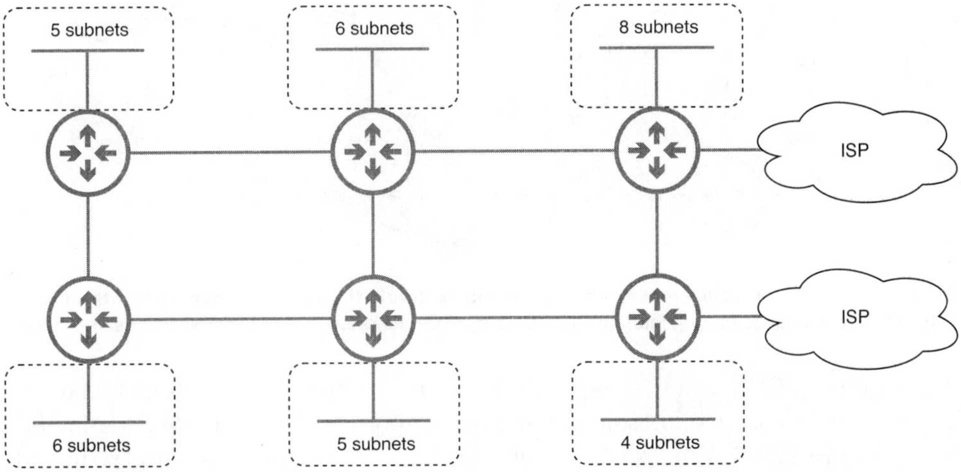

Figure 17.4 Configuring static routes to every destination on each router, even in a fairly small network like this, is not practical; it would be both time-consuming and prone to human error.

Before we move on to examine the different types of routing protocols, it is worth mentioning that static routes have their own advantages, such as predictability and control. Because static routing involves manually configuring routes (specifying the next hop for each destination), they are useful in situations where you want to control the exact path that packets take. Fortunately, there is no need to choose between static and dynamic routing; you can use a combination of static and dynamic routing on a single router.

17.2 Types of routing protocols

Routing protocols can be divided into two main categories: *Interior Gateway Protocols* (IGP) and *Exterior Gateway Protocols* (EGP). IGPs are used to exchange routing information within a single *autonomous system* (AS)—the network of a single organization. EGPs, on the other hand, are used to exchange routing information between different autonomous systems, such as between an enterprise and an ISP or between two ISPs.

> **NOTE** *Gateway* is an old term for a router. Although we call them routers these days, the term *gateway* is still used in some contexts (such as *default gateway*, as we covered in chapter 9).

Figure 17.5 demonstrates the difference between IGPs and EGPs. Each organization in the diagram uses an IGP to exchange routing information within their organization but an EGP to exchange routing information with other organizations.

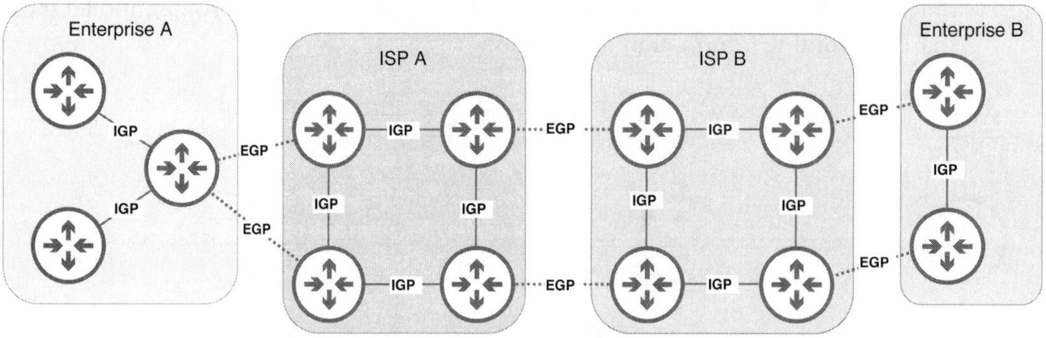

Figure 17.5 IGPs are used to exchange routing information with routers in the same AS (connected with solid lines). EGPs are used to exchange routing information with routers in a different AS (connected with dotted lines).

Although the CCNA exam focuses on one specific routing protocol (OSPF), you are also expected to understand some fundamental information about other routing protocols. Figure 17.6 lists the routing protocols that are commonly used today. In addition to being categorized as either an IGP or EGP, the routing protocols can be further categorized by *algorithm type*, which describes how the routers share information and calculate routes.

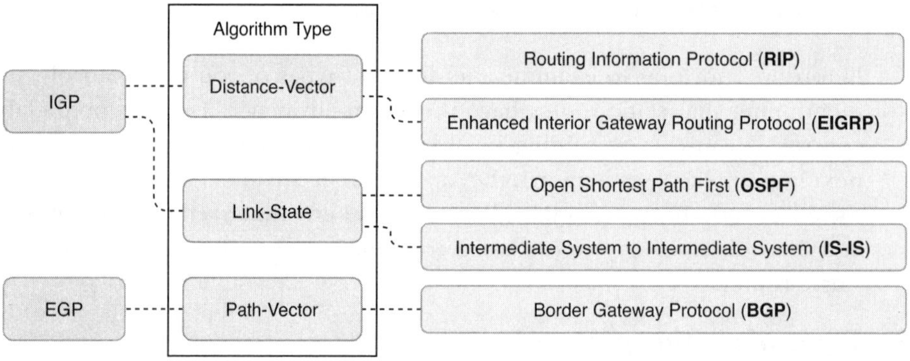

Figure 17.6 The five routing protocols in common use today. IGPs can be categorized as distance-vector or link-state. The two distance-vector IGPs are RIP and EIGRP. The two link-state IGPs are OSPF and IS-IS. The only exterior gateway protocol in use today, Border Gateway Protocol, uses a path-vector algorithm.

17.2.1 Interior gateway protocols

IGPs use one of two algorithm types: distance-vector and link-state. In this section, we'll take a look at the basic characteristics of each.

DISTANCE-VECTOR PROTOCOLS

There are two main distance-vector routing protocols in use today: the industry-standard *Routing Information Protocol* (RIP) and the Cisco-developed *Enhanced Interior*

Gateway Routing Protocol (EIGRP). RIP is a very simple protocol that is usually only used in very small networks and labs. EIGRP, on the other hand, is more advanced than RIP—in fact, it's sometimes called an *advanced distance-vector protocol*—and is in use in many large-scale networks today.

NOTE Although EIGRP was developed by Cisco, most of its functionality was released to the public in RFC 7868, so other vendors can implement it on their devices. However, very few other vendors have implemented it, so it's generally safe to say that EIGRP only runs on Cisco routers.

Routers using a distance-vector protocol share information about their known networks and their metric to reach those networks. *Metrics* are a similar concept to STP's root cost. Whereas the STP root cost is a measure of the efficiency of a path to the root bridge, a metric is a measure of the efficiency of a route to the destination network; we will cover metrics in section 17.3.1. Figure 17.7 shows how a router learns of a destination network (LAN A) with a distance-vector routing protocol. R1 learns of LAN A from two neighbors: R2 and R5. Because the route via R5 has a lower metric, R1 inserts the route via R5 into its routing table; a lower metric value is preferable.

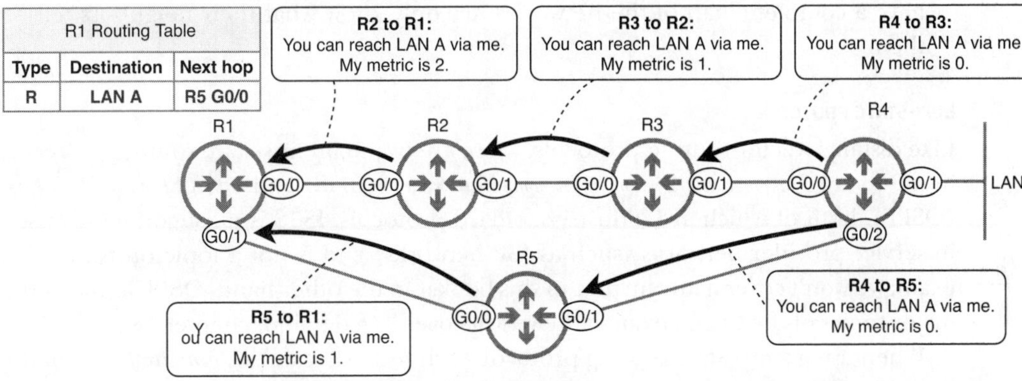

Figure 17.7 Routers share routing information with a distance-vector routing protocol. R1 learns of LAN A from both R2 and R5 but inserts the route via R5 into its routing table due to the lower metric value.

NOTE The route type of R in figure 17.7 indicates a route learned via the routing protocol RIP. The details of RIP aren't relevant to the CCNA exam.

The key characteristic of distance-vector routing protocols is that each router doesn't have a complete map of the network; for each destination network it learns about, it only knows the metric and next-hop router. Using the example of figure 17.7, R1 knows that to reach LAN A, it can forward packets to R2, which has a metric of 2, or R5, which has a metric of 1; it doesn't know the details of the network beyond R2 and R5, as shown in figure 17.8.

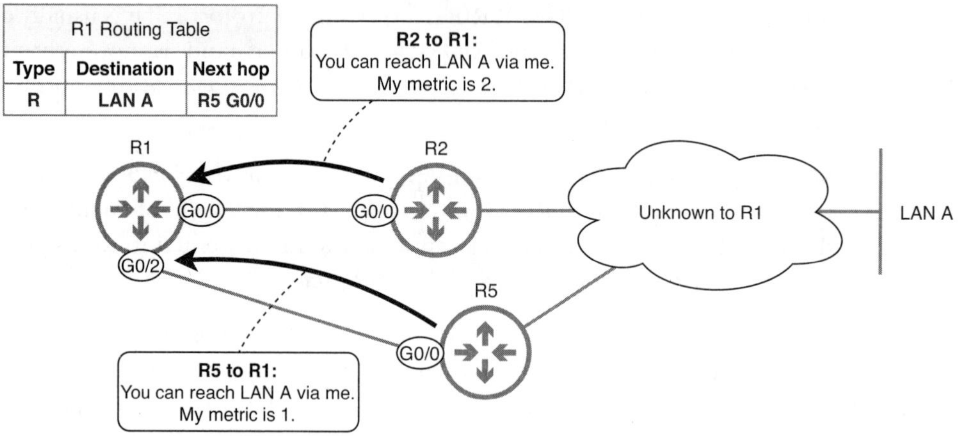

Figure 17.8 R1 learns of LAN A from R2 and R5 and selects a route based on that information. R1 is unaware of the details of the network beyond R2 and R5.

NOTE Distance-vector routing is sometimes called *routing by rumor*. Routers don't have a complete map of the network; they only know what their neighbors tell them.

LINK-STATE PROTOCOLS

Like distance-vector routing protocols, there are two main link-state routing protocols in use today: *Intermediate System to Intermediate System* (IS-IS) and *Open Shortest Path First* (OSPF), both of which are industry-standard protocols. IS-IS is most commonly used in service-provider networks (such as ISP networks) and is not a topic on the CCNA exam; we won't cover it any further in this book. On the other hand, OSPF is one of the major topics of the CCNA exam, and we will cover it in detail in chapter 18.

When using a link-state routing protocol, each router creates a *connectivity map* of the network. To allow all routers to build their connectivity map, each router shares information about its connected links and the state of those links (the connected subnets, metric cost, etc.)—hence the name *link state.* This information is not shared only with directly connected neighbors; it is shared with all routers in the network, so they can all build the same connectivity map. Each router then uses this map of the network to calculate its best route to each destination in the network. Figure 17.9 demonstrates this concept; R1 builds a connectivity map and uses it to calculate a route to LAN A.

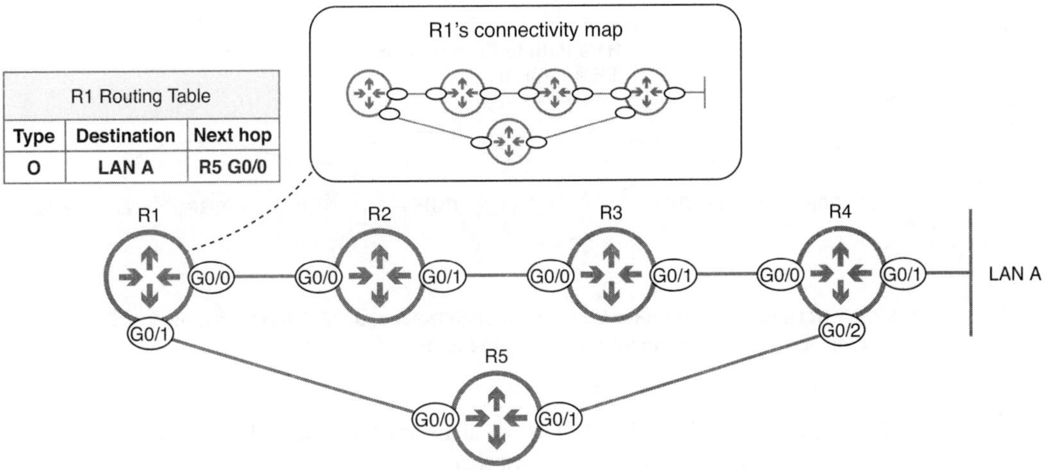

Figure 17.9 R1 builds a connectivity map of the network and uses it to calculate a route to LAN A.

NOTE The route type of O in figure 17.9 indicates a route learned via the routing protocol OSPF, the topic of chapter 18.

Building this map of the network and using it to calculate routes requires more CPU and memory resources on the router than required by distance-vector routing protocols, which can be a concern in very large networks. The map is stored in memory using a structure called the *link-state database* (LSDB), and calculating routes from the LSDB can be CPU-intensive. However, there are methods to overcome this limitation, such as dividing the network into *areas*, which we'll cover in chapter 18.

17.2.2 Exterior gateway protocols

In modern networks, only a single EGP is widely used: *Border Gateway Protocol* (BGP). BGP uses a *path-vector* algorithm to calculate routes. Like the two IGP algorithm types, the name path-vector gives us a hint about how BGP works. The path is the series of autonomous systems a packet will travel through along the route to the destination—for example, perhaps it will travel through two different ISPs before reaching the destination AS.

Figure 17.10 demonstrates path-vector logic: packets from R1 to destinations in Enterprise B will travel through ISP A and ISP B and then reach Enterprise B. R1 learns of this route by communicating with ISP A using BGP. Rather than making routing decisions based on the series of individual routers that packets will travel through, BGP makes routing decisions based on the series of autonomous systems they will travel through (each AS likely consisting of multiple routers).

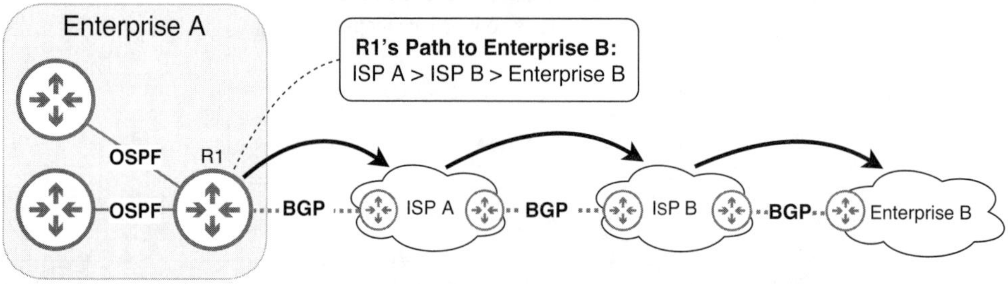

Figure 17.10 R1's path to Enterprise B passes through ISP A and ISP B and then arrives at Enterprise B. Path-vector logic is AS-to-AS, rather than router-to-router.

NOTE Figure 17.10 is a simplification of how BGP works. BGP takes multiple attributes of the path into account, not just the number of autonomous systems.

17.3 Route selection

Route selection is something we already covered in chapter 9. That definition of route selection referred to packet forwarding; when a router forwards a packet, it will select the most specific matching route in the routing table.

However, route selection can also refer to the process of selecting which routes are used to populate the routing table. Routes learned via a dynamic routing protocol aren't automatically inserted into the router's routing table. Likewise, manually configured static routes don't necessarily enter the routing table either. If a route isn't in the routing table, it can't be used to forward packets. To summarize, the following are the two meanings of the term *route selection*:

- *Routing table population*—The process of selecting which routes the router will enter into its routing table
- *Packet forwarding*—The process of selecting the best route in the routing table to forward a particular packet

If a router learns multiple routes to the same destination, it will only insert the best route to that destination into its routing table. To determine which route is best, it will compare two parameters: metric and administrative distance.

17.3.1 The metric parameter

We already saw an example of how metrics work in figure 17.7. R1 learned two routes to reach LAN A: one with a metric of 2 and one with a metric of 1. Which of the two routes did R1 insert into its routing table? R1 selected the latter route because of its lower metric.

Each routing protocol's metric is calculated differently. RIP uses a simple hop count: the number of routers between the router and the destination is the route's metric. OSPF uses a cost value that is calculated from the bandwidth of each link in the path.

EIGRP uses a more complex calculation based on bandwidth and *delay* (how long it takes bits to travel across a link), as well as other parameters. Table 17.1 summarizes how RIP, EIGRP, and OSPF calculate metrics.

Table 17.1 IGP metrics

IGP	Metric	Description
RIP	Hop count	Each router in the path counts as one hop. The total metric is the total number of hops to the destination.
EIGRP	Metric based on bandwidth and delay	A complex formula that can take into account many values. By default, bandwidth and delay are used.
OSPF	Cost	The cost of each link is calculated based on bandwidth. A route's metric is the total cost of each link in the path.

Figure 17.11 shows an example of route selection in a network of routers that use OSPF to share routing information. R1 uses its connectivity map to calculate the possible routes to reach 192.168.3.0/24 and selects the best route for its routing table.

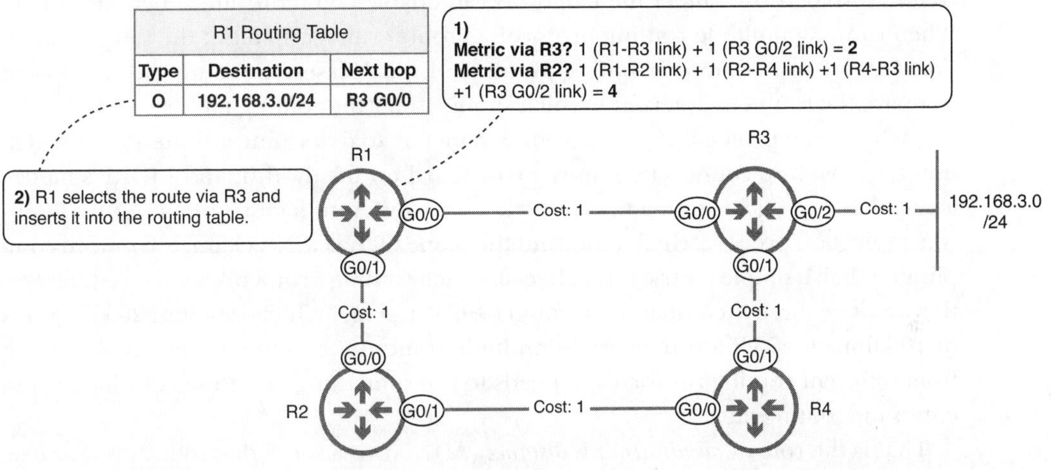

Figure 17.11 R1 inserts the best route to 192.168.3.0/24 into its routing table. (1) R1 calculates the possible routes to 192.168.3.0/24. The route via R3 has a metric of 2, and the route via R2 has a metric of 4. (2) R1 selects the route via R3 because of its lower metric and inserts the route into its routing table.

The following example shows the route in R1's routing table. Pay attention to the two values in square brackets:

```
R1# show ip route
. . .
O     192.168.3.0/24 [110/2] via 192.168.1.6, 00:08:35, GigabitEthernet0/0
```

R1 selects the route via R3 (metric 2) and inserts it into the routing table.

After the destination network of `192.168.3.0/24`, the route includes two values in square brackets: `[110/2]`. The first value (`110`) is the route's administrative distance (covered in section 17.3.2), and the second value (`2`) is the route's metric. In the following example, I disable R1's G0/0 interface, which renders the route via R3 invalid. I then check the routing table again; the alternate route via R2, with a metric of 4, is inserted into the routing table in place of the route via R3:

```
R1(config)# interface g0/0
R1(config-if)# shutdown
R1(config-if)# do show ip route
. . .
O     192.168.3.0/24 [110/4] via 192.168.1.2, 00:00:04, GigabitEthernet0/1
```

The route via R2 (metric 4) is selected after the router via R3 (metric 2) is removed.

17.3.2 The administrative distance parameter

Although most routers will only run one routing protocol, there are cases where a router will run multiple protocols—for example, if two enterprises (running different routing protocols) connect their networks to enable communication between them. When running multiple routing protocols, a router can learn about the same destination network from different routing protocols. In such cases, the router needs a way to compare the routes to determine which should enter the routing table.

Each routing protocol uses different parameters to determine a route's metric: RIP uses a simple hop count, OSPF uses a cost based on bandwidth, and EIGRP's metric is calculated using a formula that can take many different factors into account. BGP's route selection process, which is beyond the scope of the CCNA exam, is far more complicated than a simple metric value. Because each routing protocol's metric is different, they can't be directly compared; it would be like asking, "Which is better: 20 kilograms or 10 kilometers?" If a router learns multiple routes to the same destination network from different routing protocols, it needs to use something else to select which route enters the routing table.

That is the role of *administrative distance* (AD). AD is a value that indicates how preferred a routing protocol is. A lower AD value indicates a routing protocol that IOS considers more "trustworthy"—more likely to select good routes. Whereas a metric is used to compare routes learned via the same routing protocol, AD is used to compare routes learned via different routing protocols. Table 17.2 lists the default AD values of some different routing protocols (including connected and static routes).

Table 17.2 Default AD values

Route type/protocol	Default AD
Connected	0
Static	1
External BGP (EBGP)	20
EIGRP	90
OSPF	110
IS-IS	115
RIP	120
Internal BGP (IBGP)	200
Unusable route	255

EXAM TIP Make sure you know these default AD values; I recommend using flashcards to memorize them.

As when comparing metric values, the lower AD value is preferred. Connected routes (the routes that are automatically added when you configure an IP address on an interface) have an AD of 0; they are always preferred over other route types. Static routes, with an AD of 1, are preferred over routes learned from any of the dynamic routing protocols by default; however, we'll cover how you can make them less preferred later in this section. The least-preferred AD value is 255. Cisco routers can use this value to mark a route unusable; it will be removed from the routing table.

Figure 17.12 shows an example in which AD is used to select which route enters the routing table. R1 learns of the destination network 10.0.0.0/24 via EIGRP and OSPF. Although the EIGRP route's metric value (3584) is numerically higher than the OSPF route's (4), that is irrelevant in this case; EIGRP and OSPF metric values can't be directly compared. Instead, AD is used to decide which route enters the routing table. EIGRP's AD (90) is lower than OSPF's (110), so R1 inserts the EIGRP route into its routing table.

NOTE Due to the formula EIGRP uses to calculate metrics, the metric values of EIGRP routes tend to be quite large compared to those of RIP and OSPF routes. Although this route's metric is 3584 (because R1 and the destination are only separated by a few routers), it's not rare for the metric of EIGRP routes to be in the range of tens or hundreds of thousands.

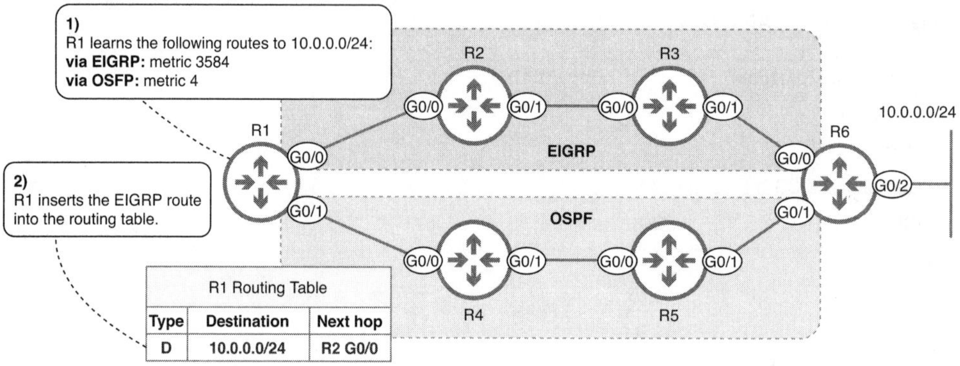

Figure 17.12 R1 uses AD to select which route enters the routing table. (1) R1 learns two routes to 10.0.0.0/24: via EIGRP (metric 3584) and via OSPF (metric 4). (2) EIGRP's AD (90) is lower than OSPF's (110), so R1 inserts the EIGRP route into its routing table. The metric values are irrelevant in this case.

The following example shows the EIGRP route in R1's routing table. Take note of the values in square brackets—EIGRP's AD is 90, and the route's metric is 3584:

```
R1# show ip route
. . .
D        10.0.0.0 [90/3584] via 192.168.12.2, 00:33:30, GigabitEthernet0/0
. . .
```

NOTE Metrics and AD are only used to compare routes to the same destination—the same destination network address with the same prefix length. If two routes have the same destination network address but a different prefix length (i.e., 192.168.0.0/24 and 192.168.0.0/25), they are considered different destinations; both routes will be inserted into the routing table. We will clarify this point in section 17.3.3.

ECMP

Metrics are used to select among routes to the same destination that were learned via the same routing protocol, and AD is used to select among routes to the same destination that were learned via different routing protocols. But what happens if a router learns multiple routes to the same destination via the same routing protocol and the routes have the same metric? In that case, all routes will be added to the routing table, and traffic will be load-balanced over them; half of the traffic will be sent using one route and the other half using the other route. This is called *equal-cost multi-path* (ECMP) routing.

NOTE By default, a maximum of four routes to the same destination can be used for ECMP routing.

Figure 17.13 shows an example of ECMP. R1 learns two routes to 10.0.0.0/24: one from R2 and one from R4. Both routes are learned via OSPF and have a metric of 4. Therefore, R1 inserts both routes into the routing table; it will load-balance traffic over the two routes.

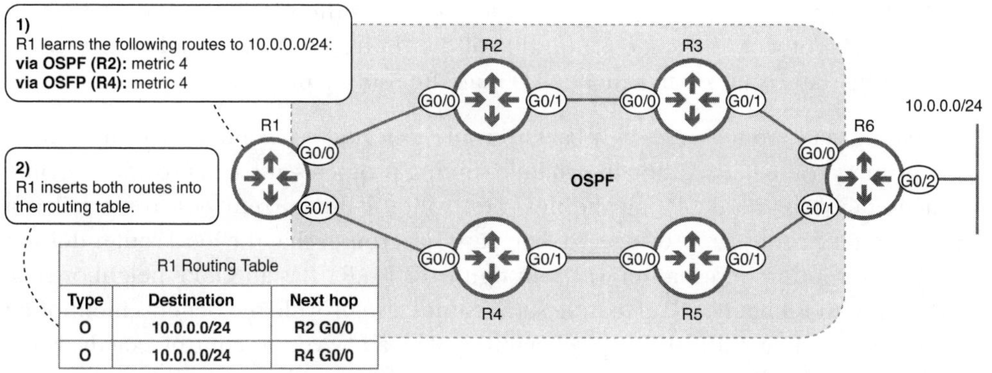

Figure 17.13 An example of ECMP routing. (1) R1 learns two routes to 10.0.0.0/24 via OSPF with the same metric: one from R2 and one from R4. (2) R1 inserts both routes into its routing table; it will load-balance traffic using the two routes.

FLOATING STATIC ROUTES

By default, static routes have an AD of 1 and are thus preferred over routes learned using a dynamic routing protocol. However, there are cases where you might want to configure a static route as a backup that only enters the routing table if the main route (learned via a routing protocol) is lost. That is the role of floating static routes.

A *floating static route* is a static route configured with an AD greater than the default of 1 for the purpose of making it less preferred. For example, to make a static route less preferred than an OSPF route to the same destination, it should be configured with an AD greater than 110 (OSPF's AD). To configure a floating static route, just add the AD value to the end of the command. For example, you can configure a floating recursive static route with the `ip route` *`destination-network netmask next-hop ad`* command. Figure 17.14 shows an example in which I configure a static route with an AD of 111 to make it less preferable than a route learned via OSPF.

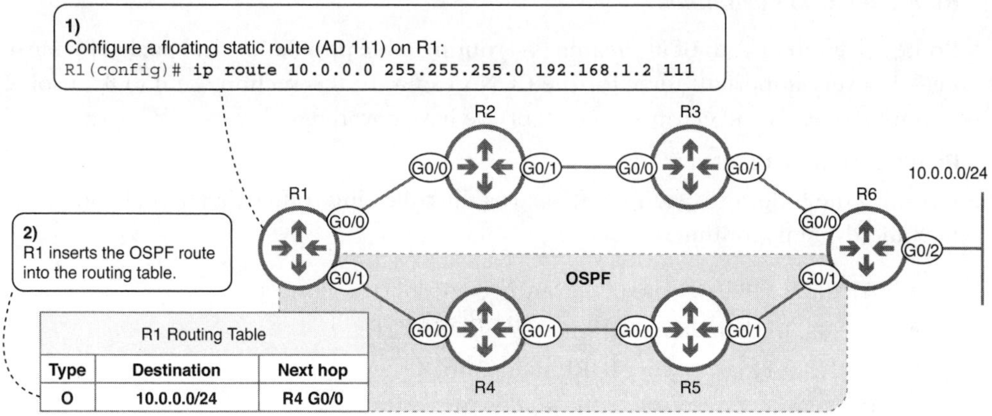

Figure 17.14 A floating static route is less preferred than an OSPF route to the same destination.

NOTE If you configure a floating static route with the same AD as a dynamic routing protocol, the static route will still be preferred. You should configure floating static routes with a higher AD than the routing protocol.

A floating static route serves as a backup route, offering a secondary path for data if the primary route fails. Although dynamic routing protocols also can provide the same functionality (by recalculating the next-best route if the current best route fails), a floating static route can provide a backup path via a router that the local router doesn't exchange routing information with—in figure 17.14, R1 has an OSPF neighbor relationship with R4 but not R2. Floating static routes also provide the benefits mentioned previously, such as control and predictability; they allow you to control exactly which path traffic will take if the primary route fails.

In the following example, I test the floating static route we saw in figure 17.14. When I first check R1's routing table, the OSPF route is present. I then disable R1's G0/1 interface (simulating a hardware failure) and check the routing table again; this time, the floating static route (with an AD of 111) has taken the place of the OSPF route:

```
R1(config)# do show ip route
. . .
O        10.0.0.0 [110/4] via 192.168.1.6, 00:25:43,
➥GigabitEthernet0/1
. . .
R1(config)# interface g0/1
R1(config-if)# shutdown
R1(config)# do show ip route
. . .
S        10.0.0.0 [111/0] via 192.168.1.2
. . .
```

The OSPF route is preferred over the floating static route.

Disables R1's G0/1 interface

The floating static route enters R1's routing table.

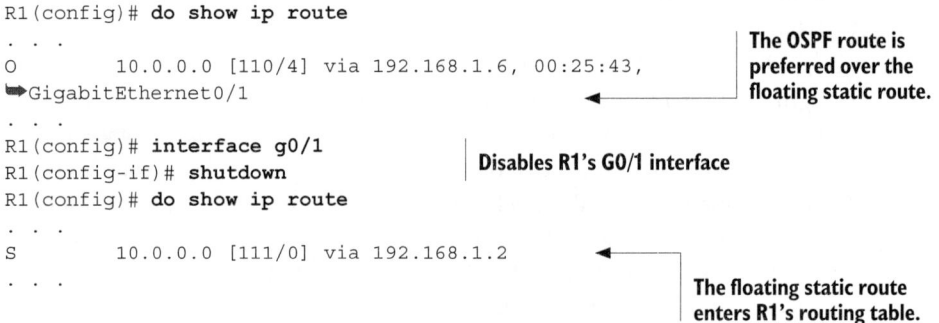

NOTE Static routes don't use the concept of metrics; their metric is always 0.

17.3.3 Route selection examples

Route selection in both of its meanings—routing table population and packet forwarding—is a very important topic for the CCNA exam. In this section, we'll look at some examples of each and clarify the concepts we have covered so far.

ROUTING TABLE POPULATION

Consider the following example. R1 learns the following routes via manual configuration and dynamic routing protocols:

- (A) 203.0.113.0/24 via static routing
- (B) 203.0.113.0/25 via RIP, metric 4
- (C) 203.0.113.0/26 via EIGRP, metric 5678
- (D) 203.0.113.0/27 via OSPF, metric 10

Which route(s) will R1 insert into its routing table? Having read up to this point, you may think that R1 will select the static route because it has the lowest AD. Or perhaps you think R1 will select the OSPF route because it has the longest prefix length (using the "most specific matching route" rule covered in chapter 9). However, the answer is that R1 will insert all four routes into its routing table.

The reason is that all four routes are to different destinations. Although they have the same destination network address (203.0.113.0), they all have different prefix lengths and are thus considered different destinations. There is no need to compare them; R1 will insert them all into the routing table.

It is worth noting that the four subnets in the example overlap, as shown in figure 17.15. The /25, /26, and /27 subnets are contained within the /24 subnet. However, when it comes to building the routing table, they are considered different destination networks and thus will all be inserted into the routing table.

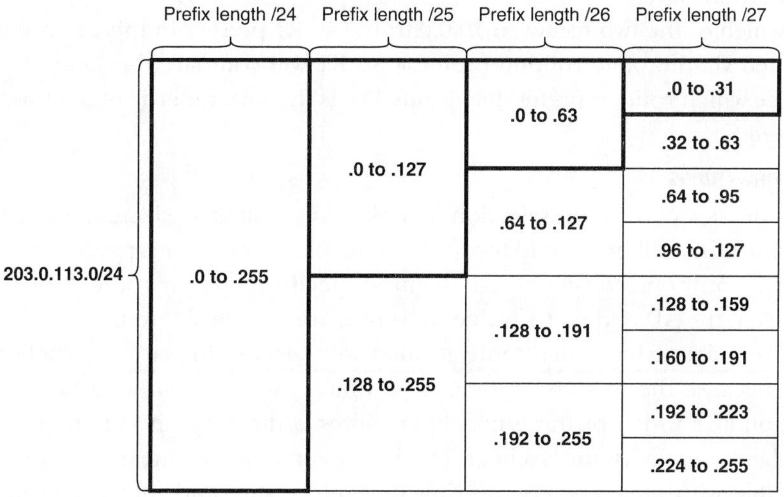

Figure 17.15 The four routes in the example overlap. 203.0.113.0/24 includes 203.0.113.0–.255, 203.0.113.0/25 includes 203.0.113.0–.127, 203.0.113.0/26 includes 203.0.113.0–.63, and 203.0.113.0/27 includes 203.0.113.0–.31. However, IOS considers them to be routes to different destinations and will insert all four routes into the routing table.

> **NOTE** The concept of "most specific matching route" is irrelevant to this question. The most specific matching route rule is used to select which route in the routing table will be used to forward a packet; it is not used to select which routes will enter the routing table.

Let's take a look at one more example. R1 learns the following routes via dynamic routing protocols:

- (A) 10.0.0.0/8 via EIGRP, metric 2345
- (B) 10.0.0.0/8 via OSPF, metric 10
- (C) 10.0.0.0/16 via OSPF, metric 20
- (D) 10.0.0.0/16 via OSPF, metric 5

Which route(s) will R1 insert into its routing table in this example? Let's walk through the logic. In this example, R1 learns two routes to each of two different destination networks: two routes to 10.0.0.0/8 and two routes to 10.0.0.0/16. Therefore, R1 must select the best of the two routes to 10.0.0.0/8 and the best of the two routes to 10.0.0.0/16.

Which of the two routes to 10.0.0.0/8 will R1 prefer? Because R1 learns the two routes via different routing protocols, it will use AD to compare the routes. EIGRP's metric (90) is lower than OSPF's (110), so R1 will select the EIGRP route; therefore, A is one of the answers.

And which of the two routes to 10.0.0.0/16 will R1 prefer? In this case, both routes are learned via the same routing protocol, so R1 will compare their metric values to determine which route is preferable. Route D has the lower metric of the two, so it will be selected.

PACKET FORWARDING

The second aspect of route selection is packet forwarding—selecting which route in the routing table will be used to forward a particular packet. This process is simpler in that there is only one consideration: the most specific matching route. When forwarding a packet, the AD and metric values of routes are not considered.

However, identifying which route a router will select to forward a packet on can be difficult because the process of identifying which routes match a particular packet's destination and which of those matching routes is the most specific requires you to convert between binary and decimal. This is why I emphasized the importance of being comfortable with binary when covering IPv4 addressing and subnetting in previous chapters.

Let's look at an example of route selection in the context of packet forwarding. Examine R1's routing table in the following. Which route will it select to forward a packet destined for 203.0.113.65?

```
R1# show ip route
. . .
S        203.0.113.0/24 [1/0] via 192.168.1.2
R        203.0.113.0/25 [120/4] via 192.168.1.6
D        203.0.113.0/26 [90/5678] via 192.168.1.10
O        203.0.113.0/27 [110/10] via 192.168.1.14
```

The first step is to identify which routes match the packet's destination. As we covered in chapter 9, if the packet's destination IP address is a part of the network specified in the route, it's a match. In the following example, I have written out each route in binary, as well as the packet's destination IP address (203.0.113.65):

/24 means the first 24 bits must match.

/25 means the first 25 bits must match.

```
203.0.113.0/24 = 11001011.00000000.01110001.00000000
203.0.113.0/25 = 11001011.00000000.01110001.00000000
203.0.113.0/26 = 11001011.00000000.01110001.00000000
203.0.113.0/27 = 11001011.00000000.01110001.00000000
203.0.113.65   = 11001011.00000000.01110001.01000001
```

/26 means the first 26 bits must match.

The packet's destination IP address

/27 means the first 27 bits must match.

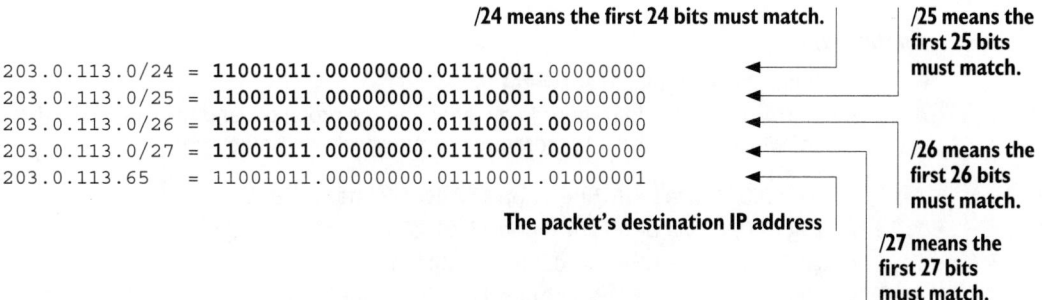

EXAM TIP To speed up the process during the exam, you don't have to write out all 32 bits of every address. In this example, the shortest prefix length is /24, and the four routes and the destination IP address all begin with 203.0.113, so there is no need to write out the first three octets of all of them (they're all the same); you can just write out the relevant octets (the final octet, in this case).

The route to 203.0.113.0/24 matches the packet's destination, and so does the route to 203.0.113.0/25. The route to 203.0.113.0/26 doesn't match the packet's destination because the 26th bit doesn't match; it's `0` in the route but `1` in the packet's destination IP address. Likewise, the /27 route doesn't match because of the mismatched 26th bit.

Out of the two matching routes, the route to 203.0.113.0/25 is more specific; it has the longer prefix length. Therefore, it is the route that will be selected to forward the packet; R1 will forward the packet to the next hop 192.168.1.6. The fact that the route has a higher AD than the other three routes is irrelevant, and so is the route's metric; when selecting which route will be used to forward a packet, the only consideration is the most specific matching route. To summarize, here are the two aspects of route selection:

- Routing table population:
  - Metrics are used to select among routes to *the same destination* that are learned via *the same routing protocol.*
  - AD is used to select among routes to *the same destination* that are learned via *different routing protocols.*
- Packet forwarding:
  - The most specific matching route is selected.

Exam scenarios

To achieve CCNA exam success, it's essential that you understand dynamic routing—especially the route selection topics covered in this chapter. We already covered a few example questions, but here are a couple more that test your knowledge of route selection:

(continued)

1 (multiple choice, multiple answers)
R1 learns the following routes via dynamic routing protocols and manual configuration. Which routes will R1 insert into its routing table? (Select three.)

- A 10.0.0.0/16 via EIGRP, next hop 172.16.1.2, metric 7812
- B 10.0.0.0/16 via EIGRP, next hop 172.16.23.2, metric 7812
- C 10.0.0.0/16 via OSPF, next hop 10.0.0.1, metric 5
- D 10.0.0.0/24 via EIGRP, next hop 172.16.1.2, metric 1098
- E 10.0.0.0/24 via static routing, next hop 10.2.2.2, default AD

In this scenario, R1 learns routes to two different destination networks: 10.0.0.0/16 and 10.0.0.0/24. Of the three routes to 10.0.0.0/16, A and B are preferred for their lower AD—EIGRP's 90 vs OSPF's 110. Both EIGRP routes have identical metric values (7812), so R1 will insert both into its routing table—an example of ECMP. So A and B are two of the correct answers.

Of the two routes to 10.0.0.0/24, E is preferred for its lower AD—as a static route, its default AD of 1 is lower than that of any dynamic routing protocol. So the third correct answer is E.

2 (multiple-choice, single answer)
R1 has built its routing table through a combination of dynamic and static routing. When forwarding a packet, which of the following is used to select which route is used to forward the packet?

- A Longest prefix length
- B Most specific matching route
- C Lowest AD
- D Lowest metric

Although a router uses AD and metrics to select which routes to insert into its routing table, packet forwarding is simpler: the router will forward the packet according to the most specific matching route in the routing table (the matching route with the longest prefix length). Option A touches on the "longest prefix length" aspect but misses the critical "matching" aspect. Having the longest prefix length doesn't necessarily mean that a route will be selected to forward a packet; the route must also match the packet's destination IP address. So B is the best answer for this question.

17.4 The network command

RIP, EIGRP, and OSPF are all configured by activating the protocol on one or more of the router's interfaces. The router will then advertise the network prefix (network address and netmask) of the interface. RIP and EIGRP configuration are out of the scope of the CCNA exam, and we will cover OSPF configuration in greater detail in chapter 18, but in this section, we will look at one command that is shared by all three protocols: the `network` command. This command tells the router to

- Look for interfaces with an IP address that is in the specified range
- Activate the routing protocol on those interfaces
- Advertise the network prefix of the interface(s) to its neighbors

Although RIP, EIGRP, and OSPF all share the **network** command, there are differences in syntax between them; we will focus on OSPF, since its configuration is a CCNA exam topic. To configure OSPF on a Cisco router, use the **router ospf** *process-id* command in global config mode to enter *router config mode*—a new configuration mode, from which you can use the **network** command.

NOTE A router can run separate OSPF processes (instances), which is why you must specify a *process-id* in the **router ospf** command. However, the use cases of multiple OSPF processes are beyond the scope of the CCNA exam.

Figure 17.16 shows how the **network** command can be used to activate OSPF on a router's interfaces. The syntax of the network command is **network** *ip-address wildcard-mask* **area** *area-id*. The key to this command is the wildcard mask, which looks like an inverted netmask but serves a different purpose.

NOTE OSPF uses *areas* to logically divide up the network; we will cover OSPF areas in chapter 18. For now, we will just specify **area 0** in the network command.

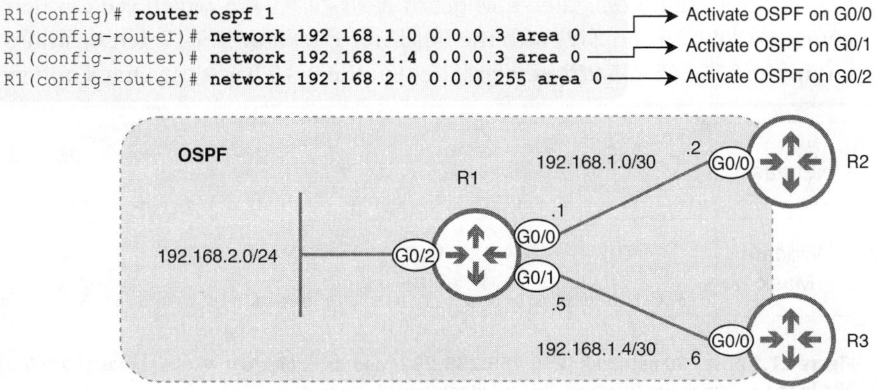
R1(config)# router ospf 1
R1(config-router)# network 192.168.1.0 0.0.0.3 area 0
R1(config-router)# network 192.168.1.4 0.0.0.3 area 0
R1(config-router)# network 192.168.2.0 0.0.0.255 area 0
Activate OSPF on G0/0
Activate OSPF on G0/1
Activate OSPF on G0/2
OSPF
R1
192.168.1.0/30
.2
G0/0
R2
.1
G0/0
192.168.2.0/24
G0/2
G0/1
.5
G0/0
R3
192.168.1.4/30
.6

Figure 17.16 Activating OSPF on a router's interfaces with the network command. The command uses a wildcard mask, which looks like an inverted netmask.

A *wildcard mask*, like a netmask, is a series of 32 bits. The purpose of a wildcard mask is to indicate which bits need to match between two IP addresses and which bits don't. The wildcard mask in the **network** command specifies which bits have to match between the IP address in the **network** command and the IP address configured on a router's interface. A 0 bit in the wildcard mask means that the bits in the same position of the **network** command's IP address and the interface's IP address must match. A 1 bit in the wildcard mask means that the bits don't have to match.

Let's examine the three **network** commands used in figure 17.16. In the following example, I show the **network** command used to activate OSPF on R1's G0/0 interface. Note that the appropriate bits match between the **network** command's IP address (192.168.1.0) and R1 G0/0's IP address (192.168.1.1)—those specified by 0 bits in the wildcard mask:

The IP address of R1's G0/0 interface

The IP address specified in the network command

```
192.168.1.1 = 11000000.10101000.00000001.00000001
192.168.1.0 = 11000000.10101000.00000001.00000000
0.0.0.3     = 00000000.00000000.00000000.00000011
```

The wildcard mask specified in the network command

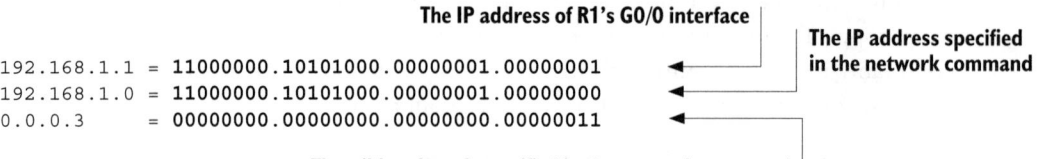

Next is the command I used to activate OSPF on R1's G0/1 interface. Once again, the appropriate bits match between the IP address specified in the **network** command and the IP address of G0/1:

The IP address of R1's G0/1 interface

The IP address specified in the network command

```
192.168.1.5 = 11000000.10101000.00000001.00000101
192.168.1.4 = 11000000.10101000.00000001.00000100
0.0.0.3     = 00000000.00000000.00000000.00000011
```

The wildcard mask specified in the network command

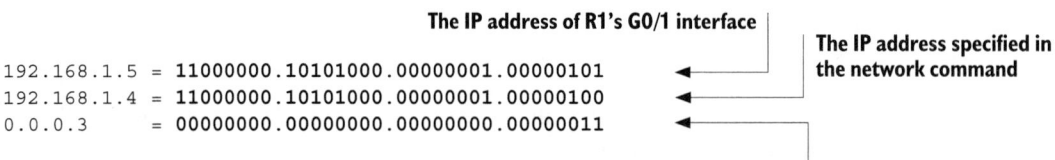

In these two examples, I used a wildcard mask of 0.0.0.3, which is equivalent to a /30 netmask (255.255.255.252) with the bits inverted. Figure 17.17 demonstrates this: all 1 bits in the 255.255.255.252 netmask are 0 in the 0.0.0.3 wildcard mask and vice versa.

Netmask	255	255	255	252
	1 1 1 1 1 1 1 1	1 1 1 1 1 1 1 1	1 1 1 1 1 1 1 1	1 1 1 1 1 1 0 0
Wildcard Mask	0	0	0	3
	0 0 0 0 0 0 0 0	0 0 0 0 0 0 0 0	0 0 0 0 0 0 0 0	0 0 0 0 0 0 1 1

Figure 17.17 A /30 netmask (255.255.255.252) and its equivalent wildcard mask (0.0.0.3). The 1 bits in the netmask are 0 in the wildcard mask and vice versa.

> **NOTE** A shortcut to calculating a netmask's equivalent wildcard mask is to subtract each octet of the netmask from 255. The first three octets of a /30 netmask are 255 and 255-255 = 0. The final octet is 252 and 255-252 = 3.

Finally, let's look at the command I used to activate OSPF on R1's G0/2 interface. This time, the interface's prefix length is /24, so I used the wildcard mask equivalent of a /24 netmask: 0.0.0.255:

The IP address of R1's G0/2 interface

The IP address specified in the network command

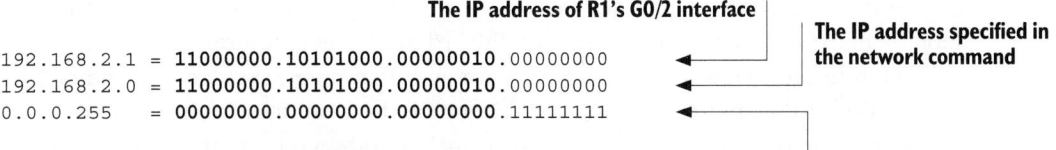

```
192.168.2.1 = 11000000.10101000.00000010.00000000
192.168.2.0 = 11000000.10101000.00000010.00000000
0.0.0.255   = 00000000.00000000.00000000.11111111
```

The wildcard mask specified in the network command

Table 17.3 lists some netmasks and their equivalent wildcard masks.

Table 17.3 /24+ netmasks and wildcard masks

Prefix length	Netmask	Wildcard mask (last octet binary)
/24	255.255.255.0	0.0.0.255 (11111111)
/25	255.255.255.128	0.0.0.127 (01111111)
/26	255.255.255.192	0.0.0.63 (00111111)
/27	255.255.255.224	0.0.0.31 (00011111)
/28	255.255.255.240	0.0.0.15 (00001111)
/29	255.255.255.248	0.0.0.7 (00000111)
/30	255.255.255.252	0.0.0.3 (00000011)
/31	255.255.255.254	0.0.0.1 (00000001)
/32	255.255.255.255	0.0.0.0 (00000000)

Why wildcard masks?

You might wonder why we use wildcard masks instead of netmasks. The key is to recall what netmasks are used for: they identify the size of a network prefix, distinguishing between the network portion and the host portion of an IP address. For example, configuring **`ip address 192.168.1.1 255.255.255.0`** on a router interface tells the router that its IP address is 192.168.1.1—the first three octets are the network portion, and the last octet is the host portion. The prefix is 192.168.1.0/24.

However, when dealing with the OSPF **`network`** command, the IP address and wildcard mask are used differently; they don't define a network prefix as a netmask would. Instead, they specify a range of IP addresses, not necessarily part of the same subnet. This range is used to determine which router interfaces will take part in OSPF, meaning which ones will send and receive OSPF routing information. Here's a quick recap:

- A netmask (or subnet mask) is used to distinguish the network and host portions of an IP address. It determines the length of a subnet's network prefix.
- In the context of the OSPF **`network`** command, an IP address and wildcard mask do not define a network prefix. Instead, they define a range of IP addresses (that aren't necessarily part of the same subnet). This range is used to determine which interfaces on the router will participate in the OSPF process (i.e., which interfaces will send and receive OSPF routing information).

In the three **network** commands we looked at, I used the network address (host portion of all 0s) of each interface and the wildcard mask that is equivalent to the netmask of each interface. However, it's important to note that the **network** command is flexible: as long as the appropriate bits match between the IP address in the **network** command and the interface's IP address (those indicated by a 0 bit in the wildcard mask), OSPF will be activated on the interface. Figure 17.18 shows a different way to activate OSPF on R1's interfaces, this time using only two **network** commands.

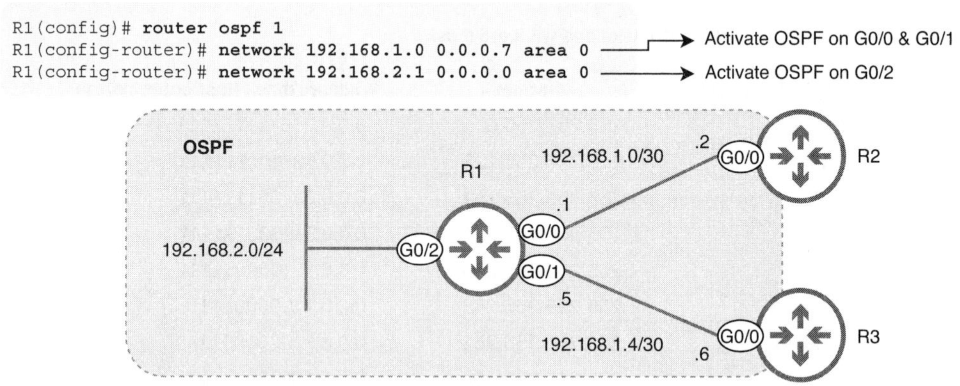

Figure 17.18 Activating OSPF on R1's interfaces with two `network` commands. The first command activates OSPF on R1's G0/0 and G0/1 interfaces, and the second activates OSPF on G0/2.

The first command activates OSPF on both G0/0 and G0/1; the appropriate bits of each interface's IP address match the IP address specified in the **network** command. By using a wildcard mask of 0.0.0.7—equivalent to a /29 netmask (255.255.255.248)—I tell R1 to activate OSPF on all interfaces with an IP address from 192.168.1.0 to 192.168.1.7, which includes G0/0 (192.168.1.1) and G0/1 (192.168.1.5):

```
192.168.1.1 = 11000000.10101000.00000001.00000001   <- The IP address of R1's G0/0 interface
192.168.1.5 = 11000000.10101000.00000001.00000101   <- The IP address of R1's G0/1 interface
192.168.1.0 = 11000000.10101000.00000001.00000000   <- The IP address specified in the network command
0.0.0.7     = 00000000.00000000.00000000.00000111   <- The wildcard mask specified in the network command
```

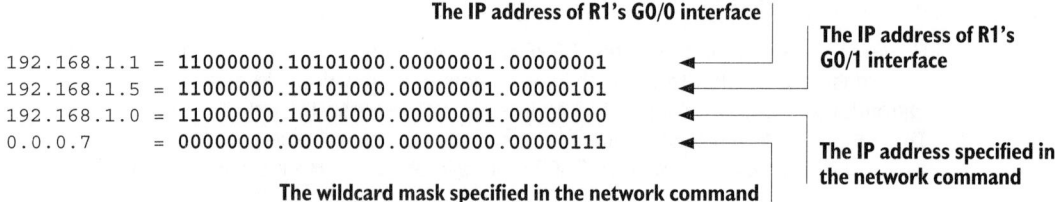

The second command activates OSPF on G0/2 in a different manner than in the previous example. By specifying G0/2's exact IP address in the **network** command and using a wildcard mask of 0.0.0.0—equivalent to a /32 netmask (255.255.255.255)—I tell R1 to activate OSPF only on the interface with IP address 192.168.2.1, R1's G0/2 interface:

The IP address of R1's G0/2 interface

The IP address specified in the network command

```
192.168.2.1 = 11000000.10101000.00000010.00000001
192.168.2.1 = 11000000.10101000.00000010.00000001
0.0.0.0     = 00000000.00000000.00000000.00000000
```

The wildcard mask specified in the network command

As we just saw, the **network** command is quite flexible. The result of the previous two examples (figures 17.17 and 17.18) is the same: OSPF is activated on R1's interfaces, and R1 will advertise the network address of its interfaces to its neighbors. However, the recommended method of using the **network** command is the last one we looked at: specify the exact IP address of the interface and use a wildcard mask of 0.0.0.0.

The reason for this recommendation is to prevent unintended activation of OSPF on interfaces. If you use a **network** command with a broader range of addresses, any interface with an IP address in that range will be included in the OSPF process. By specifying the exact IP address of the interface with a wildcard mask of 0.0.0.0, you ensure that only the desired interface is included.

> **NOTE** A shortcut to activate OSPF on all interfaces is to use **network 0.0.0.0 255.255.255.255 area 0**. A wildcard mask of 255.255.255.255 is equivalent to a netmask of 0.0.0.0 and matches all possible IP addresses. This is handy for quickly activating OSPF in a lab setting but is not recommended in a real network.

There are two major misconceptions that many students have about the OSPF **network** command. The first is that the wildcard mask in the **network** command has to match the netmask of the interface. This is not the case, as we saw in the previous examples; as long as the correct bits match between the IP address in the **network** command and the interface's IP address—the bits specified by the wildcard mask—OSPF will be activated on the interface.

The second misconception is that the **network** command specifies which networks OSPF should advertise. It does not; rather, it specifies which interfaces OSPF should be activated on. The router will then advertise the network prefix of the interface. To clarify, let's look at what the two commands in figure 17.18 do. Here is the first command:

```
R1(config-router)# network 192.168.1.0 0.0.0.7 area 0
```

Although 0.0.0.7 is equivalent to a /29 netmask, this command does not tell R1 to advertise the 192.168.1.0/29 network. It tells R1 to do the following:

- Look for interfaces with an IP address in the 192.168.1.0 to 192.168.1.7 range:
  - R1 G0/0 and G0/1's IP addresses are in this range.
- Activate OSPF on those interfaces.
- Advertise the network prefix of the interfaces to neighbors:
  - R1 will advertise G0/0's prefix of 192.168.1.0/30 and G0/1's prefix of 192.168.1.4/30.

And here is the second command, used to activate OSPF on R1's G0/2 interface:

```
R1(config-router)# network 192.168.2.1 0.0.0.0 area 0
```

This command does not tell R1 to advertise 192.168.2.1/32 but rather to activate OSPF on the interface with an IP address of 192.168.2.1 (G0/2) and advertise that interface's network prefix, which is 192.168.2.0/24.

> **EXAM TIP** In chapter 18, we will look at a more straightforward method to activate OSPF on a router's interfaces. However, for the CCNA exam, you should be familiar with the `network` command and wildcard masks.

Summary

- Dynamic routing is a process by which routers share information about the network with each other, allowing them to build their routing tables automatically. They do this by using a routing protocol.
- Dynamic routing provides several advantages over static routing, such as adaptability and scalability.
- Static routing also has advantages over dynamic routing, such as predictability and control. Fortunately, both can be used at the same time.
- Routing protocols can be divided into two main categories: *Interior Gateway Protocols* (IGP) and *Exterior Gateway Protocols* (EGP).
- IGPs are used to exchange routing information within a single *autonomous system* (AS), and EGPs are used to exchange routing information between autonomous systems.
- IGPs can be categorized by the type of algorithm they use to share routing information and calculate routes: distance-vector or link-state.
- The two distance-vector IGPs are *Routing Information Protocol* (RIP) and *Enhanced Interior Gateway Routing Protocol* (EIGRP).
- The two link-state IGPs are *Intermediate System to Intermediate System* (IS-IS) and *Open Shortest Path First* (OSPF).
- Distance-vector routing is also called *routing by rumor*. The router doesn't have a complete map of the network; it only knows what its neighbors tell it.
- Routers using a link-state routing protocol build a "connectivity map" of the network and use that map to calculate routes to each destination.
- The only EGP in common use today is *Border Gateway Protocol* (BGP). It uses a path-vector algorithm, which calculates routes using AS-to-AS logic, rather than router-to-router; it's designed for larger-scale routing.
- The term *route selection* has two main meanings, one regarding routing table population and one regarding packet forwarding.

- In routing table population, route selection is the process of selecting which routes will enter the routing table. The router will use AD and metrics to select which routes enter the routing table.
- In packet forwarding, route selection is the process of selecting the best route in the routing table to forward a packet. The router will select the most specific matching route in the routing table to forward the packet.
- Only the best route to each destination will be added to the routing table and, therefore, be a candidate for packet forwarding. Routes that do not enter the routing table cannot be used to forward packets.
- A *metric* is a measure of the efficiency of a route. It is used to select among routes to the same destination (same network address and prefix length), learned via the same routing protocol.
- Each IGP uses a different metric. RIP uses hop count, EIGRP uses a metric based on bandwidth and delay (and other parameters), and OSPF uses a cost based on the bandwidth of each link.
- Because each protocol uses a different metric, metrics cannot be used to compare routes learned via different routing protocols.
- *Administrative distance* (AD) is a value that indicates how preferred a routing protocol is. A lower AD value is preferred and means that IOS considers the protocol more trustworthy—more likely to select good routes.
- AD is used to select among routes to the same destination, learned via different routing protocols.
- The default AD values are Connected = 0, Static = 1, eBGP = 20, EIGRP = 90, OSPF = 110, IS-IS = 115, RIP = 120, iBGP = 200, unusable = 255.
- If multiple routes to the same destination are learned via the same routing protocol and have the same metric, they will all be inserted into the routing table, and the router will load-balance traffic over the routes. This is called *equal-cost multipath* (ECMP) routing.
- A *floating static route* is a static route configured with an AD greater than the default of 1 for the purpose of making it less preferred. The command syntax is **`ip route`** *`destination-network netmask next-hop ad`*.
- Even if multiple routes have the same destination network address, their destinations are considered different if they have different prefix lengths. They will all be inserted into the routing table (i.e. 192.168.0.0/16, 192.168.0.0/17, and 192.168.0.0/18).
- The **`network`** command is used by RIP, EIGRP, and OSPF to activate the protocol on the router's interfaces. It is configured in router config mode.
- To enter router config mode for OSPF, use the command **`router ospf`** *`process-id`*. The syntax of the OSPF network command is **`network`** *`ip-address wildcard-mask`* **`area`** *`area-id`*.

- The **`network`** command tells the router to
  - Look for interfaces with an IP address in the specified range
  - Activate the routing protocol on those interfaces
  - Advertise the network prefix of the interface(s) to neighbors
- A *wildcard mask* is a series of 32 bits that indicates which bits have to match between two IP addresses. A 0 bit in the wildcard mask means the bits have to match, and a 1 bit in the wildcard mask means the bits don't have to match.
- A wildcard mask looks like an inverted netmask but serves a different purpose. A netmask indicates the network and host portions of an IP address, and a wildcard mask is used to specify a range of IP addresses (not necessarily in the same subnet).
- All 1 bits of a netmask are 0 in the equivalent wildcard mask and vice versa. For example, a /24 netmask is 255.255.255.0, and the equivalent wildcard mask is 0.0.0.255.
- If the appropriate bits match between the IP address in the **`network`** command and an interface's IP address, OSPF will be activated on the interface.
- The **`network`** command is flexible. The IP address and wildcard mask of the command don't have to be the same as the IP address and netmask of the interface. If the correct bits match between the **`network`** command's IP address and the interface's IP address, OSFP will be activated on the interface.
- It is recommended to specify the interface's exact IP address and use a /32 wildcard mask (0.0.0.0) in the **`network`** command to ensure that OSPF is activated only on the intended interface.
- A shortcut to activate OSPF on all interfaces is to use **`network 0.0.0.0 255.255.255.255 area`** `0`, because this matches all possible IP addresses. This is a handy shortcut in a simulated lab, but it is not recommended in a real network.
- The IP address and wildcard mask in the **`network`** command do not determine which prefixes the router advertises. They determine which interfaces OSPF is activated on, and then the router advertises those interface's prefixes.

18 Open Shortest Path First

This chapter covers

- Open Shortest Path First link-state advertisements and database
- How OSPF routers calculate routes
- Configuring OSPF on Cisco routers
- How OSPF routers become neighbors and form adjacencies

Open Shortest Path First (OSPF) is an interior gateway protocol (IGP) that serves as a key building block of modern enterprise networks. In chapter 17, we covered dynamic routing protocols in general and also examined how to use the `network` command to activate OSPF on router interfaces. In this chapter, we will dig deeper into the topic of OSPF and see how it actually works, including how OSPF-enabled routers become neighbors with each other, share routing information, calculate routes, and many other details.

These days, two versions of OSPF are in use: OSPFv2, which is primarily used for IPv4 networks, and OSPFv3, which is primarily used for IPv6 networks (although it can be used for IPv4 as well). For the purpose of the CCNA exam, the version we are concerned with is OSPFv2; all mentions of OSPF in this book are specifically referring to OSPFv2, as stated in exam topic 3.4: Configure and verify single area OSPFv2.

The name *Open Shortest Path First* has two aspects: *Open* means that it is an open standard protocol; OSPF is not Cisco proprietary. All vendors are free to implement

OSPF on their network devices. *Shortest Path First* (SPF) is the name of the algorithm used to calculate routes; it is also called *Dijkstra's algorithm* after its creator, Edsger Dijkstra.

18.1 OSPF foundations

There are three main steps that OSPF routers go through to share routing information and build their routing tables:

1. Form neighbor relationships with other OSPF-enabled routers.
2. Exchange routing information to build a connectivity map of the network.
3. Calculate the best routes to each destination.

Let's begin by examining the second and third steps of that process, and then we'll examine the details of how OSPF routers become neighbors in section 18.3.

18.1.1 The link-state database

When using a dynamic routing protocol, routers exchange routing information with each other and then use that information to calculate routes automatically. In OSPF, routers exchange routing information using data structures called *link-state advertisements* (LSA). Each router organizes the LSAs it receives in a database called the *link-state database* (LSDB). The LSDB serves as the router's map of the network topology, which is used for calculating the shortest path to each destination network; this is the "connectivity map" of the network that I mentioned in chapter 17.

Figure 18.1 shows how OSPF-enabled routers share LSAs to build the LSDB. Each router creates an LSA that includes information about its connected networks and then sends it to its neighboring routers, which will proceed to forward it to other routers in the OSPF area; OSPF areas are logical divisions of the network that we'll cover in section 18.1.2. The process of sending LSAs to all other routers in the OSPF area is called *LSA flooding*.

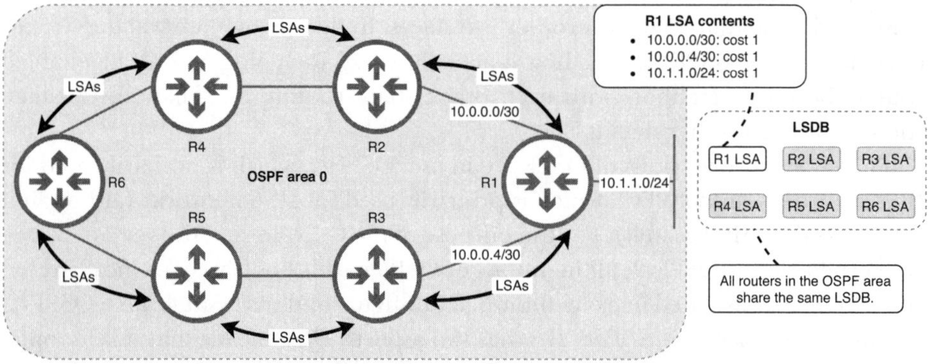

Figure 18.1 Routers flood LSAs within the OSPF area to ensure all routers have an identical LSDB. The LSAs that make up the LSDB contain information about each router's connected networks, such as their cost. R1's LSA indicates that it is connected to 10.0.0.0/30, 10.0.0.4/30, and 10.1.1.0/24, each with a cost of 1.

It is essential that all routers in the area have the same LSDB, so each router can use the SPF algorithm to calculate routes to all destination networks. For example, the routers in figure 18.1 will use the LSDB to calculate a route to the 10.1.1.0/24 network. Using the LSDB, it is as if the routers are looking at the same diagram as us but with more detailed information about each link. This is in contrast to distance-vector routing protocols like RIP and EIGRP, in which each router does not have a complete map of the network.

18.1.2 OSPF areas

The network we saw in figure 18.1 was an example of *single-area OSPF*; the network is a single logical unit, and all routers in it share the same LSDB. In small networks, a single-area approach is nice and simple and doesn't have any major downsides. However, in a large network with dozens or hundreds of routers (instead of the six in figure 18.1), a single-area design has multiple negative effects:

- The larger LSDB takes up more memory resources on the routers.
- The SPF algorithm takes more time and CPU resources to calculate routes.
- A single change in the network (i.e., an interface going up or down) causes LSAs to flood the network and causes every router to run the SPF algorithm again.

By dividing a large OSPF network into multiple smaller areas, we minimize those negative effects. Smaller LSDBs mean OSPF uses fewer resources on routers, and the SPF algorithm doesn't take as much time to calculate routes. Network changes are only advertised within the local area, and if there is network instability (interfaces going up and down), its effects are limited to a single area.

An OSPF *area* can be defined as a set of routers that share the same LSDB. Although the CCNA exam topics list states that you should be able to "configure and verify single area OSPFv2," you also need a basic understanding of what an area is and the benefits of multi-area OSPF.

Figure 18.2 shows a multi-area OSPF network consisting of four areas. OSPF employs a two-level hierarchical structure consisting of a *backbone area* (area 0) and other non-backbone areas. All non-backbone areas must be connected to area 0, and traffic between areas must pass through area 0.

NOTE In single-area OSPF, it's highly recommended that you use area 0, although it is technically possible to use another area number. Using area 0 simplifies the process of expanding into multi-area OSPF in the future, if needed.

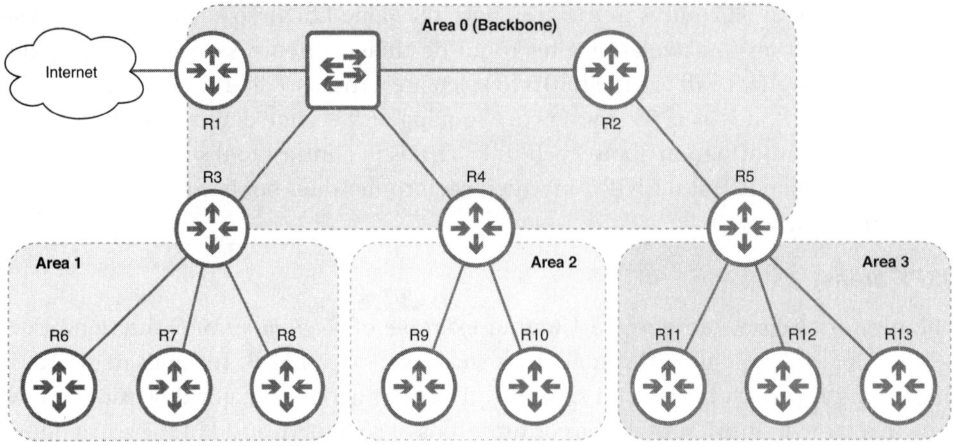

Figure 18.2 A multi-area OSPF network consisting of four areas. Area 0 is the backbone area to which other areas must connect. Areas 1, 2, and 3 are non-backbone areas, and traffic between them must pass through area 0.

OSPF distinguishes between four different types of routers. Table 18.1 summarizes these four router types and lists which routers in figure 18.2 are of each type; note that some routers fit into multiple categories.

Table 18.1 OSPF router types

Router type	In figure 18.2	Description
Internal router	R1, R2, R6, R7, R8, R9, R10, R11, R12, R13	All OSPF-enabled interfaces are in the same area.
Backbone router	R1, R2, R3, R4, R5	At least one interface is in area 0.
Area border router (ABR)	R3, R4, R5	Routers that connect one (or more) areas to area 0
Autonomous system boundary router (ASBR)	R1	Routers that connect the OSPF autonomous system to external networks (i.e., the internet)

NOTE Although R1 has an interface connected to the internet, that interface does not use OSPF and therefore does not affect its classification as an internal OSPF router.

An *internal router* has all of its OSPF-enabled interfaces in the same area, whether that is area 0 or a non-backbone area. A *backbone* router has at least one interface in the backbone area. An *area border router* connects one (or more) areas to area 0; because non-backbone areas cannot connect directly to each other, all ABRs are also backbone routers (although backbone routers aren't necessarily ABRs).

NOTE ABRs maintain a separate LSDB for each area they are connected to.

The final router type is an *autonomous system boundary router* (ASBR)—a router that connects the OSPF autonomous system (AS) to external networks, such as the internet or another enterprise's network. Note that this type is independent of the others; an ASBR can be a backbone router or not and can be an internal router or an ABR. As listed in table 18.1, figure 18.2's R1 is an internal router, a backbone router, and an ASBR, all at once. In section 18.2.4, we'll see how to configure a default route on an ASBR and advertise it to other routers in the OSPF AS.

OSPF routes can be categorized as intra-area, inter-area, or external. *Intra-area* routes are routes to destinations in the same OSPF area as the router; for example, if the router is an internal router in area 1, all routes to destinations within area 1 are intra-area routes. *Inter-area* routes are routes to destinations in an area the router does not connect to; for example, if an ABR connected to areas 0 and 1 learns a route to area 2. Finally, routes to external destinations—advertised by an ASBR—are called *external routes.*

EXAM TIP Although the exam topics list only specifies single-area OSPF, you should know the different router and route types for the CCNA exam.

18.1.3 OSPF cost

As we covered in chapter 17, OSPF's metric is called *cost,* and it's the value OSPF uses to determine the best path to each destination (the *shortest* in OSPF). Each OSPF-enabled interface has an associated cost value, and a route's cost is the cumulative cost of each interface a packet must be sent out of to reach the destination. Figure 18.3 demonstrates this concept; R1's cost to reach 192.168.3.0/24 is the cumulative cost of R1 G0/0, R2 G0/1, and R3 G0/1 (but not R2 G0/0 and R3 G0/0).

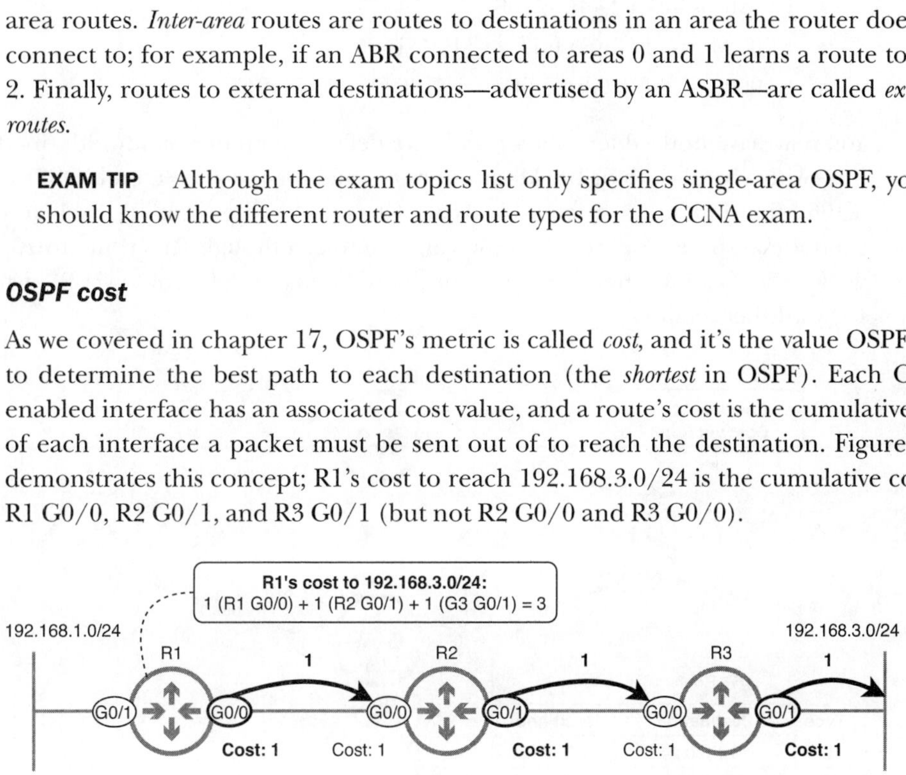

Figure 18.3 A route's cost is the cumulative cost of each interface out of which a packet must be sent to reach the destination. R1's cost to reach 192.168.3.0/24 is 3: 1 for R1 G0/0, plus 1 for R2 G0/1, plus 1 for R3 G0/1.

Although figure 18.3's depiction of OSPF cost is accurate, it's more common to refer to the cost of a link rather than the cost of each interface that makes up the link. Because both sides of the link should have the same cost—it is considered a misconfiguration if they don't—and a router considers only one side of the link when doing route cost calculations, it's simpler to think of the link as a single entity.

Using figure 18.3's example, it doesn't matter if R1 is calculating a route to 192.168.3.0/24 or R3 is calculating a route to 192.168.1.0/24; the cost is the same in either direction. Except when specifically referring to an interface's cost, I will refer to a link's cost rather than each individual interface's cost.

REFERENCE BANDWIDTH

The cost of a link is calculated by dividing a *reference bandwidth* value by the link's bandwidth; the default reference bandwidth is 100 Mbps. If this calculation results in a value less than 1, the OSPF cost is assigned as 1 because OSPF does not accept fractional or decimal values for cost. This gives the following default OSPF cost values:

- 10 Mbps link = 10 (100/10)
- 100 Mbps link = 1 (100/100)
- 1,000 Mbps (1 Gbps) link = 1 (100/1000 = 0.1)
- 10,000 Mbps (10 Gbps) link = 1 (100/10000 = 0.01)

You may have noticed a problem: with the default reference bandwidth of 100 Mbps, links with a bandwidth of 100 Mbps or greater all have the same cost. If OSPF considers a 100 Mbps link just as preferable as a 1 Gbps or 10 Gbps link, it's likely to calculate suboptimal routes. Figure 18.4 shows an example: although R1's route to 10.1.3.0/24 via R4 uses FastEthernet links, it is considered equal to R1's route via R2, which uses GigabitEthernet links.

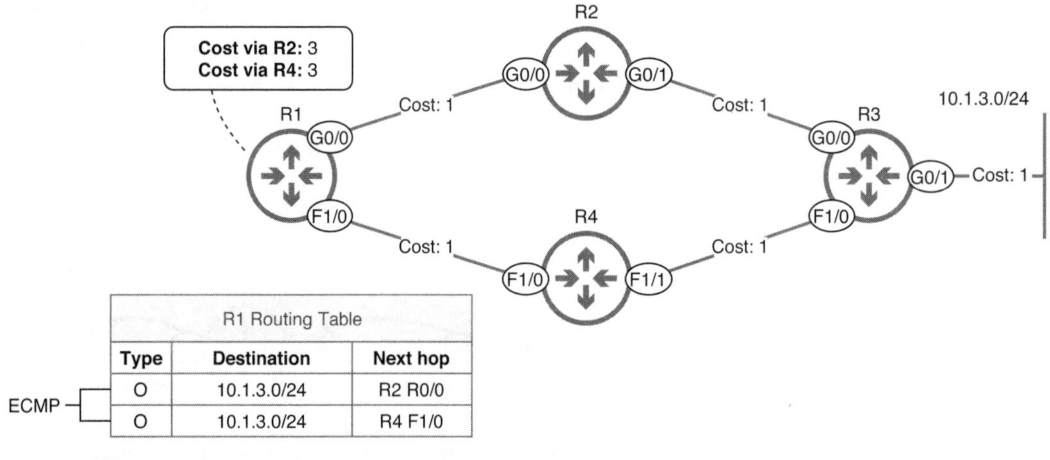

Figure 18.4 Although the route to 10.1.3.0/24 via R2 is superior to the route via R4, the OSPF cost of both routes is the same. R1 adds both routes to the routing table and will load-balance over them with ECMP.

R1 adds both routes to the routing table and will use ECMP to load-balance traffic over them. While ECMP itself isn't a bad thing, attempting to forward equal amounts of traffic over links with vastly different bandwidths could lead to congestion on the slower links, while the faster links are underutilized.

OSPF was developed decades ago when FastEthernet was considered a very high-speed link; that's why the default reference bandwidth is 100 Mbps. However, in modern networks it's better to adjust the reference bandwidth value to allow OSPF to differentiate between links of greater bandwidths. To adjust the reference bandwidth value, use the **`auto-cost reference-bandwidth`** *`mbps`* command in OSPF router config mode.

In the following example, I confirm the cost of R1's interfaces with the **`show ip ospf interface brief`** command. I then adjust the reference bandwidth to 1000 Mbps, so GigabitEthernet links have a cost of 1, and FastEtherent links have a cost of 10. Although there is no specific recommended value to use for the reference bandwidth, it's common to set it to match the bandwidth of the fastest link in the network. Another option is to set the reference bandwidth to a value greater than the current fastest link's bandwidth to allow even faster links to be added to the network without adjusting the reference bandwidth again:

```
R1# show ip ospf interface brief
Interface    PID   Area   IP Address/Mask    Cost  State Nbrs F/C
Gi0/0        1     0      10.0.0.1/30        1     DR    1/1
Fa1/0        1     0      10.0.0.5/30        1     DR    1/1
R1# configure terminal
R1(config)# router ospf 1
R1(config-router)# auto-cost reference-bandwidth 1000
% OSPF: Reference bandwidth is changed.
        Please ensure reference bandwidth is consistent
➥ across all routers.
R1(config-router)# do show ip ospf interface brief
Interface    PID   Area   IP Address/Mask    Cost  State Nbrs F/C
Gi0/0        1     0      10.0.0.1/30        1     DR    1/1
Fa1/0        1     0      10.0.0.5/30        10    DR    1/1
```

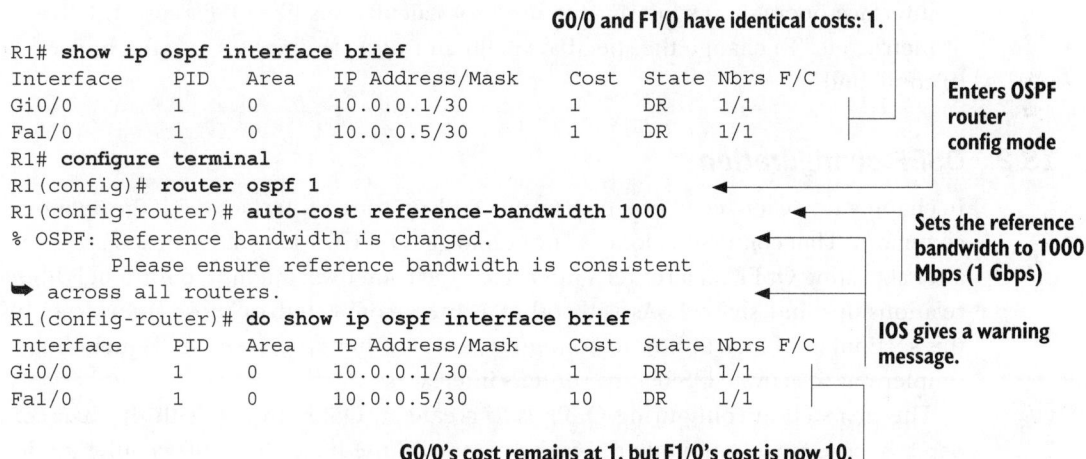

G0/0 and F1/0 have identical costs: 1.

Enters OSPF router config mode

Sets the reference bandwidth to 1000 Mbps (1 Gbps)

IOS gives a warning message.

G0/0's cost remains at 1, but F1/0's cost is now 10.

As the warning message in the previous example states, it's important that you configure the same reference bandwidth on all routers to ensure consistent route selection. In the worst-case scenario, having different reference bandwidths could result in routing loops: if router A believes the best route to a destination is via router B, but router B believes the best route is via router A, packets for that destination will loop between the two routers until their TTL expires—never reaching their intended destination.

MODIFYING THE COST OF A LINK

Although modifying the reference bandwidth is usually sufficient to allow OSPF to select the most efficient path to a destination, in some cases, you may want to modify the cost of a particular link to make it more or less preferable. There are two methods to do so:

- Configure the cost with the **`ip ospf cost`** *`cost`* command in interface config mode.

- Modify the interface's bandwidth value with the **`bandwidth`** *`kbps`* command in interface config mode.

NOTE Although the reference bandwidth is configured in megabits per second, the interface bandwidth value is configured in kilobits per second.

Of the two, the first method is preferred if you want to modify the OSPF cost of a particular link: it allows you to directly configure the interface's OSPF cost. The second method, instead, is used to influence the automatic cost calculation we covered previously: reference bandwidth/interface bandwidth. However, an interface's bandwidth value affects more than just OSPF cost values, such as QoS (quality of service) mechanisms, so it's usually best not to modify it.

NOTE Modifying an interface's bandwidth value doesn't actually affect how the interface operates; it's just a value used for calculations like OSPF cost, EIGRP metric, etc. To change the speed at which an interface operates, use the **`speed`** command.

18.2 OSPF configuration

In chapter 17, we looked at how to activate OSPF on router interfaces with the **`network`** command. That command alone is enough to get OSPF working at its most basic level; after activating OSPF on a router's interfaces, the router will attempt to form neighbor relationships and share LSAs with other routers connected to those interfaces. In this section, we'll look at how to configure various other aspects of OSPF, including a simpler way to activate OSPF on a router's interfaces.

The first step in configuring OSPF is to create an OSPF process with the **`router ospf`** *`process-id`* command; this is the command used to enter router config mode, from which you can use the **`network`** command and many other OSPF-related commands. Similar to how PVST+ creates multiple STP instances on a switch, each calculating a unique spanning tree, you can create multiple OSPF processes. Each of those processes independently calculates its own routes to destination networks. However, running multiple OSPF processes on a router is extremely rare, and the specific use cases are beyond the scope of the CCNA exam. For the purposes of this chapter, we will just use process ID 1 (although you can pick any other number you'd like).

NOTE The OSPF process ID is *locally significant*; it doesn't matter if the process ID matches neighboring routers. For example, a router running OSPF process ID 1 can become a neighbor of a router running OSPF with a process ID of 65535 (the highest possible value).

Figure 18.5 shows the topology we will configure in this section: a single-area OSPF network of four routers. The 10.1.3.0/24 subnet is connected to R3 G0/2, which we will configure as a passive interface—more about that in section 18.2.3. R1 connects to the internet, and we will configure it to advertise a default route to the other routers.

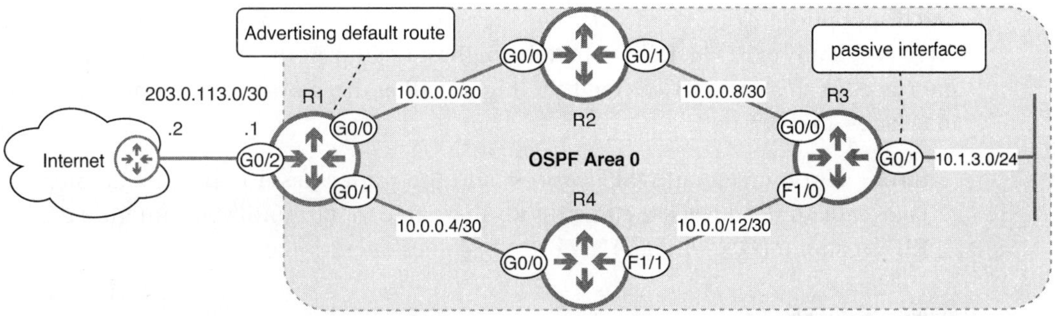

Figure 18.5 A single-area OSPF network of four routers. R3 connects to the 10.1.3.0/24 subnet on its G0/2 interface, a passive interface. R1 connects to the internet and advertises a default route to the other routers.

18.2.1 The router ID

When you first use the `router ospf` command to create the OSPF process, the router will assign itself a *router ID* (RID)—a unique 32-bit value that identifies the router in the OSPF AS. Unlike the process ID, the RID must be unique; there can't be two routers with the same RID in the AS. To view a router's RID, you can use the `show ip protocols` command; this command shows information about active routing protocols on the router. In the following example, I create OSPF process 1 on R1 and check its RID:

```
R1(config)# router ospf 1                         <-- Creates OSPF process 1
R1(config-router)# do show ip protocols
. . .
Routing Protocol is "ospf 1"
  Outgoing update filter list for all interfaces is not set
  Incoming update filter list for all interfaces is not set
  Router ID 203.0.113.1                           <-- R1 selects the IP address of G0/2 as its RID.
  Number of areas in this router is 1. 1 normal 0 stub 0 nssa
      . . .
```

R1 selected the IP address of its G0/2 interface—203.0.113.1—as its RID. The RID is assigned in the following order of priority:

1 Manual configuration with the `router-id` command
2 Highest IP address on an operational (up/up) loopback interface (we'll cover loopback interfaces in this section)
3 Highest IP address on an operational (up/up) physical interface

As indicated in the first point, you can manually configure the RID with the `router-id` command. However, this command can only be configured once you've entered router config mode. To access router config mode, you have to first create the OSPF process with the `router ospf` command.

Therefore, when you first create the OSPF process, the router can't consider any manual RID configuration: one hasn't been set yet. Instead, it only considers the second and third options to assign the RID: the highest IP address on an operational loopback interface (if any exist) or, failing that, the highest IP address on an operational physical interface. In this case, R1 selected the highest IP address on an operational physical interface—that of G0/2.

> **NOTE** If you create an OSPF process and the router has no operational interfaces with an IP address, the process won't be able to start until you configure the RID or an interface with an IP address becomes operational.

LOOPBACK INTERFACES

A *loopback interface* is a virtual router interface that is always up and reachable as long as the device is operational (although you can disable the interface with **`shutdown`**). Unlike physical interfaces (i.e., GigabitEthernet0/1), which rely on physical ports and connections, loopback interfaces are entirely software-based. The benefit of a loopback interface is that it provides a stable, reliable interface that you can use to identify and connect to the router without relying on any particular physical port. Figure 18.6 shows how R1's loopback interface provides a stable interface for an admin to connect to with *Secure Shell* (SSH).

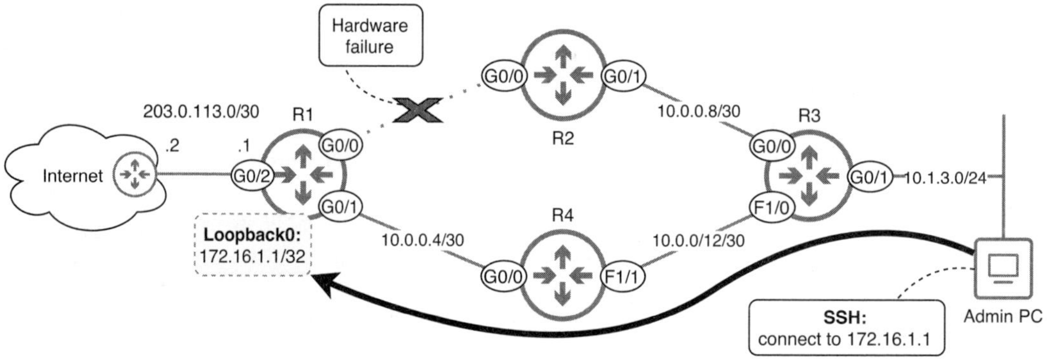

Figure 18.6 An admin uses SSH to connect to R1's Loopback0 interface. Loopback0 doesn't rely on the status of a particular physical interface, such as G0/0, which is down due to a hardware failure.

> **NOTE** SSH is a protocol used to remotely access a device's CLI in a secure manner; we will cover it in chapter 5 of volume 2 of this book.

If the admin had, for example, attempted to connect to the IP address of R1's G0/0 interface, the connection would have failed; the G0/0 interface is down due to a hardware failure. On the other hand, the Loopback0 interface provides a stable IP address that the admin can connect to regardless of the status of R1's physical ports. However, it's important to note that the admin's PC still needs a valid physical path to reach R1. If both G0/0 and G0/1 were down, the PC would not be able to connect to R1 despite the loopback interface.

Although loopback interfaces are not required, it is highly recommended that you configure them on routers and that you activate OSPF on them so all routers can reach each other's loopback interfaces. To create a loopback interface, use the **`interface loopback`** *`number`* command—it's common to start with Loopback0. In the following example, I configure a loopback interface on R1, configure an IP address on it, and check the OSPF RID once again:

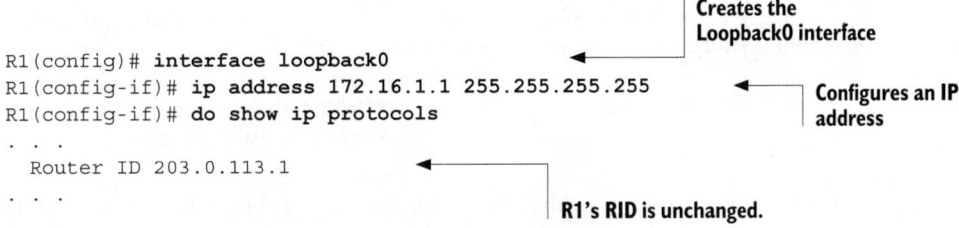

```
R1(config)# interface loopback0                          <- Creates the Loopback0 interface
R1(config-if)# ip address 172.16.1.1 255.255.255.255     <- Configures an IP address
R1(config-if)# do show ip protocols
. . .
  Router ID 203.0.113.1                                  <- R1's RID is unchanged.
. . .
```

NOTE It's standard to configure loopback interfaces with a /32 netmask (255.255.255.255). This is because a loopback interface, by its nature, doesn't need to communicate with other devices on the same subnet (as a physical interface would). Instead, it represents a single device and thus doesn't need a range of addresses.

Despite configuring a loopback interface, R1's RID remains the same; to keep the RID stable, IOS doesn't reselect it when a new interface is configured. It is possible to reset the OSPF process with the **`clear ip ospf process`** command in privileged `EXEC` mode, but even that won't cause R1 to select the loopback interface's IP address as the RID, as shown in the following example:

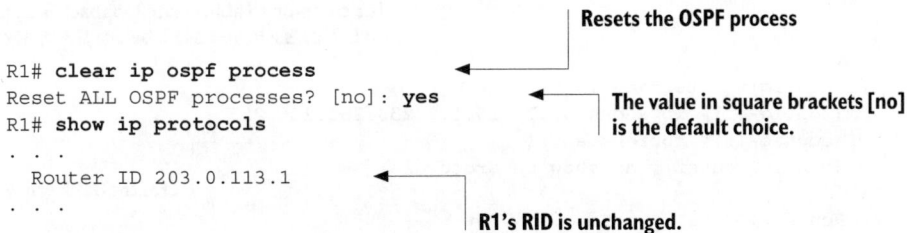

```
R1# clear ip ospf process                    <- Resets the OSPF process
Reset ALL OSPF processes? [no]: yes          <- The value in square brackets [no] is the default choice.
R1# show ip protocols
. . .
  Router ID 203.0.113.1                      <- R1's RID is unchanged.
. . .
```

NOTE The point to remember here is that once the router has selected its RID, it will maintain that RID even if you configure a loopback interface and reset OSPF. A loopback interface's IP address will only be used for the initial RID selection when you first create the OSPF process. To make a router change its RID after it has already selected one, you must manually configure the RID; we'll cover that next.

CHANGING THE RID

After R1 has selected its RID, the best way to change it is to manually configure it and then reset the OSPF process (if needed). In any case, hardcoding the router's RID with manual configuration is considered a best practice to ensure predictable RIDs on all routers. In the following example, I configure the **router-id** *router-id* command on R1, causing it to change its RID:

```
R1(config)# router ospf 1
R1(config-router)# router-id 172.16.1.1          ← Manually configures R1's RID
R1(config-router)# do show ip protocols
. . .
  Router ID 172.16.1.1          ← R1's RID is changed to the
. . .                             value we manually configured.
```

NOTE If the router has already established a neighbor relationship with one or more OSPF neighbors, you will have to reset the OSPF process with **clear ip ospf process** for the newly configured RID to take effect. But at this point in the example, I haven't activated OSPF on any of R1's interfaces yet, so it has no OSPF neighbors. That is why the new RID took effect immediately.

Although the OSPF RID is often derived from one of the router's IP addresses, it's important to note that the RID is not an IP address; it's just a 32-bit value that is formatted similarly to an IP address (dotted decimal notation). As long as the RID is unique in the OSPF AS, it can be any 32-bit value.

In the following example, I configure a loopback interface on R2 and then create the OSPF process. In this case, R2 takes the IP address of Loopback0 as its RID because I configured the loopback interface before creating the OSPF process:

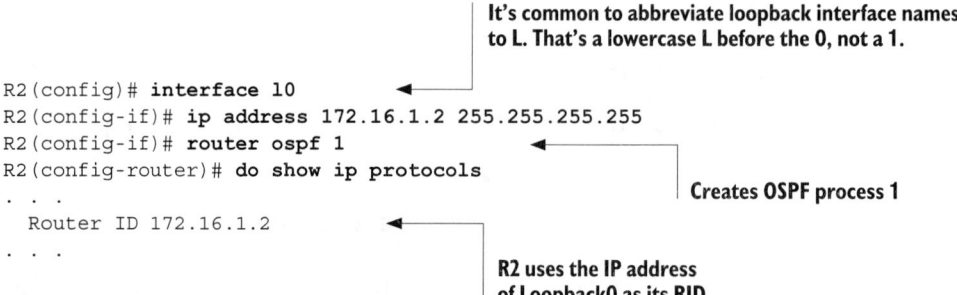

```
                                  It's common to abbreviate loopback interface names
                                  to L. That's a lowercase L before the 0, not a 1.
R2(config)# interface l0          ←
R2(config-if)# ip address 172.16.1.2 255.255.255.255
R2(config-if)# router ospf 1          ← Creates OSPF process 1
R2(config-router)# do show ip protocols
. . .
  Router ID 172.16.1.2          ← R2 uses the IP address
. . .                             of Loopback0 as its RID.
```

NOTE For the sake of space, I won't show the configurations, but I also configured Loopback0 on R3 (172.16.1.3/32) and R4 (172.16.1.4/32) and created the OSPF process.

Loopback addresses and loopback interfaces

In chapter 7, I briefly introduced the concept of loopback addresses, which are IP addresses in the reserved 127.0.0.0/8 range. Messages sent to any address in this range are "looped back" to the local device without being transmitted across the network. For example, if you issue the **`ping 127.0.0.1`** command on a PC, you'll get a response back from the PC itself. This can be used to test the device's network software.

Although they share the term *loopback*, loopback interfaces are a different concept from loopback addresses. Loopback interfaces are virtual interfaces in a router that can be assigned any valid IP address (which does not include the reserved loopback address range). Loopback interfaces provide a stable and reliable IP address that can be used to reach the router and isn't dependent on the status of a particular physical interface.

EXAM TIP The OSPF RID is exam topic 3.4.d; you should know how the RID is initially determined and how to change it.

18.2.2 Activating OSPF on interfaces

Activating OSPF on interfaces is possibly the most important part of configuring OSPF; it's what tells the router to make OSPF neighbors and share routing information. In chapter 17, we covered how to activate OSPF on interfaces with the **`network`** command. In the following example, I use the command to activate OSPF on R1's G0/0, G0/1, and L0 interfaces:

```
R1(config)# router ospf 1
R1(config-router)# network 10.0.0.1 0.0.0.0 area 0
R1(config-router)# network 10.0.0.5 0.0.0.0 area 0
R1(config-router)# network 172.16.1.1 0.0.0.0 area 0
R1(config-router)# do show ip protocols
. . .
  Router ID 172.16.1.1
  Number of areas in this router is 1. 1 normal 0 stub 0 nssa
  Maximum path: 4
  Routing for Networks:
    10.0.0.1 0.0.0.0 area 0
    10.0.0.5 0.0.0.0 area 0
    172.16.1.1 0.0.0.0 area 0
. . .
```

Activates OSPF on R1's physical interfaces

Activates OSPF on Loopback0

This section lists the configured `network` commands.

NOTE I did not activate OSPF on R1 G0/2, which is connected to the internet. Later, we will configure a default route via G0/2 on R1 and advertise it to R1's neighbors, but there is no need to activate OSPF on the interface.

However, there is a more straightforward method of activating OSPF on interfaces: the **`ip ospf`** *`process-id`* **`area`** *`area`* command in interface config mode. Whereas the **`network`** command specifies a range of IP addresses, and the router activates OSPF on all interfaces with an IP address in that range, this command allows you to explicitly specify which interfaces OSPF should be activated on. In the following example, I enable OSPF on R2's G0/0, G0/1, and L0 (Loopback0) interfaces:

```
R2(config)# interface range g0/0-1,l0          <-- Configures G0/0, G0/1 and L0 with one command
R2(config-if-range)# ip ospf 1 area 0          <-- Activates OSPF on the three interfaces
R2(config-if-range)# do show ip protocols
. . .
  Router ID 172.16.1.2
  Number of areas in this router is 1. 1 normal 0 stub 0 nssa
  Maximum path: 4
  Routing for Networks:
  Routing on Interfaces Configured Explicitly (Area 0):
    Loopback0
    GigabitEthernet0/0
    GigabitEthernet0/1
```

This section lists the interfaces OSPF is explicitly activated on.

I think you'll agree that this method is much simpler than using the **network** command, although you should know both for the CCNA exam. In the following example, I use this method to activate OSPF on R3 and R4's interfaces as well:

```
R3(config)# interface range g0/0-2,l0
R3(config-if-range)# ip ospf 1 area 0

R4(config)# interface range g0/0-1,l0
R4(config-if-range)# ip ospf 1 area 0
```

EXAM TIP If a lab simulation in the exam expects you to use one OSPF configuration method over another, it will tell you so. Cisco exam questions can be difficult, but they aren't unfair.

18.2.3 Passive interfaces

Activating OSPF on an interface causes the router to perform two key actions:

- It attempts to form neighbor relationships with routers connected to the interface.
- It advertises the network prefix of the interface to neighbors.

However, there are cases where you might want the router to perform the second action—advertising the network prefix—without attempting to form network relationships on the interface. To form neighbor relationships, OSPF-enabled routers send *hello* messages out of their interfaces. If an interface isn't connected to another router, these hello messages are wasted—using up CPU and memory resources on the router and consuming network bandwidth. Furthermore, these unnecessary OSPF messages can pose a security risk, as malicious users could gather information about the network by examining them.

NOTE We will cover OSPF hello messages and other message types in section 18.3.

This is where passive interfaces come into play. A *passive interface* in OSPF is one that doesn't send OSPF messages to initiate neighbor relationships, even though it's OSPF enabled. However, the router will still advertise the network prefix of the interface to its OSPF neighbors, allowing them to forward packets to destinations in the network.

Figure 18.7 shows a situation in which you should configure a passive interface. R3 G0/2 connects to the 10.1.3.0/24 network, but there are no other routers connected to the interface. To allow R1, R2, and R4 to learn of 10.1.3.0/24 while preventing R3 from sending OSPF hello messages out of the interface, it should be configured as a passive interface.

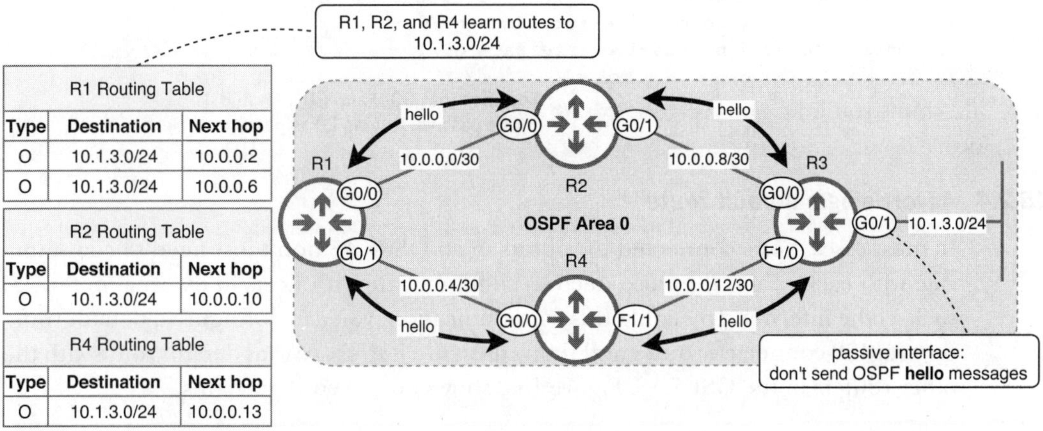

Figure 18.7 R3 advertises the network prefix of G0/2—a passive interface—but does not send OSPF hello messages out of it.

Configuring loopback interfaces as passive is also considered good practice in OSPF. Because a loopback interface is a virtual interface that isn't physically connected to any network, there's no practical need for it to send OSPF hello messages to try to form neighbor relationships. To configure a passive interface, use the **`passive-interface`** *`interface-name`* command in router config mode. In the following example, I configure R3 G0/2 and L0 as passive interfaces:

```
R3(config)# router ospf 1
R3(config-router)# passive-interface g0/2
R3(config-router)# passive-interface l0
R3(config-router)# do show ip protocols
. . .
 Routing on Interfaces Configured Explicitly (Area 0):
   Loopback0
   GigabitEthernet0/0
   GigabitEthernet0/1
   GigabitEthernet0/2
```

Configures G0/2 and L0 as passive interfaces

```
Passive Interface(s):
  GigabitEthernet0/2
  Loopback0
```

G0/2 and L0 are now passive.

Another method of configuring passive interfaces is to use the **`passive-interface default`** command, which makes all interfaces passive by default. You can then use the **`no passive-interface`** *`interface-name`* command to specify which interfaces should not be passive. This method of configuration can be convenient if a router has many OSPF-enabled interfaces but only a few interfaces that it needs to form OSPF neighbor relationships on. Although this is not the case for R2, in the following example, I use this method to configure L0 as a passive interface and G0/0 and G0/1 as nonpassive:

```
R2(config)# router ospf 1
R2(config-router)# passive-interface default
R2(config-router)# no passive-interface g0/0
R2(config-router)# no passive-interface g0/1
```

Makes R2's interfaces passive by default

Specifies that G0/0 and G0/1 should not be passive, leaving L0 as passive

18.2.4 Advertising a default route

In most cases, hosts connected to routers in an OSPF AS don't just need to communicate with each other; they also need to communicate with hosts in external networks, such as the internet. To enable this communication, you can configure a default route on your ISP-connected router and then configure it to share that default route with the other routers in the OSPF AS. Figure 18.8 shows how to configure this.

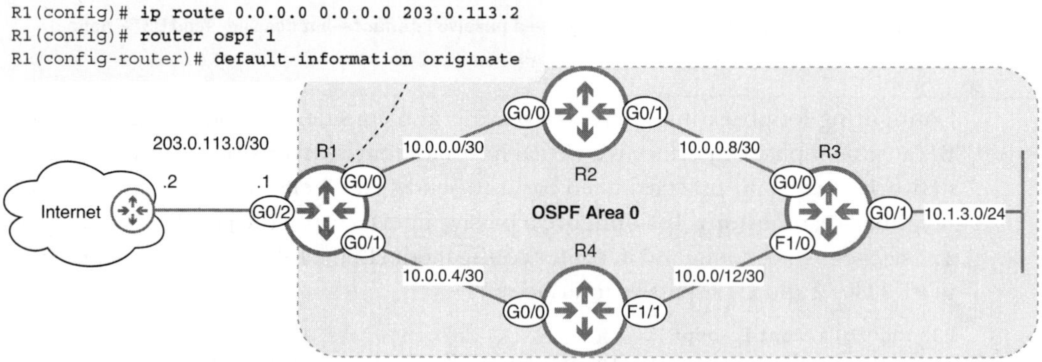

Figure 18.8 R1 functions as an ASBR, advertising a default route into the OSPF AS. After configuring a default route, use `default-information originate` to advertise the route to other routers in the OSPF AS.

To make R1 advertise a default route to R2, R3, and R4, you should first configure a static default route on R1. If you configure `default-information originate` on R1 without configuring a default route, R1 won't advertise a default route to other routers; it must have a default route in its own routing table first.

After configuring the default route, use the **`default-information originate`** command in router config mode to make R1 advertise the default route to the other routers; I do so in the following example. Notice the additional statement added to the output of **`show ip protocols`** R1 is now an ASBR:

```
R1(config)# ip route 0.0.0.0 0.0.0.0 203.0.113.2
R1(config)# router ospf 1
R1(config-router)# default-information originate
R1(config-router)# do show ip protocols
. . .
Routing Protocol is "ospf 1"
  Outgoing update filter list for all interfaces is not set
  Incoming update filter list for all interfaces is not set
  Router ID 172.16.1.1
  It is an autonomous system boundary router
. . .
```

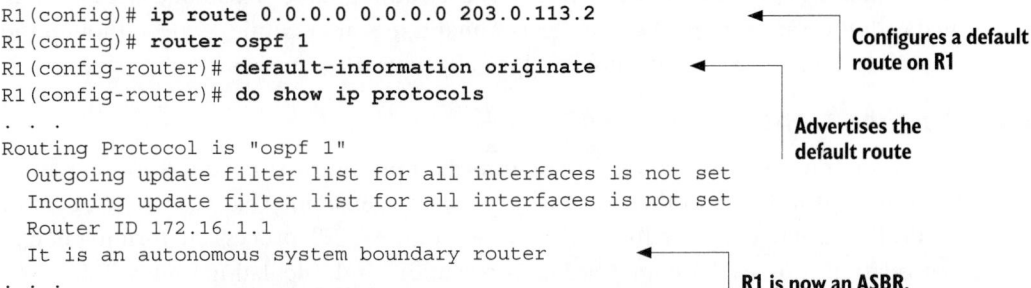

Configures a default route on R1

Advertises the default route

R1 is now an ASBR.

> **NOTE** The **`default-information originate always`** command allows a router to advertise a default route, even if it doesn't have one in its own routing table. However, the use cases of this command are beyond the scope of the CCNA exam.

In the following example, I use **`show ip route ospf`** on R2 to view routes that R2 learned via OSPF. R2 has learned a default route from R1, in addition to the other routes it has learned via OSPF:

```
R2# show ip route ospf
. . .
O*E2  0.0.0.0/0 [110/1] via 10.0.0.1, 00:37:34,
      GigabitEthernet0/0
      10.0.0.0/8 is variably subnetted, 7 subnets, 3 masks
O        10.0.0.4/30 [110/2] via 10.0.0.1, 00:02:09,
      GigabitEthernet0/0
O        10.0.0.12/30 [110/2] via 10.0.0.10, 01:11:30,
      GigabitEthernet0/1
O        10.1.3.0/24 [110/2] via 10.0.0.10, 01:11:30,
      GigabitEthernet0/1
      172.16.0.0/32 is subnetted, 4 subnets
O        172.16.1.1 [110/2] via 10.0.0.1, 01:11:30,
      GigabitEthernet0/0
O        172.16.1.3 [110/2] via 10.0.0.10, 01:11:30,
      GigabitEthernet0/1
O        172.16.1.4 [110/3] via 10.0.0.10, 00:13:54,
      GigabitEthernet0/1
                    [110/3] via 10.0.0.1, 00:02:09,
      GigabitEthernet0/0
```

Default route learned from R1

Routes to the other routers' connected networks

Routes to the other routers' loopback interfaces

NOTE Loopback interfaces add a cost of 1 to a route. For example, R2's cost to reach R1's loopback interface (172.16.1.1) is 2: 1 for the R2–R1 link, plus 1 for R1 L0 (Loopback0).

Notice that R2 has inserted two paths to 172.16.1.4 into its routing table; this is an example of ECMP, which we covered in chapter 17. By default, OSPF will insert up to four equal-cost routes to a destination into the routing table. This value can be modified with the **`maximum-paths`** *`number`* command in router config mode, although the default setting of 4 is usually sufficient for most network scenarios.

18.3 Neighbors and adjacencies

For OSPF routers to exchange routing information, they first need to form neighbor relationships with each other. In this section, we'll examine that crucial first step of OSPF. For review, the three fundamental steps of the OSPF process are forming neighbor relationships, exchanging routing information, and calculating routes. Table 18.2 summarizes the five different message types that OSPF uses in this process; we will examine each one's role in this section as we cover how OSPF routers form neighbor relationships.

Table 18.2 OSPF message types

Type	Name	Purpose
1	Hello	Neighbor discovery and maintenance
2	Database Description (DBD)	Summary of the router's LSDB. Used to check whether the LSDB of each router is the same.
3	Link-State Request (LSR)	Requests specific LSAs from a neighbor
4	Link-State Update (LSU)	Sends specific LSAs to a neighbor
5	Link-State Acknowledgment (LSAck)	Used to acknowledge that the router received an LSU

18.3.1 Neighbor states

For OSPF routers to exchange routing information with each other, they have to pass through a series of *neighbor states*, in which the routers verify that various configuration parameters match between them. Figure 18.9 outlines the OSPF neighbor states from Down to Full.

We could spend several pages covering this process. If you continue your studies of OSPF beyond the CCNA, the details of this process are essential for understanding the OSPF protocol and how to troubleshoot it. However, for the purpose of the CCNA exam, a general understanding of each state's purpose and the sequence of states is sufficient.

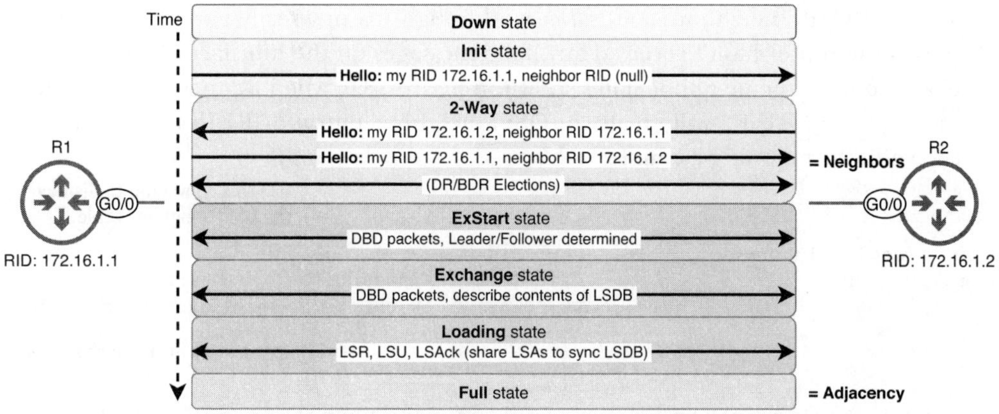

Figure 18.9 The OSPF neighbor states: Down, Init, 2-Way, ExStart, Exchange, Loading, and Full. Routers that reach the 2-Way state are OSPF neighbors. Some routers remain in this state, and some proceed to establish a full adjacency.

When OSPF is activated on an interface, the router regularly sends OSPF hello messages, which are used for dynamically discovering OSPF neighbors and for maintaining neighbor relationships after they have been established. These hello messages include various pieces of information, two of which are the local router's RID and the RIDs of any neighbor routers it is aware of on the interface.

OSPF hello messages are sent to IP address 224.0.0.5, which is a *multicast* IP address. Whereas unicast packets are one-to-one (from one host to one other host), and broadcast packets are one-to-all, multicast packets are one-to-multiple (but not necessarily all). A packet sent to the multicast IP address 224.0.0.5 will be flooded by a switch and, therefore, received by all hosts on the segment. However, only router interfaces with OSPF activated will be interested in the contents of the packet; other hosts will simply ignore it, as shown in figure 18.10.

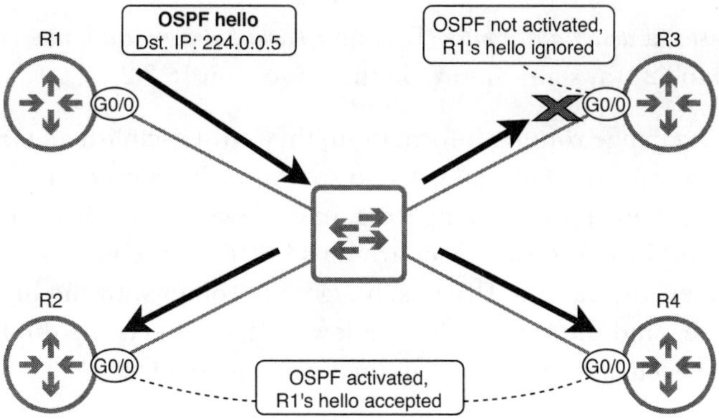

Figure 18.10 An OSPF hello message from R1 is addressed to multicast address 224.0.0.5. The switch floods the frame, and OSPF-enabled R2 G0/0 and R4 G0/0 accept the hello message. R3 ignores the hello because G0/0 is not OSPF-enabled.

The first OSPF neighbor state is *Down*, although it's not really a neighbor state—it means the router hasn't received any hello messages on the interface. Then, using an example from the neighbor states shown in figure 18.9, when R2 first receives a hello message from R1, R2 will create an OSPF neighbor entry for R1 in the *Init* state, as shown in the following example:

```
                                                          Use this command to display
                                                          the OSPF neighbor table.
R2# show ip ospf neighbor
Neighbor ID     Pri   State           Dead Time   Address         Interface
172.16.1.1        1   INIT/DROTHER    00:00:38    10.0.0.1        GigabitEthernet0/0
                                                  R2 has an entry for R1 in the Init state.
```

show ip ospf neighbor is a very useful command to check the router's OSPF neighbors and their states. The Init state means that the router has received an OSPF hello message from a neighboring router, but that hello message did not include the local router's own RID. R2 will then send its own hello message to R1, including R1's RID in the message, having learned it from R1's hello. When R1 receives this hello from R2, R1 will create an OSPF neighbor entry for R2 in the 2-Way state—bypassing the Init state. The following example shows R1's OSPF neighbor table entry for R2:

```
                                                        Displays the OSPF neighbor table
R1# show ip ospf neighbor
Neighbor ID     Pri   State           Dead Time   Address     Interface
172.16.1.2        1   2WAY/DROTHER    00:00:39    10.0.0.2    GigabitEthernet0/0
```

Having received a hello from R2—and thus having learned R2's RID—R1 sends another hello to R2, including R2's RID in the message this time. R2 then moves its neighbor table entry for R1 to the 2-Way state. At this point, R1 and R2 are considered OSPF neighbors—they see and acknowledge each other but have not exchanged any routing information.

NOTE In some cases, a *designated router* (DR) and *backup designated router* (BDR) election is held in the 2-Way state—more on that in section 18.3.2.

For OSPF routers to exchange routing information, they must establish an OSPF adjacency by progressing toward the Full state. To do so, they will proceed to the ExStart and Exchange states, where they exchange database description (DBD) messages, which are summaries of the contents of each router's LSDB. In the ExStart state, they determine which router will lead the DBD exchange; the router with the higher RID will become the Leader, and the router with the lower RID will become the Follower. Then, the actual DBD exchange takes place in the Exchange state.

NOTE Leader/Follower is a recent update to OSPF terminology, replacing the previous Master/Slave. Because it's a recent update, the old terms are still more common (and used in Cisco IOS software), so you should be aware of them.

After exchanging DBDs, the routers are aware of the contents of each other's LSDBs. They then proceed to the Loading state, where they use link-state request (LSR) messages to request specific LSAs from each other, link-state update (LSU) messages to send LSAs, and link-state acknowledgment (LSAck) messages to acknowledge receipt of LSUs.

NOTE LSAs are data structures that contain OSPF routing information, and they are sent in LSU messages. You can think of LSUs as the envelopes that carry LSAs.

The routers then enter the Full state, meaning that they have synced their LSDBs. At this point, they are called *adjacent neighbors* or *fully adjacent neighbors*, and their neighbor relationship is now called an *adjacency* or *full adjacency*. As long as the connection between the routers remains stable, they should remain in the Full state, sharing LSAs as the network changes.

Even after a neighbor relationship or adjacency is established, routers will continue sending hello messages at regular intervals, as determined by the *hello timer*, which is 10 seconds by default. The purpose of these hello messages is to maintain neighbor relationships. If a router stops receiving hellos from a neighbor, it will remove the neighbor from the neighbor table; this is determined by the *dead timer*, which is 40 seconds by default. This means that a router will remove a neighbor if the router hasn't received a hello from the neighbor for the past 40 seconds.

18.3.2 OSPF network types

OSPF uses an interface setting called *network type* to determine how OSPF behaves over a particular network. In this context, a *network* is a connection between two or more routers—a segment. The network type influences things like the OSPF message timers, whether a DR and BDR are elected, and whether all neighbor relationships will become full adjacencies.

There are various OSPF network types: broadcast, non-broadcast multi-access (NBMA), point-to-point, point-to-multipoint, point-to-multipoint non-broadcast, and loopback. The CCNA exam topics explicitly state the two network types you need to know for the exam in topics 3.3.b, Point-to-point, and 3.3.c, Broadcast (DR/BDR selection). Table 18.3 summarizes those two network types.

Table 18.3 OSPF network types

Broadcast	Point-to-point
DR/BDR elected	No DR/BDR
Establish full adjacency only with DR & BDR	Establish full adjacency
Neighbors dynamically discovered	Neighbors dynamically discovered
Default timers: hello = 10, dead = 40	Default timers: hello = 10; dead = 40

The two shared characteristics of these network types are dynamic neighbor discovery and the default timers. By sending hello messages out of OSPF-enabled interfaces, routers are able to dynamically discover which neighbors are connected to the interface, as opposed to requiring an admin to manually configure neighbor IP addresses (as required on some OSPF network types).

The default hello timer on both of these network types is 10 seconds, so interfaces send hello messages at 10-second intervals. The default dead timer is 40 seconds, so a neighbor is removed from the neighbor table if no hello message is received for 40 seconds. Other network types use longer default timers of 30 and 120 seconds.

> **NOTE** If the router detects a physical link failure (placing the interface in the down/down state), OSPF will immediately remove the neighbor—no need to wait for the dead timer to count down. The dead timer is only relevant if the interface remains up but the router stops receiving hello messages from the neighbor (for whatever reason).

Broadcast network type

Broadcast is the default OSPF network type of Ethernet interfaces (of all speeds—FastEthernet, GigabitEthernet, etc.). You can confirm that with the **`show ip ospf interface`** command, as in the following example:

OSPF is activated on the interface with the network command.

```
R1# show ip ospf interface g0/0
GigabitEthernet0/0 is up, line protocol is up
  Internet Address 10.0.0.1/30, Area 0, Attached via Network Statement
  Process ID 1, Router ID 172.16.1.1, Network Type BROADCAST, Cost: 1
. . .
```

The network type of G0/0 is broadcast.

The main defining characteristic of the broadcast network type is that a *designated router* (DR) and *backup designated router* (BDR) are elected in the 2-Way neighbor state; other routers connected to the segment become *DROthers* (usually pronounced D-R-other). While the DR and BDR establish full adjacencies with all routers in the segment, DROthers only establish a full adjacency with the DR and BDR of the segment and remain neighbors in the 2-Way state with fellow DROthers—they don't exchange LSAs with each other.

The purpose of electing a DR and BDR is to reduce the amount of OSPF traffic in the segment by only requiring routers to exchange LSAs (in LSU messages) with the DR and BDR of the segment. Figure 18.11 shows how the number of adjacencies (and, therefore, LSA exchanges) is reduced, limiting the amount of OSPF traffic in the segment and the amount of resources used on the routers.

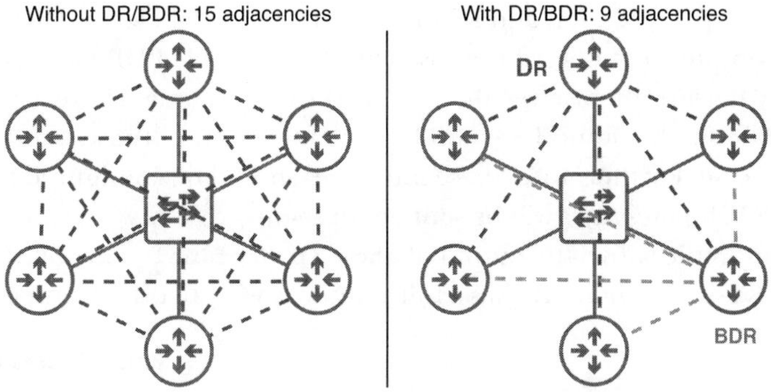

Figure 18.11 Six routers are connected to the same network segment. Without the DR/BDR, 15 OSPF adjacencies (and 15 LSA exchanges) would be required. With the DR/BDR, only 9 are required, reducing the amount of OSPF traffic.

NOTE To address messages to only the DR and BDR, DROthers send the packets to multicast IP address 224.0.0.6. Remember the two OSPF multicast IP addresses: 224.0.0.5 (all OSPF routers) and 224.0.0.6 (DR and BDR only).

Depending on the number of routers connected to the segment, the DR/BDR feature of the broadcast network type can greatly reduce the resources used by OSPF on the segment. This could be further reduced by electing only a DR, but the BDR is important for providing stability and resiliency; if the DR fails for some reason, the BDR takes over automatically as the new DR.

Figure 18.12 shows an example OSPF AS with DRs, BDRs, and DROthers labeled. Note that the DR and BDR are elected per segment, not per area. For example, R2 is the DR for the R1–R2 segment, but a DROther for the R2–R3–R4–R5 segment.

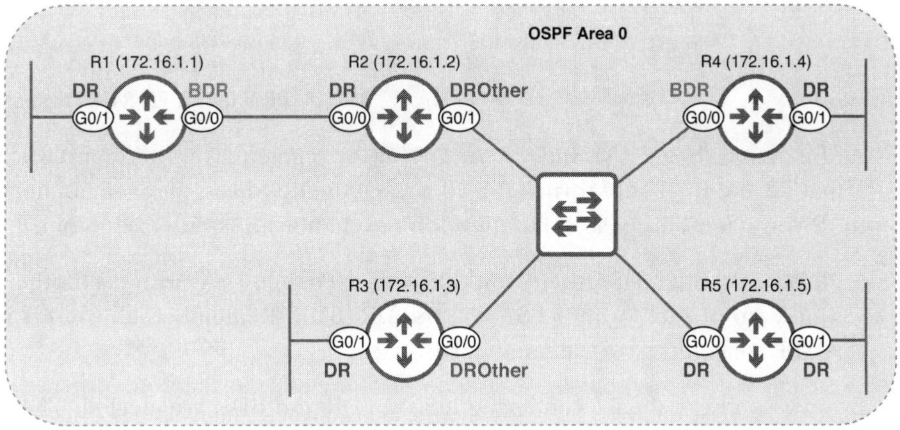

Figure 18.12 An OSPF AS consisting of six segments. The DR/BDR election is held per segment, not per area. RIDs are in parentheses.

The G0/1 interfaces of R1, R3, R4, and R5 in figure 18.12 are labeled as DRs. Because there are no other routers connected to those segments, no DR/BDR election is held; the routers simply declare themselves the DR for those segments. However, no adjacencies will be established, and no LSAs will be exchanged out of those interfaces; *DR* is just a title in this case. Furthermore, these interfaces should be configured in passive mode, so no OSPF hello messages will be sent out of them.

The following example shows the output of `show ip ospf neighbor` on R5. As the DR of the R2–R3–R4–R5 segment, R5 has a full adjacency with all other routers:

```
R5# show ip ospf neighbor
Neighbor ID   Pri  State          Dead Time  Address   Interface
172.16.1.2    1    FULL/DROTHER   00:00:34   10.0.0.1  GigabitEthernet0/0
172.16.1.3    1    FULL/DROTHER   00:00:34   10.0.0.2  GigabitEthernet0/0
172.16.1.4    1    FULL/BDR       00:00:38   10.0.0.3  GigabitEthernet0/0
```

R2 and R3 are DROthers.

R4 is the BDR.

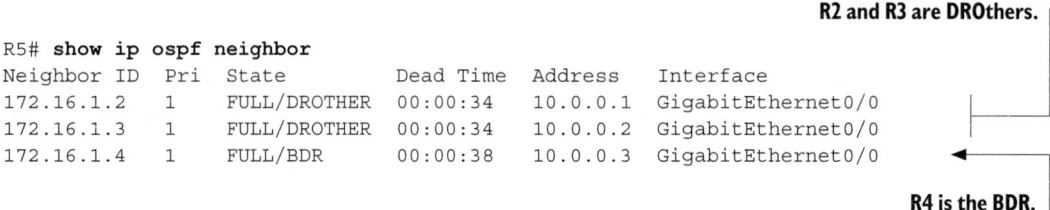

Although the output doesn't explicitly state that R5 is the DR, because none of the three other routers connected to the segment are the DR, you can conclude that R5 must be the DR for the segment. Let's confirm by using the same command on R2:

```
R2# show ip ospf neighbor
Neighbor ID   Pri  State          Dead Time  Address   Interface
172.16.1.1    1    FULL/BDR       00:00:30   10.0.0.9  GigabitEthernet0/0

172.16.1.3    1    2WAY/DROTHER   00:00:34   10.0.0.2  GigabitEthernet0/1

172.16.1.4    1    FULL/BDR       00:00:30   10.0.0.3  GigabitEthernet0/1
172.16.1.5    1    FULL/DR        00:00:31   10.0.0.4  GigabitEthernet0/1
```

R2 and R3, both DROthers, remain in the 2-Way neighbor state.

R1 is the BDR (and thus R2 is the DR) of the R1–R2 segment.

R5 is the DR of the R2–R3–R4–R5 segment.

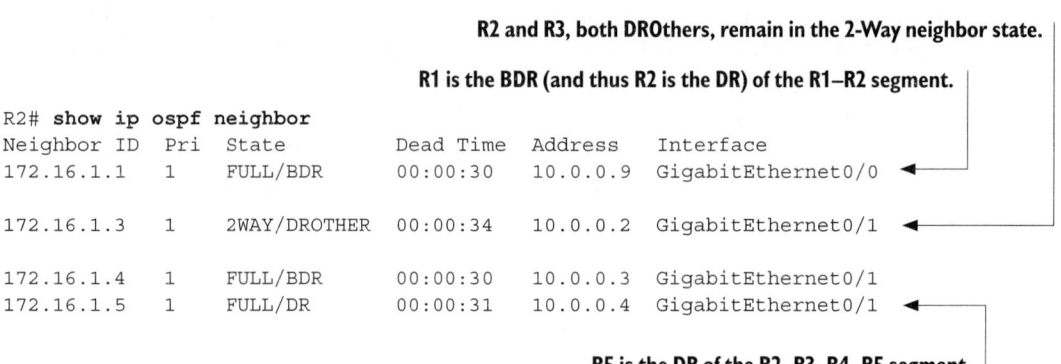

As the output shows, R5 is indeed the DR for the segment. Another point worth noting is that R2 and R3 do not form a full adjacency; as DROthers, they remain neighbors in the 2-Way state. This means that they don't exchange LSAs with each other.

> **NOTE** Although DROthers don't directly exchange LSAs with each other, they will learn of each other's LSAs via the DR/BDR. Remember, all routers in the OSPF area must have the same LSDB.

By now, you're probably wondering how the DR and BDR are elected. The DR/BDR are elected with the following two criteria:

- The highest interface priority
- The highest RID

The router with the highest interface priority will become the DR for the segment, and the router with the second highest will become the BDR. The OSPF *interface priority* is a configurable value (default 1) that can be configured with the **`ip ospf priority`** *`priority`* command in interface config mode.

NOTE If you want to ensure that a router never becomes the DR or BDR for a segment, configure **`ip ospf priority`** `0` on its interface.

In the example we saw in figure 18.12, all interfaces had the default priority of 1, so the second parameter was used to decide the DR of each segment: the OSPF RID. If interface priorities are tied, the router with the highest RID will become the DR (R5, 172.16.1.5), and the router with the second highest RID the BDR (R4, 172.16.1.4).

Let's change the interface priority of R2 G0/1 to test out the DR/BDR election. In the following example, I set R2 G0/1's interface priority to 100 and confirm the results:

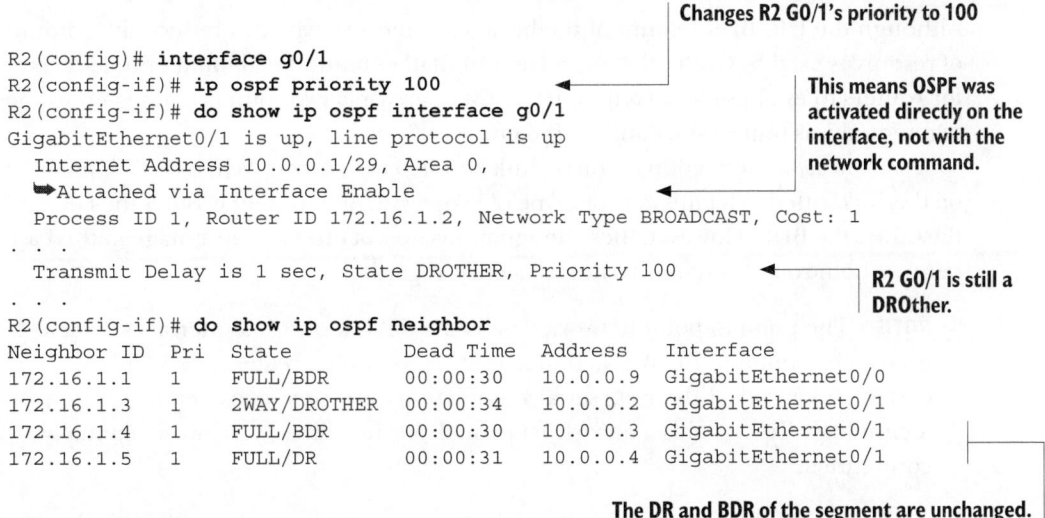

```
R2(config)# interface g0/1
R2(config-if)# ip ospf priority 100                    <-- Changes R2 G0/1's priority to 100
R2(config-if)# do show ip ospf interface g0/1
GigabitEthernet0/1 is up, line protocol is up
  Internet Address 10.0.0.1/29, Area 0,
  ➥Attached via Interface Enable                      <-- This means OSPF was activated directly on the
                                                           interface, not with the network command.
  Process ID 1, Router ID 172.16.1.2, Network Type BROADCAST, Cost: 1
. . .
  Transmit Delay is 1 sec, State DROTHER, Priority 100 <-- R2 G0/1 is still a DROther.
. . .
R2(config-if)# do show ip ospf neighbor
Neighbor ID  Pri  State          Dead Time  Address    Interface
172.16.1.1   1    FULL/BDR       00:00:30   10.0.0.9   GigabitEthernet0/0
172.16.1.3   1    2WAY/DROTHER   00:00:34   10.0.0.2   GigabitEthernet0/1
172.16.1.4   1    FULL/BDR       00:00:30   10.0.0.3   GigabitEthernet0/1
172.16.1.5   1    FULL/DR        00:00:31   10.0.0.4   GigabitEthernet0/1
                                 The DR and BDR of the segment are unchanged.
```

Although R2 G0/1 now has the highest priority of the segment, R5 and R4 remain the DR and BDR. That's because, once the DR and BDR have been elected, they won't be *preempted*—their roles won't be taken—even if the priority of an existing router is increased or a router with a higher priority connects to the segment. To make a DR or BDR give up its role, you can use the **`clear ip ospf process`** command to reset the router's OSPF process, as I do on R5 in the following example:

```
R5# clear ip ospf process                     Resets R5's OSPF process
Reset ALL OSPF processes? [no]: yes
R5# show ip ospf neighbor
Neighbor ID  Pri  State          Dead Time  Address    Interface
```

```
172.16.1.2    100  FULL/BDR       00:00:35    10.0.0.1  GigabitEthernet0/0
172.16.1.3    1    2WAY/DROTHER   00:00:31    10.0.0.2  GigabitEthernet0/0
172.16.1.4    1    FULL/DR        00:00:31    10.0.0.3  GigabitEthernet0/0
```

R4 becomes the new DR, and R2, the BDR.

After resetting R5's OSPF process, R4 (formerly the BDR) becomes the new DR, and R2 becomes the new BDR, despite having the highest priority. These results reveal an important point about how the DR and BDR function: if the DR goes down, routers connected to the segment don't hold an election for the new DR. Instead, the BDR immediately takes over as the new DR; that's why R4 becomes the new DR. Then, an election is held to determine the new BDR; R2 wins this election and becomes the new BDR. To make R2 the DR, you would have to then reset R4's OSPF process, making R2 (the BDR) immediately take over R4's role.

> **EXAM TIP** The broadcast network type is exam topic 3.4.c. You should understand the DR/BDR election in particular.

POINT-TO-POINT NETWORK TYPE

Although the DR/BDR feature of the broadcast network type can reduce the amount of resources used by OSPF, electing a DR and BDR extends the amount of time it takes for routers to establish a full adjacency; if there are only two routers connected to the segment, this is unnecessary and inefficient.

A *point-to-point* connection is a direct link between two routers. When OSPF is enabled on this link with the default network type of broadcast, one router becomes the DR, and the other, the BDR. However, these designations do not offer any advantage in this case because both routers establish a full adjacency, regardless.

> **NOTE** The point-to-point network type is the default on *serial* interfaces, which used to be common for WAN connections. Due to the greater speed and lower cost of fiber-optic Ethernet, serial connections are now considered a legacy technology. To use this network type on Ethernet links, you must manually configure it.

By using the OSPF point-to-point network type, we eliminate the DR/BDR election process, allowing the routers to establish a full adjacency in less time. This network type is designed for direct connections between two routers, and it is the most efficient option in these situations. Figure 18.13 shows a situation where the point-to-point network type should be configured. R1 and R2 have a point-to-point connection, so there is no need to elect a DR and BDR.

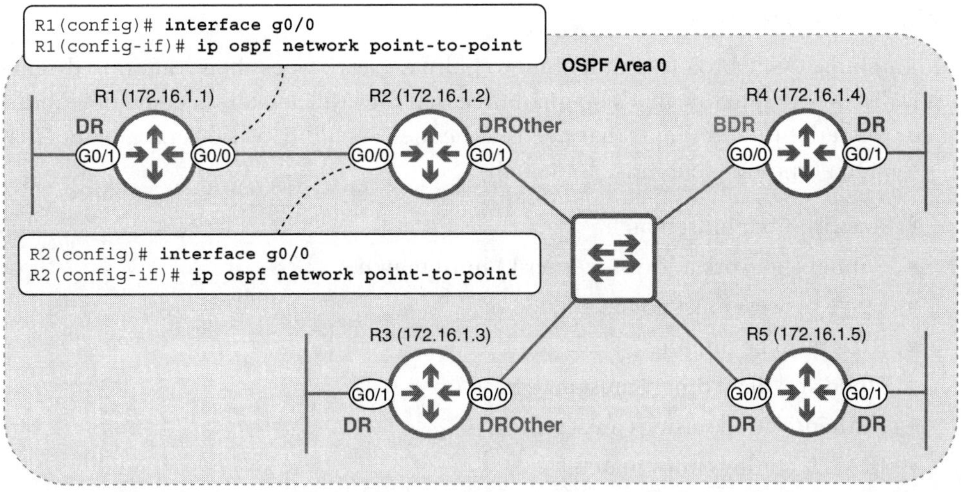

Figure 18.13 Electing a DR and BDR on a connection between two routers is unnecessary, so the R1–R2 link should use the point-to-point network type.

To configure the point-to-point network type, use the **ip ospf network point-to-point** command in interface config mode—make sure you do it on both sides of the connection! In the following example, I configure the point-to-point network type on R1 G0/0 and R2 G0/0 and then confirm. Notice that R1 and R2 establish a full adjacency, but neither is a DR or BDR, as indicated by the state of `FULL/ -`:

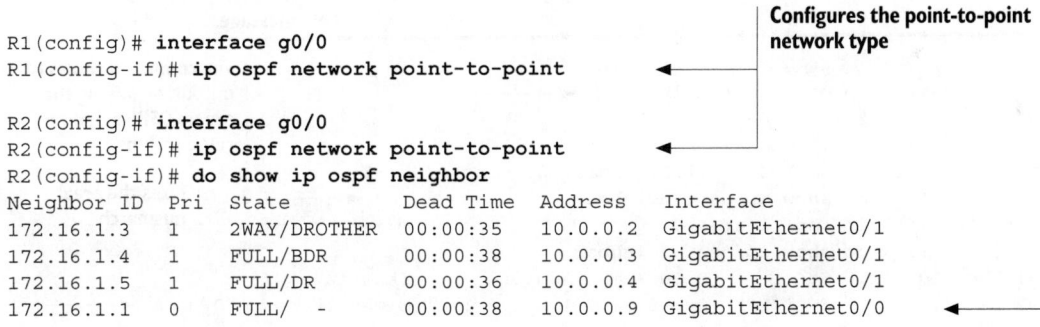

```
R1(config)# interface g0/0
R1(config-if)# ip ospf network point-to-point        ◄── Configures the point-to-point network type

R2(config)# interface g0/0
R2(config-if)# ip ospf network point-to-point        ◄──
R2(config-if)# do show ip ospf neighbor
Neighbor ID  Pri  State         Dead Time  Address   Interface
172.16.1.3   1    2WAY/DROTHER  00:00:35   10.0.0.2  GigabitEthernet0/1
172.16.1.4   1    FULL/BDR      00:00:38   10.0.0.3  GigabitEthernet0/1
172.16.1.5   1    FULL/DR       00:00:36   10.0.0.4  GigabitEthernet0/1
172.16.1.1   0    FULL/  -      00:00:38   10.0.0.9  GigabitEthernet0/0   ◄──
                                    R1 and R2 establish a full adjacency with no DR/BDR.
```

EXAM TIP The point-to-point network type is exam topic 3.4.b. You should understand the advantage it provides (no DR/BDR election) and how to configure it.

18.3.3 Neighbor requirements

Although the OSPF broadcast and point-to-point network types allow routers to dynamically discover neighbors, that's no guarantee that they will actually become neighbors; there is a set of requirements that needs to be met, including various parameters that must match (and one that must not match):

- Area number must match.
- Subnet (network address, netmask) must match.
- OSPF process must not be `shutdown`.
- RIDs must be unique.
- Hello and dead timers must match.
- Authentication settings must match.
- IP MTU settings must match.*
- Network type must match.*

A mismatch of the final two, which I've marked with asterisks (*), will not prevent routers from becoming neighbors but will prevent OSPF from operating properly. Let's go through these requirements one by one, and see how OSPF is affected. I'll use a simple connection between two routers: R1 (192.168.1.1/30) and R2 (192.168.1.2/30). In the following example, I configure an area number mismatch on R1 and R2, and they fail to become OSPF neighbors. After fixing the mismatch, the issue is resolved:

```
R1(config-if)# ip ospf 1 area 0
R2(config-if)# ip ospf 1 area 1
*Jun  9 03:40:12.255: %OSPF-4-ERRRCV:
➥Received invalid packet: mismatched area ID from
➥backbone area from 192.168.1.1, GigabitEthernet0/0
R2(config-if)# do show ip ospf neighbor
R2(config-if)# ip ospf 1 area 0
R2(config-if)# do show ip ospf neighbor
Neighbor ID  Pri  State      Dead Time   Address        Interface
192.168.1.1  1    FULL/BDR   00:00:37    192.168.1.1    GigabitEthernet0/0
```

Configures an area mismatch on R1 and R2

R2 displays an error message.

The command shows no output, signifying there are no OSPF neighbor relationships.

Fixes the area mismatch

R1 and R2 become OSPF neighbors.

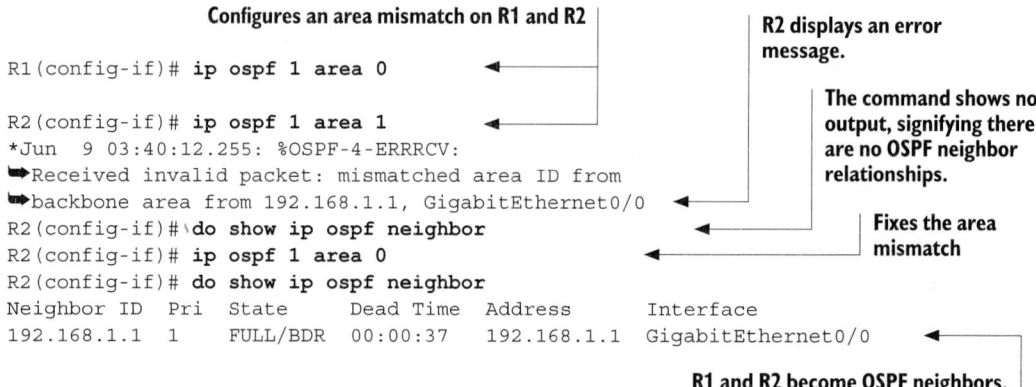

In the next example, I change the netmask of R2's interface. Even though I didn't change the IP address; just having a mismatched netmask causes the adjacency to go from Full to Down.

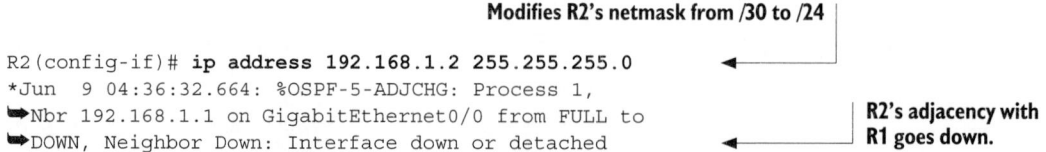

```
R2(config-if)# ip address 192.168.1.2 255.255.255.0
*Jun  9 04:36:32.664: %OSPF-5-ADJCHG: Process 1,
➥Nbr 192.168.1.1 on GigabitEthernet0/0 from FULL to
➥DOWN, Neighbor Down: Interface down or detached
```

Modifies R2's netmask from /30 to /24

R2's adjacency with R1 goes down.

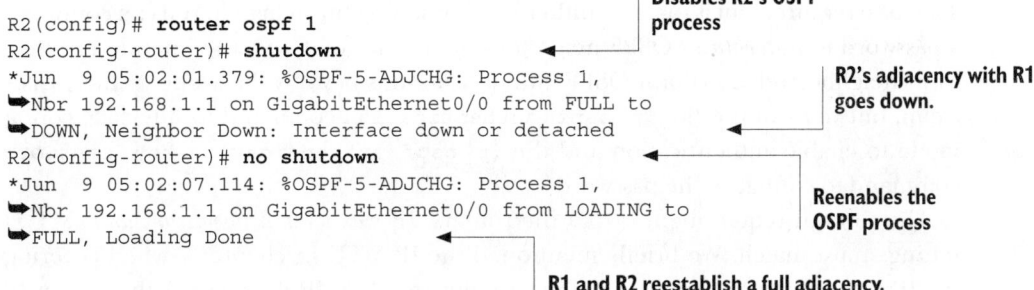

```
R2(config-if)# ip address 192.168.1.2 255.255.255.252      <-- Restores the netmask to /30
*Jun  9 04:37:36.071: %OSPF-5-ADJCHG: Process 1,
➥Nbr 192.168.1.1 on GigabitEthernet0/0 from LOADING to
➥FULL, Loading Done      <-- R1 and R2 reestablish a full adjacency.
```

The third requirement is that the OSPF process must not be **shutdown**, referring to the command you can use in router config mode to disable OSPF, much like how you use the **shutdown** command to disable an interface. I demonstrate this in the following example:

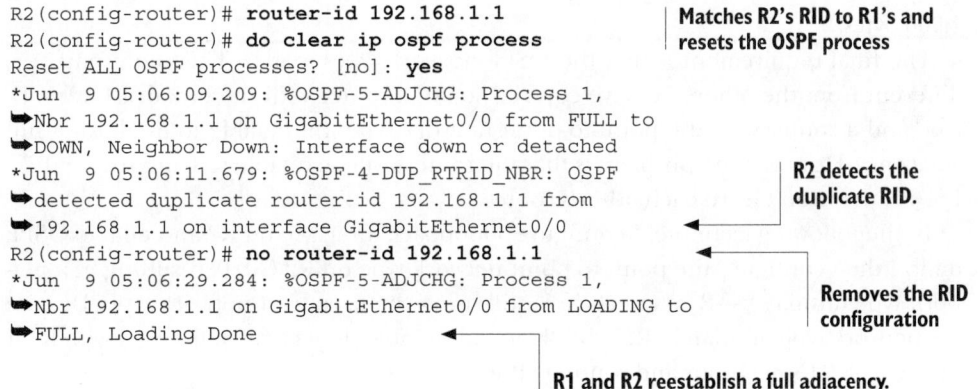

```
R2(config)# router ospf 1
R2(config-router)# shutdown      <-- Disables R2's OSPF process
*Jun  9 05:02:01.379: %OSPF-5-ADJCHG: Process 1,
➥Nbr 192.168.1.1 on GigabitEthernet0/0 from FULL to
➥DOWN, Neighbor Down: Interface down or detached      <-- R2's adjacency with R1 goes down.
R2(config-router)# no shutdown      <-- Reenables the OSPF process
*Jun  9 05:02:07.114: %OSPF-5-ADJCHG: Process 1,
➥Nbr 192.168.1.1 on GigabitEthernet0/0 from LOADING to
➥FULL, Loading Done      <-- R1 and R2 reestablish a full adjacency.
```

The fourth requirement is that the routers' RIDs must be unique—the one parameter that must not match. In the following example, I modify R2's RID to match R1's, reset the OSPF process, and they fail to become neighbors. Removing the R2's RID configuration fixes the issue:

```
R2(config-router)# router-id 192.168.1.1      <-- Matches R2's RID to R1's and resets the OSPF process
R2(config-router)# do clear ip ospf process
Reset ALL OSPF processes? [no]: yes
*Jun  9 05:06:09.209: %OSPF-5-ADJCHG: Process 1,
➥Nbr 192.168.1.1 on GigabitEthernet0/0 from FULL to
➥DOWN, Neighbor Down: Interface down or detached
*Jun  9 05:06:11.679: %OSPF-4-DUP_RTRID_NBR: OSPF
➥detected duplicate router-id 192.168.1.1 from
➥192.168.1.1 on interface GigabitEthernet0/0      <-- R2 detects the duplicate RID.
R2(config-router)# no router-id 192.168.1.1      <-- Removes the RID configuration
*Jun  9 05:06:29.284: %OSPF-5-ADJCHG: Process 1,
➥Nbr 192.168.1.1 on GigabitEthernet0/0 from LOADING to
➥FULL, Loading Done      <-- R1 and R2 reestablish a full adjacency.
```

The fifth requirement is that the hello and dead timers must match. The default hello timer is 10 seconds, and the default dead timer is 40 seconds, but they can be configured with the **ip ospf hello-interval** *seconds* and **ip ospf dead-interval** *seconds* commands in interface config mode. In the following example, I modify R2's hello timer, causing the adjacency with R1 to go down:

```
R2(config)# interface g0/0
R2(config-if)# ip ospf hello-interval 5
*Jun  9 05:14:34.525: %OSPF-5-ADJCHG: Process 1,
➥Nbr 192.168.1.1 on GigabitEthernet0/0 from FULL to
➥DOWN, Neighbor Down: Dead timer expired
R2(config-if)# ip ospf hello-interval 10
*Jun  9 05:17:25.749: %OSPF-5-ADJCHG: Process 1,
➥Nbr 192.168.1.1 on GigabitEthernet0/0 from LOADING to
➥FULL, Loading Done
```

Modifies R2's hello timer (ip ospf hello-interval 5)

R2's adjacency with R1 goes down.

Restores R2's hello timer to the default (ip ospf hello-interval 10)

R1 and R2 reestablish a full adjacency.

The sixth requirement is that the authentication settings must match. You can configure a password to *authenticate* OSPF neighbors—to ensure that only the intended routers form neighbor relationships. OSPF authentication is beyond the scope of the CCNA exam, but you can use the **`ip ospf authentication`** command in interface config mode to enable authentication and the **`ip ospf authentication-key`** *`password`* command to configure the password.

The seventh requirement is that the routers' IP *maximum transmission unit* (MTU) settings must match. We briefly mentioned the IP MTU in chapter 7 when covering the IPv4 header; it determines the maximum size of an IPv4 packet. Although an IP MTU mismatch will not prevent two OSPF routers from becoming neighbors, they will be unable to establish a full adjacency; they will not be able to advance beyond the ExStart/Exchange states. Like authentication, the details of IP MTU are beyond the scope of the CCNA exam, but you can modify an interface's IP MTU with the **`ip mtu`** *`bytes`* command in interface config mode; the default setting on Ethernet interfaces is 1,500 bytes.

The final requirement is that the OSPF network types match. This requirement is different from the others we have covered so far: a router with the broadcast network type and a router with the point-to-point network type will be able to establish a full adjacency. However, the problem is that the routers will be unable to synchronize their LSDBs; they won't learn each other's routes.

In the following example, I configure a loopback interface on R2 and enable OSPF on it. I then configure the point-to-point network type on R2 G0/0, resulting in a network type mismatch—R1's interface is still using the broadcast network type. Despite the network type mismatch, R2's OSPF neighbor table shows a full adjacency with R1. I then check R1's neighbor and routing tables:

```
R2(config)# interface l0
R2(config-if)# ip address 10.10.10.2 255.255.255.255
R2(config-if)# ip ospf 1 area 0
R2(config-if)# interface g0/0
R2(config-if)# ip ospf network point-to-point
R2(config-if)# do show ip ospf neighbor
```

Configures Loopback0 and activates OSPF

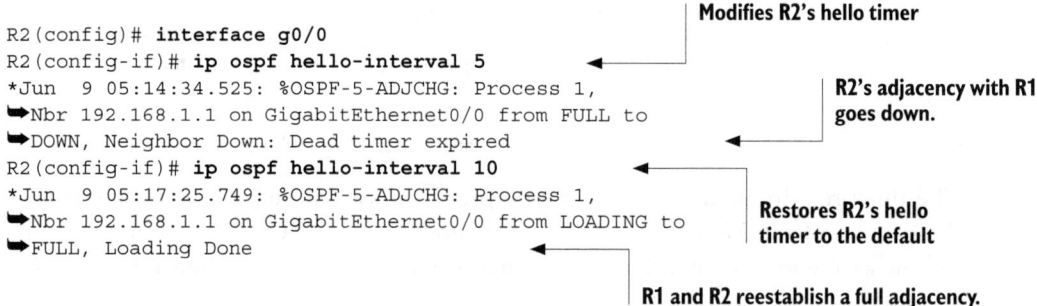

Changes R2 G0/0's network type to point-to-point

```
Neighbor ID   Pri   State       Dead Time   Address       Interface
192.168.1.2   1     FULL/  -    00:00:34    192.168.1.2   GigabitEthernet0/0

R1# show ip ospf neighbor
Neighbor ID   Pri   State      Dead Time    Address       Interface
192.168.1.2   1     FULL/DR    00:00:34     192.168.1.2   GigabitEthernet0/0
R1# show ip route ospf
. . .
```

R1 and R2 have a full adjacency.

No routes display; R1 does not learn a route to R2's loopback interface, despite having a full adjacency.

The OSPF neighbor tables for R1 and R2 both indicate a full adjacency, but there is something strange: R2's output shows a state of `FULL/ -` (as expected when using the point-to-point network type), but R1's output shows `FULL/DR`—R1 believes that R2 is the DR. Furthermore, although OSPF is activated on R2's loopback interface, R1's routing table shows no route to the interface's address (10.10.10.2/32). Despite achieving full adjacency, R1 and R2 weren't actually able to synchronize their LSDBs. The solution is to ensure that both sides of the connection are using the same network type, whether that is broadcast or point-to-point.

EXAM TIP Neighbor adjacencies are exam topic 3.4.a; make sure you know these requirements for the exam.

18.4 LSA types

OSPF routers share routing information by sending LSU messages, which contain LSAs. There are various different kinds of LSAs, each with its own purpose, but for the CCNA exam, you should be aware of three:

- *Type 1 (Router LSA)*—Generated by all routers, this LSA describes the router's links.
- *Type 2 (Network LSA)*—Generated by the DR of a broadcast network, this LSA lists all routers on the segment.
- *Type 5 (AS External LSA)*—Generated by ASBRs, this LSA advertises routes to external networks (i.e., a default route to the internet).

Figure 18.14 shows the OSPF AS we looked at in section 18.3.2, modified with a connection to the internet, which R1 advertises with **`default-information originate`**. Notice the contents of the LSDB, which are shared by all five routers.

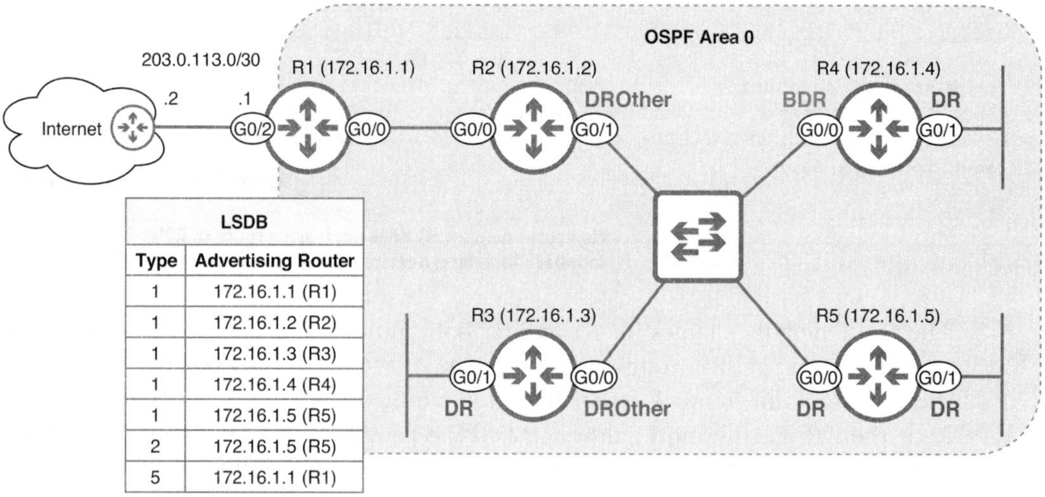

LSDB	
Type	**Advertising Router**
1	172.16.1.1 (R1)
1	172.16.1.2 (R2)
1	172.16.1.3 (R3)
1	172.16.1.4 (R4)
1	172.16.1.5 (R5)
2	172.16.1.5 (R5)
5	172.16.1.1 (R1)

Figure 18.14 An OSPF AS and the contents of its LSDB. Each router advertises a type 1 (Router) LSA. R5, as the DR of the R2–R3–R4–R5 segment, advertises a type 2 (Network) LSA. R1, as an ASBR, advertises a type 5 LSA.

> **NOTE** R3, R4, and R5 don't advertise a type 2 LSA for their G0/1 interfaces. As mentioned before, with no neighbors on those interfaces, they are DRs in name only.

To view the OSPF LSDB, use the **`show ip ospf database`** command. The output of this command should be the same on all routers; they should all have the same LSAs in their LSDB. In the following example, I use the command on R1. The specifics of how to read the output are beyond the scope of the CCNA; just note that each router advertises a type 1 LSA, R5 advertises a single type 2 LSA, and R1 advertises a single type 5 LSA:

```
R1# show ip ospf database
            OSPF Router with ID (172.16.1.1) (Process ID 1)
              Router Link States (Area 0)
Link ID       ADV Router    Age    Seq#          Checksum   Link count
172.16.1.1    172.16.1.1    1851   0x80000008    0x0015D5   3
172.16.1.2    172.16.1.2    1852   0x8000000A    0x003688   4
172.16.1.3    172.16.1.3    1825   0x80000014    0x002510   3
172.16.1.4    172.16.1.4    1824   0x80000018    0x0052D9   3
172.16.1.5    172.16.1.5    1824   0x80000015    0x008D9C   3

              Net Link States (Area 0)
Link ID       ADV Router    Age    Seq#          Checksum
10.0.0.4      172.16.1.5    1824   0x8000000E    0x00B89D

              Type-5 AS External Link States
Link ID       ADV Router    Age    Seq#          Checksum   Tag
0.0.0.0       172.16.1.1    1850   0x80000001    0x009B58   1
```

Each router advertises a type 1 (Router) LSA.

R5 advertises a type 2 (Network) LSA for the R2–R3–R4–R5 segment.

R1 advertises a type 5 (AS External) LSA.

Summary

- Two versions of OSPF are used: OSPFv2 (for IPv4) and OSPFv3 (mainly for IPv6).
- OSPF uses the *Shortest Path First* (SPF) algorithm, also called *Dijkstra's algorithm.*
- OSPF routers go through three main steps: forming neighbor relationships, exchanging routing information, and calculating routes.
- OSPF routers exchange routing information using *link-state advertisements* (LSAs), which are organized in the *link-state database* (LSDB). The process of sending LSAs to all other routers in the same OSPF area is called *LSA flooding.*
- An OSPF network can be logically divided into *areas.* Routers in an OSPF area all share the same LSDB. Area 0 is the *backbone area* to which all other areas must connect.
- In large networks, multi-area OSPF provides advantages: smaller LSDBs take up fewer memory resources, the SPF algorithm takes less time and CPU resources to calculate routes, and network changes/instability are isolated to a single area.
- An *internal router* has all OSPF-enabled interfaces in the same area. A *backbone router* has at least one interface in area 0. An *area border router* (ABR) connects one (or more) areas to area 0. An *autonomous system border router* (ASBR) connects the OSPF AS to external networks.
- *Intra-area routes* are routes to destinations in an area the router is connected to. *Inter-area* routes are routes to destinations in an area the router is not connected to. *External* routes are routes to destinations outside of the OSPF AS.
- OSPF's metric is called *cost,* and a route's cost is the cumulative cost of each interface a packet must be sent out of to reach the destination.
- A link's cost is calculated by dividing the *reference bandwidth* (default 100 Mbps) by the link's bandwidth. Values less than 1 are assigned as 1, meaning links with a bandwidth of 100 Mbps or greater all have a cost of 1 by default.
- You can change the reference bandwidth with the **`auto-cost reference-bandwidth`** *`mbps`* command in router config mode.
- You can modify a link's cost with **`ip ospf cost`** *`cost`* on each interface or by modifying the interfaces' bandwidth with **`bandwidth`** *`kbps`*.
- Use **`show ip ospf interface brief`** to view OSPF-enabled interfaces.
- The OSPF process ID is specified with the **`router ospf`** *`process-id`* command and is locally significant; it doesn't have to match between routers.
- Use **`show ip protocols`** to view information about routing protocols on the router, such as the OSPF RID, OSPF-enabled interfaces, etc.
- Each router's OSPF *router ID* (RID) must be unique. It is determined in the following order: (1) manual configuration with the **`router-id`** command, (2) highest IP address on a loopback interface, and (3) highest IP address on a physical interface.

- A *loopback interface* is a virtual interface that is not dependent on the status of a particular physical interface. You can create a loopback interface with the **interface loopback** *number* command and configure an IP address like a physical interface.
- In addition to the network command, you can activate OSPF on interfaces with the **ip ospf** *process-id* **area** *area* command in interface config mode.
- A *passive interface* is OSPF-enabled but does not send OSPF hello messages.
- To configure a passive interface, use **passive-interface** *interface-name* in router config mode or **passive-interface default** and then **no passive-interface** *interface-name* to make specific interfaces nonpassive.
- Use **default-information originate** in router config mode to make a router advertise its default route to its OSPF neighbors (making it an ASBR).
- OSPF uses five message types: hello, database description (DBD), link-state request (LSR), link-state update (LSU), and link-state acknowledgment (LSAck).
- Hellos are used for neighbor discovery and maintenance. DBDs provide a summary of the router's LSDB. LSRs request specific LSAs from a neighbor. LSUs send specific LSAs to a neighbor. LSAcks acknowledge receipt of an LSU.
- OSPF hello messages are sent to multicast IPv4 address 224.0.0.5. This multicast address is used to send messages to all OSPF routers on the segment.
- There are seven OSPF neighbor states: Down, Init, 2-Way, ExStart, Exchange, Loading, and Full.
- OSPF routers in the 2-Way state are *neighbors* but have not yet exchanged LSAs.
- Routers in the Full state are *adjacent/fully adjacent*; they have an *adjacency/full adjacency*. They have exchanged LSAs and synced their LSDBs.
- Use **show ip ospf neighbor** to view information about OSPF neighbors.
- OSPF uses an interface setting called *network type* to determine how OSPF behaves over a particular network (a segment—a link between one or more routers).
- Use **show ip ospf interface** *interface* to view details about a particular interface.
- Ethernet interfaces use the *broadcast* network type by default. This network type allows neighbors to dynamically discover each other and uses these default timers: hello = 10, dead = 40.
- OSPF routers elect a *designated router* (DR) and *backup designated router* (BDR) on each broadcast network segment. The remaining routers are *DROthers*. The DR/BDR election occurs in the 2-Way state.
- All routers on the segment establish a full adjacency with the DR/BDR, but DROthers remain neighbors in the 2-Way state with each other.
- The DR and BDR are determined using (1) the highest interface priority or (2) the highest RID. The default interface priority is 1. It can be configured with **ip ospf priority**.

- Increasing a router's interface priority/RID or connecting a new router with a higher interface priority/RID will not cause the router to *preempt* the DR/BDR. To make the DR or BDR give up its role, use **`clear ip ospf process`**.
- If the DR is lost, the BDR immediately takes over its role, and an election is held for the new BDR.
- The *point-to-point* network type is ideal for connections between two routers. The routers establish a full adjacency without a DR/BDR election. Use **`ip ospf network point-to-point`** in interface config mode to configure this network type.
- For routers to become OSPF neighbors, the OSPF process must not be **`shutdown`**, the RIDs must be unique, and the following parameters must match: area number, subnet, hello/dead timers, authentication settings, IP MTU settings, and network type.
- If the IP MTU settings don't match, the routers will be stuck in the ExStart/Exchange states. If the network type doesn't match, the routers will establish a full adjacency but will not sync their LSDBs.
- There are various kinds of LSAs, including type 1 (Router LSA), type 2 (Network LSA), and type 5 (AS External LSA).
  - *Type 1 (Router LSA)*—Generated by all routers, this LSA describes the router's links.
  - *Type 2 (Network LSA)*—Generated by the DR of a broadcast network, this LSA lists all routers on the segment.
  - *Type 5 (AS External LSA)*—Generated by ASBRs, this LSA advertises routes to external networks (i.e., a default route to the internet).

19 First hop redundancy protocols

This chapter covers

- How FHRPs provide a redundant default gateway for end hosts
- The three FHRPs used by Cisco routers and their characteristics
- How to configure Cisco's Hot Standby Router Protocol

When covering STP in chapter 14, I emphasized the importance of redundancy in a LAN. In modern enterprise networks, redundancy plays an essential role in ensuring network reliability and resilience. As businesses increasingly rely on digital operations and processes, network downtime can result in substantial financial losses and damage to one's reputation. Redundancy safeguards against this by eliminating single points of failure.

Redundancy doesn't just mean having multiple potential paths to reach destinations within the same LAN; it also means having multiple potential paths to reach destinations outside of the LAN. First hop redundancy protocols (FHRPs), the topic of this chapter, facilitate this by enabling multiple routers to work together, providing a redundant default gateway for hosts in a LAN. FHRPs constitute CCNA exam topic 3.5: Describe the purpose, functions, and concepts of first hop redundancy protocols.

Cisco routers support three different FHRPs: Hot Standby Router Protocol (HSRP), Virtual Router Redundancy Protocol (VRRP), and Gateway Load Balancing Protocol (GLBP). They all serve the purpose of providing a redundant default gateway for hosts but also have their own unique characteristics. We will begin by covering FHRPs as a whole and then cover the characteristics of each FHRP that you should know for the CCNA exam.

19.1 FHRP concepts

First hop redundancy protocol (FHRP) is a category of protocol that allows multiple routers to work together to provide a redundant default gateway for hosts in a LAN, minimizing downtime in the event of a hardware failure. This is the reason for the name: the default gateway is the first hop in the packet's path to its destination.

19.1.1 Providing a redundant default gateway

An end host's default gateway is an IP address that is either manually configured or automatically learned via DHCP (the topic of chapter 4 in volume 2). End hosts use the Address Resolution Protocol (ARP) to learn the MAC address of the default gateway and then encapsulate packets to external destinations in frames addressed to the default gateway's MAC address. Because hosts rely on the default gateway to reach external destinations, the default gateway must be resilient to failures.

At first glance, the network in figure 19.1 might look like it deserves a perfect score when it comes to redundancy; there are multiple connections between switches, providing multiple paths to destinations within the LAN, and there are two routers, providing multiple paths to external destinations. However, without an FHRP, the two routers are unable to coordinate with each other to provide a redundant default gateway.

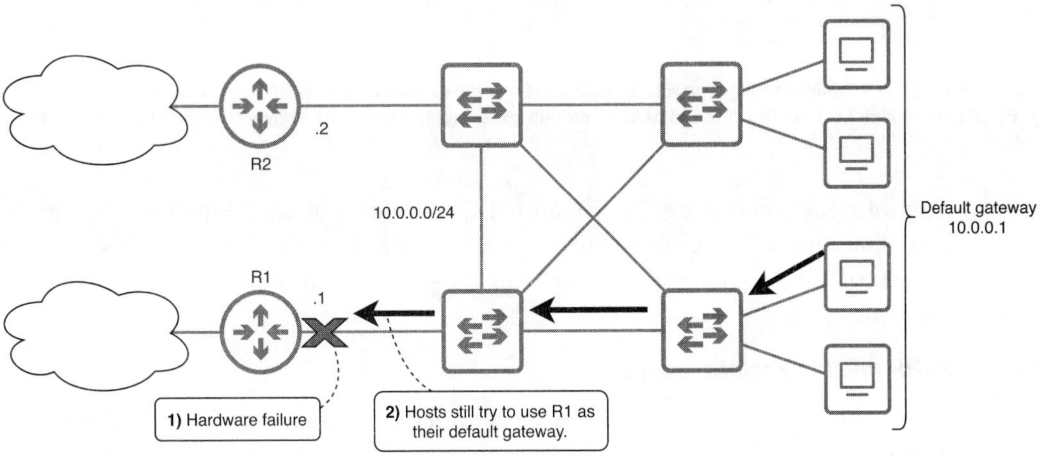

Figure 19.1 Despite the hardware failure on R1, hosts in the LAN still try to use R1 as their default gateway. Without an FHRP, R2 is unable to take over R1's role.

Because the end hosts still use IP address 10.0.0.1 as their default gateway, they will continue to send packets destined for external destinations in frames addressed to R1, despite the hardware failure preventing R1 from fulfilling its role as default gateway. You could reconfigure each host's default gateway to 10.0.0.2 or R2's IP address to 10.0.0.1, but this kind of manual intervention is not acceptable in modern networks; it is expected that the network will recover automatically and with minimal downtime.

Figure 19.2 shows how an FHRP allows R2 to take over as the default gateway after R1's hardware failure. R1 and R2 both share a *virtual IP* (VIP) address, which is configured as the default gateway of hosts in the LAN. Under normal circumstances, R1 responds to ARP requests directed to the VIP (10.0.0.1), so end hosts will use R1 as their default gateway. However, when a hardware failure prevents R1 from performing its role, R2 will take over as the default gateway; R2 will respond to ARP requests for the VIP.

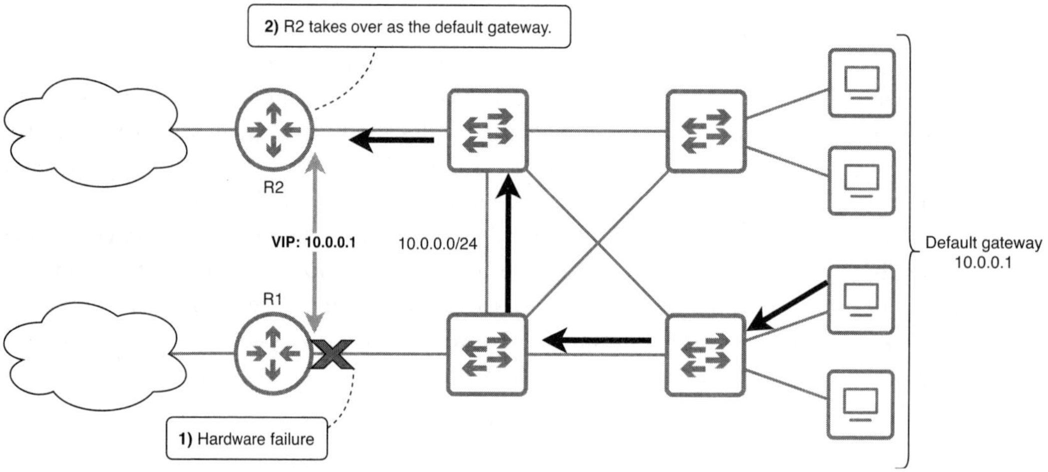

Figure 19.2 After a hardware failure on R1, R2 takes over as the default gateway. R1 and R2 share a virtual IP (VIP) address, which hosts in the LAN use as their default gateway. The hosts are unaware of the change from R1 to R2.

A set of routers configured to use an FHRP is called a *group*. A single router can be part of multiple FHRP groups. This comes in handy when a LAN has multiple subnets, as each subnet can have its own FHRP group—its own redundant default gateway IP address.

19.1.2 FHRP neighbor relationships

To coordinate with each other, routers using an FHRP communicate via multicast *hello* messages. Routers send hello messages at regular intervals, and these messages are used both for establishing FHRP neighbor relationships and for maintaining those relationships. If a router stops receiving hello messages from a neighbor, it will assume that the neighbor has gone down and will act accordingly (e.g., by taking over the role of default gateway). This mechanism is similar to OSPF's mechanism for establishing and maintaining neighbor relationships that we covered in chapter 18.

NOTE The exact multicast address to which hello messages are sent depends on the FHRP. We will cover such details in section 19.2.

As mentioned in chapter 18, multicast messages are flooded by switches, so all hosts in the LAN receive them. However, only routers running the FHRP are interested in the contents of the messages; other hosts simply ignore them. On the other hand, when a device receives a broadcast message, it has to de-encapsulate it and use up processing power to determine if the message is relevant. This is why FHRPs (and dynamic routing protocols) send multicast messages, rather than broadcast; they take up fewer resources on hosts that are not interested in the contents of those messages. Figure 19.3 shows how routers use hello messages to establish and maintain their FHRP neighbor relationship and also introduces a few new concepts.

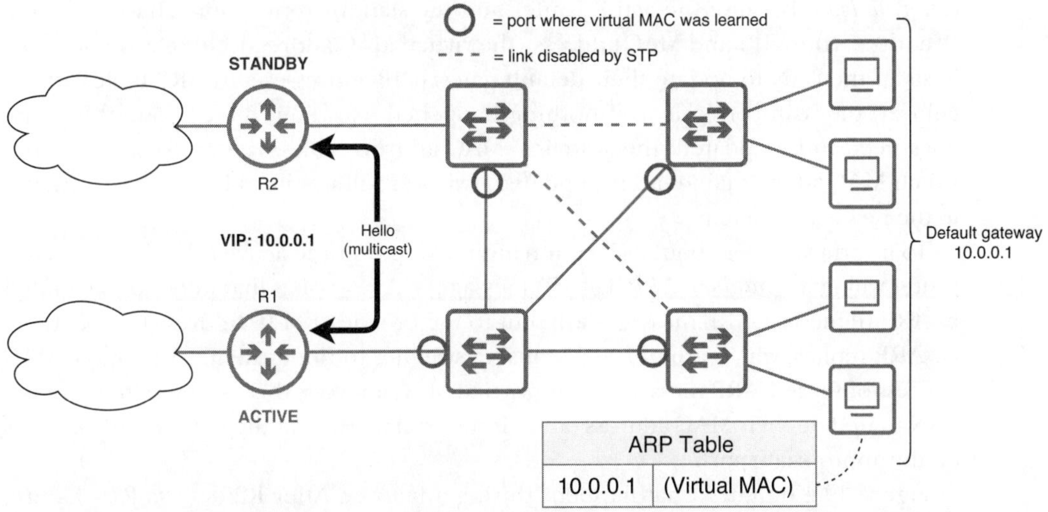

Figure 19.3 R1 and R2 communicate with multicast hello messages to establish and maintain their FHRP neighbor relationship. R1 becomes the active router, and R2, the standby. When a host sends an ARP request to the VIP, R1 will reply with the virtual MAC address, allowing the host to create an appropriate ARP table entry. Switches will also learn the virtual MAC address on the appropriate port.

Through their hello messages, the routers elect an active router and a standby router. As the names suggest, the *active* router serves as the default gateway, while the *standby* router is ready to take over if the active router fails. Note that the terms *active* and *standby* are used by HSRP; other FHRPs use different terms that we will cover in section 19.2.

In addition to sharing a VIP, the active and standby routers also share a *virtual MAC address*. When a host sends an ARP request to the VIP, the active router will reply with the virtual MAC address—not the MAC of its own interface. This results in two actions:

- The host that receives the ARP reply will create an ARP table entry mapping the VIP to the virtual MAC address. To send packets to external destinations, the host will encapsulate the packets in frames destined for the virtual MAC address.
- Switches will learn the virtual MAC address on the appropriate port—the port leading toward the current active router.

NOTE Each FHRP uses a different format for the virtual MAC address. We will cover the virtual MAC address formats in section 19.2.

19.1.3 Failover

The process of the active router failing and the standby router taking over its role is called *failover*. Because the active router and the standby router both share the same IP address (the VIP) and MAC address (the virtual MAC address), there is no need for hosts in the LAN to update their default gateway IP addresses and ARP tables after a failover; they can continue as if nothing happened. However, there is one thing that does need to be updated: the switches' MAC address tables. If a failover occurs but switch MAC address tables aren't updated, switches will not be able to forward frames to the new active router.

To inform switches about its location after taking over the active role, the new active router will send *gratuitous ARP* (GARP) messages—ARP replies that were not prompted by ARP requests. GARP messages are sent to the broadcast MAC address (unlike regular ARP replies, which are unicast), causing switches to flood them. The source MAC address of these GARP messages is the virtual MAC address; this causes switches in the LAN to update their MAC address tables if necessary, learning the virtual MAC address on the appropriate port.

Figure 19.4 outlines what happens during a failover. After R2 detects R1's failure, it takes over as the active router and sends GARP messages, allowing the switches to re-learn the virtual MAC address on the appropriate port (if necessary—not all switches need to update their MAC address table entry for the virtual MAC). This process is transparent to the end hosts; their default gateway remains 10.0.0.1 (the VIP), and 10.0.0.1 is still mapped to the same virtual MAC address in their ARP tables.

After R1 recovers from its hardware failure—perhaps a faulty power supply is replaced—there are two things that can happen: R1 can reclaim its role as the active router, or it can become the new standby router. If a router (R1) takes over the role of the current operational active router (R2), it is called *preemption*—the same term is used with regard to OSPF's designated router (DR) and backup designated router (BDR) elections, as covered in chapter 18.

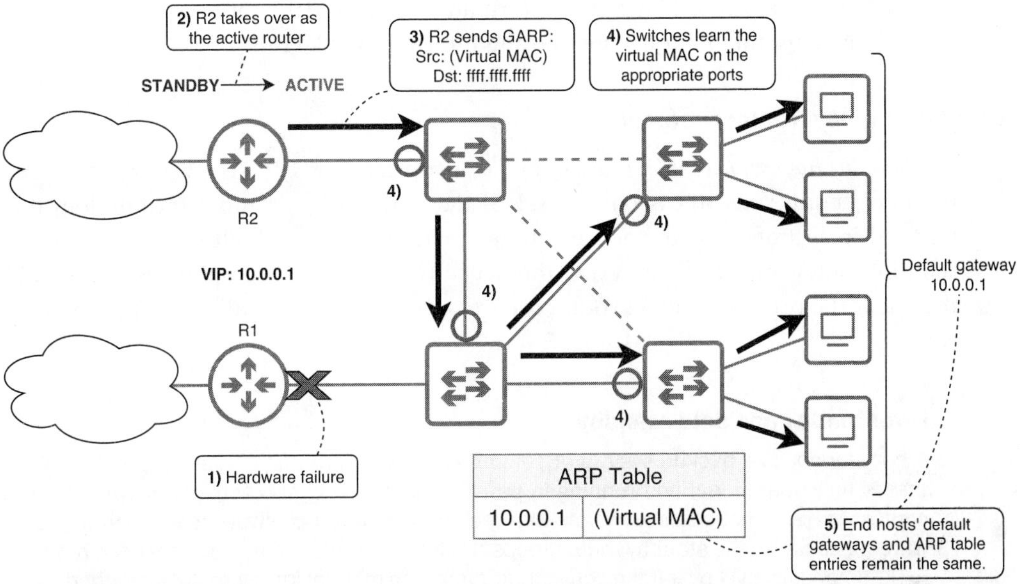

Figure 19.4 An FHRP failover. (1) A hardware failure occurs on R1. (2) R2 takes over as the active router. (3) R2 sends GARP messages, sourced from the virtual MAC and destined for the broadcast MAC. (4) The switches learn the virtual MAC on the appropriate ports—those leading toward the new active router. (5) End hosts' default gateways and ARP table entries for the VIP remain the same.

19.2 Comparing FHRPs

Cisco routers support three different FHRPs, each with its own characteristics: Hot Standby Router Protocol (HSRP), Virtual Router Redundancy Protocol (VRRP), and Gateway Load Balancing Protocol (GLBP). For the purpose of the CCNA exam, you should understand the basic characteristics of each. Table 19.1 lists some essential characteristics of each FHRP that we will cover in this section.

Table 19.1 FHRP characteristics

	HSRP	VRRP	GLBP
Terminology	Active/Standby	Master/Backup	AVG/AVF
Multicast IP	v1: 224.0.0.2 v2: 224.0.0.102	224.0.0.18	224.0.0.102
Virtual MAC format	v1: 0000.0c07.acXX v2: 0000.0c9f.fXXX	0000.5e00.01XX	0007.b400.XXYY
Cisco proprietary?	Yes	No	Yes
Load balancing	Per subnet	Per subnet	Per host
Preemption (default)	Disabled	Enabled	AVG: Disabled AVF: Enabled

EXAM TIP You should know the information in table 19.1 for the exam. Flashcards are a useful tool for remembering information like this.

19.2.1 Hot Standby Router Protocol

Hot Standby Router Protocol (HSRP) is a Cisco-proprietary FHRP. As a Cisco-proprietary protocol, it only runs on Cisco routers. HSRP uses the active/standby terminology that we used in section 19.1; the active router functions as the default gateway, while the standby router waits to take over if the active router fails. Preemption is disabled by default; if the previously active router recovers from a failure, it will not retake its active role.

> **Hot standby and cold standby**
>
> A *hot standby* is a backup system (it could be a server, a router, or some other device) that is fully operational and running in parallel with the primary (active) system. In the context of HSRP, *hot standby* means that the standby router is always ready to start forwarding packets. The standby router keeps track of the status of the active router, ready to automatically take over if the active router fails—no manual intervention is required.
>
> A *cold standby* is a backup system that is not operational under normal circumstances. If the primary system fails, the backup system may need to be started up, configured, cabled, etc. An example of a cold standby router is a spare router kept in storage. Should the active router fail, the standby router is retrieved from storage and used to replace the failed active router. Clearly, this approach is less desirable than using an FHRP like HSRP, which ensures continuous network availability and a smooth transition from active to standby.

There are two versions of HSRP: version 1 and version 2. The two versions are largely similar, but there are some key differences that you should be aware of. HSRPv1 hello messages are sent to multicast IP address 224.0.0.2; this address is not reserved for HSRP but is used to address messages to all routers in the LAN. HSRPv2, on the other hand, uses multicast IP address 224.0.0.102, which is reserved exclusively for HSRPv2 and GLBP (the topic of section 19.2.3).

Another difference is the format of the virtual MAC address. HSRPv1 uses the format 0000.0c07.acXX, where XX is the HSRP group number. For example, HSRPv1 group 1 will use virtual MAC address 0000.0c07.ac01, and HSRPv1 group 15 will use 0000.0c07.ac0f (as covered in chapter 6, 0d15 is equivalent to 0xf). HSRPv2 uses the format 0000.0c9f.fXXX. Using the same examples as previously, HSRPv2 group 1 will use virtual MAC address 0000.0c9f.f001, and group 15 will use 0000.0c9f.f00f.

NOTE Because the HSRPv2 virtual MAC format leaves three hex digits to represent the group number, instead of HSRPv1's two hex digits, HSRPv2 supports more groups. In total, HSRPv1 supports 256 groups (0–255), and HSRPv2 supports 4,096 (0–4,095).

As mentioned in section 19.1.1, a single router can be part of multiple FHRP groups. When there are multiple subnets in a LAN, there should be one HSRP group per subnet. Instead of one router being active in all subnets, you can configure one router to be active in half of the subnets and the other to be active in the remaining subnets. This achieves load balancing, avoiding congestion on any single link in the network.

Figure 19.5 shows an example of load balancing with HSRP. There are two subnets in the LAN: subnet 1 (10.0.0.0/24) and subnet 2 (10.0.1.0/24). R1 is the active router in subnet 1 and the standby router in subnet 2, and vice versa. As a result, hosts in subnet 1 will use R1 as their default gateway (unless it fails), and hosts in subnet 2 will use R2 as their default gateway.

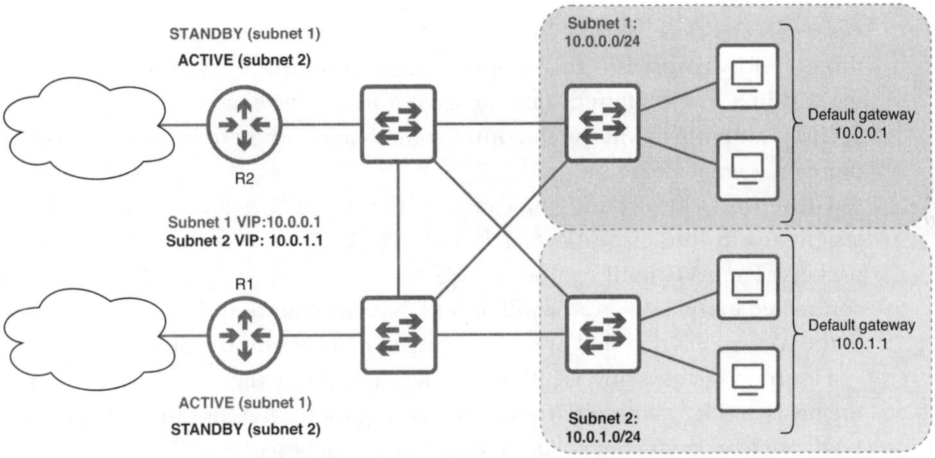

Figure 19.5 HSRP load balancing. R1 is the active router in subnet 1 and the standby router in subnet 2. R2 is the standby router in subnet 1 and the active router in subnet 2.

One final major difference between versions 1 and 2 is that HSRPv2 adds support for IPv6, whereas HSRPv1 only supports IPv4. So far in this book, we have only covered IPv4, but we will begin looking at IPv6 in chapter 20.

19.2.2 Virtual Router Redundancy Protocol

Virtual Router Redundancy Protocol (VRRP) is the Internet Engineering Task Force's industry-standard answer to HSRP. At a high level, HSRP and VRRP are nearly identical. However, you should know the differences between them for the CCNA exam. One difference is terminology; instead of HSRP's active and standby routers, VRRP calls them *master* and *backup* routers. Furthermore, although HSRP preemption is disabled by default, VRRP preemption is enabled by default.

VRRP's multicast IP and virtual MAC addresses are also different. VRRP routers send hello messages to multicast IP address 224.0.0.18—a reserved address that only VRRP-enabled routers use. The VRRP virtual MAC address format is 0000.5e00.01XX, where XX is the VRRP group number. For example, VRRP group 12 will use the virtual MAC address 0000.5e00.010c.

Perhaps the most significant difference between HSRP and VRRP is that VRRP is an industry-standard protocol, and therefore any vendor is free to implement it on its devices. If a Cisco router and a Juniper router must cooperate to provide a redundant default gateway for a LAN, they must use VRRP; the Juniper router can't run HSRP.

Like HSRP, VRRP can provide load balancing on a per-subnet basis. This can be achieved by configuring one router to be the master router in half of the subnets and the other router to be the master router in the remaining subnets. However, neither HSRP nor VRRP can efficiently achieve load balancing within a single subnet. To achieve that, you'll have to use the next FHRP: GLBP.

19.2.3 Gateway Load Balancing Protocol

Gateway Load Balancing Protocol (GLBP) is another Cisco-proprietary FHRP. Of the three FHRPs covered in this chapter, GLBP is unique in that it enables load balancing within a single subnet; some hosts in a subnet will use one router as their default gateway, and others will use the other router (assuming two routers); load balancing is done on a *per-host* basis.

GLBP works by electing one router as the *Active Virtual Gateway* (AVG), which then assigns up to four *Active Virtual Forwarders* (AVF)—the routers that actively forward packets. The AVG itself can be an AVF too. That means that if there are four routers connected to the LAN, traffic will be load-balanced among all four routers. Preemption of the AVG role is disabled by default, but AVF preemption is enabled by default.

Figure 19.6 shows how GLBP works. R1, the AVG, assigns itself as the AVF for half of the hosts and R2 as the AVF for the remaining half. There is only a single subnet in the LAN, but load balancing is achieved on a per-host basis.

Although there is only a single VIP (10.0.0.1), load balancing is achieved by assigning each AVF a unique virtual MAC address. The AVG is responsible for answering ARP requests, but instead of replying with its own MAC address, it replies with the virtual MAC of one of the AVFs, in a round-robin manner. As a result, in a LAN with two AVFs, half of the hosts in the LAN will address frames to one AVF's virtual MAC and the other half to the other AVF's virtual MAC.

DEFINITION *Round-robin* is a simple method for distributing tasks evenly in a cyclical manner. In the context of GLBP, if there are two AVFs, the AVG will reply with the virtual MAC of AVF 1, then AVF 2, then AVF 1, etc.

Like HSRPv2, GLBP sends hello messages to the reserved multicast IP address 224.0.0.102. The GLBP virtual MAC address format is 0007.b400.XXYY, where XX is the GLBP group number and YY is the AVF number. For example, AVF 1 in group 1 will use virtual MAC 0007.b400.0101, and AVF 2 in group 11 will use virtual MAC 0007.b400.0b02.

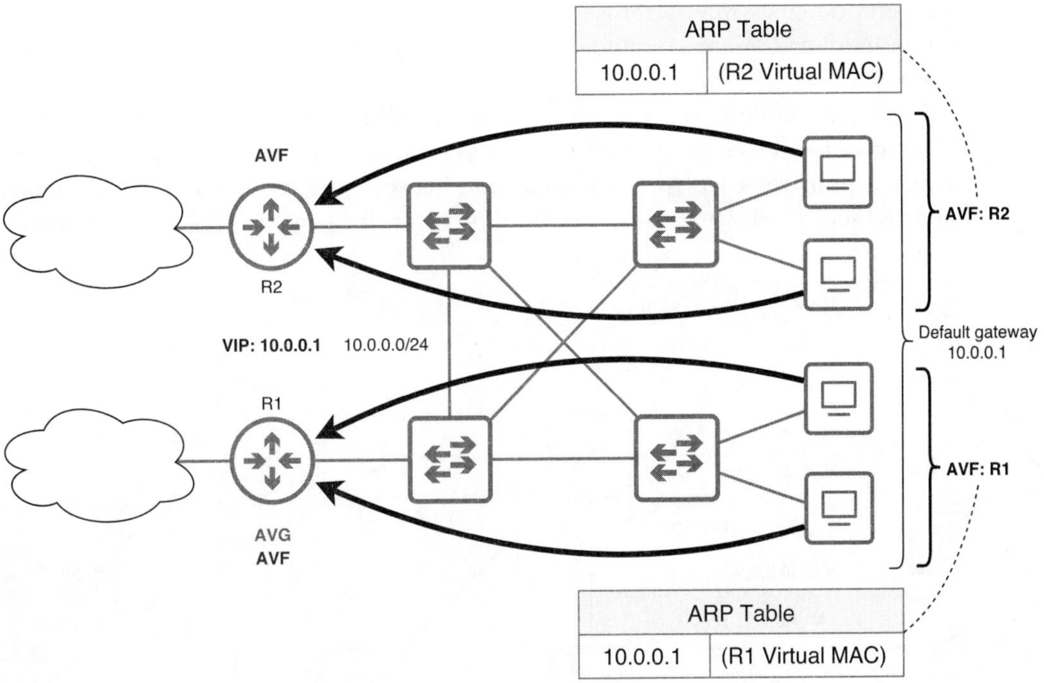

Figure 19.6 GLBP enables load balancing among hosts in the same subnet. Half of the hosts in 10.0.0.0/24 use one AVF (R1) as their default gateway, and the other half use the other AVF (R2). Each AVF has a unique virtual MAC address.

19.3 Basic HSRP configuration

CCNA exam topic 3.5 uses the verb *describe*, not *configure* (i.e., Describe the purpose, functions, and concepts of first hop redundancy protocols). However, Cisco exams can occasionally be liberal in their interpretation of the exam topics. HSRP is the most commonly used FHRP on Cisco routers, and its basic configuration is worth knowing for the CCNA exam. Furthermore, getting a bit of hands-on practice configuring HSRP in a lab can help you understand the concepts that you have studied. For those reasons, in this section, we'll briefly cover how to configure HSRP.

Before we delve into how to configure HSRP, let's first consider why you would want to implement it in the first place. Think back to figure 19.1, where hosts were sending packets to a router that was down due to a hardware failure, despite there being another functional router connected to the LAN. The result of such a failure is that end users lose connectivity to destinations outside of the LAN: they can't access files on corporate servers, can't access the internet, can't join an important call with a client, etc.

In modern enterprises, the inability to access crucial resources over the network often means an inability to perform required tasks—it's more than a simple inconvenience. Although hardware failures are rare, they are almost inevitable over the lifespan of a network. That's where HSRP comes into play. To minimize the disruption caused by router hardware failures, redundant routers should be configured with an FHRP, such as HSRP.

Figure 19.7 shows how to configure HSRP on two Cisco routers: R1 and R2. Note that although R1 and R2 share the VIP, each router still requires its own unique IP address, which is primarily used for communication between the two routers. For example, when R1 sends HSRP hello messages, it sources them from its own IP address (10.0.0.2).

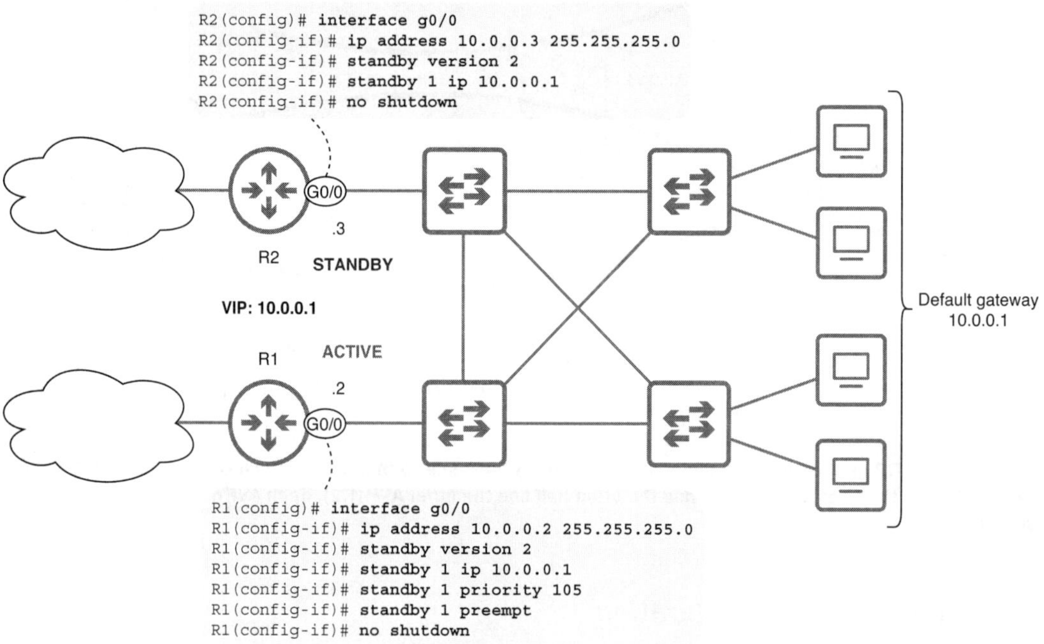

Figure 19.7 An HSRPv2 group of two routers. R1 is the active router, and R2 is the standby. If R1 fails, R2 will become the active router. However, because preemption is enabled on R1, it will retake its role after it recovers from the failure.

Let's examine those configurations, specifically the HSRP configurations—you should be familiar with configuring an interface's IP address and enabling it with `no shutdown` by now. The following example shows how to configure R1, the active router of the HSRP group:

```
R1(config)# interface g0/0
R1(config-if)# ip address 10.0.0.2 255.255.255.0
R1(config-if)# standby version 2           ← Enables HSRP version 2
R1(config-if)# standby 1 ip 10.0.0.1       ← Configures the VIP for HSRP group 1
R1(config-if)# standby 1 priority 105      ← Increases R1's priority value
R1(config-if)# standby 1 preempt           ← Enables preemption
R1(config-if)# no shutdown
```

The first HSRP command is **`standby version 2`**. As you probably guessed, this command enables HSRP version 2. If you enable HSRPv2 on one router, you must enable it on the other router; HSRPv1 and HSRPv2 aren't compatible.

The second command is **`standby`** *`group`* **`ip`** *`vip`*, used to configure the VIP. When configuring an HSRP group, it is important that both of these parameters—the group number and the VIP—match on both routers. If either of these don't match, the routers won't be able to work together to function as a redundant default gateway.

The third command is **`standby`** *`group`* **`priority`** *`priority`*. This command is used to influence which router becomes active and which becomes standby. The HSRP active router is determined in the following manner:

1. The router with the highest priority
2. The router with the highest IP address

In this example, R1 G0/0's IP address is 10.0.0.2, and R2 G0/0's is 10.0.0.3. As a result, if both routers use the default HSRP priority (100), R2 will become the active router; it has a higher IP address. To ensure that R1 becomes the active router, I used the command **`standby 1 priority 105`**, raising R1's priority above R2's.

Finally, I enabled preemption—which is disabled by default—with the command **`standby 1 preempt`**. Preemption determines what happens when a higher-priority router comes back online after a failure. Enabling preemption ensures that R1 is the active router as long as it is up and running. If R1 were to fail, leading to R2 taking over as the active router, R1 would take over the active role again after recovering from the failure.

The following example shows R2's configurations, highlighting the HSRP-related commands. Two commands that I used on R1 are missing: I didn't configure R2's priority, and I didn't enable preemption. By increasing R1's priority to 105, I ensured that it becomes the active router; there is no need to modify R2's priority. And preemption only needs to be configured on the higher-priority router that retakes its role after a failure; the command is not necessary on the lower-priority router (although it would do no harm to configure it anyway):

```
R2(config)# interface g0/0
R2(config-if)# ip address 10.0.0.3 255.255.255.0
R2(config-if)# standby version 2                  <-- Enables HSRP version 2
R2(config-if)# standby 1 ip 10.0.0.1              <-- Configures the VIP for HSRP group 1
R2(config-if)# no shutdown
```

> **NOTE** The commands we have covered here can also be used to configure VRRP and GLBP, replacing **`standby`** with **`vrrp`** or **`glbp`** (except **`standby version 2`**). However, I wouldn't expect any questions about VRRP or GLBP configuration on the exam.

After configuring HSRP, you can use **`show standby brief`** to verify its operation. In the following example, I use the command on R1:

```
R1# show standby brief
                     P indicates configured to preempt.
                     |
Interface   Grp  Pri P State   Active          Standby         Virtual IP
Gi0/0       1    105 P Active  local           10.0.0.3        10.0.0.1
```

The `State` of `Active` indicates that R1 is the active router. This is confirmed by the value of `local` in the `Active` column. The `Standby` column states `10.0.0.3`—R3's IP address. For comparison, in the following example, I use the same command on R2:

```
R2# show standby brief
                     P indicates configured to preempt.
                     |
Interface   Grp  Pri P State   Active          Standby         Virtual IP
Gi0/0       1    100   Standby 10.0.0.2        local           10.0.0.1
```

This time, the `State` is `Standby`, which is confirmed by the value of `local` in the `Standby` column. The `Active` column states `10.0.0.2`—R1's IP address. For more detailed information about HSRP, you can remove the **`brief`** keyword; the following example shows the output of **`show standby`** on R1, pointing out some additional information not shown in the output of the previous command:

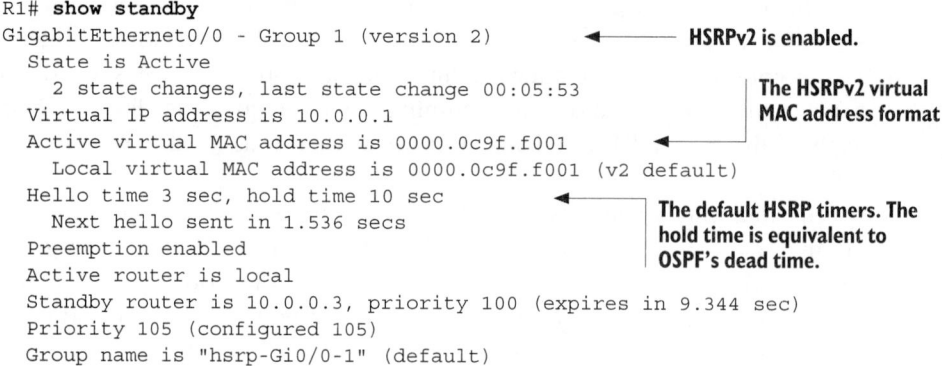

```
R1# show standby
GigabitEthernet0/0 - Group 1 (version 2)
  State is Active
    2 state changes, last state change 00:05:53
  Virtual IP address is 10.0.0.1
  Active virtual MAC address is 0000.0c9f.f001
    Local virtual MAC address is 0000.0c9f.f001 (v2 default)
  Hello time 3 sec, hold time 10 sec
    Next hello sent in 1.536 secs
  Preemption enabled
  Active router is local
  Standby router is 10.0.0.3, priority 100 (expires in 9.344 sec)
  Priority 105 (configured 105)
  Group name is "hsrp-Gi0/0-1" (default)
```

HSRPv2 is enabled. (GigabitEthernet0/0 - Group 1 (version 2))

The HSRPv2 virtual MAC address format (Active virtual MAC address is 0000.0c9f.f001)

The default HSRP timers. The hold time is equivalent to OSPF's dead time. (Hello time 3 sec, hold time 10 sec)

Summary

- *First hop redundancy protocol* (FHRP) is a category of protocol that allows multiple routers to work together to provide a redundant default gateway for hosts in a LAN.
- The active router actively forwards packets between hosts in the LAN and external destinations. The standby router is ready to take over if the active router fails.
- Routers using an FHRP share a *virtual IP* (VIP) address, which is configured as the default gateway of hosts in the LAN. They also share a virtual MAC address.
- The active router uses the virtual MAC when replying to ARP requests sent to the VIP. When hosts send packets to external destinations, the frames encapsulating the packets will be sent to the active router.

- Routers using an FHRP communicate via multicast hello messages, which are sent at regular intervals. Hello messages are used to establish and maintain neighbor relationships.
- When the active router fails and the standby router takes over the active role, it is called a *failover*.
- After a failover, the new active router sends *gratuitous ARP* (GARP) messages—ARP replies that were not prompted by ARP requests.
- GARP messages are addressed to the broadcast MAC address (ffff.ffff.ffff) in order to update switches' MAC address tables.
- Because the VIP and virtual MAC addresses remain the same, FHRP failovers are transparent to end hosts; the end hosts are not aware that a failover has occurred.
- Cisco routers support three FHRPs: HSRP, VRRP, and GLBP.
- *Hot Standby Router Protocol* (HSRP) is a Cisco-proprietary FHRP with two versions: HSRPv1 and HSRPv2.
- *Preemption* is an FHRP feature that allows a higher-priority router to take over as the active router, even if there is another active router present.
- HSRP elects one *active* router, and other routers become *standby* routers. HSRP preemption is disabled by default.
- HSRPv1 uses the multicast IP address 224.0.0.2, and HSRPv2 uses 224.0.0.102.
- The HSRPv1 virtual MAC address format is 0000.0c07.acXX, where XX is the HSRP group number. The HSRPv2 format is 0000.0c09.fXXX, where XXX is the group.
- HSRPv2 adds IPv6 support, whereas HSRPv1 only supports IPv4.
- HSRP supports per-subnet load balancing by configuring a different active router for different subnets.
- *Virtual Router Redundancy Protocol* (VRRP) is an industry-standard FHRP, which can be implemented on any vendor's routers.
- VRRP elects one *master* router, and other routers become *backup* routers. Unlike HSRP, preemption is enabled by default.
- VRRP uses the multicast IP address 224.0.0.18.
- The VRRP virtual MAC address format is 0000.5e00.01XX, where XX is the VRRP group number.
- Like HSRP, VRRP supports per-subnet load balancing.
- *Gateway Load Balancing Protocol* (GLBP) is a Cisco-proprietary FHRP that enables load balancing within a single subnet; load balancing is done on a per-host basis.
- GLBP elects one *Active Virtual Gateway* (AVG), which assigns up to four *Active Virtual Forwarders* (AVF). The AVG itself can be an AVF. AVG preemption is disabled by default, but AVF preemption is enabled.

- Although there is a single VIP, GLBP achieves load balancing by assigning each AVF a unique virtual MAC address. The format is 0007.b400.XXYY, where XX is the group number and YY is the AVF number.
- The AVG replies to ARP requests using the virtual MAC of one of the AVFs in a round-robin manner.
- Although routers using an FHRP share a VIP, each router still needs its own unique IP address. It uses this IP address when communicating with other routers.
- Enable HSRP version 2 with **`standby version 2`** in interface config mode.
- Configure the HSRP VIP with **`standby`** *`group`* **`ip`** *`vip`* in interface config mode.
- Configure the HSRP priority (default 100) with **`standby`** *`group`* **`priority`** *`priority`* in interface config mode.
- Enable HSRP preemption with **`standby`** *`group`* **`preempt`** in interface config mode.
- Use **`show standby brief`** and **`show standby`** to verify HSRP operation.

Part 5

IPv6

For decades, the dominant version of the Internet Protocol has been IPv4. Also for decades, however, another version has been slowly gaining adoption: Internet Protocol version 6 (IPv6), the topic of part 5 of this book. As the pool of available IPv4 addresses has all but dried up in recent years, IPv6 adoption has accelerated, and modern network professionals must be familiar with both IPv4 and IPv6.

Chapter 20 starts with a look at IPv6 addresses. We will explore the concepts of global unicast, unique local, link-local, and multicast addresses in IPv6, as well as how to configure them in Cisco IOS. For CCNA students, who have often just become comfortable with IPv4, IPv6 can seem intimidating. But rest assured that they are actually quite similar, with the most significant differences being the address sizes (32 bits for IPv4 versus 128 bits) and representation (decimal versus hexadecimal).

The similarities between IPv4 and IPv6 will become clear when we cover IPv6 routing in chapter 21, which covers familiar IPv4 concepts from an IPv6 perspective: connected and local routes, static route configuration, default routes, floating static routes, and others. The knowledge and skills you acquire in these two chapters are critical for the CCNA exam, but on top of that, they will be invaluable in your journey as a network professional; IPv6 is the future, and its adoption is consistently growing year after year.

20 IPv6 addressing

This chapter covers

- Why IPv6 is needed
- How to convert between binary, decimal, and hexadecimal number systems
- The structure of IPv6 addresses
- How to configure IPv6 addresses on Cisco routers
- The various IPv6 address types

IPv4, the version of the Internet Protocol that we have focused on up to this point in the book, was developed at a time when no one knew the internet would be as ubiquitous as it is today; the current IPv4 standard was published in 1981. As a result, IPv4 has limitations, the most significant one being insufficient address space; there aren't enough IPv4 addresses available for all of the devices in the world that require network connectivity.

In this chapter, we will cover the next version of the Internet Protocol: IPv6. IPv6 provides several benefits over IPv4, the most significant one being a much larger address space. Although IPv4 is still the dominant version in use today, IPv6 adoption is growing, and the modern network engineer must be familiar with both. Specifically, we will cover the following CCNA exam topics:

- 1.8: Configure and verify IPv6 addressing and prefix
- 1.9: Describe IPv6 address types

What about IPv5?

Given that IPv6 follows IPv4, "What about IPv5?" is a natural question. *Internet Stream Protocol* (ST), a family of experimental protocols designed to work with applications such as real-time video and voice, used version number 5 in the Version field of the IP header. Although ST was never referred to as IPv5, IPv4's successor was named IPv6 to avoid any confusion with ST.

20.1 The need for IPv6

The main reason IPv6 is needed is that there simply aren't enough IPv4 addresses available. IPv4 addresses' 32-bit length allows for 4,294,967,296 (2^{32}) unique IPv4 addresses. However, not all of those addresses are available to assign to hosts. For example, the class D range is reserved for multicast addresses, and the class E range is reserved for experimental purposes and research.

Even with all of the reserved addresses removed, there are still billions of IPv4 addresses available for hosts. However, in our era of unprecedented connectivity, even those billions of addresses are not enough. We're running out of IPv4 addresses and have been for a long time; this problem is called *IPv4 address exhaustion.* The problem is exacerbated by inefficient use of the available address space, but even with the most efficient use, it would only be a matter of time before we run out of IPv4 addresses.

IP address assignments are controlled by an organization called the *Internet Assigned Numbers Authority* (IANA). IANA distributes IP address space to various *Regional Internet Registries* (RIR), which then assign addresses to organizations (such as Internet Service Providers) as needed. Figure 20.1 shows the five RIRs and the regions they serve.

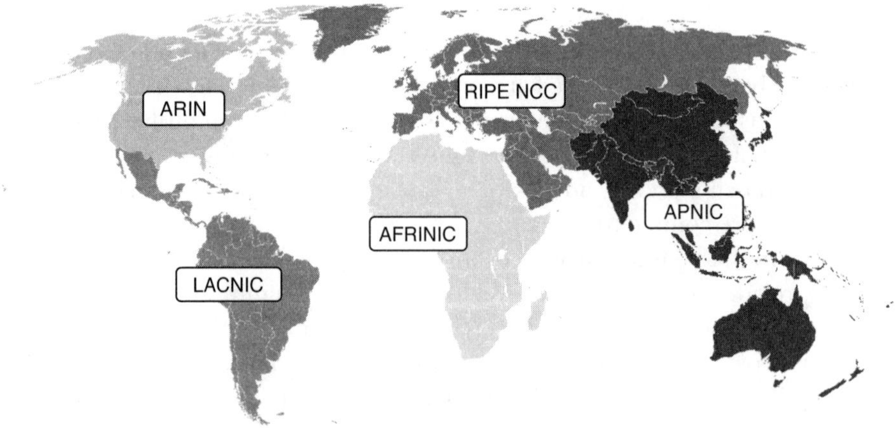

Figure 20.1 The five RIRs. AFRINIC serves Africa. APNIC serves the Asia-Pacific region. ARIN serves Canada, the United States, parts of the Caribbean, and Antarctica. LACNIC serves most of the Caribbean and all of Latin America. RIPE NCC serves Europe, West Asia, Central Asia, and Russia.

Unfortunately, the RIRs are running out of IPv4 addresses. For example, ARIN announced exhaustion of its IPv4 address pool in 2015, RIPE NCC announced the same in 2019, and LACNIC in 2020.

In addition to subnetting with CIDR (as we covered in chapter 11), which allows for more efficient use of the IPv4 address space, two particular technologies—*private IPv4 addresses* and *network address translation* (NAT)—have been instrumental in extending the lifespan of IPv4. We will cover private IPv4 addresses and NAT in chapter 9 of volume 2, but in this chapter, we'll focus on the long-term solution to IPv4 address exhaustion: IPv6.

IPv6 addresses are four times the size of IPv4 addresses: 128 bits. With that information, you might assume that IPv6 provides four times as many addresses as IPv4, but that is not the case; each additional bit doubles the number of addresses. Let's compare the number of IPv4 and IPv6 addresses:

- 4,294,967,296 (2^{32}) IPv4 addresses
- 340,282,366,920,938,463,463,374,607,431,768,211,456 (2^{128}) IPv6 addresses

The number of grains of sand on Earth is estimated to be between 10^{20} to 10^{24}, so the number of IPv6 addresses is between 340 trillion and 3.4 quintillion times larger than the estimated number of grains of sand on Earth. This enormous number ensures that the IPv6 address space is more than sufficient to accommodate the current and foreseeable future needs of the growing internet.

Although there are various differences between IPv4 and IPv6 (the size and format of their addresses being just one of them), their general purpose is the same. Just like IPv4, IPv6 encapsulates Layer 4 segments (i.e., TCP or UDP) with a header to make packets, providing end-to-end addressing from a message's source host to its destination host. Likewise, an IPv6 packet is encapsulated in an Ethernet frame at each hop in the path to its final destination, just like an IPv4 packet.

IPv6 adoption

Google keeps track of the percentage of users that access Google over IPv6 at https://www.google.com/intl/en/ipv6/statistics.html. At the time of writing, it is nearly 45%—a major increase from roughly 1% just a decade ago.

20.2 Hexadecimal

Whereas IPv4 addresses are written in dotted-decimal notation, IPv6 addresses are written in hexadecimal. Before we cover the details of how IPv6 addresses are written in section 20.3, let's review hexadecimal notation and look at how to convert between decimal, binary, and hexadecimal.

As we covered in chapter 6, the hexadecimal number system uses the same 10 digits as the decimal number system (0–9), and the first 6 letters of the alphabet (A–F)—a total of 16 digits. In effect, this means that a single hexadecimal digit contains four bits of information because $2^4 = 16$. Table 20.1 demonstrates this: 0b0000–0b1111 can be represented by 0x0–0xF (the equivalent decimal values are included for reference).

Table 20.1 Decimal, binary, and hexadecimal numbers

Decimal	Binary	Hex.	Decimal	Binary	Hex.
0	0000	0	8	1000	8
1	0001	1	9	1001	9
2	0010	2	10	1010	A
3	0011	3	11	1011	B
4	0100	4	12	1100	C
5	0101	5	13	1101	D
6	0110	6	14	1110	E
7	0111	7	15	1111	F

NOTE A group of four bits (a half-byte) is also called a *nibble.*

IPv6 addresses are split into groups of four hexadecimal characters (16 bits) when written (a string of 128 bits is not very human-readable), so let's practice converting 16-bit values between binary and hexadecimal. This skill is necessary for mastering IPv6, just as converting 8-bit values between binary and decimal is necessary for IPv4.

Converting from binary to hexadecimal can be done with a three-step process. To demonstrate, let's convert 0b1101101100101111 to hexadecimal:

1. Split the number into four-bit groups: 1101, 1011, 0010, 1111.
2. Convert each four-bit group into decimal: 13, 11, 2, 15.
3. Convert each decimal number into hexadecimal: D, B, 2, F.

NOTE Memorizing the decimal values of hexadecimal A–F is very helpful: 0d10 = 0xA, 0d11 = 0xB, 0d12 = 0xC, 0d13 = 0xD, 0d14 = 0xE, 0d15 = 0xF.

We now have the answer: 0b1101101100101111 is equivalent to 0xDB2F. As you can see, hexadecimal is much more compact than binary; the same value can be expressed with one quarter the number of digits.

To convert from hexadecimal to binary, you can use a similar process. Let's do that with the number 0x41AE:

1. Split up the hexadecimal digits: 4, 1, A, E.
2. Convert each hexadecimal digit to decimal: 4, 1, 10, 14.
3. Convert each decimal digit to binary: 0100, 0001, 1010, 1110.

That's the answer: 0x41AE is equivalent to 0b0100000110101110. For further practice, write some random 16-bit numbers in binary and convert them to hexadecimal. Then, do the same in the opposite direction: write some random four-digit hexadecimal numbers and convert them to binary. You can check your answers with a free converter online: try a Google search for "binary to hexadecimal converter."

> **NOTE** Make sure you can do these conversions confidently before moving on. For some fun practice converting 1-byte numbers, which follows the same process we just covered, you can try the game "Flippy Bit And the Attack of the Hexadecimals from Base 16" at https://mng.bz/PZRv. A browser game, Android app, and iOS app are available.

20.3 IPv6 addressing

Now that you're comfortable converting between binary and hexadecimal, let's move on to IPv6 addressing. IPv6 addresses can be intimidating to many students at first, primarily because they are quite large and because they are written in hexadecimal, rather than decimal. However, there is no need to be afraid of IPv6; after the initial period of unfamiliarity, you'll grow to love it! I, for one, welcome our new IPv6 overlords. Both IPv4 and IPv6 are just binary represented in two different ways: dotted decimal versus hexadecimal.

20.3.1 IPv6 header

Before looking at IPv6 addresses themselves, let's take a brief look at the header that they are part of. As with the IPv4 header, don't expect any questions about the specifics of the IPv6 header on the CCNA exam. However, a basic understanding of the header provides valuable context for understanding IPv6 as a whole. Figure 20.2 shows the format of the IPv6 header.

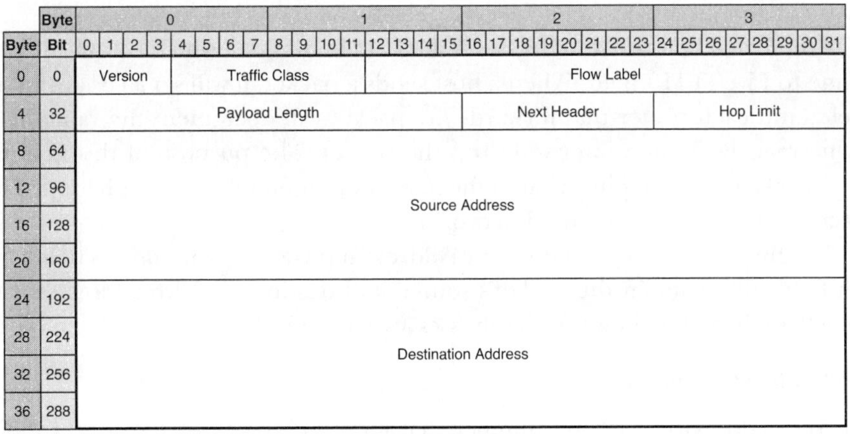

Figure 20.2 The format of the IPv6 header. The fields are Version, Traffic Class, Flow Label, Payload Length, Next Header, Hop Limit, Source Address, and Destination Address. The header is 40 bytes in size.

Just like the IPv4 header, the first field of the IPv6 header is the Version field. This field is four bits in length and is always set to 0b0110 (0d6) to indicate IPv6. The next field is the Traffic Class field, an 8-bit field that is used for Quality of Service (QoS)—the topic of chapter 10 of volume 2. This field is split up into two parts: the 6-bit Differentiated Services Code Point (DSCP) and the 2-bit Explicit Congestion Notification (ECN)—just like in the IPv4 header. We'll cover how this field is used in chapter 10 of volume 2.

Next is a 20-bit field called *Flow Label.* This field is, as the name suggests, used to label flows; a *flow* is a sequence of packets sent from a particular source to a particular destination (i.e., a TCP session between two hosts). The potential uses of this field are beyond the scope of the CCNA exam, but it can also play a role in QoS.

The fourth field is Payload Length, a 16-bit field that is used to indicate the length of the packet's encapsulated payload (i.e., the encapsulated TCP or UDP segment). Whereas the IPv4 header is variable in length (20–60 bytes), the IPv6 uses a fixed 40-byte header. As a result, whereas IPv4 uses two separate length fields—*Internet Header Length* to indicate the header's length and *Total Length* to indicate the entire packet's length—IPv6 only requires a single length field, indicating the size of the payload.

The next field of the IPv6 header is Next Header, which indicates the type of message encapsulated in the packet; this is equivalent to IPv4's Protocol field. For example, a value of 6 in this field indicates that a TCP segment is encapsulated inside. Following are some common values you can expect in the IPv6 Next Header and IPv4 Protocol fields:

- 1: ICMP
- 6: TCP
- 17: UDP
- 58: ICMPv6 (ICMP for IPv6)
- 88: EIGRP
- 89: OSPF

The final field before the addresses is the Hop Limit field, which is equivalent to IPv4's Time to Live (TTL) field. When a host sends a packet, it will set a certain value in this field, and each router that forwards the packet will decrement the value by 1. If the value reaches 0, the router will drop the packet. The purpose of this field is to prevent packets from looping around the network indefinitely (although loops should not occur in a properly configured network).

The final two fields are the Source Address and Destination Address fields—two 128-bit fields that contain the packet's source and destination IPv6 addresses. In section 20.3.2, we'll explore how these addresses are structured.

20.3.2 IPv6 address structure

An IPv6 address is a 128-bit number that identifies a host at Layer 3 of the TCP/IP model. As the following example shows, a string of 128 bits is not very human-readable:

00100000000000010000110110111000010110010001011111101010101111010110010101100010000101111110101011001001001011010101100110111101

IPv4 addresses are divided into four groups of 8 bits and written in dotted decimal to make them more human-readable. For demonstration purposes, here's what the previous IPv6 address would look like written in dotted decimal:

32.1.13.184.89.23.234.189.101.98.23.234.201.45.89.189

Although the dotted-decimal address is more manageable than the binary address, it's still quite long. To allow the same address to be written in even fewer digits, IPv6 addresses are divided into eight groups of 16 bits, separated by colons, and written in hexadecimal. That same IPv6 looks like this when written in hexadecimal:

2001:0db8:5917:eabd:6562:17ea:c92d:59bd

NOTE Hexadecimal can be written using uppercase or lowercase letters (A–F or a–f). However, IPv6 addresses should be written using lowercase letters—more on this later.

There is no official or standard term for each group of 16 bits in an IPv6 address. I previously preferred *quartet* because each group results in four hexadecimal digits. Another common term is *hextet*, although the term implies 6 bits, not 16 bits; the precise term is *hexadectet*. However, *hextet* is more common—probably because it's easier to pronounce. Although it is an informal term, I will use *hextet* as a convenient way to refer to each group of 16 bits in an IPv6 address.

Figure 20.3 shows the previous IPv6 address along with the binary of each hextet. It also introduces the IPv6 prefix length, which is always written with slash notation (/64)—no more dotted-decimal netmasks!

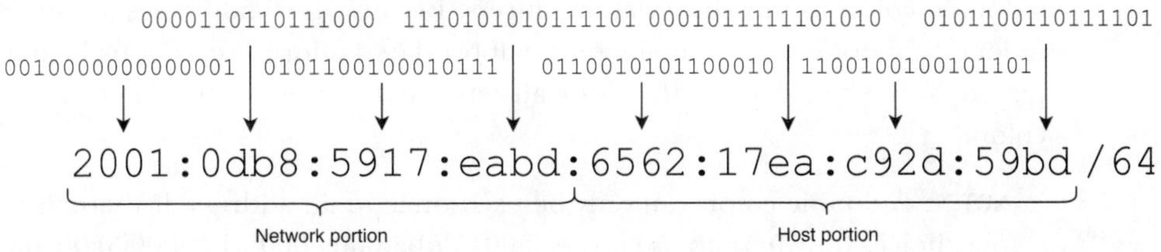

Figure 20.3 An IPv6 address written in hexadecimal and binary. The prefix length is /64, meaning that the first half (64 bits) of the address is the network portion, and the second half (64 bits) is the host portion.

NOTE IPv6 typically uses /64 prefix lengths. Although this is extremely inefficient—each subnet contains about 18 quintillion addresses—the IPv6 address space is so large that /64 prefix lengths are preferred due to their simplicity.

20.3.3 Abbreviating IPv6 addresses

Although hexadecimal notation makes IPv6 addresses much more manageable than a simple string of 128 bits, it still results in 32 digits—much longer than an IPv4 addess, which is 4–12 digits in dotted decimal. Fortunately, IPv6 provides two methods for abbreviating addresses, which can significantly reduce their length and complexity:

- Removing leading zeros
- Omitting consecutive all-zero hextets

Leading zeros—any hexadecimal 0 digits on the left side of a hextet—can be removed to shorten the hextet. Here is an example:

- *Original address*—2001:**0**db8:**000**0:**00**1b:20a1:**00**20:**00**80:34bd
- *Abbreviated address*—2001:db8:0:1b:20a1:20:80:34bd

In the abbreviated address, I removed leading zeros from five hextets. Note that the 0020 and 0080 hextets were abbreviated to 20 and 80, respectively. *Trailing zeros*—those on the right side of a hextet—cannot be removed. Furthermore, the 0000 octet was abbreviated to 0—only three of the four zeros can be removed, not all four.

The second method is to omit consecutive all-zero hextets—two or more hextets of all zeros (0x0000); the omitted hextets are represented by a double colon. Here is an example of this method:

- *Original address*—2001:2db8:**0000:0000:0000:0000**:1280:34bd
- *Abbreviated address*—2001:2db8::1280:34bd

The original address has four consecutive all-zero hextets, which were replaced with a double colon in the abbreviated address. Because IPv6 addresses are eight hextets in length, there is no ambiguity in the abbreviated address; only four hextets are displayed, so we can deduce that four all-zero hextets were abbreviated by the double colon.

NOTE A double colon can only be used once in an address. If there are multiple choices for where to use it (i.e., 2001:0db8:0000:0000:1234:0000:0000:0001), only one series of all-zero hextets can be shortened (i.e., 2001:0db8::1234:0000:0000:0001).

The two address-abbreviation methods can be combined if the address permits it. Following is an example of abbreviating an address both by removing leading zeros and by omitting consecutive all-zero hextets:

- *Original address*—2001:0db8:0000:0000:002f:0001:0000:34bd
- *Abbreviated address*—2001:db8::2f:1:0:34bd

RFC 5952: IPv6 address representation

IPv6 address representation—how we write IPv6 addresses—is addressed in RFC 5952. Its status is "proposed standard," meaning it has not been implemented as a true internet standard. However, it provides some useful guidelines for how to write IPv6 addresses that I recommend following for consistent and accurate IPv6 address representation:

- All leading zeros must be removed. 2001:0db8::0001 is incorrect; it must be written as 2001:db8::1
- The double colon must abbreviate the address as much as possible. For example, 2001:db8:0:0:0:0:2:1 cannot be abbreviated as 2001:db8::0:2:1; it must be abbreviated as 2001:db8::2:1.
- An individual all-zero hextet cannot be omitted with a double colon. For example, 2001:db8::1:2:3:4:5 is incorrect; it must be written as 2001:db8:0:1:2:3:4:5.
- If there are multiple choices for the placement of a double colon, it must be used to replace the longest series of all-zero hextets. For example, 2001:0:0:1:0:0:0:1 must be abbreviated as 2001:0:0:1::1.
  If the two choices are of equal length, the leftmost series must be replaced. For example, 2001:db8:0:0:1:0:0:1 must be abbreviated as 2001:db8::1:0:0:1.
- Hexadecimal characters a–f must be written in lowercase, not uppercase.

Table 20.2 shows some more full and abbreviated IPv6 addresses for your reference. For the rest of this chapter and chapter 21, I will abbreviate IPv6 addresses by default.

Table 20.2 IPv6 address abbreviation

Full address	Abbreviated address
2e09:2100:0222:00f0:1000:0000:0000:011f	2e09:2100:222:f0:1000::11f
fd00:af89:0010:01df:ac80:0000:0000:0000	fd00:af89:10:1df:ac80::
ff02:0000:0000:0000:0000:0000:0000:0002	ff02::2
fe80:0000:0000:0000:1010:000a:0bad:cafe	fe80::1010:a:bad:cafe
0000:0000:0000:0000:0000:0000:0000:0001	::1

20.3.4 *Identifying the IPv6 prefix*

A network *prefix* is the combination of a network address and prefix length. For example, if a host has IPv4 address 192.168.1.10/24, the prefix is 192.168.1.0/24. You should be comfortable with this process by now—we covered it in detail in chapter 11.

The concept is exactly the same in IPv6: an IPv6 prefix is the combination of a network address (an IPv6 address with an all-zero host portion) and a prefix length. For example, if a host has IPv6 address 2001:db8:1:2:a:b:c:d/64, what is the network prefix?

Because IPv6 almost exclusively uses /64 prefix lengths, you don't even need to convert to binary: simply convert the final four hextets—the host portion of the address—to all zeros: 2001:db8:1:2::/64 (abbreviating the host portion's zeros with ::). Table 20.3 lists some example IPv6 host addresses and their prefixes.

Table 20.3 IPv6 network prefixes

Host address	Prefix
fd00:af89:1234:1200:0:123:4567:beef/64	fd00:af89:1234:1200::/64
2001:db8:babe:cafe:2100:101:0:1/64	2001:db8:babe:cafe::/64
fd00:1234:5678:9012::feed:dad/64	fd00:1234:5678:9012::/64
2333::efd:1212:1:1/64	2333::/64
3100:ab00:1f26::2000:1/64	3100:ab00:1f26::/64

NOTE Identifying the IPv6 prefix when using non-/64 prefix lengths (i.e., /55, /73, /97) can be a useful exercise for converting between hexadecimal and binary but is not very practical in reality; IPv6 usually uses /64.

20.4 IPv6 address configuration

Although IPv6 involves learning many new concepts, I have some good news: many IPv6 configuration and verification commands are identical to IPv4 configuration commands, simply replacing `ip` with `ipv6`. Here are some examples:

- IPv4—`ip address`, IPv6—`ipv6 address`
- IPv4—`ip route`, IPv6—`ipv6 route`
- IPv4—`show ip interface brief`, IPv6—`show ipv6 interface brief`
- IPv4—`show ip route`, IPv6—`show ipv6 route`

In this section, we'll look at a couple of methods for configuring IPv6 addresses on Cisco router interfaces: manual configuration and a method that allows the router to automatically generate the address's host portion. Figure 20.4 shows the simple network we will use: a single router (R1) connected to three networks.

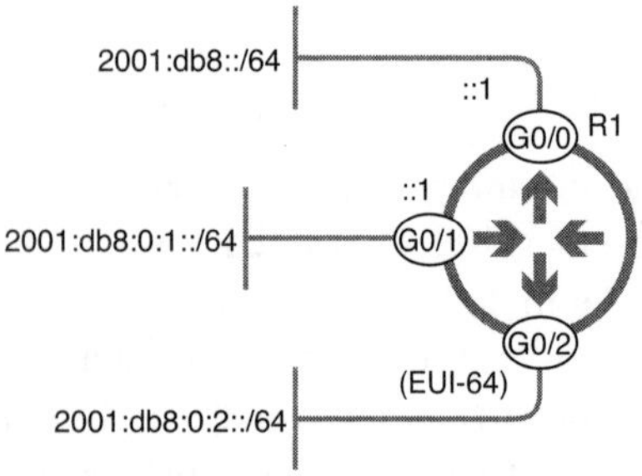


```
R1(config)# ipv6 unicast-routing
R1(config)# interface g0/0
R1(config-if)# ipv6 address 2001:db8::1/64
R1(config-if)# no shutdown
R1(config-if)# interface g0/1
R1(config-if)# ipv6 address 2001:db8:0:1::1/64
R1(config-if)# no shutdown
R1(config-if)# interface g0/2
R1(config-if)# ipv6 address 2001:db8:0:2::/64 eui-64
R1(config-if)# no shutdown
```

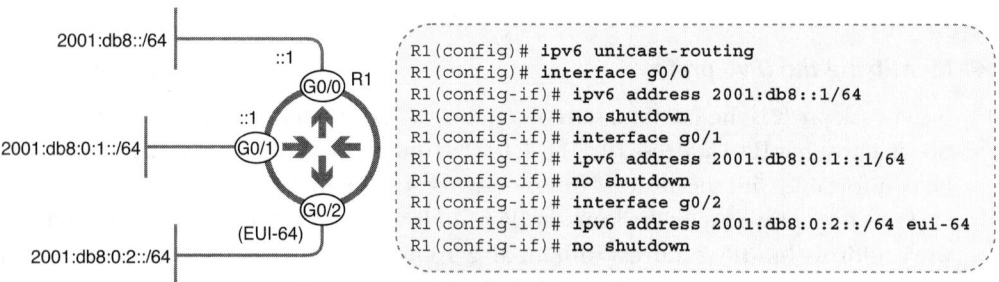

Figure 20.4 A router with three connected IPv6 networks. `ipv6 unicast-routing` allows the router to forward IPv6 packets. `ipv6 address` configures an IPv6 address on each interface. Modified EUI-64 is used to automatically generate the host portion of G0/2's IPv6 address.

The first command you should use when configuring IPv6 on a Cisco router is **`ipv6 unicast-routing`** in global config mode. Without this command, you will be able to configure IPv6 addresses on the router, but it won't be able to route IPv6 packets. For example, R1 won't be able to forward packets between hosts in 2001:db8::/64 and 2001:db8:0:1/64 without this command.

> **EXAM TIP** Don't forget **`ipv6 unicast-routing`**! It's easy to overlook because IPv4 routing is enabled by default, but IPv6 routing isn't.

20.4.1 Manually assigning an IPv6 address

The command to manually assign an IPv6 address is **`ipv6 address`** *`address/prefix-length`*. In addition to using **`ipv6`** instead of **`ip`**, another major difference is that you have to specify the prefix length using slash notation (**`/64`**), instead of a dotted-decimal netmask like in IPv4. In the following example, I configure R1 G0/0's IPv6 address and confirm with **`show ipv6 interface brief`**:

```
R1(config)# interface g0/0
R1(config-if)# ipv6 address 2001:db8::1/64
R1(config-if)# no shutdown
R1(config-if)# do show ipv6 interface brief
GigabitEthernet0/0          [up/up]
    FE80::260:2FFF:FE62:B801
    2001:DB8::1
GigabitEthernet0/1          [administratively down/down]
    Unassigned
GigabitEthernet0/2          [administratively down/down]
    Unassigned
```

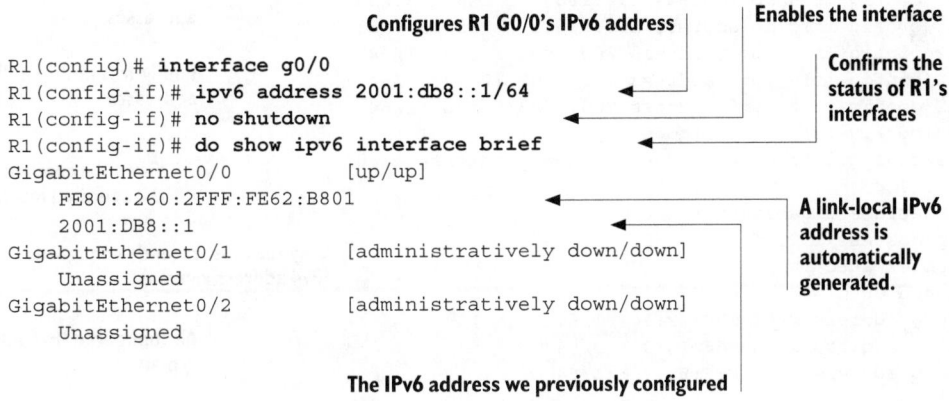

Configures R1 G0/0's IPv6 address

Enables the interface

Confirms the status of R1's interfaces

A link-local IPv6 address is automatically generated.

The IPv6 address we previously configured

> **NOTE** Cisco IOS **`show`** commands display IPv6 addresses using uppercase A–F. RFC 5952 isn't a full internet standard, so its recommendations aren't always followed.

There are a few main things to point out about the previous example. First, notice that you can configure abbreviated IPv6 addresses; as long as you abbreviate the address correctly, Cisco IOS will be able to interpret it as the proper address. Second, after configuring the 2001:db8::1/64 address on G0/0, a second address is automatically generated—a *link-local* address. We will cover this address type in section 20.5.3.

For demonstration purposes, in the following example, I configure G0/1's full, unabbreviated IPv6 address. Notice that, in the output of **`show ipv6 interface brief`**, Cisco IOS automatically abbreviates the address to its shortest possible version:

```
R1(config)# interface g0/1
R1(config-if)# ipv6 address 2001:0db8:0000:0001:0000:0000:0000:0001/64
R1(config-if)# no shutdown
R1(config-if)# do show ipv6 interface brief
GigabitEthernet0/0 [up/up]
    FE80::260:2FFF:FE62:B801
    2001:DB8::1
GigabitEthernet0/1 [up/up]
    FE80::260:2FFF:FE62:B802
    2001:DB8:0:1::1
GigabitEthernet0/2 [administratively down/down]
Unassigned
```

Configures R1 G0/1's IPv6 address

Cisco IOS automatically abbreviates the address.

One practical difference between configuring IPv4 and IPv6 addresses in Cisco IOS is that IPv4 addresses overwrite each other, but IPv6 addresses don't. In the following example, I configure multiple IPv4 and IPv6 addresses on another router (R2); notice the results afterward:

```
R2(config)# interface g0/0
R2(config-if)# ip address 192.168.1.1 255.255.255.0
R2(config-if)# ip address 192.168.1.2 255.255.255.0
R2(config-if)# ip address 192.168.2.1 255.255.255.0
R2(config-if)# ipv6 address 2001:db8:12:34::1/64
R2(config-if)# ipv6 address 2001:db8:12:34::2/64
R2(config-if)# ipv6 address 2001:db8:56:78::1/64
R2(config-if)# no shutdown
R2(config-if)# do show running-config interface g0/0
. . .
interface GigabitEthernet0/0
ip address 192.168.2.1 255.255.255.0
duplex auto
speed auto
ipv6 address 2001:DB8:12:34::1/64
ipv6 address 2001:DB8:12:34::2/64
ipv6 address 2001:DB8:56:78::1/64
```

Configures multiple IPv4 addresses

Configures multiple IPv6 addresses

Views the configuration of the specified interface

Only the most recently configured IPv4 address remains.

All configured IPv6 addresses remain.

Notice that only the most recently configured IPv4 address (192.168.2.1/24) remains; it overwrites the previously configured addresses. However, configuring additional IPv6 addresses doesn't overwrite the previous ones; R2 now has three IPv6 addresses on the same interface. Keep this difference in mind as you practice configuring IPv6: if you want to change an interface's IPv6 address, you must use the `no` command to remove the existing IPv6 address.

There are use cases for configuring multiple IP addresses on an interface, but they are beyond the scope of the CCNA exam. One example use case is when you have run out of addresses in a particular subnet: you can add another subnet to the same router interface by configuring an additional IP address in the new subnet. However, for the purpose of the CCNA exam, you can assume that each router interface has one IP address.

Multiple IPv4 addresses on an interface

You can also configure multiple IPv4 addresses on an interface by adding the **`secondary`** keyword to the end of the **`ip address`** command. For example, the first IP address might be configured as **`ip address 192.168.1.1 255.255.255.0`**, and the second **`ip address 192.168.10.1 255.255.255.0 secondary`**. There is no limit to the number of secondary addresses you can configure on an interface.

20.4.2 Modified EUI-64

Modified Extended Unique Identifier 64 (EUI-64) is a method of automatically generating a 64-bit IPv6 interface identifier—the host portion of the address. To configure an IPv6 address using Modified EUI-64, specify a /64 IPv6 prefix and add the **`eui-64`** keyword to the end of the **`ipv6 address`** command. In the following example, I use EUI-64 to configure R1's G0/2 interface:

```
R1(config)# interface g0/2
R1(config-if)# ipv6 address 2001:db8:0:2::/64 eui-64
R1(config-if)# no shutdown
R1(config-if)# do show ipv6 interface brief
GigabitEthernet0/0 [up/up]
    FE80::260:2FFF:FE62:B801
    2001:DB8::1
GigabitEthernet0/1 [up/up]
    FE80::260:2FFF:FE62:B802
    2001:DB8:0:1::1
GigabitEthernet0/2 [up/up]
    FE80::260:2FFF:FE62:B803
    2001:DB8:0:2:260:2FFF:FE62:B803
```

Configures R1 G0/2 with Modified EUI-64

R1 automatically generates the host portion of the address.

NOTE The host portion of the address I configured on G0/2 and that of its automatically configured link-local address are the same; both use Modified EUI-64.

How does Modified EUI-64 generate a 64-bit interface identifier? It takes the interface's 48-bit MAC address and adds 0xfffe (a reserved 16-bit value) to make it 64 bits in total. Here is the three-step process:

1. Divide the MAC address in half.
2. Insert 0xfffe in the middle.
3. Invert the seventh bit.

Figure 20.5 demonstrates this three-step process using G0/2's MAC address (0060.2f62.b803). Let's see how R1 turned the 48-bit MAC address into the 64-bit interface identifier 0260:2fff:fe62:b803.

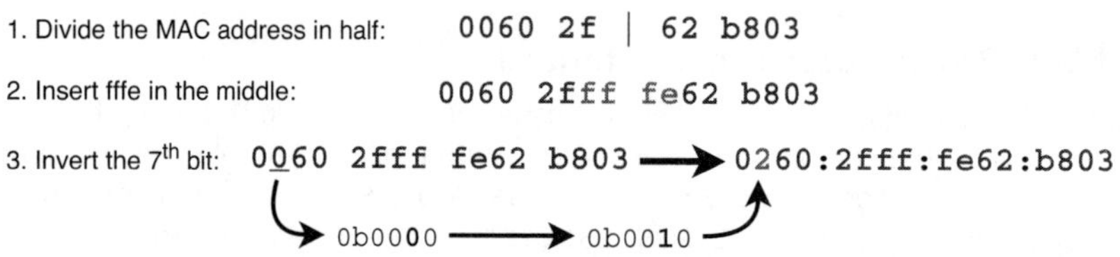
1. Divide the MAC address in half:
0060 2f | 62 b803
2. Insert fffe in the middle:
0060 2fff fe62 b803
3. Invert the 7th bit:
0060 2fff fe62 b803
0260:2fff:fe62:b803
0b0000
0b0010

Figure 20.5 Generating a 64-bit interface identifier using Modified EUI-64. (1) Divide the MAC address in half and (2) insert `fffe` in the middle to make it 64 bits. Then, (3) invert the seventh bit—the third bit of the second hex digit.

The third step, in which you must invert the seventh bit of the 64-bit identifier, probably requires some explanation. Because each hexadecimal digit is 4 bits, the seventh bit of the interface identifier is the third bit of the second hexadecimal digit—the second hexadecimal 0, in this case. Inverting the seventh bit of R1 G0/2's MAC address—changing it from 0b0 to 0b1—changes the second hexadecimal digit from 0x0 (0b0000) to 0x2 (0b0010). This results in the interface identifier 0260:2fff:fe62:b803. That interface identifier, combined with the 64-bit prefix specified in the **`ipv6 address`** command, results in IPv6 address 2001:db8:0:2:260:2fff:fe62:b803.

Table 20.4 shows some example MAC addresses and Modified EUI-64 interface identifiers. For practice, I recommend writing out each MAC address and doing the conversions yourself.

Table 20.4 Example Modified EUI-64 interface IDs

MAC address	Modified EUI-64 Interface ID
7f2b.cbac.1813	7d2b:cbff:feac:1813
1548.4fff.2101	1748:4fff:feff:2101
3150.c012.1212	3350:c0ff:fe12:1212
84ec.4389.fd23	86ec:43ff:fe89:fd23
9eba.1112.9900	9cba:11ff:fe12:9900

EXAM TIP Modified EUI-64 is exam topic 1.9.d. For the CCNA exam, you should be comfortable converting a MAC address to a Modified EUI-64 interface identifier using the three-step process outlined in this section.

Why invert the seventh bit?

The term *Modified* in the name *Modified EUI-64* refers to the inversion of the seventh bit that is done when using EUI-64 to generate a 64-bit interface identifier for an IPv6 address. Although it's beyond the scope of the CCNA exam, let's take a look at why this is done.

MAC addresses can be divided into two types: a *Universally Administered Address* (UAA) is a MAC address that is uniquely assigned to the device by the manufacturer, and a *Locally Administered Address* (LAA) is assigned locally and doesn't have to be globally unique. You can identify a UAA or LAA by the seventh bit of the MAC address, called the *U/L bit* (Universal/Local bit):

- U/L bit of 0 = UAA
- U/L bit of 1 = LAA

In the context of IPv6 addresses and EUI-64, the meaning of this bit is reversed:

- U/L bit of 0 = The MAC address the EUI-64 ID was generated from was an LAA.
- U/L bit of 1 = The MAC address the EUI-64 ID was generated from was a UAA.

The exact reasoning for this reversal is not worth delving into here. Just remember that this bit is always flipped when using EUI-64 to generate an interface ID for IPv6 (the host portion of the address). This process is called Modified EUI-64, although it's often casually referred to simply as EUI-64.

20.5 IPv6 address types

Like IPv4, there are various IPv6 addresses and address ranges that are reserved for specific purposes. In this section, we will cover those address types and their IPv4 equivalents. For some of these IPv6 address types, we have covered the IPv4 equivalent previously in this book. In other cases, this will be their first introduction.

Figure 20.6 outlines the five main address types we will delve into in this section:

- *Global unicast*—Globally unique addresses that can be used for communication over the internet.
- *Unique local*—Addresses that don't have to be globally unique; they can be freely used in internal networks but can't be used for communication over the internet.
- *Link-local*—Used for communication between directly connected hosts.
- *Multicast*—Used for one-to-multiple communication, allowing a single packet to be addressed to multiple hosts.
- *Anycast*—Used for one-to-one-of-multiple communication, an anycast address is a unicast address that is assigned to multiple hosts. Packets are delivered to the nearest host configured with the address, often used on servers to provide services over the internet with low latency.

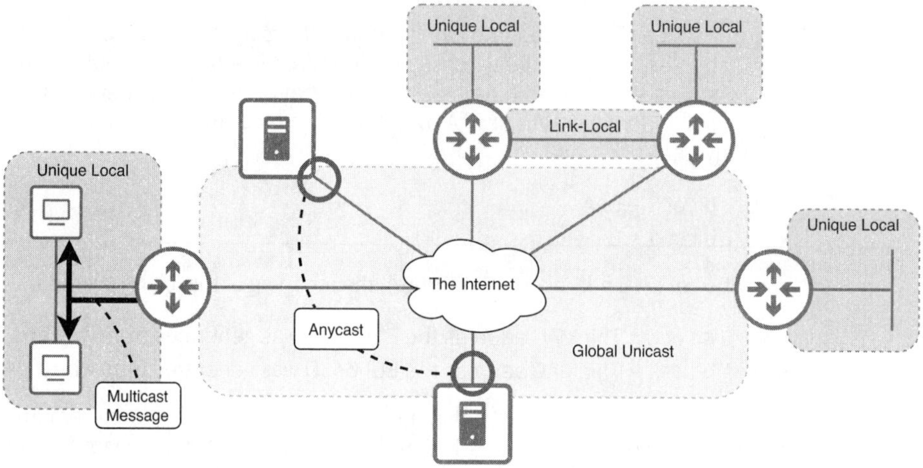

Figure 20.6 IPv6 address types: global unicast, unique local, link-local, multicast, and anycast.

20.5.1 Global unicast

IPv6 *global unicast* addresses are globally unique addresses used for communication over the public internet. Their allocation is controlled by IANA, as mentioned in section 20.1. Because they are public and must be globally unique, an enterprise is not free to use whichever global unicast addresses they want; the enterprise will typically be assigned an address block from an ISP or from the appropriate RIR, depending on the type and size of the business.

The global unicast address range was originally defined as 2000::/3, which includes all addresses from 2000:: through 3fff:ffff:ffff:ffff:ffff:ffff:ffff:ffff. However, the definition of global unicast addresses has expanded to include any address that is not specifically reserved for other purposes.

An enterprise that requests IPv6 global unicast addresses will typically be assigned a /48 address block from the RIR or ISP; this is called the *global routing prefix*. Because IPv6 prefix lengths are typically /64, the /48 global routing prefix leaves 16 bits free for the enterprise to use to make different subnet addresses; this 16-bit section of the address is called the *subnet identifier*. The remaining 64 bits are the interface identifier—the host portion. Figure 20.7 shows the structure of an IPv6 global unicast address.

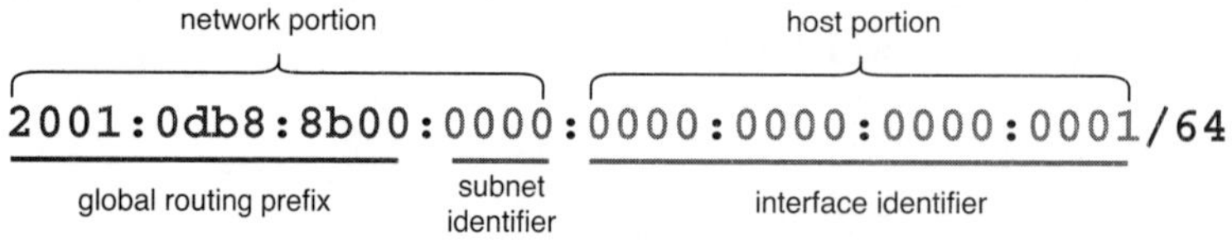

Figure 20.7 The structure of an IPv6 global unicast address. The first 48 bits are the global routing prefix, assigned to the enterprise by the ISP. The next 16 bits are the subnet identifier, which the enterprise can use to make various subnets. The remaining 64 bits are the interface identifier—the host portion of the address.

The IPv6 subnetting process is the same as IPv4 subnetting; the bits of the subnet identifier are equivalent to the borrowed bits when subnetting IPv4 networks. Following are the first few subnets that can be made with the 2001:db8:8b00::/48 address block:

- 2001:db8:8b00::/64 (subnet identifier 0x0000)
- 2001:db8:8b00:1::/64 (subnet identifier 0x0001)
- 2001:db8:8b00:2::/64 (subnet identifier 0x0002)

The IPv4 equivalent of an IPv6 global unicast address is a *public IPv4 address.* The ranges for public IPv4 addresses are all the addresses that are not part of the reserved private or other special-purpose ranges. I will mention the IPv4 private address ranges in section 20.5.2 and then cover them in greater detail in chapter 9 of volume 2.

> **NOTE** The 2001:db8::/32 address range is reserved for use in examples in books, documentation, etc. Most examples of global unicast IPv6 addresses in this book will be from this reserved range.

20.5.2 Unique local

IPv6 *unique local* addresses (ULAs) are very similar to global unicast addresses. Like global unicast addresses, they are used for unicast communications; they are meant to identify a single host on the network. The main difference in use is that ULAs are *private* addresses; they do not have to be globally unique, and enterprises are free to use them in their internal networks. However, they cannot be used for communications over the internet—a public network that relies on each destination having a unique address. ISPs will drop packets sourced from or destined for ULAs.

IPv6 ULAs are equivalent to *private IPv4 addresses,* which are addresses included in one of the following three ranges:

- 10.0.0.0/8 (10.0.0.0–10.255.255.255)
- 172.16.0.0/12 (172.16.0.0–172.31.255.255)
- 192.168.0.0/16 (192.168.0.0–192.168.255.255)

You'll probably recognize the three private IPv4 address ranges; I use them in most examples in this book. We will cover these addresses in greater detail in chapter 9 of volume 2.

The IPv6 ULA range is defined as fc00::/7, which includes all addresses from fc00:: through fdff:ffff:ffff:ffff:ffff:ffff:ffff:ffff. However, the range is divided into two /8 blocks:

- fc00::/8—Currently reserved and not defined for any specific purpose
- fd00::/8—The active range for IPv6 ULAs

Because the fc00::/8 range is currently reserved, all ULAs should begin with fd. Figure 20.8 shows the structure of an IPv6 ULA, similar to that of a global unicast address.

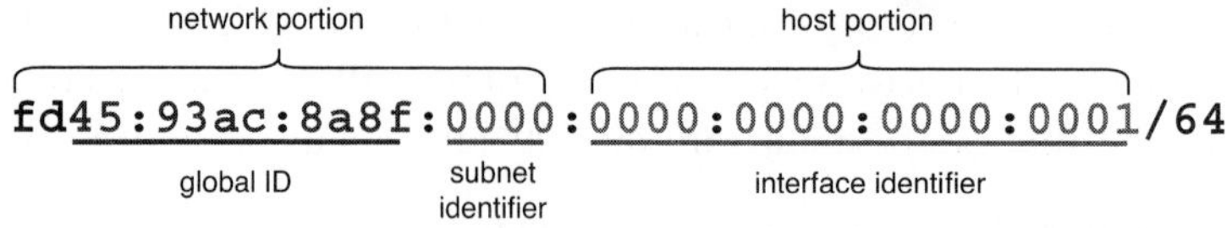

Figure 20.8 The structure of an IPv6 unique local address. After the prefix fd, there is a 40-bit global ID, which should be randomly generated. The following 16 bits are the subnet identifier, and the remaining 64 bits are the interface identifier.

After the prefix fd, ULAs have a 40-bit *global ID*, which should be randomly generated; this makes it highly likely that the global ID will be globally unique, resulting in each enterprise having unique ULAs. The rest of the address is identical to a global unicast address: a 16-bit subnet identifier and a 64-bit interface identifier.

> **Randomly generated global IDs**
>
> Randomly generating global IDs for ULAs to make them globally unique may seem to contradict the fact that ULAs are private addresses and don't have to be globally unique. Even though that is true, there are benefits to avoiding overlapping addresses between enterprises. For example, in business scenarios, mergers and acquisitions often require the integration of two or more previously separate networks. If ULAs use randomly generated global IDs, the likelihood of overlapping addresses is minimized, making the integration process much smoother.

20.5.3 Link-local

IPv6 *link-local addresses* (LLA), as we saw in section 20.4, are automatically generated on IPv6-enabled interfaces—those with an IPv6 address (i.e., a global unicast address) configured.

> **NOTE** You can enable IPv6 on an interface without configuring an IPv6 address by using the **`ipv6 enable`** command. In this case, the interface will only have an automatically generated LLA.

LLAs are unicast addresses used to identify a single host. However, as the name implies, LLAs can only be used for communication on the local link—between devices connected to the same network segment. Devices that aren't connected to the same segment cannot communicate using LLAs. Figure 20.9 demonstrates this concept.

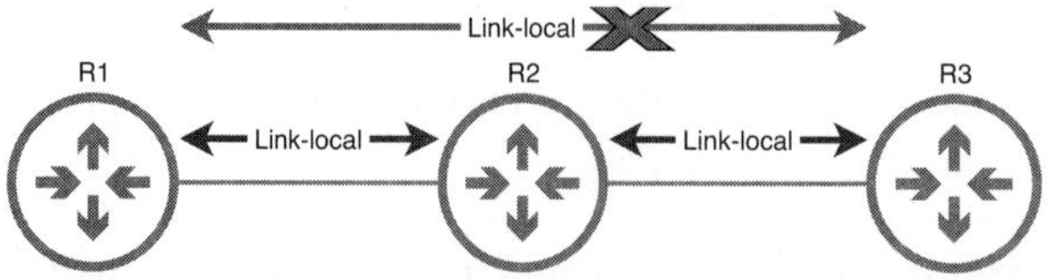

Figure 20.9 Link-local addresses can only be used for communication between hosts connected to the same link (segment). R1–R2 and R2–R3 communication can be sourced from/destined for each other's LLA, but R1–R3 communication cannot.

IPv6 LLAs use the fe80::/10 range, but the standard also states that the following 54 bits must be 0. As a result, all LLAs use the fe80::/64 prefix. The remaining 64 bits—the interface identifier—are automatically generated using Modified EUI-64 rules. However, it is also possible to manually configure the interface's LLA with the **`ipv6 address`** *`address`* **`link-local`** command (without specifying a prefix length), as in the following example:

```
R1(config)# do show ipv6 interface brief
GigabitEthernet0/0          [up/up]
    FE80::260:2FFF:FE62:B801            <-- R1's automatically configured LLA
    2001:DB8::1
. . .
R1(config)# interface g0/0
R1(config-if)# ipv6 address fe80::1 link-local        <-- Manually configure the LLA
R1(config-if)# do show ipv6 interface brief
GigabitEthernet0/0          [up/up]
    FE80::1                             <-- R1's LLA has changed.
    2001:DB8::1
```

> **NOTE** Each IPv6 interface must have exactly one link-local address. Configuring a new one will overwrite the old one, unlike global unicast and unique local addresses, which do not overwrite each other.

IPv4 also uses link-local addresses; the reserved range is 169.254.0.0/16. However, the major difference between IPv4 and IPv6 is that IPv6 requires each interface to have an LLA. We'll explore the role of LLAs in IPv6 in chapter 21.

IPv4 doesn't require each interface to have an LLA, but one situation in which you may encounter IPv4 LLAs is when a host attempts to receive an IPv4 address using *Dynamic Host Configuration Protocol* (DHCP) but is unable to; in many operating systems, the host will then automatically generate an IPv4 LLA for itself. We'll cover DHCP in chapter 4 of volume 2.

20.5.4 Multicast

Unicast addresses, such as global unicast, unique local, and link-local IPv6 addresses, are used for one-to-one communication—from one host to another. Multicast addresses, on the other hand, provide one-to-multiple communication—from one host to multiple destinations; all hosts that have joined the relevant *multicast group*. For example, as we covered in chapter 18, OSPF routers accept packets destined for 224.0.0.5 on their OSPF-activated interfaces; in other words, they join the 224.0.0.5 multicast group. IPv4 multicast addresses are from the class D range (224.0.0.0–239.255.255.255).

IPv6 uses the ff00::/8 range for multicast addresses; if an address begins with ff, it's a multicast address. However, IPv6 defines several multicast *scopes* that determine how far the multicast packets should travel; these scopes are determined by the final digit of the first hextet. Table 20.5 lists and briefly describes some of the IPv6 multicast scopes.

Table 20.5 IPv6 multicast scopes

Scope	First hextet	Description
Interface-local	ff01	The packet doesn't leave the local device. Can be used to send traffic to a service within the local device.
Link-local	ff02	The packet remains on the local segment. Routers will not route the packet.
Site-local	ff05	The packet can be forwarded by routers. Should be limited to a single physical site (location).
Organization-local	ff08	Wider in scope than site-local (an entire enterprise/organization).
Global	ff0e	No boundaries. Possible to be routed over the internet.

NOTE Don't mix up unicast link-local addresses (LLAs) as covered in section 20.5.3 and the link-local multicast scope. The term *link-local address* typically refers to a unicast address, and *link-local multicast* refers to the multicast scope.

Figure 20.10 gives a visual representation of each of the multicast scopes (aside from interface-local), representing how far each kind of multicast packet sent by PC1 may travel.

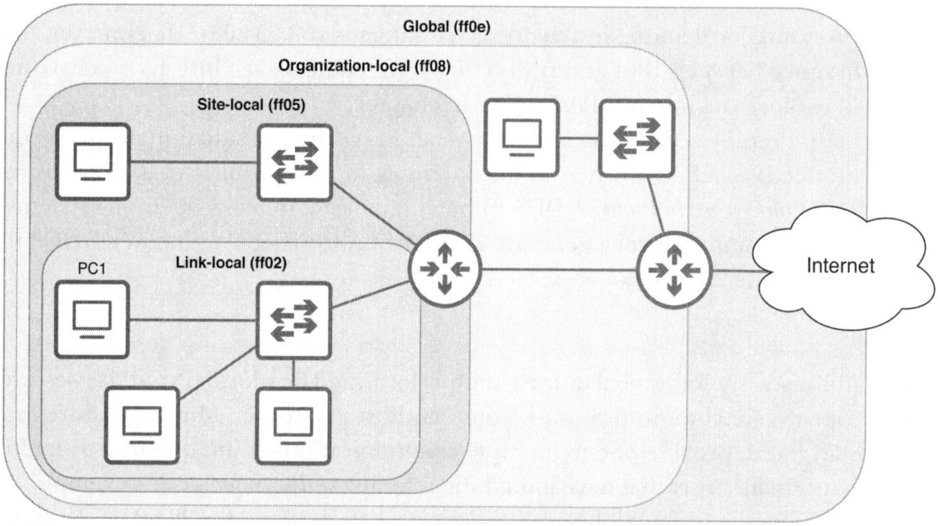

Figure 20.10 IPv6 multicast scopes from the perspective of PC1. Link-local multicast remains within the local link. Site-local multicast may be forwarded within the local site. Organization-local multicast may be forwarded within the organization. Global multicast has no boundaries and may be forwarded over the internet.

EXAM TIP The specifics of how site-local, organization-local, and global multicast packets are forwarded by routers are well beyond the scope of the CCNA exam. I recommend just memorizing their names and first hextet patterns (ff05, ff08, ff0e).

The one multicast scope you should be familiar with for the CCNA exam is link-local: multicast messages that are sent to other hosts in the same network segment. Table 20.6 lists some common IPv6 link-local multicast addresses and their IPv4 equivalents (a couple of which we saw when covering OSPF in chapter 18). Switches will flood these messages to all hosts on the local segment by default, and it is up to those hosts to decide if they are interested in the contents or not.

Table 20.6 Common link-local multicast addresses

Purpose	IPv6 address	IPv4 address
All nodes	ff02::1	224.0.0.1
All routers	ff02::2	224.0.0.2
All OSPF routers	ff02::5	224.0.0.5
All OSPF DRs/BDRs	ff02::6	224.0.0.6
All RIP routers	ff02::9	224.0.0.9
All EIGRP routers	ff02::a	224.0.0.10

NOTE In IPv6, there is no such thing as a broadcast address. Instead, IPv6 hosts can use the all-nodes multicast address (ff02::1) to send a message to all hosts on the local segment. In effect, this is like a broadcast message: from one host to all other hosts connected to the same segment.

You can check which multicast groups a Cisco router interface has joined—which types of multicast messages it is interested in—with the `show ipv6 interface` command. In the following example, I use the command on R1, which we configured in section 20.4:

```
R1# show ipv6 interface g0/0
GigabitEthernet0/0 is up, line protocol is up
IPv6 is enabled, link-local address is FE80::2D0:97FF:FE92:B401
No Virtual link-local address(es):
Global unicast address(es):
2001:DB8:1:1::1, subnet is 2001:DB8:1:1::/64
Joined group address(es):
FF02::1
FF02::2
FF02::1:FF00:1
FF02::1:FF92:B401
. . .
```

The all-nodes multicast address

The all-routers multicast address

Two solicited-node multicast addresses

R1 has joined four multicast groups on its G0/0 interface: ff02::1 (all nodes), ff02::2 (all routers), as well as two *solicited-node* multicast addresses; we will cover those soon in chapter 21. If R1 receives a packet addressed to any of those four multicast addresses, it will examine the contents. If it receives a packet addressed to any other multicast address, it will discard the packet; it's not interested in the contents.

20.5.5 Anycast addresses

We have covered unicast (one-to-one), broadcast (one-to-all), and multicast (one-to-multiple), but *anycast* (one-to-one-of-multiple) is a new concept. Anycast was already present in IPv4, but with IPv6, the concept was more formally defined and integrated. Figure 20.11 visually illustrates the concepts of unicast, broadcast, multicast, and anycast.

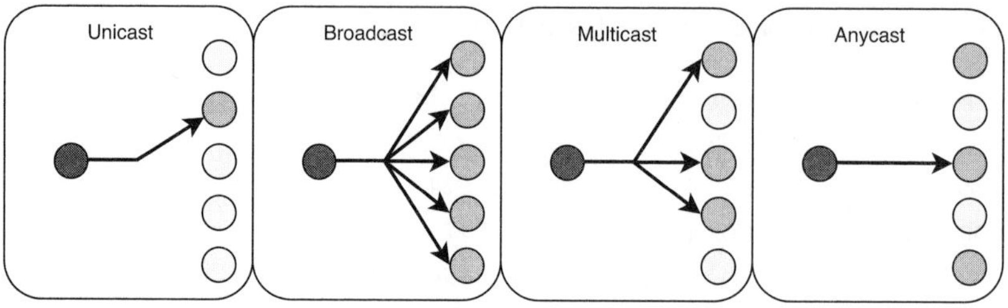

Figure 20.11 Different routing/addressing methodologies. Unicast is one-to-one, broadcast is one-to-all, multicast is one-to-multiple, and anycast is one-to-one-of-multiple.

When using anycast, the same IP address is shared by multiple hosts. The address itself is indistinguishable from a unicast address (i.e., a global unicast address); there is no reserved range for anycast addresses.

Normally, unicast addresses should be unique—not shared by multiple hosts. Anycast is an exception to that rule; the same address is configured on multiple hosts. Packets destined for the anycast address will be delivered to one of the hosts configured with the address. Which of those hosts the packets will be delivered to depends on the routers in the path; each router will forward the packets according to the best route in its routing table. As a result, the packets should reach the destination host closest to the source.

Anycast is useful when providing services over the internet. By configuring the same IP address on servers in different global locations, users can access the server closest to their location; this can result in lower latency. *Content Delivery Network* (CDN) services such as Cloudflare use anycast for this purpose.

Because anycast addresses are identical to unicast addresses, they can be configured like any other unicast address with the **ipv6 address** command. However, if you add the **anycast** keyword to the end of the command, the address will be marked as such in the output of some **show** commands. This doesn't affect the behavior of the router (and is therefore not necessary), but it is helpful for making the intent of the configuration clear for others (and your future self). In the following example, I configure an anycast address and verify with a **show** command:

```
R1(config)# interface g0/0
R1(config-if)# ipv6 address 2001:db8:0:100::1/64 anycast
R1(config-if)# show ipv6 interface g0/0
GigabitEthernet0/0 is up, line protocol is up
IPv6 is enabled, link-local address is FE80::260:2FFF:FE62:B801
```

Configures an IPv6 address and specifies it as anycast

```
No Virtual link-local address(es):
Global unicast address(es):
2001:DB8::1, subnet is 2001:DB8::/64
2001:DB8:0:100::1, subnet is 2001:DB8:0:100::/64 [ANY]
. . .
```

[ANY] indicates an anycast address.

20.5.6 Other reserved addresses

Both IPv4 and IPv6 have many other reserved addresses and address ranges. For the CCNA exam, there are two more reserved IPv6 addresses you should be aware of: the unspecified address and the loopback address.

The *unspecified* IPv6 address is the all-zeros address: 0000:0000:0000:0000:0000:0000:0000:0000. When abbreviated, it is simply written as "::". This address can be used as a source address when a device doesn't yet know its IPv6 address. Also, IPv6 default routes are configured to destination ::/0—more on that in chapter 21. The IPv4 equivalent of this address is also all zeros: 0.0.0.0.

The *loopback* IPv6 address is the address immediately after the unspecified address; it's usually written as ::1. Messages sent to this address are looped back to the local device; they are not sent out of any interfaces. This can be used to test the networking software on the local device. The IPv4 equivalent is the reserved 127.0.0.0/8 range.

Summary

- IPv4 address exhaustion—running out of IPv4 addresses—is a major problem in our era of unprecedented connectivity; IPv6 is the long-term solution.
- IPv4 addresses are 32 bits in length, providing 2^{32} (over 4 billion) addresses, but IPv6 addresses are 128 bits in length, providing 2^{128} (over 340 undecillion) addresses.
- To convert a binary number to hexadecimal, (1) split the number into 4-bit groups, (2) convert each 4-bit group to decimal, and (3) convert each decimal number to hexadecimal.
- To convert a hexadecimal number to binary, (1) split up the hexadecimal digits, (2) convert each hexadecimal digit to decimal, and (3) convert each decimal digit to binary.
- The IPv6 header is 40 bytes in length and consists of eight fields: Version, Traffic Class, Flow Label, Payload Length, Next Header, Hop Limit, Source, and Destination.
- IPv6 addresses are divided into eight groups of 16 bits (usually called *hextets*) and written in hexadecimal, with a colon between each group.
- For simplicity, IPv6 addresses typically use /64 prefix lengths—the first 64 bits are the network portion, and the last 64 bits are the host portion.
- IPv6 addresses can be abbreviated by removing leading zeros from each hextet and by abbreviating two or more consecutive all-zero hextets with a double colon (::).

- A network prefix is a combination of a network address and prefix length. If a host has IPv4 address 192.168.1.10/24, the prefix is 192.168.1.0/24. If a host has IPv6 address 2001:db8:1:2:a:b:c:d/64, the prefix is 2001:db8:1:2::/64.
- Many IPv6 configuration and verification commands are similar to IPv4 equivalents: **ipv6 address, ipv6 route, show ipv6 interface brief, show ipv6 route**.
- When configuring IPv6 on a Cisco router, you should first enable IPv6 routing with the **ipv6 unicast-routing** command. IPv6 routing is not enabled by default.
- You can manually assign an IPv6 address to an interface with **ipv6 address** *address/prefix-length*. Unlike IPv4, IPv6 prefix lengths are configured with slash notation, not dotted-decimal netmasks.
- Even if you configure a full (or partially abbreviated) IPv6 address, IOS will display the fully abbreviated address in the output of **show** commands.
- If you configure an IPv4 address on an interface that already has an IPv4 address, the new address will overwrite the old one. If you do the same in IPv6, the new address will not overwrite the old one; the interface will have multiple addresses.
- Modified Extended Unique Identifier 64 (Modified EUI-64) is a method of automatically generating a 64-bit interface identifier (host portion of the address) by adding 16 bits (0xfffe) to the interface's 48-bit MAC address.
- Use **ipv6 address** *prefix* **eui-64** to configure an IPv6 with Modified EUI-64.
- To convert a MAC address to a Modified EUI-64 interface ID, (1) divide the MAC address in half, (2) insert fffe in the middle, and (3) invert the seventh bit.
- IPv6 global unicast addresses are globally unique addresses used for communication over the public internet. The global unicast range was originally defined as 2000::/3, but now includes any address not specifically reserved for other purposes.
- Global unicast addresses consist of a 48-bit global routing prefix (assigned by an RIR or ISP), a 16-bit subnet identifier (used to make subnets), and a 64-bit interface identifier (the host portion of the address).
- The IPv4 equivalent of a global unicast address is a public IPv4 address. Public IPv4 addresses include all addresses that are not part of the reserved private or other special-purpose ranges.
- IPv6 unique local addresses (ULAs) are private addresses; they do not have to be globally unique, and enterprises are free to use them in their internal networks. However, they cannot be used for communication over the internet.
- The ULA range is defined as fc00::/7 but is divided into two /8 ranges: fc00::/8 (reserved) and fd00:/8 (the active ranges for ULAs).

- After the fd prefix, a ULA has a 40-bit global ID, which should be randomly generated to avoid overlap with other enterprises. The next 16 bits are the subnet identifier, and the last 64 bits are the interface identifier.
- ULAs are equivalent to IPv4 private addresses, in the ranges 10.0.0.0/8, 172.16.0.0/12, and 192.168.0.0/16.
- IPv6 link-local addresses (LLAs) are automatically generated on IPv6-enabled interfaces using Modified EUI-64. The LLA range is fe80::/10, but the following 54 bits should be set to 0, resulting in the fe80::/64 prefix.
- The IPv4 equivalent is the 169.254.0.0/16 range. IPv6-enabled interfaces require an IPv6 LLA, but IPv4-enabled interfaces don't require an IPv4 LLA.
- You can enable IPv6 on an interface without configuring an IPv6 address with **`ipv6 enable`**. In that case, the interface will have only the automatically generated LLA.
- You can manually configure an interface's LLA with **`ipv6 address`** *`address`* **`link-local`**.
- LLAs can only be used for communication with devices on the same segment.
- IPv6 multicast addresses are from the ff00::/8 range. They are used to provide communication from one host to multiple others. The IPv4 equivalent is the class D range (224.0.0.0–239.255.255.255).
- Several scopes define how far the multicast packets should travel: *interface-local* (ff01), link-local (ff02), site-local (ff05), organization-local (ff08), and global (ff0e).
- Some common link-local IPv6 and IPv4 multicast addresses are all nodes (ff02::1, 224.0.0.1), all routers (ff02::2, 224.0.0.2), all OSPF routers (ff02::5, 224.0.0.5), all OSPF DRs/BDRs (ff02::6, 224.0.0.6), all RIP routers (ff02::9, 224.0.0.9), and all EIGRP routers (ff02::a, 224.0.0.10).
- Unicast communication is one-to-one, broadcast is one-to-all, multicast is one-to-multiple, and anycast is one-to-one-of-multiple.
- An anycast address is a unicast address configured on multiple hosts. Packets destined for the address will be delivered to the closest host with the address, as determined by routers' routing decisions.
- You can specify an IPv6 address as anycast with the **`ipv6 address`** *`address/prefix-length`* **`anycast`** command.
- The unspecified IPv6 address is all zeros, usually written as ::. It is used in default routes or when the device doesn't know its IPv6 address yet. The IPv4 equivalent is 0.0.0.0.
- The loopback IPv6 address is ::1. Messages sent to this address are looped back to the local device without being sent out of an interface. This can be used to test the device's network software. The IPv4 equivalent is the 127.0.0.0/8 range.

21 IPv6 routing

This chapter covers

- How IPv6 uses Neighbor Discovery Protocol for address resolution (and more)
- The IPv6 routing table
- How routers forward IPv6 packets
- How to configure IPv6 static routes

In chapter 20, we covered IPv6 addressing, including how to configure IPv6 addresses on Cisco routers and the various IPv6 address types. In this chapter, we'll build upon that knowledge and look at IPv6 routing, including how routers forward IPv6 packets and how to configure IPv6 static routes. Specifically, we will cover the following exam topics:

- 3.1 Interpret the components of routing table
- 3.2 Determine how a router makes a forwarding decision by default
- 3.3 Configure and verify IPv4 and IPv6 static routing

We have already covered these exam topics from an IPv4 perspective, particularly in chapter 9. The good news is that the fundamentals of IPv6 routing are largely identical to those of IPv4 routing, so many of the concepts in this chapter will not be new to you. One point worth mentioning is that IPv6 dynamic routing is not included in the CCNA exam—only static routing; the exam topics list mentions OSPFv2 (which only supports IPv4), not OSPFv3 (which supports both IPv4 and IPv6).

21.1 Neighbor Discovery Protocol

When an end host sends an IPv4 packet, or when a router forwards an IPv4 packet, it must encapsulate the packet in an Ethernet frame destined for the packet's next hop; that might be the packet's final destination host, or it might be the next router in the path to the final destination. And how does it learn the MAC address of the next hop? The answer is ARP.

A host's ARP table maps Layer 3 (IPv4) addresses to Layer 2 (MAC) addresses. To encapsulate a packet in a frame with the proper destination MAC address, a host will look in its ARP table for an entry matching the next hop's IPv4 address and use the mapped MAC address as the frame's destination. If no such entry exists, the host will broadcast an ARP request to learn the next hop's MAC address.

NOTE The term *host* as I use it in this book includes both end hosts, such as servers and PCs, and network infrastructure devices, such as routers.

End hosts sending IPv6 packets and routers forwarding IPv6 packets also need to encapsulate those packets in frames addressed to the next hop. But there's a major difference between IPv4 and IPv6: IPv6 doesn't use ARP! Instead, IPv6 uses a protocol called *Neighbor Discovery Protocol* (NDP), which plays a similar role to ARP, mapping Layer 3 (IPv6) addresses to Layer 2 (MAC) addresses. However, NDP also has some additional functions, two of which we'll cover in this section: router discovery and duplicate address detection.

21.1.1 Solicited-node multicast

Some NDP functions use a particular kind of multicast address called a *solicited-node multicast* address, which is generated from a host's unicast address (global unicast, unique local, or link-local). To generate a solicited-node multicast address, prepend ff02:0000:0000:0000:0000:0001:ff (abbreviated to ff02::1:ff) to the last six hexadecimal digits of the unicast address. Figure 21.1 shows how to generate a solicited-node multicast address.

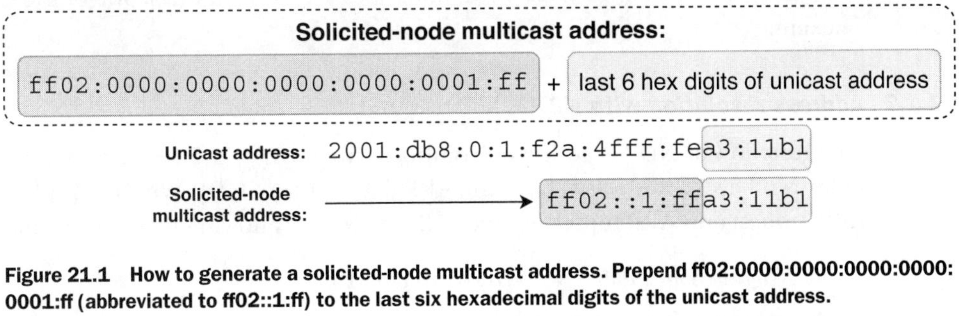

Figure 21.1 How to generate a solicited-node multicast address. Prepend ff02:0000:0000:0000:0000:0001:ff (abbreviated to ff02::1:ff) to the last six hexadecimal digits of the unicast address.

NOTE The scope of a solicited-node multicast address is link-local, as indicated by ff02.

For reference, table 21.1 lists some unicast addresses and their equivalent solicited-node multicast addresses. In sections 21.1.2 and 21.1.4, we'll see some examples of this message type in action.

Table 21.1 Solicited-node multicast addresses

Unicast address	Solicited-node multicast address
2001:db8:123::1	ff02::1:ff00:1
fd12:3456:78:1df:ac80:0:3ab:fff1	ff02::1:ffab:fff1
fe80::99ff:fe12:1234	ff02::1:ff12:1234

In chapter 20, I showed the following output when demonstrating multicast IPv6 addresses. In addition to joining the ff02::1 and ff02::2 multicast groups, note that R1 has joined two additional multicast groups for the solicited-node multicast address of each of its unicast addresses (global unicast and link-local):

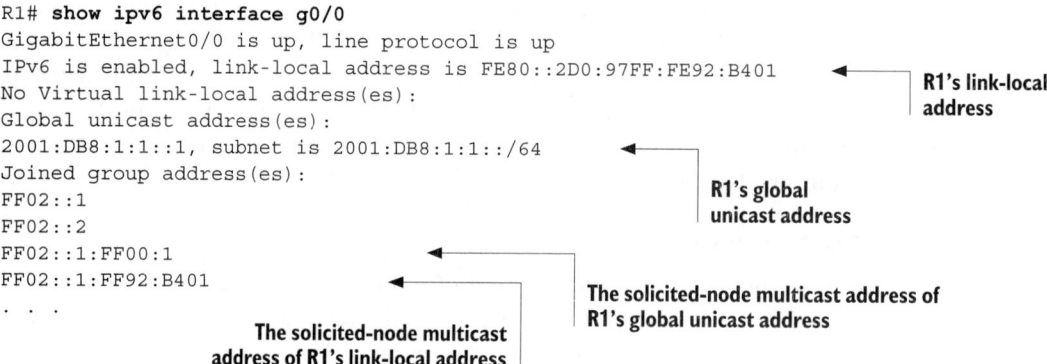

```
R1# show ipv6 interface g0/0
GigabitEthernet0/0 is up, line protocol is up
IPv6 is enabled, link-local address is FE80::2D0:97FF:FE92:B401
No Virtual link-local address(es):
Global unicast address(es):
2001:DB8:1:1::1, subnet is 2001:DB8:1:1::/64
Joined group address(es):
FF02::1
FF02::2
FF02::1:FF00:1
FF02::1:FF92:B401
. . .
```

- R1's link-local address (IPv6 is enabled, link-local address is FE80::2D0:97FF:FE92:B401)
- R1's global unicast address (2001:DB8:1:1::1)
- The solicited-node multicast address of R1's global unicast address (FF02::1:FF00:1)
- The solicited-node multicast address of R1's link-local address (FF02::1:FF92:B401)

NOTE Multicast packets, such as those destined for a solicited-node multicast address, are encapsulated in frames destined for an equivalent multicast MAC address. The details of these MAC addresses are beyond the scope of the CCNA exam.

21.1.2 Address resolution with NDP

One function of NDP is address resolution—mapping a known Layer 3 address to an unknown Layer 2 address. This is the ARP-like aspect of NDP. Whereas IPv4's ARP uses ARP request and ARP reply messages, NDP uses the following two ICMPv6 messages:

- *Neighbor Solicitation* (NS)—ICMPv6 type 135
- *Neighbor Advertisement* (NA)—ICMPv6 type 136

ICMP and ICMPv6 message types

NDP can be considered a component of ICMPv6—ICMP for IPv6. ICMP and ICMPv6 perform various functions in IPv4 and IPv6 networks, respectively, and they define various message types (each identified by a number) that they use to perform those functions.

Two example ICMP messages that we've covered are Echo Request (type 8) and Echo Reply (type 0), which are used for IPv4 ping messages. ICMPv6 uses its own Echo Request (type 128) and Echo Reply (type 129) messages for the same purpose.

NDP uses five different ICMPv6 messages: Router Solicitation (type 133), Router Advertisement (type 134), Neighbor Solicitation (type 135), Neighbor Advertisement (type 136), and Redirect (type 137). We'll cover the first four of those messages in this section.

Figure 21.2 shows the NDP address resolution process, consisting of an NS message from the requester and an NA message in response.

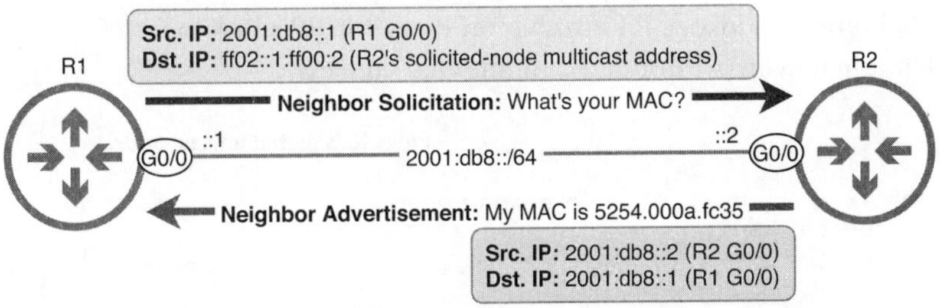

Figure 21.2 An NDP exchange between two routers. R1 sends an NS message to learn R2 G0/0's MAC address, and R2 sends an NA message in response.

ARP request messages are broadcast to all hosts on the local segment. However, as we covered in chapter 20, the concept of "broadcast" doesn't exist in IPv6; there is no broadcast address. This is where the solicited-node multicast address comes into play.

To learn a neighbor's MAC address, a host will send a *Neighbor Solicitation* (NS) message (equivalent to an ARP request) to the neighbor's solicited-node multicast address. The target of the NS message will then reply with a *Neighbor Advertisement* (NA) message (equivalent to an ARP reply), informing the requester of its MAC address. Unlike the NS message, the NA message is a simple unicast message from the responder to the requester.

Overlapping solicited-node multicast addresses

Although very unlikely, it's possible for two hosts to have different IPv6 addresses but identical solicited-node multicast addresses. For example:

- *Host A*—2001:db8:1:1::1100:1234/64
- *Host B*—2001:db8:1:1::2200:1234/64

> ***(continued)***
>
> Although the two addresses are unique, both result in the same solicited-node multicast IPv6 address: ff02::1:ff00:1234. So how can Host A and Host B differentiate between an NS destined for Host A and an NS destined for Host B?
>
> The answer lies within the NS message body itself—the payload of the IPv6 packet. NS messages include a Target Address field in which the unicast IPv6 address of the message's target (i.e., 2001:db8:1:1::1100:1234 for Host A) is specified. By examining this field, the hosts can identify which NS messages are meant for them and which should be ignored.

Just as a host using IPv4 stores L3–L2 address mappings in its ARP table, a host using IPv6 stores L3–L2 address mappings in its *IPv6 neighbor table*, which you can check with the command **`show ipv6 neighbors`**. In the following example, I send a ping from R1 to R2 and then check R1's neighbor table. Notice that in addition to an entry for R2's global unicast address, R1 also has an entry for R2's link-local address, which R1 created automatically (without me pinging that address):

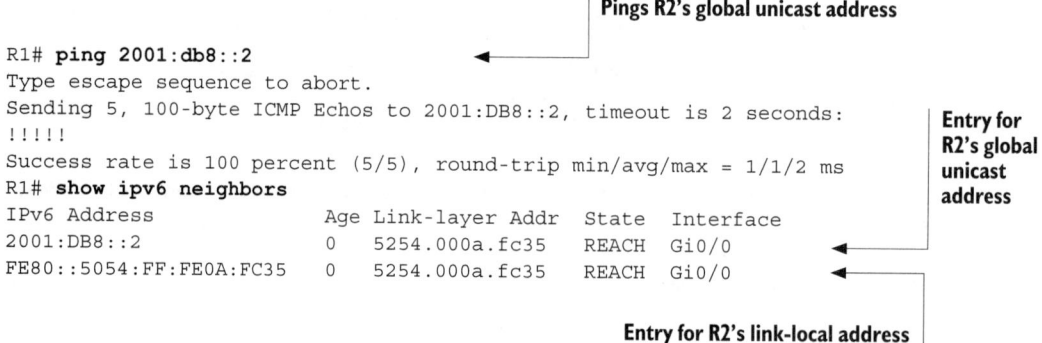

```
R1# ping 2001:db8::2                          <-- Pings R2's global unicast address
Type escape sequence to abort.
Sending 5, 100-byte ICMP Echos to 2001:DB8::2, timeout is 2 seconds:
!!!!!
Success rate is 100 percent (5/5), round-trip min/avg/max = 1/1/2 ms
R1# show ipv6 neighbors
IPv6 Address              Age Link-layer Addr  State  Interface
2001:DB8::2                 0  5254.000a.fc35   REACH  Gi0/0     <-- Entry for R2's global unicast address
FE80::5054:FF:FE0A:FC35     0  5254.000a.fc35   REACH  Gi0/0     <-- Entry for R2's link-local address
```

The `IPv6 Address` column lists each neighbor's IPv6 address, and the `Age` column indicates how many minutes have passed since each entry was created or refreshed. The `Link-Layer Addr` column lists each neighbor's MAC address, and the `State` columns indicate the state of each neighbor; the IPv6 neighbor states are beyond the scope of the CCNA exam (`REACH` means the neighbor is reachable—that's what you want to see). Finally, the `Interface` column lists the interface where each neighbor is connected.

21.1.3 Router discovery with NDP

In addition to its ARP-like address resolution functionality, NDP also provides *router discovery*, allowing hosts to automatically discover routers connected to the local network, as well as other characteristics of the local network (such as the network prefix). The following two message types are used for this purpose:

- *Router Solicitation* (RS)—ICMPv6 type 133
- *Router Advertisement* (RA)—ICMPv6 type 134

Router Solicitation (RS) messages are used to ask all routers on the local network to identify themselves; these messages are sent to the "all routers" link-local multicast address ff02::2. *Router Advertisement* (RA) messages are sent in response to RS messages and are also periodically sent by all routers (even without receiving an RS); RA messages are typically sent to the "all nodes" link-local multicast address ff02::1.

NDP's router discovery functionality is used to facilitate *Stateless Address Autoconfiguration* (SLAAC—pronounced "slack"). SLAAC allows a host to automatically generate its own IPv6 address and also learn other information such as the default gateway.

NOTE SLAAC is stateless because there is no central server keeping track of information such as which host has which address. This is in contrast to *Dynamic Host Configuration Protocol* (DHCP), in which a server manages address assignments; this is stateful. DHCP is the topic of chapter 4 of volume 2.

Figure 21.3 shows a Cisco router (R2) using SLAAC to generate an IPv6 address for its G0/0 interface; you can configure this with the **`ipv6 address autoconfig`** command. R2 then sends an RS message, and R1 replies with an RA message. From this RA message, R2 learns the network prefix of the link (2001:db8::/64) and uses Modified EUI-64 to generate the host portion of its IPv6 address.

NOTE Instead of Modified EUI-64, some operating systems randomly generate the host portion of the address. Cisco IOS, however, uses Modified EUI-64.

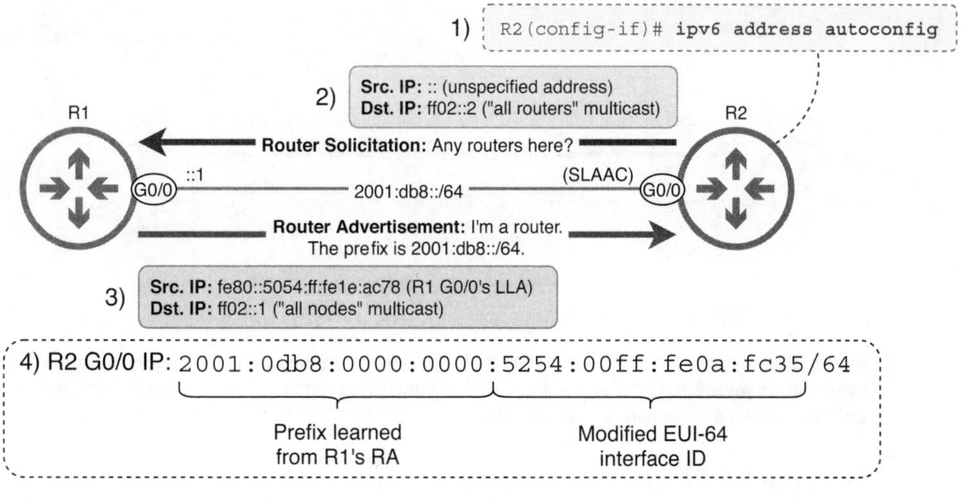

Figure 21.3 R2 uses SLAAC to generate an IPv6 address. (1) Issue the `ipv6 address autoconfig` command. (2) R2 sends an RS message. (3) R1 responds with an RA message. (4) R2 combines the learned prefix with a Modified EUI-64 interface ID to make its IPv6 address.

The **ipv6 address** *prefix* **eui-64** command (covered in chapter 20) and the ipv6 **address autoconfig** commands both use Modified EUI-64 to generate the host portion of the address. However, the former command requires you to manually specify the prefix, whereas the latter automatically learns the prefix via NDP RS/RA messages.

> **NOTE** If you use the **ipv6 address autoconfig default** command on a Cisco router, in addition to generating an IPv6 address, it will insert a default route into its routing table using the link-local address of the responding router as the next hop. Using the example of figure 21.3, R2 would insert a default route with R1 as the next hop.

21.1.4 Duplicate Address Detection

NDP's *Duplicate Address Detection* (DAD) is a feature that checks if an Ipv6 address is unique on the network before a host uses it. Whenever an interface is configured with an IPv6 address, whether it's automatically assigned or manually entered, it uses DAD. Also, any time a host's interface initializes (enters an up/up state), DAD checks all of its IPv6 addresses to make sure none of them are duplicates on the network.

> **NOTE** An IPv6 address is considered tentative until the DAD process completes; it cannot be used for communication until it has been proven unique on the network.

DAD is performed using two NDP messages that we covered previously: Neighbor Solicitation (NS) and Neighbor Advertisement (NA). Figure 21.4 shows how a Cisco router (R2) uses DAD to determine whether its newly configured IPv6 address is unique.

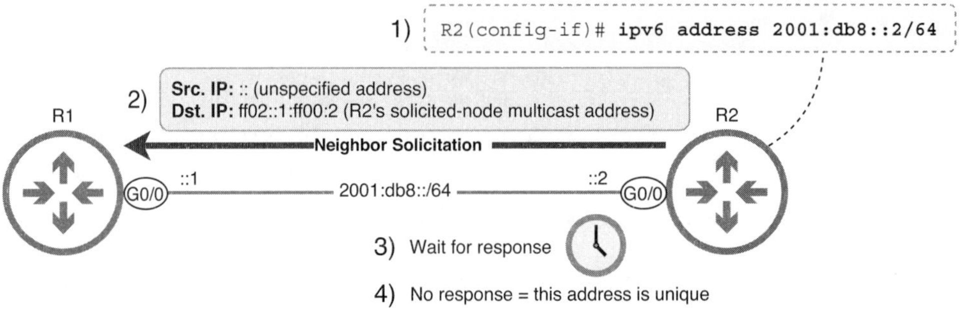

Figure 21.4 R2 uses DAD to verify that its Ipv6 address is unique. (1) Configure R2's address. (2) R2 sends an NS message to its own solicited-node multicast address. (3) R2 waits for a response. (4) R2 doesn't receive a response, so the address is unique.

To perform DAD, a host will send an NS message to its own solicited-node multicast address. If it receives no response after waiting a certain period of time, the host can safely declare that the address is unique; it can now use the address for communication. However, if it receives an NA message in response, it means another device on the network is already using the same IPv6 address; the address will be marked as a duplicate, and the host will not be able to use it to communicate over the network.

The following example shows what happens if, instead of a unique address, I configure the same IPv6 address as R1 on R2. A warning message is displayed, and the address is marked as `[DUP]` (duplicate) in the output of **`show ipv6 interface`**; R2 cannot use this address:

```
R2(config)# interface g0/0
R2(config-if)# ipv6 address 2001:db8::1/64
R2(config-if)# no shutdown
%IPV6_ND-4-DUPLICATE: Duplicate address 2001:DB8::2
➥on GigabitEthernet0/0
R2(config-if)# do show ipv6 interface g0/0
GigabitEthernet0/0 is up, line protocol is up
  IPv6 is enabled, link-local address is FE80::5054:FF:FE0A:FC35
  No Virtual link-local address(es):
  Global unicast address(es):
    2001:DB8::1, subnet is 2001:DB8::/64 [DUP]
. . .
```

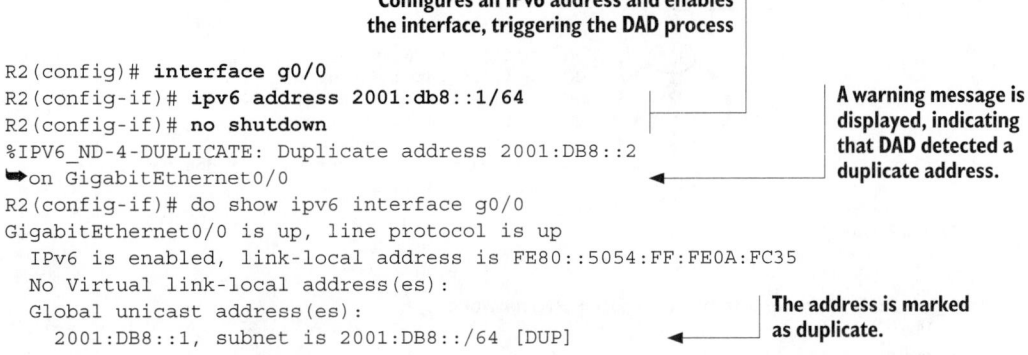

Configures an IPv6 address and enables the interface, triggering the DAD process

A warning message is displayed, indicating that DAD detected a duplicate address.

The address is marked as duplicate.

The solution for a duplicate address is simply to fix the configuration error: use **`no`** to remove the duplicate address, and reconfigure the interface with a unique address.

> **NOTE** DAD is not a standardized feature in IPv4, although some mechanisms can be used to detect duplicate addresses. IPv6 made DAD mandatory as a component of NDP.

21.2 The IPv6 routing table

Routers using IPv6 build a routing table—a database of the best route(s) to each destination known by the router. A router can learn routes in multiple ways, such as manual configuration (static routing) and dynamic routing. Additionally, a router automatically learns connected and local routes when you configure IP addresses on its interfaces.

All of this should sound familiar; it's the same as in IPv4. In this section, we will look at the routing table and review some fundamental routing concepts from an IPv6 perspective. Although the concepts are not new to you, understanding them in the context of IPv6 is crucial.

21.2.1 Connected and local routes

A *connected route* is a route to the network an interface is connected to; these routes are automatically added to the routing table for each interface that has an IP address and is in an up/up state. These routes tell the router that if a packet is destined for an IP address in this network, the router should forward the packet directly to the destination host.

A *local route* is a route to the exact IP address configured on the router's interface; the router automatically adds one of these routes to its routing table for each IP address that it has. These routes tell the router that if a packet is destined for this IP address, the router should receive the packet for itself—continue to de-encapsulate the message and examine the contents.

To demonstrate IPv6 connected and local routes, let's use the simple network shown in figure 21.5: one router with two connected networks.

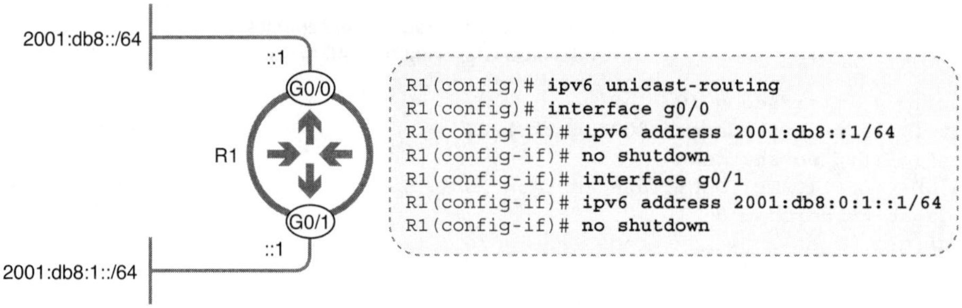

Figure 21.5 A router with two connected IPv6 networks

> **NOTE** As I noted in chapter 20, don't forget **ipv6 unicast-routing**! Forgetting this command is a very common mistake when configuring IPv6.

The following example shows the output of **show ipv6 interface brief** on R1. Notice that in addition to the global unicast address configured on each interface, R1 has two automatically generated (using Modified EUI-64) link-local addresses:

```
R1# show ipv6 interface brief
GigabitEthernet0/0      [up/up]
    FE80::5054:FF:FE06:1B6F
    2001:DB8::1
GigabitEthernet0/1      [up/up]
    FE80::5054:FF:FE09:A180
    2001:DB8:1::1
. . .
```

Now let's take a look at R1's IPv6 routing table with **show ipv6 route**. The output is very similar to what you're used to from the IPv4 routing table:

```
R1# show ipv6 route
IPv6 Routing Table - default - 5 entries
Codes: C - Connected, L - Local, S - Static, U - Per-user Static route
. . .
C   2001:DB8::/64 [0/0]
     via GigabitEthernet0/0, directly connected       | G0/0's connected route
L   2001:DB8::1/128 [0/0]
     via GigabitEthernet0/0, receive                  | G0/0's local route
C   2001:DB8:1::/64 [0/0]
     via GigabitEthernet0/1, directly connected       | G0/1's connected route
L   2001:DB8:1::1/128 [0/0]
     via GigabitEthernet0/1, receive                  | G0/1's local route
```

```
L    FF00::/8 [0/0]
      via Null0, receive
```

A route that discards multicast traffic

R1 added a connected route and a local route for each address configured on its interfaces. A local route is an example of a *host route*—a route to a single destination IP address (R1's own IP address, in this case). IPv6 host routes use a /128 prefix length. A connected route is an example of a *network route*—a route to more than one destination IP address. Any IPv6 route with a prefix length of /127 or shorter is a network route.

EXAM TIP Network and host routes are exam topics 3.3.b and 3.3.c, respectively. Make sure you can identify and configure them in both IPv4 and IPv6. We will cover how to configure IPv6 static routes in section 21.3.

However, R1 did not add any connected or local routes for its link-local addresses—this is expected. Traffic to and from link-local addresses doesn't need to be routed in the traditional sense because it never leaves the local link; there's no need for a routing table entry. A link-local address can be used as the next-hop address of a route (as we'll cover in section 21.3.2), but never as the destination of a route.

The final route in R1's routing table is a route to ff00::/8—the multicast address range. This route is inserted automatically by the router. The route specifies `Null0`, a virtual interface; packets sent to this interface are dropped. Cisco routers don't forward multicast packets by default, so this route ensures that multicast packets are dropped.

NOTE The ff00::/8 route doesn't prevent the router from sending or receiving multicast packets, such as those used in NDP exchanges with its neighbors. It prevents the router from forwarding multicast packets.

21.2.2 Route selection

When a router receives a packet, it looks up the packet's destination IP address in its routing table and selects the best route; this is called *route selection.* The router will forward the packet according to the *most specific matching route*—the matching route with the longest prefix length. Once again, this is identical to IPv4.

NOTE As covered in chapter 17, the term *route selection* can also refer to the process of selecting which routes enter the router's routing table (using metric and administrative distance).

Figure 21.6 shows a route selection decision by R1; a packet arrives on one of its interfaces, so R1 has to make a decision about what to do with the packet. Two of R1's routes match the packet's destination IP address, and R1 selects the more specific of the two—the route with the longer prefix length (/128 vs. /64).

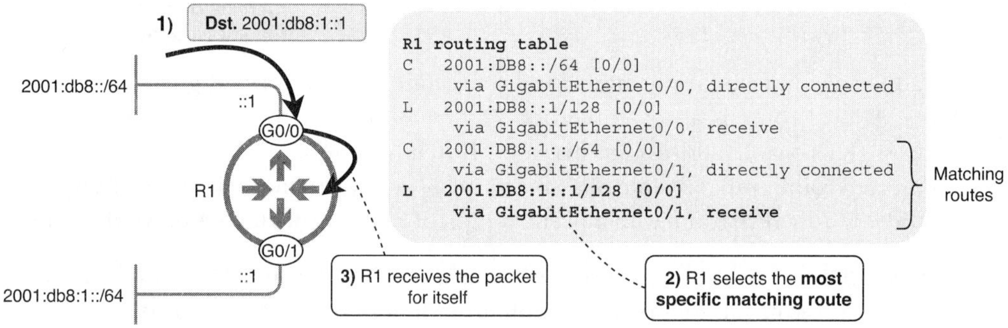

Figure 21.6 R1 makes a route selection decision. 1) R1 receives a packet destined for 2001:db8:1::1. 2) R1 performs a routing table lookup and selects the most specific matching route—the local route to 2001:db8:1::1/128. 3) R1 receives the packet for itself.

What happens if there is no route in the routing table that matches the packet's destination IP address? The answer is the same as in IPv4: the router drops the packet.

21.3 IPv6 static routing

Connected routes allow a router to forward packets destined for hosts in its connected networks, and local routes allow the router to receive packets destined for itself. However, most routers also need to be able to forward packets to remote destinations—those that aren't directly connected to the router itself. To achieve that, we need to either manually configure routes to those destinations (static routing) or enable a dynamic routing protocol and allow the router to automatically share routing information with other routers.

Although IPv4 dynamic routing is included in the CCNA exam topics, IPv6 dynamic routing is not. IPv6 static routing, however, is a CCNA exam topic, so let's look at how to configure IPv6 static routes on Cisco routers. Figure 21.7 shows the network we'll use for this section; this is the same topology we used when covering IPv4 static routing in chapter 9.

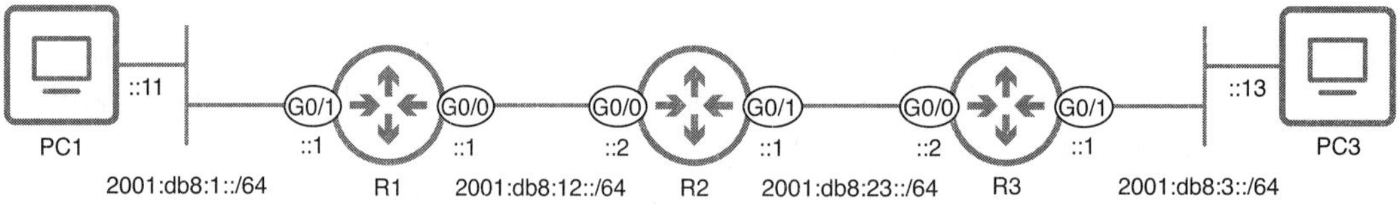

Figure 21.7 An IPv6 network consisting of three routers. Which static routes must be configured to enable communication between PC1 and PC3?

For the goal of enabling communication between PC1 and PC3, each router needs a route to PC1's network (2001:db8:1::/64) and a route to PC3's network (2001:db8:3::/64). R1 has a connected route to 2001:db8:1::/64, and R3 has one to 2001:db8:3::/64, leaving four static routes that we must configure—table 21.2 lists those routes.

Table 21.2 IPv6 static routes required to enable communication between PC1 and PC3

Router	Required routes	Next hop
R1	2001:db8:3::/64	2001:db8:12::2 (R2 G0/0)
R2	2001:db8:1::/64	2001:db8:12::1 (R1 G0/0)
	2001:db8:3::/64	2001:db8:23::2 (R3 G0/0)
R3	2001:db8:1::/64	2001:db8:23::1 (R2 G0/1)

21.3.1 Configuring IPv6 static routes

The command to configure an IPv6 static route is **`ipv6 route`**. After specifying the destination network prefix, you can specify the next-hop IP address, the exit interface, or both. In this section, we'll examine each of those configuration methods:

- **`ipv6 route`** *`destination-prefix next-hop`*
- **`ipv6 route`** *`destination-prefix exit-interface`*
- **`ipv6 route`** `destination-prefix exit-interface next-hop`

Recursive static routes

A static route that specifies only the next-hop IP address is called a *recursive static route.* Figure 21.8 shows how to configure four recursive static routes to enable communication between PC1 and PC3.

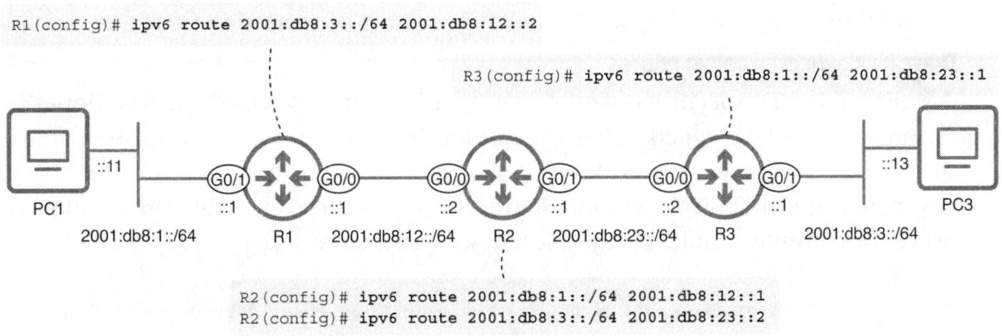

Figure 21.8 Configuring recursive static routes on R1, R2, and R3 to enable PC1–PC3 communication. Each route's next-hop IP address is specified.

> **NOTE** Like configuring IPv6 addresses on interfaces, IPv6 static routes use slash notation (i.e. /64), not dotted-decimal netmasks.

In the following example, I configure the necessary routes on R2 and check its routing table with **`show ipv6 route static`** (to display only static routes):

```
R2(config)# ipv6 route 2001:db8:1::/64 2001:db8:12::1
R2(config)# ipv6 route 2001:db8:3::/64 2001:db8:23::2
```

```
R2(config)# do show ipv6 route static
. . .
S   2001:DB8:1::/64 [1/0]
     via 2001:DB8:12::1
S   2001:DB8:3::/64 [1/0]
     via 2001:DB8:23::2
```

This type of route is called *recursive* because it requires recursive (repeated) routing table lookups:

1. A lookup to find the IP address of the next hop
2. A lookup to find which interface the next hop is connected to

If R2 receives a packet destined for PC3, the second static route we configured tells R2 which next hop to forward the packet to (2001:db8:23::2). R2 would then need to do a second routing table lookup to determine which interface 2001:db8:23::2 is connected to. In the following example, I use **show ipv6 route connected** to show R2's connected routes:

```
R2# show ipv6 route connected
. . .
C   2001:DB8:12::/64 [0/0]
     via GigabitEthernet0/0, directly connected
C   2001:DB8:23::/64 [0/0]
     via GigabitEthernet0/1, directly connected
```

R2 has a connected route to 2001:db8:23::/64 on its G0/1 interface; this route matches next hop 2001:db8:23::2. R2 now knows how to forward the PC3-destined packet: it should forward it to next hop 2001:db8:23::2, which is connected to G0/1.

DIRECTLY CONNECTED STATIC ROUTES

A static route that specifies only the exit interface—the interface packets should be forwarded out of—is called a *directly connected static route.* The reason for the name is that this kind of route makes the router believe that it is directly connected to the destination specified in the route. Figure 21.9 shows the same routes we configured previously—this time only specifying each route's exit interface.

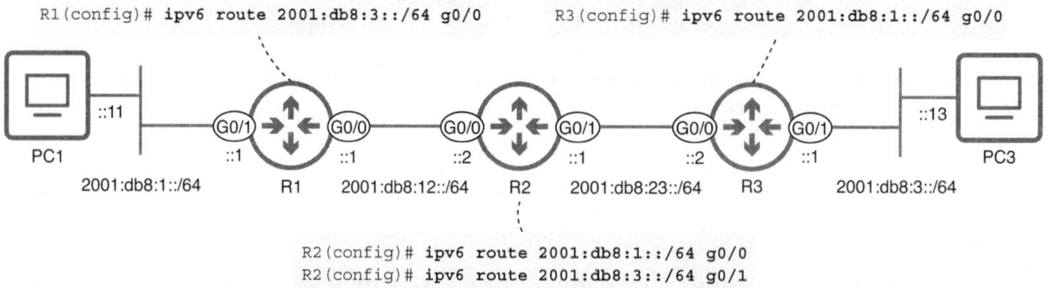

Figure 21.9 Configuring fully specified static routes on R1, R2, and R3. Each route's exit interface is specified.

There is one major problem with these routes: they don't work! The routers will accept the commands, and the routes will appear in the routers' routing tables, but communication via these routes will fail.

IPv4 directly connected static routes rely on a mechanism called *proxy ARP*, in which a router responds to ARP requests on behalf of another host. Cisco routers don't support an equivalent proxy NDP, so these routes won't work as intended. In the following example, I configure R1's route to 2001:db8:3::/64 and check its routing table; at first glance, there doesn't seem to be anything wrong with the route:

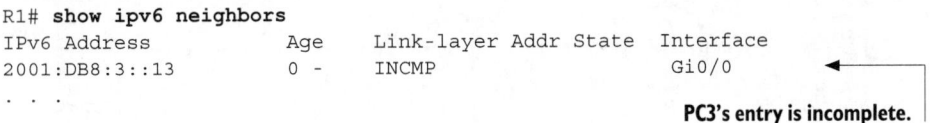

```
R1(config)# ipv6 route 2001:db8:3::/64 g0/0          <-- Configures a directly
R1(config)# do show ipv6 route static                    connected static route
. . .
S    2001:DB8:3::/64 [1/0]
     via GigabitEthernet0/0, directly connected       <-- The route appears as directly connected.
```

After looking at R1's routing table, you might assume that it's ready to forward packets between PC1 and PC3; if this were an IPv4 network, it would be. However, in this case, a ping from PC1 to PC3 fails, and R1's IPv6 neighbor table shows why:

```
R1# show ipv6 neighbors
IPv6 Address              Age    Link-layer Addr State   Interface
2001:DB8:3::13            0 -    INCMP                    Gi0/0      <-- PC3's entry is incomplete.
. . .
```

R1's neighbor table shows an `INCMP` (incomplete) entry for PC3 (2001:db8:3::13). This entry means that R1 sent a neighbor solicitation message out of G0/0 to try to learn PC3's MAC address, but it failed to resolve the address; R2 didn't reply on behalf of PC3. As a result, R1 was unable to encapsulate PC1's pings to PC3 in properly addressed Ethernet frames; R1 had no choice but to drop them.

EXAM TIP If an exam question requires you to configure, verify, or troubleshoot IPv6 static routes, remember that directly connected static routes don't work on Ethernet interfaces, even though they appear as valid routes in the routing table—a potential trick question!

Serial interfaces

Directly connected IPv6 static routes don't work on Ethernet interfaces (including Fast Ethernet, Gigabit Ethernet, etc.), but they do work on *serial* interfaces. Serial interfaces are a legacy technology used for point-to-point connections between two devices. Due to their exclusively point-to-point nature, they don't need any Layer 2 addressing to indicate which device frames are destined for; a frame sent by one device must be destined for the other device.

(continued)

As a result, serial interfaces don't use MAC addresses and don't require ARP/NDP address resolution, so directly connected IPv6 (and IPv4) routes work on these connections. Serial interfaces used to be common for *Wide Area Network* (WAN) connections and were on previous versions of the CCNA exam but were removed from the exam topics list in 2020.

FULLY SPECIFIED STATIC ROUTES

A *fully specified static route* specifies both the exit interface and the next hop. Figure 21.10 shows the same four routes we configured in the previous two examples—this time specifying each route's exit interface and next-hop IP address.

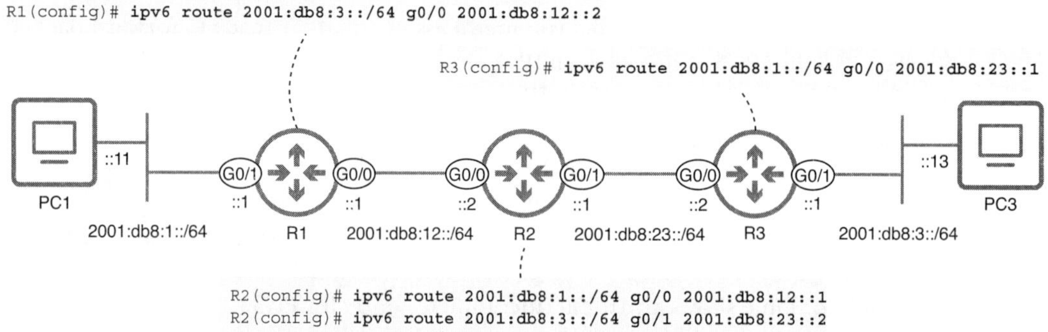

Figure 21.10 Configuring fully specified static routes on R1, R2, and R3 to enable PC1–PC3 communication. Each route's exit interface and next-hop IP address are specified.

In the following example, I show the configuration of R3's route to 2001:db8:1::/64 and then check its routing table:

```
R3(config)# ipv6 route 2001:db8:1::/64 g0/0 2001:db8:23::1    <-- Configures a fully specified static route
R3(config)# do show ipv6 route static
. . .
S 2001:DB8:3::/64 [1/0]
via 2001:DB8:12::2, GigabitEthernet0/0    <-- The route shows both the next hop and the exit interface.
```

In practice, you can configure either recursive or fully specified static routes; there is no significant difference in performance between them. Just remember that IPv6 directly connected static routes don't work on Ethernet connections.

21.3.2 Link-local next hops

Packets sourced from or destined for link-local addresses are not routable; a router will not forward them. However, a link-local address can be used as the next hop of a route. This may seem counterintuitive—how can an unroutable address be used in a route? Link-local next hops work because the link-local address is only used to direct the packet to the next immediate destination on the local link, not to route it across multiple hops or network segments.

Figure 21.11 shows the same example network as before, with the same four routes configured to enable communication between PC1 and PC3. This time, I used link-local next-hop addresses.

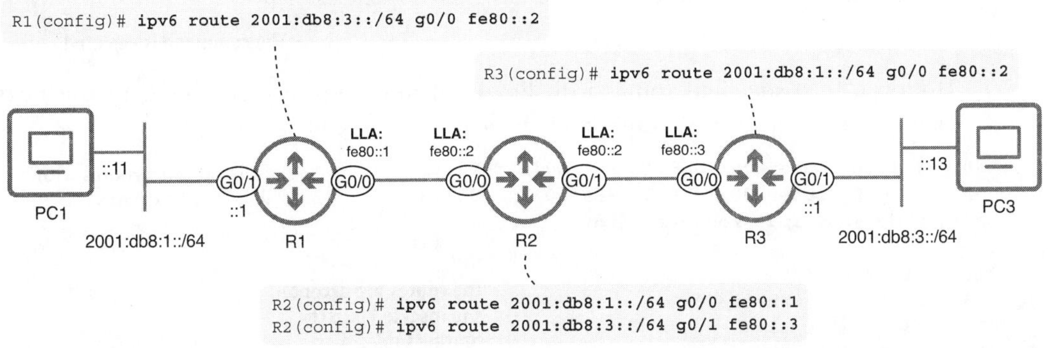

Figure 21.11 Configuring static routes using link-local next hops on R1, R2, and R3 to enable PC1–PC3 communication

You may have noticed that global unicast addresses are not shown for the R1–R2 and R2–R3 links in figure 21.11. These connections are examples of *transit links*—links that only serve to carry traffic between different parts of a network. Because these links don't serve as destinations for data, there's often no need to be able to communicate with them from remote networks; link-local addressing is sufficient for them to serve their purpose.

Although all IPv6-enabled interfaces automatically generate a link-local address using Modified EUI-64 rules, I manually configured the routers' link-local addresses to simplify them. In the following example, I configure R2's link-local addresses as fe80::2:

```
R2(config)# interface range g0/0-1
R2(config-if-range)# ipv6 address fe80::2 link-local
```

If configuring the same IP address on two different interfaces seems strange to you, you're right! Because a router's role is to connect different networks, no two interfaces should be in the same subnet, let alone have the exact same IP address. However, link-local addresses are an exception to that rule.

Because link-local addresses are significant and must be unique only within the context of a single network link, the same link-local address can be used on different interfaces as long as they are on separate links. This allows for configurations like the previous example: identical link-local addresses on multiple interfaces of the same router.

All of the static routes shown in figure 21.11 are fully specified; that's for a good reason. All link-local addresses share the same fe80::/64 prefix, and it's possible for the same IP address to exist on multiple links. For that reason, a route specifying a link-local next-hop IP address without specifying the exit interface is ambiguous; the router has no way to know which interface the correct next hop is connected to. In fact, IOS won't let you configure such a route, as shown in the following example:

```
R2(config)# ipv6 route 2001:db8:1::/64 fe80::1
% Interface has to be specified for a link-local nexthop
```

Configures only a link-local next-hop IP address

The command is rejected.

However, fully specified routes with link-local next hops are accepted. In the next example, I configure R2's routes and check its routing table:

```
R2(config)# ipv6 route 2001:db8:1::/64 g0/0 fe80::1
R2(config)# ipv6 route 2001:db8:3::/64 g0/1 fe80::3
R2(config)# do show ipv6 route static
. . .
S 2001:DB8:1::/64 [1/0]
via FE80::1, GigabitEthernet0/0
S 2001:DB8:3::/64 [1/0]
via FE80::3, GigabitEthernet0/1
```

Fully specified routes with link-local next hops

The routes are accepted and inserted into the routing table.

To summarize, here are three takeaways regarding link-local IP addresses:

- Link-local addresses alone can be sufficient on transit links. Global unicast/unique local addresses might be unnecessary.
- Link-local addresses have to be unique only in the context of the local link.
- Routes with link-local next hops must be fully specified.

21.3.3 Configuring a default route

An IPv6 *default route* is a route to ::/0, which matches every possible IPv6 address—all 340,282,366,920,938,463,463,374,607,431,768,211,456 of them. This is equivalent to 0.0.0.0/0 in IPv4. By being the least specific route possible, a default route is used as a catch-all, only selected to forward a packet if no other routes match the packet's destination IP address.

Default routes are most commonly used to provide a route to the internet. The logic is that packets destined for hosts in the enterprise's internal network should have a more specific route in the routing table; if the router receives a packet that doesn't match any internal destination, it's probably destined for the internet. Figure 21.12 shows an example of a default route to the internet.

EXAM TIP Default static routes are exam topic 3.3.a, and you should know how to configure them in both IPv4 and IPv6.

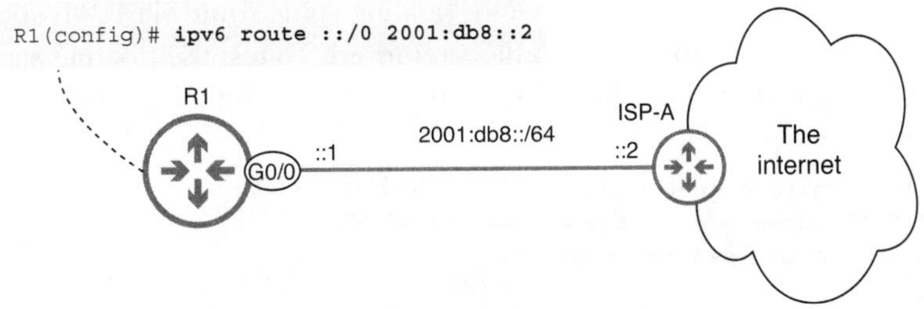

Figure 21.12 Configuring a default route to the internet

21.3.4 Floating static routes

As in IPv4, specifying an administrative distance (AD) value at the end of an IPv6 static route allows you to create a *floating static route*—a route that is made less preferable by using a non-default AD value. Figure 21.13 shows an example of a floating static route. Continuing from the example we saw in figure 21.12, R1 is now connected to a second ISP (ISP-B). A floating static route using ISP-B as the next hop provides a backup route to the internet.

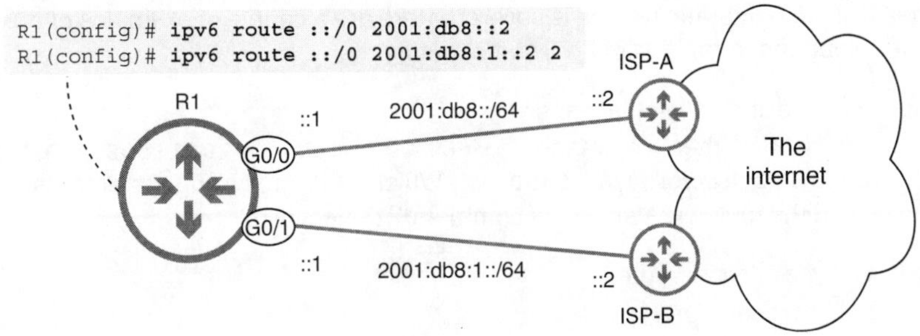

Figure 21.13 Configuring default routes to the internet. The route via ISP-A serves as the primary route, and the floating route via ISP-B serves as a backup.

Let's examine the effect of this configuration. In the following example, I configure the two routes on R1 and check its routing table:

```
R1(config)# ipv6 route ::/0 2001:db8::2          <- Configures a default route via ISP-A
R1(config)# ipv6 route ::/0 2001:db8:1::2 2      <- Configures a floating default route via ISP-B
R1(config)# do show ipv6 route static
. . .
S ::/0 [1/0]                                     R1 inserts only the
via 2001:DB8::2                                  route via ISP-A.
```

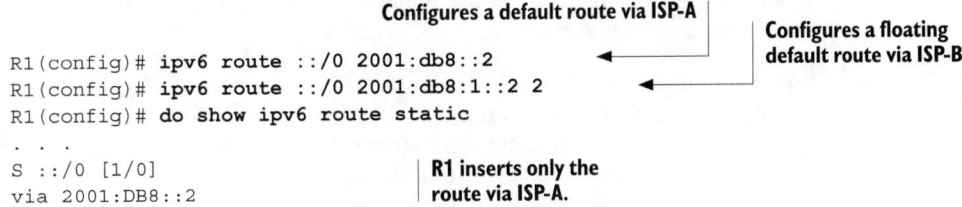

Static routes have an AD value of 1 by default. By configuring the ISP-B route with an AD value of 2, I made it less preferable than the ISP-A route. As a result, R1 inserts only the ISP-A route into its routing table. The floating static route via ISP-B should only enter the routing table if the ISP-A route is removed. To test the floating static route, in the following example, I disable R1's G0/0 interface, simulating a hardware failure on the connection:

```
R1(config)# interface g0/0
R1(config)# shutdown
R1(config)# do show ipv6 route static
. . .
S ::/0 [2/0]
via 2001:DB8:1::2
```

Disables R1's G0/0 interface

The floating static route enters the routing table.

As expected, the floating static route entered the routing table only after the ISP-A route was removed. Floating static routes are used as backup routes, whether that is a backup to another static route (as in this example) or another kind of route.

EXAM TIP Floating static routes are exam topic 3.3.d, so make sure you know how to configure them in both IPv4 and IPv6.

Exam scenarios

Just like IPv4 routing, IPv6 routing is a critical part of the CCNA exam, although when it comes to IPv6, only static routing is covered. Here are a couple of examples of questions that test your understanding of IPv6 static routing:

1 (multiple choice, multiple answers)
You issue the command **`ipv6 route 2001:db8:1:1::1/128 GigabitEthernet0/1 fe80::2`**. Which of the following statements are true about the route created by the command? (Select two.)

- A It is a network route.
- B It is a host route.
- C It is a recursive route.
- D It is a directly connected route.
- E It is a fully specified route.

This question tests your understanding of the different IPv6 route types we covered in this chapter. The destination of the route uses a /128 prefix length; it is a route to a single destination IPv6 address, making it a host route. So B is correct. The route specifies both an exit interface and a next-hop IP address, so it is a fully specified route. Therefore, E is the second correct answer.

2 (lab simulation)
A lab simulation might require you to configure IPv6 static routes to enable connectivity between hosts in a network. You could be given a network diagram and be required to configure the appropriate routes on one or more routers—perhaps with a floating static route or two thrown in for an additional challenge! Remember that the principles of IPv4 and IPv6 static routes are the same; the only major differences are the first word of the command (**`ip`** vs **`ipv6`**) and the format of the addresses.

Summary

- IPv6 uses *Neighbor Discovery Protocol* for various essential functions like ARP-esque Layer 2 address resolution, router discovery, and duplicate address detection.
- Some NDP functions, such as address resolution and duplicate address detection, use a *solicited-node multicast* address, which is generated from a unicast address.
- To generate a solicited-node multicast address, prepend ff02:0000:0000:0000:0000:0001:ff (ff02::1:ff) to the last six hexadecimal digits of the unicast address. For example, 2001:db8::12:3456 results in ff02::1:ff12:3456.
- NDP address resolution uses two ICMPv6 messages: *Neighbor Solicitation* (NS) and *Neighbor Advertisement* (NA). These are equivalent to ARP Request and ARP Reply.
- To learn a neighbor's MAC address, a host will send an NS message to the neighbor's solicited-node multicast address. The neighbor will reply with a unicast NA message, informing the sender of its MAC address.
- An IPv6 host stores its L3–L2 address mappings in the *IPv6 neighbor table*, which can be viewed with **`show ipv6 neighbors`**.
- NDP's router discovery function allows hosts to automatically discover routers connected to the local network, as well as other characteristics of the local network (such as the prefix).
- Router discovery uses two message types: *Router Solicitation* (RS) and *Router Advertisement* (RA).
- RS messages are sent to the "all routers" multicast address (ff02::2) to ask all routers on the local link to identify themselves. Routers typically send RA messages to the "all nodes" multicast address (ff02::1) in reply.
- NDP router discovery facilitates *Stateless Address Autoconfiguration* (SLAAC), which allows a host to automatically generate its own IPv6 address.
- A SLAAC-enabled host will send an RS message to discover routers on the local link, and routers will reply with RA messages.
- The host will combine the prefix information learned from the RA with an EUI-64 interface identifier to automatically generate its IPv6 address.
- You can configure a Cisco router to learn its IPv6 address via SLAAC with **`ipv6 address autoconfig`**.
- NDP's Duplicate Address Detection (DAD) is a feature that checks if an IPv6 address is unique on the network before a host uses it.
- Whenever an interface is configured with an IPv6 address, the host uses DAD. Likewise, when an IPv6-enabled interface initializes, it uses DAD.
- To perform DAD, a host sends an NS message to its own solicited-node multicast address. If there is no response, the address is determined to be unique. If the host receives an NA message in response, the address is a duplicate.
- If DAD detects a duplicate IPv6 address, the address cannot be used.

- IPv6-enabled routers build a routing table in which they store the best route(s) to each known destination. You can view the IPv6 routing table with **`show ipv6 route`**.
- A router will insert a connected route to each network its interfaces are connected to and a local route to the exact IP address of each of its interfaces.
- A local route is an example of a *host route*—a route to a single destination IP address. IPv6 host routes use a /128 prefix length.
- A connected route is an example of a *network route*—a route to more than one destination IP address, with a /127 or shorter prefix length.
- Routers forward IPv6 packets according to the *most specific matching route* in the routing table—the same as IPv4 packets.
- A static route that specifies only the next-hop IP address is called a *recursive static route* because it requires recursive (repeated) routing table lookups to forward a packet. The command syntax is **`ipv6 route`** *`destination-prefix next-hop`*.
- A static route that specifies only the exit interface is called a *directly connected static route* because it makes the router believe that it is directly connected to the destination network. The syntax is **`ipv6 route`** *`destination-prefix exit-interface`*.
- Directly connected IPv6 static routes don't work on Ethernet interfaces. Directly connected IPv4 static routes rely on proxy ARP to work, but Cisco routers don't support an equivalent proxy NDP.
- A static route that specifies both the exit interface and the next-hop IP address is called a *fully specified static route*. The syntax is **`ipv6 route`** *`destination-prefix exit-interface next-hop`*.
- Although packets sourced from and destined for link-local addresses are not routable, link-local addresses can be used as next-hop addresses of routes.
- *Transit links* are links that only serve to carry traffic between different parts of a network—they often do not need global unicast/unique local addresses. Link-local addresses are often sufficient.
- Link-local addresses must be unique only within the context of a single link, so multiple interfaces on the same router can share the same link-local address.
- Static routes with link-local next hops must be fully specified; IOS will reject the command otherwise.
- An IPv6 default route is a route to ::/0, which matches every possible IPv6 address. This is equivalent to 0.0.0.0/0 in IPv4.
- Default routes are most commonly used to provide a route to the internet. Packets that don't match any internal destinations are forwarded to the internet.

- An administrative distance (AD) value can be specified at the end of the `ipv6 route` command to configure a *floating static route*—a route that is made less preferable by configuring it with a non-default AD.
- Floating static routes act as backup routes, only entering the routing table if a more desirable route (i.e., another static route with the default AD value) is removed.

Part 6

Layer 4 and IP access control lists

Having covered several key Layer 2 and Layer 3 concepts in previous parts of this book, in part 6, we now move up to Layer 4: the Transport Layer. Whereas Layers 1, 2, and 3 are focused on carrying messages between hosts with the help of the switches and routers that form the network infrastructure, Layer 4 runs on top of those lower layers and is responsible for ensuring that messages are delivered to the correct application in an efficient and reliable manner. Chapter 22 of this book delves into the two primary protocols that operate at this layer—TCP and UDP—comparing and contrasting their features, benefits, and drawbacks.

Chapters 23 and 24 move our focus to IP access control lists (ACLs), an essential tool for network security, controlling the flow of traffic by selectively permitting and denying packets. Standard ACLs, discussed in chapter 23, enable traffic filtering based on source IP addresses, providing a basic level of security and traffic control. Chapter 24 covers extended ACLs, providing a chance to apply the Layer 4 knowledge acquired in chapter 22; extended ACLs enable traffic filtering based not only on source and destination IP addresses but also Layer 4 TCP/UDP port numbers and other parameters.

Part 6 is a critical section that bridges the gap between the lower-level networking functions of Layers 1, 2, and 3 and the higher-level applications they support. TCP, UDP, and standard/extended ACLs have wide applications in networking and are critical CCNA exam topics; they will come up several times in volume 2 of this book. So let's get started!

22 Transmission Control Protocol and User Datagram Protocol

This chapter covers

- How the Transmission Control Protocol and User Datagram Protocol provide Layer 4 addressing and session multiplexing
- How TCP provides features like reliable communication and flow control
- Comparing TCP and UDP, and the situations in which each is preferred

In chapter 3 of this book, we covered physical cables, connectors, and ports—Layer 1 of the TCP/IP model. In other chapters, we covered the Data Link Layer (Layer 2): MAC addresses, frame switching, VLANs, STP, and other related topics. We have also spent many pages on the Network Layer (Layer 3): IPv4 and IPv6 addressing, subnetting, packet forwarding, static and dynamic routing, first-hop redundancy protocols, etc. In this chapter, we will venture beyond those first three layers and take a look at Layer 4 of the TCP/IP model: the Transport Layer. Specifically, we will examine the two major Layer 4 protocols: Transmission Control Protocol (TCP) and User Datagram Protocol (UDP), which are exam topic 1.5: Compare TCP to UDP.

22.1 The role of Layer 4

In chapter 4 of this book, we took a high-level look at the role of each layer of the TCP/IP model. For review, figure 22.1 summarizes the role of each layer.

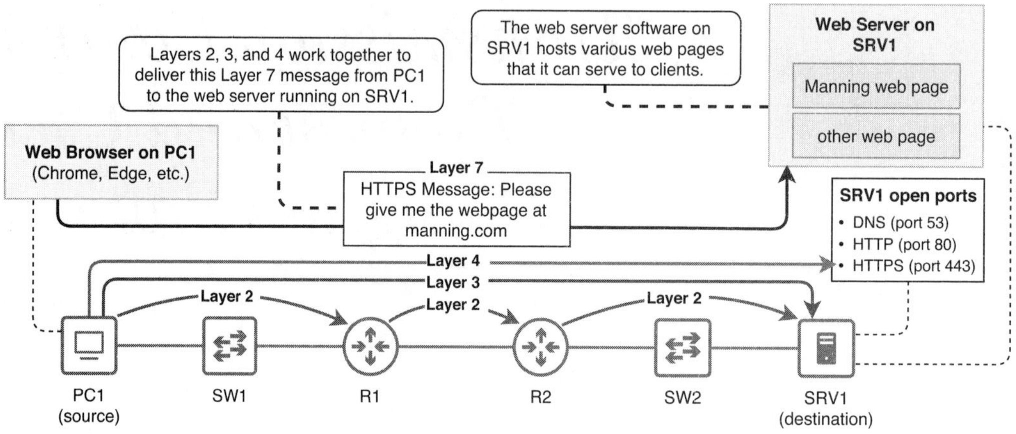

Figure 22.1 A web browser on PC1 uses a Layer-7 protocol (HTTPS) to request a web page from the web server on SRV1. Layers 2, 3, and 4 work together to deliver the message to the appropriate application on SRV1. Layer 1 provides the medium over which the communication occurs.

> **NOTE** *Hypertext Transfer Protocol Secure* (HTTPS) is an Application Layer protocol often used for transmitting web pages over a network, such as the internet.

Layer 1 encompasses the physical components required for communication: the cables connecting the devices and the signals that travel over them. Layer 2 deals with hop-to-hop communication between intermediate nodes in the path to the destination. Switches use Layer 2 information (MAC addresses) to make forwarding decisions, and end hosts and routers must encapsulate packets in frames destined for the MAC address of the next hop.

Layer 3 provides end-to-end addressing from the source host to the destination host, and routers use Layer 3 information (IP addresses) to make forwarding decisions, ensuring packets reach their correct destinations. However, it's not enough for the data to reach the correct destination host; the data has to reach the correct application process on the destination host, and that's one of the major roles of Layer 4. However, Layer 4 can also provide many other services that we will examine when looking at the specifics of TCP and UDP in section 22.2.

In this chapter, we will focus primarily on Layer 4 communication between hosts, but don't forget that Layer 4 operates on top of Layers 1, 2, and 3; the lower layers are necessary to deliver Layer 4 segments between the communicating hosts. Likewise, keep in mind that Layer 4's purpose is to provide services to the Application Layer protocols that run above Layer 4, although we won't focus on the specifics of those protocols in this chapter.

22.1.1 Port numbers

Like Ethernet and IP, Layer 4 protocols such as TCP and UDP use their own system of addressing, called *ports*. The term *port*, in this case, does not refer to a physical port on a device; a Layer 4 port is a number ranging from 0 to 65535 that is used to address a message to a specific application process on the destination host.

Figure 22.2 shows how PC1 addresses data to a specific application service on SRV1. Data prepared by the Application Layer is encapsulated in a TCP header, making a TCP segment. The segment is sourced from a random port (more on this later) and destined for port 443; this addresses the message to the HTTPS service running on SRV1. This segment is encapsulated in an IP header destined for SRV1's IP address. This packet is then encapsulated in a new Ethernet header/trailer at each hop in the path from PC1 to SRV1—a process we've covered a few times in this book.

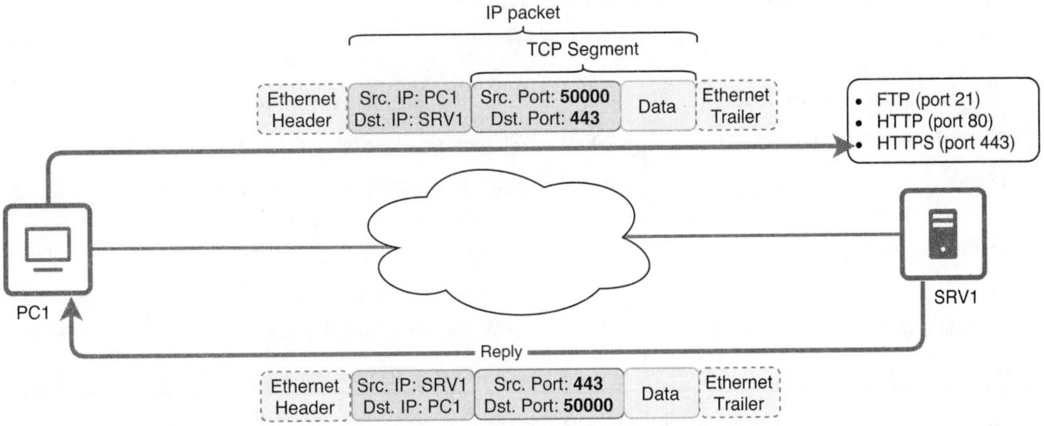

Figure 22.2 PC1 sends a TCP segment to SRV1. The segment is sourced from port 50000 on PC1 and destined for port 443 on SRV1. SRV1's reply reverses the ports: it is sourced from port 443 on SRV1 and destined for port 50000 on PC1.

When SRV1 replies to PC1, SRV1 reverses the port numbers; SRV1's TCP segment to PC1 is sourced from port 443 and destined for port 50000. This is similar to how the IP addresses are reversed; the reply is sourced from SRV1's IP address and destined for PC1's IP address.

Some Application Layer protocols use TCP as their Layer 4 protocol, and some use UDP; as we'll cover in section 22.2, TCP and UDP have different characteristics that make them suitable for different kinds of Application Layer protocols. In addition to using a specific Layer 4 protocol, each Application Layer protocol also uses a different port number. As we saw in figure 22.2, HTTPS uses TCP as its Layer 4 protocol, with its port number being 443. To address a message to the web server running on SRV1 (which uses HTTPS), PC1 must send the message in a TCP segment destined for port 443.

NOTE Although TCP and UDP are the most common Layer 4 protocols, they are not the only ones. However, for the purpose of the CCNA exam, you just need to know TCP and UDP.

A server running a particular application service is said to "listen on" the relevant port, meaning it waits for incoming messages addressed to the specific TCP or UDP port number. For example, a web server using HTTPS listens on TCP port 443. Table 22.1 lists the Layer 4 protocols and port numbers of some common Application Layer protocols. Note that some protocols can use both TCP and UDP, depending on what kind of communication is required. For example, *Domain Name System* (DNS)—used to translate names like google.com to IP addresses—uses either TCP or UDP; we'll cover DNS in chapter 3 of volume 2 of this book.

Table 22.1 Port numbers of common Application Layer protocols

TCP		UDP	
Application Layer Protocol	**Port**	**Application Layer Protocol**	**Port**
FTP (File Transfer Protocol) data	20	DNS (Domain Name System)	53
FTP control	21	DHCP (Dynamic Host Configuration Protocol) server	67
SSH (Secure Shell)	22	DHCP client	68
Telnet	23	TFTP (Trivial File Transfer Protocol)	69
SMTP (Simple Mail Transfer Protocol)	25	NTP (Network Time Protocol)	123
DNS (Domain Name System)	53	SNMP (Simple Network Management Protocol) agent	161
HTTP (Hypertext Transfer Protocol)	80	SNMP manager	162
POP3 (Post Office Protocol version 3)	110	Syslog	514
IMAP (Internet Message Access Protocol)	143		
HTTPS (HTTP Secure)	443		

EXAM TIP Make sure you know the Layer 4 protocol (TCP/UDP) and port number of each Application Layer protocol we cover in this book. Table 22.1 would be a good reference for flashcards to help you memorize the port numbers for each protocol. Several chapters in volume 2 of this book will also give you a chance to review most of these protocols as we cover them in more detail.

Port numbers are assigned by an organization called the *Internet Assigned Numbers Authority* (IANA, pronounced as "eye-AN-uh"). IANA divides port numbers into three ranges, each with its own purpose. *Well-known* ports (0–1023) are reserved for the most common protocols; all of the port numbers in table 22.1 are from this range. *Registered ports* (1024–49151) are not as strictly controlled as well-known ports, but an enterprise may register its protocol with IANA to use a port number in this range to avoid conflicts; different protocols should not use the same port number.

The remaining ports are *ephemeral ports* (49152–65535). These ports are not controlled by IANA, so registration is not required to use them. They are most commonly used by client devices as the source ports for connections. For example, in the example we saw in figure 22.2, a client (PC1) used port 50000 (an ephemeral port) as the source port of its message to a server (SRV1). The following is a summary of the three port ranges:

- *Well-known ports*—0–1023
  - Reserved for use by the most common protocols.
  - Controlled and assigned by IANA.
  - Also called *system ports.*
- *Registered ports*—1024–49151
  - Protocols may be registered with IANA to use a port number in this range.
  - Registration is done to avoid conflicts, so that two different protocols don't use the same port number.
  - Also called *user ports.*
- *Ephemeral ports*—49152–65535
  - Not controlled or assigned by IANA.
  - Dynamically selected by client devices as the source port for connections.
  - Also called *dynamic* or *private ports.*

22.1.2 Session multiplexing

Imagine you have three web browsers open on your PC: Chrome, Firefox, and Edge. In Chrome, you visit wikipedia.org and click around, viewing a few articles. Then you do the same on Firefox and Edge. Each browser on your PC is a client using HTTPS to interact with a Wikipedia web server, and each of these interactions is called a *session*—an exchange between two communicating devices. How does your PC keep track of these sessions? Why does a link clicked in Chrome not open in Firefox?

When a client, like one of your web browsers, initiates communication with a server, it selects a random number from the ephemeral port range (49152–65535) to use as the source port for that particular session. This port is used to uniquely identify the session for the duration of its communication with the server. This process of keeping track of each communication session is called *session multiplexing.*

This is why when you click a link in Chrome, the resulting page doesn't appear in Firefox—each browser selects a unique port associated with its connection to the server. Figure 22.3 shows how these ephemeral ports are used to keep track of each session between your PC and the Wikipedia server.

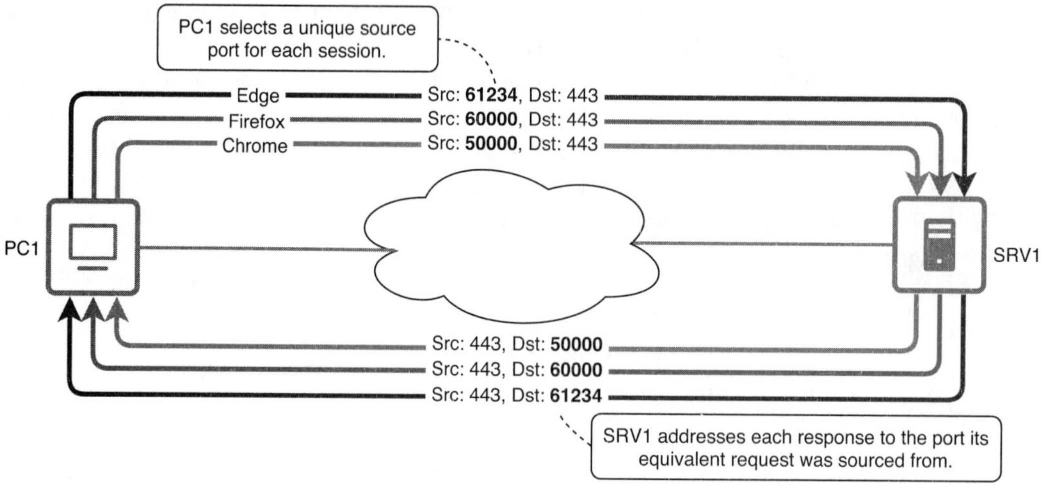

Figure 22.3 Session multiplexing is achieved through port numbers. PC1 selects a unique source port for each communication session with SRV1, which addresses each response to the same port from which the corresponding request originated.

Sockets and sessions

The combination of an IP address, a port number, and Layer 4 protocol is called a *socket*. A web server with IP address 203.0.113.1 that listens on TCP port 443 has the following socket: 203.0.113.1, TCP port 443. When a client wants to connect to this server, it opens its own socket. Let's say a client with IP address 192.168.1.1 uses port 50000 for this purpose—its socket is 192.168.1.1, TCP port 50000.

A session can be thought of as a combination of the two sockets. In our example, that means the following two sockets:

- *Client socket*—192.168.1.1, TCP port 50000
- *Server socket*—203.0.113.1, TCP port 443

This pair of sockets is sometimes called a *five-tuple*, because it consists of five elements: the client IP, the client port number, the server IP, the server port number, and the Layer 4 protocol (TCP or UDP). You may or may not encounter the terms *socket* and *five-tuple* on the CCNA exam, but they are terms commonly used in networking.

22.2 TCP and UDP

As mentioned previously, there are two main Layer 4 protocols in use today: TCP and UDP. Because exam topic 1.5 states that you must be able to "compare TCP to UDP," it's important that you understand the characteristics of these two protocols.

22.2.1 Transmission Control Protocol

Transmission Control Protocol (TCP) is a Layer 4 protocol that, in addition to providing addressing and session multiplexing, offers a variety of benefits, such as connection-oriented communication, data sequencing, reliable communication via acknowledgment and retransmission, and flow control; we will cover these benefits in this section.

Figure 22.4 shows the format of the TCP header. Although I will refer to some of these fields as we cover TCP's features, don't worry about memorizing the header; I include it here only for reference.

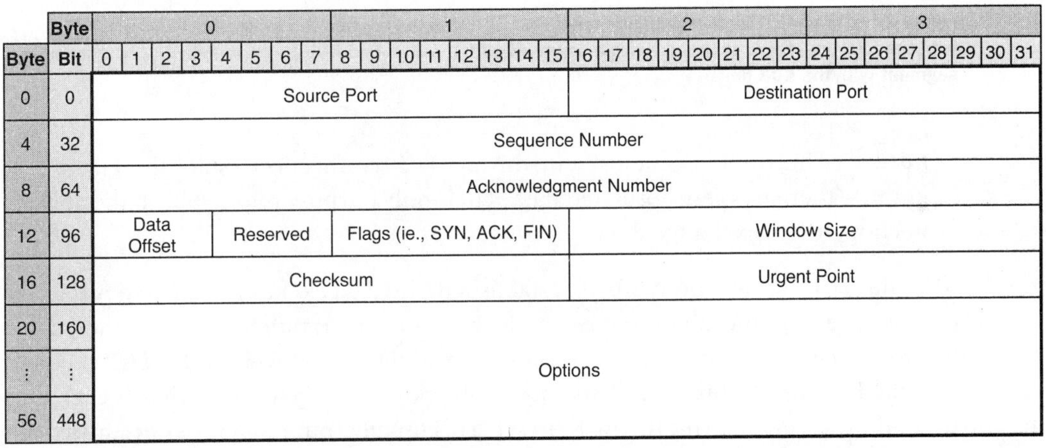

Byte
0
1
2
3
Byte
Bit
0 1 2 3 4 5 6 7 8 9 10 11 12 13 14 15 16 17 18 19 20 21 22 23 24 25 26 27 28 29 30 31
0 0
Source Port
Destination Port
4 32
Sequence Number
8 64
Acknowledgment Number
12 96
Data Offset
Reserved
Flags (ie., SYN, ACK, FIN)
Window Size
16 128
Checksum
Urgent Point
20 160
⋮ ⋮
Options
56 448

Figure 22.4 The format of the TCP header. Like the IPv4 header, it is a minimum of 20 bytes in size but can be up to 60 bytes if Options are included.

> **NOTE** The Source Port and Destination Port fields are each 16 bits in length. That's why there are 65,536 port numbers (from 0–65535) in total: $2^{16} = 65,536$.

TCP CONNECTIONS

TCP is a *connection-oriented* protocol. That means that, before exchanging data, hosts must first establish a connection. Furthermore, after the necessary data has been exchanged, the hosts will terminate the connection. Therefore, exchanging data via TCP is a three-step process:

1. Connection establishment
2. Data exchange
3. Connection termination

The Flags field of the TCP header is 8 bits in length, meaning there are eight different flags, each with a different function. A *flag* is an individual bit that indicates or controls a particular behavior in a protocol. To activate ("set") a flag, the sending host will set the flag's binary value to 1. TCP connections are established using two flags in the Flags field of the TCP header: SYN (synchronize) and ACK (acknowledge). The process is called the *three-way handshake,* because it involves three messages, as shown in figure 22.5.

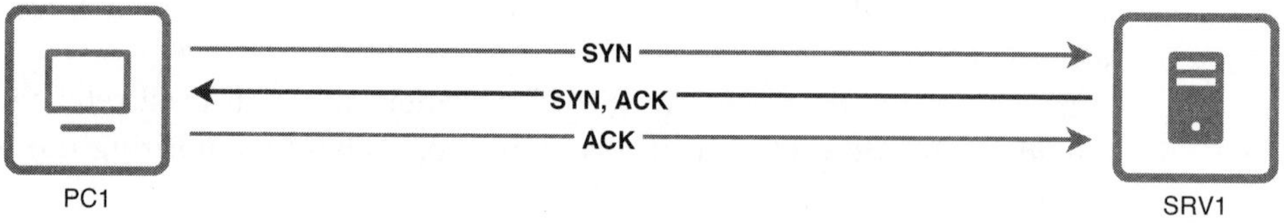

Figure 22.5 The TCP three-way handshake. PC1 initiates the connection by sending a TCP segment with the SYN flag, SRV1 responds with a segment with the SYN and ACK flags, and finally, PC1 sends a segment with the ACK flag.

> **NOTE** The three segments sent during TCP connection establishment are empty—there is no encapsulated data. Their only purpose is to establish the connection, not to exchange data.

After the TCP connection has been established, the data exchange can take place. For example, perhaps the client requests a file from the server, which the server then transfers to the client. After each device is done sending data, it will send a TCP segment with the FIN (finish) bit set, and the hosts will acknowledge each other's FIN segments by sending a segment with the ACK bit set. This usually (but not always) occurs in four separate messages and thus is often called the *four-way handshake* (in contrast with the three-way handshake used for connection establishment). Figure 22.6 shows the TCP connection termination process after connection establishment and data exchange.

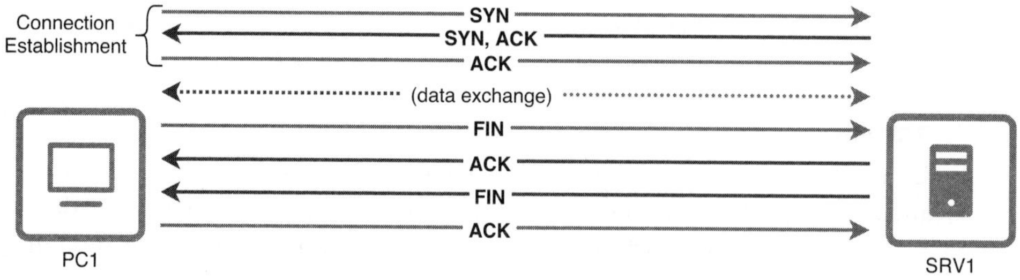

Figure 22.6 TCP connection termination. After the connection establishment and data exchange, PC1 sends a segment with the FIN flag to terminate the connection. SRV1 replies with an ACK segment and then sends its own FIN segment, to which PC1 replies with an ACK segment.

> **EXAM TIP** Remember the TCP connection establishment (SYN, SYN-ACK, ACK) and termination (FIN, ACK, FIN, ACK) sequences for the exam.

Unlike TCP connection establishment, which always occurs in three sequential messages, connection termination doesn't always occur as stated previously. For example, in some cases, the server might send a single segment with both the ACK and FIN flags set, resulting in the sequence FIN, ACK-FIN, ACK. However, the details of this are beyond the scope of the CCNA exam, so I recommend learning the typical four-way handshake for now.

DATA SEQUENCING AND ACKNOWLEDGMENT

Another feature of TCP is *data sequencing*, meaning that even if segments arrive at their destination out of order, TCP provides the means to rearrange them in the correct order. This is achieved using the Sequence Number field of the TCP header. Furthermore, each segment is acknowledged by the receiver using the Acknowledgment Number field, providing *reliable communication*; TCP confirms that each segment is received. Figure 22.7 shows this process.

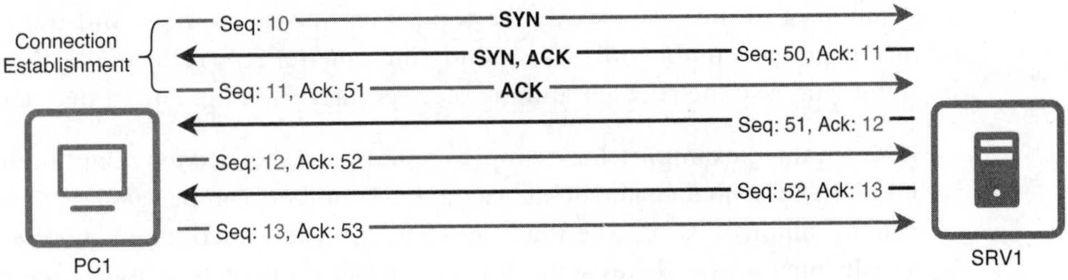

Figure 22.7 TCP data sequencing and acknowledgment. During connection establishment, each host sets a random initial sequence number. Each segment is acknowledged by the receiver by indicating the sequence number of the next segment it expects to receive.

During the TCP connection establishment process, each host sets a random *initial sequence number* that it increments as it sends data to the other host. In figure 22.7's example, PC1 selected 10 as its initial sequence number, and SRV1 selected 50.

To acknowledge receipt of a particular segment, the receiving host will set its next segment's acknowledgment number to the sequence number of the next segment it expects to receive (not the sequence number of the segment it just received). For example, after SRV1 receives PC1's segment with sequence number 10, SRV1's reply uses acknowledgment number 11. Likewise, after PC1 receives SRV1's segment with sequence number 50, PC1 acknowledges its receipt by using acknowledgment number 51.

The exchange in figure 22.7 shows PC1 and SRV1 sending and receiving segments in turn, one segment at a time. Before sending a new segment, each host waits for its previously sent segment to be acknowledged. However, for the sake of efficiency, it's possible for multiple segments to be acknowledged with a single segment. Figure 22.8 shows an example: PC1 and SRV1 send each other two segments at a time before waiting for acknowledgment.

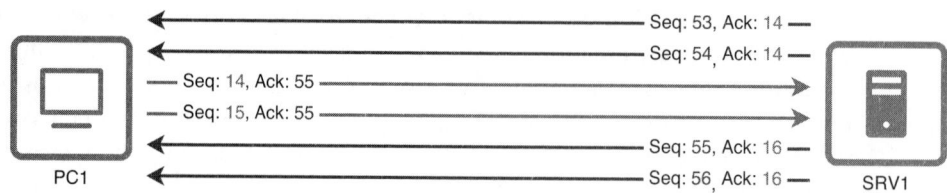

Figure 22.8 PC1 and SRV1 send each other two segments at a time before waiting for acknowledgment. Segments sent consecutively without receiving a new segment from the other host have identical acknowledgment numbers.

TCP connections operate bidirectionally, with each host maintaining its own sequence and acknowledgment numbers. The incrementation of these numbers is determined by the communication dynamics between the hosts. In scenarios where one host predominantly sends data while the other predominantly receives—such as a file transfer from one host to the other—only the sender's sequence number and the receiver's acknowledgment number will consistently increment. This reflects the flow of data from the sender to the receiver and the receiver's acknowledgment of that data.

> **NOTE** In these examples, I use simple sequence and acknowledgment numbers, but real TCP sequence and acknowledgment numbers can be very large (on the scale of billions). Also, note that sequence and acknowledgment numbers are actually measures of bytes sent and received, not values that are incremented by 1 with each segment. For the purpose of the CCNA, just understand the concepts—don't worry about the exact numbers.

RETRANSMISSION

We just covered how TCP acknowledges receipt of each segment, but how does this provide the "reliable communication" that I mentioned previously? What happens if the sender does not receive acknowledgment for a segment that it sent? If the sender of a segment does not receive an acknowledgment within a certain period of time (called the *retransmission timeout*), it will *retransmit* the segment, as shown in figure 22.9.

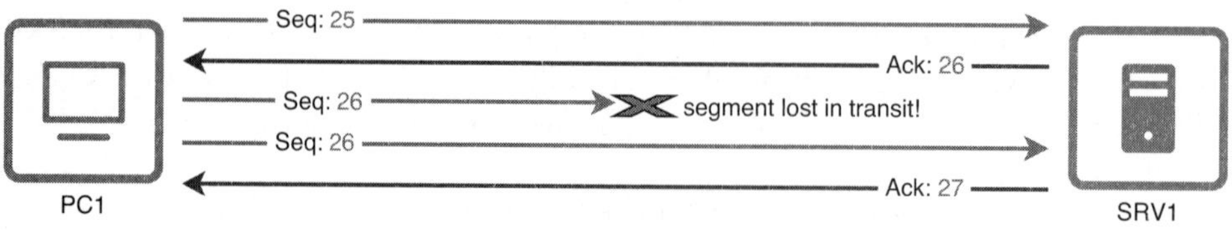

Figure 22.9 TCP retransmission. PC1's first segment with sequence number 26 does not reach SRV1. Because PC1 doesn't receive an acknowledgment for the segment, it retransmits the segment, which is then received and acknowledged by SRV1.

NOTE For simplicity's sake, figure 22.9 focuses on the data transfer from PC1 to SRV1, showing only PC1's sequence numbers and SRV1's acknowledgment numbers.

Another event that could trigger a retransmission is a host receiving a segment with a faulty checksum. Similar to Ethernet's Frame Check Sequence field, which checks for errors in a frame, and IPv4's Header Checksum field, which checks for errors in the IPv4 header, TCP uses its Checksum field to check for errors in segments.

When a device constructs a TCP segment, it uses an algorithm to calculate a checksum, which is included in the TCP header's Checksum field. The host that receives the segment will calculate its own checksum value from the segment. If the two values don't match, it means that the data has been corrupted in transit. As a result, the receiver discards the segment and does not send an acknowledgment, which triggers a retransmission from the sender.

Flow control

The final TCP feature we will cover is *flow control*, a mechanism that prevents a sender from overwhelming a receiver by sending too much data too quickly. It ensures that the sender only sends as much data as the receiver is able to handle at a given time. This is critical in situations where the sender can transmit data faster than the receiver can process it.

The appropriate data transfer rate depends on multiple things, such as the speed of the receiver's network connection, its processing capability, and the current load on both. If the sender sends data too quickly, either the receiver or the network it is connected to could be overloaded, resulting in dropped segments (and lots of retransmissions—bad for performance!). Note that the appropriate rate is not fixed; it can vary within a session, and TCP provides the ability to adjust depending on the current conditions.

Flow control is implemented in TCP primarily through the Window Size field of the TCP header, through which a receiver tells a sender how much data the sender should send before waiting for an acknowledgment. Figure 22.10 demonstrates the concept: PC1 (the receiver) uses the Window Size field of its segments to tell SRV1 how much data to send before waiting for the next acknowledgment.

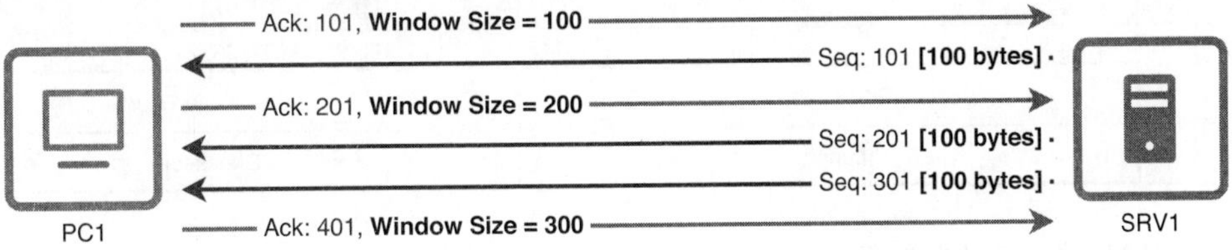

Figure 22.10 TCP flow control is achieved through the Window Size field of the TCP header. In its segments to SRV1, PC1 specifies how much data SRV1 should send before waiting for the next acknowledgment. This can be adjusted dynamically to find an appropriate rate.

NOTE Figure 22.10 focuses only on the data transfer from SRV1 to PC1. Keep in mind that each host specifies its own window size, although SRV1's specified window size isn't shown. Each host specifies its window size in every single TCP segment it sends.

In the first message from PC1 to SRV1 shown in figure 22.10, PC1 specifies a window size of 100 bytes. SRV1 then sends a segment with 100 bytes of encapsulated data and waits for acknowledgment from PC1. In its segment acknowledging receipt of SRV1's segment, PC1 specifies a greater window size: 200 bytes. SRV1 then sends 200 bytes of data (in two TCP segments) before waiting for PC1's acknowledgment. In the final message shown, PC1 specifies a window size of 300 bytes.

NOTE Because TCP is able to dynamically adjust the window size to find an appropriate rate, it is said that TCP uses a *sliding window*.

22.2.2 User Datagram Protocol

Just like TCP, the *User Datagram Protocol* (UDP) provides Layer 4 addressing and session multiplexing via port numbers. However, when compared to TCP, the defining characteristics of UDP stem more from what it doesn't provide rather than what it does:

- UDP is not connection oriented. Hosts do not establish a connection before communication; the sending host simply sends the data.
- UDP does not provide reliable communication. UDP does not provide a mechanism for acknowledging received messages or retransmitting lost messages.
- UDP does not provide data sequencing. There is no sequence number in the UDP header. If messages arrive out of order, UDP provides no mechanism to put them back in order.
- UDP does not provide flow control; it has no mechanism like TCP's window size to control the flow of data. UDP simply sends data as quickly as it can.

Figure 22.11 shows the UDP header. Whereas the TCP header is 20–60 bytes in size, the UDP header is very simple and lightweight—only 8 bytes in size.

	Byte	0								1								2								3							
Byte	Bit	0	1	2	3	4	5	6	7	8	9	10	11	12	13	14	15	16	17	18	19	20	21	22	23	24	25	26	27	28	29	30	31
0	0	Source Port																Destination Port															
4	32	Length																Checksum															

Figure 22.11 The UDP header. Compared to the TCP header, the UDP header is very lightweight, being only 8 bytes in size.

NOTE Because UDP has a checksum field, it is able to provide error detection. However, unlike TCP, there is no mechanism for retransmission, so messages with errors are discarded and forgotten by UDP.

Defining UDP by what it doesn't provide may make UDP seem inferior to TCP, but that is not the case. There are many instances where UDP is preferred, and we will cover them in section 22.2.3.

Datagrams and data streams

A *datagram* (the D in UDP) is a basic unit of transfer that is self-contained and independent of other messages. In the case of UDP, "datagram" is in the name because UDP uses a datagram model for transmission, which means it sends data in discrete chunks (datagrams) that are independent of each other.

This is in contrast to TCP, which treats data as a continuous stream. It breaks this stream up into manageable chunks (segments) for transmission, but the boundaries of these segments have no correlation with the structure of the data itself.

As an analogy, you can think of the data that must be sent as a chapter of a book. UDP might send the data one sentence (or paragraph—whatever fits into a single datagram) at a time; each is a coherent unit. TCP, on the other hand, treats the chapter (the data) as a continuous stream, and the boundary between segments might be in the middle of a paragraph, a sentence, or even a word. Although a half sentence doesn't make sense on its own, TCP provides the mechanisms to ensure that all of the data is received and is in the correct order.

22.2.3 Comparing TCP and UDP

Although all of TCP's features may seem great, they come at the cost of additional *overhead*—the additional data and processing required to manage and ensure the transmission of the actual user data inside each segment. TCP's overhead comes in three main forms:

- *Data overhead*—The extra bytes of the TCP header (20–60 bytes versus UDP's 8) means that the ratio of encapsulated data to headers is reduced. Headers are necessary for the protocols to function but do not carry actual user data.
- *Processing overhead*—This refers to the additional computing resources required to implement the protocol. TCP, with its features such as connection establishment, reliable communication, and flow control, requires more processing power and memory than UDP, which provides none of these features.
- *Time overhead*—Establishing TCP connections introduces additional latency; unlike UDP, in which a host immediately sends data, hosts using TCP must first perform the three-way handshake to establish a connection. Furthermore, the need to wait for acknowledgments of transmitted data can slow down transmission.

EXAM TIP The material in this section is especially important for the CCNA exam since it directly addresses exam topic 1.5: Compare TCP to UDP.

Table 22.2 summarizes the differences between TCP and UDP. We will examine these differences in greater detail as we cover the situations in which each protocol is preferred.

Table 22.2 Comparing TCP and UDP

TCP	UDP
Connection-oriented	Not connection-oriented
Data sequencing	No data sequencing
Reliable	Unreliable
Flow control	No flow control
More overhead	Less overhead
Preferred in situations where data integrity is critical and delivery of all segments is required	Preferred in situations where speed or efficiency is a priority and some packet loss is acceptable

NOTE Although we are discussing Layer 4, where the term *segment* (TCP) or *datagram* (UDP) is more accurate, the term *packet* (which includes the Layer 3 header) is often used more broadly. For example, *packet loss* refers to the loss or discard of messages in a network during transmission.

QUIC

Although not a CCNA exam topic, there is a third Layer 4 protocol that is gaining in popularity: QUIC, which was originally developed by engineers at Google. QUIC is officially not an acronym; it's just the protocol's name (although it originally stood for Quick UDP Internet Connections). QUIC is built on top of UDP but provides TCP-like functionality with reduced latency and built-in encryption for secure connections. QUIC is now used for the majority of connections from Chrome to Google web servers and is currently used by roughly 7% of all websites.

SCENARIOS WHERE TCP IS PREFERRED

TCP, with its various features, is preferred in situations where data integrity is critical and the delivery of all segments is required. For example, TCP is usually the preferred choice for file transfers. When downloading a file, minor latency due to connection establishment, retransmissions, and other TCP features is acceptable; it's more important that the entire file arrives intact, with all of its bytes in the correct order.

Web browsing is another scenario where TCP is typically preferred. When a user accesses a website, the underlying HTTP or HTTPS protocols use TCP to ensure that all of the web content (text, images, etc.) is reliably delivered and displayed in the correct order. Similarly, email protocols like SMTP, POP3, and IMAP use TCP to ensure that emails are not lost in transmission and that they arrive correctly at their destinations.

Scenarios where UDP is preferred

UDP, simple and lightweight, is preferred in several situations, such as these:

- Real-time applications
- Simple query/response protocols
- When reliability is provided by other means

Real-time applications like video streaming, online gaming, and voice/video calling (i.e., Zoom) typically use UDP. These applications need fast data transmission and can tolerate some loss of data; the most recent data is the most valuable, and lost data quickly becomes irrelevant. For example, in a video call, if some packets are lost, it's usually better to have minor temporary visual or audio degradation rather than a delay while waiting for the missing packets to be retransmitted.

UDP is also often preferred for simple query–response protocols, such as DNS. Figure 22.12 shows an example: PC1 uses DNS to learn the IP address of google.com before it is able to use HTTPS to access the website.

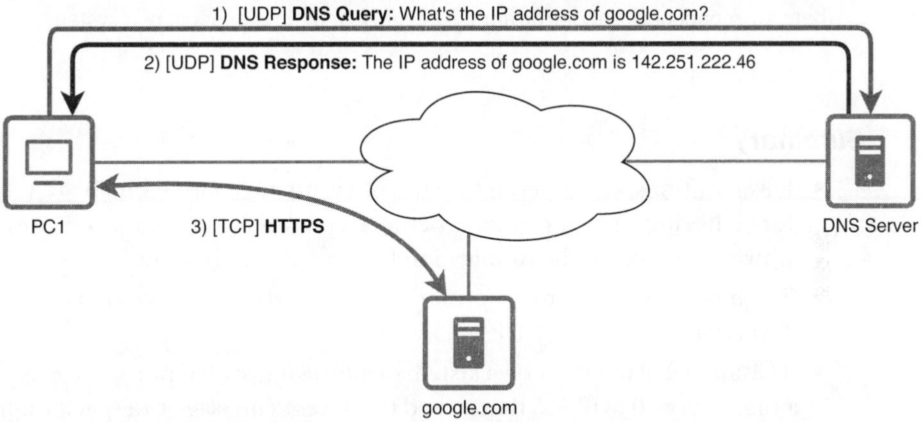

Figure 22.12 Simple DNS exchanges like the one in steps (1) and (2) use UDP. Having learned google .com's IP address, in step 3, PC1 uses HTTPS to access the website.

A protocol like DNS, which usually involves short requests (queries) and responses, does not require the various features of TCP. The overhead of setting up a TCP connection isn't worth it for a single, small request and response; it would only delay the exchange by introducing latency.

> **NOTE** As mentioned previously, DNS uses TCP in some cases, although we will not cover those cases in this chapter.

A third situation where UDP may be preferred is when reliability is provided by other means. Although UDP itself doesn't provide reliability, the underlying Application Layer protocol might; *Trivial File Transfer Protocol* (TFTP) is one example. Although I previously stated that TCP is usually preferred for file transfers, the TFTP protocol—which, as the name suggests, is used for transferring files—has its own built-in reliability mechanism. When using TFTP, the receiver must acknowledge each TFTP message it receives. For that reason, TFTP does not need to rely on TCP to provide reliable delivery of messages; it uses UDP instead. We will cover TFTP in chapter 8 of volume 2 of this book.

Although voice/video calling applications fall into the category of "real-time applications," you could say that they have their own built-in reliability too. If you are on a call and packet loss causes a short disruption, you can ask the speaker to repeat what they said. This is reliability at Layer 8—the User Layer!

Layer 8

Layer 8 isn't an officially recognized layer of the OSI or TCP/IP models. It's just a term used humorously or ironically in networking and other IT fields to acknowledge that, beyond the technical issues handled within the layers of the OSI and TCP/IP models, there are often factors like user error, organizational politics, and other human factors that can impact network performance, security, and other aspects of a system.

Summary

- Layer 4 (Transport) operates on top of Layers 1, 2, and 3, which are responsible for delivering Layer 4 segments between communicating hosts. Likewise, Layer 4 provides services to the Application Layer protocols that run above it.
- The most common Layer 4 protocols are *Transmission Control Protocol* (TCP) and *User Datagram Protocol* (UDP).
- TCP and UDP use their own system of addressing called ports. A *port* is a number ranging from 0 to 65535 that is used to address a message to a specific application process on the destination host.
- Application Layer protocols run on top of either TCP or UDP (or both in some cases). Each also *listens* on a specific port number. For example, HTTPS listens on TCP port 443.
- Port numbers are assigned by the *Internet Assigned Numbers Authority* (IANA). IANA divides port numbers into three ranges: well-known, registered, and ephemeral.
- *Well-known* ports (0–1023) are reserved for the most common protocols and are strictly controlled and assigned by IANA.
- *Registered* ports (1024–49151) are not as strictly controlled as well-known ports but can be registered for use with a specific protocol.

- *Ephemeral* ports (49152–65535) are not controlled by IANA, and registration is not required to use them. They are most commonly used by client devices as the source ports for connections.
- Port numbers also allow for *session multiplexing*, which allows hosts to keep track of communication sessions by associating them with their unique source and destination IP addresses and port numbers.
- In addition to addressing and session multiplexing, TCP provides benefits like connection-oriented communication, data sequencing, reliable communication, and flow control.
- Exchanging data via TCP is a three-step process: (1) connection establishment, (2) data exchange, (3) connection termination.
- TCP connection establishment uses two flags in the TCP header: SYN and ACK. It involves three messages (SYN, SYN-ACK, ACK) and is often called the *three-way handshake*.
- TCP connection termination uses FIN and ACK flags, usually in a four-message exchange that is sometimes called the *four-way handshake*: FIN, ACK, FIN, ACK.
- TCP provides data sequencing and reliable communication using sequence and acknowledgment numbers. Each TCP segment that a host sends must be acknowledged by the receiver.
- Each host randomly selects an *initial sequence number* in the three-way handshake.
- A host acknowledges receipt of one or more segments by sending a segment with the acknowledgment number set to the sequence number of the next segment it expects to receive.
- If the sender of a segment does not receive an acknowledgment within a certain period of time (the *retransmission timeout*), it will retransmit the segment. This provides reliable delivery of segments.
- *Flow control* is a mechanism that prevents a sender from overwhelming a receiver by sending too much data too fast. It is implemented in TCP through the Window Size field, which specifies how many bytes the sender should send before waiting for an acknowledgment.
- Each host in a TCP exchange specifies its own window size, which it adjusts throughout the exchange. For this reason, it is said that TCP uses a *sliding window*.
- Like TCP, UDP provides Layer 4 addressing and session multiplexing via port numbers. However, UDP is not connection oriented and does not provide reliable communication, data sequencing, or flow control.
- Although TCP provides more features than UDP, they come at the cost of additional *overhead*—the additional data and processing required to manage and ensure the transmission of the actual user data in each segment.
- TCP is preferred in situations where data integrity is critical and the delivery of all segments is required, such as file transfers, web browsing, and email.

- For example, in file transfers, minor latency due to connection establishment, retransmissions, and other TCP features is acceptable. It's more important that the entire file arrives intact, with all of its bytes in the correct order.
- UDP is preferred for real-time applications, for simple query–response protocols, and when reliability is provided by other means.
- Real-time applications use UDP because the most recent data is the most valuable, and lost data quickly becomes irrelevant. If packet loss occurs in a voice/video call, it's better to have minor temporary visual or audio degradation than a delay while waiting for missing packets.
- Simple query–response protocols (i.e., DNS, which usually uses UDP) prefer UDP because the overhead of setting up a TCP connection isn't worth it for a single, small query and response.
- UDP is also preferred when reliability is provided by other means, such as the Application Layer protocol. For example, *Trivial File Transfer Protocol* (TFTP) provides basic reliability by requiring acknowledgment of each message.

23 Standard access control lists

This chapter covers

- How access control lists filter packets by matching and acting on them
- Configuring standard numbered and named ACLs
- Applying ACLs to interfaces to filter inbound or outbound packets

By default, a Cisco router forwards any packet that has a matching route in its routing table. However, this default behavior may not align with an organization's security needs. In many cases, access to specific resources—such as servers containing sensitive information—should be restricted to authorized individuals or devices.

In a networking role, it's typically not your responsibility to define the security requirements of your organization—most organizations above a certain size will have a dedicated security team. However, it is your responsibility to build and maintain a network that meets your organization's security requirements, and *access control lists* (ACLs) are an essential tool to help you achieve that goal. In this chapter, we'll examine ACLs from the perspective of a network engineer who must fulfill such requirements: users in department A shouldn't be able to access resources on server B, users in departments X and Y shouldn't be able to communicate with each other over the network, etc.

ACLs function as packet filters, examining each packet as it enters or exits a router's interface and then determining if the packet should be allowed or blocked based on a set of predefined rules. ACLs are CCNA exam topic 5.6: Configure and verify access control lists. In this chapter, we will cover standard ACLs, which filter packets based on their source IP address. In the next chapter, we will cover extended ACLs, which enable the router to filter packets based on various other parameters such as Layer 4 protocol and port numbers.

23.1 How ACLs work

An ACL is an ordered list of rules that filters packets as they are received by or forwarded out of an interface. If you're familiar with programming concepts, you may find ACLs fairly simple to grasp; they are very similar to if-then-else conditionals, which evaluate conditions and take different actions based on the results. ACLs examine certain criteria within a packet (such as the source IP address) and then take specific actions. For example:

1. If the packet matches rule 1, then take the corresponding action.
2. Otherwise, if the packet matches rule 2, then take the corresponding action.
3. Otherwise, discard the packet (if no rules are matched).

If you don't have any programming experience—I didn't when I got my CCNA—don't worry: we'll walk through the logic of ACLs step by step in this section. We'll explore the mechanics of how ACLs operate: the process of matching packets, the role of the implicit deny, how ACLs are applied to interfaces, and the various types of ACLs available.

> **NOTE** Don't worry about Cisco IOS command syntax in this section; I will represent ACLs with simple English sentences. The goal is to understand ACL concepts before learning how to configure them.

23.1.1 Matching and acting on packets

Each ACL consists of a series of rules called *access control entries* (ACEs). Each ACE specifies a matching condition (an IP address or range of IP addresses) and an action (permit or deny). Packets that are *permitted* are forwarded, and packets that are *denied* are discarded.

Imagine that your organization uses the 192.168.0.0/16 address range for its internal network, from which you create various subnets to be used by different departments; perhaps 192.168.1.0/24 is reserved for users in the engineering department. The requirements from the security team state that users in the engineering department must not be able to access a particular group of servers containing customer information, but users in other departments should be able to. Here's an example of an ACL, consisting of two ACEs, that fulfills this requirement:

1. If the source IP address matches 192.168.1.0/24, then deny the packet.
2. If the source IP address matches 192.168.0.0/16, then permit the packet.

A router evaluating a packet against this ACL will process the ACEs in order, from top to bottom. Figure 23.1 shows a flow chart demonstrating how the router would evaluate a packet against this ACL.

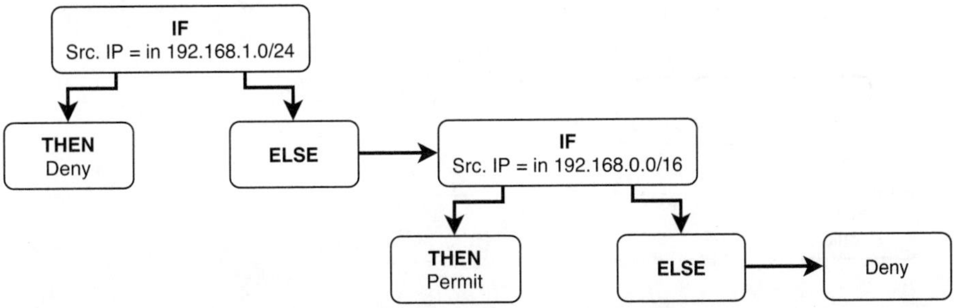

Figure 23.1 How a router evaluates a packet against an ACL. If the source IP matches 192.168.1.0/24, then deny the packet. Otherwise, if the source IP matches 192.168.0.0/16, then permit the packet. Otherwise, deny the packet.

> **NOTE** The final deny action is not defined in either of the ACEs. It is known as the *implicit deny*; we will cover it in section 23.1.2.

Packets are evaluated against each ACE in order, from top to bottom. If a packet matches an ACE's condition, the router takes the action specified in the ACE—permit or deny—and doesn't process the rest of the ACL; the remaining ACEs will be ignored. For this reason, the order of the ACEs is very important; it influences the overall effect of the ACL.

So what's the effect of our example ACL? Packets from IP addresses in the 192.168.1.0/24 range (the engineering department) will be denied—the router will discard them. Then, packets from other IP addresses in the 192.168.0.0/16 range (the rest of the internal network) will be permitted—the router will forward them. Finally, packets from all other source IP addresses (hosts outside of the internal network) will be denied.

> **NOTE** Even though the 192.168.1.0/24 range is included in the 192.168.0.0/16 range, packets from IP addresses in 192.168.1.0/24 will not be permitted by the second ACE; they will be denied by the first ACE before the router processes the second ACE.

Let's reverse the two ACEs in our example ACL to see how this changes the effect of the ACL. Here is the ACL now:

1. If the source IP address matches 192.168.0.0/16, then permit the packet.
2. If the source IP address matches 192.168.1.0/24, then deny the packet.

Figure 23.2 shows how a router would evaluate a packet from 192.168.1.1 against this ACL; the effect of this ACL would be quite different from the first.

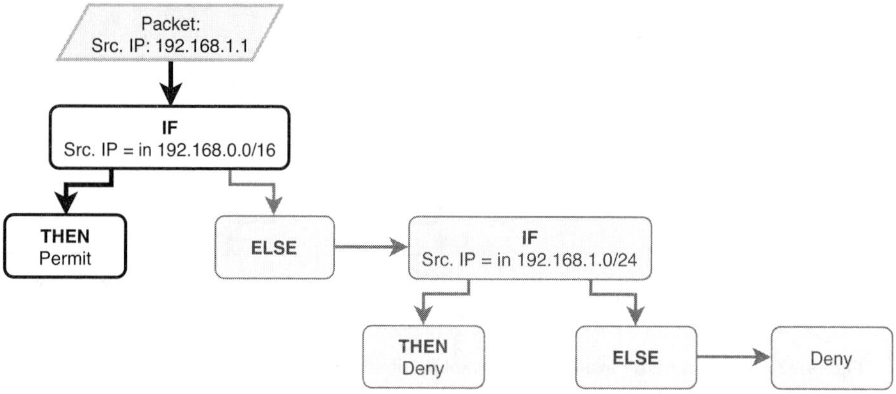

Figure 23.2 A router evaluates a packet from 192.168.1.1 against the ACL. The packet is permitted by the first ACE. It is never evaluated against the second ACE, which would deny the packet.

Even though the second ACE specifies that packets with a source IP in 192.168.1.0/24 (such as 192.168.1.1) should be denied, the packet from 192.168.1.1 is permitted because it matches the first ACE. The overall effect of this ACL is that all packets sourced from IP addresses in 192.168.0.0/16 (including those in 192.168.1.0/24) will be permitted, and all other packets will be denied.

NOTE The second ACE is an example of a *shadowed rule*—a rule (ACE) that will never be acted upon because it is preceded by a less specific rule covering its matching condition (192.168.0.0/16 includes 192.168.1.0/24). This shouldn't occur in a properly configured ACL; you should always configure more specific rules first.

23.1.2 The implicit deny

As mentioned at the beginning of this chapter, a Cisco router will forward any packet with a valid route by default. However, when using ACLs, the behavior changes: any packet not explicitly permitted by the ACL is denied by default.

At the end of every ACL, there is a hidden rule that denies any packets not previously matched by the ACL's configured ACEs; this is called the *implicit deny*. If a packet doesn't match any explicitly defined conditions, it will be denied by this hidden rule. The implicit deny ensures a secure stance, where only the traffic explicitly permitted by the ACL will be forwarded and everything else will be automatically discarded. This is the example ACL from the previous section, with the implicit deny explicitly stated:

1 If the source IP address matches 192.168.1.0/24, then deny the packet.
2 If the source IP address matches 192.168.0.0/16, then permit the packet.
3 If the source IP address doesn't match any preceding entry, deny the packet.

Figure 23.3 shows an example of a packet being denied by the implicit deny. The packet's source IP is 172.16.1.1, which is outside of the range used for the internal networks of our fictional organization (192.168.0.0/16). Although the ACL doesn't explicitly deny packets from this IP address, the packet is discarded thanks to the ACL's implicit deny rule.

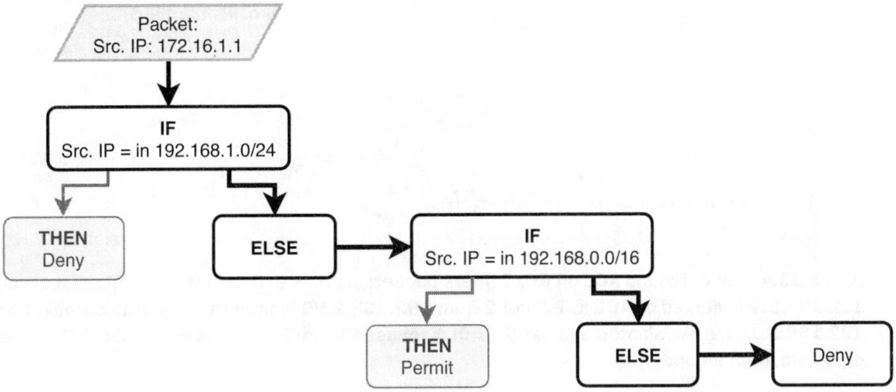

Figure 23.3 A packet is denied by the implicit deny. The packet's source IP (172.16.1.1) doesn't match the first ACE (192.168.1.0/24) or the second ACE (192.168.0.0/16), so it is denied by the implicit deny; the router will discard it.

23.1.3 Applying ACLs

The act of creating an ACL doesn't affect the router's behavior on its own; the ACL must be applied to one (or more) of the router's interfaces to take effect. You can apply ACLs in either the inbound or outbound direction (or both), depending on the desired result.

An inbound ACL evaluates packets as they enter the interface the ACL is applied to; every time the router receives a packet on the interface, the router will evaluate the packet against the ACL. If the ACL permits the packet, the router will then continue to process the packet. If the ACL denies the packet, the router will discard it.

Outbound ACLs evaluate packets as they exit the interface; if the router determines that a packet should be forwarded out of the interface, the router will first evaluate the packet against the ACL. If the ACL permits the packet, the router will forward the packet, but if the ACL denies the packet, the router will discard it.

NOTE You may encounter the terms *ingress* and *egress* instead of *inbound* and *outbound*, respectively—they mean the same thing.

Figure 23.4 demonstrates an outbound ACL filtering packets destined for the 192.168.3.0/24 LAN. The ACL is applied outbound on R1's G0/2 interface and, therefore, filters packets as they are forwarded out of G0/2—as they exit the interface. The ACL does not filter packets that are received by G0/2—packets that enter the interface.

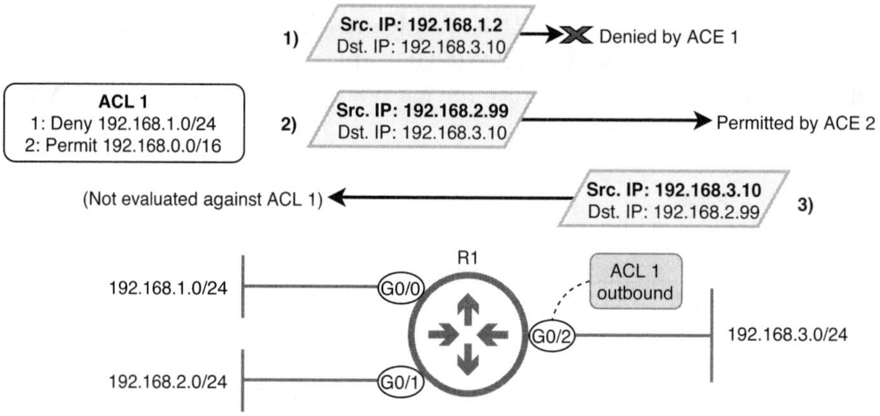

Figure 23.4 An outbound ACL on G0/2 filters packets as they exit the interface. Packet 1 from 192.168.1.2 is denied by ACE 1. Packet 2 from 192.168.2.99 is permitted by ACE 2. Packet 3 from 192.168.3.10 isn't evaluated against the ACL because the packet enters G0/2; the ACL is applied outbound, not inbound.

Figure 23.5 shows the same ACL applied inbound on R1 G0/2. Because the ACL is applied inbound, it is not used to filter packets sent out of G0/2. As a result, the first two packets are forwarded without being evaluated against ACL 1. The third packet, from 192.168.3.10 to 192.168.2.99, is permitted by ACE 2.

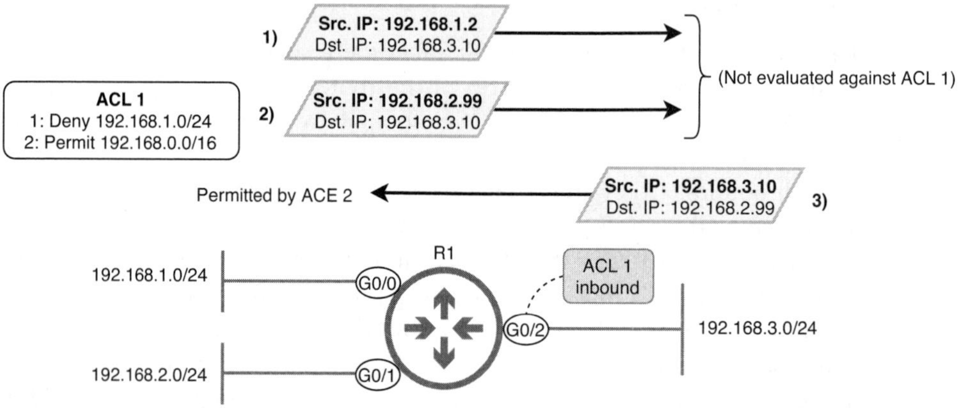

Figure 23.5 An inbound ACL on G0/2 filters packets as they enter the interface. Packets 1 and 2 are forwarded out of G0/2 without being evaluated against ACL 1. Packet 3 is evaluated as it enters G0/2 and is permitted by ACE 2.

The ideal location and direction to apply an ACL depends on the desired result; applying ACL 1 inbound on G0/2, as in figure 23.5, doesn't make sense. The effect of ACL 1 is to deny packets sourced from the 192.168.1.0/24 LAN, but packets sourced from that LAN will never be received by G0/2, to which the 192.168.3.0/24 LAN is connected. In effect, ACL 1 in figure 23.5 is useless.

However, applying ACL 1 outbound on G0/2, as we saw in figure 23.4, does make sense: it blocks packets sourced from 192.168.1.0.24 from reaching destinations in G0/2's connected LAN (192.168.3.0/24); they will be discarded before being forwarded out of the interface.

Standard ACLs should usually be applied outbound on the interface connected to the destination LAN you want to protect; this serves to filter packets destined for that LAN. However, we will see an example in which applying an ACL inbound is useful in section 23.2, allowing you to block unwanted traffic from entering a router and therefore from accessing any of the router's connected LANs.

NOTE Each interface can have a maximum of one ACL applied in each direction: one inbound and one outbound. The same ACL can be applied to multiple interfaces.

23.1.4 ACL types

ACLs can be categorized based on two characteristics—their matching parameters and their identification method:

- *Matching parameters*—Standard ACLs, extended ACLs
- *Identification method*—Numbered ACLs, named ACLs

Standard ACLs, the topic of this chapter, match packets based on a single parameter: source IP address. *Extended ACLs,* the topic of the next chapter, allow for more granular packet-filtering; they match packets based on additional parameters, such as source/destination IP addresses, source/destination port numbers, and others.

Numbered ACLs are identified by a number, and *named ACLs* are identified by a name. By combining the two methods of categorization, we can identify the four ACL types you should know for the CCNA exam, as shown in table 23.1.

Table 23.1 ACL types

	Numbered ACL	Named ACL
Standard ACL	Standard numbered ACL	Standard named ACL
Extended ACL	Extended numbered ACL	Extended named ACL

EXAM TIP Only *IP ACLs*—ACLs that filter IP packets—are covered in the CCNA exam. The four ACL types in table 23.1 are all examples of IP ACLs. Specifically, you are expected to know IPv4 ACLs; IPv6 ACLs are not covered in the CCNA exam.

In section 23.2, we'll see how to configure and apply standard numbered and named ACLs in Cisco IOS. Then, in the next chapter, we'll do the same for extended ACLs.

23.2 Configuring standard ACLs

Configuring ACLs, whether standard or extended, numbered or named, consists of two steps:

1. Creating the ACLs
2. Applying the ACLs

In this section, we will examine how to create standard numbered and named ACLs and how to apply them to interfaces to filter packets. Figure 23.6 shows the network we will use for this section, as well as the commands we will use to configure and apply the ACLs:

- ACL 1, applied outbound on R2 G0/0, blocks the engineering department (192.168.1.0/24) from accessing Server LAN A, which includes SRV1.
- ACL BLOCK_MARTHA_BOB, applied inbound on R2 G0/2, prevents two users from accessing either of R2's connected LANs.

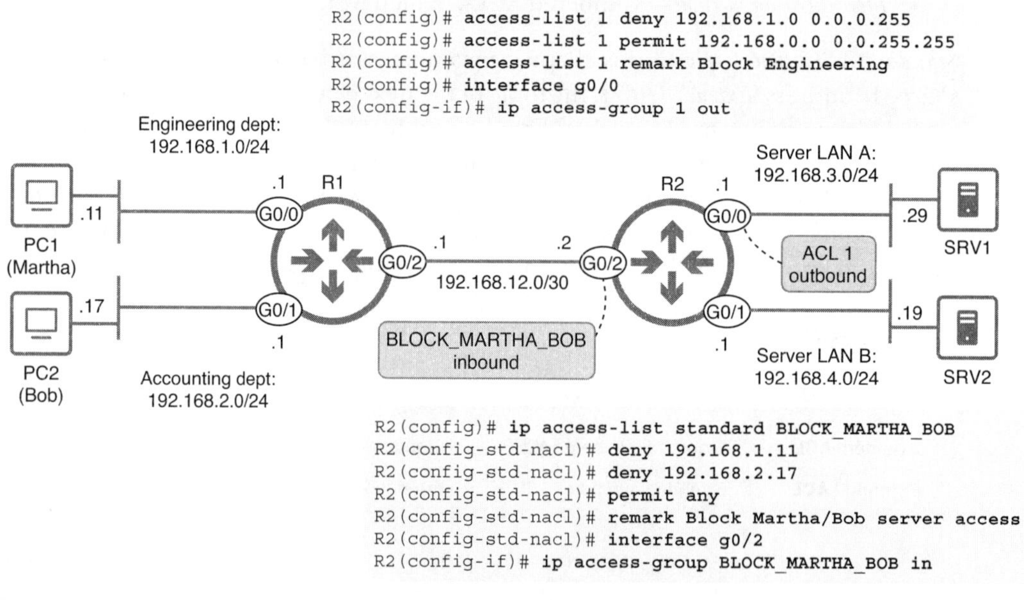

Figure 23.6 Configuring and applying standard numbered and named ACLs to control traffic in the network

EXAM TIP The exam topics list states that you must be able to configure ACLs and verify them with **show** commands. For practice, I recommend recreating the network shown in figure 23.6 in a lab (i.e., in Cisco Packet Tracer) and following along as you read this section. You can also experiment with configuring and testing other ACLs using the same network.

23.2.1 Numbered ACLs

Numbered ACLs, as the name implies, are identified with numbers. However, you can't just pick any number to identify an ACL; there are reserved ranges that can only be used for specific kinds of ACLs. For example:

- *Standard IP ACLs*—1–99 and 1300–1999
- *Extended IP ACLs*—100–199 and 2000–2699

The original ranges for standard and extended ACLs are 1–99 and 100–199, respectively. However, those ranges were later expanded to allow for a greater number of ACLs, giving us the 1300–1999 and 2000–2699 ranges. Because we are covering standard ACLs in this chapter, we must pick our ACL numbers from the appropriate ranges.

EXAM TIP Make sure you know the ranges for standard and extended ACLs. As always, I recommend flashcards to help with memorization.

Creating the ACL

In our example network, R1 and R2 are connected by a point-to-point link, and each router is connected to two LANs: R1 is connected to 192.168.1.0/24 (the engineering department) and 192.168.2.0/24 (the accounting department), and R2 is connected to 192.168.3.0/24 (Server LAN A) and 192.168.4.0/24 (Server LAN B), which contain servers used by the organization. To demonstrate numbered ACL configuration, we will create an ACL that limits access to Server LAN A, blocking the engineering department from accessing the LAN.

When configuring a numbered ACL, you must configure each ACE sequentially, from top to bottom. The order in which you configure the ACEs is very important, as the router will process the ACEs in the order they were configured in when evaluating a packet against the ACL.

The primary command to configure an ACE as part of a standard numbered ACL is **`access-list`** *`number`* {**`permit`** | **`deny`**} *`source-ip wildcard-mask`*. The *`number`* argument is the number used to identify the ACL—make sure it's in one of the correct ranges (1–99 or 1300–1999). In the following example, I configure ACL 1 on R2, consisting of two ACEs (and an optional remark, identifying the ACL's purpose):

```
R2(config)# access-list 1 deny 192.168.1.0 0.0.0.255
R2(config)# access-list 1 permit 192.168.0.0 0.0.255.255
R2(config)# access-list 1 remark Block Engineering
```

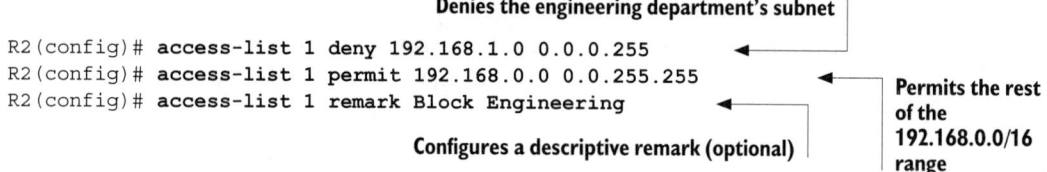

- Denies the engineering department's subnet
- Permits the rest of the 192.168.0.0/16 range
- Configures a descriptive remark (optional)

NOTE The remark is optional but can be useful for indicating the ACL's purpose to others who look at the config (or to your future self).

ACLs use wildcard masks, which we covered in chapter 17. For review, wildcard masks indicate bits that must match with a 0 and bits that don't have to match with a 1. In practice, you can generally think of them as inverse netmasks: 0.0.0.255 is the wildcard mask equivalent of 255.255.255.0, a /24 netmask.

NOTE A shortcut to calculating a netmask's equivalent wildcard mask is to subtract each octet of the netmask from 255. The first three octets of a /24 netmask are 255 and 255 – 255 = 0. The final octet is 0 and 255 – 0 = 255. That gives us 0.0.0.255.

After configuring an ACL, you can verify it with either **`show access-lists`** (which shows all ACLs) or **`show ip access-lists`** (which shows only IP ACLs); since we are configuring only IP ACLs, the output of both commands should be the same. In the following example, I verify ACL 1 on R2:

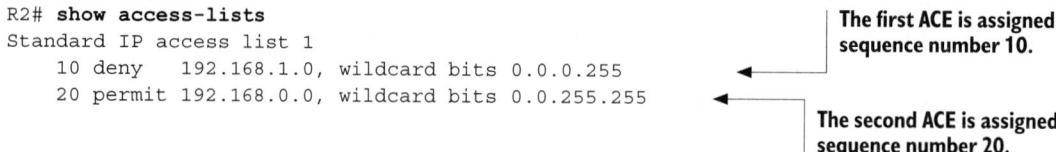

```
R2# show access-lists
Standard IP access list 1
    10 deny   192.168.1.0, wildcard bits 0.0.0.255
    20 permit 192.168.0.0, wildcard bits 0.0.255.255
```

- The first ACE is assigned sequence number 10.
- The second ACE is assigned sequence number 20.

NOTE The remark doesn't appear in **`show access-lists`**, only in the config.

Notice the *sequence numbers* that were automatically added to the beginning of each ACE: 10 and 20. When configuring ACLs, the first ACE is given sequence number 10, and the default increment is 10. This leaves plenty of room between each ACE, which enables you to configure new ACEs in between existing ACEs if needed. However, that is only possible in named ACL config mode, which we will cover in section 23.2.2.

APPLYING THE ACL

For an ACL to take effect, it must be applied to an interface. The command to do so is **`ip access-group`** *`number`* {**`in`** | **`out`**}. In the following example, I apply ACL 1 outbound on R2's G0/0 interface and verify with **`show ip interface g0/0`**:

```
R2(config)# interface g0/0
R2(config-if)# ip access-group 1 out
R2(config-if)# do show ip interface g0/0
```

- Applies ACL 1 outbound on G0/0

```
GigabitEthernet0/0 is up, line protocol is up (connected)
Internet address is 192.168.3.1/24
. . .
Outgoing access list is 1
Inbound access list is not set
. . .
```

ACL 1 is applied outbound (outgoing).

Figure 23.7 shows the effect of this configuration: packets are filtered as R2 forwards them out of G0/0, controlling access to Server LAN A.

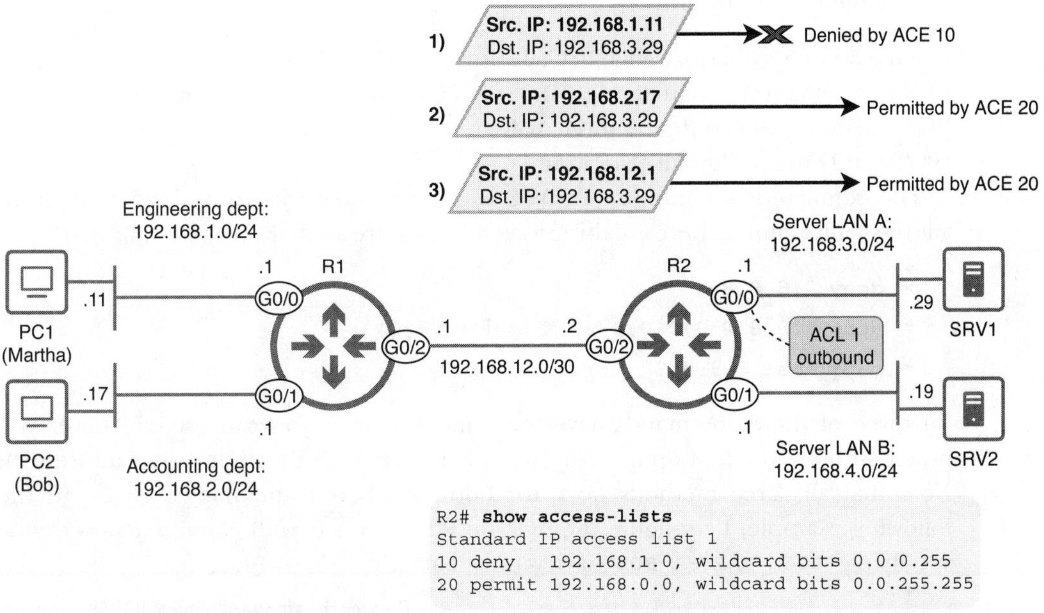

Figure 23.7 Packets filtered by R2's ACL 1, applied outbound on G0/0. Packet 1, from the engineering department, is denied by ACE 10. Packets 2 and 3 are permitted by ACE 20.

The general rule when applying standard ACLs is to apply them as close to the destination as possible; the destination is the LAN you want to protect with the ACL. In this case, the destination is Server LAN A—we want to filter traffic destined for that LAN. By placing the standard ACL outbound on R2 G0/0, you ensure that only traffic destined for G0/0's connected LAN is filtered by the ACL; other traffic is not affected.

23.2.2 Named ACLs

Numbered and named ACLs differ not only in how they identify ACLs (with a number or a name) but also in how they are configured. Whereas numbered ACLs are configured entirely from global config mode, named ACLs are first created in global config mode, but each ACE is configured in a separate config mode. You can enter *standard named ACL config mode* and configure each ACE with the following commands:

- Enter standard named ACL config mode: **`ip access-list standard`** *`name`*
- Configure ACEs: `[`*`seq-num`*`]` `{`**`permit`** `|` **`deny`**`}` *`source-ip wildcard-mask`*

NOTE In named ACL config mode, you can optionally specify a *`seq-num`* (sequence number) to control where the ACE is inserted in the ACL. By default, ACEs will start at sequence 10 and increment by 10 for each new ACE, but this option is useful for inserting new ACEs in between existing ACEs (for example, at sequence number 15).

In our example scenario, we'll block two users from accessing Server LAN A and Server LAN B: Martha from engineering (who uses PC1) and Bob from accounting (who uses PC2). To do so, let's configure three ACEs: one to deny Martha (PC1), one to deny Bob (PC2), and one to allow all other traffic.

The command to configure an ACE is quite flexible when matching a single IP address. For example, here are three ways to configure an ACE denying 8.8.8.8:

- **`deny 8.8.8.8`**
- **`deny 8.8.8.8 0.0.0.0`** (a /32 wildcard mask)
- **`deny host 8.8.8.8`**

All three of these commands have the same effect, so you can use whichever you prefer—I'll use the first option (replacing **`8.8.8.8`** with the appropriate addresses). Note that all three methods work for both numbered and named ACLs. In the following example, I configure the ACL on R2 and verify with **`show access-lists`**, specifying **`BLOCK_MARTHA_BOB`** to view only that ACL:

```
R2(config)# ip access-list standard BLOCK_MARTHA_BOB      <-- Creates the standard named ACL
R2(config-std-nacl)# deny 192.168.1.11                    | Denies Martha and Bob
R2(config-std-nacl)# deny 192.168.2.17                    |
R2(config-std-nacl)# permit any                           <-- Permits all other traffic
R2(config-std-nacl)# do show access-lists BLOCK_MARTHA_BOB
Standard IP access list BLOCK_MARTHA_BOB
    10 deny   192.168.1.11
    20 deny   192.168.2.17
    30 permit any
```

NOTE The **`any`** keyword used in the third ACE is a handy way to match all IP addresses; alternatively, you could configure **`permit 0.0.0.0 255.255.255.255`**. You can use it in both numbered and named ACLs.

Applying a named ACL is identical to applying a numbered ACL: you can apply it inbound on R2's G0/2 interface with **`ip access-group BLOCK_MARTHA_BOB in`**. By applying the ACL inbound on G0/2, packets are filtered as R2 receives them from R1. This filters packets destined for both destinations that we want to protect: Server LAN A and Server LAN B. Figure 23.8 shows the result of applying our new ACL. Note that ACL 1, which we configured and applied previously, is still in effect.

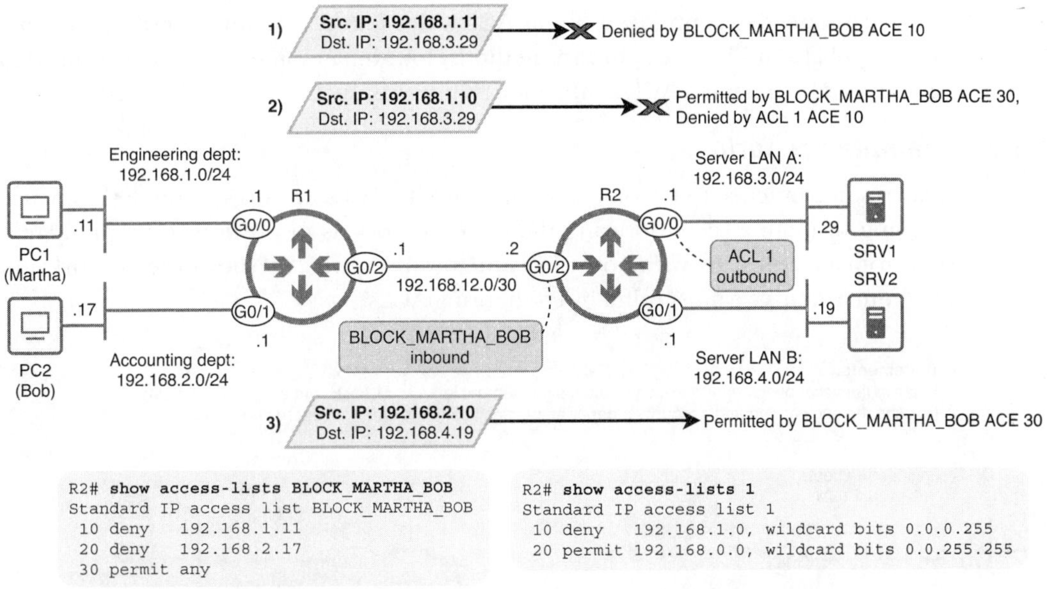

Figure 23.8 Packets filtered by R2's ACLs. Packet 1 is denied by `BLOCK_MARTHA_BOB`'s ACE 10 as it enters R2 G0/2. Packet 2 is permitted by `BLOCK_MARTHA_BOB`'s ACE 30 as it enters R2 G0/2 but denied by ACL 1's ACE 10 as it exits R2 G0/0. Packet 3 is permitted by `BLOCK_MARTHA_BOB`'s ACE 30 as it enters R2 G0/2 and not evaluated against an ACL as it exits R2 G0/1—no ACL is applied to that interface.

In modern versions of Cisco IOS, you can also configure numbered ACLs in named ACL config mode by specifying a number instead of a name after **`ip access-list standard`**. In the following example, I configure the previous ACL, using a number instead of a name:

```
R2(config)# ip access-list standard 99
R2(config-std-nacl)# deny 192.168.1.11
R2(config-std-nacl)# deny 192.168.2.17
R2(config-std-nacl)# permit any
```

However, after configuring the ACL, it will appear in the running config as if it was configured using the traditional method. The following example shows ACL 99 in R2's config:

```
R2# show running-config | include access-list 99
access-list 99 deny 192.168.1.11
access-list 99 deny 192.168.2.17
access-list 99 permit any
```

Named ACL config mode provides some benefits, such as the ability to specify sequence numbers and easier ACL editing—we'll cover that in the next chapter. However, keep in mind that ACLs configured using both methods function identically after they have been configured; both are standard ACLs, filtering packets based on source IP addresses.

If you just need to configure a simple ACL with a few ACEs, a numbered ACL configured in global config mode is an easy method. However, in some cases, you may need to take advantage of named ACL config mode's benefits, such as when editing ACLs.

23.3 Example scenario

It takes some practice to become comfortable with ACLs. In this section, let's practice by going through a scenario using the same network as in previous examples. We'll start from a blank slate, with no ACLs configured. Figure 23.9 shows the network and the requirements we must fulfill by configuring ACLs.

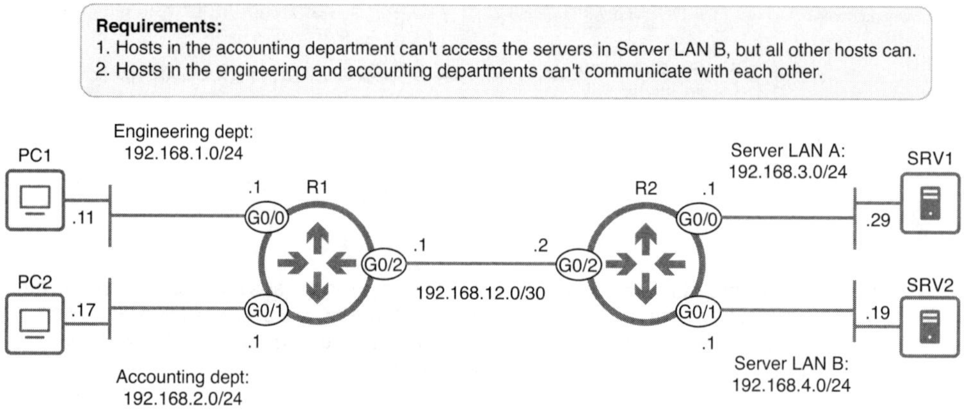

Figure 23.9 Requirements to be fulfilled by configuring standard ACLs

> **NOTE** You can fulfill these requirements using numbered or named ACLs; the destination is more important than how you get there. For demonstration purposes, I will configure both types.

The first requirement states that "Hosts in the accounting department can't access the servers in Server LAN B, but all other hosts can." To fulfill that requirement, I will configure an ACL on R2 that denies the accounting subnet (192.168.2.0/24) but permits all other IP addresses. I will then apply it as close to the destination as possible: outbound on R2's G0/1 interface. In the following example, I configure and apply the ACL:

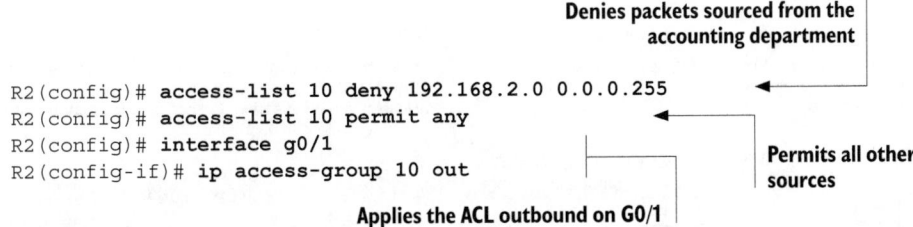

```
R2(config)# access-list 10 deny 192.168.2.0 0.0.0.255
R2(config)# access-list 10 permit any
R2(config)# interface g0/1
R2(config-if)# ip access-group 10 out
```

Denies packets sourced from the accounting department (line 1)

Permits all other sources (line 2)

Applies the ACL outbound on G0/1 (lines 3–4)

That ACL fulfills the first requirement. The second requirement states that "Hosts in the engineering and accounting departments can't communicate with each other." This can be achieved by configuring two ACLs on R1:

1. An ACL that denies 192.168.1.0/24 but permits all other IP addresses
2. An ACL that denies 192.168.2.0/24 but permits all other IP addresses

By applying the first ACL outbound on R1 G0/1, packets from hosts in the engineering department will be blocked from reaching destinations in the accounting department. In the following example, I configure and apply the ACL on R1:

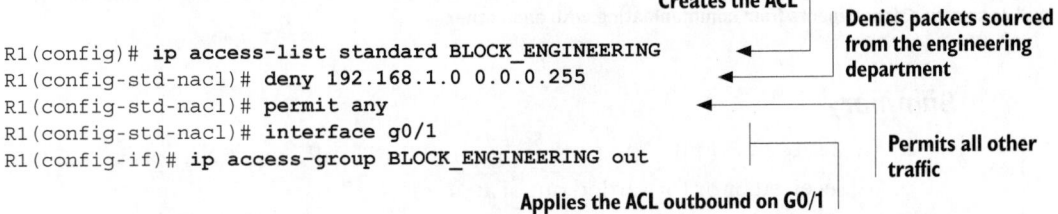

```
R1(config)# ip access-list standard BLOCK_ENGINEERING
R1(config-std-nacl)# deny 192.168.1.0 0.0.0.255
R1(config-std-nacl)# permit any
R1(config-std-nacl)# interface g0/1
R1(config-if)# ip access-group BLOCK_ENGINEERING out
```

Creates the ACL (line 1)

Denies packets sourced from the engineering department (line 2)

Permits all other traffic (line 3)

Applies the ACL outbound on G0/1 (lines 4–5)

Likewise, by applying the second ACL outbound on R1 G0/0, packets sourced from hosts in the accounting department will be blocked from reaching hosts in the engineering department. I configure and apply the second ACL in the following example:

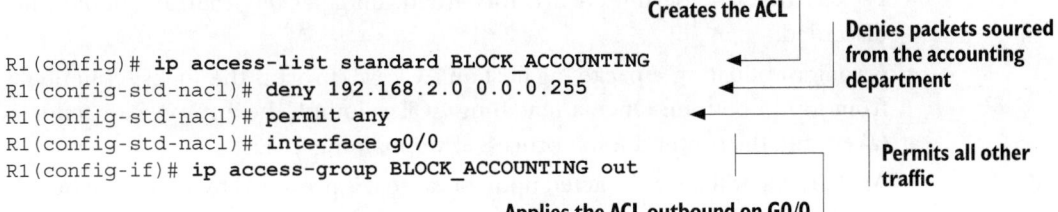

```
R1(config)# ip access-list standard BLOCK_ACCOUNTING
R1(config-std-nacl)# deny 192.168.2.0 0.0.0.255
R1(config-std-nacl)# permit any
R1(config-std-nacl)# interface g0/0
R1(config-if)# ip access-group BLOCK_ACCOUNTING out
```

Creates the ACL (line 1)

Denies packets sourced from the accounting department (line 2)

Permits all other traffic (line 3)

Applies the ACL outbound on G0/0 (lines 4–5)

We have now fulfilled the requirements! For review, figure 23.10 shows the requirements and the ACLs we configured to fulfill those requirements.

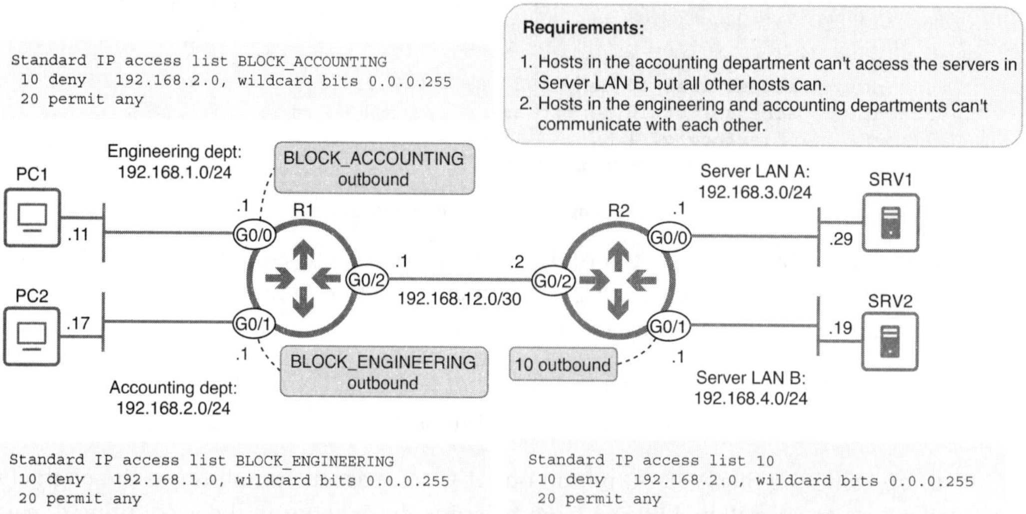

Figure 23.10 Three ACLs configured on R1 and R2 fulfill the requirements. ACL 10, configured on R2, prevents hosts in 192.168.2.0/24 from accessing 192.168.4.0/24. The two named ACLs on R1 prevent the engineering and accounting departments from communicating with each other.

Summary

- An access control list (ACL) is an ordered list of rules that filters packets as they are received by or forwarded out of an interface.
- ACLs function like if-then-else conditionals in programming, evaluating conditions and taking actions based on the results.
- Each ACL consists of a series of rules called *access control entries* (ACEs). Each ACE specifies a matching condition and an action (permit or deny).
- Packets that are permitted are forwarded, and packets that are denied are discarded.
- A router evaluating a packet against an ACL will process the ACEs sequentially from top to bottom. Once a matching ACE is found, the appropriate action is taken, and the router doesn't process any remaining ACEs.
- An ACE that will never be acted upon because it is preceded by a less specific rule covering its matching condition is an example of a *shadowed rule.*
- If a packet doesn't match any of an ACL's explicitly defined conditions, it will be denied by a hidden rule called the *implicit deny.*
- The act of creating an ACL doesn't affect the router's behavior on its own; the ACL must be applied to one (or more) interfaces to take effect.
- ACLs can be applied to an interface inbound and/or outbound. An inbound ACL filters packets as they are received by the interface. An outbound ACL filters packets as they are forwarded out of the interface.

- Each interface can have a maximum of one ACL applied in each direction: one inbound and one outbound.
- ACLs can be categorized based on their matching parameters: *standard ACLs* match packets based only on their source IP address. *Extended ACLs* can match packets based on source/destination IP addresses, source/destination ports, and others.
- ACLs can also be categorized by how they are identified. *Numbered ACLs* are identified by a number. *Named ACLs* are identified by a name.
- You should know four ACL types for the CCNA: standard numbered, standard named, extended numbered, and extended named.
- Numbered ACLs are identified by a number that indicates whether the ACL is standard or extended. Standard ACLs use ranges 1–99 and 1300–1999, and extended ACLs use ranges 100–199 and 2000–2699.
- Standard numbered ACLs are configured one ACE at a time in global config mode with the **`access-list`** *`number`* {**`permit`** | **`deny`**} *`source-ip wildcard-mask`* command.
- The order in which you configure ACEs is important. The ACEs will be processed in the order you configure them.
- You can configure an optional descriptive remark with **`access-list`** *`number`* **`remark`** *`remark`*. This is useful to clarify the purpose of the ACL.
- You can view all ACLs with **`show access-lists`** and all IP ACLs with **`show ip access-lists`**.
- Each ACE is automatically assigned a *sequence number*, starting from 10 and incrementing by 10 for each ACE.
- You can apply an ACL to an interface with **`ip access-group`** {*`number`* | *`name`*} {**`in`** | **`out`**}.
- Named ACLs are created in global config mode, but ACEs are configured in a separate config mode.
- You can create a standard named ACL with **`ip access-group standard`** *`name`*.
- You can configure ACEs in standard named ACL config mode with `[seq-num]` {**`permit`** | **`deny`**} *`source-ip wildcard-mask`*.
- You can match a single IP address in three ways:
  - {**`permit`** | **`deny`**} **`8.8.8.8`**
  - {**`permit`** | **`deny`**} **`8.8.8.8 0.0.0.0`**
  - {**`permit`** | **`deny`**} **`host 8.8.8.8`**
- The **`any`** keyword can be used to match all IP addresses, such as **`permit any`**.
- Numbered ACLs can also be configured in named ACL config mode.
- Named ACL config mode provides some benefits, such as the ability to specify sequence numbers and easier ACL editing. However, both types function identically once they have been configured.

24 Extended access control lists

This chapter covers

- The various parameters extended access control lists use to match packets
- Configuring extended numbered and named ACLs
- Editing ACLs by deleting and resequencing ACEs

In the previous chapter, we covered standard ACLs, which filter packets based on a single parameter: the source IP address. Although standard ACLs have their uses, they are a blunt instrument; they don't provide precise control over exactly which kinds of traffic are permitted and denied. Extended ACLs, the topic of this chapter, are a more precise tool: they allow you to filter packets based on many more parameters, providing more granular control over traffic.

Although extended ACLs can be more complex than standard ACLs, the good news is that the fundamentals of how ACLs work, as we covered in the previous chapter, remain the same. Like standard ACLs, the access control entries (ACEs) of an extended ACL are processed in order from top to bottom. Extended ACLs include an implicit deny that discards all traffic that isn't matched by an explicitly configured ACE. Extended ACLs also need to be applied to an interface in the inbound and/or outbound directions to take effect.

Given these similarities, in this chapter we will jump right into looking at how to configure extended ACLs—how to configure ACEs that match packets based on their protocol, source/destination IP addresses, and source/destination ports. As in the previous chapter, we will cover CCNA exam topic 5.6: Configure and verify access control lists.

24.1 Configuring extended ACLs

Extended ACLs can filter packets based on a variety of different parameters, such as

- The protocol of the packet's payload (TCP, UDP, ICMP, etc.)
- Source and/or destination IP addresses
- Source and/or destination TCP/UDP ports

Configuring extended ACLs is very similar to configuring standard ACLs: you can configure numbered ACLs in global config mode with the **`access-list`** command or create and configure ACLs in named ACL config mode with the **`ip access-list`** command. However, due to the additional parameters that extended ACLs can use to match packets, there are additional keywords and arguments to familiarize yourself with.

24.1.1 Matching protocol, source, and destination

Let's begin by configuring ACLs that match packets based on the encapsulated protocol, source IP address, and destination IP address. The following example shows the command syntax for how to configure a numbered ACL with these parameters:

```
R1(config)# access-list number {permit | deny} protocol source destination
```

> **NOTE** Extended numbered ACLs must use a number from one of the appropriate ranges: 100–199 or 2000–2699.

The following example shows how to configure an extended ACL in named ACL config mode. As with standard ACLs, modern versions of Cisco IOS allow you to configure both extended numbered and extended named ACLs in named ACL config mode:

```
R1(config)# ip access-list extended {name | number}
R1(config-ext-nacl)# [seq-num] {permit | deny} protocol source destination
```

The *`protocol`*, *`source`*, and *`destination`* arguments in these commands are the matching parameters; this is where you specify which packets should match—and be acted upon by—the ACE. For a packet to match an ACE, it must match all of the specified values: the specified *`protocol`*, *`source`*, and *`destination`*. Partial matches don't count! Figure 24.1 gives more detail about which values you can configure for these arguments.

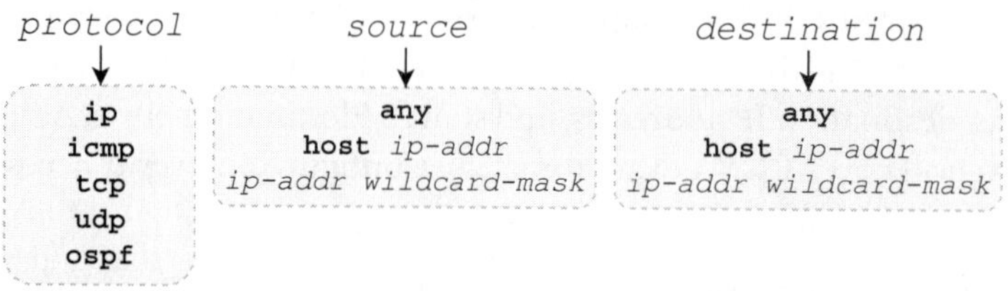

Figure 24.1 Possible matching parameters. The *`protocol`* argument specifies the protocol of the packet's payload. The *`source`* and *`destination`* arguments specify the packet's source and destination IP addresses, respectively.

The *`protocol`* argument warrants some additional explanation. You can specify a keyword like **`icmp`**, **`tcp`**, **`udp`**, or **`ospf`** to match packets that carry an ICMP, TCP, UDP, or OSPF payload, respectively. Another common keyword is **`ip`**, which matches all IPv4 packets; use this if you don't care what the protocol of the encapsulated message is and you want to match only based on source/destination IP addresses.

You should be familiar with the options for the *`source`* and *`destination`* arguments: we covered them in the previous chapter. By providing an IP address and wildcard mask (*`ip-addr wildcard-mask`*), you can specify a range of IP addresses to match. The **`any`** keyword matches all possible IP addresses—equivalent to **`0.0.0.0 255.255.255.255`** (that's a /0 wildcard mask, not a /32 netmask). **`host`** *`ip-addr`* allows you to specify a single IP address to match—equivalent to an IP address and a /32 wildcard mask (**`0.0.0.0`**).

> **NOTE** When configuring a standard ACL, you can match a single IP address by simply specifying the IP address, without the **`host`** keyword or a wildcard mask. However, that doesn't work in extended ACLs. To match a single IP address in an extended ACL, for example 8.8.8.8, use **`host 8.8.8.8`** or **`8.8.8.8 0.0.0.0`**.

With these three parameters, you can fulfill more precise security requirements than with standard ACLs–for example, "block all TCP traffic from host A to LAN B" or "permit only ICMP traffic from LAN X to LAN Y." Table 24.1 lists and explains some example ACEs. Compare each ACE and its explanation to familiarize yourself with the logic of ACEs that match packets based on protocol, source, and destination.

Table 24.1 Example ACEs for extended ACLs

ACE	Explanation
`permit ip any any`	Permits all IPv4 packets from any source to any destination
`deny udp 10.0.0.0 0.0.0.255 192.168.1.0 0.0.0.255`	Prevents 10.0.0.0/24 from sending UDP messages to 192.168.1.0/24
`deny icmp any 203.0.113.0 0.0.0.255`	Prevents all hosts from sending ICMP messages (i.e., ping) to 203.0.113.0/24
`permit ip host 172.16.1.1 any`	Permits all IPv4 packets from 172.16.1.1 to any destination

Now let's examine an entire extended ACL and consider its effect on traffic. Figure 24.2 shows an example network—the same one we looked at in the previous chapter—and an extended named ACL, applied outbound on R1's G0/2 interface.

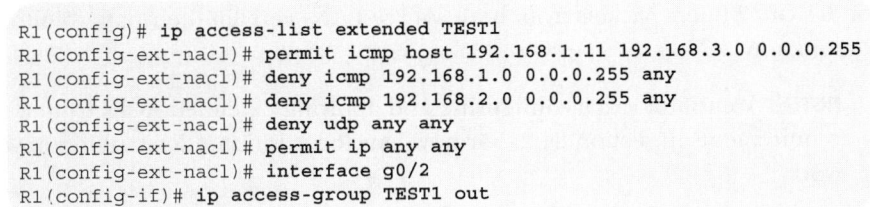

```
R1(config)# ip access-list extended TEST1
R1(config-ext-nacl)# permit icmp host 192.168.1.11 192.168.3.0 0.0.0.255
R1(config-ext-nacl)# deny icmp 192.168.1.0 0.0.0.255 any
R1(config-ext-nacl)# deny icmp 192.168.2.0 0.0.0.255 any
R1(config-ext-nacl)# deny udp any any
R1(config-ext-nacl)# permit ip any any
R1(config-ext-nacl)# interface g0/2
R1(config-if)# ip access-group TEST1 out
```

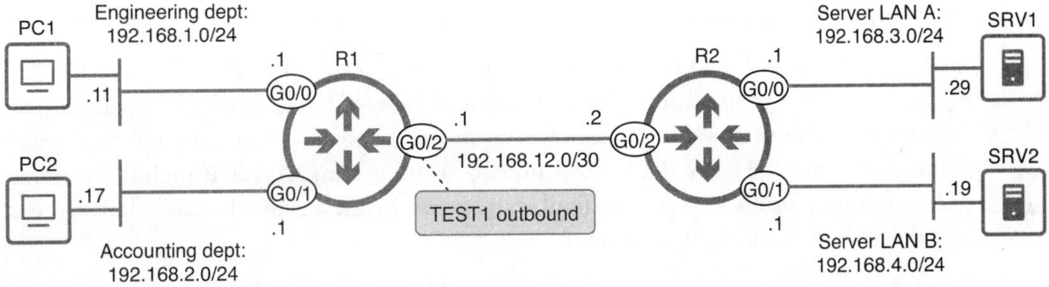

Figure 24.2 Extended ACL TEST1 is applied outbound on R1 G0/2. TEST1 permits ICMP traffic from PC1 to 192.168.3.0/24, denies ICMP traffic from 192.168.1.0/24 and 192.168.2.0/24, denies all UDP traffic, and permits all other IPv4 packets.

TEST1's first ACE permits ICMP traffic from PC1 (192.168.1.11) to hosts in Server LAN A, such as SRV1; this would allow PC1 to test connectivity by pinging SRV1, for example. The second and third ACEs, however, deny all ICMP traffic from hosts in the engineering and accounting subnets (except for PC1's ICMP traffic that is matched by the first ACE).

The fourth ACE denies all UDP traffic, and the final ACE permits all other IPv4 packets. The **any any** keywords in both ACEs mean they will match packets from any source IP address to any destination IP address. Keep in mind that the ACL is applied outbound on R1's G0/2 interface, so it only filters packets that are to be forwarded out of that interface, toward R2 and its connected LANs.

As covered in chapter 23, standard ACLs should be applied as close to the destination as possible. Standard ACLs don't provide granular control of which packets are filtered, so if you apply them too close to their source, you could inadvertently block legitimate traffic from the source.

Extended ACLs, however, provide more control over exactly which types of packets are permitted and which should be denied. For that reason, it's more efficient to apply extended ACLs as close to the source as possible. A properly configured extended ACL will only block the intended traffic, and applying the ACL close to the source is more efficient, because it prevents packets from traveling all the way across the network just to be discarded right before reaching their destination.

In this example, we are filtering packets from the engineering and accounting departments' LANs to Server LAN A and Server LAN B. Applying TEST1 outbound on R1 G0/2 filters packets from both source LANs early in their path to either of the destination LANs.

NOTE We will practice configuring and applying extended ACLs from a set of requirements in section 24.2. For now, our focus is on understanding how they work.

24.1.2 Matching TCP/UDP port numbers

Matching packets based on protocol, source, and destination provides much more granular control than standard ACLs provide. However, by adding TCP and UDP port numbers to the mix, we can achieve even more control over which packets are permitted or denied. Figure 24.3 shows how to configure an ACE that includes ports in its matching parameters; pay particular attention to the keyword values that you can provide for the `operator` arguments.

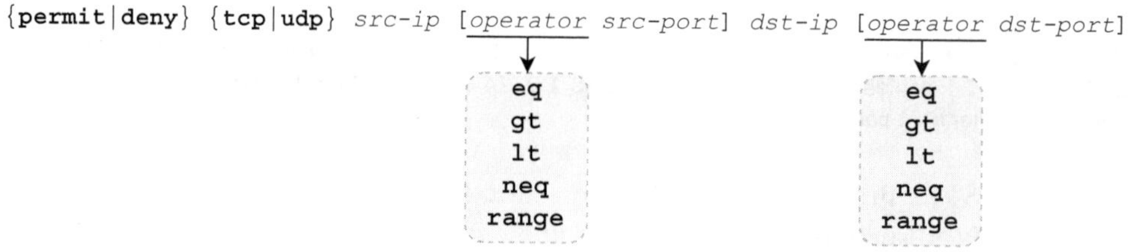

Figure 24.3 Configuring an ACE that matches packets based on protocol (TCP/UDP), source/destination IP addresses, and source/destination ports

Here is an example and explanation of each of the keywords you can provide for the `operator` arguments:

- **`eq 80`** = Equal to 80
- **`gt 80`** = Greater than 80 (but not including 80)
- **`lt 80`** = Less than 80 (but not including 80)
- **`neq 80`** = Not equal to 80 (anything other than 80)
- **`range 80 100`** = From 80 to 100 (including 80 and 100)

Table 24.2 lists some example ACEs that include the source and/or destination port numbers in their list of matching parameters. Once again, compare each ACE and its explanation to familiarize yourself with their logic. Make sure you can identify each part of each ACE: the protocol, source IP addresses, source ports, destination IP addresses, and destination ports. Some ACEs specify both source and destination port numbers, but others specify only one. If you don't specify a source port number, all source port numbers will count as a match, and the same applies for the destination port number.

Table 24.2 Example ACEs including port numbers

ACE	Explanation
`permit tcp 10.0.0.0 0.0.0.255 any eq 443`	Allows hosts in 10.0.0.0/24 to access all web servers using HTTPS (port 443)
`deny udp any gt 50000 host 203.0.113.1`	Prevents all hosts with a UDP source port greater than 50000 from accessing 203.0.113.1
`permit tcp 10.0.0.0 0.0.0.255 gt 9999 host 203.0.113.1 neq 23`	Allows hosts in 10.0.0.0/24 with a TCP source port greater than 9,999 to access all TCP ports on 203.0.113.1 except port 23
`deny tcp any lt 1024 any gt 1023`	Denies all TCP messages with a source port lower than 1,024 and a destination port greater than 1,023

NOTE Remember that a packet must match all parameters in the ACE to be considered a match. If the ACE specifies the protocol, source IP, source port, destination IP, and destination port, all five parameters must match.

Figure 24.4 shows each of the ACEs from table 24.1 and identifies each part: protocol, source IP, source port, destination IP, and destination port.

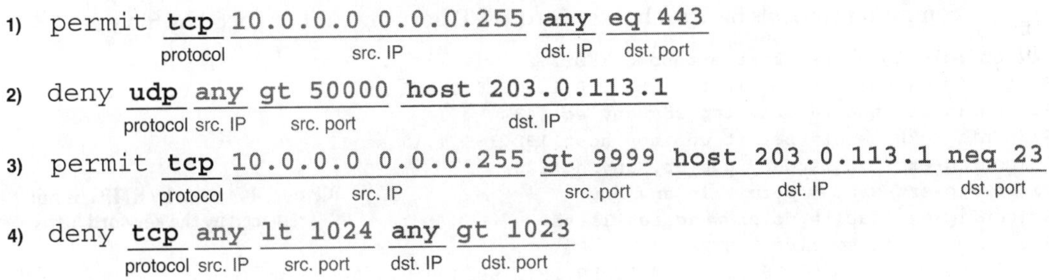

Figure 24.4 ACEs that match packets based on protocol, source IP, source port, destination IP, and destination port. Not all ACEs specify both the source and destination ports.

Now let's examine an extended ACL that uses ACEs like these, filtering packets based on source and/or destination ports. Examine the ACL shown in figure 24.5—applied outbound on R1 G0/2—and consider which traffic is allowed and which isn't.

```
R1(config)# ip access-list extended TEST2
R1(config-ext-nacl)# permit tcp 192.168.1.0 0.0.0.255 192.168.3.0 0.0.0.255 eq 443
R1(config-ext-nacl)# deny tcp any any eq 443
R1(config-ext-nacl)# permit udp any host 192.168.4.19 eq 123
R1(config-ext-nacl)# deny udp any any eq 123
R1(config-ext-nacl)# permit ip any any
R1(config-ext-nacl)# interface g0/2
R1(config-if)# ip access-group TEST2 out
```

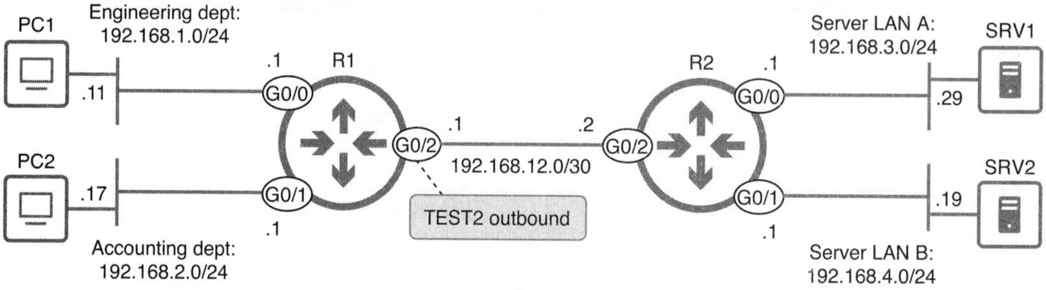

Figure 24.5 Extended ACL TEST2 is applied outbound on R1 G0/2. TEST2 permits HTTPS traffic from the engineering department to Server LAN A, denies all other HTTPS traffic, permits all NTP traffic to SRV2, denies all other NTP traffic, and permits all other IPv4 packets.

In the following example, I configure the ACL shown in figure 24.5 and confirm with **show access-lists**. Notice that UDP port 123, as specified in the third and fourth ACEs, is replaced by the keyword `ntp`, because NTP uses UDP port 123. You can configure some well-known port numbers by specifying either the port number itself or the equivalent keyword. Whichever you configure, the keyword (i.e., `ntp`) will appear in the output of **show** commands. However, as the example also demonstrates, not all common protocols have such a keyword; TCP port 443 isn't replaced by **https**:

```
R1(config)# ip access-list extended TEST2
R1(config-ext-nacl)# permit tcp 192.168.1.0 0.0.0.255 192.168.3.0 0.0.0.255 eq 443
R1(config-ext-nacl)# deny tcp any any eq 443
R1(config-ext-nacl)# permit udp any host 192.168.4.19 eq 123
R1(config-ext-nacl)# deny udp any any eq 123
R1(config-ext-nacl)# permit ip any any
R1(config-ext-nacl)# do show access-lists
Extended IP access list TEST2
    10 permit tcp 192.168.1.0 0.0.0.255 192.168.3.0 0.0.0.255 eq 443
    20 deny tcp 192.168.2.0 0.0.0.255 any eq 443
    30 permit udp any host 192.168.4.19 eq ntp
    40 deny udp any any eq ntp
    50 permit ip any any
```

TCP port 443, used by HTTPS, is not replaced by the keyword https.

UDP port 123, used by NTP, is replaced by the keyword ntp.

Because ACLs in CCNA exam questions may use keywords instead of port numbers, I recommend getting familiar with a few common ones, such as the following:

- TCP 20 (FTP data) = **ftp-data**
- TCP 21 (FTP control) = **ftp**

- TCP 23 (Telnet) = `telnet`
- TCP/UDP 53 (DNS) = `domain`
- UDP 67 (DHCP server) = `bootps`
- UDP 68 (DHCP client) = `bootpc`
- UDP 69 (TFTP) = `tftp`
- TCP 80 (HTTP) = `www`

EXAM TIP Make sure you know the Layer 4 protocol and port numbers of common protocols, such as those listed here. I listed them in chapter 22 and will mention them as we cover each protocol in volume 2 of this book, but it's worth emphasizing the importance of knowing them.

24.2 Example security requirements

Now that we've examined extended ACLs and their components, let's practice configuring them to fulfill a set of requirements as defined by the security team of our fictional organization. Extended ACLs add a few layers of complexity on top of standard ACLs, so this practice is especially important. Figure 24.6 shows the scenario, with three requirements we must fulfill by configuring extended ACLs.

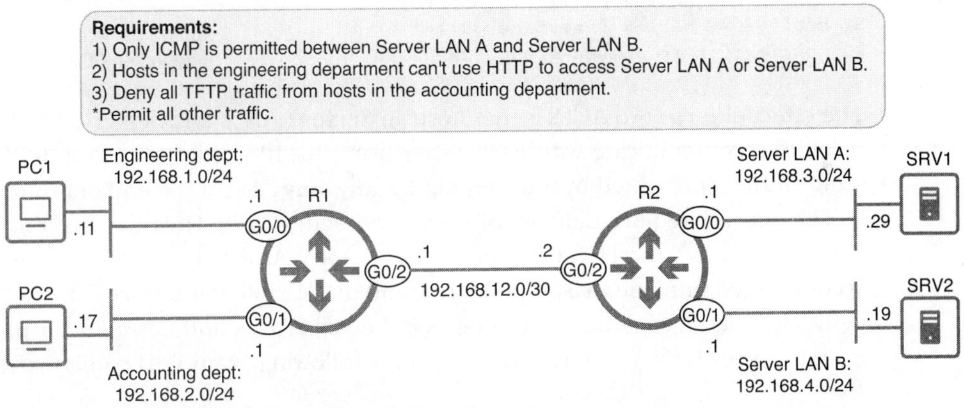

Figure 24.6 Requirements to be fulfilled by configuring extended ACLs

The first requirement states that "Only ICMP is permitted between Server LAN A and Server LAN B." I will accomplish this with two ACLs:

- An ACL that permits ICMP traffic from Server LAN A to Server LAN B and denies other traffic between them but allows all traffic to other destinations
- An ACL that permits ICMP traffic from Server LAN B to Server LAN A and denies other traffic between them but allows all traffic to other destinations

In the following example, I configure the first ACL and apply it inbound on R2 G0/0; this filters packets sent from hosts in Server LAN A:

```
R2(config)# ip access-list extended ICMP_1
R2(config-ext-nacl)# permit icmp 192.168.3.0
➥0.0.0.255 192.168.4.0 0.0.0.255
R2(config-ext-nacl)# deny ip 192.168.3.0
➥0.0.0.255 192.168.4.0 0.0.0.255
R2(config-ext-nacl)# permit ip any any
R2(config-ext-nacl)# interface g0/0
R2(config-if)# ip access-group ICMP_1 in
```

Permits ICMP traffic from Server LAN A to Server LAN B

Denies all other traffic from Server LAN A to Server LAN B

Permits all other traffic

Applies the ACL inbound on G0/0

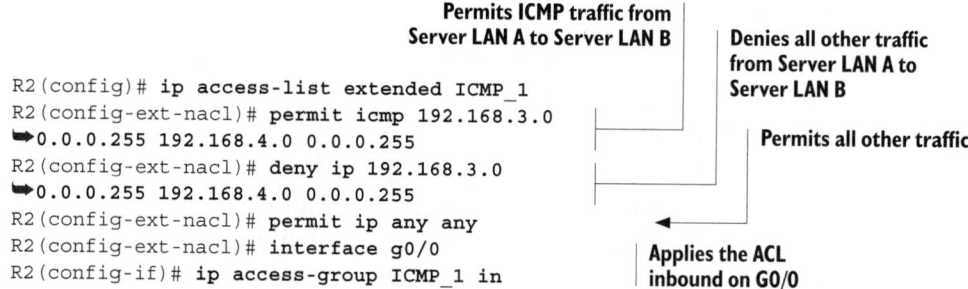

That fulfills one half of the first requirement. In the next example, I configure the second ACL, this time applying it inbound on R2 G0/1:

```
R2(config)# ip access-list extended ICMP_2
R2(config-ext-nacl)# permit icmp 192.168.4.0
➥0.0.0.255 192.168.3.0 0.0.0.255
R2(config-ext-nacl)# deny ip 192.168.4.0
➥0.0.0.255 192.168.3.0 0.0.0.255
R2(config-ext-nacl)# permit ip any any
R2(config-ext-nacl)# interface g0/1
R2(config-if)# ip access-group ICMP_2 in
```

Permits ICMP traffic from Server LAN B to Server LAN A

Denies all other traffic from Server LAN B to Server LAN B

Permits all other traffic

Applies the ACL inbound on G0/1

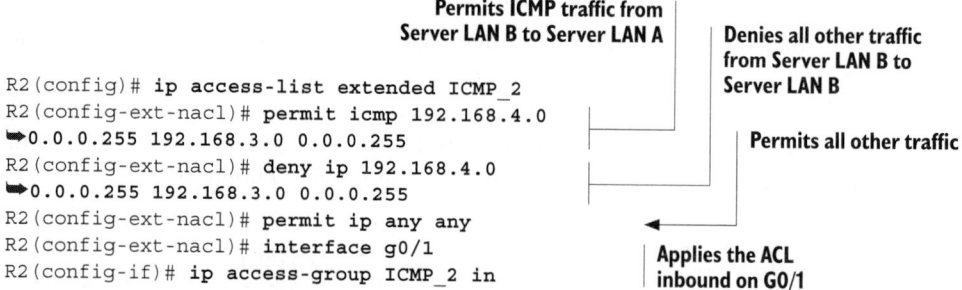

The effect of these two ACLs is that hosts in Server LAN A and Server LAN B will only be able to communicate with each other using ICMP—ping, for example. However, other traffic is permitted by the `permit ip any any` ACE at the end of both ACLs.

The second requirement in our scenario states that "Hosts in the engineering department can't use HTTP to access Server LAN A or Server LAN B." This can be accomplished with one ACL applied inbound on R1's G0/0 interface. The ACL should deny TCP messages sourced from hosts in Server LAN A and destined for port 80 on hosts in Server LAN A or Server LAN B. In the following example, I configure that ACL:

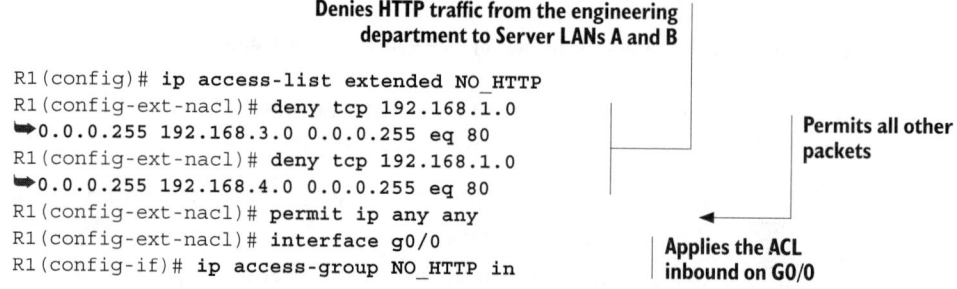

```
R1(config)# ip access-list extended NO_HTTP
R1(config-ext-nacl)# deny tcp 192.168.1.0
➥0.0.0.255 192.168.3.0 0.0.0.255 eq 80
R1(config-ext-nacl)# deny tcp 192.168.1.0
➥0.0.0.255 192.168.4.0 0.0.0.255 eq 80
R1(config-ext-nacl)# permit ip any any
R1(config-ext-nacl)# interface g0/0
R1(config-if)# ip access-group NO_HTTP in
```

Denies HTTP traffic from the engineering department to Server LANs A and B

Permits all other packets

Applies the ACL inbound on G0/0

NOTE When a host uses HTTP to access resources on another host (a server), it uses port 80 as the destination port, not the source port. Therefore, to filter HTTP traffic from a client to a server, make sure to match based on the destination port—not the source port. This applies to other protocols too; the following example filters TFTP traffic by matching destination port 69.

The final requirement states, "Deny all TFTP traffic from hosts in the accounting department." We can fulfill this requirement with a simple two-ACE ACL: one ACE to deny TFTP traffic and one to permit all other traffic. In the following example, I configure that ACL and apply it inbound on R1 G0/1. For demonstration purposes, I'll configure this one as a numbered ACL from global config mode:

```
R1(config)# access-list 100 deny udp 192.168.2.0 0.0.0.255 any eq 69
R1(config)# access-list 100 permit ip any any
R1(config)# interface g0/1
R1(config-if)# ip access-group 100 in
```

Denies all TFTP traffic from the accounting department (line 1)
Permits all other packets (line 2)
Applies the ACL inbound on G0/1 (lines 3–4)

We have now fulfilled all three requirements. For review, figure 24.7 shows the requirements again and the four ACLs we configured to fulfill them.,

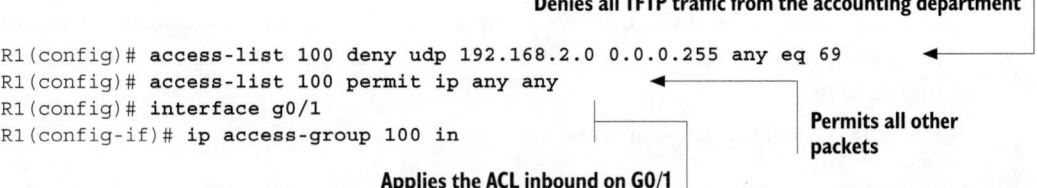

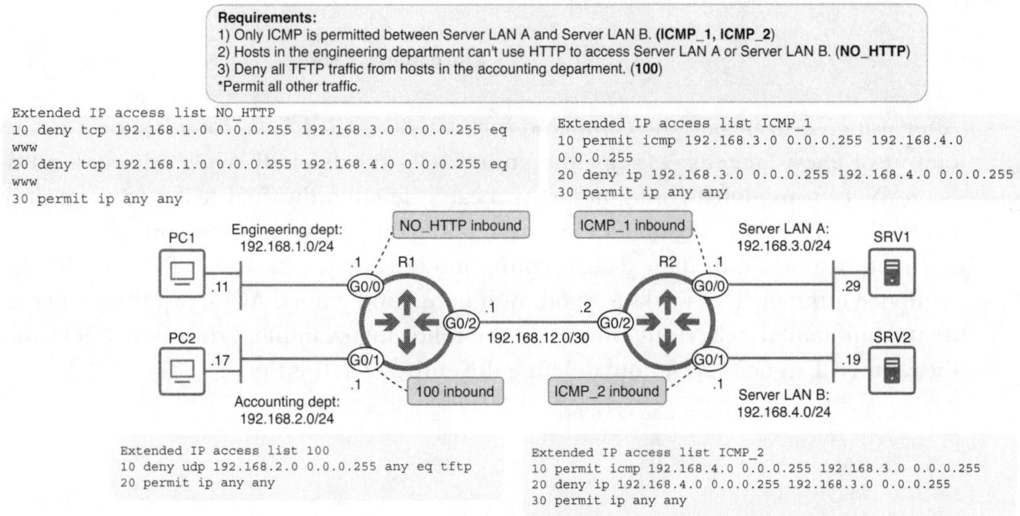

Figure 24.7 Four ACLs configured on R1 and R2 fulfill the requirements. ACLs ICMP_1 and ICMP_2 fulfill requirement 1, ACL NO_HTTP fulfills requirement 2, and ACL 100 fulfills requirement 3.

24.3 Editing ACLs

The order in which you configure an ACL's ACEs is very important, because it determines the order the router will process them when evaluating a packet against the ACL. However, even if you configure the ACEs in the proper order, in some cases you may have to edit the ACL later. For example, you may have to delete an ACE or insert a new ACE in between existing ones. In this section, we'll examine how to do that.

> **NOTE** Everything in this section applies to both standard and extended ACLs. To keep the ACLs simple, I'll use standard ACLs.

24.3.1 Deleting ACEs

Negating a command in Cisco IOS is as simple as inserting the **no** keyword in front of it. However, let's see what happens when we use that method to delete an ACE from a numbered ACL:

```
R1(config)# do show access-lists
Standard IP access list 1
    10 deny   192.168.1.1
    20 deny   192.168.2.1
    30 deny   192.168.3.0, wildcard bits 0.0.0.255
    40 permit any
R1(config)# no access-list 1 deny 192.168.3.0 0.0.0.255
R1(config)# do show access-lists
R1(config)#
```

Negates the command for ACE 30

No output is shown.

After using **no** to negate the command for ACE 30, ACL 1 is no longer shown in the output of **show access-lists**—the entire ACL was deleted! When editing a numbered ACL from global config mode, you can't delete individual ACEs; you can only delete the entire ACL. Fortunately, named ACL mode fixes this limitation.

Deleting an ACE in named ACL config mode is easy: just use **no** followed by the sequence number. This works for both numbered and named ACLs; just remember to do it from named ACL config mode. In the following example, I delete ACE 30 from the same ACL as before, without deleting the entire ACL this time:

```
R1(config)# do show access-lists
Standard IP access list 1
    10 deny   192.168.1.1
    20 deny   192.168.2.1
    30 deny   192.168.3.0, wildcard bits 0.0.0.255
    40 permit any
R1(config)# ip access-list standard 1
R1(config-std-nacl)# no 30
R1(config-std-nacl)# do show access-lists
Standard IP access list 1
    10 deny   192.168.1.1
    20 deny   192.168.2.1
    40 permit any
```

Enters named ACL config mode and deletes ACE 30

ACE 30 was removed from ACL1.

Named ACL config mode also provides the benefit of allowing you to insert new ACEs in between existing ones by specifying a sequence number at the beginning of the configuration command. In the following example, I insert a new ACE 30 to the same ACL as before in place of the ACE 30 that I just deleted:

```
R1(config-std-nacl)# 30 deny 192.168.4.0 0.0.0.255
R1(config-std-nacl)# do show access-lists
Standard IP access list 1
    10 deny   192.168.1.1
    20 deny   192.168.2.1
    30 deny   192.168.4.0, wildcard bits 0.0.0.255
    40 permit any
```

24.3.2 Resequencing ACEs

Named ACL config mode allows you to configure new ACEs between existing ones by specifying each ACE's sequence number, but what if there is no space between ACEs? By default, sequence numbers begin at 10 and increment by 10, so this problem is rare. However, if you do run out of space between ACEs, Cisco IOS provides a handy command that will automatically adjust the sequence numbers. The syntax of the command is **`ip access-list resequence`** {*`name`*|*`number`*} *`starting-seq-num increment`*. Figure 24.8 shows an example command and explains the final two arguments (*`starting-seq-num`* and *`increment`*):

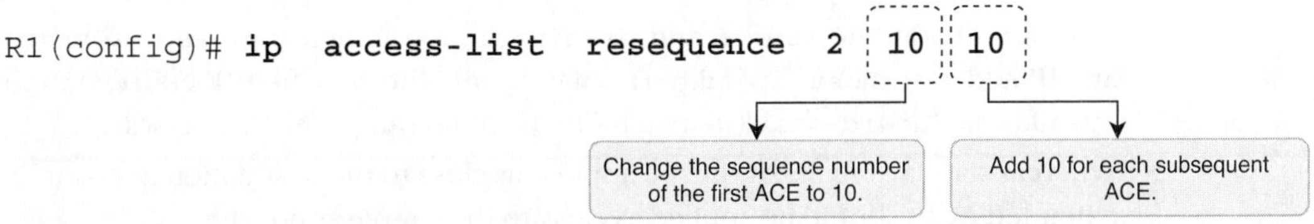

Figure 24.8 The `ip access-list resequence` command. The `starting-seq-num` argument specifies the new sequence number of the ACL's first ACE, and the `increment` argument specifies the increment for each subsequent ACE.

In the following example, I view an example ACL (ACL 2) that has four ACEs with sequence numbers 10, 18, 19, and 20. I then use **`ip access-list resequence`** to adjust the sequence numbers. After issuing the command, there is room between the ACEs to insert new ones as needed:

```
R1(config)# do show access-lists
Standard IP access list 2
    10 deny 192.168.1.0 0.0.0.255
    18 deny 192.168.3.0 0.0.0.255
    19 deny 192.168.4.0 0.0.0.255
    20 permit any
R1(config)# ip access-list 2 resequence 10 10
R1(config)# do show access-lists
Standard IP access list 2
```

Sets the first ACE to sequence 10 and adds 10 for each subsequent ACE

```
10 deny 192.168.1.0 0.0.0.255
20 deny 192.168.3.0 0.0.0.255
30 deny 192.168.4.0 0.0.0.255
40 permit any
```

Sequence 10 remains 10, 18 becomes 20, 19 becomes 30, and 20 becomes 40.

Summary

- Extended ACLs can filter packets based on parameters such as the protocol of the packet's payload (TCP, UDP, ICMP, OSPF, etc.), source/destination IP addresses, and source/destination ports.
- Extended ACL configuration is similar to standard ACL configuration. You can configure extended ACLs in global config mode with the **`access-list`** command (numbered only) or in named ACL config mode with **`ip access-list`**.
- You can configure an extended numbered ACL with **`access-list`** *`number`* {**`permit`** | **`deny`**} *`protocol source destination`*. Extended numbered ACLs must use a number from ranges 100–199 or 2000–2699.
- You can configure an extended ACL in named ACL config mode with **`ip access-list extended`** {*`name`* | *`number`*}. From there, configure each ACE with [*`seq-num`*] {**`permit`** | **`deny`**} *`protocol source destination`*.
- For the *`protocol`* argument, you can specify a keyword like **`icmp`**, **`tcp`**, **`udp`**, or **`ospf`** to match packets that carry the specified protocol in its payload. Or you can specify **`ip`** to match all IPv4 packets, regardless of the encapsulated protocol.
- The options for the *`source`* and *`destination`* arguments are **`any`** (to match any IP address), **`host`** *`ip-addr`* (to match only the specified IP address), and *`ip-addr wildcard-mask`* (to match the specified range of IP addresses).
- Whereas standard ACLs should be applied as close to the destination as possible, extended ACLs should be applied as close to the source as possible.
- When **`tcp`** or **`udp`** are specified for the *`protocol`* argument, you can also specify TCP/UDP port number(s) as matching conditions.
- The command syntax to configure an ACE that specifies a port number is {**`permit`**|**`deny`**} {**`tcp`**|**`udp`**} *`src-ip`* [*`operator src-port`*] *`dst-ip`* [*`operator dst-port`*].
- The options for the *`operator`* argument are **`eq`** (equal to X), **`gt`** (greater than X), **`lt`** (lower than X), **`neq`** (not equal to X), and **`range`** (from X to Y). Some examples are
  - **`eq 80`** = Equal to 80
  - **`gt 80`** = Greater than 80 (but not including 80)
  - **`lt 80`** = Less than 80 (but not including 80)
  - **`neq 80`** = Not equal to 80 (anything other than 80)
  - **`range 80 100`** = From 80 to 100 (including 80 and 100)

- An ACE can specify only the source port, only the destination port, both, or neither. If you don't specify the source/destination ports as matching conditions, all source/destination ports will match.
- A packet must match all of an ACE's conditions to be considered a match. If the ACE specifies the protocol, source IP, source port, destination IP, and destination port, all five parameters must match.
- When specifying port numbers in an ACE, some common protocols have keywords that can be used instead of numbers. Some examples are
  - TCP 20 (FTP data) = **`ftp-data`**
  - TCP 21 (FTP control) = **`ftp`**
  - TCP 23 (Telnet) = **`telnet`**
  - TCP/UDP 53 (DNS) = **`domain`**
  - UDP 67 (DHCP server) = **`bootps`**
  - UDP 68 (DHCP client) = **`bootpc`**
  - UDP 69 (TFTP) = **`tftp`**
  - TCP 80 (HTTP) = **`www`**
- When a host uses a protocol to access resources on another host (a server), it uses the protocol's port number as the destination port, not the source port. To filter that traffic, make sure to filter based on the destination port, not the source port.
- When editing a numbered ACL from global config mode, you can't delete individual ACEs; you can only delete the entire ACL.
- Deleting an ACE in named ACL config mode is easy: use **`no`** followed by the sequence number, such as **`no 30`** to delete the ACE with sequence number 30.
- Named ACL config mode also allows you to insert new ACEs in between existing ones by specifying a sequence number at the beginning of the command.
- You can renumber an ACL's ACEs with the **`ip access-list resequence`** *`{name | number} starting-seq-num increment`* command. *`starting-seq-num`* specifies the sequence number of the first ACE, and *`increment`* specifies the increment for each additional ACE. For example, **`ip access-list 1 resequence 5 5`** will set ACL 1's first ACE to sequence number 5, the second to 10, the third to 15, etc.

A Exam topics reference table

The following table lists the CCNA exam topics and the chapters in this book that cover each of them. However, keep in mind that Cisco occasionally (but rarely) makes minor, unannounced changes to the exam topics, so I recommend going straight to the source to verify the official list: https://learningnetwork.cisco.com/s/ccna-exam-topics.

Furthermore, Cisco publishes its Certification Roadmaps at https://learningnetwork.cisco.com/s/cisco-certification-roadmaps. I recommend bookmarking that page; it will give you information about Cisco's yearly certification review process and any scheduled changes coming to the CCNA exam (and Cisco's other exams).

The first time you read this book, I recommend following the chapters in order. However, it's important to carefully examine the CCNA exam topics and make sure you know all of them before taking the CCNA exam. This resource should be helpful in that process; if there are any exam topics that you don't feel confident about, refer to the table to know which chapters you should review.

Exam topic	Chapter(s)
1.0 Network fundamentals—20%	
1.1 Explain the role and function of network components	2 (vol. 1)
1.1.a Routers	2 (vol. 1)
1.1.b Layer 2 and Layer 3 switches	2 (vol. 1), 12 (vol. 1)
1.1.c Next-generation firewalls and IPS	2 (vol. 1), 11 (vol. 2)
1.1.d Access points	18 (vol. 2)
1.1.e Controllers	19 (vol. 1), 22 (vol. 2)
1.1.f Endpoints	2 (vol. 1)
1.1.g Servers	2 (vol. 1)
1.1.h PoE	10 (vol. 2)
1.2 Describe characteristics of network topology architectures	15-17 (vol. 2)
1.2.a Two-tier	15 (vol. 2)
1.2.b Three-tier	15 (vol. 2)
1.2.c Spine-leaf	15 (vol. 2)
1.2.d WAN	16 (vol. 2)
1.2.e Small office/home office (SOHO)	15 (vol. 2)
1.2.f On-premises and cloud	17 (vol. 2)
1.3 Compare physical interface and cabling types	3 (vol. 1)
1.3.a Single-mode fiber, multimode fiber, copper	3 (vol. 1)
1.3.b Connections (Ethernet shared media and point-to-point)	3 (vol. 1), 8 (vol. 1)
1.4 Identify interface and cable issues (collisions, errors, mismatch duplex, and/or speed)	8 (vol. 1)
1.5 Compare TCP to UDP	22 (vol. 1)
1.6 Configure and verify IPv4 addressing and subnetting	7 (vol. 1), 11 (vol. 1)
1.7 Describe private IPv4 addressing	9 (vol. 2)
1.8 Configure and verify IPv6 addressing and prefix	20 (vol. 1)
1.9 Describe IPv6 address types	20 (vol. 1)
1.9.a Unicast (global, unique local, and link local)	20 (vol. 1)
1.9.b Anycast	20 (vol. 1)
1.9.c Multicast	20 (vol. 1)
1.9.d Modified EUI 64	20 (vol. 1)
1.10 Verify IP parameters for Client OS (Windows, Mac OS, Linux)	4 (vol. 2)
1.11 Describe wireless principles	18 (vol. 2), 20 (vol. 2)
1.11.a Nonoverlapping Wi-Fi channels	18 (vol. 2)
1.11.b SSID	18 (vol. 2)
1.11.c RF	18 (vol. 2)
1.11.d Encryption	20 (vol. 2)
1.12 Explain virtualization fundamentals (server virtualization, containers, and VRFs)	17 (vol. 2)

1.0 Network fundamentals—20% *(continued)*	
1.13 Describe switching concepts	6 (vol. 1)
1.13.a MAC learning and aging	6 (vol. 1)
1.13.b Frame switching	6 (vol. 1)
1.13.c Frame flooding	6 (vol. 1)
1.13.d MAC address table	6 (vol. 1)
2.0 Network access—20%	
2.1 Configure and verify VLANs (normal range) spanning multiple switches	12 (vol. 1), 13 (vol. 1)
2.1.a Access ports (data and voice)	12 (vol. 1), 13 (vol. 1)
2.1.b Default VLAN	12 (vol. 1)
2.1.c InterVLAN connectivity	12 (vol. 1), 13 (vol. 1)
2.2 Configure and verify interswitch connectivity	12 (vol. 1), 13 (vol. 1)
2.2.a Trunk ports	12 (vol. 1), 13 (vol. 1)
2.2.b 802.1Q	12 (vol. 1), 13 (vol. 1)
2.2.c Native VLAN	12 (vol. 1)
2.3 Configure and verify Layer 2 discovery protocols (Cisco Discovery Protocol and LLDP)	1 (vol. 2)
2.4 Configure and verify (Layer 2/Layer 3) EtherChannel (LACP)	16 (vol. 1)
2.5 Identify basic operations of Rapid PVST+ Spanning Tree Protocol	14 (vol. 1), 15 (vol. 1)
2.5.a Root port, root bridge (primary/secondary), and other port names	14 (vol. 1), 15 (vol. 1)
2.5.b Port states and roles	14 (vol. 1), 15 (vol. 1)
2.5.c PortFast	14 (vol. 1), 15 (vol. 1)
2.5.d Root guard, loop guard, BPDU filter, and BPDU guard	14 (vol. 1), 15 (vol. 1)
2.6 Compare Cisco Wireless Architectures and AP modes	19 (vol. 2)
2.7 Describe physical infrastructure connections of WLAN components (AP, WLC, access/trunk ports, and LAG)	19 (vol. 2), 21 (vol. 2)
2.8 Describe network device management access connections (Telnet, SSH, HTTP, HTTPS, console, TACACS+/RADIUS, and cloud managed)	19 (vol. 2), 21 (vol. 2)
2.9 Interpret the wireless LAN GUI configuration for client connectivity, such as WLAN creation, security settings, QoS profiles, and advanced settings	21 (vol. 2)
3.0 IP Connectivity—25%	
3.1 Interpret the components of routing table	9 (vol. 1), 17 (vol. 1), 21 (vol. 1)
3.1.a Routing protocol code	9 (vol. 1), 17 (vol. 1)
3.1.b Prefix	9 (vol. 1), 21 (vol. 1)
3.1.c Network mask	9 (vol. 1), 21 (vol. 1)
3.1.d Next hop	9 (vol. 1), 21 (vol. 1)
3.1.e Administrative distance	17 (vol. 1)
3.1.f Metric	17 (vol. 1)
3.1.g Gateway of last resort	9 (vol. 1), 21 (vol. 1)

3.2 Determine how a router makes a forwarding decision by default	9 (vol. 1), 17 (vol. 1), 21 (vol. 1)
3.2.a Longest prefix match	9 (vol. 1), 17 (vol. 1), 21 (vol. 1)
3.2.b Administrative distance	17 (vol. 1)
3.2.c Routing protocol metric	17 (vol. 1)
3.3 Configure and verify IPv4 and IPv6 static routing	9 (vol. 1), 17 (vol. 1), 21 (vol. 1)
3.3.a Default route	9 (vol. 1), 21 (vol. 1)
3.3.b Network route	9 (vol. 1), 21 (vol. 1)
3.3.c Host route	9 (vol. 1), 21 (vol. 1)
3.3.d Floating static	17 (vol. 1), 21 (vol. 1)
3.4 Configure and verify single area OSPFv2	17 (vol. 1), 18 (vol. 1)
3.4.a Neighbor adjacencies	18 (vol. 1)
3.4.b Point-to-point	18 (vol. 1)
3.4.c Broadcast (DR/BDR selection)	18 (vol. 1)
3.4.d Router ID	18 (vol. 1)
3.5 Describe the purpose, functions, and concepts of first hop redundancy protocols	19 (vol. 1)
4.0 IP Services—10%	
4.1 Configure and verify inside source NAT using static and pools	9 (vol. 2)
4.2 Configure and verify NTP operating in a client and server mode	2 (vol. 2)
4.3 Explain the role of DHCP and DNS within the network	3 (vol. 2), 4 (vol. 2)
4.4 Explain the function of SNMP in network operations	6 (vol. 2)
4.5 Describe the use of syslog features including facilities and severity levels	7 (vol. 2)
4.6 Configure and verify DHCP client and relay	4 (vol. 2)
4.7 Explain the forwarding per-hop behavior (PHB) for QoS such as classification, marking, queuing, congestion, policing, shaping	10 (vol. 2)
4.8 Configure network devices for remote access using SSH	5 (vol. 2)
4.9 Describe the capabilities and functions of TFTP/FTP in the network	8 (vol. 2)
5.0 Security fundamentals—15%	
5.1 Define key security concepts (threats, vulnerabilities, exploits, and mitigation techniques)	11 (vol. 2)
5.2 Describe security program elements (user awareness, training, and physical access control)	11 (vol. 2)
5.3 Configure and verify device access control using local passwords	5 (vol. 1), 5 (vol. 2), 11 (vol. 2)
5.4 Describe security password policy elements, such as management, complexity, and password alternatives (multifactor authentication, certificates, and biometrics)	11 (vol. 2)
5.5 Describe IPsec remote access and site-to-site VPNs	16 (vol. 2)
5.6 Configure and verify access control lists	23 (vol. 1), 24 (vol. 1)

5.0 Security fundamentals—15% *(continued)*	
5.7 Configure and verify Layer 2 security features (DHCP snooping, dynamic ARP inspection, and port security)	12-14 (vol. 2)
5.8 Compare authentication, authorization, and accounting concepts	11 (vol. 2)
5.9 Describe wireless security protocols (WPA, WPA2, and WPA3)	20 (vol. 2)
5.10 Configure and verify WLAN within the GUI using WPA2 PSK	21 (vol. 2)
6.0 Automation and Programmability—10%	
6.1 Explain how automation impacts network management	22 (vol. 2)
6.2 Compare traditional networks with controller-based networking	22 (vol. 2)
6.3 Describe controller-based and software defined architecture (overlay, underlay, and fabric)	22 (vol. 2)
6.3.a Separation of control plane and data plane	22 (vol. 2)
6.3.b Northbound and Southbound APIs	22 (vol. 2)
6.4 Explain AI (generative and predictive) and machine learning in network operations	22 (vol. 2)
6.5 Describe characteristics of REST-based APIs (authentication types, CRUD, HTTP verbs, and data encoding)	23 (vol. 2)
6.6 Recognize the capabilities of configuration management mechanisms such as Ansible and Terraform	25 (vol. 2)
6.7 Recognize components of JSON-encoded data	24 (vol. 2)

B CLI command reference table

Most chapters of this book introduce several Cisco IOS CLI commands—totaling about 300. Being proficient with these commands is essential for success on the CCNA exam. The following table lists the various commands covered in this volume, organized by chapter, and gives a brief description of each. For a more complete explanation of a command's purpose and its usage, refer back to the relevant chapter.

Several commands are covered in multiple chapters in this book. In most cases, I have listed the command only under the chapter in which it was covered first or covered in greatest depth. Furthermore, a few commands in this book were introduced for demonstration purposes rather than as commands you need to know for the CCNA exam; for completeness, I include these commands in the table as well.

Mode	Command	Description
Chapter 5: The Cisco IOS CLI		
>	**enable**	Enter privileged EXEC mode.
#	**disable**	Return to user EXEC mode.
#	**reload**	Reboot the device.
#	**show running-config**	View the running-config.
#	**show startup-config**	View the startup-config.
#	**write**	Save the device configuration by copying the running-config to the startup-config.
#	**write memory**	
#	**copy running-config startup-config**	
#	**write erase**	Erase the startup-config. The device will load a factory-default configuration after the next reboot.
#	**erase startup-config**	
#	**erase nvram:**	
#	**show** *command* **| include** *string*	Limit **show** command output to lines that include the specified string.
(config)#	**hostname** *name*	Set the device's hostname.
(config)#	**enable password** *password*	Configure an unhashed enable password.
(config)#	**enable secret** *password*	Configure a hashed enable secret.
(config)#	**service password-encryption**	Encrypt passwords in the configuration with type-7 encryption (weak).
(config)#	**exit**	Return to the previous level in the IOS CLI hierarchy.
(config)#	**end**	Return to privileged EXEC mode from any configuration mode.
Chapter 6: Ethernet LAN switching		
#	**show mac address-table**	View the switch's MAC address table.
#	**clear mac address-table dynamic**	Remove all dynamic MAC addresses.
#	**clear mac address-table dynamic address** *address*	Remove the specified dynamic MAC address.
#	**clear mac address-table dynamic interface** *interface*	Remove all dynamic MAC addresses learned on the specified interface.
#	**ping** *ip-address*	Ping the specified host (ICMP echo/reply).
Chapter 7: IPv4 addressing		
#	**show ip interface** [*interface*]	View detailed Layer 3 information about interfaces.
#	**show ip interface brief**	View a concise summary of interface IP addresses and status.
(config)#	**interface** *interface*	Enter interface config mode for the specified interface.
(config-if)#	**ip address** *ip-address netmask*	Set the interface's IP address/netmask.
(config-if)#	[**no**] **shutdown**	Enable/disable the interface.

Chapter 8: Router and switch Interfaces		
#	**show interfaces** [*interface*]	View interface Layer 1/2 information.
#	**show interfaces description**	View interface descriptions and status.
#	**show interfaces status**	View interface status, speed, and duplex.
(config)#	**interface range** *interface-list*	Configure multiple interfaces at once.
(config-if)#	**description** *description*	Set the interface's description.
(config-if)#	**speed** {**auto** | *speed*}	Set the interface's speed.
(config-if)#	**duplex** {**auto** | **full** | **half**}	Set the interface's duplex.
Chapter 9: Routing fundamentals		
#	**show ip route**	View the routing table.
(config)#	**ip route** *destination-network netmask next-hop*	Configure a recursive static route.
(config)#	**ip route** *destination-network netmask exit-interface*	Configure a directly connected static route.
(config)#	**ip route** *destination-network netmask exit-interface next-hop*	Configure a fully specified static route.
Chapter 12: VLANs		
#	**show vlan brief**	View a list of VLANs and associated ports.
#	**show interfaces trunk**	View a list of trunk ports.
(config)#	**vlan** *vlan-id*	Configure a VLAN.
(config-vlan)#	**name** *name*	Name the VLAN.
(config-vlan)#	[**no**] **shutdown**	Enable/disable the VLAN.
(config-if)#	**switchport mode** {**access** | **trunk**}	Manually configure access or trunk mode.
(config-if)#	**switchport access vlan** *vlan-id*	Set the port's access VLAN.
(config-if)#	**switchport trunk encapsulation dot1q**	Set the port's trunk encapsulation protocol.
(config-if)#	**switchport trunk allowed vlan** {*vlans* | **add** *vlans* | **remove** *vlans* | **except** *vlans* | **all** | **none**}	Specify or modify the port's list of allowed VLANs (when in trunk mode).
(config-if)#	**switchport trunk native vlan** *vlan-id*	Specify the port's native VLAN.
(config)#	**interface** *interface.subif-number*	Configure a subinterface (ROAS).
(config-subif)#	**encapsulation dot1q** *vlan* [**native**]	Specify the subinterface's VLAN ID.
(config)#	**ip routing**	Enable IP routing on a multilayer switch.
(config)#	**interface vlan** *vlan-id*	Configure a switch virtual interface (SVI).
(config-if)#	**no switchport**	Make the port a Layer 3 routed port.
Chapter 13: Dynamic Trunking Protocol and VLAN Trunking Protocol		
#	**show interfaces switchport**	Show port operational and administrative modes.

Chapter 13: Dynamic Trunking Protocol and VLAN Trunking Protocol *(continued)*		
`(config-if)#`	**`switchport mode dynamic {auto	desirable}`**	Use DTP to determine the port's operational mode.
`(config-if)#`	**`switchport nonegotiate`**	Disable DTP on the port.
`#`	**`show vtp status`**	View VTP information.
`(config)#`	**`vtp domain`** *`name`*	Set the VTP domain name.
`(config)#`	**`vtp mode {server	client	transparent	off}`**	Set the VTP mode.
`(config)#`	**`vtp version {1	2	3}`**	Set the VTP version.
`#`	**`vtp primary`**	Make this switch the VTP primary server (VTP version 3 only).
Chapter 14: Spanning Tree Protocol; Chapter 15: Rapid Spanning Tree Protocol		
`#`	**`show spanning-tree`**	View STP status and information.
`(config)#`	**`spanning-tree vlan`** *`vlan`* **`priority`** *`priority`*	Set the STP bridge priority.
`(config)#`	**`spanning-tree vlan`** *`vlan`* **`root primary`**	Set the bridge priority to 24576, or the lowest increment of 4096 needed to become the root bridge.
`(config)#`	**`spanning-tree vlan`** *`vlan`* **`root secondary`**	Set the bridge priority to 28672.
`(config-if)#`	**`spanning-tree vlan`** *`vlan`* **`port-priority`** *`priority`*	Set the STP port priority.
`(config-if)#`	**`spanning-tree portfast enable`**	Enable PortFast on the port.
`(config)#`	**`spanning-tree portfast default`**	Enable PortFast on all access ports.
`(config-if)#`	**`spanning-tree bpduguard enable`**	Enable BPDU Guard on the port.
`(config)#`	**`spanning-tree portfast bpduguard default`**	Enable BPDU Guard on all PortFast-enabled ports.
`(config)#`	**`spanning-tree mode {pvst	rapid-pvst}`**	Set the STP mode (standard or rapid).
`#`	**`show spanning-tree pathcost method`**	View the port cost calculation method.
`(config)#`	**`spanning-tree pathcost method {short	long}`**	Set the port cost calculation method.
`(config-if)#`	**`spanning-tree link-type {point-to-point	shared}`**	Set the port's RSTP link type.
Chapter 16: EtherChannel		
`(config-if)#`	**`channel-group`** *`group`* **`mode {desirable	auto}`**	Configure a PaGP EtherChannel.
`(config-if)#`	**`channel-group`** *`group`* **`mode {active	passive}`**	Configure an LACP EtherChannel.
`(config-if)#`	**`channel-group`** *`group`* **`mode on`**	Configure a static EtherChannel.
`(config)#`	**`interface port-channel`** *`number`*	Configure the port-channel interface.
`#`	**`show etherchannel summary`**	View EtherChannel status.
`#`	**`show pagp neighbor`**	View PAgP neighbor status.

#	**show lacp neighbor**	View LACP neighbor status.
(config)#	**port-channel load-balance** *parameters*	Modify the EtherChannel load-balancing parameters.
#	**show etherchannel load-balance**	View the load-balancing parameters.
	Chapter 17: Dynamic routing; Chapter 18: Open Shortest Path First	
(config)#	**ip route** *destination-network netmask next-hop administrative-distance*	Configure a floating static route.
(config)#	**router ospf** *process-id*	Create/configure an OSPF process.
(config-router)#	**network** *ip-address wildcard-mask* **area** *area*	Activate OSPF on interfaces with an IP address in the specified range.
(config-router)#	**auto-cost reference-bandwidth** *mbps*	Modify the OSPF cost reference bandwidth.
(config-router)#	**passive-interface** *interface*	Configure a passive interface.
(config-router)#	**passive-interface default**	Make all interfaces passive by default.
(config-router)#	**default-information originate** [**always**]	Advertise a default route to other routers.
(config-router)#	**maximum-paths** *number*	Set the maximum number of routes inserted into the routing table for ECMP.
(config-router)#	**router-id** *rid*	Manually set the OSPF router ID (RID).
(config-if)#	**ip ospf** *process-id* **area** *area*	Activate OSPF on the interface.
(config-if)#	**ip ospf network** {**point-to-point** | **broadcast**}	Set the interface's OSPF network type.
(config-if)#	**ip ospf priority** *priority*	Set the interface's OSPF priority (for the DR/BDR election).
(config-if)#	**ip ospf cost** *cost*	Set the interface's OSPF cost.
(config-if)#	**bandwidth** *kbps*	Set the interface's bandwidth.
(config-if)#	**ip ospf hello-interval** *seconds*	Set the interface's hello timer.
(config-if)#	**ip ospf dead-interval** *seconds*	Set the interface's dead timer.
(config-if)#	**ip ospf authentication**	Enable OSPF authentication.
(config-if)#	**ip ospf authentication-key** *password*	Set the OSPF authentication password.
(config-if)#	**ip mtu** *bytes*	Set the interface's IP MTU.
(config)#	**interface loopback** *number*	Create/configure a loopback interface.
#	**show ip protocols**	View information about the router's active routing protocols.
#	**show ip ospf interface brief**	View OSPF-activated interfaces.
#	**show ip ospf neighbor**	View OSPF neighbors and their status.
#	**show ip ospf interface** *interface*	View information about an OSPF interface.
#	**show ip ospf database**	View the OSPF LSDB.
#	**clear ip ospf process**	Reset the OSPF process.

Chapter 19: First Hop Redundancy Protocols		
(config-if)#	**standby** *group* **ip** *virtual-ip*	Set the HSRP virtual IP address.
(config-if)#	**standby** *group* **priority** *priority*	Set the HSRP priority.
(config-if)#	**standby** *group* **preempt**	Enable HSRP preemption.
(config-if)#	**standby version 2**	Enable HSRP version 2.
#	**show standby** [**brief**]	View HSRP status and information.
Chapter 20: IPv6 Addressing; Chapter 21: IPv6 Routing		
(config)#	**ipv6 unicast-routing**	Enable IPv6 routing.
(config-if)#	**ipv6 address** *address*/*prefix-length*	Configure an IPv6 address.
(config-if)#	**ipv6 address** *prefix*/*prefix-length* **eui-64**	Configure an IPv6 address, using EUI-64 to generate the host portion.
(config-if)#	**ipv6 address** *address*/*prefix-length* **link-local**	Configure a link-local IPv6 address.
(config-if)#	**ipv6 address** *address*/*prefix-length* **anycast**	Configure an anycast IPv6 address.
(config-if)#	**ipv6 address autoconfig** [**default**]	Use SLAAC to generate an IPv6 address.
(config-if)#	**ipv6 enable**	Enable IPv6 on the interface without configuring an IPv6 address.
#	**show ipv6 interface brief**	View a concise summary of interface IPv6 addresses and status.
#	**show ipv6 interface** [*interface*]	View detailed Layer 3 information about IPv6 interfaces.
#	**show ipv6 neighbors**	View the IPv6 neighbor table (like ARP).
#	**show ipv6 route**	View the IPv6 routing table.
(config)#	**ipv6 route** *destination-prefix next-hop* [*ad*]	Configure a recursive static route.
(config)#	**ipv6 route** *destination-prefix exit-interface* [*ad*]	Configure a directly connected static route.
(config)#	**ipv6 route** *destination-prefix exit-interface next-hop* [*ad*]	Configure a fully specified static route.
Chapter 23: Standard access control lists; Chapter 24: Extended access control lists		
(config)#	**access-list** *number* {**permit** | **deny**} *src-ip wildcard*	Configure an ACE in a standard numbered ACL.
(config)#	**access-list** *number* **remark** *remark*	Configure an ACL remark.
(config)#	**ip access-list standard** *name*	Configure a standard named ACL.
(config-std-nacl)#	[*seq*] {**permit** | **deny**} *src-ip wildcard*	Configure an ACE in the standard named ACL.
(config)#	**access-list** *number* {**permit** | **deny**} *protocol source destination*	Configure an ACE in an extended numbered ACL, matching based on protocol and source/destination IP.
(config)#	**access-list** *number* {**permit** | **deny**} {**tcp**|**udp**} *source* [*operator src-port*] *destination* [*operator dst-port*]	Configure an ACE in an extended numbered ACL, matching based on protocol, src/dst IP, and src/dst port.

(config)#	**ip access-list extended** *name*	Configure an extended named ACL.
(config-ext-nacl)#	[*seq*] {**permit** | **deny**} *protocol source destination*	Configure an ACE in the extended named ACL, matching based on protocol and source/destination IP.
(config-ext-nacl)#	[*seq*] {**permit** | **deny**} {**tcp**|**udp**} *source* [*operator src-port*] *destination* [*operator dst-port*]	Configure an ACE in the extended named ACL, matching based on protocol, src/dst IP, and src/dst port.
(config-if)#	**ip access-group** *acl* {**in** | **out**}	Apply an ACL to an interface.
(config)#	**ip access-list resequence** *acl starting-seq-num increment*	Resequence an ACL.
#	**show access-lists**	View all ACLs.
#	**show ip access-lists**	View all IP ACLs.

C Chapter quiz questions

This appendix includes several quiz questions for each chapter of this volume. The goal of these questions is not necessarily to simulate real CCNA exam questions, but simply to test your knowledge of each chapter's contents. With that said, many of these questions are similar to what you might find on the CCNA exam; these questions target the CCNA exam topics and aim for a similar level of detail.

In any case, these questions will help you evaluate your readiness for the exam and identify some of your weak points—topics that you should focus on before taking on the CCNA exam itself. For the correct answers and a brief explanation of each question, refer to appendix D. I recommend attempting each chapter's questions after you have studied the chapter, and then once more for review after you have finished the book.

Chapter 2: Network devices

1 Which device enables hosts to communicate with hosts in other LANs?

   A Switch
   B Firewall
   C Router
   D Server

2 Which of the following device types typically has many physical ports for end hosts to connect to?

   A Router
   B Switch
   C Server
   D Client

3 What type of software runs on an end host and filters traffic entering the host?

   A Host-based firewall
   B Network firewall
   C Client
   D Server

4 What kind of network is used to connect remote locations?

   A LAN
   B WAN

5 Which role describes a device that accesses services provided by another host?

   A Router
   B Server
   C User
   D Client

Chapter 3: Cables, connectors, and ports

1 What is the standard maximum cable length of a copper UTP cable?

   A 1 kilometer
   B 100 meters
   C 100 feet
   D 1000 feet

2 Which technology allows a device to automatically adjust which pin pairs it uses to transmit and receive data in a copper UTP cable?

   A Crossover
   B Straight-through

   C Auto MDI-X
   D Tx/Rx
3. Which of the following cable types supports connections over the greatest distances?
   A Copper UTP
   B Multimode fiber
   C Single-mode fiber
4. How many bits can a 1 Gbps interface transmit per second?
   A 1000 bps
   B 1,000,000 bps
   C 1,000,000,000 bps
   D 1,000,000,000,000 bps
5. Which of the following is equivalent to 1 Mbps?
   A 1000 kbps
   B 1024 kbps
   C 1000 bps
   D 1024 bps
6. Which of the following is NOT an advantage of fiber-optic cables over copper UTP cables?
   A Less vulnerable to EMI
   B Lower cost
   C Greater maximum distances
   D Less security risk
7. What is the minimum copper UTP cable standard that supports 1 Gbps Ethernet?
   A Cat 6a
   B Cat 5e
   C Cat 5
   D Cat 3

Chapter 4: The TCP/IP networking model

1. Which of the following define standards at Layers 1 and 2 of the TCP/IP Model? (select two)
   A IPv4
   B HTTP
   C Ethernet
   D 802.11 (Wi-Fi)

2 Which layer of the TCP/IP Model defines standards related to the physical medium and how data should be encoded into signals sent over the medium?

A Layer 1
B Layer 2
C Layer 3
D Layer 7

3 Which layer of the TCP/IP Model is responsible for end-to-end delivery of a message from the source host to the destination host?

A Layer 1
B Layer 2
C Layer 3
D Layer 4

4 Which layer of the TCP/IP Model is responsible for delivering a message to the next node in the path to the final destination?

A Layer 1
B Layer 2
C Layer 3
D Layer 4

5 Which word describes a frame's payload?

A Packet
B Segment
C L2PDU
D L4PDU

6 Which layer provides a service to the Application Layer by delivering data to the appropriate application process on the destination host?

A Layer 2
B Layer 3
C Layer 4
D Layer 7

7 Signals sent out of a physical port of one device are received by a physical port of another device. Which term describes this interaction?

A Same-layer interaction
B Adjacent-layer interaction

8 Which layer of the TCP/IP Model provides an interface between a web browser like Google Chrome and the network?

A Application Layer
B Transport Layer

C Network Layer

D Data Link Layer

Chapter 5: The Cisco IOS CLI

1 What kind of cable is typically used to connect to the console port of a Cisco router or switch?

A Fiber-optic

B Crossover

C Straight-through

D Rollover

2 What mode in the IOS hierarchy is indicated by the prompt `hostname>`?

A Privileged EXEC mode

B Global configuration mode

C User EXEC mode

D Enable mode

3 Which of the following commands can be used to return to privileged EXEC mode from global configuration mode? (select two)

A **`disable`**

B **`exit`**

C **`escape`**

D **`end`**

4 Which command can be used to view the device's active configuration from global configuration mode?

A **`do show running-config`**

B **`show running-config`**

C **`do show startup-config`**

D **`show startup-config`**

5 Where is a device's startup-config file stored?

A Flash

B RAM

C NVRAM

6 Which of the following commands cannot be used to save a device's configuration?

A **`write`**

B **`write memory`**

C **`copy running-config startup-config`**

D **`copy startup-config running-config`**

7 Which of the following commands configures a password to limit access to privileged EXEC mode and stores the password as a secure hash?
   - A **`enable password`** *`password`*
   - B **`enable secret`** *`password`*
   - C **`service password-encryption`**
   - D **`exec password`** *`password`*

8 What is the effect of the **`service password-encryption`** command?
   - A Currently configured passwords are encrypted.
   - B Passwords configured in the future will be encrypted.
   - C A and B
   - D None of the above

Chapter 6: Ethernet LAN switching

1 What is the OUI of the BIA "0cf5.a452.b103"?
   - A b103
   - B 52.b103
   - C 0cf5
   - D 0cf5.a4

2 What is the only field of the Ethernet trailer?
   - A EtherType
   - B Destination
   - C FCS
   - D SFD

3 Which field of an Ethernet frame does a switch use to dynamically learn MAC addresses?
   - A FCS
   - B Type/Length
   - C Destination
   - D Source

4 Which of the following frames are flooded by a switch? (select two)
   - A Broadcast
   - B Unknown unicast
   - C Known unicast

5 Which of the following statements accurately describes ARP?
   - A ARP maps a known Layer 3 address to an unknown Layer 2 address.
   - B ARP maps a known Layer 3 address to a known Layer 2 address.

C ARP maps an unknown Layer 3 address to an unknown Layer 2 address.

D ARP maps an unknown Layer 3 address to an unknown Layer 2 address.

6 What is the destination MAC address of an unknown unicast frame?

A ffff.ffff.ffff

B The MAC address of the frame's destination host

C The MAC address of the frame's sender

7 Which utility involves ICMP echo requests and responses?

A ARP

B ping

C broadcasting

8 In an ARP exchange, which of the following messages is unicast?

A ARP request

B ARP reply

C A and B

D None of the above

Chapter 7: IPv4 addressing

1 What bit pattern is found at the beginning of an IPv4 packet?

A 0110

B 0100

C 1000

D 0001

2 What is indicated by the Total Length field of the IPv4 header?

A The length of the Frame

B The length of the Packet

C The length of the IPv4 header

D The length of the Ethernet header and trailer

3 Which field of the IPv4 header is used to prevent packets infinitely looping around the network?

A DSCP

B ECN

C IHL

D TTL

4 Which netmask is equivalent to a /16 prefix length?

A 255.0.0.0

B 255.255.0.0

- C 255.255.255.0
- D 255.255.255.255

5 In the output of **show ip interface brief**, what are the default Status and Protocol of a Cisco router interface?

- A `administratively down/down`
- B `down/down`
- C `up/down`
- D `up/up`

6 A PC's IP address is 172.16.12.27/24. What is the first usable address of its network?

- A 172.16.12.0
- B 172.16.12.1
- C 172.16.12.254
- D 172.16.12.255

7 Which of the following is a loopback address?

- A 203.0.113.107
- B 192.0.5.50
- C 127.20.67.1
- D 10.11.11.10

8 Which of the following commands configures an IPv4 address on a router's interface?

- A `R1(config)#` **`ipv4 address 10.0.0.1 255.255.255.0`**
- B `R1(config)#` **`ip address 10.0.0.1 255.255.255.0`**
- C `R1(config-if)#` **`ipv4 address 10.0.0.1 255.255.255.0`**
- D `R1(config-if)#` **`ip address 10.0.0.1 255.255.255.0`**

Chapter 8: Router and switch interfaces

1 Which of the following statements are true? (select two)

- A Cisco router interfaces have **no shutdown** applied by default.
- B Cisco switch interfaces have **shutdown** applied by default.
- C Cisco router interfaces have **shutdown** applied by default.
- D Cisco switch interfaces have **no shutdown** applied by default.

2 Which of the following is the default setting on a Gigabit Ethernet interface?

- A **`speed 1000`**
- B **`speed 1g`**
- C **`speed auto`**

3 Which term describes two-way communication in which devices take turns transmitting and receiving?

 A Half duplex

 B Full duplex

 C Simplex

4 Two PCs and two servers are connected to a hub. How many collision domains are there in the LAN?

 A One

 B Two

 C Three

 D Four

5 Two PCs and two servers are connected to a switch. How many collision domains are there in the LAN?

 A One

 B Two

 C Three

 D Four

6 Which technology is used by Ethernet hosts operating in half-duplex to detect and recover from collisions?

 A Auto MDI-X

 B CSMA/CD

 C CSMA/CA

 D Autonegotiation

7 SW1 F0/1 and SW2 F0/1 are connected and have the default settings. What speed and duplex settings will appear in the output of **`show interfaces status`**?

 A `100, full`

 B `100, half`

 C `a-100, half`

 D `a-100, a-full`

8 Which error counter in the output of **`show interfaces`** counts frames that failed the FCS check?

 A Collisions

 B Input errors

 C CRC

 D Runts

9 What is the result of a speed mismatch on two connected interfaces?

 A The interfaces will operate at the slower of the two speeds.

 B The interfaces will be in a down/down state.

- C Collisions and late collisions will occur.
- D Communications will be unaffected.

10 When there is a duplex mismatch between two connected devices, which error counters will likely increment on the half-duplex device? (select two)

- A Collisions
- B Runts
- C CRC
- D Late collisions

Chapter 9: Routing fundamentals

1 After configuring an IP address on and enabling a router interface, which route(s) will be automatically added to the router's routing table?

- A C and L
- B L
- C S and C
- D C

2 Which type of route represents the exact IP address of a router's interface with a /32 prefix length?

- A S
- B L
- C C
- D O

3 If a packet's destination IP address doesn't match any routes in the routing table, what action will the router take on the packet?

- A It will drop the packet.
- B It will broadcast the packet out of all interfaces.
- C It will use ARP to identify the next hop.
- D It will receive the packet for itself.

4 Which of the following is a host route?

- A A route to 10.0.0.0/8
- B A route to 203.0.113.0/24
- C A route to 8.8.8.8/32
- D A route to 172.25.0.0/16

5 Which of the following commands configures a recursive static route?

- A `ip route 10.0.0.0 255.0.0.0 gigabitethernet0/0`
- B `ip route 10.0.0.0 255.0.0.0 192.168.1.1`
- C `ip route 10.0.0.0 255.0.0.0 gigabitethernet0/0 192.168.1.1`

6 Which route in its routing table will a router select to forward a packet?
   - A The most specific matching route
   - B The route with the longest prefix length
   - C The route with the shortest prefix length
   - D The route that matches the most IP addresses

7 Which of the following commands configures a default route?
   - A `ip route 0.0.0.0 0.0.0.0 203.0.113.1`
   - B `ip route 8.0.0.0 255.255.255.0 default`
   - C `ip route default 203.0.113.1`

8 Which of the following static routes relies on proxy ARP?
   - A `ip route 5.0.0.0 255.0.0.0 192.0.2.2`
   - B `ip route 5.0.0.0 255.0.0.0 gigabitethernet0/1`
   - C `ip route 5.0.0.0 255.0.0.0 gigabitethernet0/2 203.0.113.2`

Chapter 10: The life of a packet

1 Which of the following statements is true about a message traversing multiple network hops to reach its final destination?
   - A The message's destination IP address remains the same at each hop, but its destination MAC address changes.
   - B The message's destination IP address and MAC address remain the same at each hop.
   - C The message's destination IP address changes at each hop, but its destination MAC address remains the same.
   - D The message's destination IP address and MAC address change at each hop.

2 Which of the following tables maps MAC addresses to physical ports?
   - A ARP table
   - B MAC address table
   - C Routing table

3 A router receives a packet destined for 10.0.0.1. The most specific matching route's next-hop IP address is 172.16.12.2. Which IP address will the router send an ARP request to?
   - A 10.0.0.1
   - B 172.16.12.2

4 A PC sends a packet destined for a host in a remote network. What is the destination MAC address of the frame the PC sends out of its network port?
   - A The PC's own MAC address
   - B The destination host's MAC address
   - C The default gateway's MAC address

5 Which of the following tables maps destination networks to next hops?
   - A ARP table
   - B MAC address table
   - C Routing table

Chapter 11: Subnetting IPv4 networks

1 Given a /25 address block, what prefix length is appropriate to create 16 subnets of equal size?
   - A /27
   - B /28
   - C /29
   - D /30

2 Given a /23 address block, how many subnets can you create that support at least 16 usable host addresses in each subnet?
   - A 8 subnets
   - B 16 subnets
   - C 32 subnets
   - D 64 subnets

3 A server's IP address is 172.19.209.178/29. What is the network address of its subnet?
   - A 172.19.209.168
   - B 172.19.209.176
   - C 172.19.209.180
   - D 172.19.209.192

4 PC1's IP address is 192.168.222.101/26. What is the broadcast address of its subnet?
   - A 192.168.222.127
   - B 192.168.222.128
   - C 192.168.222.255
   - D 192.168.222.254

5 Given a /12 address block, how many subnets can you create that support at least 200 usable host addresses in each subnet?
   - A 512 subnets
   - B 1024 subnets
   - C 2048 subnets
   - D 4096 subnets

6 Given a /15 address block, what prefix length is appropriate to create 1024 subnets of equal size?

A /25

B /24

C /23

D /22

7 A printer's IP address is 10.109.211.107/28. What is the network address of its subnet?

A 10.109.211.106

B 10.109.211.96

C 10.109.211.112

D 10.109.211.104

8 R1's IP address is 203.0.113.237/27. What is the broadcast address of its subnet?

A 203.0.113.238

B 203.0.113.239

C 203.0.113.247

D 203.0.113.255

9 You have been given the 192.168.27.0/24 address block to create subnets of appropriate sizes for your organization. You have already assigned the first subnet to support 109 hosts. The second subnet must support 60 hosts. What is the usable host address range of the second subnet?

A 192.168.27.129 to 192.168.27.190

B 192.168.27.65 to 192.168.27.126

C 192.168.27.128 to 192.168.27.191

D 192.168.27.129 to 192.168.27.254

10 You have been given the 10.0.2.0/23 address block to create subnets of appropriate sizes for your organization. You have already assigned the first subnet to support 40 hosts. The second subnet must support 29 hosts. What is the broadcast address of the second subnet?

A 10.0.2.111

B 10.0.2.79

C 10.0.2.95

D 10.0.2.127

Chapter 12: VLANs

1 Which of the following statements about VLANs is true?

A VLANs divide a collision domain into multiple collision domains.

B VLANs divide a broadcast domain into multiple broadcast domains.

- C VLANs segment a LAN at Layer 3 of the TCP/IP Model.
- D Switches can flood frames to hosts in different VLANs, but cannot forward frames to hosts in different VLANs.

2 You issue **`switchport access vlan 10`** on a switch port, but VLAN 10 doesn't exist yet on the switch. What is the result of the command?

- A The port is disabled until you create VLAN 10.
- B The command is rejected.
- C The switch automatically creates VLAN 10.
- D The port is assigned to the default VLAN.

3 Which VLANs exist on a Cisco switch by default and cannot be deleted?

- A VLANs 1, 1002, 1003, 1004, and 1005
- B VLANs 1, 1001, 1002, 1003, 1004, and 1005
- C VLANs 1, 1003, 1004, and 1005
- D VLAN 1

4 Which VLAN is untagged on a trunk port?

- A The default VLAN
- B The native VLAN
- C The access VLAN
- D VLAN 1

5 How many VLANs are there in total, including reserved VLANs?

- A 4092
- B 4094
- C 4095
- D 4096

6 Which VLANs are allowed on a trunk port by default?

- A 1–4094
- B 1–1001
- C 1
- D No VLANs are allowed by default.

7 A LAN you are managing includes VLANs 1, 2, and 3. VLAN 4, a new VLAN, is added and it is your job to make sure that all trunk links allow it. Which command is appropriate to add VLAN 4 to each trunk's list of allowed VLANs?

- A **`switchport trunk allowed vlan 4`**
- B **`switchport trunk allowed vlan add 4`**
- C **`switchport trunk allowed vlan allow 4`**
- D **`switchport trunk vlan allow 4`**

8 Which of the following is a security best practice related to VLANs?

A Leave VLAN 1 as the native VLAN but don't assign hosts to it.

B A port's native VLAN should be the same as its access VLAN.

C Configure a non-default unused VLAN as the native VLAN.

D The default and native VLANs should be the same.

9 In a ROAS configuration, which command tells the router which VLAN to tag frames with?

A `R1(config)# interface g0/1.10`

B `R1(config-subif)# switchport trunk vlan 10`

C `R1(config-subif)# vlan tag dot1q 10`

D `R1(config-subif)# encapsulation dot1q 10`

10 Which of the following is NOT a requirement for an SVI to be in an up/up state?

A The VLAN associated with the SVI must exist on the switch.

B The SVI must be enabled.

C The VLAN must be enabled.

D The switch must have both an access port associated with the VLAN and a trunk port that allows the VLAN.

Chapter 13: Dynamic Trunking Protocol and VLAN Trunking Protocol

1 If two Cisco switches are connected with the default settings, what will be the operational mode of their ports?

A Access

B Trunk

2 Which of the following **`switchport mode`** command combinations configured on two connected ports will result in a valid trunk link?

A **`dynamic auto + trunk`**

B **`dynamic auto + dynamic auto`**

C **`dynamic desirable + access`**

D **`trunk + access`**

3 Which administrative modes result in a port not sending DTP frames?

A Trunk and access

B Dynamic auto and access

C Access

D Trunk

4 Which VTP mode(s) will cause a switch to sync its VLAN database to other switches in the VTP domain?

A Server

B Transparent

- C Client
- D Server and client

5 What will a switch without a VTP domain name do upon receiving a VTP message on one of its trunk ports?

- A It will ignore the message.
- B It will forward the message but not join the VTP domain.
- C It will join the sender's VTP domain.

6 Which VTPv3 modes allow a switch to create VLANs and propagate them to other switches in the VTP domain?

- A Server
- B Server and transparent
- C Primary server and transparent
- D Primary server

7 Which VTP versions support extended-range VLANs?

- A VTPv3
- B VTPv2
- C VTPv1, VTPv2, and VTPv3
- D VTPv2 and VTPv3

8 Which ports do switches send VTP messages out of?

- A Access ports
- B Trunk ports
- C All ports

Chapter 14: Spanning Tree Protocol

1 Which of the following are negative effects of Layer-2 loops? (select two)

- A MAC address flapping
- B Broadcast storms
- C Expired TTL
- D Routing loops

2 In a four-switch LAN, which of the following switches would be selected as the STP root bridge?

- A SW1, BID: 32769:5254.00fa.abcd
- B SW2, BID: 32769:5254.0000.0002
- C SW3, BID: 36865:5254.0000.0001
- D SW4, BID: 1:5254.00ff.f012

3 How many root ports will there be in a four-switch LAN?

- A 1
- B 2

- C 3
- D 4

4 Which STP port roles send BPDUs?

- A Designated ports
- B Root ports
- C Designated and root ports
- D Designated, root, and non-designated port

5 When you connect an end host to a switch port without PortFast, how long does it take for the port to enter the STP forwarding state?

- A 15 seconds
- B 20 seconds
- C 30 seconds
- D 35 seconds

6 What happens when a switch port configured with **`spanning-tree bpduguard enable`** receives a BPDU?

- A The port ignores the BPDU.
- B The port is error-disabled.
- C BPDU Guard is disabled on the port.
- D The port immediately moves to the forwarding state.

7 Two switches, SW1 and SW2, are connected by two links using the default STP cost values. SW2 is the root bridge. SW1 G0/1 is connected to SW2 G0/2, and SW1 G0/2 is connected to SW2 G0/1. Which port will SW1 select as its root port?

- A G0/1
- B G0/2

8 SW3 and SW4 are part of a larger LAN. They are connected by their G0/1 ports, neither of which is a root port. Both switches have equal root costs. How will they determine which port becomes designated and which becomes non-designated?

- A The port with the lowest port ID will become designated.
- B The port with the highest port ID will become designated.
- C The port on the switch with the lowest BID will become designated.
- D The port on the switch with the highest BID will become designated.

9 How many STP designated ports will there be in a four-switch LAN with a total of seven links?

- A 1
- B 4
- C 7
- D 14

10 Which STP port role points away from the root bridge and is in a forwarding state?

- A Designated
- B Non-designated
- C Root

11 Which command is most likely to ensure that a switch becomes the root bridge for VLAN 1?

- A **`spanning-tree vlan 1 root primary`**
- B **`spanning tree vlan 1 root 0`**
- C **`spanning-tree vlan 1 priority root`**
- D **`spanning-tree vlan 1 priority 0`**

Chapter 15: Rapid Spanning Tree Protocol

1 The output of **`show spanning-tree`** on a Cisco switch states `Spanning tree enabled protocol ieee`. Which version of STP is the switch running?

- A IEEE-standard Rapid STP
- B Rapid PVST+
- C IEEE-standard STP
- D PVST+

2 You configure **`spanning-tree pathcost method long`** on a Cisco switch. Which of the following accurately represent the default port costs after issuing that command? (select two)

- A 1 Tbps: 2
- B 10 Gbps: 2,000
- C 10 Mbps: 20,000,000
- D 100 Mbps: 200,000

3 If the RSTP sync mechanism succeeds, how long does it take for a port to transition from the discarding state to the forwarding state?

- A 6 seconds
- B 15 seconds
- C 30 seconds
- D It transitions immediately.

4 SW1 G0/1 is not a root port or a designated port, and SW1 is not the designated bridge for the segment G0/1 is connected to. What is SW1's G0/1's RSTP port role?

- A Alternate
- B Backup
- C Non-designated

5 Which RSTP port type will not trigger a topology change notification if the port's status changes?

A Point-to-point

B Shared

C Edge

D Backup

6 If the RSTP root bridge has two ports connected to the same segment via a hub, what will the role be of the port that is not designated?

A Root

B Alternate

C Blocking

D Backup

7 Which command configures the RSTP edge link type on a port?

A **`spanning-tree link-type edge`**

B **`spanning-tree portfast`**

C **`spanning-tree link-type portfast`**

D **`spanning-tree edge`**

8 SW1's G0/1 port is in the up/up state but has stopped receiving BPDUs from its RSTP neighbor. How long will SW1 wait before reacting and initiating a topology change?

A 6 seconds

B 15 seconds

C 20 seconds

D 30 seconds

9 Which RSTP link type is default on full-duplex ports?

A Full

B Shared

C Point-to-point

D Independent

10 Four switches are interconnected, with a total of six links between them. How many of each RSTP port role are there?

A 4 root, 4 designated, 4 alternate

B 3 root, 6 designated, 3 alternate

C 3 root, 3 designated

D 3 root, 3 designated, 6 alternate

11 Which optional STP feature disables a port if it stops receiving BPDUs?

A BPDU Guard

B BPDU Filter

C Root Guard

D Loop Guard

12 BPDU Filter has been enabled globally for all PortFast-enabled ports. What happens when one of the BPDU Filter-enabled ports receives a BPDU?

A PortFast and BPDU Filter are disabled on the port.

B The port is error-disabled.

C The port ignores the BPDU.

D The port enters the discarding state.

Chapter 16: EtherChannel

1 Which of the following statements about EtherChannel is false?

A EtherChannel combines multiple physical links into a single logical link.

B EtherChannel eliminates the need for STP in a LAN.

C A frame flooded out of a port-channel interface will only be flooded out of one of the member ports.

D EtherChannel formation can be dynamically negotiated or statically configured.

2 Which of the following dynamic EtherChannel mode combinations will result in a valid EtherChannel? (select two)

A auto + auto

B desirable + active

C passive + active

D desirable + desirable

3 Which of the following settings doesn't have to match among the member ports of an EtherChannel?

A Description

B Duplex

C Speed

D Operational mode (access or trunk)

4 Which dynamic EtherChannel modes can form a valid EtherChannel with a neighbor configured with `channel-group 1 mode on`?

A Desirable or active

B Desirable or auto

C Active only

D None of the above

5 Which protocol can be used to negotiate an EtherChannel with a non-Cisco switch?

   A PAgP
   B LACP
   C Neither

6 Port-channel 1 and its member ports currently operate in access mode. What will happen after you configure **`switchport mode trunk`** on the port-channel 1 interface?

   A The port-channel is disabled until you configure trunk mode on the member ports.
   B The configuration is inherited by the member ports.
   C The member ports are disabled until you configure trunk mode on them.
   D The command is rejected.

7 When connecting two switches with a Layer-3 EtherChannel, where should each switch's IP address be configured?

   A On the port-channel interface
   B On the member ports
   C On both the port-channel interface and the member ports

Chapter 17: Dynamic routing

1 Which type of dynamic routing protocol is used to exchange routing information within an AS?

   A IGP
   B EGP
   C BGP
   D ISP

2 Which of the following dynamic routing protocols use a link-state algorithm? (select two)

   A IS-IS
   B RIP
   C OSPF
   D EIGRP

3 Which type of routing protocol is also known as "routing by rumor"?

   A IGP
   B Link-state
   C Distance-vector
   D Path-vector

4 When multiple routes to the same destination network are learned via the same routing protocol, which parameter is used to select which route(s) will enter the routing table?

A Prefix length

B Metric

C AD

D Specificity

5 When multiple routes to the same destination network are learned via different routing protocols, which parameter is used to select which route(s) will enter the routing table?

A Prefix length

B Metric

C AD

D Specificity

6 Which of the following accurately represent IOS default AD values? (select two)

A Static = 0

B EIGRP = 90

C OSPF = 110

D RIP = 115

7 If a Cisco router learns multiple routes to the same destination via the same routing protocol, and all routes have the same metric, what is the maximum number of routes to that destination that the router will insert into its routing table by default?

A 1

B 2

C 4

D 8

8 What kind of static route acts as a backup for another route, only entering the routing table if the more preferred route is removed from the routing table?

A Default static route

B Floating static route

C Recursive static route

D Backup static route

9 A router learns the following routes via manual configuration and dynamic routing protocols. Which route(s) will it insert into its routing table? (select all that apply)

A 10.0.0.0/8 via RIP, metric 6

B 10.0.0.0/16 via OSPF, metric 5

- C 10.0.0.0/16 via static routing
- D 10.0.0.0/24 via EIGRP, metric 10127

10 A router learns the following routes via manual configuration and dynamic routing protocols. Which route(s) will it insert into its routing table? (select all that apply)

- A 192.168.1.0/24 via RIP, metric 2
- B 192.168.1.0/24 via OSPF, metric 15
- C 192.168.1.0/24 via EIGRP, metric 2345
- D 192.168.1.0/24 via static routing, AD 89

11 A router receives a packet destined for 192.0.2.29. It has the following four routes in its routing table. Which route will it select to forward the packet?

- A `R 192.0.2.0/27 [120/5] via 10.0.0.2`
- B `S 192.0.2.0/28 [1/0] via 10.0.0.6`
- C `O 192.0.2.16/29 [110/20] via 10.0.0.10`
- D `D 192.0.2.24/30 [90/1012] via 10.0.0.14`

12 A router receives a packet destined for 10.23.107.126. It has the following four routes in its routing table. Which route will it select to forward the packet?

- A `S 10.23.107.0/25 [1/0] via 172.16.1.1`
- B `O 10.23.107.0/26 [110/10] via 172.16.1.5`
- C `D 10.23.107.96/27 [90/2345] via 172.16.1.9`
- D `D 10.23.107.112/28 [90/3456] via 172.16.1.13`

13 R1's G0/1 interface has the IP address 192.168.209.101/30. Which of the following **network** commands would activate OSPF on the interface? (select all that apply)

- A **`network 192.168.209.100 0.0.0.3 area 0`**
- B **`network 192.168.209.101 0.0.0.0 area 0`**
- C **`network 192.168.0.0 0.0.255.255 area 0`**

Chapter 18: Open Shortest Path First

1 R1 is part of an OSPF network, and all of its OSPF-enabled interfaces are in area 1. Furthermore, it connects to the Internet and advertises a default route to other OSPF routers. What OSPF router types apply to R1? (select all that apply).

- A Internal router
- B Backbone router
- C ABR
- D ASBR

2 What command should you configure on a router to ensure that all GigabitEthernet interfaces have an OSPF cost of 10?

A **auto-cost reference-bandwidth 100**

B **auto-cost reference-bandwidth 1000**

C **auto-cost reference-bandwidth 10000**

D **auto-cost reference-bandwidth 100000**

3 What is the effect of the **passive-interface** command on an OSPF-activated interface?

A The router will attempt to form OSPF neighbor relationships on the interface, but won't send hello messages out of the interface.

B The router will advertise the interface's network to other OSPF routers, but won't send hello messages out of the interface.

C The router will send hello messages out of the interface, but won't advertise the interface's network to other OSPF routers.

D The router will send hello messages out of the interface, but won't attempt to form OSPF neighbor relationships on the interface.

4 Which of the following represents the order of priority when a router decides its OSPF RID?

A 1) Manual configuration, 2) Highest IP address on a loopback interface, 3) Highest IP address on a physical interface

B 1) Manual configuration, 2) Lowest IP address on a loopback interface, 3) Lowest IP address on a physical interface

C 1) Manual configuration, 2) Highest IP address on a physical interface, 3) Highest IP address on a loopback interface

D 1) Manual configuration, 2) Lowest IP address on a physical interface, 3) Lowest IP address on a loopback interface

5 R1 has multiple OSPF neighbor relationships. R1's OSPF RID is 192.168.1.1, which was inherited from a physical interface's IP address. You then configure the IP address 10.0.0.2 on a loopback interface and configure **router-id 1.1.1.1** in router config mode for the OSPF process. What is R1's RID after you issue the **router-id 1.1.1.1** command?

A 192.168.1.1

B 10.0.0.2

C 1.1.1.1

6 Which of the following commands activates OSPF on an interface without using the **network** command?

A **R1(config)# ip ospf 1 area 0**

B **R1(config-if)# ip ospf 1 area 0**

C **R1(config-router)# ip ospf 1 area 0**

D **R1(config-ospf)# ip ospf 1 area 0**

7 Four routers connected to a segment with the OSPF broadcast network type have the default OSPF priority. R4 is the DR and R3 is the BDR. You configure **ip ospf priority 100** on R2's interface connected to the segment and reset OSPF on R4 with **clear ip ospf process**. Which of the following statements is true after you reset R4's OSPF process?

A R2 is the DR and R3 is the BDR.

B R3 is the DR and R2 is the BDR.

C R2 is the DR and R4 is the BDR.

D R3 is the DR and R4 is the BDR

8 Which of the following commands can be used to prevent routers from electing a DR/BDR?

A `Router(config-if)#` **ip ospf network point-to-point**

B `Router(config-if)#` **ip ospf network broadcast**

C `Router(config-if)#` **ip ospf priority 1**

D `Router(config-if)#` **ip ospf network direct**

9 Which of the following are requirements for two routers to become OSPF neighbors? (select two)

A Area numbers must be unique.

B RIDs must be unique.

C Hello and dead timers must match.

D RIDs must match.

10 Which of the following represents the order of priority when routers elect a DR/BDR?

A 1) Lowest interface priority, 2) Lowest RID

B 1) Lowest RID, 2) Lowest interface priority

C 1) Highest interface priority, 2) Highest RID

D 1) Highest RID, 2) Highest interface priority

Chapter 19: First hop redundancy protocols

1 Which of the following statements about the virtual IP and virtual MAC used by HSRP are true?

A The active and standby routers share a VIP, but each uses a different virtual MAC address.

B The active and standby routers each use a different VIP, but share a virtual MAC address.

- **C** The active and standby routers share a VIP and virtual MAC address.
- **D** The active and standby router each use different VIPs and virtual MAC addresses.

2 During HSRP failover, what is the purpose of the new active router sending GARP messages?

- **A** To make end hosts update their ARP table.
- **B** To make end hosts update their default gateway IP address.
- **C** To make switches update their MAC address table.
- **D** To inform the former active router of the failover.

3 Which virtual MAC address is used by VRRP group 12?

- **A** 0000.5e00.010c
- **B** 0000.5e00.0112
- **C** 0000.0c07.ac0c
- **D** 0000.0c07.ac12

4 R1 is a master router, actively forwarding packets between the LAN and external networks. R2 is a backup router, waiting to take over in case R1 fails. Which FHRP are R1 and R2 using?

- **A** HSRP
- **B** VRRP
- **C** GLBP

5 Which FHRP facilitates load balancing of traffic within a single subnet?

- **A** HSRP
- **B** VRRP
- **C** GLBP

6 R1 and R2 use VRRP to provide a redundant default gateway for end hosts. R1 was the master router, but a hardware failure on R1 caused R2 to take over the master role. Given the default settings, what happens when R1 recovers from its hardware failure?

- **A** R1 becomes the master router again.
- **B** R2 remains the master router.

7 Which command configures the HSRP VIP?

- **A** `R1(config-if)# `**`hsrp 1 vip 10.0.0.1`**
- **B** `R1(config-if)# `**`hsrp 1 ip 10.0.0.1`**
- **C** `R1(config-if)# `**`standby 1 vip 10.0.0.1`**
- **D** `R1(config-if)# `**`standby 1 ip 10.0.0.1`**

8 What is the correct order of priority when electing the HSRP active router?

- **A** 1) Lowest interface priority, 2) Lowest interface IP address
- **B** 1) Lowest interface IP address, 2) Lowest interface priority

C 1) Highest interface IP address, 2) Highest interface priority
D 1) Highest interface priority, 2) Highest interface IP address

Chapter 20: IPv6 addressing

1 Which of the following are not valid IPv6 addresses? (select two)
A 2607:f8b0:4005:800::1004
B 2607:f8b0:4005:800:1111:0:1:2:3
C 2607:f8b0:4005:800:gh::1004
D fe80::204:61ff:fe9d:f156

2 Which of the following is a correctly abbreviated version of the IPv6 address 2001:0db8:85a3:0000:0000:8a2e:0370:7334?
A 2001:db8:85a3::8a2e:37:7334
B 2001:db8:85a3::0:8a2e:37:7334
C 2001:0db8:85a3::8a2e:370:7334
D 2001:db8:85a3::8a2e:370:7334

3 Which command configures an IPv6 address using the specified prefix and an automatically generated interface ID?
A **`ipv6 address eui-64`**
B **`ipv6 address 2001:db8:0:1::/64 auto`**
C **`ipv6 address autoconfig`**
D **`ipv6 address 2001:db8:0:1::/64 eui-64`**

4 R1's G0/1 interface's MAC address is 7ea2.1097.ff27. What is its Modified EUI-64 interface ID?
A 7ea2:10ff:fe97:ff27
B 7ca2:10ff:fe97:ff27
C 7da2:10ff:ff97:ff27
D 7fa2:10ff:fe97:ff27

5 Which MAC address was used to generate the Modified EUI-64 interface ID 1f7d:2aff:fedd:611c?
A 1b7d.2add.611c
B 1c7d.2add.611c
C 1d7d.2add.611c
D 1e7d.2add.611c

6 Which type of IPv6 address is equivalent to a private IPv4 address?
A ULA
B LLA
C EUI
D GUA

7 Which kind of IPv6 address is not routable?

A ULA

B LLA

C Multicast

D GUA

8 Which kind of IPv6 address must be configured on every IPv6-enabled interface?

A ULA

B LLA

C Anycast

D GUA

9 Which IPv6 multicast scope remains on the local segment?

A ff01

B ff02

C ff05

D ff08

10 Which IPv6 multicast address can be used to achieve the same effect as a message to the IPv4 address 255.255.255.255?

A ff02::1

B ff02::2

C ff02::5

D ff02::a

11 Which IPv6 address is equivalent to an IPv4 address in the 127.0.0.0/8 range?

A ::

B ::1

C ::127

D 127::1

12 Which IPv6 address type involves configuring the same address on multiple hosts?

A Unicast

B Broadcast

C Multicast

D Anycast

Chapter 21: IPv6 routing

1 What is the IPv4 equivalent of an IPv6 neighbor table?

A ARP table

B Routing table

- C MAC address table
- D IPv4 neighbor table

2 What scope is used by IPv6 solicited-node multicast addresses?

- A Interface-local
- B Link-local
- C Site-local
- D Organization-local

3 What solicited-node multicast address is generated from the unicast address df56:9098:1010:fd:ab29::f892?

- A ff02::1:ff:f892
- B ff02:1::ff00:f892
- C ff02:1::ff:f892
- D ff02::1:ff00:f892

4 Which message types does NDP use for Layer-2 address resolution? (select two)

- A RS
- B NS
- C RA
- D NA

5 Which command can be used to view a list of IPv6-address-to-Layer-2-address mappings?

- A **`show ipv6 arp`**
- B **`show ndp`**
- C **`show ipv6 neighbors`**
- D **`show ipv6 ndp`**

6 Which command can be used to configure an IPv6 with a prefix learned via RA and an automatically generated interface ID?

- A **`ipv6 enable`**
- B **`ipv6 address eui-64`**
- C **`ipv6 address autoconfig`**
- D **`ipv6 address 2001:db8::/64 eui-64`**

7 Which NDP messages are used in the DAD process? (select two)

- A RS
- B NS
- C RA
- D NA

8 Which of the following IPv6 static routes will not function properly, despite appearing in the routing table?

   A `ipv6 route 2001:db8::/64 GigabitEthernet0/1`
   B `ipv6 route 2001:db8::/64 2001:db8:12::2`
   C `ipv6 route 2001:db8::/64 GigabitEthernet0/1 2001:db8:12::2`

9 Which of the following commands configures a recursive host route?

   A `ipv6 route 2001:db8::1/128 2001:db8:23::3`
   B `ipv6 route 2001:db8::/64 2001:db8:23::3`
   C `ipv6 route 2001:db8::1/128 GigabitEthernet0/1`
   D `ipv6 route 2001:db8::/64 GigabitEthernet0/1`

10 Which of the following commands configures a fully specified default route?

   A `ipv6 route :: GigabitEthernet0/1`
   B `ipv6 route ::/0 GigabitEthernet0/1`
   C `ipv6 route ::/0 GigabitEthernet0/1 2001:db8::1`
   D `ipv6 route :: GigabitEthernet0/1 2001:db8::1`

Chapter 22: Transmission Control Protocol and User Datagram Protocol

1 Which of the following protocol and port pairs are correct? (select three)

   A DNS = TCP/UDP port 53
   B SSH = TCP port 23
   C HTTPS = TCP port 80
   D Syslog = TCP port 514
   E DHCP server = UDP port 67
   F DHCP client = UDP port 68

2 Which TCP field does a host use to indicate how much data it can receive before sending an ACK?

   A Maximum Segment Size
   B Acknowledgment Number
   C Sequence Number
   D Window Size

3 Which of the following is provided by TCP, but not UDP?

   A Best-effort communication
   B Data sequencing
   C Session multiplexing
   D Error detection

4 In which of the following cases is UDP usually preferred? (select two)
   - A When reliable delivery of messages is required.
   - B Real-time applications
   - C Simple query/response protocols
   - D File transfer protocols

5 What is the correct sequence of the TCP three-way handshake?
   - A SYN, ACK, SYN, ACK
   - B SYN, ACK, SYN-ACK
   - C SYN, SYN-ACK, ACK
   - D SYN, SYN, ACK

6 What does the value in a TCP segment's Acknowledgement Number field represent?
   - A The sequence number of the last segment the host received.
   - B The sequence number of the next segment the host expects to receive.
   - C The sequence number of the first segment the host received.

7 When a client sends a request to a server, which type of port does the client typically source the request from?
   - A A registered port
   - B An ephemeral port
   - C A well-known port

8 Which of the following protocols use a Layer-4 protocol that provides reliable delivery of messages? (select two)
   - A Telnet
   - B NTP
   - C SNMP
   - D FTP

Chapter 23: Standard access control lists

1 Which of the following commands permit only the specified host's IP address? (select three)
   - A `access-list 1 permit 8.8.8.8`
   - B `access-list 1 permit 8.8.8.8 0.0.0.0`
   - C `access-list 1 permit 8.8.8.8 255.255.255.255`
   - D `access-list 1 permit host 8.8.8.8`

2 Where should standard ACLs generally be applied?
   - A As close to the source as possible
   - B As close to the destination as possible

3 Which of the following are valid standard ACL numbers? (select three)

A 100

B 1301

C 1999

D 2000

E 99

F 199

4 Which command can be used to create a standard named ACL?

A **ip access-list TEST_ACL**

B **access-list TEST_ACL**

C **ip access-list standard TEST_ACL**

D **access-list standard TEST_ACL**

5 Which parameters can standard ACLs use to match packets? (select all that apply)

A Source IP address

B Destination IP address

C Protocol

D Source and/or destination port numbers

6 You create an ACL with a single ACE: **deny 192.168.1.0 0.0.0.255**. You then apply the ACL to an interface. What is the effect of this ACL?

A Packets sourced from 192.168.1.0/24 are denied.

B All packets are denied.

C All packets are permitted.

D Packets sourced from 192.168.1.0/24 are permitted.

7 Which command applies ACL 1 to an interface, filtering packets received by the interface?

A **ip access-list 1 in**

B **ip-access-list 1 out**

C **ip access-group 1 in**

D **ip-access-group 1 out**

8 What is the effect of an ACL that has been created, but not applied to an interface?

A The ACL has no effect.

B The ACL filters all packets received by the router.

C The ACL filters all packets forwarded by the router.

D The ACL filters all packets sent by the router itself.

Chapter 24: Extended access control lists

1 Which of the following are valid extended ACL numbers? (select three)

A 99

B 2000

C 1999

D 199

E 2599

F 200

2 Which of the following extended ACL entries blocks requests from clients to an HTTPS server?

A `deny tcp any eq 443 host 192.0.2.1`

B `deny tcp any host 192.0.2.1 eq 443`

C `deny tcp any eq 80 host 192.0.2.1`

D `deny tcp any host 192.0.2.1 eq 80`

3 Which of the following extended ACL entries permits all messages from the server with IP address 203.0.113.1 except its responses to SSH clients?

A `permit tcp 203.0.113.1 0.0.0.0 neq 22 any`

B `permit tcp 203.0.113.1 0.0.0.0 eq 22 any`

C `permit tcp 203.0.113.1 0.0.0.0 any neq 22`

D `permit tcp 203.0.113.1 0.0.0.0 any eq 22`

4 Which of the following extended ACL entries denies connections from clients to port 21 of an FTP server?

A `deny tcp any host 198.51.100.1 eq ftp-data`

B `deny udp any host 198.51.100.1 eq ftp-data`

C `deny tcp any host 198.51.100.1 eq ftp`

D `deny udp any host 198.51.100.1 eq ftp`

5 Which of the following is an accurate description of the effect of this ACE: `deny icmp 172.16.24.0 0.0.1.255 any`

A Deny all ICMP messages from hosts in the 172.16.24.0/24 subnet.

B Deny all ICMP messages from hosts in the 172.16.24.0/23 subnet.

C Deny all ICMP messages destined for hosts in the 172.16.24.0/24 subnet.

D Deny all ICMP messages destined for hosts in the 172.16.24.0/23 subnet.

6 Which of the following extended ACL entries permits Telnet connections from hosts in the 192.168.2.0/25 subnet to hosts in the 10.0.0.0/9 subnet?

A `permit tcp 192.168.2.0 0.0.0.127 10.0.0.0 255.128.0.0 eq 23`

B `permit tcp 192.168.2.0 0.0.0.127 10.0.0.0 0.127.255.255 eq 22`

- C `permit tcp 192.168.2.0 0.0.0.127 10.0.0.0 0.127.255.255 eq 23`
- D `permit tcp 192.168.2.0 255.255.255.128 10.0.0.0 255.128.0.0 eq 23`

7 Which command can be used to create an extended named ACL?

- A `access-list TEST_ACL`
- B `ip access-list TEST_ACL`
- C `access-list extended TEST_ACL`
- D `ip access-list extended TEST_ACL`

8 What is the effect of the command **`ip access-list resequence 100 10 5`**?

- A Change the sequence number of ACL 100's first ACE to 10 and add 5 for each subsequent ACE.
- B Change the sequence number of the ACL's first ACE to 100, add 10 for the second ACE, and 5 for the third ACE.
- C Change the sequence numbers of ACL 100's first 10 ACEs to use increments of 5.
- D Change the sequence number of ACL 5's first ACE to 1000 and add 10 for each subsequent ACE.

Appendix D: Chapter quiz answers

This appendix lists the answers to the chapter quiz questions in appendix C and gives explanations for each answer. The explanations are brief (one or two sentences); for more thorough explanations of the concepts, refer back to the relevant chapter.

Chapter 2: Network devices

1. Which device enables hosts to communicate with hosts in other LANs?
C: Router
A router is a networking device that forwards data packets between computer networks, enabling communication between hosts in different local area networks (LANs).
2. Which of the following device types typically has many physical ports for end hosts to connect to?
B: Switch
A switch is a device in a computer network that connects other devices together. It has multiple ports to which computers, printers, and other networking devices can be connected. A switch is used within a LAN to connect multiple devices and manage their network traffic.

3. What type of software runs on an end host and filters traffic entering the host?
A: Host-based firewall
A host-based firewall is a software application installed on a single computer (the host) in a network. It monitors and filters incoming and outgoing network traffic based on a set of rules.
4. What kind of network is used to connect remote locations?
B: WAN
A wide area network (WAN) is a network that extends over a large geographical area, often connecting multiple smaller networks like LANs. WANs are used to connect remote or geographically dispersed locations.
5. Which role describes a device that accesses services provided by another host?
D: Client
A client is a computer or a program that accesses services provided by another computer (the server). The client uses the network to send requests to the server and to receive data and services in return. This client-server model is a fundamental concept in networking.

Chapter 3: Cables, connectors, and ports

1. What is the standard maximum cable length of a copper UTP cable?
B: 100 meters
The standard maximum length for copper unshielded twisted pair (UTP) cables in an Ethernet network is 100 meters (328 feet). Attempts to use UTP cables longer than 100 meters can result in signal attenuation and decreased performance.
2. Which technology allows a device to automatically adjust which pin pairs it uses to transmit and receive data in a copper UTP cable?
C: Auto MDI-X
Automatic Medium-Dependent Interface Crossover (Auto MDI-X) is a technology that allows devices to automatically adjust their pin configurations without needing specific crossover or straight-through cables.
3. Which of the following cable types supports connections over the greatest distances?
C: Single-mode fiber
Single-mode fiber optic cables are designed for long-distance communication, often over many kilometers. They have a smaller core diameter than multimode fiber, allowing only one mode of light to travel along the cable. This reduces signal attenuation and allows data to travel longer distances.
4. How many bits can a 1 Gbps interface transmit per second?
C: 1,000,000,000 bps
The prefix "giga" means "billion", so a 1 Gbps (gigabit per second) interface can transmit 1,000,000,000 (one billion) bits per second.
5. Which of the following is equivalent to 1 Mbps?
A: 1000 kbps

The term Mbps stands for megabits per second, and kbps stands for kilobits per second. The prefix "mega" means "million" and the prefix "kilo" means "thousand", so 1 Mbps is equivalent to 1000 kbps.

6. Which of the following is NOT an advantage of fiber-optic cables over copper UTP cables?

B: Lower cost

The main advantages of fiber-optic cables over copper UTP cables include being less vulnerable to electromagnetic interference (EMI), supporting greater maximum transmission distances, and posing less security risk due to leaked signals. However, fiber-optic connections are generally more expensive due to both the cables and the small form-factor pluggable (SFP) transceivers.

7. What is the minimum copper UTP cable standard that supports 1 Gbps Ethernet?

B: Cat 5e

While the original Cat5 standard could theoretically support gigabit speeds, Cat5e is specifically designed to support 1 Gbps and is generally considered the minimum requirement for Gigabit Ethernet.

Chapter 4: The TCP/IP networking model

1. Which of the following define standards at Layers 1 and 2 of the TCP/IP Model? (select two)

C: Ethernet

D: 802.11 (Wi-Fi)

Ethernet and 802.11 (Wi-Fi) are standards that operate at Layers 1 (Physical) and 2 (Data Link) of the TCP/IP model. They both define standards relating to a physical medium (cables or electromagnetic radio waves) and sending messages over that medium.

2. Which layer of the TCP/IP Model defines standards related to the physical medium and how data should be encoded into signals sent over the medium?

A: Layer 1

Layer 1, the Physical Layer, is responsible for the physical connections between devices and how to encode messages into signals (such as electrical or light signals) that are sent over those connections.

3. Which layer of the TCP/IP Model is responsible for end-to-end delivery of a message from the source host to the destination host?

C: Layer 3

Layer 3, the Network Layer, is responsible for the end-to-end delivery of messages across a network. It uses IP addressing to determine routes for data, ensuring that packets are delivered from the source host to the destination host.

4. Which layer of the TCP/IP Model is responsible for delivering a message to the next node in the path to the final destination?

B: Layer 2

Layer 2, the Data Link Layer, is responsible for delivering a message to the next node in the network path. It handles communication between adjacent network nodes and can include protocols like Ethernet or Wi-Fi, dealing with the MAC addresses of the devices.

5. Which word describes a frame's payload?

A: Packet

A frame is a Layer 2 Protocol Data Unit (L2PDU), and its payload (the message it encapsulates) is typically a packet. A packet is an L3PDU and contains the Layer 3 header (like an IP header) and its payload.

6. Which layer provides a service to the Application Layer by delivering data to the appropriate application process on the destination host?

C: Layer 4

Layer 4, the Transport Layer, provides services to the Application Layer by delivering data to the appropriate application process on the destination host. This is an example of adjacent-layer interaction—a layer servicing the layer above it.

7. Signals sent out of a physical port of one device are received by a physical port of another device. Which term describes this interaction?

A: Same-layer interaction

"Same-layer interaction" refers to the process where a layer in one device communicates with the same layer in another device. For example, when signals are sent from a physical port of one device and are received by a physical port of another device, it's an instance of same-layer interaction, as each device's Physical Layer is involved in the communication.

8. Which layer of the TCP/IP Model provides an interface between a web browser like Google Chrome and the network?

A: Application Layer

The Application Layer provides an interface between application software, like a web browser, and the underlying network.

Chapter 5: The Cisco IOS CLI

1. What kind of cable is typically used to connect to the console port of a Cisco router or switch?

D: Rollover

A rollover cable is typically used to connect a computer to the console port of a Cisco router or switch. This cable has a unique pinout where the wire connected to pin 1 on one end is connected to pin 8 on the other end, pin 2 to pin 7, pin 3 to pin 6, etc.

2. What mode in the IOS hierarchy is indicated by the prompt `hostname>`?

C: User EXEC mode

The prompt `hostname>` indicates that the device is in User EXEC mode. This mode provides limited access to the device and doesn't support any configurations or disruptive commands.

3. Which of the following commands can be used to return to privileged EXEC mode from global configuration mode? (select two)

B: **`exit`**

D: **end**

The **exit** command returns you to the previous level in the IOS hierarchy, which, from global configuration mode, would be privileged EXEC mode. The **end** command also takes you directly back to privileged EXEC mode from any point in the configuration hierarchy.

4. Which command can be used to view the device's active configuration from global configuration mode?

A: **do show running-config**

The running-config is the device's active configuration—the configuration that determines the device's current operation—and it can be viewed with **show running-config**. To use **show** commands from global config mode, you must add **do** in front of the command.

5. Where is a device's startup-config file stored?

C: NVRAM

The startup configuration file of a Cisco device is stored in Non-Volatile Random-Access Memory (NVRAM). Unlike standard RAM, NVRAM retains its contents even when the device is powered off.

6. Which of the following commands cannot be used to save a device's configuration?

D: **copy startup-config running-config**

To save a device's configuration, you must copy the contents of the running-config in RAM to the startup-config in NVRAM, but this command does the opposite. It copies the contents of the startup-config to the running-config.

7. Which of the following commands configures a password to limit access to privileged EXEC mode and stores the password as a secure hash?

B: **enable secret** *password*

The "enable secret" is a password for accessing privileged EXEC mode. The device stores the enable secret as a secure hash, providing better security than the "enable password".

8. What is the effect of the **service password-encryption** command?

C: A and B

The **service password-encryption** command has two effects: it encrypts currently configured cleartext passwords and ensures that any passwords configured in the future are automatically encrypted. Note that this encryption is not secure, but it does provide basic protection against someone looking at the configuration over your shoulder.

Chapter 6: Ethernet LAN switching

1. What is the OUI of the BIA "0cf5.a452.b103"?

D: 0cf5.a4

The Organizationally Unique Identifier (OUI) is the part of the burned-in address (BUA—another name for a MAC address) that uniquely identifies the manufacturer. It consists of the first 24 bits (the first half) of the MAC address.

2. What is the only field of the Ethernet trailer?

C: FCS

The only field in the Ethernet trailer is the Frame Check Sequence (FCS). The frame's receiver uses the FCS to detect errors in the frame.

3. Which field of an Ethernet frame does a switch use to dynamically learn MAC addresses?

D: Source

A switch dynamically learns MAC addresses by examining the source MAC address field of each frame it receives. It then adds the MAC address to its MAC address table, associating it with the switch port on which it received the frame.

4. Which of the following frames are flooded by a switch? (select two)

A: Broadcast

B: Unknown unicast

Broadcast frames are addressed to the broadcast MAC address (ffff.ffff.ffff) and are flooded out of all ports except the one the frame was received on. Unknown unicast frames are addressed to a single host, but the switch doesn't have a matching entry in its MAC address table, so the switch floods the frame like a broadcast frame.

5. Which of the following statements accurately describes ARP?

A: ARP maps a known Layer 3 address to an unknown Layer 2 address.

Address Resolution Protocol (ARP) is used to learn the unknown MAC address of another host by sending an ARP request to the host's known IP address.

6. What is the destination MAC address of an unknown unicast frame?

B: The MAC address of the frame's destination host

An unknown unicast frame is addressed to a single intended recipient (not to the broadcast MAC address "ffff.ffff.ffff"). However, because the switch does not have the intended recipient's MAC address in its table, the switch's only option is to flood the frame.

7. Which utility involves ICMP echo requests and responses?

B: ping

The ping utility involves sending Internet Control Message Protocol (ICMP) echo requests and waiting for echo responses. It is used to test the reachability of hosts on an IP network.

8. In an ARP exchange, which of the following messages is unicast?

B: ARP reply

In an ARP exchange, the ARP request is broadcast to all devices on the local network, but the ARP reply is a unicast message sent back to the requester with the needed MAC address information.

Chapter 7: IPv4 addressing

1. What bit pattern is found at the beginning of an IPv4 packet?

B: 0100

The first field of the IPv4 header is the four-bit Version field, which indicates the IP version of the packet. IP version 4 is indicated with 0b0100 (which is equal to 0d4).

2. What is indicated by the Total Length field of the IPv4 header?
B: The length of the Packet
The Total Length field in the IPv4 header specifies the entire packet's length, including both the header and the encapsulated payload, in bytes.
3. Which field of the IPv4 header is used to prevent packets infinitely looping around the network?
D: TTL
The Time To Live (TTL) field in the IPv4 header is used to prevent packets from looping infinitely around the network. The TTL value is decremented by one by each router that forwards the packet. If the TTL reaches zero, the packet is discarded.
4. Which netmask is equivalent to a /16 prefix length?
B: 255.255.0.0
A /16 prefix length is indicated with a netmask consisting of 16 1s followed by 16 0s: 11111111.11111111.00000000.00000000, which is 255.255.0.0 in dotted decimal.
5. In the output of **`show ip interface brief`**, what are the default Status and Protocol of a Cisco router interface?
A: `administratively down/down`
Cisco router interfaces have the **`shutdown`** command applied by default, which means they will be in the "administratively down/down" state. To enable a router interface, use **`no shutdown`** on the interface.
6. A PC's IP address is 172.16.12.27/24. What is the first usable address of its network?
B: 172.16.12.1
With a /24 prefix length, the network address of the network is 172.16.12.0—a reserved address. The first usable address is the next address, 172.16.12.1.
7. Which of the following is a loopback address?
C: 127.20.67.1
In IPv4, the address range 127.0.0.0/8 (127.0.0.0–127.255.255.255) is reserved for loopback addresses, used to test network functionality on the local host.
8. Which of the following commands configures an IPv4 address on a router's interface?
D: `R1(config-if)#` **`ip address 10.0.0.1 255.255.255.0`**
The command to configure an IPv4 address on a router's interface is **`ip address`** *`ip-address netmask`* in interface config mode.

Chapter 8: Router and switch interfaces

1. Which of the following statements are true? (select two)
C: Cisco router interfaces have **`shutdown`** applied by default.
D: Cisco switch interfaces have **`no shutdown`** applied by default.
By default, Cisco router interfaces are disabled with the **`shutdown`** command. Cisco switch interfaces, on the other hand, are enabled; they have **`no shutdown`** applied by default.
2. Which of the following is the default setting on a Gigabit Ethernet interface?
C: **`speed auto`**

The default setting on interfaces of all speeds is typically **`speed auto`**, using autonegotiation to determine the speed at which the interface will operate.

3. Which term describes two-way communication in which devices take turns transmitting and receiving?

A: Half duplex

Half duplex refers to two-way communication where devices take turns transmitting and receiving. In half-duplex mode, a device must wait for the other to finish transmitting before it can start.

4. Two PCs and two servers are connected to a hub. How many collision domains are there in the LAN?

A: One

When devices are connected to a hub, there is only one collision domain. This means that only one of the devices can transmit at once; the others must wait their turn.

5. Two PCs and two servers are connected to a switch. How many collision domains are there in the LAN?

D: Four

When devices are connected to a switch, each port on the switch is a separate collision domain. Therefore, with four devices connected to a switch, there are four collision domains.

6. Which technology is used by Ethernet hosts operating in half-duplex to detect and recover from collisions?

B: CSMA/CD

Carrier Sense Multiple Access with Collision Detection (CSMA/CD) is used by Ethernet hosts operating in half-duplex mode to detect and recover from collisions. The device senses whether other devices are transmitting or not and detects when collisions have occurred.

7. SW1 F0/1 and SW2 F0/1 are connected and have the default settings. What speed and duplex settings will appear in the output of show interfaces status?

D: `a-100, a-full`

With default settings of **`speed auto`** and **`duplex auto`**, both switches will use autonegotiation to determine their speed and duplex settings. The interfaces will show `a-100` for speed and `a-full` for duplex, with the `a-` prefix meaning "auto".

8. Which error counter in the output of show interfaces counts frames that failed the FCS check?

C: CRC

Cyclic Redundancy Check (CRC) errors are recorded with the `CRC` error counter in the output of **`show interfaces`**. These errors occur when the frame fails the Frame Check Sequence (FCS) check in the Ethernet trailer.

9. What is the result of a speed mismatch on two connected interfaces?

B: The interfaces will be in a down/down state.

If there is a speed mismatch, the connection will not be operational; the devices will be unable to communicate. You can expect the connected interfaces to be in a down/down state.

10. When there is a duplex mismatch between two connected devices, which error counters will likely increment on the half-duplex device? (select two)
A: Collisions
D: Late collisions
If there is a duplex mismatch and the connected devices transmit at the same time, the half-duplex device will interpret it as a collision, which can lead to incrementing collision and late collision counters.

Chapter 9: Routing fundamentals

1. After configuring an IP address on and enabling a router interface, which route(s) will be automatically added to the router's routing table?
A: C and L
When an IP address is configured on an active router interface, two types of routes are automatically added to the router's routing table: a connected route (C) and a local route (L). The connected route indicates the network directly connected to the router, and the local route indicates the exact IP address of the router's interface with a /32 prefix length.
2. Which type of route represents the exact IP address of a router's interface with a /32 prefix length?
B: L
A local (L) route in the routing table represents the exact IP address of a router's interface with a /32 prefix length. A local route is automatically created by the router for each of its active interfaces.
3. If a packet's destination IP address doesn't match any routes in the routing table, what action will the router take on the packet?
A: It will drop the packet.
If a packet's destination IP address does not match any entries in the router's routing table, the router doesn't know how to forward the packet. As a result, the router will drop the packet. Routers don't flood messages like switches.
4. Which of the following is a host route?
C: A route to 8.8.8.8/32
A host route is a route to a single IP address, represented by a /32 prefix length. The route to 8.8.8.8/32 is a host route as it specifies a single IP address: 8.8.8.8.
5. Which of the following commands configures a recursive static route?
B: `ip route 10.0.0.0 255.0.0.0 192.168.1.1`
A recursive static route specifies the next-hop IP address, not the exit interface. It is "recursive" because it requires an additional routing table lookup: after the router has determined the next-hop IP address, it must perform an additional lookup to determine which interface the next hop is connected to.
6. Which route in its routing table will a router select to forward a packet?
A: The most specific matching route
When forwarding a packet, a router will choose the most specific matching route in its routing table; this is the matching route with the longest prefix length.

7. Which of the following commands configures a default route?

A: **`ip route 0.0.0.0 0.0.0.0 203.0.113.1`**

A default route is a route to 0.0.0.0/0—a route that matches all possible IP addresses. When the router has a default route in its routing table, it will use the route to forward packets that don't match any more specific routes.

8. Which of the following static routes relies on proxy ARP?

B: **`ip route 5.0.0.0 255.0.0.0 gigabitethernet0/1`**

This route relies on proxy ARP because it specifies only the exit interface; it's a directly connected static route. This makes the router behave as if it were directly connected to the destination, and it will therefore send an ARP request directly to the destination IP address (instead of to the next-hop router's IP address). This will only work if the next-hop router has proxy ARP enabled and can reply to the ARP request.

Chapter 10: The life of a packet

1. Which of the following statements is true about a message traversing multiple network hops to reach its final destination?

A: The message's destination IP address remains the same at each hop, but its destination MAC address changes.

As a message travels across multiple network hops to reach its final destination, the destination IP address remains constant throughout its journey. However, the destination MAC address changes at each hop. Each router changes the destination MAC address to that of the next hop on its path to the final destination.

2. Which of the following tables maps MAC addresses to physical ports?

B: MAC address table

A switch's MAC address table maps MAC addresses to physical ports. When a frame arrives at a switch, the switch uses this table to determine the port that the frame should be forwarded out of.

3. A router receives a packet destined for 10.0.0.1. The most specific matching route's next-hop IP address is 172.16.12.2. Which IP address will the router send an ARP request to?

B: 172.16.12.2

When a router forwards a packet, it needs to encapsulate the packet in a frame addressed to the next hop. To do so, it needs to send an ARP request for the next-hop IP address to determine the next hop's MAC address (unless the router already has a corresponding entry in its ARP table).

4. A PC sends a packet destined for a host in a remote network. What is the destination MAC address of the frame the PC sends out of its network port?

C: The default gateway's MAC address

When a PC sends a packet to a host in a remote network, the PC encapsulates the packet in a frame destined for the default gateway. The default gateway is responsible for routing the packet beyond the local network to reach the remote network.

5. Which of the following tables maps destination networks to next hops?
C: Routing table
A router's routing table maps destination networks to their corresponding next hops. This is how the router determines how to forward packets toward their destination.

Chapter 11: Subnetting IPv4 networks

1. Given a /25 address block, what prefix length is appropriate to create 16 subnets of equal size?
C: /29
To create 16 subnets, you need to borrow 4 bits from the host portion (since $2^4 = 16$). This results in a /29 prefix length, adding 4 to the original /25 prefix length.
2. Given a /23 address block, how many subnets can you create that support at least 16 usable host addresses in each subnet?
B: 16 subnets
A /23 address block has 9 host bits (32 – 23 = 9). To support at least 16 usable host addresses, 5 host bits are needed, which supports $2^5 - 2 = 30$ host addresses. 9 host bits minus the 5 needed for host addresses leaves 4 bits that you can borrow to make subnets, allowing for $2^4 = 16$ subnets.
3. A server's IP address is 172.19.209.178/29. What is the network address of its subnet?
B: 172.19.209.176
To calculate this, write the final octet in binary: 0d178 = 0b10110010. Then, change the bits of the host portion (the last 3 bits) all to 0: 10110000. Then convert back to decimal: 0b10110000 = 0d176. Therefore, the network address is 172.19.209.176.
4. PC1's IP address is 192.168.222.101/26. What is the broadcast address of its subnet?
A: 192.168.222.127
To calculate this, write the final octet in binary: 0d101 = 0b01100101. Then, change the bits of the host portion (the last 6 bits) all to 1: 01111111. Then convert back to decimal: 0b01111111 = 0d127. Therefore, the broadcast address is 192.168.222.127.
5. Given a /12 address block, how many subnets can you create that support at least 200 usable host addresses in each subnet?
D: 4096 subnets
A /12 address block has 20 host bits (32 – 12 = 20). To create subnets that support at least 200 usable host addresses, 8 host bits are needed ($2^8 - 2 = 254$). That leaves 12 bits that you can borrow to make subnets (20 – 8 = 12), allowing for $2^{12} = 4096$ subnets.
6. Given a /15 address block, what prefix length is appropriate to create 1024 subnets of equal size?
A: /25
Making 1024 subnets requires 10 borrowed bits (since $2^{10} = 1024$). Therefore, the answer is /25, adding 10 to the original /15 prefix length.
7. A printer's IP address is 10.109.211.107/28. What is the network address of its subnet?
B: 10.109.211.96

To calculate the network address, write the final octet in binary: 0d107 = 0b01101011. Then, change the hosts bits (the final 4 bits) to 0: 01100000. Finally, convert back to decimal: 0b01100000 = 0d96. Therefore, the network address is 10.109.211.96.

8. R1's IP address is 203.0.113.237/27. What is the broadcast address of its subnet?

D: 203.0.113.255

To determine the broadcast address, write the final octet in binary: 0d237 = 0b11101101. Then, change the host bits (the last 5 bits) to 1: 11111111. Then, convert back to decimal: 0b11111111 = 0d255. Therefore, the broadcast address is 203.0.113.255.

9. You have been given the 192.168.27.0/24 address block to create subnets of appropriate sizes for your organization. You have already assigned the first subnet to support 109 hosts. The second subnet must support 60 hosts. What is the usable host address range of the second subnet?

A: 192.168.27.129 to 192.168.27.190

The first subnet, which must support 109 hosts, is 192.168.27.0/25 (a /25 prefix length leaves 7 host bits and supports $2^7 - 2 = 126$ hosts). The second subnet, which must support 60 hosts, should use a /26 prefix length (leaving 6 hosts bits and supporting $2^6 - 2 = 62$ hosts). Therefore, the second subnet is 192.168.27.128/26, with a usable address range of 192.168.27.129–192.168.27.190.

10. You have been given the 10.0.2.0/23 address block to create subnets of appropriate sizes for your organization. You have already assigned the first subnet to support 40 hosts. The second subnet must support 29 hosts. What is the broadcast address of the second subnet?

C: 10.0.2.95

The first subnet must use a /26 prefix length, which leaves 6 host bits, to support 40 hosts ($2^6 - 2 = 62$); it is 10.0.2.0/26. The second subnet should use a /27 prefix length, leaving 5 hosts bits and supporting $2^5 - 2 = 30$ hosts. Therefore, the second subnet is 10.0.2.64/27, and its broadcast address is 10.0.2.95 (host bits all set to 1).

Chapter 12: VLANs

1. Which of the following statements about VLANs is true?

B: VLANs divide a broadcast domain into multiple broadcast domains.

Virtual Local Area Networks (VLANs) divide a single broadcast domain into multiple smaller broadcast domains. This improves network performance and security by reducing the size of the broadcast domains and isolating network traffic.

2. You issue **`switchport access vlan 10`** on a switch port, but VLAN 10 doesn't exist yet on the switch. What is the result of the command?

C: The switch automatically creates VLAN 10.

On Cisco switches, if you assign a port to a VLAN that does not exist, the switch will automatically create that VLAN.

3. Which VLANs exist on a Cisco switch by default and cannot be deleted?

A: VLANs 1, 1002, 1003, 1004, and 1005

VLAN 1 and several VLANs reserved for FDDI and Token Ring support (1002–1005)—old technologies that are no longer used—exist on Cisco switches by default. These VLANs cannot be deleted.

4. Which VLAN is untagged on a trunk port?

B: The native VLAN

When a trunk port receives untagged frames, it assigns them to the native VLAN, and when sending frames in the native VLAN, it sends them untagged. The native VLAN is VLAN 1 by default, but it can be changed with **`switchport trunk native vlan`** *`vlan`* in interface config mode.

5. How many VLANs are there in total, including reserved VLANs?

D: 4096

The VLAN Identifier (VID) field of the 802.1Q tag is 12 bits in size, allowing for $2^{12} = 4096$ VLANs (0–4095). However, VLANs 0 and 4095 are reserved for special purposes, so a Cisco switch can have a maximum of 4094 VLANs (1–4094).

6. Which VLANs are allowed on a trunk port by default?

A: 1–4094

By default, all VLANs (1–4094) are allowed on a trunk port. You can use the **`switchport trunk allowed vlan`** command to allow only the necessary VLANs.

7. A LAN you are managing includes VLANs 1, 2, and 3. VLAN 4—a new VLAN—is added, and it is your job to make sure that all trunk links allow it. Which command is appropriate to add VLAN 4 to each trunk's list of allowed VLANs?

B: **`switchport trunk allowed vlan add 4`**

Use **`switchport trunk allowed vlan add`** *`vlans`* to add VLANs to a trunk's list of allowed VLANs. The **`add`** keyword is very important. If you configure **`switchport trunk allowed vlan 4`**, it won't add VLAN 4 to the list of allowed VLANs; it will replace the current list with only VLAN 4.

8. Which of the following is a security best practice related to VLANs?

C: Configure a non-default unused VLAN as the native VLAN.

A security best practice for VLANs is to configure a non-default, unused VLAN as the native VLAN on trunk ports. This helps mitigate security exploits related to the native VLAN; it is recommended that you do not use the native VLAN in your networks.

9. In a ROAS configuration, which command tells the router which VLAN to tag frames with?

D: `R1(config-subif)#` **`encapsulation dot1q 10`**

In a router-on-a-stick (ROAS) configuration, the command **`encapsulation dot1q`** *`vlan-id`* is used in subinterface configuration mode to specify the VLAN ID for tagging frames. The VLAN ID doesn't have to match the subinterface ID (i.e. GigabitEthernet0/1.10), but it's best to match them for simplicity's sake.

10. Which of the following is NOT a requirement for an SVI to be in an up/up state?

D: The switch must have both an access port associated with the VLAN and a trunk port that allows the VLAN.

For a switch virtual interface (SVI) to be in an up/up state, the switch must have either an access port associated with the VLAN or a trunk port that allows the VLAN; it is not necessary to have both.

Chapter 13: Dynamic Trunking Protocol and VLAN Trunking Protocol

1. If two Cisco switches are connected with the default settings, what will be the operational mode of their ports?
A: Access
Cisco switch ports default to **`switchport mode dynamic auto`**. Two connected ports in dynamic auto mode will not form a trunk; they will operate as access ports.
2. Which of the following **`switchport mode`** command combinations configured on two connected ports will result in a valid trunk link?
A: **`dynamic auto`** + **`trunk`**
Although a port configured with **`switchport mode trunk`** does not use DTP to determine its own operational mode, it will still send DTP messages to encourage its connected neighbor to operate in trunk mode. This means the port in dynamic auto mode will also operate in trunk mode, forming a valid trunk link.
3. Which administrative modes result in a port not sending DTP frames?
C: Access
Ports configured with **`switchport mode access`** will not send DTP frames. Switch ports in other modes will, including those configured with **`switchport mode trunk`** (unless you also configure **`switchport nonegotiate`**).
4. Which VTP mode(s) will cause a switch to sync its VLAN database to other switches in the VTP domain?
D: Server and client
In VTP, both server and client modes will synchronize VLAN information upon receiving a VTP message with a higher revision number. Server mode allows a switch to create, modify, and delete VLANs and propagate those changes to other switches, while client mode switches receive and apply these changes but cannot create, change, or delete VLANs.
5. What will a switch without a VTP domain name do upon receiving a VTP message on one of its trunk ports?
C: It will join the sender's VTP domain.
A switch that does not have a VTP domain name configured will adopt the domain name from a received VTP message and sync its VLAN database.
6. Which VTPv3 modes allow a switch to create VLANs and propagate them to other switches in the VTP domain?
D: Primary server
In VTP version 3, only the "primary server" mode allows a switch to create VLANs and propagate them across the VTP domain; regular VTPv3 servers cannot. Use **`vtp primary`** in privileged EXEC mode to make a switch the primary server.
7. Which VTP versions support extended-range VLANs?
A: VTPv3

Only VTP version 3 supports extended-range VLANs (VLANs 1006–4094). VTPv1 and VTPv2 support only normal-range VLANs (1–1005).

8. Which ports do switches send VTP messages out of?

B: Trunk ports

VTP messages are only sent out of a switch's trunk ports, not access ports.

Chapter 14: Spanning Tree Protocol

1. Which of the following are negative effects of Layer-2 loops? (select two)

A: MAC address flapping

B: Broadcast storms

Layer-2 loops can cause MAC address flapping, where a switch cannot determine the correct port for a MAC address due to the address repeatedly appearing on different ports. They can also cause broadcast storms, where looping broadcast frames consume network bandwidth and overwhelm network devices.

2. In a four-switch LAN, which of the following switches would be selected as the STP root bridge?

D: SW4, BID: 1:5254.00ff.f012

The switch with the lowest Bridge ID (BID) will be selected as the root bridge in STP. The BID is a combination of the priority value and the MAC address. SW4 has the lowest priority (1) and therefore the lowest BID, so it would be the root bridge.

3. How many root ports will there be in a four-switch LAN?

C: 3

In a network with four switches, there will be one root bridge and three non-root bridges. Each non-root bridge will select one root port—the port with the lowest cost to reach the root bridge. Therefore, there will be three root ports in total.

4. Which STP port roles send BPDUs?

A: Designated ports

STP BPDUs are only sent out of designated ports. The root bridge, which has only designated ports, sends BPDUs out of all ports every 2 seconds. Then, other switches use their designated ports to propagate those BPDUs out to other switches.

5. When you connect an end host to a switch port without PortFast, how long does it take for the port to enter the STP forwarding state?

C: 30 seconds

When an end host is first connected to a switch port without PortFast, the port must transition through the STP listening and learning states before entering the forwarding state. How long the port spends in each state is determined by the forward delay timer, which is 15 seconds by default; this means it will take 30 seconds in total (15*2).

6. What happens when a switch port configured with `spanning-tree bpduguard enable` receives a BPDU?

B: The port is error-disabled.

When BPDU Guard is enabled on a port and it receives a BPDU, the port is put into an error-disabled state to prevent potential STP topology changes. This is a protective measure typically used on access ports that should be connected to end hosts.

7. Two switches, SW1 and SW2, are connected by two links using the default STP cost values. SW2 is the root bridge. SW1 G0/1 is connected to SW2 G0/2, and SW1 G0/2 is connected to SW2 G0/1. Which port will SW1 select as its root port?

B: G0/2

A switch selects its port with the lowest root cost as its root port. If multiple ports are tied, it will select the port connected to the switch with the lowest BID. If multiple ports are still tied, it will select the port connected to the port with the lowest port ID. In this question, SW1 G0/2 (connected to SW2 G0/1) is connected to a port with a lower port ID than SW1 G0/1 (connected to SW2 G0/2), so SW1 G0/2 will become SW1's root port. It's important to note that SW1 doesn't compare its own port IDs; it compares the neighbor's (SW2's) port IDs.

8. SW3 and SW4 are part of a larger LAN. They are connected by their G0/1 ports, neither of which is a root port. Both switches have equal root costs. How will they determine which port becomes designated and which becomes non-designated?

C: The port on the switch with the lowest BID will become designated.

When two switches have equal root costs, the switch with the lower BID will have its port become the designated port. The other switch's port will be non-designated (blocking).

9. How many STP designated ports will there be in a four-switch LAN with a total of seven links?

C: 7

In an STP network, every network segment (link) will have one designated port. With seven links, there will be seven designated ports.

10. Which STP port role points away from the root bridge and is in a forwarding state?

A: Designated

STP root and designated ports are in a forwarding state once the LAN has converged. Root ports point toward the root bridge; they provide each switch's active path to the root bridge. Designated ports, on the other hand, point away from the root bridge. Each root port always connects to a designated port.

11. Which command is most likely to ensure that a switch becomes the root bridge for VLAN 1?

D: **`spanning-tree vlan 1 priority 0`**

The best way to ensure that a switch becomes the root bridge for a particular VLAN is to use **`spanning-tree vlan`** *`vlan-id`* **`priority 0`** to make its bridge priority 0—the lowest possible value. This way, it can only be usurped by another switch with a lower MAC address that also has its priority set to 0.

Chapter 15: Rapid Spanning Tree Protocol

1. The output of **`show spanning-tree`** on a Cisco switch states `Spanning tree enabled protocol ieee`. Which version of STP is the switch running?

D: PVST+

`Spanning tree enabled protocol ieee` means that the switch is running Cisco's Per-VLAN Spanning Tree Plus (PVST+), not IEEE-standard STP. If the switch is running Rapid PVST+, it will state `Spanning tree enabled protocol rstp`. Cisco switches don't run the IEEE-standard versions of these protocols.

2. You configure **`spanning-tree pathcost method long`** on a Cisco switch. Which of the following accurately represent the default port costs after issuing that command? (select two)

B: 10 Gbps: 2,000

D: 100 Mbps: 200,000

The long port costs are: 10 Mbps = 2,000,000, 100 Mbps = 200,000, 1 Gbps = 20,000, 10 Gbps = 2,000, 100 Gbps = 200, 1 Tbps = 20, and 10 Tbps = 2.

3. If the RSTP sync mechanism succeeds, how long does it take for a port to transition from the discarding state to the forwarding state?

D: It transitions immediately.

In RSTP, when the sync mechanism succeeds, a port can transition from the discarding state to the forwarding state immediately, bypassing the 30 second wait that is necessary in classic STP. This is the primary advantage of RSTP.

4. SW1 G0/1 is not a root port or a designated port, and SW1 is not the designated bridge for the segment G0/1 is connected to. What is SW1's G0/1's RSTP port role?

A: Alternate

In RSTP, a port that is neither a root port nor a designated port, and is not the designated bridge for its segment, is an alternate port. Alternate ports provide an alternate path to the root bridge and remain in a discarding state while they are not needed.

5. Which RSTP port type will not trigger a topology change notification if the port's status changes?

C: Edge

An edge port in RSTP connects to an end device (like a PC or server)—not to another switch. If an edge port's status changes (goes up or down), it does not trigger a topology change notification because it does not affect the RSTP topology among the switches.

6. If the RSTP root bridge has two ports connected to the same segment via a hub, what will the role be of the port that is not designated?

D: Backup

In RSTP, if the root bridge has multiple ports connected to the same segment via a hub, one port will be the designated port and the others will be backup ports. The backup port role is used for ports that provide a redundant path to the same segment as another port on the same switch. This is an exception to the general rule that all ports on the root bridge must be designated.

7. Which command configures the RSTP edge link type on a port?

B: **`spanning-tree portfast`**

The **`spanning-tree portfast`** command is used to configure an RSTP edge port. Unlike the point-to-point and shared link types, you cannot use the **`spanning-tree link-type`** command to configure an edge port.

8. SW1's G0/1 port is in the up/up state but has stopped receiving BPDUs from its RSTP neighbor. How long will SW1 wait before reacting and initiating a topology change?

A: 6 seconds

In RSTP, if a switch stops receiving BPDUs on a port, it waits for three times the Hello time before initiating a topology change. The default Hello time is 2 seconds, so the switch will wait 6 seconds (3*2 seconds) before reacting and initiating a topology change. Note that the switch will only wait 6 seconds if the port remains up/up; if a hardware failure or something else causes the port to go down, the switch will react immediately—no need to wait 6 seconds.

9. Which RSTP link type is default on full-duplex ports?

C: Point-to-point

Full-duplex ports use the RSTP point-to-point link type by default; this is the only link type that can use RSTP's sync mechanism for rapid convergence. This link type should be used for direct connections between two switches.

10. Four switches are interconnected, with a total of six links between them. How many of each RSTP port role are there?

B: 3 root, 6 designated, 3 alternate

Because there are 6 links, there are a total of 12 ports (2 connected to each link). There are 4 switches, and each non-root switch must have 1 root port, so there are 3 root ports. Each link must have one designated port, so there are 6 designated ports. The remaining ports are alternate ports - they enter the discarding state to prevent loops. So, there are 3 alternate ports. There are no backup ports; hubs are extremely rare in modern networks, and no hubs are mentioned in the question.

11. Which optional STP feature disables a port if it stops receiving BPDUs?

D: Loop Guard

When a Loop Guard-enabled port stops receiving BPDUs, it will enter the loop-inconsistent state, effectively disabling the port. This protects against loops caused by a port erroneously transitioning to the forwarding state.

12. BPDU Filter has been enabled globally for all PortFast-enabled ports. What happens when one of the BPDU Filter-enabled ports receives a BPDU?

A: PortFast and BPDU Filter are disabled on the port.

BPDU Filter can be enabled in two ways: in interface config mode with **`spanning-tree bpdufilter enable`**, or globally on all PortFast-enabled ports with **`spanning-tree portfast bpdufilter default`**. When enabled in interface config mode, the port doesn't send BPDUs and ignores all received BPDUs. When enabled globally, the port doesn't send BPDUs, but if it receives a BPDU, PortFast and BPDU Filter will be disabled; the port then operates as a normal STP or RSTP port.

Chapter 16: EtherChannel

1. Which of the following statements about EtherChannel is false?

B: EtherChannel eliminates the need for STP in a LAN.

EtherChannel does not eliminate the need for STP in a LAN. While EtherChannel can aggregate multiple physical links into a single logical link, reducing the number of ports that need to be blocked by STP, STP still plays a critical role in the larger network topology for loop prevention.

2. Which of the following dynamic EtherChannel mode combinations will result in a valid EtherChannel? (select two)

C: passive + active

D: desirable + desirable

When using Link Aggregation Control Protocol (LACP), the mode combinations that will result in a valid EtherChannel are passive+active and active+active. When using Port Aggregation Protocol (PAgP), they are auto+desirable and desirable+desirable. PAgP and LACP modes don't mix; a switch using PAgP won't form an EtherChannel with a switch using LACP.

3. Which of the following settings doesn't have to match among the member ports of an EtherChannel?

A: Description

A description doesn't affect a port's operation, so each member port of an EtherChannel can have a unique description. However, settings like speed, duplex, and access/trunk mode must match among all ports in an EtherChannel.

4. Which dynamic EtherChannel modes can form a valid EtherChannel with a neighbor configured with **`channel-group 1 mode on`**?

D: None of the above

Just as PAgP and LACP modes can't form an EtherChannel with each other, neither can form an EtherChannel with a switch configured to use static EtherChannel. To form a working static EtherChannel, both sides must be configured with **`mode on`**.

5. Which protocol can be used to negotiate an EtherChannel with a non-Cisco switch?

B: LACP

Link Aggregation Control Protocol (LACP) is an IEEE standard and can be used to negotiate an EtherChannel with a non-Cisco switch. PAgP, on the other hand, is a Cisco-proprietary protocol and can only be used on Cisco devices.

6. Port-channel 1 and its member ports currently operate in access mode. What will happen after you configure **`switchport mode trunk`** on the port-channel 1 interface?

B: The configuration is inherited by the member ports.

When you configure the port-channel interface, the member ports inherit this configuration. Changing the port-channel interface to trunk mode automatically updates the member ports to match this configuration, ensuring consistency across the EtherChannel.

7. When connecting two switches with a Layer-3 EtherChannel, where should each switch's IP address be configured?

A: On the port-channel interface

In a Layer-3 EtherChannel, IP addressing is configured on the port-channel interface rather than on the individual member ports. This setup allows the EtherChannel to function as a single logical interface at Layer 3.

Chapter 17: Dynamic routing

1. Which type of dynamic routing protocol is used to exchange routing information within an AS?

A: IGP

Interior gateway protocols (IGPs) are used to exchange routing information within an autonomous system (AS). Examples include OSPF, EIGRP, RIP, and IS-IS. This is in contrast to exterior gateway protocols (EGPs) like BGP, which are used to exchange routing information between ASs.

2. Which of the following dynamic routing protocols use a link-state algorithm? (select two)

A: IS-IS

C: OSPF

IS-IS and OSPF are both link-state routing protocols. They maintain a complete map of the network topology to make routing decisions.

3. Which type of routing protocol is also known as "routing by rumor"?

C: Distance-vector

Distance-vector routing protocols are often referred to as "routing by rumor" because the router doesn't build a complete map of the network; it only knows what its neighbors tell it.

4. When multiple routes to the same destination network are learned via the same routing protocol, which parameter is used to select which route(s) will enter the routing table?

B: Metric

When a router learns multiple routes to the same destination from the same routing protocol, the route with the lowest metric is selected for the routing table.

5. When multiple routes to the same destination network are learned via different routing protocols, which parameter is used to select which route(s) will enter the routing table?

C: AD

When routes to the same destination are learned via different routing protocols, the administrative distance (AD) is used to determine the preferred route. The route with the lowest AD is selected. Each routing protocol calculates route metric values differently, so they can't be directly compared.

6. Which of the following accurately represent IOS default AD values? (select two)

B: EIGRP = 90

C: OSPF = 110

Here are some default AD values in Cisco IOS: connected = 0, static = 1, External BGP (EBGP) = 20, EIGRP = 90, OSPF = 110, IS-IS = 115, RIP = 120, Internal BGP (IBGP) = 200, unusable = 255.

7. If a Cisco router learns multiple routes to the same destination via the same routing protocol, and all routes have the same metric, what is the maximum number of routes to that destination that the router will insert into its routing table by default?

C: 4

By default, Cisco routers can load-balance across up to four equal-cost paths; this is called equal-cost multi-path (ECMP) routing. If multiple routes to the same destination have the same metric, up to four of them can be inserted into the routing table for load balancing.

8. What kind of static route acts as a backup for another route, only entering the routing table if the more preferred route is removed from the routing table?

B: Floating static route

A floating static route is a static route with a higher AD than the primary route. It acts as a backup and is used only if the primary route is unavailable.

9. A router learns the following routes via manual configuration and dynamic routing protocols. Which route(s) will it insert into its routing table? (select all that apply)

A: 10.0.0.0/8 via RIP, metric 6

C: 10.0.0.0/16 via static routing

D: 10.0.0.0/24 via EIGRP, metric 10127

The router has learned routes to three different destination networks: 10.0.0.0/8, 10.0.0.0/16, and 10.0.0.0/24. It has only learned one route to each of 10.0.0.0/8 and 10.0.0.0/24, so it will insert both routes as is—no need to compare them with other routes. Then, the router will select which route to 10.0.0.0/16 to insert. The static route has a lower AD (1) than the OSPF route (110), so it will insert the static route into its routing table. Note that "select all that apply" questions will not appear on the CCNA exam; if you need to select multiple answers, it will state exactly how many you need to select (select two, select three, etc).

10. A router learns the following routes via dynamic routing protocols. Which route(s) will it insert into its routing table? (select all that apply)

D: 192.168.1.0/24 via static routing, AD 89

The router has learned four different routes to a single destination network: 192.168.1.0/24. So it will only insert one route into its routing table (unless ECMP comes into play). The static route has been configured with a non-default AD (89). However, its AD is still lower than that of the EIGRP route (90), so the router will insert the static route into its routing table. When configuring a floating static route, make sure to configure it so that its AD is sufficiently high to make it less preferred than other routes.

11. A router receives a packet destined for 192.0.2.29. It has the following four routes in its routing table. Which route will it select to forward the packet?

A: `R 192.0.2.0/27 [120/5] via 10.0.0.2`

When selecting which route should be used to forward a particular packet, the router only considers one thing: the most specific matching route. AD and metric are not considered. In this case, only the route to 192.0.2.0/27 (option A) matches the packet's destination IP address, so the router will forward the packet according to that route's instructions.

12. A router receives a packet destined for 10.23.107.126. It has the following four routes in its routing table. Which route will it select to forward the packet?

D: `D 10.23.107.112/28 [90/3456] via 172.16.1.13`

In this case, three routes match the packet's destination IP address: the route to 10.23.107.0/25 (A), the route to 10.23.107.96/27 (C), and the route to 10.23.107.112/28 (D). The route to 10.23.107.112/28 has the longest prefix length, so it is the most specific matching route; the router will forward the packet according to that route's instructions.

13. R1's G0/1 interface has the IP address 192.168.209.101/30. Which of the following **`network`** commands would activate OSPF on the interface?

A: **`network 192.168.209.100 0.0.0.3 area 0`**

B: **`network 192.168.209.101 0.0.0.0 area 0`**

C: **`network 192.168.0.0 0.0.255.255 area 0`**

The OSPF **`network`** command is quite flexible; as long as the appropriate bits match between the interface's IP address and the address in the **`network`** command (those indicated by a "0" bit in the wildcard mask), OSPF will be activated on the interface. In this case, all three **`network`** statements match the appropriate bits in the interface's IP address, so all three commands would activate OSPF on the interface.

Chapter 18: Open Shortest Path First

1. R1 is part of an OSPF network, and all of its OSPF-enabled interfaces are in area 1. Furthermore, it connects to the Internet and advertises a default route to other OSPF routers. What OSPF router types apply to R1? (select all that apply).

A: Internal router

D: ASBR

R1 is an internal router because all of its OSPF-enabled interfaces are in a single area (area 1). It's also an autonomous system boundary router (ASBR) because it connects to an external network (the Internet) and advertises a default route to other OSPF routers. It is not area border router (ABR) because it does not connect to multiple OSPF areas, nor is it a backbone router because it's not in area 0.

2. What command should you configure on a router to ensure that all GigabitEthernet interfaces have an OSPF cost of 10?

C: **`auto-cost reference-bandwidth 10000`**

OSPF's automatic cost calculation uses the formula "reference bandwidth/interface bandwidth". The **`auto-cost reference-bandwidth`** command is configured in Mbps, so to make a 1 Gbps (1000 Mbps) interface have a cost of 10, the reference bandwidth should be 10000 Mbps (10000/1000 = 10).

3. What is the effect of the **`passive-interface`** command on an OSPF-activated interface?

B: The router will advertise the interface's network to other OSPF routers, but won't send hello messages out of the interface.

The **`passive-interface`** command in OSPF stops the router from sending OSPF hello packets out of the interface, preventing OSPF neighbor relationships from forming on that interface. However, the network connected to the interface will still be advertised to other OSPF routers.

4. Which of the following represents the order of priority when a router decides its OSPF RID?

A: 1) Manual configuration, 2) Highest IP address on a loopback interface, 3) Highest IP address on a physical interface

The OSPF Router ID (RID) is determined in this order of priority: first, a manually configured router ID; second, the highest IP address on any active loopback interface; third, the highest IP address on any active physical interface.

5. R1 has multiple OSPF neighbor relationships. R1's OSPF RID is 192.168.1.1, which was inherited from a physical interface's IP address. You then configure the IP address 10.0.0.2 on a loopback interface and configure **`router-id 1.1.1.1`** in router config mode for the OSPF process. What is R1's RID after you issue the **`router-id 1.1.1.1`** command?

A: 192.168.1.1

Once a router has determined its RID and established an OSPF neighbor relationship with another router, the only way to change the RID is to manually configure it with the **`router-id`** *`rid`* command and then reset the OSPF process with **`clear ip ospf process`**. However, the scenario does not indicate that you reset the OSPF process, so R1's RID remains 192.168.1.1.

6. Which of the following commands activates OSPF on an interface without using the network command?

B: `R1(config-if)#` **`ip ospf 1 area 0`**

You can use the **`ip ospf`** *`process-id`* **`area`** *`area-id`* in interface config mode to activate OSPF on the interface. This is generally preferred over the **`network`** command due to its simplicity.

7. Four routers connected to a segment with the OSPF broadcast network type have the default OSPF priority. R4 is the DR and R3 is the BDR. You configure ip ospf priority 100 on R2's interface connected to the segment and reset OSPF on R4 with **`clear ip ospf process`**. Which of the following statements is true after you reset R4's OSPF process?

B: R3 is the DR and R2 is the BDR.

When the OSPF process of R4 (the DR) is reset, R3 (the BDR) immediately takes over its role as the DR, even though R2's interface now has the highest priority (100, whereas others have the default of 1). Then, an election is held to determine the new BDR; R2 wins this due to its higher priority and becomes the BDR.

8. Which of the following commands can be used to prevent routers from electing a DR/BDR?

A: `Router(config-if)#` **`ip ospf network point-to-point`**

Whereas OSPF neighbors using the broadcast network type hold DR/BDR elections, those using the point-to-point network type do not. The default network type of Ethernet interfaces is broadcast, but you can use **`ip ospf network point-to-point`** to configure the point-to-point network type.

9. Which of the following are requirements for two routers to become OSPF neighbors? (select two)
B: RIDs must be unique.
C: Hello and dead timers must match.
For two routers to become OSPF neighbors, their RIDs must be unique, and their hello and dead timers must match. The other two options are incorrect because the area numbers must match (not be unique) and the RIDs must be unique (not match).
10. Which of the following represents the order of priority when routers elect a DR/BDR?
C: 1) Highest interface priority, 2) Highest RID
The router with the highest interface priority is elected as the DR of an OSPF broadcast network. If there is a tie, the router with the highest RID becomes the DR. Then, an election using identical rules is held to determine the BDR.

Chapter 19: First hop redundancy protocols

1. Which of the following statements about the virtual IP and virtual MAC used by HSRP are true?
C: The active and standby routers share a VIP and virtual MAC address.
The Hot Standby Router Protocol (HSRP) active and standby routers share a virtual IP address (VIP) and virtual MAC address. This allows for a seamless failover from the active router to the standby router; end hosts don't have to update their default gateway IP address or ARP table when a failover occurs.
2. During HSRP failover, what is the purpose of the new active router sending GARP messages?
C: To make switches update their MAC address table.
As the previous explanation mentioned, end hosts don't have to update their default gateway IP address or ARP table when a failover from active to standby occurs. Instead, the gratuitous ARP (GARP) messages sent by the new active router serve to make switches update their MAC address tables. This allows them to correctly forward frames to the new active router.
3. Which virtual MAC address is used by VRRP group 12?
A: 0000.5e00.010c
The Virtual Router Redundancy Protocol (VRRP) virtual MAC uses the format 0000.5e00.01XX, where XX is the VRRP group number. However, because MAC addresses are written in hexadecimal, the virtual MAC format for VRRP group 12 is 0000.5e00.010c (0d12 = 0xc), not 0000.5e00.0112.
4. R1 is a master router, actively forwarding packets between the LAN and external networks. R2 is a backup router, waiting to take over in case R1 fails. Which FHRP are R1 and R2 using?
B: VRRP
In VRRP, the terms "master" and "backup" are used. HSRP uses the terms "active" and "standby", and GLBP uses "Active Virtual Gateway (AVG)" and "Active Virtual Forwarder (AVF)".

5. Which FHRP facilitates load-balancing of traffic within a single subnet?
C: GLBP
Gateway Load Balancing Protocol (GLBP) facilitates load balancing of traffic from hosts across multiple routers in a single subnet. GLBP elects up to four AVFs, each with a unique virtual MAC address, and traffic is load-balanced among the AVFs.
6. R1 and R2 use VRRP to provide a redundant default gateway for end hosts. R1 was the master router, but a hardware failure on R1 caused R2 to take over the master role. Given the default settings, what happens when R1 recovers from its hardware failure?
A: R1 becomes the master router again.
In VRRP, preemption is enabled by default. This means that if the master router (R1, in this case) recovers from a failure, it will preempt the backup router and take back its role as the master router. This ensures that the router with the highest priority always serves as the master router when it is operational.
7. Which command configures the HSRP VIP?
D: `R1(config-if)#` **`standby 1 ip 10.0.0.1`**
The command to configure the HSRP VIP is **`standby`** *`group-number`* **`ip`** *`vip`* in interface config mode.
8. What is the correct order of priority when electing the HSRP active router?
D: 1) Highest interface priority, 2) Highest interface IP address
The active router in HSRP is determined first by the highest interface priority. If there is a tie in priority, the router with the highest IP address on the HSRP-enabled interface becomes the active router.

Chapter 20: IPv6 addressing

1. Which of the following are not valid IPv6 addresses? (select two)
B: 2607:f8b0:4005:800:1111:0:1:2:3
C: 2607:f8b0:4005:800:gh::1004
Option B has too many hextets (9), and option C contains invalid characters ("g" and "h"). Hexadecimal only uses 0–9 and a–f.
2. Which of the following is a correctly abbreviated version of the IPv6 address 2001:0db8:85a3:0000:0000:8a2e:0370:7334?
D: 2001:db8:85a3::8a2e:370:7334
This option correctly abbreviates the IPv6 address by removing leading zeros and consecutive all-zero hextets. Make sure to avoid common pitfalls like removing trailing zeros, failing to remove all leading zeros, and improperly abbreviating all-zero hextets.
3. Which command configures an IPv6 address using the specified prefix and an automatically generated interface ID?
D: **`ipv6 address 2001:db8:0:1::/64 eui-64`**
The command **`ipv6 address`** *`prefix`***`/64 eui-64`** allows you to specify a /64 network prefix and automatically generate a 64-bit interface ID from the interface's MAC address using Modified EUI-64 rules.
4. R1's G0/1 interface's MAC address is 7ea2.1097.ff27. What is its Modified EUI-64 interface ID?

B: 7ca2:10ff:fe97:ff27

The Modified EUI-64 format inverts the 7th bit of the MAC address, and inserts 'ff:fe' in the middle to expand the MAC to a 64-bit interface ID. The MAC address 7ea2.1097. ff27 becomes 7ca2:10ff:fe97:ff27.

5. Which MAC address was used to generate the Modified EUI-64 interface ID 1f7d:2aff:fedd:611c?

C: 1d7d.2add.611c

To find the original MAC address, remove "ff:fe" and then invert the 7th bit back to its original state. The interface ID 1f7d:2aff:fedd:611c corresponds to the MAC address 1d7d.2add.611c.

6. Which type of IPv6 address is equivalent to a private IPv4 address?

A: ULA

Unique local addresses (ULAs) in IPv6 are equivalent to private IPv4 addresses. They are used for local communications within a private network and are not routable over the Internet (although they are routable within the private network).

7. Which kind of IPv6 address is not routable?

B: LLA

Link-local addresses (LLAs) are not routable beyond their local network segment. They are used for communication on a single link or network segment. IPv6 LLAs use the fe80::/10 range.

8. Which kind of IPv6 address must be configured on every IPv6-enabled interface?

B: LLA

Every IPv6-enabled interface must have an LLA. These addresses are used for various functions on the local network segment, so they are mandatory on all IPv6-enabled interfaces.

9. Which IPv6 multicast scope remains on the local segment?

B: ff02

IPv6 multicast addresses that begin with "ff02" have the "link-local" scope. These packets remain on the local segment; routers will not route them.

10. Which IPv6 multicast address can be used to achieve the same effect as a message to the IPv4 address 255.255.255.255?

A: ff02::1

ff02::1 is the "all nodes" link-local multicast address. Although IPv6 doesn't use the concept of "broadcast", a packet sent to this multicast address has the same effect as a packet sent to the IPv4 broadcast address 255.255.255.255; it addresses the packet to all nodes on the local segment.

11. Which IPv6 address is equivalent to an IPv4 address in the 127.0.0.0/8 range?

B: ::1

This is the IPv6 loopback address. Whereas IPv4 reserves a whole range (127.0.0.0/8) for loopback addresses, IPv6 uses only ::1. Messages sent to this address are "looped back" to the local device; they are not sent out of any interface.

12. Which IPv6 address type involves configuring the same address on multiple hosts?
D: Anycast
An anycast address is indistinguishable from a unicast address; the only difference is that an anycast address is configured on multiple hosts. This is useful when providing services over the internet; by configuring the same IP address on servers in different global locations, client devices can access the server closest to their location.

Chapter 21: IPv6 routing

1. What is the IPv4 equivalent of an IPv6 neighbor table?
A: ARP table
In IPv4, the Address Resolution Protocol (ARP) table is used to map IPv4 addresses to MAC addresses. IPv6 doesn't use ARP; instead, it uses Neighbor Discovery Protocol (NDP), storing IPv6-address-to-MAC-address mappings in the neighbor table.
2. What scope is used by IPv6 solicited-node multicast addresses?
B: Link-local
IPv6 solicited-node multicast addresses have a link-local scope (beginning with "ff02"); they are only used for communication within the local segment.
3. What solicited-node multicast address is generated from the unicast address df56:9098:1010:fd:ab29::f892?
D: ff02::1:ff00:f892
The solicited-node multicast address is formed by appending the last 24 bits of the unicast address to ff02::1:ff. Therefore, df56:9098:1010:fd:ab29::f892 generates ff02::1:ff00:f892. Note that, in the original address, two all-zero hextets were abbreviated; don't forget to include two of those abbreviated zeros after the "ff02::1:ff" prefix—ff02::1:ff:f892 is incorrect.
4. Which message types does NDP use for Layer-2 address resolution? (select two)
B: NS
D:NA
NDP uses Neighbor Solicitation (NS)—like ARP request—and Neighbor Advertisement (NA)—like ARP reply—messages for Layer-2 address resolution.
5. Which command can be used to view a list of IPv6-address-to-Layer-2-address mappings?
C: **`show ipv6 neighbors`**
IPv6-address-to-Layer-2-address mappings are stored in the IPv6 neighbor table, which can be viewed with **`show ipv6 neighbors`**.
6. Which command can be used to configure an IPv6 with a prefix learned via RA and an automatically generated interface ID?
C: **`ipv6 address autoconfig`**
The **`ipv6 address autoconfig`** command configures an IPv6 address using the prefix advertised by Router Advertisements (RA) and automatically generates the interface ID using Modified EUI-64 rules.
7. Which NDP messages are used in the DAD process? (select two)
B: NS

D: NA

For Duplicate Address Detection (DAD), a host will send an NS message to its own IPv6 address. If it doesn't receive a reply, it determines that the address is unique on the network. But if it receives an NA in reply, it determines that the address is a duplicate; it won't be able to use the address.

8. Which of the following IPv6 static routes will not function properly, despite appearing in the routing table?

A: **`ipv6 route 2001:db8::/64 GigabitEthernet0/1`**

Although Cisco IOS will allow you to configure this route, it will not function properly. Directly connected static routes can work in IPv4 because of proxy ARP, but Cisco IOS doesn't implement an equivalent proxy NDP.

9. Which of the following commands configures a recursive host route?

A: **`ipv6 route 2001:db8::1/128 2001:db8:23::3`**

A host route is a route to a single destination address, using a /128 prefix length (/32 in IPv4). A recursive route is configured by specifying a destination network and a next-hop address, so A is the correct answer.

10. Which of the following commands configures a fully specified default route?

C: **`ipv6 route ::/0 GigabitEthernet0/1 2001:db8::1`**

A default route is a route to ::/0, matching all possible IPv6 addresses. A fully specified route includes both the exit interface and the next-hop address, so option C is correct.

Chapter 22: Transmission Control Protocol and User Datagram Protocol

1. Which of the following protocol and port pairs are correct? (select three)

A: DNS = TCP/UDP port 53

E: DHCP server = UDP port 67

F: DHCP client = UDP port 68

DNS uses both TCP and UDP on port 53. DHCP servers use UDP port 67, and DHCP clients use UDP port 68. SSH uses TCP port 22 (not 23), HTTPS uses TCP port 443 (not 80), and Syslog typically uses UDP port 514.

2. Which TCP field does a host use to indicate how much data it can receive before sending an ACK?

D: Window Size

The Window Size field in the TCP header specifies the amount of data the sender can transmit before it must receive an acknowledgment from the receiving host.

3. Which of the following is provided by TCP, but not UDP?

B: Data sequencing

TCP provides data sequencing, ensuring that packets arrive in the correct order. UDP, being a simpler and more lightweight protocol, does not provide this feature. Both protocols support error detection (both headers include a "Checksum" field for that purpose), but only TCP ensures reliable delivery and ordered data sequencing.

4. In which of the following cases is UDP usually preferred? (select two)

B: Real-time applications

C: Simple query/response protocols

UDP is often chosen for real-time applications (like streaming and online gaming) due to its lower latency, and for simple query/response protocols like DNS due to its simplicity and lower overhead. TCP is most often used for reliable data transfer, like file transfers.

5. What is the correct sequence of the TCP three-way handshake?

C: SYN, SYN-ACK, ACK

The TCP three-way handshake involves a SYN packet sent from the client to the server, a SYN-ACK response from the server, and finally an ACK from the client to the server.

6. What does the value in a TCP segment's Acknowledgement Number field represent?

B: The sequence number of the next segment the host expects to receive.

The Acknowledgement Number in a TCP segment indicates the sequence number of the next expected byte from the sender, effectively acknowledging receipt of all preceding bytes.

7. When a client sends a request to a server, which type of port does the client typically source the request from?

B: An ephemeral port

Clients typically select a random ephemeral port for the source port when initiating communication to a server. Ephemeral ports are temporary ports assigned for the duration of the session.

8. Which of the following protocols use a Layer-4 protocol that provides reliable delivery of messages? (select two)

A: Telnet

D: FTP

Both Telnet and FTP use TCP, which provides reliable delivery of messages. SNMP and NTP, on the other hand, use UDP, which does not provide reliable delivery.

Chapter 23: Standard access control lists

1. Which of the following commands permit only the specified host's IP address? (select three)

A: **`access-list 1 permit 8.8.8.8`**

B: **`access-list 1 permit 8.8.8.8 0.0.0.0`**

D: **`access-list 1 permit host 8.8.8.8`**

When configuring a standard ACL, there are three ways to specify a single IP address: {**`permit`**|**`deny`**} *`ip-address`*, {**`permit`**|**`deny`**} *`ip-address`* **`0.0.0.0`**, and {**`permit`**|**`deny`**} **`host`** *`ip-address`*. Option C is incorrect because it specifies the wildcard mask **`255.255.255.255`**, which is equivalent to a /0 netmask; it matches all possible IP addresses.

2. Where should standard ACLs generally be applied?

B: As close to the destination as possible

Standard ACLs should generally be applied as close to the destination of the traffic you want to filter. Because standard ACLs filter packets based only on their source IP address, applying a standard ACL too close to the source can filter more traffic from the host/network than intended.

3. Which of the following are valid standard ACL numbers? (select three)

B: 1301

C: 1999

E: 99

Standard ACLs can use numbers from 1 to 99 and 1300 to 1999. Therefore, 1301, 1999, and 99 are valid standard ACL numbers.

4. Which command can be used to create a standard named ACL?

C: **`ip access-list standard TEST_ACL`**

The correct command to create a standard named ACL is **`ip access-list standard`** *`name`*. This command brings you to standard named ACL configuration mode, where you can configure rules for the ACL.

5. Which parameters can standard ACLs use to match packets? (select all that apply)

A: Source IP address

Standard ACLs can only match packets based on the source IP address. They cannot filter based on destination IP, protocol, or port numbers.

6. You create an ACL with a single ACE: **`deny 192.168.1.0 0.0.0.255`**. You then apply the ACL to an interface. What is the effect of this ACL?

B: All packets are denied.

Since the only ACE in the ACL denies packets from 192.168.1.0/24, and ACLs have an implicit "**`deny any`**" at the end, all packets will be denied. The ACL needs an explicit **`permit`** statement to allow other traffic.

7. Which command applies ACL 1 to an interface, filtering packets received by the interface?

C: **`ip access-group 1 in`**

The correct command to apply an ACL to an interface to filter incoming traffic is **`ip address-group`** *`acl`* **`in`**.

8. What is the effect of an ACL that has been created, but not applied to an interface?

A: The ACL has no effect.

An ACL that has been created but not applied to any interface has no effect on traffic. ACLs must be applied to interfaces to filter traffic.

Chapter 24: Extended access control lists

1. Which of the following are valid extended ACL numbers? (select three)

B: 2000

D: 199

E: 2599

Extended ACLs can use numbers from 100–199 and 2000–2699. Therefore, 2000, 199, and 2599 are valid extended ACL numbers.

2. Which of the following extended ACL entries blocks requests from clients to an HTTPS server?

B: **`deny tcp any host 192.0.2.1 eq 443`**

HTTPS uses TCP port 443. When clients send requests to an HTTPS server, they use destination port (not source port) 443. So, B is correct because it denies requests destined for port 443 on the server.

3. Which of the following extended ACL entries permits all messages from the server with IP address 203.0.113.1 except its responses to SSH clients?

A: **`permit tcp 203.0.113.1 0.0.0.0 neq 22 any`**

SSH uses TCP port 22. This time, we are filtering the server's responses, so the ACE must filter based on source port 22, not destination port 22—the opposite of the previous example. Use **`neq 22`** (not equal to 22) to permit everything except responses to SSH clients (which would be sourced from port 22).

4. Which of the following extended ACL entries denies connections from clients to port 21 of an FTP server?

C: **`deny tcp any host 198.51.100.1 eq ftp`**

FTP uses TCP (not UDP) port 21 for control connections, and the equivalent keyword when configuring an ACE is **`ftp`** (**`ftp-data`** matches port 20).

5. Which of the following is an accurate description of the effect of this ACE: **`deny icmp 172.16.24.0 0.0.1.255 any`**

B: Deny all ICMP messages from hosts in the 172.16.24.0/23 subnet.

The ACE specifies the ICMP protocol, the source subnet 172.16.24.0/23, and any destination; option B is an accurate description.

6. Which of the following extended ACL entries permits Telnet connections from hosts in the 192.168.2.0/25 subnet to hosts in the 10.0.0.0/9 subnet?

C: **`permit tcp 192.168.2.0 0.0.0.127 10.0.0.0 0.127.255.255 eq 23`**

Telnet uses TCP port 23. This ACE correctly specifies source subnet 192.168.2.0/25 (wildcard mask 0.0.0.127) and destination subnet 10.0.0.0/9 (wildcard mask 0.127.255.255).

7. Which command can be used to create an extended named ACL?

D: **`ip access-list extended TEST_ACL`**

The correct command to create a standard named ACL is **`ip access-list extended`** *`name`*. This command brings you to extended named ACL configuration mode, where you can configure rules for the ACL.

8. What is the effect of the command **`ip access-list resequence 100 10 5`**?

A: Change the sequence number of ACL 100's first ACE to 10 and add 5 for each subsequent ACE.

The syntax for the command is **`ip access-list resequence`** {*`name`*|*`number`*} *`starting-seq-num increment`*. The command specifies ACL 100, a starting sequence number of 10, and an increment of 5.

index

Numbers

Symbols

A

B

C

D

E

F

S

T